THE

SELECTED

WORKS OF

GORDON

TULLOCK

VOLUME 10

Economics without Frontiers

THE SELECTED WORKS OF GORDON TULLOCK

VOLUME 1 *Virginia Political Economy*

VOLUME 2 *The Calculus of Consent: Logical Foundations of Constitutional Democracy* (with James M. Buchanan)

VOLUME 3 *The Organization of Inquiry*

VOLUME 4 *The Economics of Politics*

VOLUME 5 *The Rent-Seeking Society*

VOLUME 6 *Bureaucracy*

VOLUME 7 *The Economics and Politics of Wealth Redistribution*

VOLUME 8 *The Social Dilemma: Of Autocracy, Revolution, Coup d'Etat, and War*

VOLUME 9 *Law and Economics*

VOLUME 10 *Economics without Frontiers* (includes a cumulative index for the series)

Gordon Tullock

THE SELECTED WORKS

OF GORDON TULLOCK

VOLUME 10

Economics without Frontiers

GORDON TULLOCK

Edited and with an Introduction by

CHARLES K. ROWLEY

Liberty Fund

Indianapolis

Introduction copyright © 2006 Liberty Fund, Inc.
All rights reserved

Printed in the United States of America

Paperback cover photo courtesy of the
American Economic Review

Frontispiece courtesy of Center for Study of Public Choice,
George Mason University, Fairfax, Virginia

10   09   08   07   06   C   5   4   3   2   1
10   09   08   07   06   P   5   4   3   2   1

Library of Congress Cataloging-in-Publication Data

Tullock, Gordon.
    Economics without frontiers / Gordon Tullock ; edited and
with an introduction by Charles K. Rowley.
        p. cm. — (The selected works of Gordon Tullock ; v. 10)
    Includes bibliographical references and index.
    ISBN 0-86597-529-9 (hardcover : alk. paper) — ISBN 0-86597-540-X
    (paperback : alk. paper)
        1. Social choice.   2. Rational choice theory.   3. Economics —
    Sociological aspects.   4. Economics — Psychological aspects.
    I. Rowley, Charles Kershaw.   II. Title.   III. Series:
    Tullock, Gordon. Selections. 2006 ; v. 10.
HB846.8.T814 2006
302'.13 — dc22

                                            2005040806

LIBERTY FUND, INC.
8335 Allison Pointe Trail, Suite 300
Indianapolis, Indiana 46250-1684

CONTENTS

Introduction, *by Charles K. Rowley* ix

I. THE ECONOMIC APPROACH TO HUMAN BEHAVIOR
   (*Richard B. McKenzie and Gordon Tullock*) 3

2. THE NEW WORLD OF ECONOMICS
Marriage, Divorce, and the Family
   (*Richard B. McKenzie and Gordon Tullock*) 25
Child Production (*Richard B. McKenzie and Gordon Tullock*) 39
The Economic Aspects of Crime
   (*Richard B. McKenzie and Gordon Tullock*) 56
The Economic versus the Sociological Views of Crime
   (*Richard B. McKenzie and Gordon Tullock*) 73
Why Government (*Gordon Tullock and Richard B. McKenzie*) 85
Rationality in Human and Nonhuman Societies
   (*Gordon Tullock and Richard B. McKenzie*) 95
Universities Should Discriminate against Assistant Professors III

3. BIOECONOMICS
Sociobiology (*Gordon Tullock and Richard B. McKenzie*) 115
Economics and Sociobiology: A Comment 133
Sociobiology and Economics 139
Territorial Boundaries: An Economic View 155
Evolution and Human Behavior 159

The Economics of Nonhuman Societies 171
   1. Introduction 173
   2. The Genetics of Society 181
   3. Coordination and the Prisoner's Dilemma 197
   4. Consider the Ant 206
   5. Termites and Bees 225
   6. Mole Rats, Sponges, and Slime Molds 236
   7. A Theory of Cooperation 250
   8. A Society of Cells 264

4. PUBLIC FINANCE

Science Fiction and the Debt 271

Subsidized Housing in a Competitive Market: Comment 275

Optimal Poll Taxes 277

Optimal Poll Taxes: Further Aspects 285

Bismarckism 289

5. MONETARY ECONOMICS

Hyperinflation in China, 1937–49
 (*Colin D. Campbell and Gordon C. Tullock*) 307

Paper Money—A Cycle in Cathay 321

Some Little-Understood Aspects of Korea's Monetary and Fiscal Systems
 (*Colin D. Campbell and Gordon Tullock*) 343

Competing Monies 359

Competing Monies: A Reply 367

When Is Inflation Not Inflation? 373

6. SIZE AND GROWTH OF GOVERNMENT

An Empirical Analysis of Cross-National Economic Growth, 1951–80
 (*Kevin B. Grier and Gordon Tullock*) 379

Provision of Public Goods through Privatization 399

7 THE THEORY OF GAMES

An Economic Theory of Military Tactics: Methodological Individualism
 at War (*Geoffrey Brennan and Gordon Tullock*) 405

Jackson and the Prisoner's Dilemma 425

Adam Smith and the Prisoners' Dilemma 429

Games and Preference 438

Index 447

Series Indexes
 Titles of Works Included in the Series 461
 Cumulative Index 467

INTRODUCTION

Economics without Frontiers, the concluding volume in the Selected Works of Gordon Tullock, brings together, in seven parts, an eclectic set of Tullock's essays, many of which significantly expanded the frontiers of economic science, always within the underlying framework of the rational-choice model. This volume highlights intellectual qualities that have directed a great deal of Tullock's scholarship throughout a lengthy and highly productive career, namely, the use he makes of his powers of observation to engage in successful economic imperialism.

Successful Economic Imperialism

In 1992, the Royal Swedish Academy of Sciences awarded the Bank of Sweden Prize in Economic Sciences in Memory of Alfred Nobel to Gary S. Becker *"for having extended the domain of microeconomic analysis to a wide range of human behavior and interaction, including nonmarket behavior."*

In the view of the Swedish Academy, Becker's contribution consisted *"primarily in having extended the domain of economic theory to aspects of human behavior which had previously been dealt with—if at all—by other social science disciplines such as sociology, demography and criminology."* In so doing, he had stimulated economists to tackle new problems.

Central to Becker's use of the economic approach is his contention that "the economic approach is uniquely powerful because it can integrate a wide range of human behavior."[1] To this end, Becker's research program is founded on the idea that the behavior of individuals and groups adheres to the same set of fundamental principles in a wide range of different circumstances.

Specifically, Becker deploys maximizing behavior explicitly and extensively across all areas of human behavior, be they the utility or wealth function of the household (and its separate components), firm, labor union, special interest group, or government bureau. He assumes the existence of equili-

---

1. Gary S. Becker, *The Economic Approach to Human Behavior* (Chicago: University of Chicago Press, 1976), 5.

[ix]

brating markets (usually viewed as being efficient) that both coordinate and constrain the desires of different participants so that their behavior becomes mutually consistent. The preferences of individuals are assumed to be homogeneous across individuals and not to change substantially over time.[2] Becker also assumes that all individuals and groups are well informed about the market (or nonmarket) environment in which they participate.

The assumptions that underpin Becker's economic approach reflect the more general approach of the Chicago School in offering a tight prior equilibrium theory of human behavior in which markets clear quickly and efficiently and in which changes in outcomes are driven not by changes in tastes but by changes in constraints.[3] In this manner, Becker has successfully invaded other disciplines in the social sciences and has used the rational-choice approach to advance understanding of human behavior.

Over the past forty years, Tullock has matched Gary Becker in the successful imperialistic invasion of rational-choice economics into contiguous social science territories as well as, even more ambitiously, into the natural sciences. As earlier volumes in this series clearly demonstrate, Tullock has deployed the rational-choice approach of economics to disturb conventional thinking not only in economics but also in the disciplines of political science, social studies, the law, biology, and scientific method.

Tullock's economic approach, however, differs in significant respects from that of Becker and, as a result, provides different insights into the predictable implications of human (and nonhuman) interaction. Tullock retains the *Homo economicus* assumption of maximizing and self-seeking man, while being much more willing than Becker to recognize the importance of non-wealth arguments in the individual's utility function.

Tullock allows for the possibilities that markets will not always clear and that when they do clear they may do so inefficiently (especially political markets). He allows for the possibility that information will not be widely dispersed (especially in political markets). He allows for differences in individual preferences and for changes in those preferences over time, not least in response to persuasive advertising (especially in political markets).

2. George J. Stigler and Gary S. Becker, "De Gustibus Non Est Disputandum," *American Economic Review* 67 (March 1977): 76–90.

3. Melvin W. Reder, "Chicago Economics: Permanence and Change," *Journal of Economic Literature* 20 (March 1982): 1–38.

In combination, these assumptions define a diffuse rather than a tight prior equilibrium as the hallmark of Tullock's scholarship.[4] Markets are not always in equilibrium, though they do adjust dynamically toward equilibrium. Market outcomes may be inefficient in allocating resources, and they may offer high-cost solutions. Institutions matter and cannot be ignored. Ideas are important and shape outcomes. In all these respects, Tullock's analysis diverges sharply from that of the Chicago School.

Economics without Frontiers: Tullock's Contributions at the Frontier of Economics

Part 1, "The Economic Approach to Human Behavior" (coauthored with Richard McKenzie), sets the scene for the volume. It begins with the provocative statement: "Economics is not what it used to be!" The authors outline just how rational-choice economics should be applied to areas, such as criminal behavior and the production and rearing of children, that traditionally fell outside the scope of the discipline.

Part 2, "The New World of Economics," applies the rational-choice model to a diverse range of previously off-limit fields, clearly demonstrating the relevance of the economic approach to all human decision-making over the allocation of scarce resources.

"Marriage, Divorce, and the Family" (coauthored with Richard B. McKenzie) analyzes dating and courtship as investments in information concerning the suitability for the contract of marriage. The authors view the marriage contract as necessarily incomplete and as conditioned by the ease or difficulty of subsequent breach and the expected cost of divorce. They analyze the division of labor within the household from the perspective of economic efficiency conditioned by the comparative advantages of the marriage partners. Love plays a role in all this analysis, primarily as a reciprocal or unilateral externality that reduces the cost and improves the efficiency of household decision making.

"Child Production" (coauthored with Richard B. McKenzie) analyzes the process of child production and child rearing within the family as a joint

---

4. Charles K. Rowley, *The Right to Justice* (Aldershot and Brookfield, Vt.: Edward Elgar, 1993), 42–43.

household investment and consumption decision. The authors recognize that choices of this kind are more boundedly rational (i.e., subject to information and cognitive limitations) than most investment and consumption decisions, not least because children have wills of their own that cannot be foreseen at the point of reproduction. Such decisions are also more subject to error (not least because of the fallibility of contraceptive devices). At the margin, however, they are predictably responsive to change in perceived costs and benefits.

"The Economic Aspects of Crime" (coauthored with Richard B. McKenzie) deploys simple demand and supply analysis to evaluate the predictable behavior of potential criminals under alternative cost conditions. They demonstrate that criminal behavior will decline as the expected cost, measured in terms of the probability of apprehension, conviction, and the extent of punishment, increases. This prediction holds even if a significant proportion of criminals are irrational. The authors also evaluate the predictable behavior of rational individuals in seeking to remain nonvictims. The authors conclude that the police, at most, play a secondary role in crime prevention. They provide statistical support for their hypotheses.

"The Economic versus the Sociological Views of Crime" (coauthored with Richard B. McKenzie) compares the economic view that crime is a profession whose size is driven by the magnitude of expected net returns, with the sociological view that criminals are individuals who are deformed by environmental disadvantages and who are incapable of rational decision-making. McKenzie and Tullock survey compelling statistical evidence in favor of the economic hypothesis. This has important implications for controlling crime, namely, that increased punishment will deter crime much more than attempts at the rehabilitation of criminals.

"Why Government" (coauthored with Richard B. McKenzie) outlines criteria for determining rationally the respective roles of private markets and democratic governments as mechanisms for allocating scarce resources among competing ends. The authors suggest that the division of labor should be determined by the magnitude of externalities and public goods. When these are low, private markets are more efficient. When they are high, democratic governments are more efficient. The authors warn that government actions often impose negative external effects upon third parties.

"Rationality in Human and Nonhuman Societies" (coauthored with Richard B. McKenzie) evaluates the results of pioneering experimental economic studies in a search for evidence of rational behavior. The authors conclude that experimental evidence strongly supports the hypothesis that sane human beings, as well as the inhabitants of mental institutions, birds, rats, and microscopic animals, are rational in that they typically choose to buy in the cheapest market and that they respond predictably, at the margin, to changes in benefits and costs.

"Universities Should Discriminate against Assistant Professors" attempts to justify the common practice of discriminating in favor of more senior faculty in the allocation of research and secretarial support. Tullock points out that senior faculty have less economic incentive to publish, given tenure, than do more junior, untenured faculty. Positive discrimination is therefore necessary to obtain research output from senior faculty.

Part 3, "Bioeconomics," applies the rational-choice approach to a diverse range of nonhuman decision-makers. The essays brought together here constitute part of Tullock's pathbreaking and highly successful application of the rational-choice approach to biology.[5]

"Sociobiology" (coauthored with Richard B. McKenzie) demonstrates that nonhuman societies are endowed with many of the characteristics endemic to human societies. Animals, insects, and even plants are real-estate owners that engage in such apparently rational decisions as whether or not to defend their estates or to predate on the estates of others. Such nonhuman societies are often characterized by dominance structures that provide for the efficient protection of the followers by the leaders. Insects such as ants, bees, and termites organize themselves into groups that provide for an efficient division of labor. While there is little reason to suppose that humans can learn to organize themselves more efficiently by studying nonhuman behavior, the behavior of nonhuman species appears to conform, nevertheless, to the principle of rationality.

"Economics and Sociobiology: A Comment" notes that modern biology was, in a sense, founded by the economist Thomas Malthus, whose writings inspired Charles Darwin's seminal text, *On the Origin of Species*.[6] Not surprisingly, therefore, a number of economists attempt to explain human behavior in terms of nonhuman behavior. Tullock takes issue with the attempt by Gary

5. A number of Tullock's most famous bioeconomics papers are published in *Virginia Political Economy*, volume 1 of the series.

6. Thomas R. Malthus, *An Essay on the Principle of Population* (1798; London: Cambridge University Press, 1992); Charles Darwin, *On the Origin of Species by Means of Natural Selection, Or the Preservation of Favoured Races in the Struggle for Life* (London, 1859; Norwalk, Conn.: Easton, 1963).

Becker to explain altruism within the human species as the consequence of narrowly self-interested rational calculation.[7] Not so, explains Tullock. Direct altruism, in the sense of voluntary gifts, is an expression of tastes or, perhaps, of inborn drives.

"Sociobiology and Economics" discusses the fact that both economics and modern biology use the methodology of Karl Popper, who emphasized that theories should be tested against their predictions rather than their assumptions.[8] Tullock also notes that modern biology assumes that species act through natural selection as if to maximize utility subject to constraints. In consequence, surviving species exhibit efficient behavior. However, because humans are at the top of the predator chain, they face quite different evolutionary conditions than other species, most notably because their main causes of unnatural deaths are attacks by members of their own species. For this reason, human society has little to learn from the study of animal behavior.

"Territorial Boundaries: An Economic View" demonstrates the rational behavior of birds in determining their property boundaries. Tullock analyzes, from the perspective of rational choice, the efficient geographic nest location of a second bird given that one bird has already made its nest in an adjacent area and may be prepared to defend that location against perceived invasion. Tullock develops a testable model of the shape and size of each bird's nesting territory, relevant in periods of either high or low bird populations.

"Evolution and Human Behavior" draws upon behavior patterns evident among nonhuman species to explain the existence within the human species of behavior patterns that do not satisfy the narrow self-interest postulate. Tullock shows that such apparently deviant behaviors as altruism toward strangers and the willingness to risk one's life for one's tribe were and are frequently important for the evolutionary survival of more-primitive species.

"The Economics of Nonhuman Societies" is a monograph that represents Tullock's most significant contribution to bioeconomics. Here we see Tullock at his observing best, developing important economic theories on the basis of his careful tracking of animal, insect, and plant life.

Tullock shows how numerous nonhuman species, including animals, insects, and even plants, accomplish extraordinary feats of cooperation and of adaptation to changes in their environment. They do so without either of the

---

7. Gary S. Becker, "Altruism, Egoism, and Genetic Fitness: Economics and Sociobiology," *Journal of Economic Literature* 14 (September 1976): 817–26.

8. Karl R. Popper, *The Logic of Scientific Discovery* (New York: Basic Books, 1959).

two major organizational techniques used by human beings, namely, central control or the market. Students of human societies normally do not even know about the nature of these nonhuman societies. Biologists, although impressed by the efficiency of large ant and large bee communities, do not seem to realize how difficult such coordination is for species with such microscopic brains, to say nothing about the apparently rational behavior of plants that have no brains at all. It is not without significance that Tullock's favorite non-human species is the slime mold, surely one of the most primitive organisms ever to inhabit the planet.

Part 4, "Public Finance," brings together five papers by Tullock that explore important issues of public finance from the perspectives of methodological individualism and public choice.

"Science Fiction and the Debt," originally published in Italian in 1963, uses an ingenious example to demonstrate why government debt is always and exclusively a burden on the future generations.[9]

"Subsidized Housing in a Competitive Market: Comment" notes that housing vouchers issued to the poor are likely to be illegally discounted by landlords of lower-priced housing who will remit a cash payment to cover part of the differential. Instead of housing-specific vouchers, Tullock argues, a somewhat lower, but non-housing-specific, cash payment to the poor is more welfare enhancing.

"Optimal Poll Taxes" and "Optimal Poll Taxes: Further Aspects" evaluate the efficiency implications of imposing negative or positive poll taxes, respectively, on individuals who do not vote or who do vote in democratic elections. Tullock makes a convincing welfare economics argument against the imposition of negative poll taxes and in favor of the imposition of positive poll taxes designed to cover the overall cost of running an election.

"Bismarckism" is a critique of the current system of social security in the United States. Tullock shows the harmful consequences of this system both for the poor and for the well-off and the significantly declining benefits to the median-income group. He outlines the fiscal illusion, if not the outright fraud, perpetrated by successive U.S. governments to "protect" social security. Tullock is doubtful about the long-term political viability of the system.

Part 5, "Monetary Economics," comprises six papers that reflect Tullock's

---

9. Gordon Tullock, "Who Bears the Burden?" *Revista di Diritto Finanziaro e Scienza della Finanze* 22 (June 1963): 207–13.

early thinking on the relationship between the supply of money and price inflation in China and South Korea.

"Hyperinflation in China, 1937–49" (coauthored with Colin D. Campbell) is Tullock's first scholarly paper, published in 1954, several years before he entered the American academy. The paper is based on Tullock's personal observations during his spell as a foreign service officer in Tientsin, from 1948 to 1950. The authors demonstrate that the Chinese experience over the period 1937–49 shows that people are prepared to retain currency as a medium of exchange under conditions of hyperinflation, while discarding it as a store of value and as a unit of account. The Chinese were willing to pay a high price to avoid the disadvantages of barter during a lengthy period of volatile inflation and hyperinflation.

"Paper Money—A Cycle in Cathay" charts the history of inflation and the rise and fall of paper money in China through seven dynasties, each with its own monetary institutions. Because paper, ink, and printing were all invented in China, it is not surprising that paper currency also first appeared there in the ninth century. Tullock clearly shows how the abuse of the printing press by successive Chinese dynasties culminated in inflation, the collapse of the dynasty, the temporary abandonment of paper money, its reinstatement, further abuse, dynasty collapse, paper currency abandonment, and reinstatement until 1500, when the old Chinese system broke down under Western influence.

"Some Little-Understood Aspects of Korea's Monetary and Fiscal Systems" (coauthored with Colin D. Campbell) is based on Tullock's experience of monetary expansion and price inflation in South Korea during his spell as foreign service officer from September 1953 to December 1954. Tullock notes that many U.S. advisers simply failed to recognize the endemic nature of inflation in South Korea following the expulsion of the Japanese, in 1945. The Koreans adapted well to high and variable rates of inflation. The *won* (subsequently the *hwon*) remained in use as a medium of exchange and even as a unit of account, though not as a store of value. Resort to barter was largely avoided.

"Competing Monies" and "Competing Monies: A Reply" both draw on Tullock's experiences in China and South Korea. In China, between 1948 and 1950, two kinds of silver dollar, small gold bars, and the Chinese Nationalist paper currency (later the Chinese Communist paper currency) all circulated at the same time. In Korea, between 1952 and 1953, there were, once again, three currencies. Tullock demonstrates how inflation, and varying rates of inflation, will influence the demand by individuals across each of these competing currencies.

"When Is Inflation Not Inflation?" focuses on the situation of rising prices induced by the discovery of some highly valued resource (diamonds, gold, or oil). If the value of a country's currency remains stable or appreciates in terms of foreign currencies, Tullock questions whether the observed phenomenon should be designated as inflation from the perspective of those living and working in that country.

Part 6, "Size and Growth of Government," brings together two of Gordon Tullock's contributions to understanding the positive and negative roles of government in influencing the rate of economic growth of the economy and in dealing effectively with the provision of public goods.

"An Empirical Analysis of Cross-National Economic Growth, 1951–80" (coauthored with Kevin B. Grier) provides a comprehensive econometric analysis of the determinants of economic growth over the period 1951–80 in Organisation for Economic Co-operation and Development (OECD) countries, Asia, Africa, and the Americas. The authors find a persistent negative correlation between the growth in a government's share in gross domestic product and economic growth for the OECD, Latin America, and Africa, but not for Asia. Inflation variability adversely affects economic growth in all sectors except in Latin America. Although there is evidence of convergence of growth rates within the OECD, this does not hold for the rest of the world.

"Provision of Public Goods through Privatization" argues that the provision of public goods by for-profit firms, at least in the case of pharmaceutical research, is more efficient than public provision. Governments typically provide the benefits of such research at a zero price, primarily to their own citizens. Private corporations, on the other hand, provide patented products at a market price worldwide. Arguably, the latter solution dispenses outputs more efficiently, if world welfare is the relevant criterion.

Part 7, "The Theory of Games," brings together four papers that deal with prisoners' dilemma situations and their possible resolution.

"An Economic Theory of Military Tactics" (coauthored with Geoffrey Brennan) analyzes armies as collections of individuals who may be as much at war with one another and with their own leaders as they are with enemy forces. The authors model the situation as a prisoners' dilemma in which the rational choice for each individual is to desert unless the enemy forces desert first, whereas the rational choice for the group is to stand and fight. In such circumstances, the chief element in winning the war is to convince the opponent of one's determination to fight. If so convinced, the opposition will be tempted to desert. Positive incentives, such as the spoils system, and negative incentives, such as torture and execution for those who desert, play essential roles in mitigating the prisoners' dilemma.

"Jackson and the Prisoner's Dilemma" attempts to explain the relatively low rate of rifle firing by infantrymen during battle in terms of a prisoners' dilemma situation. Firing one's weapon attracts the attention of the enemy to the infantryman in question, raising his probability of injury or death. Yet, firing one's weapon provides a public good for one's colleagues. By grouping infantrymen closely together, the prisoners' dilemma can be eased, since the group as a whole and not the individual becomes the target for enemy return fire. Mechanisms such as grouping are far more likely to reduce shirking than are attempts at morale-building by generals.

"Adam Smith and the Prisoners' Dilemma" suggests that the artificial nature of the prisoners' dilemma is not usually replicated in the real world. In the real world, individuals typically select those with whom they contract on the basis of reputation and prior experience. In such circumstances, opportunities for cooperation exist, even in environments imbued with distinct prisoners' dilemma characteristics. Specialists in game theory typically underestimate the capacity of individuals for realizing gains-from-trade in the real world.

"Games and Preference" challenges the usefulness of game theory, other than in its simplest prisoners' dilemma format, as a formal body of mathematics allegedly applying to human action. Tullock claims that game theory has provided genuine insights into only a very small collection of special cases. The end product of game theory is, in Tullock's judgment, its contribution to our vocabulary and to our methods of thinking about certain kinds of economic problems. As a solution device, it is severely crippled.

In its breadth and diversity, *Economics without Frontiers* is an apt representation of Tullock's half-century of contributions to economic science. His testament is in his life and in his work. It is fitting, therefore, to end the introduction—and the series—with the epitaph engraved on the tomb of Sir Christopher Wren in St. Paul's Cathedral: *Lector, si monumentum requiris, circumspice* (Reader, if you seek his monument, look around).

PART I

THE ECONOMIC
APPROACH TO
HUMAN BEHAVIOR

THE ECONOMIC APPROACH
TO HUMAN BEHAVIOR
Richard B. McKenzie and Gordon Tullock

Economics is not what it used to be! This can be said about most disciplines, but it is particularly applicable to economics. At one time students could think of economics as being neatly contained within the sphere of "commercial life," and most courses and books on the subject have traditionally revolved around such topics as money, taxes and tariffs, stocks and bonds, and the operation of the market as it pertains to the production and sale of automobiles and toothpaste. In recent years, however, economists have greatly expanded their field of concern, and, as a result, the boundaries of economics as a discipline are rapidly expanding outward, encroaching on areas of inquiry that have historically been the exclusive domain of other social sciences. The change in direction and scope of the discipline has been so dramatic that the economists who have been involved in bringing about the change are no longer inclined to debate the issue of what is or is not economic in nature. They merely ask "What can economics contribute to our understanding of this or that problem?"

This book reflects this expanded vision. Accordingly, we will introduce you to topics and points of discussion you may never have imagined would be included in an economics book. We will talk about family life, child rearing, dying, sex, crime, politics, and many other topics.[1] We do this not because such topics add a certain flair to the book, but rather because we believe that these are extraordinarily important areas of inquiry and that economic analysis can add much to our understanding of them. In addition, we are convinced that you will learn a good deal about economics through their consideration.

In dealing with such topics, we cannot avoid coming to grips with human behavior and making it the focus of our concern. The simple reason is that crimes cannot be committed, children cannot be reared, sex cannot be had,

Reprinted, with permission, from *The New World of Economics: Explorations into the Human Experience* (Homewood, Ill.: Richard D. Irwin, 1975), 3–22.

1. Actually, Adam Smith was concerned with several of these problem areas in *The Wealth of Nations*, which was published in 1776. He would not be surprised that economists are now giving such topics more attention.

and governments cannot operate without people "behaving" in one respect or another. We argue that before we can ever hope to understand social phenomena we must understand why people behave the way they do. To do this we must have some perception, or model, of how behavior is motivated and organized, from which the revealed actions of people can be interpreted. Economists have such a model, which has been developed and refined since the days of Adam Smith, and it is because we employ this model in our discussion that we consider this to be an economic treatise. All we intend to do here is to extend the application of this model into unconventional areas.

This is not to say, however, that economics can give a complete understanding of these problem areas. Other social scientists have long considered many of the topics included in this book, and their contributions to our understanding of human behavior cannot be overlooked. By viewing these topics through the thinking process of economists, we must be ever mindful that what we are dealing with is *one* particular point of view, which can be complemented by many of the findings in other disciplines.

You may at times have reservations about accepting what we have to say, but this is not necessarily unwelcome to us. We could easily write a book with which the reader would readily agree; however, we imagine that such a book might deal only with trivial issues and very well be a monumental bore. We take the view that at any given time there are many important issues that are to some degree unsettled; we believe that learning requires that an individual not only know the settled issues but also be able to explore those issues over which there may be some disagreement.

You do not need to have a large reservoir of economic knowledge in order to understand what we have to say. We will provide you with the necessary principles on which later discussion will be founded. Furthermore, we do not intend to waste your time with a lot of esoteric theory that will never be used. We understand that you want to make as efficient use of your time as possible, and we intend to cooperate with you. (Remember, this is a book on economics!) The principles that we do develop and the points that we make will at times be very subtle and a little tricky to handle—we cannot escape this. You may be pleasantly surprised, however, at how few in number these principles are and at how useful they will be in thinking about topics that are and are not included in this book. First, we need to lay the foundation—to explain how economists look at their subject and at human behavior.

For nearly two hundred years economists have periodically struggled with the problem of defining economics, and it is still a live issue. At times the subject has been defined as "what economists do," as that part of human experience that involves money, or as a study of how men attempt to maximize their material well-being. Different people perceive a discipline in different ways; therefore, no one can ever claim to offer readers *the* definition of the subject. All we can hope to accomplish is to lay out our own perception of the subject and in that way suggest how we will proceed.

The approach taken in this book is to define economics as a *mental skill* that incorporates a special view of human behavior characteristic of economists.[2] It is, in short, a thought process, or the manner in which economists approach problems, rather than an easily distinguishable group of problems that sets an economist apart from others. Sociologists and political scientists have dealt with many of the problems considered in this book, but the reader may notice that our approach to these problems is substantially different from theirs. This mental skill or approach has several distinctive characteristics that can be discussed as follows.

Abstractions

First and foremost, the economist is prone to think, as are all other scientists, in terms of *abstractions*, not in the sense that the notions he handles are vague or nebulous, but rather in the sense that his first impulse is to reduce reality to the relationships that are important and that bring the inquiry down to manageable proportions. The ideal approach to the study of human and social phenomena would be to treat the world as we confront it. However, the world is terribly complex; at any point in time it encompasses literally billions of bits of information and tens of thousands (if not millions) of relationships. On the other hand, man's mind has a limited capacity to handle such data; it can only consider so much at any one time. It is, therefore, literally impossible for a person to think about the world in its totality and deduce anything meaningful.

---

2. In fact, it is the thought process or the mental skill developed below that defines an economist. Indeed, in the context of the discussion that follows, there are no doubt many people who call themselves economists but who do not meet the description offered here, and there are many persons in other disciplines who can, according to our definition, accurately be classified as "economists." However, given the differences in policy conclusions of "economists" and "non-economists," it is apparent that the mental skill developed here is possessed by only a small fraction of the population.

As a consequence, the scientist must restrict the information he does consider; he must *abstract* in the sense that he pulls out from the total mass of information a limited number of relationships that he thinks are important and that he can handle.

This means that the analysis that then follows will lack a certain degree of realism. The analysis is based on abstractions that represent only a small portion of what we might call the "real world." The expectation is, however, that such an approach will increase man's understanding of the "real world" and will increase his ability to predict events in it. Economists heed the principle concisely laid out by Kenneth Boulding: "It is a very fundamental principle indeed that knowledge is always gained by the orderly loss of information; that is, by condensing and abstracting and indexing the great buzzing confusion of information that comes from the world around us into a form which we can appreciate and comprehend."[3] (Take a moment and think about this.) If you have difficulty understanding the world we live in, we suggest that your problem is likely to be that you are attempting to consider too much information, *not too little*.

Since the theory or model that is handled is by its very nature "unreal," the test of its acceptability is not the degree of its "realism" but the extent to which the model is able to accomplish its purpose; that is, to explain events in the real world and to make correct predictions. At times, the reader is likely to think to himself that our analysis is, in one respect or another, unreal or that the model we employ does not represent the "fullness of the human experience." To such a comment we agree, but we must follow with the question, "Are our conclusions not borne out in the real world?"

There is a story of an economics professor who was lecturing on a very esoteric topic before his graduate class. In the middle of the lecture, the professor was interrupted by a student who said, "Sir, I hate to break in, but in the real world. . ." The professor snapped back, "Mr. Waldorf, you must remember that the real world is a special case and, therefore, we need not consider it!" Before one gets the impression that we may be taking the same view as this professor, let us emphasize that everything we say, although it may be discussed in terms of models, is directed at our understanding of the real world, and we believe that economics has a very efficient way of doing that.

3. Kenneth E. Boulding, *The Skills of the Economist*, Cleveland: Howard Allen, 1958, 2.

Values

The approach of the economist is *amoral*. Economics is not concerned with what *should be*, or how individuals should behave, but rather with understanding why people behave the way they do. Accordingly, our analysis is devoid (as much as possible) of our own personal values. We treat each topic as something that is to be analyzed and understood, and in order to do that we must avoid the temptation to judge a given form of behavior as contemptuous, immoral, good, or bad. Therefore, in the context of our analysis, the services of a prostitute are treated no differently than the services of a butcher; they are neither good nor bad—they exist and are subject to analysis. Criminal activity is considered in a manner similar to that of legitimate enterprise, and religion is treated as a "good" (for some) that is sought after and procured.

Our reason for taking this tack is that in this book we are not interested in telling people how they should behave or what is good or evil; we are interested in gaining understanding of the behavior of others, *given their values*. Further, we are interested in evaluating the effects of institutional settings on human behavior and in suggesting how institutions may be rearranged to accomplish whatever objective is desired. Note that our intention is to suggest changes in institutions and not in behavior.

Like everyone else, we have our own value systems, and we could easily make recommendations regarding how people's behavior *should be* changed to accomplish what we, as humanists, think is "right." We also recognize that you have your own values, and we in no way wish to suggest that you dispense with them. You may violently disagree with prostitution or with political corruption—we do not quarrel with this. All we ask is that you allow us the opportunity to address the question of why such phenomena occur. In the process, you may find a solution to the problem that is more consistent with your values than the solution you now perceive.

The Individual

The focal point of the study of economics is the *individual*. It is the individual who possesses values, makes choices, and, if given the freedom, takes actions. All group decisions and actions are thought of in terms of the collective decisions and actions of individuals. Social goals are considered only to the extent that they reflect the collective values or choices of individuals. All too often we hear such expressions as "society disapproves of this or that," "Congress is considering legislation," or "government has made a decision to enforce a given policy." If the expressions are meant to suggest that individuals are involved, we have no qualms; if, on the other hand, the expressions are intended to suggest that these bodies have a behavior of their own that is independent of the behavior of individuals, we must take issue. We ask how can a "group" *act*? What is group behavior if it is not the behavior of individuals? How can a society, as an independent organism, have a value? Where must the values come from?

Do not misinterpret us; we are interested in understanding group behavior. However, we argue that to do this, we must first understand the behavior of the individuals that make up the group. We take it as a given that only individuals can act.

Rational Behavior

The economist begins his analysis of human behavior with the assertion that *man acts* and that he does so with a purpose. That purpose is to improve his lot—to change his situation from something less desired to something better, or as one economist put it:

> Acting man is eager to substitute a more satisfactory state of affairs for a less satisfactory. His mind imagines conditions which suit him better, and his actions aim at bringing about this desired state. The incentive that impels a man to act is always some uneasiness. A man perfectly content with the state of his affairs would have no incentive to change things. He would have neither wishes nor desires; he would be perfectly happy. He would not act; he would simply live free from care.[4]

This is the ultimate foundation of economics as a discipline. Philosophers and social scientists in general still debate the issue of whether or not man has "free will." We do not mean to detract from the importance of the debate.

---

4. Ludwig von Mises, *Human Action: A Treatise on Economics*, New Haven: Yale University Press, 1949, 13.

From our point of view, it is not necessary to discuss it. Whether man makes free decisions or whether he is "programmed" to make the decisions is irrelevant from the economics standpoint. We only need note that he does make decisions. Such a position has several implications. First, in economics the individual is assumed to be "rational" in the sense that he is able to determine within limits what he wants and will strive to fulfill as many of his wants as possible. He is able to offset environmental, social, and biological forces that would otherwise determine what he does. To what extent he is able to accomplish this depends on the resources at his command and the intensity of his desire to overcome these forces. Although taken for granted by many, these points need to be made because not all social scientists agree with this perspective. Many will argue, at least for purposes of their theories, that a factor such as the environment *determines*—not influences—man's behavior. The economist, on the other hand, looks at such factors as constraints within which the individual's preference can operate.

This position implies that the individual will always choose more of what he wants rather than less. It also means that he will choose less of what he does *not* want than more. For example, if the individual desires beer and pretzels and is presented with two bundles of these goods, both with the same amount of pretzels and one with more beers, the rational individual (i.e., college student!) will take the bundle with the greater number of beers. If he does not like beer, then that is another matter. In a similar vein, if one bundle contains a greater variety of goods or goods with a higher "quality" than the other bundle, the individual will choose that bundle with the greater variety or higher quality.[5]

If there is some uncertainty surrounding the available bundles, the individual will choose that bundle for which the *expected value* is greatest. People do make mistakes, mainly because they have incomplete information, but this does not negate the assumption of rational behavior. We only assume that the individual's motivation is to do that which improves his station in life, not that he always accomplishes this. There are such things as losers.

Economists are often criticized for assuming that man is wholly materialistic—that man wants "material things." The criticism is unjustified. All we have assumed from the start of this section is that an *individual has desires*. These desires may be embodied in material things, such as cocktails and

---

5. For all intents and purposes, goods of differing quality can be treated as distinctly different goods.

clothes; however, we also fully recognize that men *want* things that are aesthetic, intellectual, and spiritual in nature. Some people do want to read Shakespeare and Keats and to contemplate the idea of beauty. Others want to attend church and worship as they choose. Even a few may want to read this book! We have no quarrel with this (particularly with those who are interested in this book). We accept these as values with which we must deal in our analysis. They are a part of the data we handle. We emphasize, however, that what we have to say regarding "material things" is also applicable to those values that are not material. We may talk in terms of "goods," but what we really mean are those things people value.

Cost

Another implication of our basic position is that as far as the individual is concerned, he will never reach Nirvana. He will never obtain a perfect world; and as a result, he must accept second best, which is to maximize his utility through his behavior. This suggests that the individual will undertake to do that for which there is some expected net gain. He will in this sense pursue his own self-interest. This does not mean that the individual will necessarily lack concern for his fellow man. One of the things that he may want is to give to others. Such behavior can yield as much pleasure as anything else, and if so, he will do it. Why do people give gifts, say, at Christmas time? There are many motives that can be separated out; however, we suggest that the overriding reason is that the person involved gets some pleasure (gain), in one form or another, from doing it. Even the Bible admonishes that "it is better to give than to receive," indicating that there are gains to be had for acts of charity. Can you think of anything you or anyone else has done for which you or they did not *expect* some gain? (Remember, you have, no doubt, made a mistake and lost, but this is not involved in the question.)

If the individual is seeking to maximize his utility, then it follows that he must make choices among relevant alternatives. It also follows that in the act of choosing to do one thing, the individual *must* forgo doing or having something else. There is no escaping this. Although often measured in terms of dollars, *the cost of doing or having something is that which is forgone*. Therefore, for every act there is a cost, and it is this cost that will determine whether or not (or how much) something will be done. Cost is the constraint on action. In other words, is there anything such as a "free lunch"? Free TV? Free love or sex? How can these things be had if choices are involved? No money may have changed hands, but, again, *cost is not money*. Money or, more properly, dollars—is just one means of *measuring* cost. To have such things, we have to give up something in the way of time, psychic benefits, and/or resources that may be used for other purposes.

In an attempt to explain social phenomena we will, throughout this book, address the question of the costs and benefits of any given form of behavior. In understanding behavior, cost is a very powerful explanatory factor, as we will see. Consider the following problems:

1. Why do the poor tend to ride buses, and the rich tend to fly? It may be that there are differences in the educational and experience levels of the two groups, resulting in different behavior patterns. It may also be that being rich, the rich can "afford" such "extravagancies" as airplane tickets. All these factors may explain *part* of the behavior; but we wish to stress that it may be cheaper for the poor to take a bus than to fly and for the rich to fly than take the bus. Both rich and poor pay the same price for their tickets; and, consequently, the difference in cost must lie partly in the difference in the value of the time of the rich and poor. If by rich person we mean someone whose wage rate is very high, it follows that the rich man's time is much more valuable (in terms of wages forgone) than the poor man's time. Since it generally takes longer to take a bus than to fly, the cost of taking the bus, which includes the value of one's time, can be greater to the rich than the cost of flying. The poor man's time may be worth, in terms of what he could have earned, very little. Therefore, the total cost of a bus ride can be quite inexpensive to him. As a case in point, consider Johnny Carson, who makes over $1 million per year, and a poor man who is unemployed. Determine the *total* cost for each to take the bus and plane from Washington to Chicago. You may think that Johnny Carson has a lot of "free time" for sunbathing on the beach. Regardless of how you view the situation, it is still true that Carson can sell his time for a considerable sum to many willing buyers. Given your calculations, would you ever expect Carson to take the bus?

2. Why do the British use linen table napkins more often than Americans? In part, the answer may be that the differences in culture have had an effect on the willingness of people to use one form of napkins or another. However, one should also realize that the British have to import virtually all of their paper or pulpwood and that paper is relatively expensive there. Paper napkins are much less costly in the United States. Furthermore, linen napkins require washing and ironing; and since American wages are generally higher in the United

States, the cost of using linen napkins is much greater to Americans than to people in Britain. Again, the difference in cost provides an explanation.

3. Why do some people resist cheating on their examinations? It may be that they fear being caught and suspended from school, which means they attribute a cost to cheating. Barring this, they may have a moral code that opposes cheating, at least in this form. If they cheat, they would have to bear the psychic cost of going against what they consider right. This does not mean that all those with a moral code or conscience will not cheat to some degree. (Why?)

4. Why do some men forgo asking women out on dates? They may be shy (or gay), but they may feel that the cost of the date in terms of the money and time expenditures is too great. They may also be reluctant to ask women out because in doing so they have to incur the *risk cost* of being turned down.

5. Why are people as "courteous" as they are on the highway? They may have a streak of kindness in their hearts, but they may also be fully aware of the very high cost they can incur if their rudeness ends in an accident.

Marginal Cost

In determining how many units of a *given good* he will consume, the individual must focus on the additional cost of each additional unit. Another name for this cost concept is *marginal cost*. In other words, before the rational individual can proceed to the consumption of the next unit, he must at each step along the way ask how much does that additional unit cost?

If the individual is allowed time to make choices, there is substantial reason to believe that, as a general rule, the marginal cost of successive units he provides for himself or others will rise. At any point where a choice must be made, the individual is likely to have a whole array of opportunities he can choose to forgo to do this one thing. These opportunities are likely to vary in their value to the individual. In making the choice to consume the *first* unit of a good, which opportunity will he give up? The rational man will forgo that opportunity he values least. Since cost, or, as in this case, marginal cost, is the value of that opportunity given up, this means that the cost of the first unit is as low as possible. If the individual then wishes to produce or consume a second unit, he will have to give up that opportunity that is second to the bottom in value. This means that the marginal cost of the second is greater than the first. Given this choice behavior, we should expect the marginal cost

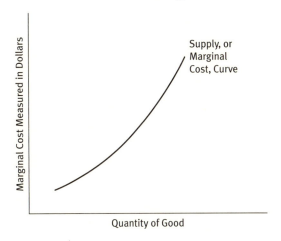

FIGURE 1

of successive units to rise progressively. Therefore, if we were to describe the relationship between the unit of the good provided and the marginal cost, we would expect to have a curve that is upward sloping to the right as in Figure 1. In this graph marginal cost is on the vertical axis, and the quantity of the good is on the horizontal axis. We economists refer to such a curve as the *supply curve*. Because of this relationship, we can argue that the higher the benefits (or price) received per unit, the more units of the good that the individual can justify providing.

There are cases in which the marginal cost of providing additional units is constant. More units of the good can be provided by forgoing alternatives that are equal in value. (Can you think of such cases?) In this event the supply curve could be horizontal. See Figure 2.

There is no reason to believe that the supply curve will remain stationary over time and under all conditions. Basically, the curve is set where it is because of a given cost structure of providing the good. It follows that anything that changes this cost structure will cause the curve to shift in one direction or the other. If the cost (which means the value of alternatives) of providing the good rises, then the curve will shift upward and to the left. If the cost goes down, the curve will move downward and to the right.[6] (Can you think of changes that would change the cost structure?)

6. For a more detailed discussion of the concept of supply, see any standard textbook on principles of economics. For example, see Armen A. Alchian and William R. Allen, *University*

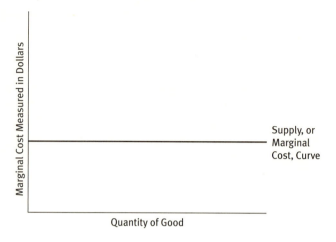

FIGURE 2

Demand

The assumption that the rational individual maximizes his utility implies that he will fully allocate his income among those things he wants. When we say income, we mean *full income*, which includes not only what a person can earn on a conventional job and which may be *measured* in terms of dollars, but also what a person can earn by doing things for himself, such as cooking meals, outside of his job. How can a person not fully allocate his income? Even when a person saves, the individual is allocating his income and is doing it for a purpose. That purpose may be to acquire a certain degree of security for himself or his family or to buy something he wants in the future. By saving, we might rightfully argue, the person is buying something.

The assumption also implies that the individual will continue to consume a given good until the marginal cost (*MC*) of the last unit obtained is equal to the marginal utility (*MU*). (Like the concept of marginal cost, marginal utility, or benefit, is the additional utility on each additional unit of the good.) If this were not the case and the marginal cost of the next unit of the good were less than the marginal utility of it, the individual could increase his level

---

Economics: Elements of Inquiry, 3rd ed., Belmont, Calif.: Wadsworth Publishing Company, 1972, or Campbell R. McConnell, *Economics: Principles, Problems, and Policies*, 5th ed., New York: McGraw-Hill Book Company, 1972, especially Chapter 4.

of satisfaction by consuming additional units. He could get more additional satisfaction from the additional unit or units than he would forgo by not consuming something else. Note that the marginal cost is the value of that which is forgone. If the marginal cost exceeds the marginal utility, the individual can increase his satisfaction by consuming at least one unit less. (Can you explain why?)

This rule is readily applicable to production and consumption decisions involving, say, carrots or candy; but we suggest that it has a much broader application than may be first realized. If you are a student, what rule do you follow in determining how much you study for a given course? We expect that you will follow the $MC = MU$ rule developed above. You will continue to study until the marginal cost of an additional minute spent studying is equal to the marginal utility gained from studying that unit of time. If the marginal utility of an additional minute is greater than the marginal cost, is not this another way of saying that you would gain more by studying this particular course than doing whatever else you could do with the time? Would you, therefore, not study that additional minute?

In determining the length of her skirt, what rule does a woman follow? Again, we argue that she will shorten the skirt until the marginal utility of taking it up one additional inch is equal to the additional cost. (What are the costs and benefits of shortening the skirt?) For different people in the same situation and for the same people in different situations, the costs and benefits of a skirt's length are different. Therefore, we would anticipate a variety of skirt lengths.

Consider a person—yourself, if you like—who is preparing to eat dinner. What rule does he use in determining how many beans he will dish onto his plate? By now, you should have it; he will add beans to his plate until the marginal cost of the additional bean is equal to the marginal utility.

No individual is really able to act in as precise a manner as the above discussion may imply. He may not have the capacity to do so, and the benefits to be gained from such precision may not be worthwhile. (Explain.) Actually, we are interested only in making the point that the individual will approximate this kind of behavior.

When considering more than one good, say, two goods such as beer and pretzels, the utility-maximizing condition of $MC = MU$ translates into the following condition:

$$MU_b/P_b = MU_p/P_p$$

where

$$MU_b = \text{marginal utility of beer}$$
$$MU_p = \text{marginal utility of pretzels}$$
$$P_b = \text{price of beer}$$
$$P_p = \text{price of pretzels}$$

If this is not the case, and MU_b/P_b is greater than MU_p/P_p, then we can show that the person will not be maximizing his utility. No one really knows what a "util" of satisfaction is, but for purposes of illustration, let us assume that utils exist and that the additional satisfaction acquired from the last unit of beer (MU_b) is 30 utils, the additional satisfaction of the last unit of pretzels (MU_p) consumed is 10 utils, and that the price of both beer and pretzels is $1. It follows that

$$MU_b/P_b > MU_p/P_p \qquad (30/\$1 > 10/\$1)$$

The individual can change his consumption behavior, consume one less unit of pretzels and use the $1 to consume one additional unit of beer. He would give up 10 utils of satisfaction in the consumption of pretzels, but he would gain 30 utils of satisfaction in beer. He would be better off, and he would continue to reorganize his purchases until the equality set forth above is met. (You may find this a little tricky. Do not hesitate re-reading what you have just finished. It is imperative that you understand what has been said above before going ahead to the next point.)

Now, let us suppose that the individual has fully maximized his satisfaction and that $MU_b/P_b = MU_p/P_p$. Further, suppose that MU of beer and of pretzels is 20 utils and that the price of beer falls to, say, $.50 and the price of pretzels remains at $1. This means that the individual can get two units of beer (40 utils) for the price of one unit of pretzels; he can gain utility by switching to beer. Notice what we have said: *if the price of beer goes down, the rational individual will buy more beer.* This all falls out of our general assumption that the individual is simply out to maximize his utility.

This inverse relationship between price and quantity is extremely important in economic theory and in the analysis presented. It is so important that economists refer to it as the "law of demand." It is important because it adds predictive content to economic analysis. We can say with a great deal of confidence that if the price of a good or service falls, *ceteris paribus*, people will buy more of it. It is, perhaps, the strongest predictive statement a social

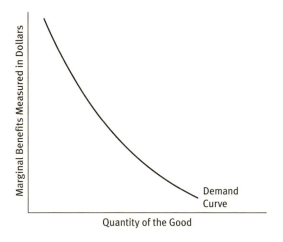

FIGURE 3

scientist can make with regard to human behavior.[7] The law of demand can be graphically depicted by a downward sloping curve as in Figure 3.

Courses in economics generally deal with the law of demand in the context of conventional goods and services such as peanut butter, detergent, and meals at a restaurant. Although we agree with such application, we wish to stress that the law has a much broader application. In fact, we go so far as to assert that the law of demand applies to anything which people value and the procurement of which is revealed in human behavior. Consequently, we argue that the law of demand is readily applicable to sex, honesty, dates, highway speeding, babies, and life itself! We predict that if the price of any one of these things goes up, the quantity demanded will diminish and vice versa.

We will spend much of our time in this book discussing how the law of demand applies to areas such as these; for purposes of illustration at this point, let us consider the demand for going to church. Many people do place a value on going to church, and as strange as it may seem, there is a price to church attendance. The church may not have a box office outside its doors selling tickets, but people have to pay the price of their time, and they do understand

7. The relationship is held with such complete confidence that one prominent economist has reportedly argued that if an empirical study ever reveals that people buy more when the price is increased, there must be something wrong with the empirical investigation. Other economists, taking a more moderate view, may recognize possible exceptions to the rule, but argue that they are extremely few.

that they are expected to contribute something to the operations of the church. (How many well-established people in the community would feel comfortable taking their families to church week after week without contributing anything to the church?) Through stewardship sermons and visitations, the church does apply pressure, as mild as it might be, to get people to contribute. To that extent they extract a price. Suppose the minister and the board of elders decide to raise significantly their demands on the congregation. What do you think will happen to the church's membership, holding all other things constant? The membership may be on the rise for a number of reasons. What we maintain is that because of the greater price, the membership will rise by less than otherwise. In that sense, the "price" increase reduces the membership. This does not necessarily mean that people would be less religious; it may only mean that some will react to the price change and make use of other ways of expressing and reinforcing their beliefs.

Suppose we return to the days when men were expected to be the ones who asked women out on dates. (In recent years, this social institution has broken down to a significant degree.) Given all the attributes of a given group of women, men placed, as they do now, some value on having dates with them. They, in other words, had a demand for dates. (In the event that you are concerned with the approach we are taking, we could easily reverse the example and talk about women's demand for dates. We only intend to use this situation as an example. We do not wish to judge it as being good or bad.)

Clearly, the utility-maximizing men will date women, if they can get the dates, until the marginal utility of the last date during some specified period of time is equal to the marginal cost of the date. There is a price for dating. For the man, if he is expected to bear the expense, it is equal to the money spent on transportation, the entertainment, and refreshment plus the value of the individual's time. (There is also a price to the woman.) Suppose that during this epoch when men were expected to pay for dates, a group of women collude; they get together and decide that the humdrum dates of yesterday are no longer up to their standards. They decide collectively to require the men to spend more on them. They, in effect, agree to raise the price of dates. If such a collusive arrangement were to stick, what do you think would have happened to the number of invitations issued to this group of women? No doubt it would fall. It may fall because the men would then have an incentive to substitute other women for the women that were taking part in the cartel. Additionally, the increase in price of dates can induce several men to consume other goods, such as watching Saturday night television or having a cold beer at a local tavern.

(As the number of calls for dates begins to fall off, there would very likely be women who would begin to chisel on the collusive agreement by effectively lowering their demands [i.e., price]. Thus, the agreement would tend to break down. Competition, as we will see on a number of occasions, will play a role in determining exactly what demands are made in areas of social interaction.)

Many people value speeding in their cars. If caught speeding they may pay a fine of, say, $50. If they expect to be caught one out of every hundred times that they speed, the price they pay per time speeding averages out to $.50. Given this price, they will find a certain quantity of speeding desirable. Suppose, now, that the fine is raised to $10,000 per speeding conviction. The average price paid per time speeding would then rise to $100. Do you think that the people would speed less, as the concept of demand predicts? (Suppose that the probability of being caught is increased. This can be accomplished by putting more patrolmen on the roads. What would be the effect?)

Supply and Demand

Measuring marginal costs and benefits in terms of dollars, we can draw both the demand and supply (i.e., marginal cost) curves on the same graph (see Figure 4). In taking this step we have constructed an *abstract* model of human behavior, but one that can be quite revealing and useful in many

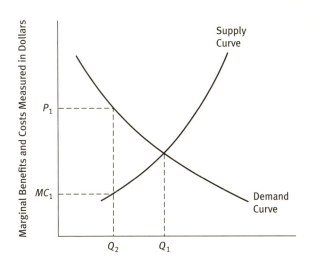

FIGURE 4

contexts. We will repeatedly demonstrate this throughout the book. For now, we need only point out that the maximizing individual will choose to produce and consume Q_1 units of this particular good. It does not matter what the good is or where the curves are positioned; the individual will choose that consumption level at the intersection of the two curves. It is at this point that marginal cost is equal to marginal utility. If the individual chooses to restrict his consumption to Q_2, note that the marginal benefit, which is indicated by the demand curve and represented by P_1, is greater than the marginal cost, which is indicated by the supply curve and is MC_1. This is true of every unit between Q_2 and Q_1. Therefore, the maximizing individual can raise his utility by consuming them. Beyond Q_1, the reverse is true; the marginal cost is greater than the marginal benefit. (Can you see this?)

Quite often, people find that it is less costly to trade with someone else than to produce the good themselves. To understand a social setting in which there are many producers and consumers trading for a particular good, we need to construct a model involving a *market* supply curve and a *market* demand curve. We can derive a market supply curve by adding together what all producers are willing to offer on the market at each possible price. If each individual producer is willing to offer a larger quantity at higher prices, the market supply curve, like the individuals' supply curves, will be upward sloping.[8] To obtain the market demand curve, we can add the amounts demanded by all consumers at each and every price. Since the individuals' demand curves are downward sloping, the same will be true of the market demand curve. The market supply and demand curves are depicted in Figure 5. The quantities involved in this graph are much greater than in Figure 4.

In a highly competitive market situation, one in which consumers have many sources for obtaining a given good, we will still expect the market to offer that quantity of the good (Q_1) which is at the intersection of the market supply and market demand curves. The simple reason is that if only Q_2 units (which is less than Q_1) are provided on the market, there will be many more units demanded (Q_3) than will be available (Q_2). Also, note that there are consumers who are willing to offer the producers a price that exceeds the marginal cost of producing the additional units. As a result, the suppliers can be induced to expand their production from Q_2 to Q_1. Beyond Q_1, the marginal

---

8. Strictly speaking, the market supply curve is not equal to the horizontal summation of the individuals' supply curves. Nothing is lost for our purposes, however, by leaving this refinement for more advanced treatments of the theory of supply.

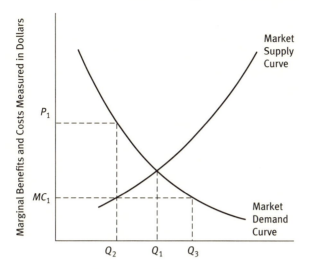

FIGURE 5

cost of providing an additional unit is greater than what any consumer is willing to pay for it. If one producer refuses to expand production to Q_1, the consumers can, since we are talking about a competitive market, turn to other producers who may be in the market or may be enticed into it. In a monopoly market, one in which there is only one producer of the good, the consumers do not have the option of turning to another producer (i.e., competitor). To that extent, the monopolist has control over the market: he can restrict the number of units provided and thereby demand a higher price from the consumer. By restricting output, the monopolist can reduce his total cost of production and can receive greater revenues. (Why?)

Similarly, suppose that the suppliers offer more than Q_1. The only way they can justify doing that is to charge a price higher than what consumers are willing to pay. Note that at Q_3 the marginal cost of the last unit is greater than the price the consumers are willing to pay for it. There will, as a result, be more units offered than will be purchased by consumers. Hence, the suppliers will be in a dilemma. Either they can cut back on production and lower the price to the point that consumers will buy what is produced, or they can continue to produce more than can be sold at the price necessary to cover the cost of production. The suppliers can also produce the good and sell it at a price less than the cost incurred. Which option do you think the rational producers will choose? They will cut production back to Q_1, of course. To the extent that the competitive market produces where marginal cost equals marginal benefit, which is the optimizing condition of individuals as explained above, economists say that it is "efficient."

Now that we have outlined the basic framework of the economist's model, we can use it to consider *changes* in market conditions (meaning environmental, social, or whatever). We consider such changes in the discussion of most topics in this book.

Concluding Comments

How a person views the world and interprets the information he receives from it depends upon the preconceived model he has of it. The preceding has been an outline of how the economist perceives the real world. For sure, this has been an incomplete description of the economist's way of thinking; there are many more refinements that can be made. (Because of space restrictions a book of this nature forces upon the authors, we have attempted to extend and refine the model until we thought the marginal benefits of an additional point were equal to the marginal cost of making the point.)

Because of this model—because of the concepts of supply and demand—the economist never thinks in terms of absolutes, of whether or not something will be done or left undone, or whether or not a goal will be sought. Everything has a price at which it may be obtained, and adjustments in behavior are made according to the price (benefits) that is charged (received). By concentrating on the general goal of utility maximization (and when talking about the firm, profit maximization) rather than on specific objectives, the economist is continually seeking out new and non-obvious alternatives and thinking in terms of the substitutability, on the margin, of specific means of reaching the general goal. Years of life are, therefore, viewed as a possible substitute for cigarette smoking; low-quality medical service in large quantities is one alternative to high-quality service in more limited quantities; ice cream is a possible substitute for good dental care. Because the economist views the individual as fundamentally seeking ways of gaining, whenever a person proposes a solution for any problems, the economist instinctively asks: Are there private interests involved? The economist is trained to separate private interests from the fabric of proposals offered as solutions for social concerns, and he is trained to pull out value judgments from arguments that are put forth as matters of logic. The economist's proclivity to think in this way sets him and his discipline apart from others.

PART 2

THE NEW WORLD
OF ECONOMICS

MARRIAGE, DIVORCE, AND THE FAMILY

Richard B. McKenzie and Gordon Tullock

The family is generally considered to be the basic building block on which social order is founded. However, even with all the attention that social scientists and others have given it, the family remains perhaps one of the least understood institutions. The purpose of this chapter is to develop insights into the marriage and family processes. Our approach is somewhat unusual. Certainly we recognize the importance of "love" in marriage and the family. However, we also recognize that in considering the establishment of a family, individuals are driven by a variety of motives. Some of these are not fundamentally different from those that lead people to buy a car or new clothes.

In addition, we will treat the family in its function as a producing unit. It is a "firm" that takes resources, including labor from within the family and the goods that are purchased, and produces things desired by family members. We want to look inside the family unit and analyze its behavior in terms of the behavior of its members. In the process we are able to make observations regarding the importance of the marriage contract, the difficulty of divorce, the economic implications of "love," and organizational principles underlying the family structure.[1]

The Marriage Contract and Divorce

Marriage can be defined in many different ways,[2] but for our purposes we view it as a contract between a man and woman (or between two parties of the same sex if homosexual marriages are ever legalized). Each party explicitly

Reprinted, with permission, from *The New World of Economics: Explorations into Human Experience* (Homewood, Ill.: Richard D. Irwin, 1975), 95–107.

1. Because of his pioneering efforts, we are indebted to Gary Becker for his work in the area. Gary S. Becker, "A Theory of Marriage: Part I," *Journal of Political Economy*, 81 (July/August 1973), 813–46, and "A Theory of Marriage: Part II," *Journal of Political Economy*, 82, supplement (March/April 1974), s11–s26.

2. Webster's defines marriage as "the institution whereby men and women are joined in a special kind of social and legal dependence for the purpose of founding and maintaining a family" (*Webster's Seventh New Collegiate Dictionary*, Springfield, Mass.: G&C Merriam Company, 1967).

or implicitly makes certain commitments as to his or her responsibilities within the family. He and she agree to recognize certain rights and privileges of the other, and both agree, again explicitly or implicitly, to a set of rules by which household decisions and changes in the contract are to be made. This last provision is necessary because not all issues concerning the relationship are ever likely to be settled before the vows are said and because conditions do change.

Such provisions of the contract may only be vaguely understood and recognized as such; but nevertheless, they are generally present in one fashion or another. The couple may simply have an understanding that they will "work things out together," tacitly realizing from their knowledge of the other's behavior what this means. The "process of marriage" may be compared to the development of a constitution and bylaws for any firm or organization; and as in the case of any one organization, the rules of the game can be as restrictive or as flexible as the people involved desire. In fact, the central purpose of dating and engagement may be to give the couple a chance to work out such provisions and to develop the contract by which both agree to live. (All couples do not, however, avail themselves of this chance to the same degree.) The contract, for example, may incorporate a provision on whether or not to have children and how many children, who will do the housework and mow the lawn, and which decisions will be democratically determined by the whole family and which decisions will be administratively determined. Although we might like to think that everything regarding the marriage *should* hinge on love, the division of the responsibilities and rewards may be greatly influenced by the relative bargaining power of the two involved.

Without the opportunity to develop such provisions, or if they are left undetermined, considerable disagreement can arise in the future, resulting in divorce. Because people have different views on what a marriage should be, the marriage may never take place, and very often does not. This is because the couple involved cannot agree on what the contract should be. In this sense the dating process screens out some of those marriages that will otherwise fold. Resources are used in dating, but at the same time the process saves resources from being tied up (albeit temporarily) in an unsatisfactory marriage.

Divorce can often be the result of insufficient resources (time, energy, and emotional hassle) being invested by the couple in developing the marriage contract. This may be because the two misjudged how many resources are required; it may also be that either or both of the parties calculate that the expected gain from spending more time and energy on the contract will not be worth the cost.

Except in the case of divorce, most provisions of the marriage contract generally do not have the force of law. Occasionally, there are cases in which a wife or husband takes her or his spouse to court (e.g., for lack of support), but these are indeed relatively rare events. One reason is that the mutually agreed-upon contract is vague and rarely written down. Another is that the cost of one spouse's taking the other to court can be considerable in terms of time and lawyers' fees and can be easily greater than any benefits that may be achieved. So many of the violations of the contract are of a trivial nature, such as one party's refusal to take out the garbage, to spend time with the children, or to refrain from flirting with other men or women. The potential benefits are just not that great, even if the court will consider the case. In addition, the court fight itself, which may generate a great deal of antagonism, can represent considerable cost.

If the provisions have any meaning, it is mainly because of the moral obligation such agreement engenders, the pressures that can be brought to bear on the parties involved by either party or by friends and others, and the threat of one party's retaliating by shirking his/her responsibilities. The main role of the court has generally been one of refereeing the division of the family assets (children included) between the husband and wife at the time of divorce. On occasion the court does attempt to bring about reconciliation.

This role of the court in the divorce process is one that is not unimportant and without economic implications. The reason is that the court's intrusion insures that the husband and wife both have *some* property rights in the family assets, both tangible and intangible. To this extent, the husband and wife have a greater incentive to "invest" their time and other resources in the development of family assets and in building a strong marital relationship. The family is an investment project in the sense that returns can be received over the span of years.

An analogy of an investment in a business is useful here. Suppose an entrepreneur is considering an investment in an office building. Will he be willing to make the investment if he knows that after doing so he has no property rights to the building—that is, someone else can take it over without any objection from the courts? Although he may be willing to make some investment in the enterprise and to protect it, he will probably be more willing to do so and to invest a larger amount if he has some rights that are protected by the state. The whole investment project will be less costly to him. The same can be applied to the willingness of the partners in a marriage to invest in the union. To the extent that the stability and durability of the marriage are favorably affected by such investments, the legal status of the marriage yields benefits to all parties in the family.

There is one problem here. That is, by giving each partner property rights over the family assets and, to some extent, over the other and by making the dissolution of the marriage costly, the husband or wife *can*, if he or she desires, abuse the other. Since there is a cost involved in divorce, one may allow himself or herself to be "exploited" because he/she may then be better off than if he/she incurs the cost. If the abuse is greater than the cost of going through with divorce, it goes without saying that the marriage will be dissolved. If the parties are single and living together, any one party can walk away without legal constraints. This may force the other party to be more considerate.

The Costs and Benefits of Marriage and the Family

In the sense that all behavior is *rational*, people's behavior with regard to marriage must also be rational. (Can you think of any reason we should assume differently?) This, of course, means that in choosing a spouse, both sexes are out to maximize their utility. It also means that in the process of becoming married, each individual must address two fundamental questions:

1. What are the costs and benefits in general of being married as opposed to remaining single?
2. Given these benefits and costs, how long and hard should he or she search for an appropriate mate?

THE COSTS OF MARRIAGE

In assessing the pros and cons of marriage, the individual must reckon with several major cost considerations. One of the most important for some but by no means all persons is the loss (cost) of independence. An individual is never completely free to do exactly what he pleases; he must consider the effects his actions have on others. However, in the proximity of the family, the possible effects which any one person's action can have on another in the family are more numerous and direct than for the person who lives alone. The result can be that everyone may willingly agree to restrict their own behavior to a much greater extent than would be necessary if they all lived alone. They may, and very likely will, also agree to make many decisions by democratic or collective action. In taking this step, the members of the household essentially agree to incur future decision costs, which include the time and trouble of reaching a decision. This is because it is generally more costly to make decisions with a larger number of people involved.

For example, it is more costly for one of the authors, McKenzie, who is married, to purchase a new car than for Tullock, who is single. All Tullock has to do in buying a car is consider his own preferences. McKenzie, on the other hand, must consider not only his own preference, but also those of his wife and children. The result can be, and almost always is, that buying a car is a long-drawn-out process for the McKenzies. Note that if McKenzie and his wife had identical preferences, which, to be sure, is never the case in marriages, their decision cost would be the same as Tullock's. In such an event, McKenzie would not have to bring his wife in on the decision to buy the car or anything else, and she would not care that he did not. Because of identical preferences, they both could be assured that whatever he bought, each would like it as well as the other. We have used just one example of the numerous times in which decision costs are incurred in a family. (If the reader thinks that such costs are unimportant, he should try marriage for a convincing empirical study!)

It is because of such decision costs that husbands and wives often agree to have many decisions made administratively by one party or the other. One party can be allowed, without consulting the other, to make decisions with respect to, say, the family meals, except under unusual circumstances. The other party can determine what clothes will be purchased for the children and what types of flowers to plant in the yard. Each party may make decisions not agreeable with the other; however, the savings in decision costs can yield benefits that more than offset the effects of "wrong" decisions.

Wives often have the responsibility of making decisions with respect to meals and the interior of the house in general, and husbands make decisions with respect to the yard and the exterior of the house, and this fact has been attributed to inculturated values; that is, spouses are merely role-playing. Although there may be some truth in the statements, we suggest that such argument does not explain why the responsibilities for decisions are divided in the first place. Our analysis indicates that the division of decision-making power within the home can be added efficiency to the operation of the household and that if roles are not assumed to begin with, they would tend to evolve. The division of powers may not end up in the same way that we now observe them, but given what they are, there may then be the criticism that inculturated roles are being assumed.

As suggested above, the family is involved to a considerable extent in the production of goods and services shared by all members of the family. These are basically of one type and available in one quantity and quality. Such a good—take, for example, the car considered above—may not be perfectly suitable for any one individual's tastes, but it is the good everyone agrees to buy. In this instance, and there are many of them, each individual must bear the cost of not getting the good in the amount and quality that are most suitable to his preferences.

This type of cost not only is incurred because of the goods produced by the family—such as cars, television programs, recreation, and "family life" (which tends to defy definition)—but is also applicable to relationships with other people. Both spouses may agree to associate with certain people, not because either finds the people to be *best* suited to what they find desirable in friends, but because the selected friends represent compromises for them both. This is not to say that each person will not have several friends of his/her own, but only that they are likely to agree on "mutual friends." To the extent that they associate with their mutual friends, there is less time for them to be with their individual friends. We submit that this can be a legitimate cost calculation in marriage.

To the extent that household decisions are democratically determined, members of the household have a say on how the burden of the production of the household goods is to be distributed. In this way they can determine who pays, either in terms of contribution of money income or time, and effort. The family can effectively "tax" family members in a way that is similar to any other collective, governmental entity. Any family member can, like any citizen, be forced to pay for collective goods and projects with which they may not be in perfect agreement. This can be considered a potential cost to a family member. This is evident from the complaints that one may hear in a home when the decision is made to go on a picnic and the burden of preparation is distributed, or when one is asked to take out the garbage or mow the lawn.

Other costs associated with marriage and the family in general include the risk cost of developing strong emotional ties with one specific group of individuals and the forgoing of the opportunity to date and in other ways associate with other people. These factors may be of no consequence to some, and may in fact be an advantage to others. Further, the cost of marrying one particular person can be the loss of the opportunity to have married someone else who is not known at the time of marriage but who, if he/she were sought out, would be a more desirable spouse. The list of cost provided can, of course, be extended.

THE BENEFITS OF MARRIAGE AND FAMILY

The benefits of marriage and the family are derived mainly from the ability of the family to produce goods and services wanted. First, the spouses have the opportunity to produce things not readily duplicated in non-marriage situations. Such a list may include children (at least ones that cannot legitimately be called bastards), prestige and status that can affect employment and the realm of friends, companionship that is solid and always there, a "family-styled sex life" that may be more desirable than sexual associations of which the individual may disapprove, and "family life" in general, which we indicated above defies definition. Granted, many of these goods can be had in certain quantities and qualities outside of the family; we are only suggesting that they take on special characteristics within the family and for that reason are valuable to people. (We recognize that to some these are costs.)

Secondly, the family operating as a single household—that is, more than one individual—can produce many goods and services more efficiently than can several single-person households. This is because there are economics of scale in household production. Take, for example, the problem of cleaning the household rug. Although there may be some selection in size and power of vacuum cleaners, generally speaking, the machines available are capable of handling the dirt of several people. However, *one* cleaner must be *purchased*. If more people are added to the house, the household need not increase the number, size, or power of the vacuum cleaner proportionally. The same can be said of many of the resources that go into the production of a garden, meals, and other household goods such as washing machines, rakes, mixers, brooms, electric toothbrushes.

Indeed, many of the goods and services provided by individuals in the home are *public goods*: they benefit everyone involved and do not diminish in quantity or quality if additional people are added to the household. For example, many things done to beautify the house are this kind of good. If a picture that all like is hung on the wall, one person's enjoyment of it does not detract in any significant way from the enjoyment by others. Because they all live under the same roof, they do not have to provide such goods for themselves individually, meaning that they can raise the quality of the goods that are had or they can divert resources to other purposes. Such goods may not be enjoyed or appreciated by a very large group of people, and because of the decision costs involved, as explained, there is some point at which the collective group would be too large. Therefore, we would expect some unit in society to develop that would be small enough that people of similar tastes can be together to have them and large enough that they can be provided efficiently. The family, in our view, is that unit. It is large enough to provide such goods as these efficiently yet small enough that the decision costs incurred are minimized. By having provision for numerous such family units, individuals are given considerable choice over the type, amount, and quality of these goods.

The efficiency of household production can also be greater because of the opportunities for the parties to specialize and effectively trade with one another. In this way the parties can take advantage of their comparative efficiency in production. Suppose, for simplicity's sake only, that there are only two things for the household to do, clean a given size house and mow its lawn which is of a given size. Suppose also that we are given the following information about the abilities of a husband and wife in doing these two things:

	CLEANING THE HOUSE	MOWING THE LAWN
Wife	60 minutes	100 minutes
Husband	100 minutes	300 minutes

What this table shows is that the wife can clean the house in 60 minutes and can mow the lawn in 100 minutes. It takes the husband 100 minutes for the house and 300 minutes for the lawn. If they both live separately and have lawns to mow and houses to clean, it would take them a total of 560 minutes. If they lived together and each cleaned half the house and mowed half of the lawn, it would take them a total of 280 minutes (80 minutes for the house cleaning and 200 minutes for the lawn). However, there is a possibility here for the two to specialize, one cleaning the house and one mowing the lawn. Since each will be doing something for the other, we can, in a sense, say they are trading.

To see this prospect, recognize that every time the wife cleans the house she gives up 3/5 of the lawn being mowed. If she spends 60 minutes on the house, those are minutes she cannot be mowing the lawn. Since it takes her 100 minutes to mow the lawn, we can assume that she could have mowed 3/5 of the lawn. On the other hand, each time the husband cleans the house, he gives up 1/3 of the lawn being mowed. (Why?) We can thereby argue that it is more costly (in terms of the portion of the lawn not mowed) for the wife to clean the house.

If we want the cost of production to be minimized, we would then argue that the wife should mow the lawn, the husband clean the house. If they do this, the total time spent by both of them would be 200 minutes. If the wife cleans the house and the husband mows, the total time would be 360 minutes.

Notice what we have demonstrated here: with the family under one common roof, the cost of the goods demanded by the members can be minimized by the husband and wife specializing and effectively trading. Notice also that we have made this demonstration even though one spouse, the wife, is actually more efficient in the production of both the mowed lawn and the cleaned house. By specializing, the wife and husband can also avoid many of the costs associated with developing the same skills. Each can concentrate his/her attention on a more limited number of household tasks, improving the efficiency with which they can be done.

This demonstration is important because it indicates that if husband and wife are interested in maximizing household production or minimizing the cost of household production, which amounts to the same thing, then they will specialize to some degree in the functions of the household. They will have what many derogatively call *roles*. However, *these roles need not be what they presently are*. Further, it indicates that certain roles may be assumed by, say, the wife not because she is necessarily less efficient than the husband in the production of those things which the husband does, but rather because her comparatively greater efficiency lies in what she does.[3] The same is true for the husband. To acquire the efficiency benefits described here, the husband and wife need to have the appropriate preferences for the assigned tasks.

Furthermore, if the decision facing the family is the allocation of members' time between work internal to the home and work external to the home and if the family is interested in minimizing the cost of goods produced in the home, then it should use that labor with the lowest value outside of the home. The cost of cleaning the house is equal to the cost of the materials and supplies and the value of the individual's time outside the home who does the cleaning. Assume that it takes two hours to clean the house, that the wage the wife can earn outside the home is $3 per hour, and that the wage of the

---

3. If the wife takes as much as 180 minutes to mow the lawn, and everything else about the example above is the same, it would still be most efficient for the wife to mow the lawn and for the husband to cook the meals.

husband is $5 per hour. (Here, we are only attempting to use a realistic example; it is a fact, which is the subject of considerable complaint by women, that husbands do tend to earn more than their wives.) It follows that it would be cheaper for the wife to do the cleaning. If the man did the cleaning it would cost an additional $4 since his wage is $2 per hour higher.[4]

Many sociologists and psychologists contend that roles are assumed within the house, such as for child care, because of socially determined values. We are unwilling to argue that such forces have *no* effect on the organization of many households. All we wish to add is that much of what we observe in household relationships may very often be the result of a conscious, rational choice on the part of the couples. Clearly, women do tend to earn less than men in the market, a point made above and in Chapter 6, either because they are the victims of discrimination or because they are less productive. Given this, which is not something individual households can do much about, it is reasonable to expect households to delegate many responsibilities, such as child care, to wives. In this way, the cost of the child care is minimized, and the output of the family is maximized. If the household production is greater by the wife staying at home, then one can suggest that the output of the wife is actually greater than what is indicated by her work in the home; she should get some credit for the greater output of the household.

If discrimination which women face outside of the home is reduced and/or they are able to raise their productivity relative to men, we should expect their wages to rise relative to their husbands'. We should then expect to see more and more wives working outside the home and *relatively* more time being spent by husbands in housework. It is clear that the labor force participation rate of women has been on the rise over the decades. There are many reasons for this, including changes in attitudes of men and women toward women working in jobs; the greater wages of women can be another explanatory factor.

---

4. The same allocation of wife- and husband-time would result if the wife is substantially more efficient in the production of household goods. Consider the case of the wife being able to earn $5 per hour and the husband earning $3 per hour. Suppose that it takes the wife an hour to do some household task and it takes the husband two hours. If the husband stayed at home to do it, it would cost the family $6 (two hours at $3 per hour). However, it would only cost them $5 (one hour at $5 per hour) for the wife to do it. In such a case the family would choose to have the wife stay at home if it was interested in minimizing production costs. Inculturated values would perhaps come into play as an explanatory factor if the couple did not obey rules for time allocation that have been developed.

There are other possible benefits to marriage and the family, like the benefit of making communication less expensive. Communication is an important aspect of any production process. (Can you name other benefits?)

Spouse Selection

The rational individual, in search of a spouse, will attempt to maximize his utility as he does in all other endeavors. He will not pretend to seek the "perfect mate," but only that one individual among those whom he knows and who are willing to marry him that *best* (not perfectly) suits his preferences. (Whom do you know who has married the *perfect person*?) This means that he will seek to minimize the cost incurred through marriage and the family.[5] If he/she marries someone who agrees with him/her, the cost associated with arriving at the marriage contract is less than otherwise. There is not as great a need for (implicit) bargaining. If he/she marries someone who agrees with him/her as to what the family should do, what kinds of recreation they should have, and the number of children and the way in which they should be reared, then the cost of having to give up friends and goods that suit his/her preferences better will be minimized. In other words, we would expect rational individuals to tend to marry persons who have similar values and preferences and who are in other ways like themselves. Interestingly enough, this is generally what researchers have found.[6]

Rational behavior has other implications with regard to search for a mate. It implies that the greater the benefits from marriage, the greater the costs that a person will be willing to incur in searching for the spouse. This means that the greater the efficiency benefits that are to be achieved in family production or the greater the esteem people give those who marry, the more costs, in terms of time and effort, that a person will apply in looking. Greater costs may take the form of later marriages and a smaller fraction of the population married. Also, the longer the individual expects the marriage to last and the more stable he expects it to be, the more careful he will be in his search. This does

---

5. In searching for a mate, he will extend his search until the marginal cost extending the search is equal to the marginal benefits.

6. See, for example, R. F. Winch, *Mate Selection*, New York: Harper and Row, 1958. This conclusion, of course, does not apply to the situation in which one party prefers a mate who will dominate him/her.

not mean that mistakes will not be made; it only means that greater costs will be incurred in trying to avoid mistakes.

It also follows that the difficulty (cost) of divorce should affect the extent to which people search for a spouse.[7] It may affect the extent to which people marry, the extent of more informal arrangements, and the availability and economic well-being of prostitution as an institution. If a divorce is made impossible, a person knows that if he chooses the "right" person then there are more benefits to be had than if divorce were easier to come by. The impossibility of divorce will assure him/her that his/her spouse cannot freely marry someone else whom he/she may later prefer. If, on the other hand, he/she chooses the "wrong" person, the impossibility of divorce will mean that the decision would carry with it greater cost than if the marriage could be easily dissolved by divorce. Therefore, as Gary Becker has argued, we would expect the resources applied to search for a mate, to be directly correlated with the difficulty of obtaining a divorce, and he writes that "Search may take the form of trial living together, consensual unions, or simply prolonged dating. Consequently, when divorce becomes easier, the fractions of the persons legally married may actually *increase* because of the effect on the age at marriage."[8] Alan Freiden has in part corroborated this hypothesis by demonstrating in a cross-state study the effects of different state divorce laws. He found that the more costly the divorce process, the smaller was the fraction of women married.[9]

If divorce is made easier, this line of analysis indicates that people will tend to incur fewer search costs, perhaps reflected in a declining age at which people marry; and aside from the experience of the last few years, the age at which men and women marry has generally been on the decline. One might reasonably assume that the durability of marriages in general is positively related to the extent to which people search the "marriage market" before they choose *the* one. If this can be accepted, and it might be a poor assumption, then making divorce easier can result in more divorces because they are less costly and also because people are expending fewer resources in search of a spouse and, therefore, making more wrong choices.

7. Becker, "A Theory of Marriage: Part II," s22–s23.

8. Ibid., s22.

9. Alan Freiden, "The United States Marriage Market," *Journal of Political Economy*, 82, supplement (March/April 1974), s34–s54.

The Implications of Love

For our purposes we say that a person "loves" another if his or her level of satisfaction is in part dependent upon the satisfaction level of the other person.[10] In this sense one person genuinely "cares" for the other person and cares what happens to him (or her). This is because he (or she) will have greater utility if it is known that the other person is in some sense better off. He will, therefore, be motivated to help improve the situation of the person who is loved. The more intense the "love" the stronger is this motivation.

As we have explained, responsibilities are typically delegated to family members, and each member is dependent upon the others fulfilling their end of the bargain. In this way the welfare of the family members will diminish if any one member shirks his responsibilities.[11] Because shirking hurts others, the person who loves the others will be less inclined to shirk than the person who does not. It is for this reason that a person, if given the choice, would naturally want to marry someone who loves him. He would also naturally want to marry someone whom he loves, because what he does for the family will also give him satisfaction to the extent that it makes everyone better off.

Where love does not exist, we will be more likely to find individuals shirking family responsibilities.[12] This in turn means that family resources will have to be diverted into the "policing" of family members. In this way love has an economic dimension. This does not mean that a person will not marry someone he does not love or who does not love him. Because of the benefits of being in a family situation, the person may prefer that to the single life. Many people do marry for money as well as for other benefits.

All of this adds up to one interesting conclusion, and that is that the *efficient* marriage is one in which the two are in love and are, in terms of values and preferences, alike. Oddly enough, this is what most people would readily argue. The interesting thing about this conclusion is that it is derived from the perspective of economics and the family as a producing unit. The

10. Here we are following Gary Becker in defining "love." The central point we make is also his. See "A Theory of Marriage: Part II," s12–s17.

11. A person can "shirk" by failing to carry out any part of the contract or by making it more difficult (costly) for the other person to see that the contract is obeyed.

12. In the jargon of economics, love can be said to internalize the externalities generated from family living.

greater the "love" and the closer the preferences of the couple, the closer will the marriage approximate what may be considered the ideal. However, in the realistic world in which we live, it is clear that the maximizing individual does not always have the opportunity to choose a spouse who both loves him and has similar preferences, or at least to any great degree. He must often choose between a person who may love him very little, but who may be in many ways like himself, and the person who loves him, but who is very unlike himself. All the individual can do is maximize over the range of opportunities he has.

The discussion suggests that love adds to the efficiency of the household; we also argued earlier that differences in preferences can detract from the efficiency with which the household is operated. If this is the case and the individual is seeking to maximize the output from being in a family, then we must conclude that love is not all that is necessary for a successful family and marriage. Marriages have been known to break up in which the parties professed to love each other dearly; the problem was that they violently disagreed over what the marriage should be and do and the roles that each was to play. The gulf in preferences could have been so wide that the love, as intense as it was, could not bridge it. This seems to be fairly descriptive of the marriage and breakup of Cher and Sonny Bono, who during the 1973–74 television season had one of the top ten programs. They broke up telling reporters that they still loved each other but that they both had such markedly different interests that they had to go their own ways. In the same way we might expect that many marriages are held together with little love, but because their preferences are so much alike, they still find their relationship very beneficial, at least given their next best opportunities.

Concluding Comment

Marriage and the family are terribly complex subjects to discuss, and the readers probably detect there is a lot that has been left unsaid. We definitely agree. We believe that the field is wide open for future research. This has only been a sample of what economists are beginning to say about such basic social institutions, and we think that the economic approach shows great promise of contributing much to our understanding of the subject.

CHILD PRODUCTION

Richard B. McKenzie and Gordon Tullock

Children may be "little darlings" in their parents' eyes, but they are also economic goods. They can provide considerable benefits to their parents and relatives, and they are the result of a continuously evolving production process. This process involves resource expenditures like everything else that is produced in the home.[1]

Children as Economic Goods

From children parents obtain a good deal of companionship, resulting in benefits not unlike those received from other goods, such as a new car or a good martini. Children can be someone to talk to or go on a walk with, and they can be ready-made partners for a game of Ping-Pong or checkers (if one can bear the hassle of getting them to do it). Their existence gives parents some hope that they will not be left alone later in life. Children also provide parents with the pleasure that comes from being respected and needed and, at least at some stages of a child's development, adored by someone else. There are very few parents who are not touched when their small children run to them when they return from work or a trip. Rightly or wrongly, children are used to fulfill parents' goals and to extend themselves beyond their own physical limitations. By having children parents are able to negate the unspoken criticism of relatives and friends that they are incapable of having or in some way loving them. The motivation for having children may include a means of fulfilling a sincerely felt need to make a contribution to society, to explore the unknown, or to test the hypothesis that they can do a better job in rearing children than others.

Reprinted, with permission, from *The New World of Economics: Exploration into the Human Experience* (Homewood, Ill.: Richard D. Irwin, 1975), 108–23.

1. We are again indebted to Gary Becker for his work in the economics of fertility, which underpins the discussion in this chapter and the work of many other economists. Gary S. Becker, "An Economic Analysis of Fertility," in *Demographic and Economic Change in Developed Countries*, Princeton: Princeton University Press, 1960, 209–40. For a critical evaluation of this literature, see Harvey Leibenstein, "An Interpretation of the Economic Theory of Fertility: Promising Path or Blind Alley?" *Journal of Economic Literature*, 12 (June 1974), 457–70.

Children at one time in our history, and this is still true in many undeveloped areas of the world, were a means by which parents could develop their own old-age pension plan. As the children grew up, parents paid into the plan by feeding and clothing their children; in later years, the children took care of their parents when they were unable to provide for themselves. This, incidentally, was at a time when security markets and insurance companies were not very well developed, particularly in newly opened territories. This kind of arrangement has not completely dissipated; however, for the most part, today people in the industrialized countries rely much more heavily on the impersonal financially based retirement plans for old-age income. The reason may be in part due to the fact that the market has provided alternative retirement schemes that are cheaper than those incorporated in children. As we will see, children can be extremely expensive. Further, the benefits in the financially based plans are contractual and to that degree are more certain or less risky. Another reason may be that the government has forced people to become a part of the social security system which may have contributed to reduced reliance on children for retirement maintenance.

Last but not least, children can be an important source of labor, particularly for families living on farms and where child labor is less expensive than mechanization. The parents in the beginning stages of the children's lives "invest" resources in their growth and development in order that they can become workers. When the child is old enough to work, they reap the returns from their investment.

Granted, parents in general may not have children for the sole purpose of seeing them become good and loyal workers or for the purpose of gaining a sense of immortality. All of the benefits that can be listed are fused in the typical decision to have a child. But, this is true in the decision to buy a new car or house; there are a multiplicity of reasons for buying or producing almost anything. All of the benefits of having children that can be enumerated add up to one total level of parental satisfaction and, to that degree, to the parents' demand for children. This demand for children — or, perhaps more properly, "child services" — can be reflected in the total *number* of children that are had or in the *quality* of the children born and reared. The one thing that can be said at this point is that the greater the benefits reaped from children, the greater the number and/or quality of children that will be had. This assumes, of course, that the cost of the children is held constant and that parents, or at least some of them, look upon the decision to have children in the same rational way that they do everything else. Because some readers will doubt the reasonableness of this latter assumption, we will return to it later.

The cost of rearing a child includes the family expenditures on giving birth, food, clothing, shelter, education, entertainment, medical expenses, insurance, transportation, etc. Other major cost items, which are often overlooked, are the emotional drain and the value of the parents' time spent on rearing the child. Estimating the cost of children is a difficult problem at best. The actual cost of a child will depend on exactly how much the parents want to spend, and all costs will vary with the economic status and location of the parents. Given these problems, however, Ritchie Reed and Susan McIntosh have made estimates of a child reared on a "modest-cost" budget in an urban setting.[2] A summary of their estimates, by the education level of the mother, is included in Table 1. The cost of giving birth, which includes prenatal and hospital care and the maternity wardrobe of the mother, is estimated at $1,534 in 1969. The expenses associated with rearing the child until the age of 18 are estimated at $32,830. Reed and McIntosh made the simplifying assumptions that the parents' incomes and the prices of the things that go into determining these figures are held constant throughout the 18 years. The cost of four years of college education for the child is estimated at being $5,560 in a public institution. The total of these costs (referred to as "total direct costs" in the table) is $39,924, and they are held constant for all education levels of the mother. The reason for this is that Reed and McIntosh wanted to focus on the impact of the different educational levels of the mother.

The opportunity cost of the mother's time is dependent upon the wage she could have earned and the number of weeks she would have worked had she not had children. In the case of the mother who has an elementary school education, the estimated opportunity cost is $44,121. For the mother who had a four-year college education, the opportunity cost is estimated at $58,904.[3] This means that the total calculated cost for the first child is a whopping $84,045 for the mother with the elementary school education, and $98,828 for the mother with four years of college.[4] The marginal cost for each additional child is $46,497 and $48,867 for the mothers with the elementary

2. Ritchie H. Reed and Susan McIntosh, "Costs of Children," in *Economic Aspects of Population Change: The Commission on Population Growth and the American Future*, ed. Elliot R. Morss and Ritchie H. Reed, Washington, D.C.: Government Printing Office, 1972, 330–50. The authors in their report provide more detailed information than can be given here.

3. For a description of how these figures were determined see ibid., 341–44.

4. Note that we have not included an estimate for the opportunity cost of the father's time, the emotional drain, risk cost, or the cost which may be associated with the depreciation of the mother's market skills.

TABLE 1. *Total Cost of a Child by Educational Level of Mother, 1969*

TYPE OF COST	ALL WOMEN	ELEMENTARY	HIGH SCHOOL	COLLEGE, 4 YEARS OR LESS	COLLEGE, 5 YEARS OR MORE
Undiscounted					
Cost of giving birth	1,534	1,534	1,534	1,534	1,534
Cost of raising a child	32,830	32,830	32,830	32,830	32,830
Cost of a college education	5,560	5,560	5,560	5,560	5,560
Total direct costs*	39,924	39,924	39,924	39,924	39,924
Opportunity costs	58,437	44,121	58,904	58,904	103,023
Total costs of first child	98,361	84,045[†]	98,828	98,828	143,947
Marginal cost of each additional child spaced two years apart[‡]	48,793	46,497	48,867	48,867	55,939
Discounted					
Cost of giving birth	1,534	1,534	1,534	1,534	1,534
Cost of raising a child	17,576	17,576	17,576	17,576	17,576
Cost of a college education	1,244	1,244	1,244	1,244	1,244
Total direct costs*	20,354	20,354	20,354	20,354	20,354
Opportunity costs	39,273	29,647	39,583	55,419	69,001
Total costs of first child	59,627	50,001[†]	59,937	75,773	89,355
Marginal cost of each additional child spaced two years apart[‡]	28,924	26,701	28,995	32,652	35,841

* These costs may be somewhat overestimated because of possible duplication occurring when the cost of giving birth as calculated by perspective is added to the USDA figures on the cost of raising a child to age 18.

[†] For a woman with only an elementary school education, a low income figure for the cost of raising a child may be more appropriate. This would reduce the total discounted cost to $44,181 and the total undiscounted cost to $72,845.

[‡] Differs from cost of first child in that the opportunity cost and the cost of giving birth are less. For additional children, the $500 cost of nursery supplies is subtracted from the cost of giving birth to the first child.

SOURCE: Ritchie H. Reed and Susan McIntosh, "Costs of Children," in *Economic Aspects of Population Change: The Commission on Population Growth and the American Future*, ed., Elliot R. Morss and Ritchie H. Reed, Washington, D.C.: Government Printing Office, 1972, 345.

school education and college education, respectively. The reason the cost for the second and following child is lower than the cost for the first is mainly due to the fact that if the children are spaced closely together, the opportunity cost of the mother's time is not duplicated with additional children. Since 1969, prices have risen considerably, and if the same study were redone today, the figure would be substantially inflated. Clearly, the cost of a child is by most standards substantial.

The costs given above are the result of the simple summation of the expenditures made and the earnings forgone during the rearing phase of the child's life. However, $1,000 spent today is worth more than $1,000 spent several years in the future. The reason is that the $1,000 spent today can earn interest during the course of years if it is deposited in a savings account or invested in interest bearing securities. Therefore, to determine the *present value* of the expenditures made on the child and the earnings forgone in the future, Reed and McIntosh discounted the yearly costs by 8 percent, and the new cost figures are recorded in the lower half of Table 1. The result is that the *discounted* total cost is $50,001 for the mother who has an elementary school education and $75,773 for the mother with four years of college. The marginal cost of each additional child is reduced to $26,701 and $32,652, respectively. Certainly, for most people the first child is the biggest single "good" they are likely to buy during their life!

The Demand and Supply of Children

By pointing out the costs and benefits of children, the authors do not mean to imply that children are just like every other good a family purchases. There is substantially more risk and uncertainty in having a child than in buying a new house or almost anything else. Parents are not able to see the good (i.e., child) before they buy it; in fact, their task is to produce it from scratch. The child comes with a will of his own from birth, which adds an element of surprise, which is not a feature of a new house. In the case of the house, the buyers can sell if they decide later that it is not what they want, perhaps recouping their investment and then some. In modern American society, to do the same with a child is frowned upon.

All of this means that the decision to have a child is more difficult than other decisions a family confronts and that there is more room for error in child production than in the production of other things. It does not follow that some parents will not attempt to approach the problem with the same rational *intentions* that they approach everything else.

Parents may conceive a child they did not plan to have, because the momentary importance of sex was so great that they forgot to take the necessary precautions. This seems to be very likely if it is recognized that, based on a

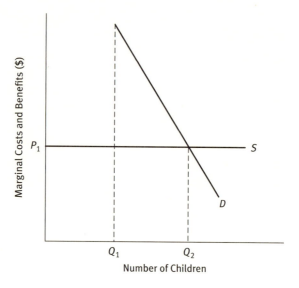

FIGURE 1

study in 1965, there are approximately two billion acts of sexual intercourse between married couples in the United States each year.[5] One could add a substantial number of acts between those who are unmarried. It is simply a matter of probability that some "goofs" will occur; no contraceptive is foolproof. To the degree that accidents occur, there will be children born and reared who are not the result of the conscious consideration of the expected costs and benefits. However, to the extent that there are parents who consider the costs and benefits in child-bearing decisions, the demand curve for children will be downward sloping. The cost of a child will influence the fertility level; more children will be had the lower the cost or price. Parents will, in addition, rationally balance off the numbers of children conceived with the quality.

In Figure 1 we have illustrated the total market demand for children (D). In our example Q_1 children will be born and reared because of impulsive or in other ways non-rational behavior on the part of parents. However, how many children will be had in total will depend also on the supply, which means cost, of children. If, for simplification, the supply of children is assumed to be

5. Leslie Aldridge Westoff and Charles F. Westoff, *From Now to Zero: Fertility, Contraception, and Abortion in America*, Boston: Little, Brown, and Company, 1971, 24. The estimate is based on a coital frequency of 6.7 times per month for all couples.

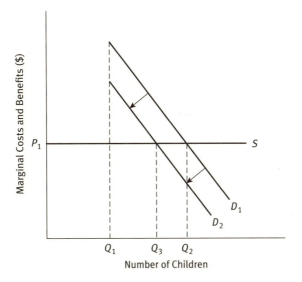

FIGURE 2

horizontal (S); that is, the marginal cost is constant at P_1, the total number of children had will be Q_2. Of this total, Q_1 will be the result of "accidents," and $Q_2 - Q_1$ will be the result of cost-benefit calculations.[6] If the reader is inclined to doubt our assumption that many child-bearing decisions are conscious rational acts, he should reflect on the number of times he has heard someone, or himself, say, "Not me! I can't afford to have another child. There is just not enough time in the day to handle the two that I've got." This is just another way of saying that the cost of the additional child is too great for the expected benefits. We might expect the people who make such statements often go to great extents trying to avoid conceiving again.

If the demand for children falls, the economist would predict that the number of children had will fall. This situation is described in Figure 2 by a shift in the demand curve from D_1 to D_2. The number of children drops from Q_2 to Q_3. The number of accidentally conceived children remains at Q_1; however, the number of "rationally determined" children falls, causing the drop in the total.[7]

6. It is quite likely that many of the births that are unplanned take the place of births that were planned for a later date. If this is the case, the demand curve will move in to the left to account for it. This does not affect the analysis.

7. The change causing the drop in the demand may make unwanted children *more* undesirable and may induce parents to take greater precautions in their coital relations.

This change in demand can result from an exogenous drop in people's "taste" for children. It can also result from a decrease in the relative prices of other goods produced and consumed in the home. If the latter happened, rational couples would tend to reallocate their resources toward the cheaper goods and away from children. It may be that one explanation for the declining birth rate has been the growing relative cheapness of goods, such as cars and all forms of entertainment, which may be substitutes for children.

In general, the location of the demand curve is dependent upon the *relative* benefits attributable to children and upon the family resources. Children who grow up on farms have many more opportunities to contribute to the family's income than the children who grow up in an urban setting. One explanation for this is the child labor laws which do not restrict children from working on farms but do restrict them from working in industry. For this reason alone economists would expect the benefits attributable to children and their parents' demand for children to be greater for farm families than for families living in the cities. In other words, the farm family's demand for children (D_1 in Figure 2) will be greater than the demand of urban families (D_2). The result is a tendency for farm families to be larger. If there is a migration of people from the farms to the cities, as there has been over the decades, one would expect birth rates to fall and the population growth rates to taper off somewhat. Interestingly, this is precisely what demographers and economists who have tested these hypotheses have found.[8]

Over time, if there is a reduction in the price of mechanized equipment, *ceteris paribus*, there may be a decrease in the size of farm families if the equipment can take the place of child labor. Cheaper farm equipment would encourage families to buy more equipment and use less labor, i.e., have fewer children.

The leftward shift in demand can also be the effect of the availability of cheaper and better contraceptives. Because they are cheaper we may anticipate more extensive use of them and fewer accidental births; the summation of the accidental plus rationally determined births would fall. Also, people's preferences for children may turn away from *numbers* to *quality*, causing the demand curve based on the number of children to shift in.

8. John D. Kasarda, "Economic Structure and Fertility: A Comparative Analysis," *Demography*, 8 (August 1971), 307–17; Stanley Kupinsky, "Non-Familial Activity and Socio-Economic Differentials in Fertility," *Demography*, 8 (August 1971), 353–67.

The reader should understand that for parents there is the ever-present decision between using their resources for the purpose of having more children and using them for the purpose of giving the number they have more attention: this can be reflected in what the parents consider a quality improvement.

We have concentrated in this section on a drop in demand for children, because that appears to us the current trend. The reader may want to extend the discussion himself by considering possible causes for an increase in demand and the consequences of such developments.

Given our model, anything that reduces the cost of children, *ceteris paribus*, will shift the supply curve downward and increase the number of children had. In the case of Figure 3, the supply goes from S_1 to S_2, and the number of children demanded goes from Q_2 to Q_3. The reason for the expansion is that prior to the cost reduction, the cost of the additional children, $Q_3 - Q_2$, exceeds the benefits indicated by the demand curve between Q_2 and Q_3. Once the supply curve shifts down, the benefits of the additional children become greater than the cost. It is therefore rational for the couple to divert more resources into child production.

Such a change may have been the consequence of an increase in efficiency of rearing children, making the whole process less costly. It may have also

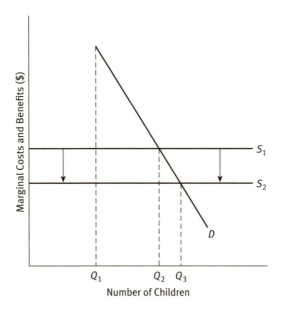

FIGURE 3

been attributable to a decrease in the prices of those resources purchased from the market that are peculiar to the production of children, or it may be attributable to changes in such exogenous forces as government policy.

As an example of a proposed change in government policy that can affect fertility rates, take the proposal of Senator Vance Hartke, who in 1974 introduced a bill to increase the personal exemption for federal income tax purposes. Senator Hartke argued that the allowable personal exemption of $750 is too low to accommodate the high cost of rearing a child today and that it should be raised to $1,000. Clearly, such a policy effectively lowers the cost of having children. If a person were in a tax rate bracket of 30 percent, Hartke's proposal reduces a person's tax liability by $75 ($250 × 30 percent) per year. In this way, the proposal reduces the cost of having a child by $1,350 (undiscounted) over the first 18 years of the child's life. This may not seem like much of a saving, since the undiscounted cost of an additional child can be upward of $50,000.

Even though such a change in the tax structure is not likely to have an effect on everyone's decision to have a child, it can affect those marginal couples whose estimated costs and benefits of having an additional child are very close or who are more or less indifferent to the idea of having a child but are inclined to hold off. For illustration, suppose a couple figures that with the $750 exemption per child the undiscounted marginal cost of the additional child is $50,000 and the marginal benefits are $49,500. Since the marginal cost is greater than the marginal benefit, the couple would not have the child. However, if the Hartke proposal is adopted the marginal cost will be lowered to $48,650, an amount less than the marginal benefits of $49,500. The passage of the higher exemption will give the green light to this couple and to others in a similar position. Such a change in the tax laws will tend to make slightly more difficult the problem of population control. Welfare payments tied to the number of children, including payments to unborn fetuses (an issue in the courts at the time of this writing, 1974), and public provision of education and day care centers can, in a similar manner, encourage population growth. In a similar way, high rates of inflation like those experienced in the United States in recent years reduce the *real* value of exemptions, thus increasing the total real costs of having children. (The above analysis actually applies to increases in the real value of personal exemptions.)

As seen in Table 1, the major cost in the rearing of a child is the opportunity cost of the parents' time. The higher the potential wage of the parents' time outside the home the higher is this component of the cost. The effect of greater cost can be to reduce the number of children had. This is illustrated in

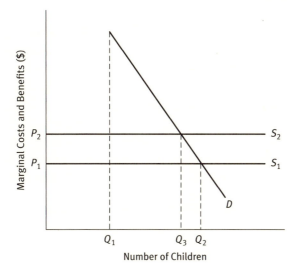

FIGURE 4

Figure 4 by the upward shift in the supply curve and the accompanying reduction in the desired children. On the other hand, the higher wage gives the couple added income to allocate to family purchases, including children. This "income effect" can have a positive influence on the production of children.[9] If this is the case, the net effect of the higher wage depends upon the relative strengths of the negative cost effect and the possible positive income effect. The empirical studies that have been done on the subject tend to find a negative correlation between family income and number of children.[10] This suggests, but does not confirm, that the negative cost effect is stronger. As opposed to being reflected in the number of children, the income effect can be realized in the *quality* of children demanded by people with higher incomes.[11]

9. We recognize the possibility that children can be "inferior goods," meaning the income effect can be negative.

10. Bruce Gardner, "Economics of the Size of North Carolina Rural Families," *Journal of Political Economy*, 81, supplement (March/April 1973), s99–s122; Dennis N. DeTray, "Child Quality and the Demand for Children," *Journal of Political Economy*, 81, supplement (March/April 1973), s70–s95.

11. Testing the relationship between income and child quality is a difficult task because of the problems associated with defining and obtaining data on *quality*. Nevertheless, Dennis N. DeTray has made an effort by defining child quality as the extent of the child's education. He finds that the education of the mother, which can be mirrored in her opportunity wage, does

The discussion of the impact of higher wages on birth rates is interesting and important because it has implications regarding population growth rate trends in developing countries. If the negative cost effect is stronger than the positive income effect, as empirical studies indicate, and this relationship holds for underdeveloped countries, then the "population explosion," which has been the concern of many in recent years, may fade *to some degree if the underdeveloped countries are ever able to develop*. The higher opportunity wage, coupled with the greater dependence on industry, could lead to a lower birth rate. All we have argued here, however, is the probable direction of the effect of development on population growth and not how strong the effect is.

Education and Child Production

The education level of parents can influence the child production process in several ways. First, it can change the parents' relative preferences for children by introducing them to things they find more valuable. Second, education can increase the opportunity wage rate of the parents and have the positive income effect and negative cost effect mentioned above. One of the more firmly established relationships in fertility literature is the negative correlation between the amount of education of the wife and the number of children she has; that is, as the wife's education level rises, the number of children tends to fall.[12] There is some evidence that shows that the relationship between the husband's education level and the number of children is positive.[13] One possible explanation for these findings is that, as many studies have found, the wife's time is relatively more important in child production than is the time of the husband, and the cost of her time will accordingly be more influential in the child production decisions. In the case of the husband, whose responsibilities have traditionally included earning the money income, his education

have an effect on the "efficiency with which child quality is produced" (p. s93). Because of the data that was used, he considers his conclusions to be weak and tentative. ("Child Quality and the Demand for Children," *Journal of Political Economy*, 81, supplement (March/April 1973), s70–s95.)

12. Gardner, "Economics of the Size of North Carolina Rural Families."

13. Masanori Hashimoto, "Economics of Postwar Fertility in Japan: Differentials and Trends," *Journal of Political Economy*, 82, supplement (March/April 1974), s170–94.

has had little cost effect, since the amount of his time involved may not be very great, but has had a positive income effect.

Third, education can increase the efficiency with which the "quality" of children can be reared. At least one empirical study tends to support this.[14] Even with a higher opportunity wage rate, greater efficiency can make a unit of "child quality," however defined by the parent, cheaper to the more educated person. For example, suppose it takes the parent with an elementary education two hours to teach his child a certain task which contributes to the child's quality. The parent's market wage rate is $2 per hour. The total cost is $4. On the other hand, if it takes the more educated parent, who earns $5 per hour, one-half hour to accomplish the same thing with his child, the cost is only $2.50. Everything else being equal, we would expect the more educated person to demand more units of child quality.

Fourth, the effects of education can show up in the parent's knowledge and use of contraceptives and in the number of unwanted children. A number of studies have found a direct relationship between parents' education and knowledge and use of contraceptives.[15] More educated parents tend to use the more effective contraceptive methods and use them to a much greater extent. Robert Michael gives three possible explanations for this: (1) Education makes the technical literature on contraception more easily understood and to that extent lowers contraception costs; (2) it raises the value of the couples' time and thereby makes more effective methods, which may be more expensive but less time-consuming, more economical (the time expenditure for a couple does vary somewhat from the pill to the use of diaphragms and foam tablets); and (3) education raises the cost of children by raising the cost of parents' time and, thereby, increases the cost of an unwanted child. This makes knowledge and use of contraceptives more valuable.[16] In the process of developing his argument, Michael makes an interesting point regarding the efficiency of contraceptive devices. He writes, "If a couple used a contraceptive technique that was 'only' 90 percent effective, in a 15-year period their expected fertility outcome would be 2.7 births. . . . Or, if a couple used a contraceptive technique that was 'only' 99 percent effective, the chance of a

---

14. Ibid.

15. Robert T. Michael, "Education and the Derived Demand for Children," *Journal of Political Economy*, 81, supplement (March/April 1973), s128–64. The author of this article refers to a number of studies connected with this point on page s140.

16. Ibid., s159.

conception in a five-year interval exceeds ten percent. 'Good' (but not perfect) contraception does not provide the long-run protection one might think." [17] He also estimated that if a fertile couple does not use any method of contraception for five years, the probability of conception is 100 percent.

Child Production and Overpopulation

Economists are in general agreement that the optimum quantity produced of anything is that quantity at which the marginal cost of the last unit is equal to the marginal benefits of it. This will be the case if all costs and benefits are actually considered by the individual making the decision on the output, and this rule of thumb holds for the production of children. However, if the person making the decision does not consider all costs in the production of, say, children—that is, someone else bears a portion of the cost—the perceived marginal cost will be lower than it really is. Using Figure 4, because not all costs are considered by the person making the child production decision, the couple will perceive that the cost of children is represented by supply curve S_1, whereas in fact the true supply curve, considering all costs, is at S_2. Couples will rationally choose to produce Q_2 children. Note that the true marginal cost (P_2), when all costs are included, between Q_2 and Q_3 is actually greater than the demand curve. This indicates that the marginal cost of the children is greater than the marginal benefits, and as a result, too many children are produced.

In our present society there are two basic ways in which couples deciding to bear children can underestimate the cost of their children. They may not consider the added congestion their children can create. This may mean that there are simply more people taking up the same limited area, reducing the freedom all persons have to move about without affecting others, or it may mean that more people are competing for resources, other than space, causing another form of congestion. This cost of an additional child is incurred in general by people not involved in the decision to have the child.

The other basic way by which the private decisions of parents can impose costs on others is through the tax system. Presently, there are many public facilities, such as schools, that are provided with tax money. If the facilities are not free to the user, they are most often subsidized. To this extent, a portion of the total cost of a child is borne by the general taxpayer. The private

17. Ibid., s141.

decision of one couple to have a child can, therefore, increase the tax bill for the rest of the community. Because these costs may not, and to a substantial degree are not, considered by the child-bearing couple, the costs they consider will be understated, resulting in overproduction of children. (It is indeed an interesting thought that the tax burden of the general public is partly dependent upon the coital frequency of couples!) One way to turn this around is to have the child-bearing couples pay the cost by imposing a tax on them for each birth. This, to put it mildly, is not likely to be a popular proposal with those who want children. They no doubt would prefer that the rest of us continue to pay the bill for their fortune or misfortune as the case may be.

Child Production and the Future

Thomas Ireland, in "The Political Economy of Child Production," has suggested some interesting, but to some, we are sure, disturbing prospects for the future course of child rearing.[18] If it were not for the rather dramatic change over the past ten years in the public's acceptance of abortions, we would indeed consider his ideas to be futuristic. But, as it is, Ireland's paper may indicate what is "just around the corner."

His paper is based on two main propositions: First, scientists now have the capability to transplant an animal fetus from its mother to a "host mother," with the birth following in due course. There is every reason to believe that if medical science is not able to do it now, the know-how will be developed in the future to accomplish the same thing in humans. Second, the problems associated with pregnancies cause some women pain and inconvenience and make many unable to work in the market for several months.

The prospect of fetus transplant provides a potential solution to the dwindling number of adoptable babies and the moral problems surrounding abortions. Because adoptable babies are becoming very expensive, the mother who would like to bear a child but who cannot because of the sterility of the husband, would have some incentive to pay to have an aborted fetus transplanted into herself.[19] This may not sound so crazy if it is remembered that women now pay handsomely for artificial insemination and for the rights to

18. Thomas R. Ireland, "The Political Economy of Child Production," paper presented at the Public Choice Society meeting, University of Maryland, March 1973.

19. Adoptable babies of minority groups are still relatively easy to obtain, but with the legalization of abortions this supply is dwindling.

adopt a child. In fact, a public interest group interested in the rights of the fetus's life may be willing to pay another mother to accept the transplant and
carry the child to term. Such a solution may be disgusting to some readers
who are concerned about the life of the fetus. Granted, this may be a less than
ideal solution, but it may be a better solution than one of standing around
discussing the question of when life begins while many fetuses are being
destroyed.

In addition, there are possibilities for payment arrangements whereby the
true mother and host mother gain by a fetus transplant. Suppose that there is
a mother who earns $20,000 per year, who wants to have a child of her own,
but who is not willing to endure the pain and loss of income associated with
pregnancy. If there is another woman who earns $8,000 per year, then the
mother can possibly agree through some institution, which is not yet established, to pay a host mother to carry the baby to term at which time the baby
would be transferred back to the original mother. If the disability associated
with the pregnancy is three months, the real mother could be willing to pay
(ignoring taxes) as much as or more than $5,000 to the host mother. By mak-
ing the payment, it will be the host mother who will lose the time at work,
which will cost her $2,000. She can receive from the real mother, say, $4,000,
and her income will rise to $10,000. Furthermore, the total output of the
economy can be $3,000 greater than what it would have been if the real
mother had lost the time from work.[20] All of this may sound a little cold-
hearted, but we really do not mean for it to be taken that way. These are, however, solutions which may be more than just attention getters in the relatively
near future.

Concluding Comments

In recent years it has been the fad to project the future course of the population trend and accompanying problems. Most of these projections are
merely statistical extrapolations of the trends of the recent past. They do not
assume that there will be adjustments made in the economy that will alter the
course of the trend. We do not wish to understate the importance of getting
the world's population growth under control. However, we suspect that the

---

20. It may be found that transferring a fetus to a host mother will affect the quality of the
child.

doomsday prophets will be mistaken in their projections, because of certain anticipated changes in the child production process. First, we expect that as the population grows larger, putting pressure on resources, the cost of producing children will become relatively greater, reflecting back on the private household decisions. Second, we suspect that as congestion becomes greater, there will be growing pressure on government to change the tax structure and to make abortion and contraceptive devices more readily and inexpensively available to the public. Third, we expect that with the growing cost of children there will be a renewed incentive to find new technology for preventing pregnancies. In fact, we view the recent public concern over population growth to be a part of the self-correcting changes we see. Those that are projecting the population are alerting the voting public to the problem and setting the stage for changes in policy.

THE ECONOMIC ASPECTS OF CRIME
Richard B. McKenzie and Gordon Tullock

The Benefits and Costs of Crime

COSTS TO THE CRIMINAL

Crime is an economic as well as a sociological and psychological problem. There are definite benefits (at least, to the criminal) and costs associated with criminal activity. The criminal can possibly increase his lifetime income even though at times he may be imprisoned. He can reduce the number of hours worked per week and, perhaps, improve his working conditions.[1] In addition, the criminal can within some socio-economic groups raise his status among his peers by commiting crimes and even by serving time.

To obtain these benefits, the criminal must incur the costs of developing the right skills (unless he wants to run the risks of bungling the job),[2] acquiring the necessary tools, such as guns and explosives, and making the contacts that may be necessary to pull off the job. In the narcotics business, the criminal must invest in raw materials, storage facilities, and processing and transportation equipment. The criminal may, like other businessmen, have to meet a payroll, which may include salesmen and administrators. In the business of shylocking, the accumulation of financial assets is important. Prostitutes may have to incur the costs of physical abuse and medical treatment.

If the criminal is a specialist in armed robbery or burglary, he must spend the time required (which implies opportunity cost) to case the site of the crime, to wait for the opportune moment, to pull off the crime itself, to fence the stolen goods, and to stay undercover until things have cooled. If caught, he has the additional costs of legal help (unless a court-appointed lawyer is

Reprinted, with permission, from *The New World of Economics: Exploration into the Human Experience* (Homewood, Ill.: Richard D. Irwin, 1975), 129–45.

1. Remember that even though you may consider the working conditions of the criminals to be bad, they may still be better than the alternative available to him.

2. As may have been suggested by the discussion in Chapter 2, there is some optimum amount of risk the criminal may rationally decide to assume. How much education, or, for that matter, any other resource input, the criminal is willing to buy depends upon the probabilities of being caught, the extent of the punishment, and the degree to which the criminal is risk averse.

secured). If convicted, he must forgo the income he could have earned while incarcerated; and because of his record, he can suffer a reduction in his earning ability after being released. There may also be for some the psychic cost of having done something wrong and the loss of respect within his family and community structure. (Consider the cases of former President Richard Nixon and former Vice President Spiro Agnew.)

The cost to the individual of committing his own crimes can be viewed as rising as the general level of criminal activity rises. As the crime rate rises, the public can be reasonably expected (beyond some threshold) to respond by applying more resources to crime prevention, making it more difficult (i.e., more costly) for the criminal to commit crimes. In addition, one might expect all criminals to commit those crimes first that will yield the largest amount of booty per resource expenditure, meaning the lower-cost crimes. This implies that to extend the level of criminal activities, criminals will have to seek out higher cost alternatives or less lucrative opportunities. Like all other production processes, one might also expect criminal activity to be subject to the law of diminishing returns. (Why?)

COSTS TO THE VICTIM

The victim of a robbery or burglary will suffer the loss of the stolen property and, possibly, bodily and mental injury, implying medical bills and loss of income. In the case of rape, the victim may be subjected not only to an extreme amount of violence but also to community gossip; and even though she may be innocent of any wrong-doing, her reputation can be damaged. This may be particularly true if the victim takes the rapist to court. The defense attorney, in an effort to make the strongest possible case for his client, may parade the victim's past (questionable) relationships before the press and community, distorting them wherever possible. The cost of legal fees and time spent in lawyers' offices and the court can be for her and other victims of other crimes a substantial portion of the total cost borne by victims; and it is because of such cost, no doubt, that many crimes go unreported. In the case of murder, the victims may be, in addition to the one murdered, the family and friends who lose income and friendship.

COSTS TO SOCIETY

The total cost of crime extends far beyond those directly involved in the crime itself. Non-victims must, in an attempt to avoid being victims, incur the costs of locks, burglary alarm systems, outside lights, and the many other devices used to make crime more costly to prospective criminals. The non-victim may also have to incur the cost required to avoid high crime areas. In early January 1974, the *Charlotte Observer* took a survey of approximately three hundred persons who had moved from Charlotte, North Carolina, to surrounding suburbs, and they found that a primary reason for over half of the respondents moving out of the city was to get away from the high incidence of crime.[3] Many of the people who had moved then had to commute longer distances to work.

Crime will also impose higher taxes on victims and non-victims alike, since police protection and judicial, penal, and (to a limited extent) rehabilitation systems are not likely to be avoided. Society may also experience a loss of social interaction. Because of fear of being sexually molested, children are taught not to speak to strangers and, above all, not to get in their cars. Women may avoid speaking to or walking on the same side of a street with men they do not know. Since policemen are given a considerable amount of discretionary power over whom to stop, search, and arrest, crime can impose on the general population a "liberty tax." Finally, people shopping in stores often go out of their way to insure that they do not give the impression that they are shoplifting.

Rationality and Crime

THE RATIONAL CRIMINAL

To the degree that crime involves benefits and costs, crime *can* be a rational act, and the amount of crime actually committed can be determined in the same manner as is the amount of any other activity. The only difference may be that crime involves behavior that is against the law. The criminal can weigh-off the benefits and costs and can choose that combination that maximizes his own utility, and he will maximize his utility if he commits those crimes for which the additional benefits exceed the additional costs.

Because of the cost of crime, the amount of crimes committed can fall far short of the amount that can, technically speaking, be committed. This would be true even if we ignore or dismiss the costs of being caught and punished. For example, suppose that the benefits of committing a particular crime, such

---

3. *Charlotte Observer*, January 6, 1974, p. 1. Charlotte, deservedly or not, has acquired the reputation among many as being the murder capital of the south.

as robbery, for a prospective criminal, are illustrated by the downward sloping demand curve in Figure 1. (Why is the demand downward sloping?) (In this graph the quantity of crimes is on the horizontal axis, and the marginal costs and benefits are on the vertical axis.) Suppose, also, that we consider only non-punishment costs such as raw materials, labor, and equipment. Further, assume that the supply curve (or marginal cost curve, S_1) in Figure 1 is upward sloping. As indicated by the graph, there are benefits to committing additional crimes until Q_1 have been committed; beyond Q_1 the additional benefits to further criminal activity become negative. However, at Q_1 the cost of committing the Q_1th crime (MC_1) is far greater than the additional benefits which, at that level of activity, are zero. The criminal, if he is operating at Q_1, can increase his personal satisfaction by reducing the number of crimes committed. If he reduces the number of crimes all the way back to Q_2, the marginal benefits from the Q_2th crime would then exceed the cost in which event it follows that he could improve his utility by increasing the number of crimes. Needless to say by now, the rational criminal can maximize his utility by committing up to Q_3 crimes, at which point the additional benefits are equal to the additional costs. The analysis can be extended to include the total "market" for crime by adding horizontally the individuals' demands and supplies. The total community crime level would then be established at the intersection of the market demand and market supply curves.

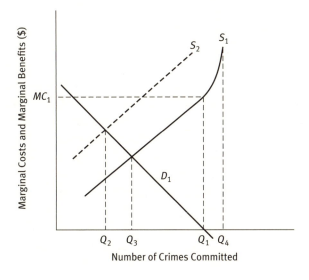

FIGURE 1

There are three important points that should be given particular attention. The first one is that the number of crimes committed by the rational criminal will not be equal to the maximum, which for our purposes can be defined as Q_1, where the demand curve intersects the horizontal axis, or Q_4, where the supply curve becomes essentially vertical. The second point that needs to be emphasized is that, given the demand for crime, the amount of crimes perpetrated is dependent upon the cost. If punishment is introduced into the analysis and the type of punishment employed represents an increase in cost to the criminal, the supply curve will decrease (i.e., move upward and to the left) to, say, S_2; and as a result, the number of crimes the criminal will *choose* to commit will be lowered. One can also suggest that anything that reduces the cost of crime, such as reduction in the cost of handguns or an increase in the leniency of the courts, can increase the supply of crime and, thereby, the number of crimes actually committed. This would also be the case if society became more tolerant of or sympathetic toward criminals. (Why?)

The third point is that although one can observe that a large number of crimes are committed, such as Q_2 in Figure 1, one cannot conclude that the severity of punishment has no effect on criminal activity. If the difference between S_1 and S_2 represents the cost imposed on the criminal by the penal system, then one can deduce that the penal system has deterred $Q_3 - Q_2$ crimes. In other words, the effectiveness of a penal system can be judged by how many crimes are committed; however, a more appropriate indication of the effectiveness of punishment, or any other policy which increases the cost of crime to the criminal, is how many crimes are never committed because of that punishment. This, we believe, is a point policemen readily see, but one which other concerned individuals often overlook.

If the booty from committing crimes increases, while the cost remains constant, one could also predict from our model that the demand for crime would rise to the upper right as in Figure 2. The number of crimes committed, we predict, would go up.

THE IRRATIONAL CRIMINAL

There is a common notion among lay and professional criminologists and sociologists that certain criminals who commit certain types of crime do not behave rationally. They do not weigh-off the benefits and costs of their actions, and we will treat this controversial issue in greater detail in the next chapter. However, at this point we want to assure the reader that we concede the point that there are "sick" criminals just as we would concede the issue

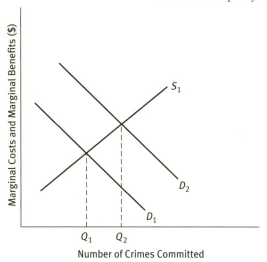

FIGURE 2

if anyone ever suggested that there are sick plumbers, businessmen, and professors.[4]

To the extent that criminals do not measure the consequences of their actions, the demand curves for sick criminals are vertical. However, this does not mean that the demand for the crime in general is not downward. The market demand curve will still be downward sloping so long as there are rational criminals in the market. The existence of the irrational criminals just moves the market demand curve for crime out to the right and does not change the slope. The supply of crimes will also increase, since there are more criminals. For example, suppose that there are rational and irrational criminals in the market and that the market demand for crime by rational criminals is equal to D_1 in Figure 3. If, for purposes of illustration, there are Q_1 crimes committed by irrational criminals, then the total market demand and supply curves would be at D_2 and S_2. The total number of crimes committed would then be Q_2, Q_1 by irrational criminals and $Q_2 - Q_1$ committed by rational criminals.

The reader should recognize that so long as the market demand for crime is downward sloping, the changes in the cost of crime as discussed above

4. We are also willing to concede the point that "sick" criminals may specialize in certain bizarre types of crimes that rational criminals do not. As we argue in the next chapters, there is presently little evidence that suggests, however, what these areas may be.

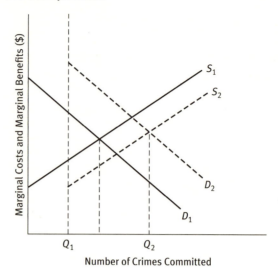

FIGURE 3

should lead to changes in the number of crimes committed *by the rational criminals*. Since the irrational criminals, by definition, do not consider costs in their behavioral decision, one should not expect their level of crime to be affected; therefore, the total market response should be in the same direction as predicted for rational criminals. (The percentage change in the amount of crime would not be as great.)

The Economics of Being a Non-victim

Victims of crimes suffer, and in that sense people can benefit by actively avoiding crimes. For certain types of crimes, such as aggravated assault, the benefits of crime avoidance can be considerable; for other types, such as having a potted petunia plant stolen from one's backyard, the benefits can be very slight, mainly because the value of the stolen property can be very low. In any event, people have a demand for crime avoidance, which implies a demand for locks and other devices and means of thwarting crimes. Furthermore, if non-victims are rational, their demand for crime avoidance is downward sloping, as is the case for everything else they value.

As illustrated in Figure 4, this means that a person will avoid more crimes the cheaper it is to do so. If the price (which must be imputed from the cost of equipment and time) of avoiding a particular crime is P_1, the number of

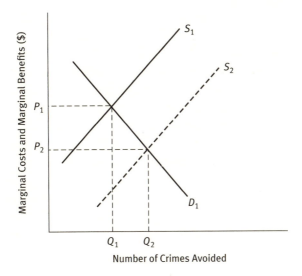

FIGURE 4

crimes avoided will be Q_1. More pointedly, the person will do only so much to reduce the risk of crimes being committed against him.[5]

This means, of course, that he will "permit," in a sense, some crimes to be committed. Granted, if there were no cost involved in crime avoidance, everyone would prefer never being a victim to, at times, being one. However, if a person did everything necessary to avoid ever being a victim, the cost (including time cost) of avoiding certain types of crimes, such as petty larceny or even burglary, can, over the long run, be greater than what he would have lost had he been less cautious and at times been a victim. To put the problem in a little different perspective, would you expect someone to spend $100,000 to avoid being robbed of $75,000? This is an extreme example, but do people not address similar questions when they consider taking measures to avoid crimes?

Clearly, people do limit the number and quality of locks on their doors; college professors (the authors included) generally have locks on their doors they know can be picked by any reasonably good thief. In fact, one of the authors is inclined to leave his door wide open when he is out on errands or in class. One reason is that any prospective thief will have to pass by a secretary and can be observed by others who may be close by. Another reason is simply that he calculates that there really is not all that much in his office to steal and

5. Operationally speaking, reducing the risk of being a victim is the same as increasing the number of crimes he avoids.

that, quite honestly, he generally figures the value of his time spent locking, searching for his keys, and unlocking the door can over the long run far exceed the value of the property likely to be stolen. You can be assured, however, that when he has an expensive calculator in his office, he closes and locks his door upon leaving. (Is his behavior inconsistent?)

People do not put bars on their windows; the major cost here is likely to be the deterioration of the outward appearance of their homes. People are also willing to walk in some areas at some times, well aware that the probability of being mugged is above zero. Admittedly, when the probability is quite high, such as may be the case in New York's Central Park at midnight, they may be willing to forgo their walks. However, just because people may not be willing to walk in Central Park, one cannot conclude that they are unwilling to assume any risk or take any chance of becoming a victim. If individuals tried to avoid *ever* being a victim of crime, we are convinced that they would lead a very dull life! In other words, rational behavior can make the criminal's work a little easier than otherwise.

Given the above discussion and Figure 4, it follows that if the cost of avoiding crime falls, the supply of crime avoidance will expand downward and to the right, resulting in an increased number of crimes avoided. That is, a person will buy more locks and/or take more time to avoid being caught in a threatening situation. Again, it should be stressed that given the cost reduction, the rational person will do only so much to avoid crimes.

It also follows that if the benefits from crime avoidance increase, the individual will expend more effort and money in an attempt to avoid crimes. This increase in demand, as illustrated in Figure 5, can be the result of an increase in the value of that which could be stolen or, perhaps, an increase in a person's assessment of the worth of his own physical condition and/or life. A person who may be depressed and care very little about living can hardly be expected to divert many resources to avoid being killed. In addition, the increase in demand can result from an increase in the probability of being a victim; in such a circumstance it is reasonable to expect a person to be willing to pay a higher price for crime avoidance. Notice that in all of these cases the increase in the cost of avoiding crimes curtails the number of crimes that the individual will attempt to avoid. In our graph if the price of crime avoidance had remained at P_1, the quantity of crimes avoided would have been Q_3; however, because the price of crime avoidance rises to P_2, the number of crimes avoided is Q_2. This quantity is higher than the original number Q_1, but still it is not as great as it would have been had the price remained at P_1.

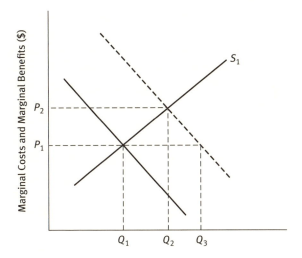

FIGURE 5

Police Protection

The individual citizen, not the police, is society's first line of defense against crime. The citizen may be an amateur, undisciplined and untrained in modern police techniques, but he does have one thing going for him, and that is his own private interest to protect those things that to him are valuable. If it were not for such motivation, we can be assured that the work of the criminal would be greatly eased. Police can contribute to crime control, but one should understand that in urban areas today there are only about two policemen for every 1,000 residents.

From this perspective, police protection and law enforcement should be viewed as a supplement to the basic protection which people provide for themselves. Generally speaking, but not always, the services of police are provided by local government, and this is done for two basic reasons. First, it may be more efficient to provide the additional protection through some collective organization. As opposed to having each store owner check to insure that his doors are locked after closing hours, the duty can be assigned to a policeman on that beat. A great deal of traveling time can be saved. Such services need not be provided publicly and often are not. Shopping centers, for example, do provide their own security guards; in a sense, they are selling police protection along with the floor space.

Second, police protection is not always the type of service that can be bought and sold in the market on a customer-by-customer basis. There are activities for which the police could *conceivably* charge in much the same way as Coca-Cola does for its drinks. This might be where the service is specifically intended to benefit one particular individual (or group), and the service can be withheld unless the individual pays the prescribed fee. An example might be a policeman's retrieval of stolen property for a particular individual; if the individual does not pay for the service, the service can be withheld.[6]

On the other hand, the benefits of police activity can be spread quite generally across the community. The presence of the police can provide an additional threat to all criminals operating in the community, and the police can contribute to the removal of criminals from the community by making crime less profitable or by putting them behind bars. In such cases all members of the community benefit (albeit in varying degrees), since the risk of becoming a victim is lowered. In addition, the community can, because of the police presence, reduce their own private actions intended to thwart crime.

If such generalized benefits are provided, then all members of the community must share in those benefits. The police can deny some benefits to some people by denying them some services, as discussed above, but they cannot deny to anyone those benefits that pervade the entire community. Consequently, it may be extremely difficult (if not impossible) for the police to charge for the generalized benefits. If a resident benefits regardless of whether or not he pays, then it is understandable why he may refuse to pay on a voluntary basis. For one thing, he can figure that he can get the protection free if it is provided. Secondly, he may reason that the amount he would be willing to contribute to the "police fund" may be so small in relation to what is needed that any contribution he makes will neither determine whether or not the police protection is provided or significantly influence the amount of protection he receives. Therefore, police protection must be financed by some extra-market means—that is, by taxation.

The members of the community may gladly consent to *some* additional taxation because they know there are benefits to be reaped from police ser-

---

6. We are merely suggesting here that the police could charge for certain types of services. The reader should not interpret our remarks as advocating such a system. Besides, the administration of such a system might be so expensive that other means of collecting may be more desirable.

vices; and without the intervention of government, meaning taxation, police protection may not be provided. This can be particularly true in the larger communities where social pressure is impotent. By voting for the additional taxes, not only may the individual acquire the very slight benefits resulting from the taxes he himself pays, but he can also benefit from the taxes paid by others.

There are limits, however, to the amount of police protection acceptable to a voting public, mainly because, as we have seen elsewhere in this chapter, there are costs involved. As the level of protection is increased, taxes must be raised, and people will have to give up other things, such as ice cream and clothes, which they value.[7] As tax rates are raised, we can reasonably assume, there will be more and more people who will find that the benefits received from the additional protection will be less than the additional costs they must incur in the form of taxes. At some point there will be a sufficient number of votes to defeat any proposal to expand police activities further. The reader should recognize that by restricting the size of the police departments, the voting public is limiting the number of crimes that will be prevented. *They are also allowing, in a sense, some crimes to be committed.* The voting public may not like to have crime in their midst, but at the same time, they may not want to see their taxes increased either. We personally see very little chance of the public ever voting to wipe out all crime, even if it were possible.

Having only limited resources with which to prevent and investigate more crimes than they can handle, the police themselves must make certain economic decisions. They must decide whether or not their resources should be applied in residential or business areas or whether they should attempt to prevent or investigate burglaries, murders, or rapes. If they apply their resources in preventing burglaries, then they must allow other crimes, such as speeding violations and murders, to occur or go unsolved. In recent times the police have been required to enforce price controls that have been mandated by the federal government. Having used their resources in this way, they cannot use them to solve other crimes. This is one aspect of wage-price controls systems that is not readily appreciated by the public who may favor controls.

---

7. You may feel that police protection is much more important than, say, ice cream. However, remember that is your preference; others may not agree with you at all levels of police protection.

TABLE 1. National Crime, Rate, and Percent Change

CRIME INDEX OFFENSES	ESTIMATED CRIME 1973		PERCENT CHANGE OVER 1972		PERCENT CHANGE OVER 1968		PERCENT CHANGE OVER 1960	
	NUMBER	RATE PER 100,000 INHABITANTS	NUMBER	RATE	NUMBER	RATE	NUMBER	RATE
Total	8,638,400	4,116.4	+5.7	+4.9	+29.7	+23.5	+157.6	+120.2
Violent	869,470	414.3	+4.9	+4.1	+47.2	+40.2	+203.8	+159.6
Property	7,768,900	3,702.1	+5.8	+5.0	+28.0	+21.9	+153.3	+116.5
Murder	19,510	9.3	+5.2	+4.5	+42.2	+34.8	+115.6	+86.0
Forcible rape	51,000	24.3	+9.7	+9.0	+62.4	+54.8	+199.2	+155.8
Robbery	382,680	182.4	+2.1	+1.3	+46.2	+39.2	+256.3	+204.5
Aggravated assault	416,270	198.4	+7.0	+6.2	+46.7	+39.7	+172.6	+132.9
Burglary	2,540,900	1,210.8	+8.0	+7.2	+38.0	+31.4	+181.3	+140.3
Larceny-theft	4,304,400	2,051.2	+4.7	+3.9	+24.8	+18.9	+134.3	+100.3
Auto theft	923,600	440.1	+4.7	+3.9	+18.5	+12.9	+183.0	+141.8

Violent crimes include murder, forcible rape, and aggravated assault. Property crimes include burglary, larceny $50 and over, and auto theft.

SOURCE: FBI, *Uniform Crime Report*, 1973, 1.

Crime Activity

We will close this chapter on crime by reviewing the statistics of major crimes in the United States. A note of caution should be made before we proceed. First, it should be understood that we are giving statistics on the *number of crimes reported*; there are, no doubt, many crimes committed each year that for one reason or another go unreported. In fact, the President's Crime Commission found that in three precincts in Washington, D.C., "six times as many crimes were committed against persons and homes as were reported to the police."[8] The number of reported crimes can also change over the years with changes in the number of reporting agencies and the number of police personnel. These two considerations suggest that the growth in criminal activity reported by the FBI can be exaggerated.

The FBI concentrates its reports on seven types of crime: murder, forcible rape, robbery, aggravated assault, burglary, larceny, and auto theft. The total number of crimes in these categories is referred to as the Crime Index. Table 1 reveals the total number of Crime Index offenses per 100,000 people in the country. The table also indicates the growth in offenses during different periods of time. Figure 6 depicts the percentage change in the number of Crime Index offenses and the crime rate over the years from 1967 to 1973. The same type of information is provided for the "crimes of violence" (which include murder, rape, robbery, and aggravated assault) and "crimes against property" (which include burglary, larceny, and auto theft) in Figures 7 and 8.

From the table and figures, several points of interest can be noted. First, the total number of index offenses has risen substantially over the long run, approximately 30 percent from 1968 to 1973. The crime rate has risen almost as much, 24 percent. Second, between 1972 and 1973, the total number of offenses, after falling between 1971 and 1972, rose by approximately 5 percent. However, as vividly revealed in Figures 7 and 8, the drop in the total number of offenses between 1971 and 1972 was due primarily to the drop in the crimes against property during that period of time. Crimes of violence, in particular, have risen continuously during the years covered by the table and charts.

8. The National Advisory Commission on Civil Disorders, "Crime in Urban Areas," in *Problems in Political Economy: An Urban Perspective*, ed. David M. Gordon, Lexington, Mass.: D. C. Heath and Company, 1971, 289.

FIGURE 6
Crime and population, 1968–1973 (percent change over 1968)

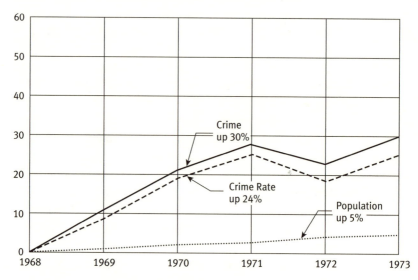

Crime = Crime index offenses.
Crime Rate = Number of offenses per 100,000 inhabitants.
SOURCE: FBI, *Uniform Crime Report*, 1973, 3.

FIGURE 7
Crimes of violence, 1967–1972 (percent change over 1967)

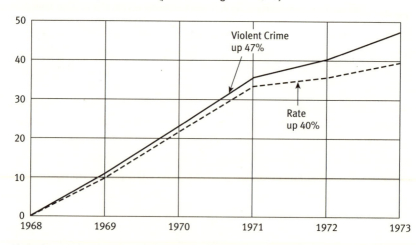

Limited to murder, forcible rape, robbery, and aggravated assault.
SOURCE: FBI, *Uniform Crime Report*, 1972, 4.

FIGURE 8
Crimes against property, 1968–1973 (percent change over 1968)

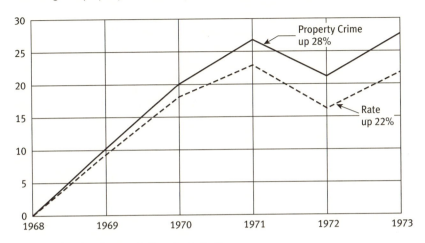

Limited to burglary, larceny-theft, and auto theft.
SOURCE: FBI, *Uniform Crime Report*, 1973, 5.

TABLE 2. *Crime Rate by Area, 1973 (rate per 100,000 inhabitants)*

| | AREA | | | |
CRIME INDEX OFFENSES	TOTAL U.S.	CITIES OVER 250,000	SUBURBAN	RURAL
Total	4,116.4	6,582.8	3,562.6	1,471.8
Violent	141.3	1,003.4	248.5	147.4
Property	3,702.1	5,579.5	3,314.1	1,324.4
Murder	9.3	20.7	5.1	7.5
Forcible rape	24.3	51.4	17.8	12.0
Robbery	182.4	571.5	76.1	17.7
Aggravated assault	198.4	359.9	149.5	110.2
Burglary	1,210.8	1,949.3	1,054.4	564.0
Larceny-theft	2,051.2	2,651.8	1,952.4	677.6
Auto theft	440.0	978.4	307.4	82.8

SOURCE: FBI, *Uniform Crime Reports*, 1973, 2.

Table 2 indicates the crime rate for the United States as a whole, for cities with populations over 250,000, for suburban areas, and for rural areas. As most readers may have anticipated, the crime rate for all crimes in the larger cities was nearly twice what it was in suburban areas and more than four times what it was in rural areas.

TABLE 3. *Disposition of Reported Crimes for Adults, 1973*

	PERCENT OF INDEX CRIMES CLEARED BY ARREST	PERCENT OF ARRESTED THAT WERE PROSECUTED	PERCENT OF PROSECUTED FOUND GUILTY ON ORIGINAL CHARGE	PERCENT OF CHARGED FOUND GUILTY ON LESSER CHARGE	PERCENT OF CHARGED ENDING IN ACQUITTAL OR DISMISSAL
Total	21	89	58	11	31
Murder	79	66	45	23	32
Forcible rape	51	76	36	17	47
Aggravated assault	63	82	61	17	44
Robberies	27	72	46	16	38
Burglaries	18	82	49	18	33
Larcenies $50 and over	19	N.A.	69	6	25
Auto thefts	16	N.A.	43	15	42

Data do not include the disposition of juvenile crimes.
N.A. denotes data was unavailable.
SOURCE: FBI, *Uniform Crime Report*, 1973, 28–35.

Table 3 provides some information on the disposition of reported crimes. Of all the index crimes committed in 1973, only 21 percent were cleared by the police, meaning the police had identified the offender, had enough information to charge him, and actually took him into custody. Of this small percentage, 89 percent were prosecuted, and 58 percent of those prosecuted were found guilty on the original charge and another 11 percent were found guilty on a lesser charge. Thirty-one percent of the cases ended in acquittal or dismissal.

The police were most effective in apprehending murderers. Seventy-nine percent of all murder cases were cleared; 45 percent ended in conviction on the original charge. Thirty-two percent, however, ended in acquittal or dismissal. The police, on the other hand, were far less successful with burglaries, larcenies, and auto thefts. Not only were the police unable to clear many of the cases, but many of the cases terminated in dismissal or acquittal. Given this information and the knowledge that many crimes go unreported, it seems reasonably clear that the risk of being caught, convicted, and punished (particularly in certain crime areas) is not as great as most laymen may believe.

THE ECONOMIC VERSUS THE
SOCIOLOGICAL VIEWS OF CRIME
Richard B. McKenzie and Gordon Tullock

Two Hypotheses on Crime

The editors of the *Washington Post* are against private ownership of guns and devote part of its editorial content to denouncing it. As part of this campaign, they found a professional robber in Washington and interviewed him quite extensively.[1] Under guarantee of anonymity, he was—as far as we can tell—very frank and explained fairly accurately his motives and *modus operandi*. His special field was armed robbery, and he was apparently making a very good income from it. He was vaguely unhappy about his occupation because he realized it was risky, but as he said, "I want to go to barber school, but I know there's not that kind of money in barbering." In general, he calculated the risks with care: "Now I know if I's gonna rob somethin' it ought to be big, because I'm gonna get the same time." "I stay in the District where the police is too busy. . . . It's too risky in Prince Georges." He read the papers daily, "for crime." "I want to know how much people out there are gittin' and who's gettin' what kind of time."

Thus, this young criminal explains his own behavior largely in terms of calculations of profits and risk of cost. It is notable that the *Washington Post* reporter seemed to pay little attention to this aspect of the matter, although he reported verbatim lengthy statements made by the criminal. The crimes in the article are blamed on the environment. The article begins by pointing out that the criminal came from a poor family background, but it devotes far more attention to the simple fact that guns are readily available in Washington, D.C., than to any other aspect of the environment. Further, there seems to be no evidence that the reporter thought of the ready availability of guns in Washington as merely a reduction in the cost of criminal activity. He regards these environmental factors as direct causes of crime, rather than as changes in technological conditions that may conceivably lead profit-seeking

Reprinted, with permission, from *The New World of Economics: Exploration into the Human Experience* (Homewood, Ill.: Richard D. Irwin, 1975), 146–56.

1. "Dodge City on the Potomac," *Washington Post*, May 11, 1969, p. D-1.

individuals to choose a life of crime. We get the impression reading the article—albeit we must read between the lines for this—that the reporter feels that the statements the criminal makes about the risks and profits are evidence of the fact that he has had a bad environment, rather than statements about the cost-benefit calculations that lead him to continue his life of crime.

It is possible we are misrepresenting the reporter's attitude by imputing to him values and positions we find in the *Washington Post* and, indeed, in a very large part of all modern discussions of crime. The conventional wisdom in this field holds that criminals either are sick persons who require treatment or are the result of environmental deprivation (which seems to amount to much the same thing operationally), and that the possibility of punishment— which plays such a large part in this criminal's calculation—actually is unimportant in determining whether a person does or does not commit any crime. It is argued that people commit crimes not because they see an opportunity for profit, but because they are somehow socially deformed. Further, it is thought that the way to deal with this problem is to change the basic environment so that no person is deformed by the environment, or to "rehabilitate" the criminal once captured. This is one of two dominant hypotheses in the criminal activity. The other hypothesis, the one that immediately occurs to any economist, is that criminals are simply people who take opportunities for profit by violating the law. Under this hypothesis, changing the costs of crime—i.e., increasing the likelihood of being put in prison, lengthening the period of imprisonment, or making prisons less pleasant— would tend to reduce the amount of crime. As discussed in the preceding chapter, the reasoning is simply that the criminals' demand for crime, like their demands for other more normal goods and activities, is downward sloping; the greater the cost or price, the lower the quantity demanded. Rehabilitation for such criminals would be relatively pointless, since the individual is not "sick."[2] He is simply behaving rationally. This point of view is held by very few professional students of crime, although it does seem to be growing in popularity.

People with economic training are apt to take the latter of these two hypotheses as true, and those with sociological training, the former. Sociolo-

---

2. Our prisons, in point of fact, devote practically no effort to "rehabilitation." This is probably wise, since those experiments in rehabilitation that have been undertaken seem to show that we do not know how to do it. See Robert Martinson, "What Works?—Questions and Answers About Prison Reform," *The Public Interest*, 35 (Spring 1974), 22–54.

gists are inclined, as does Paul Horton in the following quote, to dismiss the economic view of crime:

> This misplaced faith in punishment may rest upon the unrealistic assumption that people consciously decide whether to be criminal—that they consider a criminal career, rationally balance its dangers against its rewards, and arrive at a decision based upon such pleasure-pain calculations. It supposedly follows that if the pain element is increased by severe punishment, people will turn from crime to righteousness. A little reflection reveals the absurdity of this notion.[3]

The problem, however, is basically one for empirical research. Before turning to a discussion of what empirical research has been done in the field, we should like to clarify the two hypotheses a little bit to explain the difficulties of testing the difference between them. The economic hypothesis holds that crime would tend to occur whenever the cost fell below the receipts. The costs, in a very straightforward and simple way, would be the energy and equipment put into the actual crime—which is usually quite small—plus the probability of punishment, which in our society is apt to be imprisonment. From the sociological standpoint, these two variables would appear to be largely irrelevant. Indeed, we have never been able to understand how people who believe in the conventional wisdom favor imprisonment at all.[4]

The costs and benefits, however, are to some extent affected by the type of variable in which the sociologists are interested. First, a poor man is probably less injured by being put in jail than the wealthy man. Thus, one would anticipate that a poor man would count the cost of imprisonment as being lower than would the wealthy man, and hence—other things being equal—opportunities for crime that would attract the poor man would appear to be unprofitable from the standpoint of the wealthy man. Second, the size of the booty would be of interest. Large concentrations of wealth would attract potential criminals who would not be interested in small quantities.

These two factors, taken together, would indicate that wide disparity in income might increase crime. A wide disparity of income means that there

---

3. P. B. Horton and G. R. Leslie, *The Sociology of Social Problems*, New York: Appleton-Century-Crofts, 1960, 155.

4. Indeed, some of them have drawn the logical conclusion from their reasoning and *are* opposed to imprisonment. This opinion, however, is more apt to turn up in private conversation than in print. For one example in print, see *The Nation*, September 27, 1971, 258–59.

are some people in the community for whom imprisonment is of relatively light weight, and some targets for crime in the community that would pay off very well. Both poverty and disparity of income might increase the crime rate under *either* the sociological or the economic explanation. Lastly, life in the larger city may reduce the cost of crime as opposed to life in a smaller city. The reasons may be that crime targets are located more closely together and the lower degree of social interaction (implying lower social costs). Ethnic groups may be more willing to protect their own, and, in general, it is harder for the police to catch criminals in large cities.

It will be observed that we have listed a number of variables—which the sociologist might consider as causes of crime—as factors that affect the cost and benefit, and hence somewhat indirectly the cause of crime. This might appear to make the test of the two hypotheses difficult, and indeed it would, were it not for the fact that there are some remaining variables. If we believe that criminals are sick and are not deterred by threat of punishment, then we would predict that changes in the rate of punishment would have no effect on the crime rate. From the economic viewpoint, we would predict that such changes *would* have an effect on the crime rate. Both the sociologist and the economist would expect the same outcome if statistical tests were made of these factors; but when it came to the effect of imprisonment upon the crime rate, there would be a clear difference.

It should be noted that, although the significance or non-significance of the effect of punishment distinguishes between these two hypotheses, it cannot strictly speaking prove the economic hypothesis. A much weaker hypothesis that people respond to costs whether sick or well would lead to the same result as what we have referred to as the economic hypothesis. Indeed, Gary Becker (an economist) and his students have always used this simpler hypothesis quite explicitly. Most of the research we shall discuss below, then, goes to the question of whether or not punishment deters crime, but does not directly relate to the rationality or "sickness" of the criminal. This is, however, enough. If punishment deters crime, then the sociological approach falls to the ground, and much of the advice given to governments by sociologists over the past 50 years is clearly wrong. Indeed, such advice might well be one of the major reasons for the rising crime rate.

Before going on to the question of whether punishment deters crime, it is necessary to make a brief digression on the type of punishment to be used. At the moment, there are only two forms of punishment in general use in the United States, fines and imprisonment. Of these two, fines are clearly superior because of the immense deadweight loss involved in imprisonment. Not only is output largely lost because very little useful work is performed by prisoners, but the cost of imprisonment, which must be borne by society, is very substantial. Unfortunately, a large percentage of all criminals cannot pay fines large enough so that we would be able to regard them as having the same deterrent effect of, let us say, 10 years in prison. Under the circumstances, we are driven back on imprisonment; but we should be more than willing to explore other possible alternatives.

Prevention of crime by such things as better locks or more careful police patrols is one way of reducing the crime rate; and to some degree, in any event, it is cheaper than the imprisonment threat. Rehabilitation of criminals would be a desirable alternative.[5] Going back a little bit in time, there is, of course, the death penalty, which will be discussed below; and going back several hundred years, the use of torture and other physical punishments. The latter, of course, are constitutionally prohibited in the United States. Various African and Arab countries, however, are returning to public floggings as a basic deterrent mechanism.

Does Punishment Deter Crime?

Sociologists sometimes say that empirical tests indicate that there is no deterrent effect from imprisonment or other forms of punishment. In practice, however, little or no investigation has been undertaken by sociologists on this point. Further, the small number of tests that have been undertaken deal with the death penalty and/or are radically defective methodologically. It is not necessarily true, of course, that if the death penalty did not deter murder, then imprisonment would not deter burglary. Indeed, in our opinion, the "research" done on the death penalty largely rationalizes the moral feelings of some groups (sociologists included) without much effort to find the real truth.[6]

---

5. For a careful and exhaustive study of the published reports on rehabilitation, see Martinson, "What Works?" Although some of the techniques he discusses showed some signs of promise for future development, none has yet shown a valid statistical ability to "rehabilitate" the criminal.

6. For a survey of the conventional sociological research, see Hugo Adam Bedau, *The Death Penalty in America*, rev. ed., Garden City, N.Y.: Doubleday & Co., 1967.

Testing the deterrent effect of the death penalty on murder is rather difficult because, in the United States where most of the research has been done, death sentences have always been quite rare; even in the 1930s a murderer had only about one chance in 100 of being executed, whereas his chance of going to prison for a long period of time was 20 to 30 times as great. Under the circumstances, changes of the frequency of the death penalty would tend to be less significant by a wide margin than other variants in punishment policy. There is a modern statistical technique, multiple regression, which is suited to deal with this type of problem; but so far as we can discover, no sociologist or criminologist used this technique until the last few years. Further, they have not concerned themselves with the frequency of the death penalty in any efficient way. When they have considered the death penalty, they have mainly simply pointed out that the rank ordering of states by number of murders is highly correlated with rank ordering of states by number of executions. This brings in the size of the state as a hidden explanatory variable and obscures the actual relationship. If you are contemplating committing a murder, you should not be concerned particularly with how many other murders or how many executions have taken place in your state, but with the probability that you will be executed.

In a way, however, we are being unkind to the sociologists. Data in crime are almost incredibly bad, even for murder. Still, we can see little evidence that the sociologists have tried to apply really suitable methods to the problem. These inadequate tests of the deterrent effect of the death penalty were, however, until recently the *only* empirical investigations that had been undertaken on the deterrent effect of punishment. In spite of the fact that this evidence was extremely weak, sociologists and criminologists continued to say that it had been demonstrated that punishment had no deterrent effect.

The widely popular view that criminals are sick is based not on a few poor empirical studies, but on zero empirical studies. Some criminals are indeed mentally ill, and they are customarily segregated from the other criminals during the trial process. Thus, most states maintain facilities for the criminally insane as well as for ordinary criminals. There seems to be, however, absolutely *no* evidence that criminals who are in the ordinary prisons are more likely to be insane than people outside, or that what neuroses they do have, have much to do with their crimes.[7] In addition, if investigations deal exclusively with

7. One of our ways to investigate this subject has been to ask people if they can refer us to such empirical research. We repeat the question here.

criminals who are in prisons and who are by definition "failures" at their jobs, one can easily get a distorted picture of the criminal population. We would obtain the same type of distorted picture if we attempted to judge the intelligence and sanity of the business community as a whole by primarily observing those businessmen who go bankrupt.

What, then, have the criminologist and sociologist investigated? The answer is the environmental background of the criminal. As we have pointed out, people from poor backgrounds are apt to have a lower cost of crime, and hence, even under the economic explanation, we would anticipate that they would commit more crimes. Studies of this sort, then, do not differentiate between the two basic hypotheses, and such studies have dominated the work on the determinants of crime by sociologists and criminologists. Indeed, until very recently, those economists who turned their attention to crime simply accepted the dominant opinion of sociology and criminology and repeated the sociologists' studies, albeit with somewhat different methodology.[8] Thus, until really very recently, most "experts" on crime believed that punishment did not deter crime. This belief indicated that we were wrong to put people in prison, although this conclusion was seldom drawn. Further, it was based on an extraordinarily small quantity of very inferior work, which in turn was mostly addressed to one very special case.

Once economists began working on crime, however, it was inevitable that they would begin to investigate the possibility that crimes—like everything else—are affected by price. The deterrence theory of punishment is, after all, simply a special version of the general economic principle that raising the price of something will reduce the amount purchased.[9] Further, the first serious empirical research to test this proposition was undertaken by a master's candidate under Becker's direction. Presumably the basic research design was his, and it set the standard and style for the bulk of the empirical research that we shall discuss.

For certain types of crime, Arleen Leibowitz ran a multiple regression routine in which the crime rate by state was a dependent variable, and the

8. See, for example, Belton M. Fleisher, *The Economics of Delinquency*, Chicago: Quadrangle Books, 1966.

9. For earlier and more rigorous discussions of the economic approach to crime, see Gary S. Becker, "Crime and Punishment: An Economic Approach," *Journal of Political Economy*, 76 (March/April 1968), 169–217, and Gordon Tullock, "The Welfare Costs of Tariffs, Monopolies, and Theft," *Western Economic Journal*, 5 (1967), 224–32. The latter refers to the deterrent effects of punishment only in passing.

punishment the independent variable(s).[10] Leibowitz used three different specifications of the equation in which the likelihood of conviction and the average sentence were treated in different ways, with the objective of attempting to determine which of these was more important. For reasons that will be discussed below, she was unable to cast a great deal of light upon this subject. She did, however, find a pronounced deterrent effect.

Unfortunately, in the traditional literature, there has been some discussion as to whether the certainty of punishment is more important than the severity of punishment. Like most of the other scholars we will be citing, Leibowitz attempts to solve this problem by taking these two terms separately. Theoretically, this is unwise, since it is not obvious that individuals would have very much choice between, say, a 50-50 chance of two years in prison or a 1-4 chance of four years in prison. Further, any difference would be the effect of either risk aversion or time discounting. Both of these are apt to be small compared with the effect of the present value of the punishment.

The next study discussed was by a sociologist, Jack P. Gibbs, who apparently had not been at all influenced by Becker and who had used a somewhat different research design.[11] Gibbs took the homicide rate for each state in 1960 from the Federal Bureau of Investigation statistics and correlated it against two other variables. The first was the average time in prison for each person now in prison for homicide in each state, and the second was the likelihood of being sent to prison for homicide by state, calculated by dividing the number of people who had been imprisoned for this crime in each state by the number of homicides committed in that state (as shown in the FBI *Uniform Crime Report*). His tests also unambiguously showed the deterrent effect of punishment upon homicide.

Unfortunately, Gibbs also attempted to determine whether certainty or severity of sentence was more important. Gibbs's article set off quite a flurry of further research in the same area, and a good deal of it was devoted to this essentially irrelevant question. It should be said, however, that all of this work

10. Arleen Smigel Leibowitz, "Does Crime Pay: An Economic Analysis," M.A. thesis, Columbia University, New York, 1965. In not being published it is typical of the research in this area. Many of the papers we will discuss have not been formally published, presumably because journals regard their conclusions as beyond the pale. We have obtained copies of these, mainly in mimeographed form, through the "invisible college." It seems likely that we do not have all of them. We would appreciate being informed of further examples.

11. Jack P. Gibbs, "Crime, Punishment, and Deterrence," *Southwestern Social Science Quarterly*, 48 (March 1968), 515–30.

showed the deterrent effect for punishment. Louis Gray and David Martin reexamined Gibbs's statistics, using a different technique and, uniquely, came to the conclusion that efforts to untangle the effects of severity and certainty were a waste of time.[12] Once again, they showed the deterrent effect. Frank Bean and Robert Cushing also reexamined Gibbs's work, using still a third statistical technique and, once again, turned up deterrence effect.[13] Lastly, Charles Tittle published an expansive attack upon the severity versus certainty aspect of Gibbs's article.[14] In this study, he used basically the same sort of data but a different statistical technique than that used by Gibbs and took it for *many* crimes rather than just homicide. Once again, it clearly shows that punishment has a deterrent effect.

We now turn to a most interesting paper by Michael Block.[15] In this study, Block used Los Angeles Police districts as his observations, which meant that his data are quite different from most of the studies that use entire states as the observations. It also raises some fairly difficult problems having to do with the variables. Nevertheless, Block succeeded in making use of these data for a very elaborate series of regression operations in which the offense rate per district for each offense considered is negatively correlated with the clearance rate in that district, and positively correlated with the loot gained. It would be hard to find a more perfect expression of the economic hypothesis. Although there are some problems of a technical nature in this study, it seems to us that it offers a most intriguing opportunity for further research of the same sort in other cities. In a sense, the statewide observation data have been largely exhausted. All we can do now is try different years. Block's methods, however, can be tested in a number of different areas with completely independent data.

More recent work, in what we may call the Becker-Gibbs tradition, has been more ambitious. Phillips, Votey, and Howell, for example, produced

12. Louis N. Gray and J. David Martin, "Punishment and Deterrence: Another Analysis of Gibbs' Data," *Social Science Quarterly*, 50 (September 1969), 389–95.

13. Frank D. Bean and Robert G. Cushing, "Criminal Homicide, Punishment, and Deterrence: Methodological and Substantive Reconsiderations," *Social Science Quarterly*, 52 (September 1971), 277–89.

14. Charles R. Tittle, "Crime Rates and Legal Sanctions," *Social Problems*, 16 (Spring 1969), 409–23. It would appear to us that Tittle started out intending to demonstrate that Gibbs was totally wrong, but had to settle for bickering about this essentially irrelevant issue.

15. Michael Block, "An Econometric Approach to Theft," Stanford University, mimeographed.

a paper aimed basically at providing optimal enforcement recipes for the crime control system.[16] This goes far beyond our concern in this chapter, but it should be noted that in the process of obtaining their results, they ran a complex regression in which the deterrent effect of punishment showed up quite clearly. This study used a time series for the nation in general as its basic data, and hence it is independent of any of the previous studies. A time-series study, taken by and of itself, would not be very convincing, since various things other than deterrence change over time. Nevertheless, evidence that the time-series study leads to the same conclusion as the cross-section studies does add an element of confirmation.

Morgan Reynolds also had a good deal more ambitious goal than those we have reported so far.[17] Once again, however, his study involved—among other things—a multiple regression routine in which the deterrent effect of punishment is implicitly tested. It is a cross-section study, differing from the others only in that the other variables used in the regression were somewhat different, because it has somewhat different objectives. The deterrent effect showed up as usual. Isaac Ehrlich—once again under the supervision of Gary Becker—prepared a dissertation for a Ph.D. in economics at Columbia University.[18] The dissertation, available to us only in preliminary form, is the most ambitious study that has been attempted in this area and shows a very clear deterrent effect of punishment.

There is a very good study by R. A. Carr-Hill and N. H. Stern, "An Econometric Model of the Supply and Control of Recorded Offenses in England and Wales." We have this only as a Xerox copy of the first draft. Due to different types of statistics, the Carr-Hill/Stern research design is not identical with the ones we have discussed before, but the basic principles are the same. They show a very clear deterrent effect of imprisonment, and, indeed, the coefficients they get for imprisonment appear to be markedly higher than those in the United States. Let us hope that with time further studies in other foreign

16. Llad Phillips, Harold L. Votey, Jr., and John Howell, "Apprehension, Deterrence, Guns and Violence: The Control of Homicide," paper presented at the 46th meeting of the Western Economic Association, Vancouver, British Columbia, August 1971.

17. Morgan Reynolds, "Crimes for Profit: The Economics of Theft," Ph.D. dissertation, University of Wisconsin, 1971. We have seen only a paper he read at the Western Economic Association meeting entitled "The Economics of Theft."

18. A condensed version of this dissertation has been published; see Isaac Ehrlich, "Participation in Illegitimate Activities: A Theoretical and Empirical Investigation," *Journal of Political Economy*, 81 (May/June 1973), 521–65.

countries will become available. A good deal of further work has been done with the American data, and there is indeed room for more, but it does not seem necessary to discuss it in detail here.[19] Isaac Ehrlich returned to the problem of the death penalty in a recent article, and finds that each execution prevents somewhere between 8 and 20 murders.[20] The data problems he faced were formidable, and it is not certain in this case that his conclusions are correct, but this suggests that the repeal of the death penalty is a costly business.

There is another line of research that can be said to be indirectly related to the deterrent hypothesis. Under a grant from the National Science Foundation, a number of graduate students at Virginia Polytechnic Institute and State University have been conducting cost-benefit analyses of various types of crime in order to find out whether crime pays. As can well be imagined, the data problems are appalling. Further, it would be quite possible for deterrence to have an effect on crime, even if the criminals were so irrational that they went into the activity when the costs were greater than the benefits. Nevertheless, the general finding of this study is consistent with the deterrence hypothesis. We do find, on the whole, that professional criminals seem to have made sensible career choices. In other words, crime pays.[21] This implies but does not prove that if the cost of crime were raised, they would pick other occupations.

19. See Harold L. Votey, Jr., and Llad Phillips, *Economic Crimes: Their Generation, Deterrence, and Control*, Springfield Va.: U.S. Clearinghouse for Federal Scientific and Technical Information, 1969; Votey and Phillips, "The Law Enforcement Production Function," *Journal of Legal Studies*, 1 (June 1972); Votey and Phillips, "An Economic Analysis of the Deterrent Effect of Law Enforcement on Criminal Activity," *Journal of Criminal Law, Criminology, and Police Science*, 63 (September 1972); Votey and Phillips, "The Control of Criminal Activity: An Economic Analysis," in *Handbook of Criminology*, ed. Daniel Glaser, Chicago: Rand McNally & Co., forthcoming; Joseph P. Magaddino and Gregory C. Krohm (untitled paper, in progress); David L. Sjoquist, "Property Crime and Economic Behavior: Some Empirical Results," *American Economic Review*, 88, no. 3 (1973); Llad Phillips, Harold L. Votey, Jr., and Donald Maxwell, "Crime, Youth, and the Labor Market," *Journal of Political Economy*, 80 (May/June 1972); and Maynard L. Erickson and Jack P. Gibbs, "The Deterrence Question: Some Alternative Methods of Analysis," *Social Science Quarterly*, 53 (December 1973), 534–51.

20. Isaac Ehrlich, "The Deterrent Effect of Capital Punishment: A Question of Life and Death," *American Economic Review* (in press).

21. William E. Cobb, "Theft and the Two Hypotheses," and Gregory C. Krohm, "The Pecuniary Incentives of Property Crimes," in *The Economics of Crime and Punishment*, ed. Simon Rottenberg, Washington: American Enterprise Institute, 1973.

A Final Comment

Ideas influence the real world. The fact that most specialists in the study of crime have believed, written, and taught that punishment does not deter crime has had an effect upon public policy. Legislatures have been more reluctant to appropriate money for prisons than they otherwise would have been; judges have tended to feel that imprisonment had little effect on crime, and hence at the intellectual level, in any event, were less willing to put people in jail for long periods of time. Further, the shortage of prisons so induced has made it impossible to keep people in jail for long periods of time for serious crimes. As a result, halfway houses (which are very inexpensive), parole, and probation have been resorted to on a very large scale, and this has sharply reduced the cost of crime. This in turn leads to a rise in the crime rate that leads to further clogging of facilities, and hence further reduction in the cost of crime. The rising crime rate in the United States to a very considerable extent can be blamed upon our intellectual community.

We began this chapter with quotations from a juvenile delinquent in Washington, D.C. We suspect that he may be illiterate, or close to illiterate, and certainly has none of the academic credentials we normally require for research into the origins of crime. Nevertheless, we cannot escape the feeling that he is far better qualified to advise our government on matters of crime prevention than most professors of criminology.

WHY GOVERNMENT

Gordon Tullock and Richard B. McKenzie

A good socialist might regard the title of this chapter as showing prejudice. He would feel that the problem is "why market?" In his view, the natural state of the economy is to have government do everything, and one should have the market do only those few things that it can do well. There was, in fact, a famous debate on socialism as opposed to the market at the London School of Economics between two graduate students who later became famous economists, William Hutt and Abba Lerner. Hutt argued that we should use the market everywhere government would not be better, and Lerner argued that we should use the government everywhere the market would not be better, but they both were in substantial agreement as to which things should be allocated to the market and which should be allocated to the government. It doesn't really make any great difference which place you start from, if your ideas as to the criteria to be used in determining whether the market or the government should deal with activity are the same.

Institutions Other Than Government or Market

FAMILY

Most economists are, in fact, in agreement as to the general system to be used in determining whether the government or the market should deal with a given area. Before turning to this substantial measure of agreement, however, there are three other matters that must be dealt with. The first is that there are, in our society, institutions other than the market or the government. To take but one example, it is probable that the family is as important in allocation of resources in our economy as either the market or the government. In general, however, there's not much in the way of public policy involved here. Individual families make up their own minds as to how their collective resources shall be allocated. Different families clearly use somewhat different rules.

Reprinted, with permission, from *The New World of Economics: Explorations into the Human Experience*, 4th ed. (Homewood, Ill.: Richard D. Irwin, 1985), 191–200.

CHURCHES, PRIVATE CLUBS, AND NONPROFIT SECTOR

There are other institutions that are neither governmental nor private. The churches, the whole nonprofit sector, and private clubs are all examples which are neither, strictly speaking, market nor government, although they normally have at least some aspects which make them similar to either the government, the market, or both. Thus, in deciding whether activities should be put in the market or the government sector, we are making an incomplete analysis. But a complete analysis would be very difficult, and some of these institutions are not well understood so we will confine ourselves to that partial analysis.

Government and Private Activities

The second topic which must be discussed before turning to the basic rule for distinguishing between government and private activities is redistribution of income or wealth. In this chapter we will discuss the decision as to whether something should be government or private, without any reference to that decision's effect on income or wealth of the people, or to the fact that different distributions of wealth might lead to different decisions with respect to allocation between the government and the private sector. The reason that we are leaving it out is not that it is unimportant, but that it is to be discussed separately in the next chapter. It is easier to study these two topics if they are dealt with one at a time. The final decision as to whether any given activity will be dealt with by the government or the private sector will commonly involve both efficiency considerations (the topic of this chapter) and redistribution considerations (the topic of the next chapter).

Philosophy

The third item which must be dealt with before turning to the role of government and the market is a matter of philosophy. A democratic government does what the people want; it is not necessarily what they should want or what is good for them. The same is true with the market. It produces goods that people want and are willing to pay for. We might be better off if there were no tobacco, heroin, or alcohol. The market, however, produces all three, and if we object to them we can, of course, turn to government to prevent their being put out. But we will be able to do so only if that is widely supported.

The experiments in preventing the production and consumption of alcohol in the 1920s indicated that it was unpopular even though it had been possible to pass the Prohibition amendment through the usual democratic procedure for amending the Constitution. Currently, efforts to control drugs of a somewhat harder nature are showing almost equal difficulties.

The correct statement here is that both the market and a democratic government are mechanisms by which individual desires are implemented in a socially cooperative way. Actually, we might be better off if this were not so.[1] Nevertheless, the system that we use is one in which most people have at least some influence on the outcome, both in government and in the market.

It should be noted that it is not necessary that governments, or for that matter the market, operate in this way. In the Soviet Union, a very small group of people (during much of the history of the Soviet Union, really only one person) make all of the basic decisions, both as to government policy and as to what goods the individual will consume. Historically, some type of government depending on one person—which is called a dictatorship if it is not hereditary, and a monarchy if it is—has been the most common form of government. Further, as a general rule, these governments have had ideas as to what people should consume as well as ideas about the kind of government policies they should be subjected to. The U.S. system, however, depends basically on aggregating a large number of individual preferences. Maybe this is not a good thing. Most people who contemplate what the world's governments do or what their neighbors consume feel that these choices could be improved upon. Perhaps they could. There is no argument one way or the other in this book. We will be discussing what is the actual outcome of these two systems of aggregation rather than what we would like if good, well-informed experts were given dictatorial power in either the market or the government.

Government versus Private Enterprise

So much for preliminaries. Let us now turn to consider a very old and traditional problem in economics used to illustrate whether the government or private enterprise should be used to deal with an issue. This problem was first

---

1. I am sure that you, reader, would be better off if instead of following your own not-too-well-informed opinions, you always followed my advice. For a fee I will be glad to give you this advice, and I now inform you that the advice is valuable enough so that the $500 a year which I would charge is a bargain.

introduced by the distinguished British economist Pigou some 50 years ago, and the technology was from a modern standpoint old-fashioned. Specifically, he considered a factory which had a smoking chimney. He was not concerned, nor were the people living around the factory, with the possibility of lung cancer or all of the other problems that we now ascribe to smoke. In that era, most housewives in England washed their clothes and then hung them out on the line to dry. This, again, is old technology rather than the present-day approach. Soot from the smoke made them dirty again. This is the problem we're going to discuss. Note that this particular scheme happens to be very simple and straightforward, but it can be extended to modern situations of air and water pollution very readily.

POLLUTION

Consider the situation of the factory owner. He can reduce the amount of smoke that his factory is producing; for that matter he can eliminate it totally by the simple expedient of closing down the factory. Reducing the amount of smoke is, however, expensive. The reason he is dumping this factory waste (soot and so on) into the air is simply that that is the cheapest way of getting rid of it and is not, under the circumstances, illegal. In Figure 1 we show by line FF the cost to him of producing various amounts of pollution. Note that it is quite expensive to produce very little pollution; indeed, closing down the factory, which is the only way of reducing it to zero, would be very expensive.

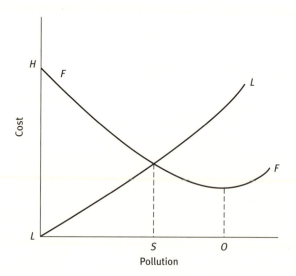

FIGURE 1

The cost to the factory owner falls steadily as he produces more and more pollution out to point O; this is his optimal point. From then on, if he wanted to produce more pollution he would have to deliberately run his factory in some inefficient way—for example, burning unnecessary fuel. The factory owner, left to himself, chooses to produce O amount of pollution. The marginal cost to the homeowners of getting their laundry dirty is shown by the line LL. It is obvious that if they had their will they would choose zero pollution. In any event, they would like less than amount O.

If we consider the total social cost of this pollution, it is obvious that it is minimized if we have S quantity of pollution. Each unit of pollution reduced beyond S costs more to reduce than the social benefit obtained by the homeowners. Whereas each unit of pollution produced beyond S benefits the manufacturer less than it injures the homemakers worried about their laundry.

Some people, on seeing this, argue that pollution should be prohibited. This is not true, and, in fact, if you talk to them for a while, it usually turns out that they really mean we should eliminate pollution insofar as it is practical. The economists respond to that by saying that point S is the practical amount to be eliminated.

EXAMPLE

As evidence that we should not eliminate pollution completely, I should perhaps mention that my secretary has a bad cold. In fact, she has had it for two days. As a result of having a bad cold, by the mere act of breathing, she is producing pollution; that is, she is expelling into the outer atmosphere various viruses and a few germs which impose real costs on other people. I, in fact, have a very mild cold which I suspect I acquired as a result of her polluting the atmosphere. (I hope that it doesn't get worse.)

Now obviously, we could design a device which would be attached to my secretary's mouth and nose and which would destroy all viruses as they come out. The reason we do not do this is simple and straightforward. The cost of the device would be greater than the benefit in reducing pollution. We prefer to have a certain number of people exposed to colds rather than compelling those who have colds to walk around with a complicated device which demolishes all viruses and bacteria in their outgoing breath.

DISEASES

With other diseases we feel differently. For many years, for example, substantially everybody was compelled to have a vaccination for smallpox, whether they wanted it or not. The motive for protection of themselves against smallpox was regarded as inadequate. Society felt that the failure to have a smallpox vaccination not only increased the risk that the individuals would be ill, but also increased the risk that they would be contagious and cause injury to other people. Currently, we are in the process of wiping small-pox out as a disease by the simple expedient of requiring everybody within many miles of any smallpox case to be vaccinated, regardless of his personal preferences in the matter. The American Civil Liberties Union has not com-plained about this, although it should be said, most of the people who have smallpox these days live in less-developed dictatorships where they do not have any rights at all. Still, back in the days when smallpox was a real problem in the United States, the courts never objected to compulsory vaccination. The difference between this and the cold is obvious. The cost of smallpox contagion is very great; the cost of a cold is modest. What we must do in all cases is to weigh the cost of the prevention against the injury which will be inflicted on other people from failing to take precautions.

BENEFIT PRODUCTION

The general rule is simple. If you, individually or with some group with whom you have a bargain, take into account only your own cost (and that is what you normally will do) and ignore the cost and benefits of other people, then you will tend to be socially too economical. This is not only true in cases where your action may injure other people, it is also true if your action might benefit them. Take a minor example of benefit production: most people who have beautiful gardens cause pleasure, not only to themselves but to their neighbors and passersby. Presumably, they don't pay much attention to this secondary pleasure and hence invest less in their gardens than they otherwise would. Here is a case where the cost of compelling them to put more money into gardens would be greater than the benefit, but there are many other cases where we do compel people to put more money into generating of benefits for others than they would do on their own.

In general, where people create benefits for others by their action, but would normally not take that benefit into account, we refer to the "problem of public goods." A surprising number of standard government activities fall in this category.[2] Some of the newer government activities, such as much environmental work, also fall here.

---

2. For mathematical reasons. Public good is normally much more rigorously and narrowly defined in advanced work. For our purposes, however, this general definition will do.

Let us return to our smoking chimney and the homemakers who worry about soot on their laundry. It is clear that if we simply let the factory owner make his own decisions as to the soot, he will release too much. There is then an argument for considering government control in this area. But it should be emphasized that this is an argument for considering, not for definitely deciding on, government intervention. Consider a simple democracy, in which the votes are counted and the outcome is simply the will of the majority. Since there is only one factory owner, and there are many homemakers whose laundry is made dirty, the probable outcome would be zero pollution. In some ways, this is as bad as the amount of pollution that the factory owner would select. In other words, a perfectly democratic government might be just as bad in controlling this activity as simply doing nothing at all—letting the factory owner pollute the air. The outcome would be different but it might be just as bad.

Of course, in the real world, the factory owner would make contributions to politicians' campaign funds, he would have a professional lobbyist working for him, and surely he would not be cut down to zero smoke. What we would expect is some kind of compromise between the desire of the homemakers and their spouses to have no smoke and the desire of the factory owner to have no restrictions on the release of smoke. There is no reason to believe that we would reach S. We would, however, reach some point to the left of the factory owner's optimum and to the right of the homemakers' optimum. This compromise would probably be better than simply leaving it to the market.

EXTERNALITIES

This should be our general rule in thinking about almost any problem where there are "large externalities." This magic phrase means simply that individual action, or action by a small group of private individuals who reach an agreement among themselves, affects other people as well as themselves, and hence their agreement will not necessarily be optimum.

When we see such a situation, and we see it all over the place, we should begin inquiring whether it would not be better to have government action than to have private control. But this is merely the start of the investigation. We must then consider what the government would probably do in this particular case. It is not obvious that the government's solution would be better than the private person's decision. As a rough rule of thumb, where the effect on other people is great, it is likely that the government will do better than the private market. Where the effect on other people is modest, it is likely that the private market will do better than government. What should be done in each case, however, is to examine the matter in detail. The objective is to obtain the optimal outcome, which in this case would be S on Figure 1. One cannot expect, however, that in the real world, with all the defects the real world has, we will in fact achieve that goal. At best, we will get a rough approximation; and whether the approximation that is obtained by the market is better than that obtained by the government requires calculation in each and every case.

So far, we have only talked about a few cases, all except the garden involving air pollution. As a matter of fact, most traditional government activities involve very severe externalities. Take military decisions. If I were to decide to protect myself against the Russians by acquiring a hydrogen bomb, the benefit (and perhaps the harm) of my decision would affect my neighbors as well as me. Indeed, military matters are a particularly clear-cut case where individual action is inefficient. This is an example of a "public good." The problem here is that investments by individuals to defend the United States will protect other individuals as well as themselves. Under the circumstances, everybody is likely to let George do it if we depend on the private market. We, therefore, in Samuelson's phrase, reach agreements to coerce each other. That is, we collectively decide on a certain amount of defense and then force ourselves to contribute.

This argument in principle is impeccable, but it has several difficulties. First, the decision as to how much defense shall be purchased is necessarily a collective decision, and many individuals may be unhappy about the decision made in a given case. In this respect it is different from the market decision, where you can decide how much you will choose to spend. This is an intrinsic inefficiency in any collective provision of goods. Once again, we must weigh this inefficiency against the inefficiency which we would suffer from the private failure to provide (or the underprovision of) this particular good. The second inefficiency, of course, is that the government may simply not get the right amount because of malfunctions of either the democratic or the bureaucratic process. We should not assume, as many economic textbooks do, that the government will make the optimal decision. It is not a choice between O in Figure 1 and S, with the government taking S, but between O in Figure 1 and some not very accurately specified other point on the horizontal axis. It is probably going to be closer to S than it is to O, but it nevertheless may not be very efficient.

Most other traditional government activities, as stated above, fall within the area where externalities are large. Police activity is an example. If I hire somebody to protect my house from burglary, and he is careful, he will check up on suspicious characters wandering in the neighborhood. This will give my neighbors protection, too, and hence I will be generating a favorable externality for them. They are, under the circumstances, unlikely to invest themselves, and once again I will probably let George do it; and with everyone else doing the same, we have an underinvestment in private protection. As shall be seen in the next chapter, there is a somewhat similar argument—interestingly enough, invented by Milton Friedman—for government provision of charity to the poor.

It is not my purpose here to go on and demonstrate that each and every government activity involves externalities. Indeed, there are a number of government activities that do not. Most economists, however, when they find the government doing something which does not involve externalities, are apt to argue that it should be transferred to the market. There are indeed some cases where the government itself is engaged in generating externalities, and they are purely negative. The Civil Aeronautics Board of unlamented memory, for example, created a cartel in the airline business and kept fares much higher than they needed to be. Still the general rule is: where there are large externalities (or public goods, which is simply an extreme case of an externality), then we should give careful consideration to the use of the government rather than the market. Where the externalities are low or nonexistent, the market will probably be better. In those unfortunately quite numerous cases where there are externalities that are significant but not gigantic, it is usually quite difficult to say whether the market or the government will perform least badly. We should, in these cases, make careful calculations.

Concluding Comments

All this may seem quite different from what you learned in your civics class. Indeed, it is a rather new idea. Adam Smith, for example, did not use this method for determining what the government should and should not do. It has become a standard lesson in economics, however. Further, if you consider those activities of the government, which almost everyone will agree are suitable for government, you will almost always find that there is a fairly severe externality. Unfortunately, there are some government activities now undertaken where there is no externality, and there are also some areas where there are externalities and no, or inefficient, government activity. Some reallocation of various activities between the market and the government seems to be called for.

RATIONALITY IN HUMAN
AND NONHUMAN SOCIETIES
Gordon Tullock and Richard B. McKenzie

Rationality in Economics: The Experimental Evidence

In Chapter 1, we outlined the economic approach to human behavior. One of the foundations of this approach is the assumption that human beings are rational. As we pointed out in that chapter, the standard of rationality is not a very high one, but nevertheless economists do believe in the essential intelligence of human beings in the very limited sense that their demand curves slant downward and that they will select the preferred choice over the less preferred.

Among scholarly critics of economics, this rationality assumption is perhaps the most frequently criticized aspect of economics. Economists have answered this criticism in a number of ways, first by pointing out that the requirement of rationality in economics is actually a very low requirement. Second, Gary Becker has argued that the demand and supply relationship can be generated by random behavior; hence, people do not have to be rational to fulfill the basic postulates of economics.[1] This argument by Becker was criticized in part by Israel Kirzner,[2] but the basic point is generally accepted. It is not true that all of the participants in a market process have to be rational.

In this chapter, we will turn to the experimental evidence of the rationality assumption. We will begin with discussion of the experimental economics in which special experiments are set up for normal human beings. The outcome of these experiments is consistent with the rationality hypothesis. Indeed, Vernon Smith, one of the pioneers in the area, regards these experiments as the first real proof of both rationality and what we normally refer to as consumption theory. It should be said, however, that these experiments

Reprinted, with permission, from *The New World of Economics: Explorations into the Human Experience*, 4th ed. (Homewood, Ill.: Richard D. Irwin, 1985), 263–78.

1. Gary S. Becker, "Irrational Behavior and Economic Theory," *Journal of Political Economy* 70 (February 1962), 1–13.

2. Israel M. Kirzner, "Rational Action and Economic Theory," *Journal of Political Economy* 70 (August 1962), 380–85. See also Gary S. Becker, "A Reply to Kirzner," *Journal of Political Economy* 71 (February 1963), 82–83.

were originally designed for other purposes, and their proof of rationality is a secondary consequence. Nevertheless, they do prove that at least a great many people behave rationally. Incidentally, these experiments can, if desired, be repeated in almost any classroom. They are an interesting game for the first one or two times they are tried but tend to be boring if run a large number of times.

After we have discussed these examples of experimental economics, we will turn to another set of experiments which deal with rationality in quite a different way. These experiments demonstrate that *rationality* in the sense that it is used in economics characterizes not only human beings but human beings who are formally judged insane (and therefore are hospitalized), birds, rats, and a group of microscopic animals called rotifers. We do not know if these animals are rational, but they certainly behave as if they were. In other words, their demand curves slope downward. They try to buy in the cheapest market, adjust consumption in terms of prices, and so on.

An Example

Let us then turn to some very simple experiments that support the idea that markets tend to equilibrium and that this equilibrium is an efficient one. These experiments were originally carried out by Vernon Smith, and they can be duplicated in any class with no great difficulty.[3] They are less enlightening than some of the later experiments we will discuss for a number of reasons, the most important of which is that the students were simply asked to play the game of buying and selling without having any real money riding on their action. Later experiments, many of them also devised by Smith, have provided the students with cash they can earn by efficient performance in this experimental market.

In the original experiment, students are divided into sellers and buyers. Then they are given cards which tell them their minimum sale prices if they are the sellers or their maximum purchase prices if they are the buyers. One student, for example, might receive a sale card with $2.50 as the lowest price at which he or she can sell, and another might receive a purchase card with $3.50 as the highest purchase price at which he or she can buy. They are

---

3. See Vernon Smith, "An Experimental Study of Competitive Market Behavior," *Journal of Political Economy* 70 (April 1962), 111–37.

also told how many units they can buy or sell. For simplicity, this is usually one unit.

The students are then instructed to buy and sell to each other in a simulated market. Each one is to attempt to maximize his or her profit. The profit is defined as the amount that the price which the seller receives exceeds his or her minimum price. The converse rule applies to the buyer.

The technique is very informal. The students simply announce an offer to buy or sell whenever they feel like it, and some other student may then accept the offer, or perhaps no student will accept it. In professional markets—for example, the grain exchange—that operate on roughly these rules, the procedure is very disorderly, with a great deal of shouting and a set of hand signals. But for classroom purposes, it is sensible to provide some rule that guarantees that everyone understands what everyone else is saying. For example, the students could hold up their hands if they want to make or accept an offer, and the professor may indicate which one of the several raised hands will be recognized. This is some departure from the real world, but it is a little easier to follow.

The cards that have been distributed to the students are normally arranged in these experiments so that there is an equilibrium price. For example, see Figure 1.[4] Each of the dashes on the line marked *DD* represents a student holding a demand card for the price shown. Similarly, each dash on the line *SS* represents a student holding a seller's card for the price shown. The equilibrium price is a trifle less than $3.50, and the number of units that will be sold is 15. A few students will be left with transactions incompleted, but this is true of the market also.

The game is played until there are no longer any acceptable offers. Normally the price and quantity at which this occurs can be predicted quite accurately by anyone who knows the shape of the demand and supply curves represented by the cards distributed to the students. The student experimental subjects do not know this; hence, their information is incomplete. Under the circumstances, it takes a little while to establish equilibrium. On the right half of Figure 1, we show the process through time of the price of transactions. You will note that the prices start at the left with considerable variance, but toward the right end of the chart (after some experience has been accumulated), they are quite stable.

The method in which these time charts are produced is fairly simple. The individuals play the game until there are no more offers that are acceptable.

---

4. This is a mildly revised version of Smith's Figure 2, ibid., 118.

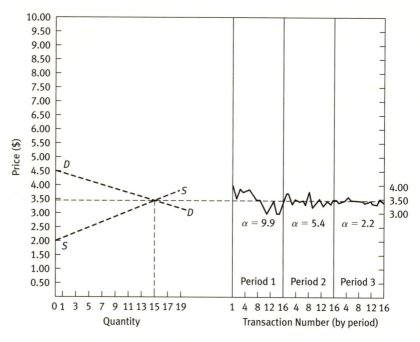

SOURCE: Vernon Smith, "An Experimental Study of Competitive Market Behavior," *Journal of Political Economy* 70 (April 1962), 118.

FIGURE 1

This is called a period, and, for example, the first such play is shown as period 1.

Once there are no more acceptable offers forthcoming, the beginning round of the game is declared finished, and each student is then told the game will start again. He will still use in the second round of the game the same prices and designation of seller and buyer that he used in the first round. In the second round of the game, however, each of the students has more information about the structure of the market than in the first round, and therefore, we would expect that the variance of prices would be lower in period 2 than in period 1. Examination of Figure 1 indicates that this is what happens. In this particular experiment, only three rounds of the game were played, and the reason is obvious from observation of the transaction chart in period 3. By period 3 with this rather simple structure, almost everyone was well enough informed so that the price was extremely stable. Smith felt that little was to be gained from further repetitions at this point, and he stopped the game.

All that we have learned so far from these experiments is that the price does indeed approach the equilibrium but that it does not do so instantaneously, because people do not have adequate information. This will surprise very few students of economics, but some noneconomists have expressed doubt on this point. However, there is a little more information to be obtained from our very simple experiment. We could make measures of the speed with which equilibrium is approached, and this is a topic upon which formal economics has very little to contribute. Economists have normally simply said that equilibrium would be achieved but not very fast.

As a matter of fact, in the article from which this experiment was drawn, Smith proceeded to test a number of hypotheses having to do with the stability of the market price and the speed at which equilibrium was approached, depending on such matters as the steepness of the demand and supply curves, whether they have roughly the same slant or one is fairly flat and the other is steep, and so forth. Not surprisingly, in general, the flatter the demand and supply curves, the faster equilibrium was approached. Although there had been speculation on this matter beforehand, the information obtained was the first real evidence.[5]

Further Experiments

Of course, a game in which nothing really rides on success in trading is really not very close to the real world. In fact, it is surprising how good the results are. After Smith had done the initial work, he was able to interest the National Science Foundation in funding more elaborate experiments in

---

5. Some of this work had been foreshadowed in S. Siegel and L. Fouraker, *Bargaining and Group Decision Making* (New York: McGraw-Hill, 1960). One nice feature of this set of experiments, however, is that they do not require any complicated setup or sizable resources; hence, any economics class that wishes can duplicate them and indeed develop more complicated hypotheses to be tested by the same method. A word of caution, however, is necessary. From my personal observation of Vernon Smith, the students playing these games tend to become bored. This is not surprising, since the games are not designed for entertainment; but a rapid boredom rate means that it is undesirable to do very much of this experimentation, even though one or two rounds of the game would probably be a good way to break up the classroom routine.

which the participants actually had something to gain from efficient behavior. Students really made a cash profit. Cards were distributed in much the same way as the earlier experiment, but the individuals received a money payment equal to the difference between their minimum sale price or maximum purchase price and the actual transaction price (if they were sellers), or below their maximum purchase price and the actual transaction price, assuming that the price was above their minimum sale price (if they were sellers), or below their maximum purchase price (if they were buyers).

Smith mainly used these funds for more complicated experiments than the one described above. But Charles Plott, building on Smith's work, duplicated the above experiment using cash payments in this manner.[6] The principal difference between Plott's experiments and Smith's is, we suppose, readily predictable. When there was something actually riding on the results, the people engaged in the game were more careful and paid closer attention, with the result that they approached equilibrium more rapidly.

Barry Keating, as a by-product of teaching managerial economics, produced some further experimental data along these same lines. In his class, the students are divided into 15 "companies," each with a small board of directors (three to five students). These companies routinely make decisions on various management policy matters including price and production schedules. The experiment is intended to be realistic in the sense that market conditions change so that the students can never be perfectly informed about the demand situation, just as real-world companies are never perfectly informed. The students are rewarded in grades if their company is "profitable."

Keating's result would surprise no economist. The companies responded to changes in the basic underlying market conditions by experimental activity with new prices and production schedules. Since different companies tried different prices and production rates, this would lead to an increase in the spread of their policies. Rather quickly, however, the spread between different companies' prices and policies narrows. Note that it never actually gets down to zero, since some of the companies are always searching to determine whether market conditions have changed. All of this, of course, is very similar to the real market.

6. All of the Plott experiments discussed in this chapter are very recent and, hence, unpublished. Since he continues to do work, anyone interested in this field can simply write to him at California Institute of Technology, Division of Humanities and Social Sciences, Pasadena, California 91109, and he will be glad to send you a large pile of papers reporting his experimental results.

POLLUTION

Plott continued his experiments into more difficult areas. One of these areas, voting procedures, was the subject of a set of experiments that rather neatly confirmed the basic proposition of Chapter 10. In that chapter, we argue that in a two-party system, even with more than one issue, the two parties tend to be very close together and at approximately the middle of the distribution. He also dealt with the problem of regulating pollution. By an ingenious technique,[7] he generated a pollutant in his experiment; that is, each individual completing a transaction imposed a cost on all other individuals, but the cost was, for him or her, lower than his or her gain. As any economist would predict, the equilibrium reached by the experiment was socially inferior, although it was privately optimal. The individuals, like real-world polluters, maximized their own profit and ignored the injury they inflicted on others, with the result that all of them were worse off than they would have been had they each taken the well-being of others into account.

In such a situation, economists usually argue that a properly calculated tax is the optimal policy, but in the real world, governments very commonly rely on regulations, a quota for example. Plott tried both of these techniques and found, as no economist would be surprised to hear, that the tax achieved the socially optimal number of sales in an efficient manner, and the quota achieved the same number but with a good deal of waste.

Another interesting and rather counterintuitive result by Plott consisted of a study of the market for advice. We are continuously in the situation where we must depend on advice from a doctor, garage mechanic, and so on, in areas which vitally concern us but where our own information is poor. Most economists, certainly the authors of this book, had always assumed that this gave these people with this special information an advantage and that at least occasionally we were cheated. Plott constructed an experiment in which some people were, in essence, customers who did not understand their car, and other people were garage mechanics who knew what was wrong. It was discovered that in his reasonably competitive market the traditional economic rule of one price was supplemented by a rule of one advice. In other words, the "mechanics" gave the best advice to their customers, apparently with the theory that the

---

7. Limitations of space, together with our lack of knowledge as to the background of our readers, make it necessary for us to condense sharply some descriptions of experimenters, such as this one. Full descriptions can be obtained, however, by writing to the author or if you are willing to wait a little while, by reading them in the published literature.

customers would just go somewhere else if they got poor advice. The result is surprising and obviously requires other testing and further experiments.[8]

Crazy but Not Irrational

The experiments discussed above were intended to demonstrate various economic propositions and test rationality as a sort of by-product. Further, normal human beings were used. Let us now turn to the evidence which indicates that abnormal human beings and at least some animals are also rational. Let us begin with people who are insane. Most patients in mental hospitals do not require any kind of physical restraint, although their behavior may be peculiar at times. Further, most are in reasonable physical health. As a consequence, the management of most mental hospitals usually tries to get a certain amount of maintenance work from their patients. For example, the patients may be asked to make up their beds, keep the area around their beds (or their room, if they have one) clean and orderly, perhaps assist in other tasks, such as mopping the hall floor. Since most of the patients are free to associate with each other, a certain amount of disciplinary control is also desirable. In particular, patients are restricted from doing things likely to irritate the other patients in their wards.

Until recently, it was always rather difficult to get the patients to cooperate. Lately, however, the introduction of "token economies" has led to significant improvements in patient behavior, with very little effort on the part of the hospital management.

The system is fairly simple. A special money (token) is issued by the hospital management. Since theft is frequently a major problem, the tokens are usually similar to traveler's checks, in the sense that each token is issued to one particular patient, and only that patient can use it.[9] Thus, if one of the patients steals the tokens of another, they do him no good.

These tokens may be used to purchase small comforts within the hospital community. For example, there may be a ward shop selling candy, cigarettes, and so forth. Further, it may be possible for the token holders to "buy"

8. Scholarly publication tends to be slow, and Plott's work has not yet been formally published. Copies may be obtained by writing to Professor Charles Plott at the California Institute of Technology.

9. Presumably the management would have no objection to bargained exchanges, but the economy is a fairly simple one, and this happens rather rarely.

better-than-standard meals, the use of recreational facilities, visits to town, and so forth.

It should be said that this new technique was not originally introduced to make the life of hospital managers easier. It began as a rather controversial method of treating patients. Although there is still some controversy about the procedure, it does seem in many cases to cure (or at least suppress the symptoms of) some mental diseases. Unfortunately, although it works in many cases, it does not work in all.

The individuals under treatment would be paid in tokens for an activity the doctors thought would benefit them. For example, an individual suffering from agoraphobia (fear of open spaces) might be given a token for walking 10 yards out into an open field and then back. After several days in which tokens were earned this way, the distance he had to go would be increased. This rather simple technique, believe it or not, does cure a fair number (unfortunately not all) of the cases of agoraphobia.

But our purpose here is to discuss the use of token economies not as a technique for curing mental illnesses but as a way of obtaining economically rational behavior from the patients in mental hospitals. After using tokens as a curative measure for a time, the caretakers of mental hospitals soon realized that the token economy could also be used for improving inmate behavior in other ways. The patient might, for example, be given a token for bedmaking or be paid in tokens for mopping the floor or assisting in other routine tasks. Indeed, in some cases the patients can actually be "employed" in simple, factory-type assembly jobs. It should be said that in general these jobs were assigned not because the institution wanted to make money but because it was thought desirable both to keep the patients busy and to give them continuing work experience in order that they can support themselves when and if they are released. Nevertheless, in a number of cases, institutions have in fact made modest profits on the operation, although in most cases there are losses if the curative aspects of the matter are disregarded.

Disciplinary problems became relatively unimportant with the token economies. Further, when difficulties did arise, in general they could be dealt with very simply and easily by changing the price. For example, in one hospital, the patients objected to mopping the floor. The caretakers simply raised the wage for floor mopping and found themselves deluged with volunteers.

Psychologists tend to be interested in improving their art; hence, they perform experiments. Changing the price of goods in the patients' shop turns out to lead to exactly the kind of behavior that economists would anticipate. For example, in one rather elaborate experiment, prices of various commodities were changed at unannounced intervals.[10] The patients in general adjusted just the way that economic theory would predict for rational beings; that is, they increased their purchases of things whose prices had gone down and reduced their purchases of those that had gone up. In some cases, the change was slow rather than immediate (which would indicate that a learning process was involved), and in some cases, errors in observation threw a good deal of sand into the procedure. Still, in general these people who had been certified as insane behaved quite rationally.[11]

In another case, the management of an institution had the patients employed in various activities for which they were paid. As an experiment, the management gave the patients a "paid vacation." The patients were given opportunities and encouragement to continue their work during their vacation, but they would be given no additional payments. Needless to say, this was an experiment, and the results are not surprising. The patients all chose not to work, thus indicating that their previous work had been a rational effort to obtain the tokens and not the result of "conditioning" or some other irrational characteristics.[12] The same management also arranged a set of experiments in which individuals were first trained for a number of different jobs and then given their choice of the jobs with token payment. After they had become accustomed to the job, they were then suddenly informed that the payment would be discontinued for their preferred job but that they could earn the same wage in a less-preferred job. As would be expected, all but one of the patients instantly changed to the less-preferred job, and the one exception changed after a day or so of experience of getting by without a "wage."[13]

R. C. Winkler, working with chronically psychotic female patients, tested more complex behavior patterns.[14] He distinguished luxury items from necessities and measured the responsiveness of the patients to price changes

---

10. R. C. Battalio, "A Test of Consumer Demand Theory Using Observation of Individual Consumer Purchases," *Western Economic Journal* 11 (December 1973), 411–28.

11. Presumably the doctors, like other people, are not perfect, and there were some errors in diagnosis among the patients; but it would be very surprising if the average patients were not in fact mentally ill.

12. T. Allyon and N. H. Azrin, "The Measurement and Reinforcement of Behavior of Psychotics," *Journal of Experimental Analysis of Behavior* 8 (November 1965), 357–83.

13. Ibid.

14. R. C. Winkler, "An Experimental Analysis of Economic Balance: Savings and Wages in a Token Economy," *Behavior Therapy* 4 (January 1973), 22–40.

of several items, reaching the standard conclusion that the demand for necessities was "price inelastic," meaning that the patients were relatively unresponsive to price changes and that the patients had greater *total expenditures* when the price of the necessities went up. They also found that the demand for luxuries was "price elastic." This means that the patients made lower total expenditures on the luxuries when their prices were raised.

In the above experiments, nothing in the way of age, IQ, educational level, type of mental disorder, or length of time in institutions seemed to affect the results. In other words, even seriously disturbed and/or very stupid people with no education who had been institutionalized for long periods of time behaved as if they were rational. It is only those people who were so seriously disturbed or so mentally impaired that they had only a few available behavior patterns—and were therefore not capable of earning and spending tokens—who did not respond to the types of experiments described above in a rational way.

In general, what these experiments indicate is that standards of rationality required for economic behavior are so low that certified patients in mental hospitals meet them. The argument that economics assumes rationality and that people are not rational is not, strictly speaking, refuted by these observations; but they certainly cast doubt on it.[15]

Rats

Let us proceed to consider some other entities normally thought to be even less rational—specifically, laboratory rats. Recently, a few economists, particularly John H. Kagel and Raymond C. Battalio of Texas A&M University, have been borrowing experimental techniques from the psychologists and using them to test whether behavior of nonhuman species is similar in restricted ways to that of human beings.[16] Since the research has only begun, they have so far tested only some of the simplest propositions of economics. It should be said at the start, however, that in these special, simple areas, rats seem to behave rationally.

15. For a general survey of token economies, see David G. Tarr, "Experiments in Token Economies: A Review of the Evidence Relating to Assumptions and Implications of Economic Theory," *Southern Economic Journal* 43 (October 1976), 1136–43.

16. John H. Kagel et al., "Demand Curves for Animal Consumers" (Paper presented at Southern Economic Association meeting, Atlanta, Georgia, November 1976).

Let us consider briefly the existing experimental technique in which the rats are confined individually in separate cages. We will in fact talk about only one rat, although Kagel and Battalio have, of course, tested their hypothesis on more than one. The box used to test the rats in these experiments is a bit of standard psychological apparatus. It consists of a box which has an internal environment wholesome enough so that the rats can be kept there indefinitely provided that food and water are supplied and the box is regularly cleaned. Attached to the box is a small computer that can be used to both meter the behavior of the experimental animal and carry out whatever provision of food or other stimuli to the animal the experimenter has planned; that is, the computer keeps track of all things going in and can be instructed to deliver various items under various conditions.

Since the rat would have great difficulty in handling token currency, the experimenters charge the rat prices not by giving it a small collection of tokens and having it insert them in a slot but by having the rat push a bar at the back of the cage. The pushes on the bar are the "payments" made by the rat, and this leads the computer to meter out to it, let us say, a small quantity of root beer, cherry cola, or whatever else the experimenters choose. They change the price of the various commodities by changing the amount delivered each time the bar is pushed. Thus, the price of 0.1cc of cherry cola might be one bar push, or two, or four.

Suppose, then, we consider one of their experiments in which a rat is given an adequate supply of food and water automatically by the machine and, in addition, is confronted with two bars—pushing one leads to root beer being provided and pushing the other provides cherry cola.

The computer can now be instructed to change the "price" of root beer and cherry cola by changing the amount received each time the bar is pressed.[17] In one experiment, for example, the amount of root beer delivered per bar push was held constant,[18] but the amount of cherry cola per bar push was

17. Note for the instructor: these experiments studied two different types of demand curves, one holding apparent real income constant and the other holding money income constant. For the purpose of this chapter, the matter is unimportant; but details of the experiment would provide a particularly easy way of explaining problems of demand curves under changes of wealth, the Slutsky-Hicks theory, and so on, if the instructor feels this material is suitable for an elementary course.

18. One of the results of this experimentation has been the discovery that rats seem to like root beer more than almost anything else. It must be genuine root beer, however. The rats apparently regard diet root beer as little better than water.

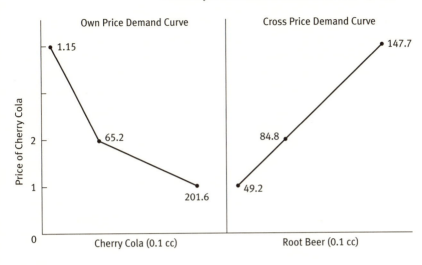

FIGURE 2

changed. It was found that when the payoff to a bar push was 0.025 cc of cherry cola, the rat consumed only a little over 0.1 cc per day. When the price was lowered so that the rat could get 0.5 cc per push, he consumed 65 cc, and at one bar push per 0.1 cc, he consumed 200 cc. Of course, the rat changed its consumption of root beer at the same time; that is, since the price of root beer was being held constant in real terms, the exchange ratio between the root beer and cherry cola for the rat was improving; hence, the rat reduced its consumption of root beer and increased its consumption of cherry cola. The rat's consumption of both cherry cola and root beer at varying prices of the cherry cola can be seen in Figure 2.[19] It can be seen that for the rat, root beer and cherry cola were substitute goods; that is, the more it consumed of one, the less it consumed of the other. There was, however, an element of complementarity (that is, the two goods are not perfect substitutes) in that the rat did not reduce its consumption of root beer at exactly the same rate as it increased its consumption of cherry cola.

Apparently the rat was behaving rationally. Its consumption of a given product increased as the price went down, and it lowered its consumption of a competing product at the same time, just as we assume rational human consumers do. The rat was equally rational in dealing with necessities. At one point, the rat, instead of being given as much water as it wished to drink and then the choice of two luxury drinks, was required to push the bar to

19. Kagel et al., "Demand Curves for Animal Consumers," Fig. 5.

get water. It turned out that the rat drank almost as much water per day at a low price as at a high price. Water was clearly a necessity to the rat, not something it drank for pleasure. Hence, it pushed the bar enough to get its daily demand for water and no more. We can say that the rat had an elastic demand for cherry cola and root beer but an extremely (almost perfectly) inelastic demand for water.

Thus, it seems that the minimum rationality assumption normally used by economists is met by quite simple animals. Those who say that human beings are not able to behave in an economically rational manner may be saying we are as dumb as or dumber than rats! Note, however, that we are discussing behavior and not the actual preferences of the rat. But we do, for subjective reasons, believe that a downward sloping demand curve reflects a desire to obtain some goal, and action is taken to that end. The other view is possible. The prominent behavior psychologist, B. F. Skinner, said:

> A rat could be said to know when to press a lever to get food, but it does not press because it knows that food will be delivered. A taxi driver could be said to know a city well, but he does not get around because he possesses a cognitive map.[20]

Skinner, of course, believes that rats and human beings are very similar in that neither one engages in what we might call *rational thought* and both respond to conditioning. The authors of this book believe that both behave rationally in attempting to achieve goals they value. From the standpoint of economics, however, the issue is not an important one, and either point of view can perhaps be held.

Birds, Snails, and Rotifers

Let us go a little further. The author investigated theoretically the behavior of an English bird called a coal tit. He explained the bird's behavior on the theory that the bird is rationally allocating its time between two different kinds of searches for food in order to get the most food with the least effort.[21] Kagel and Battalio repeated on pigeons the experiments similar to those

---

20. B. F. Skinner, *About Behaviorism* (New York: Alfred A. Knopf, 1974), 139.

21. Gordon Tullock, "The Coal Tit as a Careful Shopper," *The American Naturalist* 105 (January–February 1971), 77–80.

performed on rats. The results were similar also.[22] Even such simple animals as snails seem to have at least some ability to make rational choices.[23]

David Rapport has investigated a microscopic animal, *Stentor coeruleus*, and he finds that its behavior is simple-minded but still rational.[24] Since this very small animal has practically nothing that we would recognize as a brain or even a nervous system, it obviously has only very limited abilities to make rational choices. Nevertheless, when it was confronted with different types of food under circumstances in which the effort it had to undertake to consume each varied, it responded as would human beings or rats. When its preferred food was hard to get, the *Stentor* made do with second-rate food. However, when the cost of the "better" food was lowered, the *Stentor* would spit out the less-preferred food and concentrate on the more preferred.

Although the experiments summarized above are, as far as we know, the only formal studies of animals in which the question of whether they behave as rational consumers has been investigated, it seems to be a rather general feeling among biologists that all animals behave this way. It should be said, however, that biologists normally do not use the same language as do economists. Rapport, who performed the experiment on *Stentor* mentioned above, wrote two articles in which he attempts to introduce his fellow biologists to the vocabulary and methods of economics.[25] In these articles, he presents standard economic models, with appropriate introduction for the biologist. Towards the end of one of these articles, he says:

> The use of optimization principles has been implicit in much of theoretical biology. As Rosen points out, "that idea that nature pursues economy in all her workings is one of the oldest principles of theoretical science" (Rosen, 1967). The assumption of optimizing food selection behavior

22. Personal communication.

23. Gordon Tullock, "Switching in General Predators: Comment," *Bulletin of the Econological Society of America* 51 (September 1970), 21–24.

24. D. J. Rapport and J. E. Turner, "Determination of Predator Food Preferences," *Journal of Theoretical Biology* 26 (1970), 365–72; and David J. Rapport, Jacques Berger, and D. B. W. Reid, "Determination of Food Preference of *Stentor Coeruleus*," *Biological Bulletin* 142 (February 1972), 103–9. Since the authors assume that the readers are not much interested in either the exact nature of *Stentor coeruleus* or the details of its feeding habits, we have not described them. Any reader who finds our discussion too general can turn to the original sources.

25. David J. Rapport, "An Optimization Model of Food Selection," *American Naturalist* 105 (November–December 1971), 757–87.

appears valid provided natural selection is efficient in "weeding out" species or individuals which failed to make optimum food choices.[26]

Rapport goes on to discuss the deductions that can be drawn from this rational model for biology and methods of testing them. He then performed some of the tests in the articles listed above and confirmed the theory.

Concluding Comments

Thus, human beings in experimental situations, microscopic animals, birds, rats, and inhabitants of mental hospitals choose to buy in the cheapest market. Obviously, it does not follow directly from all of this that everyone is rational in his daily life. What we have attempted to demonstrate in this chapter is not that human beings are necessarily rational (although we do believe that they are quite rational) but that the requirement of rationality used in economics is a very modest one. We are not saying anything very complimentary about human beings when we say that they are economically rational. On the other hand, people who say that human beings are not rational are saying something extremely insulting. They are saying that microscopic animals are brighter and better able to make intelligent consumption decisions than is the average human being.

26. Rapport, "Optimization Model of Food Selection," 583–84; inner quote by Rosen refers to R. R. Rosen, *Optimality Principles in Biology* (London: Butterworths, 1967).

UNIVERSITIES SHOULD DISCRIMINATE
AGAINST ASSISTANT PROFESSORS

The "publish-or-perish" system is designed to motivate people to produce research by making their incomes depend upon their published output.[1] Granted that resources in secretarial help, research assistants, etc., are limited and that the university wants to maximize the number of published papers from its faculty, then concentration of these resources on the people who have already published a great deal is sensible. The payoff (reward) to an article differs, depending on stage in career, calendar age, and number of previous articles. A man of 28, preparing to work on his third article, can anticipate a massively greater increase in his lifetime earnings as a result of publication of that article than can a man of 50 contemplating his 50th article. Under the circumstances, the university need pay little attention to the younger man; his incentives are such that he is totally irrational (assuming he has the necessary talent to produce articles) if he is not willing to invest a great deal of his own resources in the article. Thus, if he cannot get his wife to type it, he should be willing to learn to type or to hire a private secretary even for five drafts. The senior man, on the other hand, has only a modest prospective increase in income from the article; hence, if he is to be motivated to produce it, he must be provided with facilities that lower the cost of production to him.

It would, of course, be more efficient to deal with the same problem by changing pay schedules so that the return on articles is about the same in all ranges. Universities are non-profit-making enterprises, however, and there is no reason to believe that they make any particular effort to be efficient in their decisions. Indeed, as a man who has had a good deal of experience with universities over the years, I would even argue that they have a positive preference for inefficiency. Thus, switching over to a more rational payment schedule for articles does not seem very likely behavior for universities.

This is particularly so because the efficient method of motivating senior members of the faculty to produce would not be to offer them large increases in their wages for each article, but to threaten them with large decreases in

Reprinted, with permission of the University of Chicago, publisher, from *Journal of Political Economy* 81 (September–October 1973): 1256–57. Copyright 1973 by The University of Chicago.

1. Gordon Tullock, *The Organization of Inquiry* (Durham, N.C.: Duke University Press, 1965), 34–39.

their wages if their productivity fell below some specified amount. The tenure provisions make this impossible. This "sacred custom" thus discourages research, as well as contributing massive inefficiencies in other aspects of university management.

The custom of rewarding members of the faculty for the articles they produce, but with a very substantial quantity discount—which is the present university custom—would probably be very hard to change. We do observe, however, that among their customs is that of providing senior members of the faculty research assistance that is denied to junior members. This is less efficient than using the salary scale to achieve the same end, but it is more efficient than distributing secretarial and other research resources among the faculty on an "egalitarian" basis. Granted that the university is not likely to make any large efforts to improve efficiency, at the very least it can refrain from moving to a lower level of efficiency and, perhaps, by increasing the discrimination against assistant professors, improve its efficiency in a modest way.

The above argument is, of course, reinforced by the income tax law that makes it rational for senior members of the faculty to take part of their income in the form of handsome offices, secretaries, etc.

PART 3

BIOECONOMICS

SOCIOBIOLOGY

Gordon Tullock and Richard B. McKenzie

That some animals have fairly complex social orders has been known for a very long time. The ant was held up as an example in the Old Testament, and beekeeping seems to be an immensely ancient human profession. The study of animal societies has, of course, always been part of biology. In recent years, however, a new subdiscipline within biology, called sociobiology, has been developed. It studies the social interactions of nonhuman species.

The popular press has given sociobiology a good deal of attention with prominent sociobiologists such as E. O. Wilson and Robert L. Trivers appearing on the cover of *Time* or being interviewed on talk shows. It is of great interest to economists, and indeed, economists have made contributions to the sociobiological literature.[1]

Human and Nonhuman Societies

In part, the popular interest in sociobiology is the result of a mistake. Suppose that some particular type of behavior is observed among a number of social species. It is sometimes erroneously deduced that this must also be characteristic of man. The error is, of course, particularly attractive if the social species which have the particular traits are primates and, hence, close to

Reprinted, with permission, from *The New World of Economics: Explorations into the Human Experience*, 4th ed. (Homewood, Ill.: Richard D. Irwin, 1985), 279–86.

1. For example, see Gordon Tullock, "Biological Externalities," *Journal of Theoretical Biology* 33 (December 1971), 565–76; "Altruism, Malice, and Public Goods," *Journal of Social and Biological Structures* 1 (January 1978), 3–9; "Altruism, Malice, and Public Goods; Reply to Frech," *Journal of Social and Biological Structures* 1 (January 1978), 187–89; "Switching in General Predators: A Comment," *Bulletin of the Ecological Society of America* 51 (September 1970), 21–24; "The Coal Tit as a Careful Shopper," *American Naturalist* 105 (January–February 1971), 77–80; "On the Adaptive Significance of Territoriality: Comment," *The American Naturalist* 113, no. 5 (1979), 772–75; "Comment on 'The Physiological (and Sociological) Causes of the Evolution of Man from Apes'," *Speculations in Science and Technology* 1, no. 5 (December 1978), 528. See also Paul A. Samuelson, "Complete Genetic Models for Altruism, Kin Selection, and Like-Gene Selection," *Journal of Social and Biological Structures* 6, no. 1 (January 1983), 3–16, and Jack Hirshleifer, "Natural Economy versus Political Economy," *Journal of Social and Biological Structures* 1, no. 4 (October 1978), 319–37.

men. Still, perhaps the most amusing example of this dealt with ants. In the 1890s there was a prominent student of ants and their behavior who was also a Baptist clergyman. In his articles and books on ants (which were actually very good in terms of the knowledge of the times) he occasionally inserted little sermons on how much better off humans would be if we all behaved as the ants do.

In more recent times there is less of a religious drive and more of what we might call the naturalistic fallacy. To take one example which has trapped several sociobiologists, the Hamadryas baboon is, of course, a primate and, hence, reasonably closely related to human beings. It is also a social animal, and its habits make it particularly easy to study. In consequence, we probably know more about the society of the Hamadryas baboon than that of any other social animal. It happens that the Hamadryas baboon males are about twice as big as the females. Under the circumstances, it is not surprising that the Hamadryas baboon society is completely male dominated. Several sociobiologists have come to the conclusion that male dominance is "natural," because the baboons (and other primates) have it. A very prominent sociobiologist, E. O. Wilson, who happens also to be politically in favor of women's lib, has written at length about the natural male dominance and how it can be overcome if we only work hard enough. Of course, the fact that baboon society is male dominated tells us substantially nothing about male/female relationships among human beings. Nor should we regard ants as our mentors. Jan Marais was a pioneer in the study of baboons, and there is now a Jan Marais Chair of Ecology at the University of Pretoria. Its occupant remarked that careful study of the baboon tribes would permit us to live like baboons if that is what we wanted, but that personally he preferred to live like a man.

There is, however, some small element of truth in the statement that we may learn something about human society by studying animal society. First, studying animal societies may raise new questions in our minds. The answers to these questions may be of importance to the students of human society. It is in raising questions, however, rather than giving answers that the study of nonhuman societies is of direct relevance.

More important, but a problem for the future, it may be that we will eventually develop a general theory of society in which human society, baboon society, ant society, the society of the sponges, the society of the slime molds, and so forth will all be seen as special cases. On the other hand, it may well be that the things that we refer to as societies in, let us say, humans and bees are in fact radically different institutions; hence, no general theory covering both will ever be developed. But at the moment we know too little about animal societies and, for that matter, about human societies to have much hope of developing such a general theory of society in the immediate future. Still, if we do study both our own society and the various animal societies,[2] we may someday find this general theory of society. On the other hand we may not.

Economics and Biology

What, however, are economists doing in biology? In the first place, economics and biology have a fairly old relationship. The two co-inventors of the theory of evolution, Darwin and Wallace, both specifically said they got the idea from reading Malthus's essay on population. Malthus was, of course, the world's first professor of economics.[3] From this early interaction between the two disciplines until just recently, however, biology and economics developed their separate ways with little interaction.

In the last 15 to 20 years, biology and economics have begun to come together again. The basic reasons for this encouraging development were discoveries in biology and not in economics. Traditionally, biology, with the exception of genetics, had been essentially an observational and experimental subject with little in the way of formal theory. Recently, biologists realized that the general theory of evolution could be particularized into a detailed theory which could then be tested by statistical or experimental means.

As the reader may recall, Darwin argued that the development of all existing species was a result of an evolutionary process. Modernizing his thought a little bit: the genes which control the heredity of any plant or animal change very slowly, but randomly. Each change either increases the likelihood that the particular plant or animal will leave descendants or, much more commonly, lowers it. Since those genes which increase the likelihood of leaving descendants (fitness) will be more common in future generations and those which lower fitness will be rarer, over time the world population of plants and animals will evolve. The present vast collection of different plant and animal species on the surface of the earth is simply the result of this process.

---

2. There are also plant societies, but they tend to be ignored by the sociobiologists.

3. As a matter of fact, his book was good biology but poor economics, as the history of human population since he wrote it has demonstrated.

Recently economists realized the evolutionary hypothesis tells us not only something about history, but something about the present-day world too. Animals and plants should be reasonably efficiently designed for their place in the web of life. It is possible to make calculations about efficient characteristics. Birds, for example, should have certain size beaks if they feed on particular types of insects, the teeth of animals should be adjusted to their diet, and so forth. It turns out that these very general propositions can be reduced to detailed and highly specific statements, and then one can go and look at the data and see whether they fit. The result in general has been that evolution as a hypothesis has been overwhelmingly confirmed but also that biology is becoming a theoretical rather than observational science. Biologists might not like to hear this, but as a matter of fact, the *American Naturalist* and the *American Economic Review* these days look very much alike. The average article in both begins with a theoretical discussion of some point, usually developed mathematically, and then proceeds to a statistical examination of the real world to test the theory.

The resemblance between economics and biology today is not, however, a merely superficial similarity in appearance. In both cases, theory is based on the premise that subjects will maximize subject to constraints. Human beings are assumed by economics to attempt to maximize their utility subject to various restrictions put on them by the environment. The biologists assume that plants and animals are maximizing their biological fitness subject once again to restraints put upon them by the environment. Although there are, of course, many differences, there are also very strong similarities in the two approaches. It has been possible for economists to publish articles in biology and at least one biologist, Garrett Hardin, has done excellent work in economics.[4]

The Findings of Sociobiology

But so much for generalities. What have the sociobiologists found out about nonhuman societies? The first and, in some ways, most astonishing discovery is that many animals, birds, insects, and, for that matter, plants are real estate owners. They control specific pieces of ground, sea bottom, or airspace. Sociobiologists have largely ignored the plants, but it should be said

4. Garrett Hardin and John Baden, eds., *Managing the Commons* (San Francisco: W. H. Freeman, 1977).

that plants can be real estate owners too. A number of trees, bushes, and, for that matter, even some grasses exude chemicals into the soil around their base which makes it impossible for direct competitors to grow there. This means that the particular plant does not need to be concerned about other plants growing close enough to it to seriously damage its prospects.

From the economic standpoint, there is immediately here a cost-benefit calculation. Does the plant gain enough from removing all competitors a distance—which, for a small plant, may be one inch or so away—to pay for the cost of producing and exuding into the soil chemicals which make the growth of other plants unlikely? Since some plants do this and others don't, one can deduce that sometimes this is an efficient technique which is likely to contribute to survival and sometimes it is not.

Note here a characteristic of animal "property" which they do not share with humans. The plant or animal itself must defend its living space. There is no possibility of calling in the sheriff to evict a trespasser. Clearly this is less efficient than the concept of private property in human society. We don't depend completely on our own strength to maintain our property ownership, and indeed, in any community there are some elderly people who would be unable to defend themselves against even a most modest attack who nevertheless peacefully hold large pieces of property. This would be impossible in the biological realm.

There seems to be reason to believe that the human approach to property is more efficient than the animal approach, but let us nevertheless continue talking about animal property. First, the existence of property in this sense means that the property owner, whoever he or she is, must be prepared to defend the property one way or another. Usually among the animals and birds this means fighting, and of course, there is some cost to the fighting. There are two species of ground squirrels which live in the Rocky Mountains. One, which we shall call A, is the dominant species in the higher altitudes where the trees and brush are rather open. As you move down the mountain to areas where the brush is much thicker and visibility is poor, the other, which we shall call B, becomes dominant.

The explanation for this division of property seems to be simple. A is a territorial ground squirrel which protects a given territory by patrolling and fighting intruders. B is nonterritorial, simply picks up its food where it can find it, and if attacked by a member of the A species, runs away. In the high area where trees and brush are rather sparse and, hence, visibility is good, the A species drives the B species away from all suitable sources of food because each member of the A species established territorial control over an area large enough to feed itself and there are no areas left for the B squirrel.

In the lower parts of the mountain, where the trees and brush are thick and visibility is poor, the A ground squirrel attempts to set up a territory, but it isn't able to see the boundaries easily. The result is that the B squirrels can live in an area even if there are A squirrels there, and since the B squirrels do not put any energy into patrolling territory or attempting to fight off intruders, they are, in the long run, able to survive better than the A squirrels. The A squirrels run the cost of protecting their property and don't get the protection because of the technological problem of poor visibility in this area; hence, they are less fit than the B squirrels.

An economist would immediately recognize this as a simple cost-benefit problem. It takes a certain amount of energy to patrol and guard the property. In the upper areas, where there is little brush and you can see an intruding squirrel quite a ways off, the return on this exertion of energy is positive; that is, the benefit is greater than the cost. Farther down the mountain, where the brush and other undergrowth make it hard to tell whether there is another ground squirrel intruding on a squirrel's property, the benefit is much less, but the cost is as great or even greater, with the result that the A squirrel is not viable there. Although we have said that an economist would immediately recognize this as a case of cost-benefit analysis, the biologist, of course, recognized it even before the economist and used exactly the same kind of analysis except that some of the details of the mathematics are different.

Territoriality is not confined to higher mammals and birds; ant nests frequently have a home territory which they defend. Almost certainly some members of any college class will have seen a war between two ant colonies, probably fought over a boundary question. These wars, which involve immense numbers of ants and may last for days, are normally not very conspicuous, since they are fought in the grass and brush. Occasionally, however, they occur on sidewalks or other paved areas, and then they are very conspicuous indeed.

Defense of Property

So far, we have simply talked about the owner of the property defending it, and we have not said much about how he or she does it or, indeed, how the intruder tries to take advantage of the property. In some cases, as in the example of the ground squirrel B, the intruder simply sneaks in and runs if he is detected. In most cases, however, there is a more direct confrontation between the existing owner and the trespasser, who very commonly is interested in ejecting the owner and taking over the property himself. The easiest and most obvious explanation as to who wins in such an encounter is simply that the biggest and toughest member of ground squirrel A species, or biggest and toughest bird, or biggest and toughest fish, either retains his property and ejects the intruder or seizes property from a smaller and weaker member of his or her own species. This conclusion is not unanimously held by biologists.

Biologists point out quite properly that fighting is costly and individual members of species who engage in a great deal of it lower their fitness by the energy consumed in the fighting. Of course, a fight which is quite costly but which leads to the winner obtaining possession of very attractive pieces of real estate may nevertheless pay. But over time, if he has to defend that real estate in a number of other costly fights, the end product may be that he is worse off than he would have been had he not engaged in the fights at all. The B squirrels have apparently decided that fighting doesn't pay in their environment.

If we observe patterns among animals, the first thing we note is that there is a great deal of the animal equivalent of threatening and name-calling before any actual fighting occurs, and very commonly, all that happens is a good deal of threat behavior by the two birds, shall we say, at the end of which one of them flies off, admitting defeat. Some biologists have argued that the elaborate threat behavior is a ceremony, but it seems more likely that the threats are real. During the period in which the birds maneuver, threaten, and call each other names, they (like two humans working up toward a fight) are obtaining information as to who is likely to win and the severity of the fight. Obviously they don't scientifically analyze the problem, but their genes could transmit built-in reaction patterns which would have much the same effect as if they had indeed carefully weighed the probability of success, the probability of injury, and the net benefit of engaging in a real fight.

The problem here is quite complicated. There are cases in which one can imagine a species continuing to exist with part of the members of the species being programmed to fight very easily, and part being programmed to fight not at all, and both (hawks and doves) remaining viable at a particular ratio. It is not clear whether this mathematical possibility is actually presented in nature or not.

In most cases, however, it seems that the posturing and threats of the two animals are genuine, and if one or the other doesn't decide to give up, there will be a fight; mostly the fight doesn't occur, because one or the other does decide that it is not worth the risk of injury. Professor E. O. Wilson once said that any animal species which had been observed for less than 1,000 hours had a reputation for being peaceful and nonbelligerent. As soon as the observation time rose well above 1,000 hours, however, examples of severe fights and deaths occurred.

The famous sociobiologist Jane van Lawick–Goodall was a victim of this problem, although in her case the number of hours she had put in before she discovered that the chimpanzees whom she was studying could be quite belligerent was a good deal more than 1,000. She was studying chimpanzees in Africa, and it is now clear, although it was not when she began her studies, that the particular area where she studied was completely enclosed within the boundary of a chimpanzee band (animal bands are discussed below). She found that although there was a certain amount of threat behavior and mild fighting, nothing very serious in the way of fighting occurred, and she wrote books and gave lectures about how peaceful the chimpanzees were.

Then the chimpanzee group with which she was dealing split into two, and war immediately broke out between the two groups. The larger group apparently killed every single male in the smaller group. About the same time, she discovered that two females in the tribe were systematically killing and eating the children of other females. So much for the peaceful chimpanzee. Van Lawick–Goodall is not alone in having made this kind of mistake. For a while it was thought that wolf fights were always determined rather quickly by the surrender of one or the other party without any great injury. It turned out that that does indeed happen frequently, but by no means always, and wolves can be killed in fights with other wolves. With lions it would appear that murder by another lion is actually the commonest single cause of death. It is particularly true for the juveniles. Both wolves and lions are property owners, although in their case, the property is held by a group larger than an individual or a mating pair.

But let us now go on to discuss these larger groups. The bulk of the property-owning species is not particularly social. Individuals, or pairs, or, in some cases, males with harems own a piece of real estate which they defend, but they have relatively little contact with their neighbors except occasional fighting. There are other animals which operate in larger groups which we shall call bands, although biologists would use a different name for different species (a pride of lions, for example). These larger groups sometimes are real estate owners, but they have a national or band territory rather than simple ownership of the property. In most cases no individual member of the group owns any particular subsection of the larger plot that is owned by the tribe itself. Sometimes these bands do not seem to have any particular real estate area and wander across the countryside with different bands, operating in much the same territory at different times (gorillas, for example).

In those cases in which the band does have a specific piece of real estate, however, they normally defend it, sometimes marking the boundaries much the same way as the domestic dog would mark the boundaries of his master's land, and they are willing to fight over the borders. In Hans Kruuk's study of the hyenas of the Ngorongoro crater,[5] there is an account of a quite spirited border battle at which the losing hyena band was forced to move its boundary back by a considerable distance. The real estate quarrels of these bands, however, are really very similar to those of individual property owners among animals except for their larger scale.

Dominance

The internal social organization of the mammals and birds is in general some modification of a dominance order. In the chickens in which the dominance order was first carefully studied, it was noticed that there would be one chicken in the flock who could peck on any of the others and to whom the others deferred when it came to going for food; another who could peck on anyone except the first; and so on down to the bottom where there would be a chicken which could be pecked by anyone and whose life expectancy would not really be very long in the wild (although in a farmyard, presumably it would be kept alive).

The dominance order is not stable, because there are occasional confrontations between members of the group in which a lower-ranking one beats a higher-ranking one, with the result that it moves up on the scale, and the higher-ranking one moves down. Nevertheless, the higher the rank of the individual in this scheme, the more access he or she has to food, mates, and so forth. In some cases (among the wolves, for example), the top dominant also plays a very modest policing role within the tribe by breaking up fights among his juniors.

The advantage of this system for the dominants (the ones at the top of the order) is obvious, but why do these lower-ranking animals stay in the tribe rather than striking out on their own? The answer seems to be simply that the

5. Hans Kruuk, *The Spotted Hyena* (Chicago: University of Chicago Press, 1972).

lower-ranking ones do better than they would on their own. The tribe offers them some protection against predation, since such a group is less likely to be attacked than an individual animal, and in addition, there are a number of eyes and ears watching for predators. In some cases, the hunting technique used will only work if there are a considerable number of animals. It is impossible for a single wolf to pull down a moose, but a wolf pack can do so with no great difficulty.

The final reason an animal who is far down the dominance order may stick with the band is simply that the death rate of almost all species in the world is high, and the prospect that he will rise to top rank through the death of his superiors is never zero.

Lessons for Human Society

It is perhaps sensible here to discuss one aspect of fighting between animals which we have so far sidestepped. In general, if a quarrel between two animals proceeds far enough so they actually fight, one of them realizes he is losing and gives up. The other will usually not continue the attack. (Note, we said *in general*.) There are cases in which the attacker will continue until the beaten animal is dead. There are other cases in which the beaten animal doesn't realize it is beaten until it is too late and, hence, dies of its wounds even though it did try to give up.

Some people who attempt to draw lessons for human behavior from animal behavior have pointed out the pattern of behavior in which the losing animal gives up and the winning animal stops attacking as a pattern for humans. Once it is clear who is going to win, the one that is going to lose obviously has nothing to gain from continuing the fight. His or her decision to give up at that point is therefore understandable. If, however, the winner continues the attack, presumably the potential loser would attempt to defend itself. It might well inflict serious injury on the winner during the last stage of the fight. Thus, it is, on the whole, sensible for the winner to let the loser off, having "taught him a lesson," rather than to continue with the fight. Human beings in fact behave this way, but, of course, we have institutions under which the loser can be permanently penalized for losing, let us say, a war.

Naturally, the animals may not make these complex computations. Nevertheless, those who behave according to an efficient pattern will survive and produce offspring, and those who don't, will not, with the result that over time heredity leads to behavior which, in many cases, is rather similar to that which would be recommended to the animal by a game theorist with a Ph.D. from Massachusetts Institute of Technology. If, however, the most efficient behavior is extremely complex, it may be beyond the rather limited capacity of an animal brain; hence, the animal will not behave with optimal efficiency, simply because the energy cost of carrying around the large and complicated brain necessary to provide optimal efficient behavior in unusual circumstances is greater than the benefit from the fitness standpoint.

Variable Behavior

We quite frequently find that animals are able to change their pattern of behavior from a social one to an individualistic one and from property owning to non–property owning. Sometimes they will be social or property owning in some aspect of their lives and not in others. The wolves of Isle Royale, for example, hunt moose in the winter but a large number of smaller animals in the summer. In consequence of this pattern, they organize themselves in a pack for the winter, because an individual wolf cannot bring down a moose. In the summer, on the other hand, they break up and operate individually or perhaps in sets of mated pairs. The fact that biologists aren't quite certain which pattern they use in the summer is indicative of the fact that it is harder to observe wolves in the summer, when there are leaves on the trees and bushes, than it is in the winter, when the branches are bare. Initial studies of the Isle Royale wolf pack were in fact carried on from a small plane circling over the island. This technique was only suitable for winter observation.

Similarly, most sea gulls get their food from the sea, and fish move around a good deal so that ownership of a particular piece of the sea (even if it could be marked out) would be of little value. Under the circumstances, they do not own fishing grounds.

Many gulls, however, put their nests in highly restricted areas which are apparently selected because they are protected from predators. These gulls normally have very, very strict ownership arrangements with respect to the nest area.

We tend to think of insects as having fixed behavior patterns and being unable to adjust to changes in their environment, but at least in some cases, this is not so. Most tropical wasps have several queens in the nest, while all those in the temperate zone maintain single-queen nests. It seems likely that this is an adjustment to the cold winter which will kill any but the healthiest and best-fed queen. This, however, would not apply in the tropics. There is at least one example of temperate-zone wasps which were accidentally reestablished in Tasmania (which does not have cold winters) and which promptly developed multiple-queen nests.

As a final example, Kruuk's study of the hyenas of the Ngorongoro crater shows that the hyena bands have real estate holdings. His further studies of the hyenas in the vast Serengeti Plain is not absolutely clear on the point, but it certainly seems likely that the hyenas there do not really have specific hunting ranges. They travel over very large areas, and the animals they hunt also travel over large areas, so specific hunting grounds would not be very valuable. In the more confined areas of the Ngorongoro crater, real estate ownership for the pack is worthwhile but apparently not in the Serengeti.

A sort of compromise is found among the lions of the open areas of Africa. The grass-eating animals upon which they prey move according to the seasons to areas where grazing is good. The lions must follow, but they are basically a territorial animal, with each pride maintaining, insofar as it is possible, a monopoly over its own territory. The way this has worked out in the case of the lions is that the territories hunted and guarded by each pride move with the prey animals. You have what amounts to migrating property ownership.

Termite and Ant Societies

Although we are apt to feel somewhat more at home in dealing with the societies of other warm-blooded animals, particularly the primates, and also to feel at least some fellow feeling for other vertebrates, the most interesting social organizations are probably those found among the insects. There are wasps, bees, and ants which are all related to each other, the social spiders (a little-known group), and the termites. Of these, the oldest and, in some ways, best-developed are the termites. Termites are a rather primitive family of insects related to the cockroach. Although they are something of a nuisance in the United States, their highest development can be found in the tropics. Indeed, the traveler in some parts of Africa can actually take his direction from the tall, bladelike termite nests which are always rigidly oriented north and south.

Such a nest may have up to 2 million termites in it. The nest itself is, of course, only the center from which a large number of tunnels go off in all directions to permit the termites to find and consume dead wood. The nest and the tunnels are full of busy worker termites who are engaged in collecting wood, in some cases bringing water into the nest (although that is not always necessary), and maintaining the nest itself. They will be guarded by a special caste of soldier termites who are equipped with quite a wide variety of defensive armament. Perhaps the most interesting ones are those who are provided with a sort of nozzle on the top of their heads from which they can spray a sticky substance. Others have large jaws, and in some cases, the head of the soldier is specially designed for blocking the entrance into the tunnels of the nest.

The workers have much to do in addition to bringing in wood. The nest itself requires maintenance and repair, and the ventilation of the nest is important. The termite inside the nest of one of the large African colonies lives in an environment which is remarkably stable. First, the atmosphere in the nest is a great deal more moist than the outside air and contains much more carbon dioxide. It is also quite stable in temperature. The nest is built in such a way that there is a regular circulation of air through it driven by the heat generated in the nest, and there are arrangements so that the speed of circulation can be changed by termite workers so that the amount of heat radiated through the upper portion of the bladelike structure can be adjusted; hence, the temperature of the nest is kept quite stable. The inside of a termite nest is not quite as stable in temperature as the interior of a heat-regulating mammal like the human being, but it is a good deal more stable than the interior of a lizard or a fish. Last, but by no means least, the termite reproductives are, of course, the heart of the nest. Normally, there is a king or queen, but in some cases, a number of pairs of so-called secondary reproductives may be found.

The termites have another peculiarity, which is that most of them, indeed all except the highest termites, don't actually digest the wood themselves. They have in their intestines colonies of small single-celled animals which do the actual digestion. Thus, in a way, there is a colony inside the colony. Further, some of the termites engage in gardening. They build fairly large caverns in their nest in which they raise a special type of fungus.

It can be seen that the termite nest is a complex social organization with a great deal of division of labor. Further, except for the reproductives and the specialized soldier classes,[6] the division of labor among the termites does not depend on their physical constitution. Most of the termite workers are

---

6. There may be other specialized classes in some termite nests.

capable of carrying on any of the tasks in the nest. How then are the termites allocated to their jobs?

Theoretically, it could be, of course, that they simply come out of the egg with instructions for some to repair walls, others to attend to the royal pair, and so forth. We know that this is not true, however, because the number of termites engaged in any activity changes, depending on the needs of the nest. If you damage the nest, for example, the number of termites engaged in repair and reconstruction immediately rises sharply. In times of drought, more termites are involved in obtaining water.

Again, it might, of course, be that the termites are simply randomly distributed among their various activities, but if this were so, the termite nest would be highly inefficient. We do not have any positive proof that termites, ants, and so forth are highly efficient, but there is fairly good evidence that they are from the role they play in the world. Next to man, the social insects are probably the most successful single group of species on the planet. Further, the fact that both the ants and the termites, two totally unrelated species using different food sources, have found much the same social organization is evidence of their efficiency.

There is further evidence of the efficiency of these social insects, in this case taken from the ants. E. O. Wilson examined the division of ants among the various castes, specifically workers and soldiers, in his nest. In order to understand Wilson's experiment it should be pointed out that workers and soldiers are produced by the nest by the feeding and care of otherwise identical larva. Thus, the ratio between them is something determined by the nest just as the ratio between those ants engaging in repairing the walls of the nest and those seeking food is determined by the nest.

Wilson, using linear programming techniques, investigated the efficient proportion of worker and soldier ants in a number of species. In all cases, he found the actual allocation was close to the allocation that his calculation showed to be efficient. It was not perfect, but this is as likely to be because his calculations did not perfectly fit the real world as because the ants were themselves inefficient.

Similar experiments have not been carried on with respect to most other aspects of the efficiency of ant and termite nests, but nevertheless, we think we can accept that they are indeed efficient and that the allocation of labor within the nest between the various tasks is well carried out.

How is this allocation controlled? It certainly is not controlled by a central planning board, nor is there a system of formal orders transmitted from some center of the nest which says in essence: "the temperature in the nest has risen by one half a degree, open ventilation channels 13a, 26b, and 45c." Before answering this question we should keep in mind that a somewhat similar puzzle exists inside the human body. Within us are white corpuscles which are amoebalike entities within our bloodstream. These cells attack and ingest foreign matter in the bloodstream, particularly bacteria. If a human being suffers an injury, let us say, a cut to a finger, the white blood corpuscles will immediately congregate at that spot where they provide what amounts to a guard force against infection. How are they guided to the right locations?

It is certainly not true that they are ordered to the right location by the brain, because the white corpuscles have no connection with the nervous system. They will go to areas the injury has affected, even if, due to the injury itself, the nerves have been severed in that area. The simple explanation seems to be that these corpuscles are self-motivated in the sense that they "decide" where they will go and are provided with some kind of drive or motivation[7] to ingest things in the blood that should not be there. We can regard this as a "taste." Further, they are motivated to seek out places where such things are particularly common. Probably the clues which they follow are chemical. It seems likely that a cut releases into the bloodstream various bits of cell debris and chemicals from the cells which are normally not found there, and it is these chemicals and bits of debris that attract the white corpuscles. It is easier to assume that the white corpuscles are programmed to respond to these stimuli and do so than that they receive special orders.

Probably the same is true with the termites. In part, they are no doubt responding to chemicals, particularly chemicals exuded by the queen, which get transmitted around the nest from termite to termite whenever they are in close contact. But this message system can hardly control the temperature of the nest.

If, on the other hand, we assume that termites respond to temperature, then temperature changes could affect their behavior. Assume a termite in the upper part of the nest who feels that it is too hot. There is immediately available an opportunity to lower the temperature, both for itself and for the nest, by opening a few more ventilation channels. Similarly, if he feels too cold, the reverse behavior is called for. The same termite if deep down in the nest, even

7. It is hard to talk about these things with a single-cell animal which does not even have nerves, but it is clear than an amoeba in the outside world has a drive to attack and ingest bacteria.

if he was too warm, would not be stimulated to do anything about the temperature, because there would be no ventilation channels in the immediate vicinity to deal with. By complicating this set of drives and assuming that each termite has quite a number of them, we can produce something that is roughly analogous to a human-utility function for each termite. The termite (again using the human analogy) attempts to maximize this utility function, with the particular action he undertakes being determined by his or her immediate environment. This pattern of behavior could be elaborated into a complete structure for controlling any of the social insects' behavior.[8]

But although this explains why the individual termite behaves in a manner which is efficient from the standpoint of the nest, it does not explain why evolution has given the termites this set of drives. After all, many social insects (termite soldiers, for example) will sacrifice themselves for the good of the nest without, as far as one can see, the slightest hesitation or doubt. This would superficially appear to be a counterrevolutionary pattern of behavior.

Once again, if we consider the human body, the explanation is fairly simple. The human body has a very small set of cells which are involved in reproducing other human beings, but the bulk of the body cells simply exist to keep the body as a whole alive. Your skin cells sacrifice themselves by the millions for your well-being every day. Evolution has selected the human being as a complicated mechanism in which most of the cells have the duty of protecting those few which can reproduce. The nonreproducing cells have no effect on evolution at all in the future because they simply won't be around.

The same is true with the termite. Only the reproductives are involved in transmitting the genes to future generations. Therefore, there is no reason why the genes should be programmed so that there is any self-protection drive for the workers or the soldiers, and as far as we can see, they are not.[9]

The analogy between the termite's nest and the human body is strong enough so that a great many biologists tend to think that in the case of the termite the actual nest should be regarded as the individual rather than the termite itself. They refer to a "superorganism." Certainly, the termite nest, with

---

8. Gordon Tullock, "Coordination without Command" (Blacksburg, Va.: Center for the Study of Public Choice), unpublished.

9. In the case of the bees, wasps, and ants there is another and more complicated explanation based on the peculiar hereditary mechanism used by these animals. We are dubious about this alternative mechanism, but, in any event, it is irrelevant for the termites.

its controlled internal environment, does have a great deal of resemblance to the warm-blooded animal, but there seems no point here in quarreling about words. We can easily tell a termite from a termite nest, and we can talk about them separately. But there are many gaps to fill in our knowledge of termites and, indeed, of all other social animals. In many of them, the gaps are much more prominent than the few places where we have knowledge. The social spiders would be a good example. Earlier we mentioned the theory that a general science of society can be developed, with human society and the various animal societies merely being specific instances of the theory. We cannot say for certain that this is untrue, but what we can say is that if we are going to have such a general theory, we have to know a great deal more about non-human societies than we do now.

Concluding Comments

Altogether then, what we learn from studying animal societies is that on the whole we are better off not following their example. On the other hand, the societies are interesting themselves, and they permit us to think about society in a new and different way, which may lead to additional insights about human society.

Here we have talked only about the societies of higher animals and of the social insects. But there are many other societies in nature. We mentioned the societies of plants which have been totally overlooked by the sociobiologists, probably because all of the sociobiologists are zoologists rather than botanists. Even in the animal kingdom, however, there are sizable areas about which we know very little. Jellyfish, for example, are representatives of a type of animal society which is theoretically relatively comprehensible but the details of whose organization are relatively unknown. The sponges, an immensely ancient group, are societies of great complexity, and again we know almost nothing about how this society functions.

There are two other social animals which are totally unknown to the layman but reasonably well known to the professional biologist—the slime molds and the ectoprocts. Our knowledge of the actual social behavior of these two types of societies is almost nil. Indeed, we are primarily confined in this case to observations of the behavior of the entire society rather than of the individuals which constitute it. Recently a mammal, the mole rat, which has a lifestyle rather like the termite, has been discovered.

Sociobiology is, then, a fascinating field which offers great opportunities for further research. However, it is unfortunately still a large field for further research. We have only made the smallest of starts in our study in this area. A student of human society may, by examining other societies, have new questions raised in his mind. He may get new ideas for human society from them. In the present state of our knowledge, however, it is very unlikely that he will be able to offer any real insight into human functioning from the study of slime molds, baboons, and termites.

ECONOMICS AND SOCIOBIOLOGY

A COMMENT

Economics actually predates modern biology, and, indeed, modern biology was in a sense founded by the world's first professor of economics, Malthus. Both Darwin and Wallace specifically stated that their independent discoveries of evolution came as a result of reading *On Population*. Under the circumstances, it is indeed fitting that in recent years economics and biology have begun to interact.[1] The interest of a number of modern biologists in animal behavior patterns and, in particular, social behavior has led to work that is of interest to economists. As one who reads a good deal of modern biological literature, however, I should like to say that much modern biology, which has nothing to do with sociobiology, is of interest to economists, and economists can in fact make genuine contributions to biology by using the tools that remain unfamiliar to biologists.[2]

It seems likely, however, that Edward Wilson's *Sociobiology* will introduce the field to most economists. Since it is an excellent book, this is no misfortune. The point of this comment, however, is not to praise Wilson, but to point out the deficiencies in Becker's review article.[3] Becker purports to prove that a rational human egoist might behave like an altruist. He argues that an altruist does not necessarily reduce his "own consumption" as compared with an egoist because gifts from the altruist to the egoist change the behavior of the egoist in such a way as to protect the altruist. As a result, the altruist will

Reprinted, with permission of the American Economic Association, from *Journal of Economic Literature* 15 (June 1977): 502–6.

The author wishes to thank all of his colleagues at the Center for Study of Public Choice for their assistance provided by vigorous discussion of this comment and, in particular, James M. Buchanan, Geoffrey Brennan, and David Friedman.

1. See Gordon Tullock, "Switching in General Predators: Comment," *Bulletin of the Ecological Society of America* 51 (Sept. 1970): 21–24; Tullock, "The Coal Tit as a Careful Shopper," *American Naturalist* 105 (Jan.–Feb. 1971): 77–80; Tullock, "Biological Externalities," *Journal of Theoretical Biology* 33 (Dec. 1971): 565–76.

2. The biologists have recognized the importance to their discipline of learning some of the economic tools, and indeed I have on occasion been asked to advise on efficient methods of acquiring the necessary knowledge.

3. Edward O. Wilson, *Sociobiology* (Cambridge: Harvard University Press, Belknap Press, 1975); Gary S. Becker, "Altruism, Egoism, and Genetic Fitness: Economics and Sociobiology," *Journal of Economic Literature* 14 (Sept. 1976): 817–26.

end up with a higher own consumption than if he were not an altruist. Unfortunately, his general argument to this effect does not hold up. If the altruism is of a certain pattern, Becker's result is logically possible, but only under extraordinarily restrictive conditions. It seems very dubious that any real-world situation would fit the model.[4]

To begin with, the Becker definition of the word "altruist" is much more restrictive than the usual one. An individual who is interested in helping other people and does so by tithing, adjusting his behavior in accord with the principle of the negative income tax, guaranteeing a "floor" income to some other person, or entering politics with the sole motive of helping his country would be engaging in what we tend to think of as charitable or altruistic activity. This is not, however, what Becker means by altruism in his article.

There is no reason why a complex phenomenon such as altruism or charity should not be dealt with by taking up one aspect at a time. Becker, in essence, has done this with altruism, and I have no objection; but I do feel it should be understood that his explanation deals with only part of what we normally think of as altruistic or charitable behavior.

There is a second aspect of the Becker paper that is not totally clear. When Becker says "goods consumed" by the recipient, he includes time used in various nonmarket or leisure activities and satisfaction from a pleasant job as well as goods, i.e., everything that enters into the utility function of the recipient. The analysis assumes that the altruist knows the preference ordering of the recipients. In fact, judgments of this sort seem to be impossible. The history of charitable administration is almost a continuous record of the donors' or their agents' attempting to prevent the recipients' "taking advantage of" the gifts. This is even true within the family, although to a considerably lesser degree.

The issue is important because if the altruist does make a mistake in his judgment of the behavior of the recipient, then the recipient can use the altruistic behavior to inflict exactly the kind of injury on the altruist against which the Becker-type altruism can (will, in Becker's argument) protect him. Consider, for example, an individual who is receiving a transfer from the altruist such that if some contingency lowered his income by $1, he would receive an additional supplement from the altruist of $.50. He changes the

---

4. For an argument that the standard biological altruism and kin selection is also incorrect, see Gordon Tullock, "Altruism, Malice, and Public Goods," *Journal of Social and Biological Structures* (forthcoming).

conditions of work, perhaps by working a little less hard, in such a way that his income falls by $1, but his utility falls only by the equivalent of $.25. The altruist, not making a perfect judgment in this area, assumes that this is a fall in total income of $1; hence, he gives the recipient $.50. The recipient is now $.25 better off than he was before, and the altruist is $.50 worse off. This is just the kind of thing the Becker procedure is supposed to protect against, and indeed it would protect the altruist if he had perfect judgment of the recipient's utility schedule. In this case, if he had correctly assessed the recipient's utility, he would have given the recipient only $.125 instead of $.50, with the result that the recipient would have been worse off and would not have undertaken the action.

We could stop here and simply say that the Becker-type altruism, if it is based on this narrow assumption, simply has no counterpart in the real world. Supervisors of the poor for some 5,000 years have attempted to prevent the recipients of their bounty from engaging in these kinds of acts, and their record of success is, to put it mildly, modest. It is of some interest that the standard arguments for converting our relief system to the negative income tax are based on these incentive effects. The negative income tax does not eliminate a tendency on the part of the poor to make use of the relief system for the purpose of lowering their earned income with a gain in utility, but it does weaken their incentives to do so.

Nevertheless, the possibility of Becker-type altruism exists, and the question then arises whether it benefits the altruist in the sense that his own consumption is higher if he engages in altruism of this sort, as Becker argues, or if his consumption is lower. Becker's argument that his consumption is higher is quite simply that it will lead the recipient of the altruistic payment—the egoist—to refrain from certain types of actions that might harm the altruist; hence, the altruist's income could be higher. This is true under special circumstances but, as we shall see, these are so rare as to be nearly nonexistent.

I shall begin my discussion with Becker's remarks about two persons who are otherwise equally qualified, one of whom is an altruist and one of whom is an egoist.[5] If the altruist gives part of his income *to the egoist* and the egoist is therefore motivated to refrain from certain types of action that might harm the altruist, it is *possible* that the altruist is better off. Note, however, that in any event the own consumption of the egoist would be higher than the own consumption of the altruist, because he is now receiving this gift in addition

5. Becker, "Altruism," 280.

to the rent on his equal ability. Thus, although it is conceivable that as a result of the gift the altruist's income goes up, it is clear that the egoist's income must go up more. The payoff to altruism is lower than the payoff to egoism, even under these circumstances. Those egoists who are not recipients, however, might have lower incomes than the altruist.

But even granting Becker this rather implausible ability on the part of the donor to monitor the recipient's utility, his conclusion still does not follow. In essence, the altruist's gift to the recipient leads the recipient to refrain from certain types of action that might injure the donor. For this combination to benefit the "own consumption" of the donor, a set of extremely stringent conditions must be met. In order to indicate the problem, I will introduce here a little notation.[6]

Let the potential harm that the action of the recipient might inflict upon the donor be H and the benefit that accrues to the recipient from the same act be B. The gift from the donor to the beneficiary is G. The relative magnitude of these three quantities can have six possible orderings, as shown below.

$$(1) \quad H > G > B$$
$$(2) \quad H > B > G$$
$$(3) \quad G > H > B$$
$$(4) \quad G > B > H$$
$$(5) \quad B > H > G$$
$$(6) \quad B > G > H$$

Only the first of these six orderings gives the Becker effect; i.e., only if the injury to the donor from the recipient's action (H) is greater than the gift made by the donor to the recipient (G), which in turn is greater than the benefit received by the recipient from the action (B), would the Becker-type altruism protect the donor at a reasonable price.

Presumably most actions taken by the recipient that would benefit him would fall in either inequality (4) or (6) because they would have very little effect on the donor's income. Note that these inequalities would include all cases in which the act undertaken by the recipient benefited him, but imposed zero harm on the donor, which would be a very large class. Those cases in which the recipient simply made no change in his ordinary pattern of behavior as a result of the gift would also be included here. This would cover a very large part of the total of the recipient's time, although whether we want to call

---

6. This notational scheme was first suggested to me by my colleague Geoffrey Brennan.

it an "act" or not is a matter of definition. Lastly, if the "harm" were negative—that is, if the beneficiary's act exerted a positive externality on the income of the altruist, it would fall in these inequalities. In case (4), the donor's own consumption falls as a result of his altruism. In case (6), it is usually the same as it would be if he were not altruistic. Even here, however, if the "harm" is negative (i.e., a benefit to the altruist) and significant, the altruist will lose.

The other four possible arrangements would be rarer, since they all involve a rather uncommonly strong reaction between activity on the part of the recipient to increase his own income and injury to the donor. In (2) and (5), the recipient would take the act, because the benefit from the act is greater than the loss he would suffer from reduction in the gift; and in (3), the recipient's act would indeed be prevented, but the donor would be overpaying for this protection.

Note, further, that case (1), the unique case in which the donor's gift does indeed raise his own consumption, requires that the recipient be aware of the effect of his actions on the donor. Under the circumstances, a private bargain between the two would be Pareto optimal.[7] There seems to be no reason why private arrangements could not be made, particularly granting Becker's very strong assumption on the information about the recipient's utility possessed by the donor. In the real world, where people do not have this perfect information, transactions costs might inhibit at least some such bargains.

There is another situation in which Becker-type altruism could, at least theoretically, benefit the own consumption of the altruist. The recipient might deliberately take action that inflicts injury on himself if it increased the earned income of the altruist enough so that the resulting increase in the transfer from the altruist to the recipient was great enough to more than compensate for the injury. Here again, the particular ordering of magnitudes seems rather unlikely, although I will not go through the notational system again. Further, in this case, once again a Pareto-optimal bargain between the two parties covering that particular area only would dominate the generalized Becker-type altruism from the standpoint of the own consumption of the potential altruist.

Thus, a narrow egoist would do much better in terms of own consumption than an altruist. This is particularly true if the narrow egoist is willing to enter into Pareto-optimal bargains with the potential recipient in those rare cases in which he could actually benefit from his altruism. The failure of

---

7. It has nothing to do with Becker altruism, but a similar private bargain would be sensible in cases (2) and (3).

Becker's proof, with respect to the rational altruist, means that his mathematical transfer of the results in this case to the biological world fails also.

In net, Becker has not succeeded in proving his paradox. Altruism remains something that we have to explain in terms of tastes rather than in terms of rational behavior. We should, of course, continue the search for better explanations of these "tastes." If we consider the government sector, there are a number of reasons why rational men might want the government to engage in income redistribution from the upper income groups to the lower. These motives, however, are either based on the assumption that the individuals are altruistic and are seeking an efficient method of implementing their altruistic impulses,[8] or they are based on motives such as the desire to reduce risk. Direct altruism in the sense of voluntary gifts is an expression of tastes, or, perhaps, inborn drives, not of rational calculation.

8. See Harold M. Hochman and James D. Rodgers, "Pareto Optimal Redistribution," *American Economic Review* 59 (Sept. 1969): 542–57, and the vast number of articles, etc., which followed after this.

SOCIOBIOLOGY AND ECONOMICS

It is a striking fact that the world's first professor of economics in a way founded modern biology. Both Darwin and Wallace, the two co-inventors of the evolutionary hypothesis specifically acknowledged their debt to Malthus.

In spite of this close connection at the beginnings of modern biology, however, the two disciplines had very little contact with each other until about 1960 and in fact still have far less contact than I think is desirable. It is true that colleges of agriculture normally had departments of agricultural economics as well as various applied biology specialties, and individuals from two disciplines sometimes worked together on the same project. The projects were, however, highly applied, and there is no sign of the kind of interdisciplinary fertilization which would have led the biologist to use economic methods or vice versa.

The lack of cross-fertilization between two disciplines which had been so close together at the beginning is only superficially surprising. They were indeed greatly different in structure until very recently. Economics, from the beginning, has been structurally rather similar to physics in being based on complex theoretical propositions and empirical research to validate them. Before the computer revolution, the empirical work was comparatively crude, and theory was heavily emphasized. Since the advent of the computers and the new statistical tools which have been developed to make the best use of them, empirical work in economics has come into its own. It has now become as important as theoretical work.

Biology, however, although it had the vast overarching theory of natural selection, was essentially a non-theoretical or basically empirical science at the operating level. With the exception of genetics, which became a very highly developed mathematical science early in the twentieth century, most biological work was essentially observational or experimental and had little direct connection to the theory of evolution. Indeed it had little direct connection with any very sophisticated theory at all.

The situation began to change in the 1930's, with the work of such men as Fisher, but basically the revolutionary impact of the new theoretical ideas was a development of the 1960's and 1970's.

Reprinted, with permission of the International Atlantic Economic Society, from *Atlantic Economic Journal* 8 (September 1979): 1–10.

Essentially the change was the result of a major theoretical insight. It was realized that the theory of evolution was not only a grand overarching theory but it had things to say in detail about individual species. It was possible to make theoretical deductions from the theory of evolution and then to test them by examining the detailed data.

The general form of this new work can perhaps be seen from an article in the current journal of the *American Naturalist*.[1] Needless to say, in both economics and biology, not all articles follow the pattern of theory development followed by empirical testing. As in physics, in both biology and economics, there are many articles which are only theoretical and other articles which simply test empirically propositions developed theoretically elsewhere.

The similarity between the two disciplines is not limited, however, to the fact that they are now following what we might call the Popper pattern of hypothesis and test with the hypothesis deduced from a central overarching set of theories. There is also a very close resemblance in the general structure of the theory. In both cases the theory involves maximization against constraints.

To begin with biology, one of the consequences of evolution would be that most species now existent should be at least reasonably efficient. With some knowledge of the environmental conditions faced by the species, it is possible to deduce efficient patterns of behavior or physical design and then test to determine whether this deduction is correct. Most of the theoretical biology articles do indeed follow that pattern. The close similarity between this and economics is obvious. The individual economic entities are seen as maximizing utilities subject to constraints, and a deduction as to the behavior is drawn from knowledge of the constraints. This is then tested.

The two procedures are also subject to rather similar limitations. First, the assumption that the individual species is efficient or that the individual is maximizing utility is rarely directly tested. In fact, of course, the experiment of necessity is an indirect test of it, but most biologists and economists are sufficiently convinced of these foundation stones of their work so that they use them without much skepticism. To a considerable extent, of course, this conviction is based on earlier work.

Second, in both cases the deductions are a little dubious. In economics we are never really clear in our minds as to exactly what will maximize utility for

---

1. Diane W. Davidson, "Size Variability in the Worker Caste of a Social Insect (Veromessor pergandei Mayr) as a Function of the Competitive Environment," *American Naturalist*, 112, no. 985, 1978, pp. 523–32.

some given individual. We therefore use proxies, and fortunately there is a fairly simple widely used set of proxies which appears to have enough agreement with the real world so that there is no great difficulty. In biology the problem is that we do not really know the entire environment of any species in perfect detail, and we do not know the mechanical limitations on the design of species in similar perfect detail. Thus, the hypothesis that it is efficient is not perfectly fitted to the real world. This once again makes the situation rather similar to that in economics.

It can be noted from the above that I am claiming what amounts to a mapping of biology in economics. I do not claim that they can be deduced from each other but only that the particular technical apparatus now dominant in the two disciplines happens to be almost identical, with the result that individuals can easily shift from one to the other. I myself have been writing articles, notes, comments, etc., in biology for nearly ten years now.[2] Their quantity is not great, but after all, I am not a professional biologist. It is hard for an outsider to judge quality, particularly with his own work, but there is at least one objective test available from the citation index. My articles, notes, etc., have received considerably more than the average number of footnote references.

The reason for pointing out my own success in putting articles in biology is not entirely vanity, although I will not claim that is not partly involved. The real point is to indicate that the two disciplines are close enough together so that it is fairly easy to switch from one to the other. Indeed, it could be argued that I have never left economics, that all of my "biological" articles are simply economics articles in which I have rather unusual sets of entities maximizing a rather unusual utility function.

So far I have said nothing about sociobiology. This discussion of a relationship between economics and biology in general, however, is a necessary

2. For example see "Biological Externalities," *Journal of Theoretical Biology*, 33, December 1971, pp. 379–92; "Altruism, Malice, and Public Goods," *Journal of Social and Biological Structures*, 1, January 1978, pp. 3–9; "Switching in General Predators: A Comment," *Bulletin of the Ecological Society of America*, 51, September 1970, pp. 21–24; "The Coal Tit as a Careful Shopper," *American Naturalist*, 105, January–February 1971, pp. 77–80; "Altruism, Malice, and Public Goods: A Reply to Frech," *Journal of Social and Biological Structures*, 1, April 1978, pp. 187–89; "On the Adaptive Significance of Territoriality: A Comment," *American Naturalist*, 113, no. 5, pp. 772–75; and "Economics and Sociobiology: A Comment," *Journal of Economic Literature*, 15, September 1976, pp. 502–6.

preliminary to the discussion of the relationship between economics and sociobiology.

One might call the new theoretical biology "micro" deductions about plants and animals in terms of efficiency. Natural selection is assumed to guaranty that the genes provide for efficiency in the individual animal and that we can thus make deductions. This is not true only of the physical design of the animal. Insofar as behavioral patterns are inherited, they also would be selected for efficiency in the same way, and hence, the same kind of deduction can be made. There is now quite an extensive biological literature dealing with this particular topic.

Among the many behavioral patterns which might be inherited would be those which lead to social behavior. These also are subject to the same analysis, and there is here again a considerable modern literature. This field is called sociobiology.

Since the techniques of economics map a more general biological example, it follows that they would also map the sociobiology reasoning. It is thus fairly easy for economists to make contributions in the sociobiology area. I should say that in my opinion it would be equally easy for a biologist to make the reverse transition into economics, and indeed one of them, Garrett Hardin, has done so. I have thus come to what I think is the intersection of economics and sociobiology. As we have noticed, I think it is of less total significance than the intersection of economics and modern biology in general, but it still undoubtedly exists.

Further, from the standpoint of an economist, sociobiology is undeniably more interesting than the rest of biology simply because it is closer to what he normally studies. Further, it is clear that study of non-human societies will broaden the approach that an economist has in his studies of human societies. Nevertheless, I believe for reasons which will be given shortly that there is little more direct aid which any student of human society can get from sociobiology. I should like to qualify the above statement, however, by saying that I do not feel confident this will remain true in the future.

There are two problems, one of which is that human society is clearly drastically different from most animal societies; the second is that we do not understand most animal societies very well anyway. But let me elaborate. I would like to begin with a very brief statement with respect to the first point—that is, that human societies are not very similar to animal societies—turn to a fairly lengthy discussion of the second—that we don't understand animal societies very well—and then return to a discussion of the differences between the evolutionary experience of humans and of animals.

Beginning then with the differences in human societies and animal societies, the first thing that must be noted is that it is large. The importance of this observation, however, is reduced when we realize how immense the differences are among animal societies.[3] Consider the difference between a hyena pack and a slime mold. To put it mildly, it is not obvious that the difference between human society and a hyena pack is greater than the difference between the hyena pack and the slime mold. Ectroprocts, sponges, and jellyfish are all societies which are radically different from the social insects. We observe great differences between human society and those animal societies—mainly the social insects and mammals—which we understand best. This does not prove that the differences between societies of the social insect and mammals, on the one hand, and sponges, on the other, are not even greater.

The existence of this wide range of societies raises the perfectly genuine possibility, emphasized by Wilson, that we may be able to develop a general theory of society for which all of the known social groupings would be seen as special instances. We could, in this theory, move from one type of social structure to another just by changing some of the parameters. Although this is a hope for the future, we are definitely not there now. A great deal of study of such little-known societies as the social spiders, the sponges, and the ectoprocts is needed before we can tell whether this possibility is a real one.

The difficulty of lack of knowledge in this area can be illustrated by the fact that Wilson mentions sponges only three times in his massive work on sociobiology and apparently doesn't understand them. I make this point not to criticize Wilson—certainly all of us have gaps in our knowledge—but simply to point out that even such an extremely well informed man as Wilson is ignorant of one of the major categories of animal society.

Let me now turn to a more detailed discussion of the gaps in our knowledge of animal societies. I should like to begin with a criticism of what I call the haploidy theory of society in the general category of ants, bees, and wasps. That these animals, like their non-social relatives, have an unusual method of reproduction is obvious, and it seems quite possible that this unusual method of reproduction had something to do with the development of social life in this family. There is, however, a difference between the origins of a society and how that society itself works.

---

3. As far as I can tell, there are also social plants. A cluster of blackberry bushes, for example, or an elm grove would probably be called a society if it were not that we restrict the term in ordinary usage to animals only.

The hypothesized close relationship between the sisters of a queen and her offspring depends on the assumption that the queen has not mated with more than one male. Further, in about half of all ant species there is more than one queen in the nest. Indeed, the aggressive and rapidly expanding argentine ants are a multi-queen species. If they achieve world dominance, which seems possible, we will have a theory of ant society which doesn't fit the most prominent single example of such society.

It must be admitted, of course, that the haploidy does provide a particularly simple explanation of how social life might have originated. In fact it has, however, originated in widely different areas including, of course, the termites, whose societies so closely resemble the ants. This seems to indicate that the haploidy is at best a facilitating factor in the development of social organization and not a necessity.

There is another, older theory of functioning of the social organization of such species as the ant and termite which in fact works a little bit better than the haploidy theory, since it does include the termites, but also has its defects. This theory simply points out that reproduction is confined to the queen in the ant and the royal pair in the termite. Hence the workers do not pass on their own genes. The genes which control the workers, therefore, are not designed to promote survival of the workers but promote survival of the reproductives. This means the survival of the whole nest, which is necessary for the survival of the reproductives.

This theory is, I think, somewhat wider in its potential application than the haploidy theory, since it does apply to the termites. It suffers, however, once again from the fact that a number of ant nests have more than one queen, and some termite nests have more than one royal pair.

This theory, further, like the haploidy theory, falls completely apart when applied out of social insect areas. Indeed, it doesn't even fit one particular group of social insects, the social spiders.

Explaining animal society, however, is easier with the social insects than with those much more ancient societies, the slime molds and the sponges. In both of these cases apparently undifferentiated amoeba-like single-cell animals[4] at one stage in their life cycle get together and form a reproductive body in which, as far as we can see, thousands of these cells are given an

---

4. Those which, in the case of slime molds, wander around freely in the environment and, in the case of the sponges, confine their activities to moving through the jelly-like interior of the sponge itself.

opportunity to contribute their genes to the next generation, but many more such cells are not. All of our theories of transmission of a social habit from one generation to another fail in these cases. If we are to have a general theory of sociobiology, we must at the very least explain these societies.

Thus, although we may in the long run develop a general theory of society from study of all existent social animals,[5] we are a long way from it. This does not, of course, prove that we should not attempt generalizations from our present rather inadequate database. It does, however, indicate that we should put little reliance on these generalizations until we have been able to test them with further research.

Having called for more research with respect to, in essence, the hereditary basis of social behavior among non-humans, I should now like to criticize the current theory of animal societies. Apparently this behavior is explained to a very considerable extent by references to the term "altruism." In another place I have argued that at least one potential mechanism for what biologists call "altruism" kin selection will not bear the weight put upon it.[6]

Leaving that issue aside I should like to here argue that altruism is neither necessary nor the likely explanation of social behavior in animals except in those particular cases where the society consists of a single reproductive (or single pair of reproductives) and where the remaining members of the society cannot directly reproduce. In this latter case, the relationship between the, let us say, individual bee and the hive is, from the standpoint of evolution, very similar to the relationship between a skin cell and its body. In both cases there cannot be any direct reproduction, and all genetic messages must be carried by the reproductive specialists. That the non-reproductives, whether bees or skin cells, are programmed to sacrifice for the whole nest or organism is not surprising. Even here, however, the word "altruism" has to be given a rather unusual meaning to make it apply.[7]

5. And once again I would suggest looking into the problem of social plants.

6. For example, see "Altruism, Malice, and Public Goods," *Journal of Social and Biological Structures*, 1, January 1978, pp. 3–9; H. E. Frech, III, "Altruism, Malice, and Public Goods: Does Altruism Pay?" *Journal of Social and Biological Structures*, 1, April 1978, pp. 181–85; "Altruism, Malice, and Public Goods: A Reply to Frech"; and a general symposium on the subject scheduled for an early issue of the *Journal of Social and Biological Structures*.

7. Some years ago I wrote a book, *Coordination without Command: The Organization of Insect Societies*, which explains how I think these societies work. Unfortunately I was unable to find a publisher, but anyone curious can obtain a copy for the cost of photocopying.

Since the bulk of animal societies do not meet the above test, I would like to turn here to another possible organization principle which may explain them. I do not claim, of course, to have complete explanations for them; all that will be presented here is a very brief outline of how I think we should think about them and the approach which I think might be fruitful.

I said before that altruism was not necessary or terribly useful in explaining society. Let me begin by proving that it is not necessary. The proof is ridiculously simple. The very large volume of economic research which is used to explain human society characteristically does not make any use of altruism whatsoever.[8] Outside the family (and economics have mainly dealt with relations outside the family), individuals are normally assumed to be engaged in simple straightforward selfish maximization with no regard for others. Economists are aware, of course, that this is not a 100 percent realistic assumption. Human beings are undeniably altruistic, although when we say that human beings are altruistic we are using the word in a different and more conventional sense than the biologist's use of the same word. Economists indeed have investigated human altruism and, for that matter, intrafamily relations. The bulk of economic theory, however, is based on straightforward non-altruistic assumption.

This theory without any altruism is undeniably the best available theoretical explanation of any society, probably because we are more interested in human society than in others. Further, it is by now very thoroughly validated by empirical research. Most of this research is statistical investigation of real-world behavior, but there is a fair, although not overwhelming, volume of straightforward experimental research.

The fact that the theory is empirically validated—although it tends in most applications to ignore human altruism, which is a real phenomenon—may surprise the reader, but apparently human altruism outside the family is a fairly small matter. The average person is apparently willing to give something between 1 and 3 percent of his income to help others. The deviance between the real world with this minor degree of altruism and the non-altruistic theory is small enough so that it does not interfere with the empirical tests. Of course, as I have said several times, economists do on occasion directly

---

8. In earlier days human society was also explained by altruism or, to be more precise, benevolence. See the Earl of Shaftsbury, "Characteristics of Men, Manners, Opinions," *Times*, 3 Vols., 3rd Edition (N.P. 1723), and Francis Hutcheson, "A Short Introduction to Moral Philosophy" (N.P. 1747).

investigate altruism or incorporate altruism into their investigation of other subjects if it appears that in this particular case it will be of greater significance than normal.

Since this is an example of an elaborate theoretical justification of the most complex society we know,[9] it is obvious that theoretical explanations of societies do not necessarily depend on altruism. This, of course, does not prove that animal societies do not depend on altruism, merely that it is not a necessary foundation. In this connection it is notable that towards the end of *Sociobiology* Wilson extends his altruism idea to human society and says that humans have worked out a form of reciprocal altruism called contract. Perhaps he is correct and that is why we carry out contracts, but it is certainly not the explanation normally given by other students of human society.

The conventional explanation is that human society is based not on altruism but on social arrangements which in many cases (but unfortunately not in all) change the selfish advantage of the individual so that he helps others because it is in his own self-interest even though he is uninterested in their well-being. Of course, in fact he is not completely uninterested in their well-being, but the degree to which he is altruistic is relatively small compared with his drive to aid himself. Society would collapse if it depended on the rather modest bit of extra familial altruism which we do observe among human beings for its basic functioning.

These special social arrangements, however, are not found in animal societies so far as I know.[10] This social contrivance I would like to call "government," although the use of the term will be very broad and will include those very primitive societies in which there is no formal government but in which anyone who wishes to remain active and prosperous had better be well thought of by the other members of the little tribe or community.

Basically "government" in my meaning involves some kind of apparatus which will "enforce" certain rules. The details vary immensely from society to society, and the rules which are "enforced" are equally varying, but basically, in all cases, the violating individual or group is faced not only with the

9. Notably the theory seems to work very well with simple societies too. See Sol Tax, *Penny Capitalism: A Guatemalan Indian Economy*, Washington: U.S. Government Printing Office, 1953.

10. The closest animal parallel that I know of occurred in some of the mammals who operate in packs. In these packs the dominant animal may "keep order" by attacking any of his inferiors who fight among themselves.

people whom he is directly harming but with outsiders who have over-whelming force and who will coerce him if he puts them to the test.

An example of this would be hierarchical control in which the lower official who refuses to obey orders from his duly constituted superiors faced not the possibility of a fight with that superior but coercion by a much larger body. In another example, human property is different from animal territoriality in that the trespasser does not have to be ejected by the owner himself; he can call in third parties.

This institution permits humans to engage in a great deal more cooperative activity than do animals, although in those particular cases in which all members in the given animal society are descended from the same reproductives and only these reproductives can found new societies, another principle of cooperation which is even stronger is available.

This, however, is an indication that our society is not like that of most other animal societies. How then do they work? To answer this question let us talk very briefly about the problem of agreement and cheating. Consider two entities. If they interact, there may be some gain from an agreement between them which patterns their behavior so that the total output is larger than it would be if they were acting independently. Note that although usually there is some such "agreed improvement" possible, it does not follow that it is present in all cases, and in most cases it will involve only part of the activity of the two entities.

Once the agreement has been made, it may well be to the advantage of one or the other or, indeed, both of the parties to cheat on the agreement. Putting it in human terms, they don't keep their promises. One of the functions of human government, of course, is to see to it that they do keep voluntary agreements and to compel them to carry out "social agreements" such as laws and constitutions. This kind of thing is unfortunately absent in all animal societies of which I know. Bees do not keep order in their nests by having special police bees patrol the comb. But this does not mean that cooperation is totally impossible in animal society, merely that it cannot be carried to its optimal degree.

In many cases there is an agreement optimum and an independent adjustment optimum. The independent adjustment equilibrium may involve favorable interaction or at least the avoidance of unfavorable interaction between the two entities. To see the point, consider Figure 1. Here we have a standard prisoner's dilemma, with the social optimum in the upper left-hand corner and the usual prediction that without an enforced agreement the

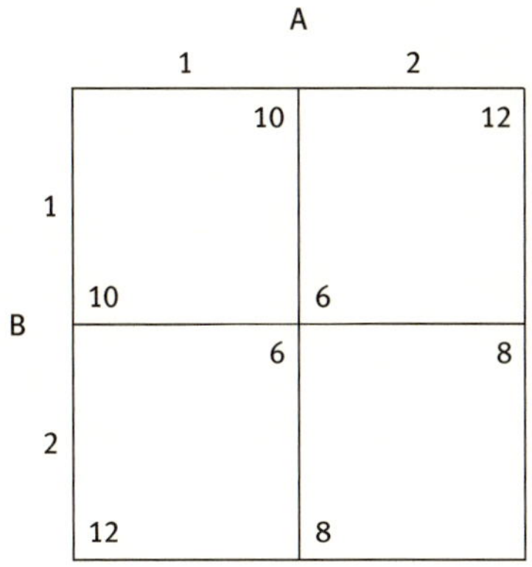

A

	1	2
B 1	10 ⎹ 10	12 ⎹ 6
2	6 ⎹ 12	8 ⎹ 8

FIGURE 1

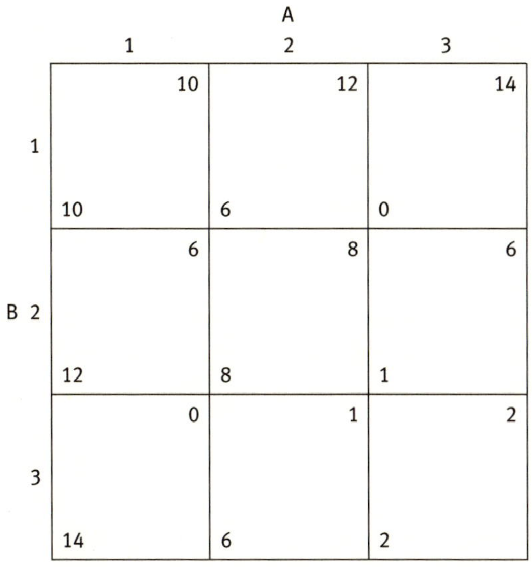

A

	1	2	3
1	10 ⎹ 10	12 ⎹ 6	14 ⎹ 0
B 2	6 ⎹ 12	8 ⎹ 8	6 ⎹ 1
3	0 ⎹ 14	1 ⎹ 6	2 ⎹ 2

FIGURE 2

outcome would be the lower right-hand corner. Both students of human society and students of biology would predict the lower right-hand corner as
the result of independent adjustment.

Now consider Figure 2, which is identical to Figure 1 except that a third
strategy has been added for each of the two players. This has a saddle point at
the middle or 2-2 square which, of course, was the solution also to Figure 1.

The parties do not play strategy 3 and thus end up worse off individually than they would with strategy 2 because the independent adjustment equilibrium of this particular game is the playing of strategy 2 by each party. Note, however, that this is the independent adjustment equilibrium and not the agreement equilibrium. A society which could enforce an agreement would achieve the 1-1 square[11] instead of the 2-2 square.

It is clear that an individual entity interacting with another will not select that strategy which injures the other entity most unless there is something in it for himself. Hence, the actual strategy chosen will of necessity not be the worst conceivable strategy from the standpoint of the two interaction entities. Thus, one can always allege that there is something in the way of cooperation in the sense that the two entities simply do not injure each other as much as possible.

Granted the immense number of species, it seems not at all improbable that there would be some of these species in which the equivalent of our 2-2 square would involve a fair amount of those species with apparent cooperation. There probably would be none which actually reached the agreement equilibrium in the upper left-hand corner, but this might be far from obvious to the observer. The observer might see only a functioning society of some sort, i.e., 2-2 and notice that it could fall to the 3-3 square. Those who are the prospects for further cooperative activity would not necessarily be visible and hence would not realize that the 1-1 square existed. Instead of looking at the 3 × 3 matrix of Figure 2 or the 2 × 2 of Figure 1, the observer would be looking at the 2 × 2 matrix of Figure 3. He might, therefore, feel that the society had reached optimal adjustment when it had not.

It seems to me that most animal societies we observe, once again leaving out those cases in which there is specialization of reproduction, would be in this independent adjustment equilibrium. Hence they would never be fully efficient, but the efficiency losses might not be very visible from the outside standpoint. We should, however, in each case seek out the reason why from a standpoint of each entity it is sensible to be in the society and not "free ride."

Let me now turn to my final subject, which is why I do not believe we can learn much about human society from animal society, although once again I am not sure this is so. Humans have had a dramatically different evolutionary experience over the last million years—perhaps over the last two million years—than any other species. Firstly, it would appear that at least as far as two

---

11. Disregarding, of course, enforcement costs.

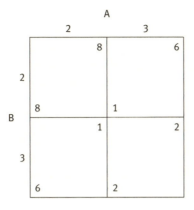

FIGURE 3

million years ago humans exercised dominance over most other species in their immediate environment. Presumably in this very early day they were rarely attacking elephants and they may well have avoided lions and tigers, but certainly they were also regarded as dangerous by these powerful animals. The bones found associated with human artifacts in periods which are recent enough so that the bones survived indicated that very early human beings were eating even the largest and most powerful of their competing species.

A species like humans or like the present-day lion [12] that is at the top of the predator chain faces quite different evolutionary conditions than other species. Lions, like human beings, are not subject to predation by other species. Their main causes of death are attacks by conspecifics (i.e., murder by another lion), disease, and starvation. Protection against disease is largely non-behavioral, e.g., such mechanism as the white corpuscles. Defense against starvation in both the lion and the human species, or at least the human species until quite recently, does involve behavioral modification.

One of the more important behavioral defenses against over-exploitation of resources leading to starvation is aggression by conspecifics. Either a lion pride or a human tribe that finds its resource base a little weak always has the alternative of turning on neighboring prides or tribes and driving them back in order to increase its own resource space. That this type of behavior is common in human history is clear. Presumably it was also common in prehistory and indeed it may have been more common, since the alternative ways of

12. Assuming he is not in competition with human beings.

dealing with the same problem were probably much less developed than they were in the historic period. Lions certainly engage in this kind of activity, although I have yet to read an account of a border war between two lion prides similar to that described by Kruuk[13] for hyenas.

It is, in general, a principle of biology that the competitors for any given entity who are most to be feared are other members of its own species. In the case of a dominant or top-of-the-food-chain animal, this takes a particularly obvious form in that the animal must fear murderous attacks from its conspecifics, and indeed, if it is to maintain control of a suitable resource base for its survival, it must be prepared to win in such battles. Putting it differently, evolution would select very strongly for efficiency in combat with conspecifics in these top-of-the-food-chain animals.

Note that I am not alleging that evolution would develop aggression or a tendency to fight when there is nothing to be gained by it. If some particular lion is aggressive, in the sense that it seeks out fights with other lions when there is nothing to be gained thereby, one can predict that its genes will be eliminated because obviously the more fights, the more likely it is to be badly injured. The same would be true with human beings. Evolution led to combat efficiency but not necessarily to any particular desire to engage in combat.

In general, however, it would appear that human beings have been for a very long time now, certainly at least 500,000 years, subject to a good deal less competitive pressure than most species. We have a fairly slow reproduction rate. In addition, our social and, for that matter, eating habits are such as to make us particularly suitable for propagation of germ diseases. Under the circumstances our effective reproduction rate, even if there were no competition for resources, would have been fairly slow until the development of modern medicine. This does not mean that we were not subject to selection, but the selective pressure was relatively weak.

Further, the principal direction of evolutionary advance in human beings was the development of a larger brain, i.e., a large, apparently non-programmed computer which could be used to solve all sorts of problems. It developed in the Old Stone Age but seems to be quite suitable for quantum mechanics, writing novels, and participating in national politics. Really, it can't have very much hardwiring and must be designed mainly for self-programming.

13. Hans Kruuk, *The Spotted Hyena, A Study of Predation and Social Behavior*, Chicago and London: University of Chicago Press, 1972, p. 335.

These facts led to a situation in which, although human beings did not, of course, escape from evolutionary selection, the selection ceased to have the tight restrictive characteristics it has on most species. The situation in which human beings found themselves did not provide a unique behavior pattern which was most efficient. It seems fairly certain that very early in the human race, individuals began to specialize in such things as making weapons or hunting. Further, technological development, although slow, does seem to have been characteristic of the human race for at least the last 500,000 years. Now consider the rule of thumb that it takes at least a hundred generations to fix a gene. In the human case that would be 2000 years. Any behavior-control gene to be selected would have to pass the test of long-run efficiency, for over a period of 2000 years the technology both of fighting and of making a living by whatever means was used by that particular tribe would certainly have changed. Further, the gene going through one hundred generations would probably pass through people who had different behavioral specialities in the tribe. The witch doctor, the maker of stone axes, and the common hunter would all have to be benefitted by that gene if it were to be selected. It does not seem likely that this would lead to tight genetic control of behavior, and, of course, in the last 50,000 years technological changes have been fast enough so that selection in general would be against any specific behavioral patterns.

As a result of this unique evolutionary background, human beings do a great many things which are contrary to the survival of their genes. The obvious single example is our tendency to put large resources into decorations of various sorts. We also spend a great deal of time in activities which have only entertainment value and which clearly do not increase the likelihood that our genes will be transmitted. We also have a rather mysterious trait, altruism, which leads us to help people who are in no way related to us. This obviously has negative survival value in any tightly evolving species. Under the loose restraints with which human beings are faced, however, it was possible for it to develop. Putting it all together, human beings have a number of traits which would not have developed had we been subject to severe selective pressure. These traits are not likely to be found in species whose evolutionary background is different from ours. This raises great doubts as to whether our societies will closely resemble non-human societies. Note, however, that it only raises great doubts, it does not prove that there is not some general science of society which covers both human society and the slime mold.

The general theme of this paper has been that we are unlikely to learn very much about human society by studying animal societies. They are fascinating subjects in and of themselves and clearly are suitable subjects for scientific investigation. In particular, a large number of them are practically unknown and could repay intensive study. I would not anticipate, however, that the result of such study would be knowledge of our own society.

TERRITORIAL BOUNDARIES

AN ECONOMIC VIEW

Burger's comment[1] is an interesting contribution to a difficult problem. My point is to suggest an alternative, more complicated, and, I hope, more realistic, formulation. The two explanations, however, are not inconsistent and will be integrated below. I will begin, however, with a model in which the bird, or whatever organism we are considering, does not engage in the Burger-type strategic calculation but simply selects the best area.

Assume an environment which is suitable for settlement of a particular bird and that at first only one bird, or one pair of birds, arrives. They should select their nest location in order to maximize their access to resources. Note that for the rest of this article, I will assume that the resource value of any given point in the area is known with certainty, thus ignoring the stochastic variables discussed in "On the Adaptive Significance of Territory."[2] This is for simplicity only. A stochastic value of each point would be readily substituted but would make the mathematics more complicated.

From any nest location, the value of any given spot is shown by equation (1), in which A is the potential resource available from the area, and D is the distance from the nest which has been selected.

$$V_j = A_j - f(D_j) \qquad j = 1, \ldots n.$$

(1)

The shape of the function $f(D_j)$ distance would depend on the use of the particular resource; for example, space for protective purposes would have a different functional shape than a food source which has to be harvested. It is, nevertheless, generally true that the farther away, the less valuable a given resource will be.

The basic problem, as shown in equation (2), is to maximize the value of the territory around the nest, the territory extending, of course, only through the domain of (3).

Reprinted, with permission of the University of Chicago Press, publisher, from *American Naturalist* 121 (March 1983): 440–42. Copyright 1983 The University of Chicago.

1. J. Burger, "Super Territories: A Comment," *American Naturalist* 118 (1981): 578–80.

2. G. Tullock, "On the Adaptive Significance of Territory: Comment," *American Naturalist* 113 (1979): 772–75.

$$\text{MAX} \sum_{j=1}^{j=n} V_j = \sum_{j=1}^{j=n} A_j - f(D_j) \tag{2}$$

$$\text{Domain } A_j - f(D) \geq 0. \tag{3}$$

Also, the area must provide enough resources to ensure survival, which is shown by the constraint Z, which is the minimum resource base which gives reasonable chance of survival and reproduction.

$$\sum_{j=1}^{j=n} V_j \geq Z \tag{4}$$

The area would be a perfect circle around the nest point if the resource were evenly distributed over space. If they were not equal, irregular shapes would presumably develop.

Assume now that other birds arrive and select nest positions and that two of the birds have chosen nest points such that the domain of (3) is satisfied for one spot for both birds. Under these circumstances conflict will occur, and each of the birds should be willing to invest in the fight up to the present value of this spot. Since I am assuming that the birds are equally big and tough (altering assumptions would be possible but make it more complicated) and that the value of any given point, that is A_j, is the same to all members of the same species, then each one would have a 50-50 chance of winning and, hence, would be willing to invest up to 50% of $A_j - f(D_j)$ in fighting over this point.

If we consider two birds whose nests are close enough together so that a number of areas satisfy domain conditions for both of them, then bird 1 will invest more resources in defense of areas nearer its nest than will bird 2; the converse holds for those areas closer to bird 2.

If we assume that the defense commitment determines the outcome, we would expect that a line would appear between the two parties connecting all points at which constraint equation (1) is the same for both parties, that the points nearer to the nest of 1 would be completely under the control of 1, and that those nearer the nest of 2 would be completely under the control of 2. There would be, however, conflict along the border, and it seems reasonable that this conflict would be proportional to the value of the various points along the border to the individual bird. Thus, if we look at figure 1 and assume the dotted line shows the border of two birds, 1 and 2, which is the line of conflict between them, there would be less fighting at point N than at point M, because N is farther from the two nests and therefore less valuable to them even though the resource produced there might be the same as that at M. This hypothesis is, of course, readily testable.

The combat cost for 1 would be shown by

$$C = \tfrac{1}{2} \sum_{j=1}^{j=m} g[A_j - f(D_j)]. \tag{5}$$

Subject to the domain limitation of

$$\text{Domain } D_1' = D_2', \tag{6}$$

a bird, in selecting a location with other birds as potential competitors for space, would try to maximize

$$\text{MAX} \sum_{j=1}^{j=m} [A_j - f(D_j)] - \tfrac{1}{2} \sum_{i=1}^{i=m} g[A_n - f(D_i)]. \tag{7}$$

It is subject to constraint 2, but the domain would be more limited, since part would be cut off by the line of conflict, hence the use of M instead of N.

$$m < n. \tag{8}$$

With this formulation we could expect irregularly shaped territories, either because resources are not evenly distributed or because the history of the arrival of birds, together with the fact that they are reluctant to move their nests once they have established them, would lead to irregularly shaped areas (see figure 1). (Note that with even distribution of resources and nest

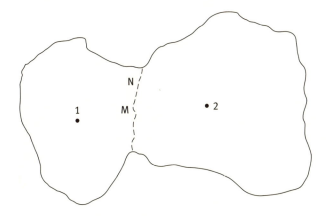

FIGURE 1
Two adjacent territories of conspecifics

movable without cost, the outcome would be the Losch system of hexagons.) It could also lead to gaps when two nests are far enough apart so that constraint 1 leaves a particular area unoccupied, but a bird settling in the area would not obtain Z. Note that if this expression is accepted, then in those years in which the bird population is low, individual territories would tend to be larger than in those years when it is large. This is also testable, but if I understand the empirical evidence, the hypothesis is already verified.

So far, the model is quite different in spirit from the Burger model. Efforts, however, in selecting nest location and in deciding whether to defend any given area might lead to the kind of strategic calculations that she emphasizes. Turning to her figure 1*B*, in which there is an opening, bird B might choose a nest location a little closer to A than is otherwise optimal in order to make certain that the area which is potentially available for C is too small to support life. If bird C does appear, bird B might also choose to invest resources in fighting (which is irrational from the standpoint of eq. [7]), on the hypothesis that this would drive bird C away, and, hence, fighting "irrationally" for one or two days would pay off in the future. I could complicate my equation to take these factors into account, but it seems to me that the first step is field observation to find out whether the behavior fits the equations I have given or whether Burger's more complicated strategic model is necessary.

EVOLUTION AND HUMAN BEHAVIOR

Introduction: The Evolution of Self-sacrificing Behavior

Most economists and most biologists believe that at least part of our behavior is inherited. Most economists use theories in which people are assumed to be selfish maximizers. For example Field says: "The standard economic model embodies an implicit theory of human nature based on the assumption that individuals are egoistic."[1] A typical support has been Darwinian. Individuals who have predispositions to act otherwise would over the eons have suffered a relative fitness disadvantage.[2] This assumption differs radically from human behavior. When some catastrophe occurs, an earthquake in Turkey or a flood in Guatemala, human beings from all over the world send gifts to the victims.

All humans presumably had common ancestors several hundred thousand years ago, but the gene overlap would be minimal. There also clearly is no chance of direct reciprocation by the victims of these catastrophes to the givers. One might hope that if you yourself suffered a similar catastrophe you also would receive gifts, but this would not be reciprocation from those to whom you had previously made gifts after a catastrophe.

This is not the only place where human beings behave in a non-selfish maximizing way. In 1945 thousands of Japanese committed suicide by attempting to crash their aircraft into American naval vessels. It's hard to see any way that this could be regarded as selfish maximization. This is particularly true because the nature of Japanese religion, for the bulk of these pilots,

Reprinted, with kind permission of Kluwer Academic Publishers, from *Journal of Bioeconomics* 4, no. 2 (2002): 99–107. Copyright 2002 Kluwer Academic Publishers.

1. Alexander Field, review of *Unto Others: The Evolution and Psychology of Unselfish Behavior*, by Elliott Sober and David Sloan Wilson, *Journal of Economic Literature* 39 (2001): 133.

2. Elliott Sober, "Unto Others: The Evolution and Psychology of Selfish Behavior," *Journal of Economic Literature* 40 (2001): 132–34. In a review of Elliott Sober and David Sloan Wilson, *Unto Others: The Evolution and Psychology of Unselfish Behavior* (Cambridge: Harvard University Press, 1998), Sober uses the group selection model which is presently being revived, notably by biologist David Sloan Wilson. Ghiselin has pointed out to me that there are other possible explanations or reinforcements to this one. See Michael T. Ghiselin, "Institutional Bioeconomics and the Division of Labor: Reflections on Yarbrough and Yarbrough's Paper," *Journal of Bioeconomics* 1 (1999): 319–22.

did not offer heavenly rewards. In a mild way I went through a similar experience. I landed in Normandy on D plus 7 as a rifle company replacement. That this was extremely dangerous, I knew, although I cannot say I realized quite how dangerous it would have been. Fortunately, I ended up in a headquarters company and ran relatively little risk. At the time that I landed, however, I had no idea that I would find the war primarily boring and not particularly dangerous. I cannot recall any strong feeling that all this was unjust or that I should do anything about it except go forward and fire my rifle. My colleagues in the replacement package with which I landed seemed to have much the same attitude. In my own case, I wasn't even enthusiastic about the war. I had read Schumpeter and thought the war was three sided. I suspected that the end would leave Russia without any other European country to hold them in check. The fact that American soldiers died to give Warsaw to the Russians did not in any way surprise me. Nevertheless I had no particular doubts about going forward and perhaps being killed. As in the case of the kamikazes, I was clearly not selfishly maximizing.

The purpose of this essay is to explain these particular kinds of behavior, which are not selfishly maximizing. Indeed, they are self-sacrificing. I am particularly interested in human behavior, but the explanation requires a deviation into biology. Human beings are not the only animals that engage in self-sacrifice. The worker bee committing suicide to defend the nest is a more comprehensive example. Biologists and bioeconomists (e.g., Landa), of course, have no difficulty explaining this.[3] The behavior of the bee protects its genes, including the gene that directs it to make the sacrifice, although it does not protect itself. It will have no descendants anyway, and by protecting the hive it makes it more likely that the gene, which directed the sacrifice, will be present in the future. Neither the bee nor the gene thinks about this; indeed the gene cannot think, and the bee's ability in that direction is minor.

For the benefit of non-biologists let me elaborate a little: any behavior which is transmitted by biological heredity goes by way of genes. A gene which directs me to take a 49 percent chance of death in order to save a brother, who has 50 percent of the same genes, from certain death will find itself statistically more numerous after I have done so than it would have been had I not taken the risk. Thus, this kind of gene has survival value, not in the sense that its holder has a higher rate of survival or higher rate of reproduction

3. Janet T. Landa, "The Political Economy of Swarming in Honeybees: Voting-with-the-Wings, Decision-Making Costs, and the Unanimity Rule," *Public Choice* 51 (1986): 25–38.

directly, but in the sense that there will be more of that gene in the next generation. Biologists have done a great deal of work with this model, and so far as I know, there's nobody who seriously doubts it.

When dealing with behavior, especially human behavior, we should keep in mind that we only know in detail a small part of the development of human beings. Most of these behavior traits that we study originated many generations ago in a society radically different from our present one. In an appendix to this article I have a discussion of the fairly detailed theories of sexual behavior among humans. These theories are based on a very small sample and a very specialized sample of human behavior, and I doubt their accuracy, but the reader should turn to the appendix for my reasoning.

I, too, am going to run a large risk here, because the traits I will discuss appear to have been produced by evolution many generations ago. Indeed they appear to have been produced before human beings crossed over from the other primates.

Charity

Let me first take up the topic of charity to people who are immensely distant from us, and then turn to risking one's life for the group. If we consider chimpanzee bands, or indeed other types of animals that live in bands, most of the members of the band will be at least distantly related to the others. This is the effect of long continued existence of the band. If we consider those bands, which have more or less continuous existence so that many individuals spend their whole adult life in one band associated with much the same comrades, then most of them would be moderately related to any randomly selected member of the same band. This would be because they are descendants, with a limitation I will discuss later, of the same collection of members of the previous generation. Thus, the genetic effects discussed above would lead them to make some, although perhaps modest, sacrifice for benefit of other members of the band. They would, for example, be willing to make small gifts to other members of the band when the sacrifice was not great. The gene that directed this would turn out to be more common in the next generation for the reasons given above.

Of course, this would apply even more strongly to direct relatives. One would anticipate that the gene for gifts to your brother would provide for much larger gifts than a gene for gifts to other members of the tribe who are not closely related. Turning to humans: parents make very large sacrifices for their children. Close relatives also receive gifts larger than those given to other members of the tribe. Indeed by observation, the sizes of the gifts we give are roughly related to the relationship, and hence the probability of gene overlaps. Gifts to other members of the tribe or village where the gene overlap is small are proportionately small. Of course, this is not the result of conscious calculation but is built into our preference function. Other members of the tribe or band are more distantly related and receive proportionately smaller gifts.

Incest

Here we come to another biological effect. Incest is dangerous, not in the sense that it kills the incestuous animal, but in the sense that it is likely to accumulate bad genes in the descendants of incestual pairing. Most non-human bands deal with this by having one or the other sex seek mates in other bands. Chimpanzees may, for example, drive out the young males who then seek mates in other tribes. This has two effects: it does make the dangerous incestual mating unusual, but it also means that any individual member of the band probably has at least some gene sharing with individuals in the next band over. Since this band also engages in outbreeding, there is a further weaker likelihood that the genes will be shared with other bands that are farther out. Thus charitable gifts, if they cost very little to the giver, may be evolutionarily selected for the area occupied by a number of bands.

The bands, however, for reasons to be discussed shortly, would tend to have few direct contacts, and those contacts that they had would tend to be unfriendly. Human tribes in such situations frequently kill people from the next tribe over if they enter their territory. The only real friendly contact they have involves sex, where outbreeding to avoid incest is necessary. Under these circumstances the information about members of other tribes would tend to fall very rapidly with distance and would reach zero for tribes farther out. The gene, however, would to some extent be shared for a considerably longer distance. Thus, gifts to people who you had no reason to believe were related to you would be feebly genetically positive. The flood victims in India in 3000 B.C. would not come to my attention. Today they do. What we would expect would be a gradual falling off in probable relationship and gene sharing from direct close relatives to the members of distant tribes. The size of the gifts and the amount of sacrifice would fall off similarly, and, of course, so we observe today. The difference is that today we know about things happening vast distances away.

The genes, of course, do not actually know the relationship of other fellow members of the species. Indeed the genes do not know anything. A gene which called for large gifts to close relatives, another gene which called for modest gifts for more distant relatives, and a third which calls for tiny gifts to anyone about whom you have information would have been genetically desirable in primitive conditions and are not dangerous now, so did not get selected out.

Villages

Of course we no longer live in tiny hunter-gatherer bands. Most human beings, however, lived in somewhat similar situations until very recently. London was a large city in 1800, but the bulk of the population of England lived in small agricultural villages. The relationship between villages was not too different from that of the relationship of two neighboring hunter-gatherer tribes. Thus, the same genes would retain their evolutionary value. Further, large cities, like London, were not only centers of population, they were also centers of disease. They required immigration from the agricultural villages to retain their population. Thus, genes that might be desirable in such a large city would have little chance of perpetuating themselves.

All of this is now changed. Not only do we have information from far off, but also very large numbers of us live safely in the cities, and we can predict that in the future those backward countries with large populations in the countryside will succumb to the same phenomenon. Further, the cities are not now massive centers of deadly disease, although the population does not seem to be increasing or even replacing itself. Thus, we would expect that with time these genes would be eliminated, but that may be a very long time off.

Extensions

To deviate slightly: people living in small communities with continuous interaction will gain from establishing a favorable reputation. Lying and breaking promises both will tend to lower the reputation and hence would tend to reduce the prosperity of the liar or promise breaker. Whether this would tend to be incorporated in the genes is obviously a difficult problem.

Further, we do sometimes lie and sometimes break our promises. There may be some formula which tells how often you should break promises and how often you should lie to get maximum survival possibility. Note, however, I've not calculated this in any way. It is an interesting but also very difficult problem which we must leave to the future.

War

Let me now turn to the kamikazes. Many animals and some plants have territories that they defend.[4] They are, in essence, using resources to preserve other resources for their use. Whether this is a good bargain or not varies a good deal, and by no means all plants or animals are territorial. Most cases of territoriality involve only a breeding pair and sometimes only one individual of either male or female sex. Animals that live in larger groups, however, may defend the territory in which they live, and I'm going to call them tribal territorial. Wolf packs, for example, defend a hunting range, although because of the size of these ranges and the sparse distribution of prey, this is not very intensive.

Origins of Group Conflict

When we turn to the early history of the human race, we are necessarily speculating. There are two possible sources of information. One of them is the behavior of our close relatives, particularly the chimpanzees and, probably, also the bonobo. They live in what we can call tribal communities. There is another close relative of ours, the gorilla, which lives in small groups, each containing an adult male, several females in his harem, and perhaps a couple of juvenile males. In all cases they seem to occupy specific territory, although I cannot say that they have been investigated carefully enough so that we can say they're truthfully territorial. There is only one case of a war between tribes of chimpanzees, but that one was particularly vicious, with the losing tribe being exterminated.[5]

---

4. Plants sometimes poison the area around their roots.

5. See Frederic L. Pryor, "What Does It Mean to Be Human? A Comparison of Primate Economics," *Journal of Bioeconomics* (forthcoming, 2003).

Wars, as among human beings, are relatively rare, and the total amount of observation of these primates is limited. Further, close observation of gorillas is dangerous and particularly so if you enter their protected space. In the case of the chimpanzees and the bonobos, the total observation is also rather limited, especially with the bonobos. In the case of the chimpanzees, the first book on them regarded them as peaceful and, indeed, held them out as models for human beings.[6] The apparent reason for this was that the study area was in the middle of the territory of one band. The war came when the population rose to the point where some of the chimpanzees broke off and tried to establish their own tribal area. As mentioned above, they were exterminated.

The bonobos are a recently discovered species and have only been moderately investigated. They are once again being held up as models for human beings, but the principal investigator admits he may be wrong.[7] Although he saw no fighting, he reports that many of the males have scars, missing fingers, even missing hands. Since wars between tribes are probably rare, the absence of direct observations does not indicate that they never occur.

Further, students are apt to put their investigative facilities where there are a lot of the animals under investigation. If the species is tribal and territorial, that is likely to be in the center of their tribal area. Thus, the rather rare combat between groups would take place some distance from the base camp and might well be missed. In any event, they are surely rare like human wars. That does not mean they are unimportant, once again like human wars.

Territoriality

The general reason for territoriality is the desirability of monopolizing a suitable supply of resources. Since there are changes in the resource availability through the year and, for that matter, from one year to the next, the area seized should be large enough to support its occupiers even in the down period. Thus trespassers must be kept out, and this would lead to fighting or at least displays from time to time. Whether the observer would see them would be a matter of chance and dependent on the length of the observations.

6. Jane Goodall, *In the Shadow of Man* (Boston: Houghton Mifflin, 1971).

7. Frans de Waal and Frans Lanting, *Bonobo, The Forgotten Ape* (Berkeley: University of California Press, 1977), 84–85.

Territoriality, although not universal among species, is not by any means remarkably rare. Most of this territoriality, however, is either individual or family. Territoriality at the tribal level is unusual, but a number of primates, including humans, use it. Its advantage is, of course, that it is easy for a group to keep individual trespassers out. Its disadvantage is that the division of resources among the members of the group must be determined and usually is determined by dominance maneuvers. These can be deadly. The human connection with the other primates was long ago and with different, although related, species. Thus the likelihood of the same genes must depend upon their evolutionary value rather than cross-breeding or other direct sharing of genes. Necessarily, the reasoning given above is speculative but can be reinforced by some further, rather speculative, evidence about primitive humans.

Primitive Tribes

We have a good deal in the way of description of tribal societies of humans. Partly that comes from historical documentation which covers primitive tribes encountered by literate peoples. Partly it comes from anthropological research on the few surviving primitive tribes in such places as the Amazon basin. They seem to be territorial in much the same sense as the chimpanzees. They have a territory occupied by each tribe and except for special occasions keep trespassers out. Usually there is some kind of overarching structure which permits the tribes to provide mates for neighboring tribes in order to avoid incest, and trading facilities may exist. Sometimes a number of villages will have an annual meeting in which nobody kills anyone else. Still, relations among the tribes are much like those of the chimpanzees.

Civilizations

Human beings are smarter than chimpanzees however. They are able to organize larger organizations, sometimes a federation of villages; more commonly, the leader of one village conquers neighboring villages and establishes an empire. With time, these things got bigger, and we had things like the Persian Empire, which tried to add Greece. It seems likely that these large organizations benefited their subject peoples. They were able to prevent local wars, and their ability to mobilize large numbers of people meant that they normally could deal with less well organized neighboring groups with ease. Domestically, they normally objected to competition in the form of local thugs or thieves and, of course, tried to prevent foreign competitors, other groups of villages, or other empires from entering. Further, they tended to improve transportation by building roads so that their armies and tax collectors could get around easily. All these things benefited their subjects probably more than the injury inflicted by their taxes. There was an even greater gain to the people who lived in the early civilized nations. Both in Mesopotamia and in Egypt, irrigation was of great importance and required the mobilization of large numbers of people. The gain to the population was great, and the need to build pyramids for their rulers was a modest price for water control, which actually kept them alive.

This may seem like a deviation from my main subject, but is not. The individual member of the tribal society would gain from the tribe's maintaining its territory or even adding some from a neighboring tribe. Of course, if he could get others to do the fighting, holding back himself, it would be even better. Tribes that had many members doing that would tend to be eliminated. Whether there would be some kind of internal structure to punish slackers or whether the tribe would itself be eliminated if there were many, with a result that those genes were also eliminated, I do not know.

Thus, in addition to genes for some types of charitable acts, we would expect genes for engaging in group fighting for territory. Thus, my landing in Normandy was simply an expression of my genetic inheritance. Surely I would not have been willing to engage in an individual landing. Landing with part of a large section of my "tribe," however, seemed perfectly normal. Thus, if I'm correct, primates organized in tribes or nations are able to fight to protect their resources or to grab other people's resources.

Primitive Human Tribes, Again

Turning to primitive human tribes: they seem to have much the same mechanism. In some cases, the Yanamo, for example, belligerency has been carried to what an outside observer is apt to think an almost insane degree. Nevertheless, they have existed for a considerable period of time in a difficult environment. Other tribes are normally not quite so belligerent as the Yanamo, but they still defend their territory and sometimes try to take neighboring territory. It would appear, then, that genes calling for participating in tribal defense or tribal aggression have been selected favorably. The kamikazes and the Americans who landed on the beaches of Normandy can most readily be explained by this mechanism.

Of course, we have ways of punishing slackers, but they are rarely used. Occasionally my co-invaders of Normandy mentioned the first sergeant and his .45 in this connection, but I never heard of its being used, and I do not think it was a major cause of their behavior. They were genetically programmed to fight for their tribe. They were also programmed to punish people who did not fight, but the second programming seems to have been mainly unnecessary and certainly seldom used. But all of this reasoning is theoretical, and the empirical tests refer to things that happened long ago or to accounts of present-day primitive people. The theory is good, and the outcome seems plausible. Nevertheless, I could easily be wrong, granted the immense distance between the theory and actual observation.

Appendix: Sexual Behavior among Humans

In pointing out an example of the type of error, which might occur, I'm going to annoy other sociobiologists by alleging that they are simply wrong in an important area. Specifically, let us consider the current theory of the relation between the sexes.

Women carry the baby before birth and nourish it for considerable periods after birth. This means a sizable capital investment by the mother. The father, however, can go on and fertilize other women freely. This has led to the theory in which the woman is very careful in order to get a father who is a good provider and who will stick with her, while the male is polygamous. Social institutions intending to make the father responsible are frequently observed but rarely prevent some extramarital sex on the part of at least some males.

All of this fits what we saw in Europe and America in the latter part of the 19th century and early part of the 20th. It doesn't fit most of history and certainly does not fit European and American behavior in the latter part of the 20th century. Let us begin abroad. Most people in the world have arranged the marriages of young people through parental contracts. Frequently there is a material payment. In any event, neither the woman nor the man has any real choice. The pattern of behavior found in many articles is simply not realistic. If we consider the situation in the United States, Sweden, and many other countries today, we find that a very large number of women produce children without any permanent arrangement with the father. Further, it is not at all obvious that a permanent arrangement with the father is even legally possible. There are frequently cases in which the male member of the family is changed, although the children usually go with the mother. Today among black families more than half of the children are fatherless. This just doesn't fit the theory discussed above.

I've no complaints about the reasoning which was used to deduce these patterns of male and female behavior. It does not, however, fit the real world today. It didn't fit the real world in, let us say, China two hundred years ago. A set of institutions prevailing in the area where most theoretical biologists lived a little while ago was used to produce a theory covering the whole world and the whole of history. Further, the biologists do not seem to notice that the changes in family structure today invalidate their theory.

The reason I brought this up is not to attack the very prominent biologists who developed the theory. My point is that this kind of theory is necessarily dubious. I've just produced a new one of my own, and I want to make it clear that I realize that it has not been tested. It's further possible that another theory would better fit what we know, and, indeed, it is possible that the whole enterprise is vacuous. Thus, in my article I may have been wasting your time. I hope you'll take comfort in the view that my wasted time and effort are even more extreme than yours. On the other hand, of course, I hope my theory is correct. If any reader can find a way to test it, I would be deeply grateful. This will be so even if the theory on testing turns out to be wrong.

THE ECONOMICS OF NONHUMAN SOCIETIES

CHAPTER I

INTRODUCTION

That humans are social is an obvious fact. We also refer to ants, or at least many species of them, as being social. If we must give a definition of the term, which includes all such "societies," the problem is difficult. Samuel Johnson has: "1, relating to a general or public interest; relating to society," which would seem to use the same general word to define one part of it. He also gives: "3, consisting in union or converse with another." Society is defined as "1, union of many in one general interest. 2, numbers united in one interest; community."

Modern dictionaries, as far as I can see, have made little progress in better defining the word. Of course, this I should say is generally true of modern dictionaries compared with Johnson. Johnson is still one of the best dictionaries ever composed. In any event, *Webster*[1] gives: "7, Living or associating in groups or concentrations; as, The ant is a social creature." "9, In botany, growing in clumps or masses."

None of these definitions is really adequate, but I cannot improve on them. Having frankly confessed to the reader that I do not have a clear definition of "society," I will proceed with my book about different kinds of societies. In this case, I do not think this will confuse the readers. All of us, even if we cannot specifically define what we mean by the word "society" or "social," nevertheless, have a pretty clear idea that—let's say an ant nest—is an example and also most human communities. Most people will accept the termite, and those who have been watching TV recently will agree that the mole rats are an example.[2]

We can draw the lines more broadly. Colonial coelenterates, from their name, are obviously a society of very small animals. The organization is more intimate than that of either the ants or the mole rats, but, nevertheless, it is social. There are also the sponges, which the nonbiologist reader will no

---

The Economics of Nonhuman Societies (Tucson, Ariz.: Pallas Press, 1979), reprinted with permission of the author.

1. *Webster's New Universal Unabridged Dictionary*, Simon & Schuster, 1979, New York.

2. Why the mole rats, a most unphotogenic species, have appeared on TV as often as they have I cannot imagine. It may be because it is so astonishing to see a mammal with a social organization very similar to that of the honeybee.

doubt be surprised to hear can be regarded as societies of single cells, many of which are amoeboid and migrate freely within the sponge.

We will give at least a skeletal discussion of several nonhuman societies, but the main purpose of the book is to develop a general theory of societies. As the reader will discover, this is a general (admittedly very vague, but nevertheless general) overtheory of all kinds of societies. The human society is a member of the family, albeit a very radically distant member. In a way, this general theory has two branches, one of which is human beings, and the other is all the rest.

There are other species. An aspen grove, for example, or, for that matter, a bamboo can, I think, be referred to as a society of semi-independent plants. Blackberry vines are normally an aggregation of independent units, which are, to some extent, interconnected and could be listed as societies.

There is also the question of whether, in order to have a society, all members must be closely related or at least members of the same species. When there is close integration and cooperative behavior of two or more species, biologists normally use the word "commensalism" or "symbiosis." Frequently, the only real difference between these and societies is just that they are different species. Lichens are a close organization of two kinds of organisms which are not even members of the same kingdom.[3] There are other such cooperative organizations of more than one species. The only reason that I can see for not calling them "societies of more than one species" is simply tradition. They raise the same problems of coordination and organization. These problems are particularly difficult, in such cases, since the genetic interests of two species must be met.

If I cannot define society, I can at least point to a few characteristics which help us to recognize it. The first of these is that the various members of the society engage in activities which are mutually helpful. Note that I am not saying they are always mutually helpful, only that, on balance, their behavior is mutually helpful. With this definition, by itself, of course "societies" could include more than one species.[4]

---

3. Lichens and their partners, usually cyanobacteria, are classified in the appropriate phylum by themselves, and then the combination is further classified as a "form phylum" of lichens. Thus, a humble cyanobacterium may be a member of two phyla while you, gentle reader, are a member of only one.

4. Most of the dogs I have known obviously regard themselves as part of a pack, which includes certain humans. Dog owners act as if they agree.

Among baboons, the normal movement of the tribe is one of a cooperative self-defensive organization jointly seeking food. There are, however, severe fights among the leading males. Thus, there is both cooperative behavior and non. But the cooperative behavior is of greater general importance than the fighting. Indeed, the only reason for the fighting is to obtain or maintain position in the larger cooperative unit. We see the same in humans, but, in general, our society is quite radically different from the other societies I will discuss.

I should say here, parenthetically, that the societies of the other large mammals—like the baboons, some monkeys which are social, wolves, etc.—are going to be discussed very little in this book. Some of them, in particular the baboons, are very interesting in themselves, but generally their society is radically different in many ways from the human society. One important difference, of course, is simply a matter of scale.

It may be that way back in the Old Stone Age human beings lived in fairly small migrating tribes which did have some structural resemblance to baboon tribes, but that stage is long past. Our current social interaction is massively more complicated, so much so that most of the traits and characteristics of that earlier society, if it did exist, are now buried and have little or no effect on our behavior.[5]

If we turn to a large ant nest or some other more complex societies I will describe, there are large-scale interactions, but nothing that really corresponds to the dominance orders that we find among the wolves and the baboons. It is true that among some social groups—bees, for example, and apparently the mole rats—there is some initial fighting to determine who should be the queen. Indeed, in some types of wasps, this is never fully determined and lower-ranking females may occasionally lay an egg. That, however, is an example of a primitive system. We will pay little attention to them, although not denying they exist.

I should like to re-emphasize that I am not suggesting that human society is something which we can understand by looking at animal societies. Indeed, my approach is the reverse. I am taking tools developed to deal with human society and using them to understand nonhuman societies. In the process, however, they will be radically generalized and, thus, a general theory of society, which fits both human and nonhuman societies, will be

---

5. Wilson would not agree. In fact, it was his disagreement on this point which made sociobiology controversial.

developed. This society will be recognizably a generalization of what we have learned about human societies to nonhuman species, but examining it may well help students of human society by clarifying some of their ideas.

The Roman soldiers practiced with weights on their swords. In a way, engaging in economic analysis of an ant nest is the same kind of thing. Economists who do so will find it much more difficult than dealing with the human societies they are accustomed to. Still, when finished, like the Roman soldier, they will find they are better equipped for their regular tasks.

Unfortunately, I cannot claim that reading this book will add anything more to the usual economists' tool kit. If economists finish, they will know a good deal about species they did not know about before, including some I am sure they never heard of. They will also have a somewhat clearer idea of some of the basic features of societies in general, including human society. They will further realize that there is a sort of general overtheory of society of which both human and nonhuman societies are examples.

For biologists, the situation is rather similar. What I am going to develop here will, to a considerable extent, be new to them, but rarely will it lead them to change their views as to how whatever species they are specializing in behaves or how it is organized. One of the complications of biology is the existence of many millions of species. This means that the average biologist can really be thoroughly familiar with only a few of them. This is, indeed, the reason that the mole rat was almost forgotten for such a long period of time.

Nevertheless, biologists who specialize in termites may find that knowledge of this overarching more general theory is of some help in clarifying their thoughts about their particular species. It is unlikely to change their views in any deep or fundamental way, but it may still be helpful.

This introduction has, by now, given a reasonable idea of what this book is about, but a little discussion of its organization may be useful. The next chapter will be essentially a discussion of the evolutionary theory of reproduction, insofar as it is relevant to societies. It will point out a number of respects in which natural selection may lead to cooperative behavior. As a complement of this, it will be necessary to indicate that it may well lead to noncooperative behavior as well.

This chapter will not be written for the biologist, who I presume already knows much of what it contains. Still, I suppose most biologists reading this book will skim through it. Therefore, I should say that it does have some features which do not appear in biological writings and which biologists may find interesting.

This points to one aspect of this book as a whole: it is not written specifically for biologists. I hope that biologists will find it interesting and helpful, but I also want it to be readable to economists. Indeed, I would like to have it readable and easy to follow for all students of human society, whether or not they are economists. I would hope the sociologists, political scientists, anthropologists, etc., would find it of some help. It is not, however, that human society is closely related to these other societies I will deal with. Their relationship is, indeed, extremely distant.

Nevertheless, there are some common features, and these common features tend to be overlooked by the students of human society basically because, like the purloined letter, they are so obvious. When you look at an ant nest, you are driven to seek explanations of how ants get cooperation and efficient division of labor. These radically different explanations may be of some help in studying human societies.

I have tried to make the book readily intelligible to people who do not have much biological background. This means that I frequently use different words than a biologist would and that my explanations, although I think there are no errors in them, may be somewhat different than those used by a biologist. I would like to ask the biologists' tolerance to this unaccustomed use of terminology. I do not think biologists will have difficulty reading it, but they may find it a bit unfamiliar because the technical vocabulary of biology is avoided where it might cause difficulties for nonbiologists.

I reverse the approach here, when I turn to economic vocabulary. I have tried to make my use of the economic language such that a biologist not trained in economics will find it easy. I should say here that biologists, in recent years, have become interested in some of the analytical tools of economics and have applied them. Indeed, they have actually invented some tools, like the hawk/dove equilibrium, which have become important in economics. Thus, I anticipate that biologists will be less put off by economic concepts than economists will be puzzled by biology. I think both can gain, and I beg the tolerance of both for language use which is intended to be readable to nonspecialists.

For the especial benefit of the economists, I have several chapters which provide a sort of survey of selected nonhuman societies. Most of the biologists reading this book will be specialists in one or the other of these societies and will have a general knowledge of the others. Even such a learned biologist as Wilson, however, did not cover all of the species in his monumental *Sociobiology*, which I will discuss here. The world which the biologist studies is a gigantic one, and it is more or less beyond the individual human mind to know all of it. Certainly it is beyond mine.

To repeat something I mentioned before, in general, I will not be much interested in the societies of the higher mammals. These are basically much simpler societies than an ant nest, although the baboon is a much more complex animal than an ant. Most of the principles and problems that I deal with fit them, too. But, frankly, I find them less interesting.

Another area that I will generally drop is what I might call the strict family. Among sexually reproducing animals in a great many species, the male and female meet only for the purpose of mating. There are others, however, in which the relationship is fairly permanent. Once again, these things can be called societies, and many of them were listed in Wilson's *Sociobiology*. I am, however, going to talk relatively little about them. These are cases of cooperative behavior which is mutually beneficial, but they are also, in my opinion, less interesting than the large societies.

After I have given the survey of existing social species, I will turn to what I think is the major contribution of this book: the exploration of how this cooperation works. Hence, for example, very small animals such as termites have very little in the way of brains. Indeed, there is some doubt as to whether we should refer to them as having brains at all. The standard ant nest has no central planning order or government. It is true that if there is only a single queen that queen will produce some pheromones which gradually get dispersed through the nest and which do have some coordinating function, but mainly the decisions as to what will be done have to be made by the individual ants.

If there is an emergency—like a human being kicks off the top of an ant nest—individual worker ants will rearrange their work very rapidly. Some of them will take the eggs and larvae down to the lower levels of the nests, and some will stop their previous work and begin repair work on the nest. Some of them may take up defensive positions in areas which previously had not been endangered. While all of this is going on, of course, they must continue collecting food and taking care of the queen. How does the individual ant "decide" to make these shifts. Again, this will be dealt with after we have looked over evolutionary theory and several social species.

As a sort of preview, however, I should say that human beings have both an economy and a government. Social insects and other social species normally have only an economy, but no government. Humans think that government is a necessary precondition for the function of the economy; thus, this proposition may seem bizarre. I am not going to argue that government is not necessary for the functioning of the human economy, but the social species I will be dealing with have built-in behavioral patterns which make government unnecessary. One might say that the great flexibility which the large brain gives human beings provides problems for which the government is necessary to solve. Less flexible social species can get by without it.

This brings me to another problem. Human societies not only have cooperative endeavors, which I have used as my definition of society, but also have command structures. They have coordination without command and coordination with command. To complete the matter, they also have vigorous noncooperation, i.e., combat, which may be either strictly individual, as in schoolboy fights, or highly hierarchical, as in two armies fighting each other.

As a general rule, the nonhuman social species do not have these hierarchies, although we will see some cases where they have something that resembles them. Human societies always have the mix of hierarchical or command structures and cooperative or noncommand structures. Even in such an apparently monolithic organization as Russia under Stalin, it was still true that a great many interactions between individual Russians were not directly ordered from on high. They were cooperative.

This cooperation might be directly counter to the desires of those on high. The black market, for example, was of great importance to the Soviet economy, even though the government made fairly strenuous efforts to stamp it out. Even within the legal part of the economy, there was a lot of cooperative behavior. Individual managers might make deals with each other which were not ordered from on high, but which fit in with the more general plans of the politburo.

The most extreme case of this need for cooperation, of course, in any hierarchical system involves the fact that the top of the hierarchy is subject to being overthrown or killed. Stalin slept in a carefully guarded area, but he did not completely trust his own secret police. His bedroom was locked, and entrance into it, even when he was not there, was very carefully restricted by Stalin himself. He was aware of the fact that when asleep he was more or less defenseless, and he did not completely trust his guard.

Indeed, it is possible that Stalin died at the time he did because of this. According to his daughter's account, when he did not come out of his bedroom in the morning, the guard commander on the spot waited a considerable period of time before breaking open the door. It is possible that medical treatment earlier might have saved Stalin's life. On the other hand, one can certainly understand the guard commander's concern for his own health if he did break the door down and found Stalin just oversleeping.

But, to repeat, such hierarchies are primarily found in human societies, although they are not unknown in other species, which I will discuss very little. The more complex societies, like those of the ants and termites, do not have this dominance. Earlier students, who thought that the bee queen[6] actually ruled, misunderstood the situation. In any event, we will give little attention to the higher species and will turn mainly to the more complex societies composed of simpler entities.

The next chapter, then, will discuss the theory of evolution and its relationship to societies. In the third chapter, there will then be an account of the basic problems of obtaining cooperation between different entities. The second will essentially be biology, and the third, drawn from economics. There will then be a number of chapters dealing with specific nonhuman societies. These are intended primarily for the nonbiologist, although biologists may find some of them interesting. With the problem laid out, we will turn to its solution. This book is intended to bridge a gap between economics and biology. I hope that people from both disciplines will find it of interest.

6. They thought she was a king.

CHAPTER 2

THE GENETICS OF SOCIETY

It is clear that much of the behavior of very simple entities is controlled by inheritance. As the entity gets more complex, the degree to which it is controlled by its genes decreases and environmental control increases. At the top of the progression, with human beings, there is a considerable dispute as to how much of our activities are inherited and how much environmental.[1]

This chapter will be devoted almost entirely to that portion of nonhuman societies' behavior which is controlled by heredity and not by different conditions under which those nonhuman societies are brought up or live. Thus, for example, the soldiers among ant species normally have the same hereditary genes as do the workers.[2] The difference is in the way they have been fed while developing. In most social species that have a queen, the queen also has the same genes as the workers, but her "upbringing" is different. On the other hand, the difference between behavior of different species of bees is clearly inherited.

Let us examine this genetic inheritance. I will begin by discussing one of the old saws of biology: the difference between group selection and individual selection. For this purpose, let me turn to a myth propounded by some early students. Baboons are preyed upon by leopards. These early students alleged that they had seen cases in which the large male baboons went out and attacked the leopard. This would be an extremely dangerous thing to do; in fact, almost suicidal. On the other hand, it surely would increase the likelihood that the baboon tribe would survive. These students were impressed by this heroism on the part of certain male baboons.

1. Adam Smith, to take an extreme case, believed that they were entirely a matter of environment and training. As a matter of fact, in this, as in so many other cases, it is very difficult to say for certain. Human beings are deeply influenced by their heredity, but also by their environment. The average height of the Japanese population, for example, has been growing fairly rapidly since about 1860. This comes from improved conditions under which children are raised and not a change in genes. On the other hand, it is extremely difficult to tell exactly what percentage of human behavior is hereditary and how much is environmentally controlled. Fortunately for this book, we know that with the simple entities, the environmental control is less important and the genetic more important than it is in human beings.

2. If they are daughters of different queens in those nests with more than one, or if the queen has been fertilized by more than one male, then the genes will vary. As far as we know, however, the mix of genes in the worker population is the same as in the soldier's.

There are two problems with this myth, one of which is that more recent students have not seen baboons attacking leopards. The other, however, is purely theoretical. In the baboon species, suppose that we have two alleles of the same gene, one of which leads males to go out and defend the group against leopards and the other which leads them not to do so. We shall call them the heroic and the cautious. Those baboon tribes which had a fair number of heroic genes in them would tend to be preyed upon less by leopards than those that had mainly cautious genes and so would tend to flourish.

On the other hand, within each of these tribes, the individual baboon that had the heroic gene would tend to be killed by leopards, while those which had the cautious gene would tend to flourish under the protection of the heroes. The baboon tribe would be selected for a high percentage of heroes within it, and the individual baboons would be selected for cautious genes.

The standard biological solution to this problem is that the individual selection of the cautious allele would outweigh the group selection of the heroic, with the result that eventually the heroes would be selected out by the leopards. As we can see, baboons, as a whole, might well be much worse off as a result of this; i.e., there might be fewer baboons in total than there would if this heroic behavior were frequent. But biology does not select what is best for a whole species, it selects for individual gene successions. If you commit suicide to protect members of society who are not related to you, your genes will not be perpetuated and theirs will be.

Now the biologist who reads this will notice that I have said nothing about inclusive fitness or Hamiltonian altruism. That is not because I do not understand it (personally, I would prefer to call it nepotism), but because I would like to defer its discussion for a few paragraphs. Let me then continue without any altruism-nepotism for a little while. I will bring it in later.

The theory of such individual versus group selection was the subject of a good deal of mathematical research as well as observation of actual behavior. This mathematical research led to a general conclusion that individual selection would always triumph over group selection unless the group's life span is similar to or shorter than the individual life span. Since there are few organized groups within the animal kingdom in which that condition exists, it was thought that this pretty much ruled out group selection.

But group selection was not actually made impossible for social species by this rule, because of the fact that the social animals, plants, etc., were occupying niches in the environment where, if there were too many egoistic individuals, the society as a whole dies. It could well die within the life span of one individual.

Most social species, including such high ones as the bees, do, indeed, have a little egoistic cheating on the part of some of their members. In some species, for example, worker honeybees will occasionally lay an egg in one of the cells. These worker-bee eggs would develop into drones that cannot contribute to the support of the nest, but would perpetuate the genes. If this happened on a large scale and if the eggs so laid were actually raised, the nest would die. In fact, in these cases, other worker bees normally eat these worker eggs. In any event, they are not usually nourished. If, however, this habit became common and the individual bees protected their eggs, it would very likely destroy the nest within one generation.

Now, obviously, this is merely a theoretical proposition and not something that we have observed. It is true, however, that there are a number of parasites which live in the nest of many social insects and which reduce its efficiency. If they become too common, the nest does die.

The social species requires a high degree of homogeneity of behavior, a part of which involves engaging in activity which does not directly benefit the individual ant, termite, etc. This would provide an opportunity for some members of the group to "free ride." To an economist, this suggests the use of some kind of police mechanism.

The individual members of a species might, for example, have a gene which would lead them to punish the free rider. If the gene existed, it would work but, unfortunately, that gene itself would be subject to the same criticism. Those particular baboons that punish other baboons for not running out and fighting with the leopards would benefit the troop, but have a lower survival than those that merely watch. It is the same problem at one stage removed.

There is a way of dealing with it in animals such as baboons and wolves which, however, requires the assumption that the gene package is not highly precise. Consider the Isle Royale wolves, which have been carefully studied, frequently from the air. In the winter, they form packs which attack moose. It is a dangerous activity, since the moose will eventually be brought to a stand and will then be surrounded by a group of wolves which attempt to dash in and take bites out of it. If the wolves are successful, the moose will die and can be eaten by the whole pack. But the moose defends itself by kicking, and because the moose is such a big animal, its well-planted kick on any wolf is apt to finish it. A free-riding wolf could make some pretense of rushing in to bite the moose but, as a matter of fact, stay well out of the reach of its hooves.

Suppose, however, that there is a gene for courage. This gene simply produces brave behavior, and it would mean not only behaving bravely when confronted by a moose, but behaving bravely within the wolf pack when confronted with another wolf interested in mating. If the alternative is a cautious gene which tells you to hold back in both situations, the brave genes could be commoner in the next generation than the cautious ones. This same mechanism could, of course, be applied to the baboons, but note that it requires the assumption that the genes are not able to distinguish between different situations where there is both a profit and a potential cost.

Although this might conceivably work for the wolves, it is hard to use this line of reasoning for ants, termites, etc. In the case of those species in which there is actually an infertile worker caste, the problem is not really very serious. Since the infertile workers could not reproduce anyway, the entire hereditary burden is carried by the breeding queen(s) or, in the case of the termites, the breeding pair(s). From the standpoint of the gene line, workers are no more important than those skin cells in your body which "cheerfully" commit suicide every day in order to protect the rest of the body, in particular, that part which engages in reproduction.

The genes that call for the skin engaging in this kind of sacrifice are not basically the parents of the next generation anyway. It is true they are "children," i.e., clones, of other nearby cells, and it could, therefore, be argued that they are perpetuating their own genes by protecting the genes of their near neighbors in the body, in particular, the sexual potential genes deep in the interior. That is the only mechanism that they could use to perpetuate their own genes.

Here I should digress briefly and say that biologists very commonly talk about individual plants, animals, cells, organs, etc., in a language which implies that they are carefully thinking out a strategy and carrying it out. Of course, this is untrue, and is not what the biologists intend. What they mean is that evolution has selected them for a particular behavior which is what they would have planned for if they had thought the matter over carefully or simply attempted to maximize the survival of their genes. The implicit "anthropomorphizing" here is simply a convenient way of dealing with a problem which is not anthropomorphic at all, but is hard to discuss in other terms (granted you are speaking English).

The protection against free riding is particularly strong if the niche occupied by a social species is not suitable for solitary members of the species. A solitary termite[3] would not be able to survive, let alone reproduce itself. Thus, any action that a worker ant took which increased its likelihood of survival within the nest but lowered the likelihood of survival of the nest would be

---

3. There are none, although there are cockroaches which are rather similar.

basically counterproductive for that individual ant's genes, unless the degree to which it endangered the safety of the nest was very slight.

The world of nature is a highly competitive one. An ant nest which contains a significant number of ants within it which were not behaving in a fully cooperative and efficient way would tend to lose out in this competition. It might take several generations, but, nevertheless, this would happen. Thus, the worker ant which somehow began to parasitize the nest and, let us assume, somehow reproduced its own genes would, in fact, be committing suicide or exterminating its own genes. Its gene line would be extinguished because it could only live in the nest and the nest would be extinguished.

Ant nests do, of course, frequently contain commensals—other insects mainly—that either do not help the ant particularly but cause no damage, damage the nest a little bit by being fed and taken care of by the ants, or, in some cases, inflict enough damage on the ant nest so that it disappears. It would, presumably, be possible for a special substrain of ants to behave the same way.

It has recently been discovered that among honeybees there are differences among different worker bees, depending on which particular drone is the father. This is possible, of course, because the queen has been fertilized by several different drones.

There is one particular ant species in which queens individually enter the nests of other ants and work their way into the royal chamber. Then they kill the resident queen and are treated by the workers as if they were the queen themselves. The new "queen" and her eggs and larvae are taken care of by the workers. They all become reproductives which, of course, leave that particular nest. Eventually, the domestic workers that were there when the new queen arrived die and she dies too. But the large number of reproductives that she has produced, under the care of the host workers, perpetuate the species.

In the war of all against all, which is nature, this is not surprising. But note that this particular ant species, in order to continue existence, must refrain from killing off all of the host ants. It is not obvious exactly how this is done. Presumably the life expectancy of the reproductives is very short, so not very many of them succeed in seizing control of a host ant nest. If that were not true, both the host ant species and the parasitic species would cease to exist. Once again, the queen would be extinguishing her own gene line when she took over the ant nest.

Cooperative effort is necessary for the survival of that particular nest. "Egoistic" behavior would lead to the death of the nest and of the individual noncooperating social insect's genes. It would not be truthfully egoistic, but misguided. Social species have found niches in which only fairly large organized groups can flourish, and hence they will disappear if they do not have the necessary behavior patterns. This does not prove that they occupy all such niches—there may be potential niches for many different social species we have not yet discovered—but the fact remains that the individual member of the social species must not be rigorously egoistic.

In addition to the problem of group selection I have mentioned above—if there are too many egoistic genes in the nest, the nest will die and not reproduce, and, therefore, those egoistic genes will not reproduce—there is also a simple and direct precaution. Many members of the society may be physically incapable of reproducing, so egoistic activity on their part would not be transmitted to the next generation.

In all of the social insects of which I am aware, the reproductive function is narrowly specialized. Spiders are thought by most laymen to be insects, but are given their own special classification by biologists. There are social spiders, and they do not seem to confine reproduction so narrowly.[4]

In the pure case, there is exactly one breeding female, a system which, unfortunately, is not as common as one might think. But it is easier to discuss than the common case in which there is more than one. In such a situation, the worker bees or worker ants, as the case may be, are unable to reproduce.[5]

Under these circumstances, clearly the individual infertile worker really does not have any egoistic traits which can be inherited, because nothing will be inherited from it. In those cases where there is more than one queen, it would still be true that most of the workers are incapable of perpetuating their genes, and so there is no way in which genetic egoism can develop. All of this, however, will be discussed more thoroughly later in the chapter when I turn to the actual reproductive procedure. For the nonce, we simply point

---

4. The social spiders seem to be a rather mysterious group. In any event, I have been unable to get a clear idea of how they are organized. We do know, however, that individual female spiders have their own nests in the great superweb which they use to trap food. In this individual nest, they raise their own eggs. For a good description, see J. W. Burgess, "Social Spiders," *Scientific American* 234, no. 3 (1976): 101–6.

5. Sometimes this is only that they are unable to reproduce as long as there is a queen present. Normally, however, if they are confronted with a dead queen and begin reproducing, they only reproduce drones and so the nest dies.

out that this kind of thing would make group selection possible by making individual selection impossible.

Many species of ants and other social insects have more than one reproductive queen or reproductive system. The termites, for example, have a royal pair, and, if something happens to the royal pair, they replace it with a collection of promoted workers. They are not as fertile as the royal pair but, by being numerous, are able to keep the nest alive. Many ants have more than one queen, and we will shortly turn to other societies where reproduction is by no means simple.

Nevertheless, the general proposition that we have developed so far would be true. In most social species, failure of coordination through "egoistic" behavior of individuals will lead the nest as a whole to die, and hence the "egoistic" individual also dies. Thus, those genes would not be perpetuated.

Now let us turn to heredity, a subject to which students of social societies have given a great deal of attention. The simplest method of reproduction is cloning, in which the cells simply split into two identical cells. This method is used by bacteria[6] and is sometimes used by some of the higher animals. It is also used by many plants. To take two obvious examples: the aspen groves which, in my opinion, should be regarded as societies, are clones and so are bamboo clumps. These groups maintain subterranean contact with each other. It is a rather mysterious characteristic of trees that many seem to have subterranean contacts with conspecifics. Whether this leads to a society or not, I do not know.

There are also animals that engage in cloning. The aphids do it for some generations, as do certain reptiles. The cloning among aphids, however, is usually interrupted after some generations for sexual reproduction. There are species in which cloning is carried on to a very large extent. The obvious cases are the colonial coelenterates, many of which are the jellyfishes (of which, I am sure, even the nonbiologist reader is familiar). These are, in fact, colonies of a very large number of rather small animals which are cloned. As the cloning proceeds, the individual polyps develop specialization, with some of them becoming stinging cells, mouth parts, etc. They are, however, all clones of the same group of genes, just as all the cells in your body are clones of the original one-celled fertilized egg.

---

6. After a number of generations, bacteria normally engage in something called "conjugation," which apparently performs the same function as sexual congress would.

The easiest way of explaining what actually happens is an analogy created by Dawkins in *The Selfish Gene.*[7] These genes create things that Dawkins called "survival machines," which are the animals and plants of which you, dear reader, are one example. This set of genes, then, perpetuates itself through time only by producing some kind of large protective mechanism of which, to repeat, you are an example. Further, these genes determine to a very large, but not complete, extent the structure of that protective mechanism. It seems likely that genes are, at least as far as mental matters are concerned, much less important for human beings than they are for ants, but that they are, at least to some extent, important even to human beings is obvious.

Looking at the matter from the standpoint of the gene, the problem of duplicate genes is simply perpetuating itself. Now, by this, I do not mean that the gene carefully thinks the matter over. The number of duplicates of a particular gene can increase or decrease in each generation. It is only those that increase or remain stable that will be around after a while. The statement that the gene tries to increase its numbers, or at least protect itself, thus implies a degree of conscious planning which is not there. Nevertheless, it fits rather well what goes on.

A gene can increase the number of its copies in the next generation either by protecting itself or by protecting other identical copies of itself. For example, suppose one particular gene sacrificed itself in order to make two other identical copies survive. This means that in the next generation there will be more of those copies present than there would be if this particular gene had not committed this heroic act.

This is the basis of what is called "inclusive fitness" or "Hamiltonian altruism." For myself, I would prefer to call it "nepotism," because, in essence, the gene is protecting its relatives. In the theory that I have stated so far, I have not referred to close relatives. As a matter of fact, in the diversity we see in the real world, the only circumstance in which genes are given an opportunity to "protect" duplicates of themselves is in situations where they are protecting relatives.

7. Dawkins's book is remarkable in being both a superb popularization and a contribution to scientific knowledge. The reason it is a contribution is because of his rigorous unwavering application of the foundations of genetics to his problems. Developments since publication have made some of his work obsolete, but it is still worth reading. R. Dawkins, *The Selfish Gene* (Oxford: Oxford University Press, 1976). In addition to Dawkins, I suggest G. C. Williams, *Natural Selection: Domains, Levels, and Challenges* (New York: Oxford University Press, 1992). Unfortunately, it is not anywhere as easy to read as Dawkins, but it is more recent.

There is an old saw that a man should be willing to take up to a 50/50 chance of death in order to protect his brother and up to a one-in-four chance in order to protect a first cousin, etc. It would be hard to test this theory, but it provides an explanation for a great deal of behavior on the part of animals, plants, etc., which is otherwise hard to explain.

I do not want to quarrel with this general biological orthodoxy, which I believe is indeed true, but I am going to argue that a particular form of group selection that I mentioned above[8] is more important in dealing with animal and, for that matter, plant societies. The reason is quite simply that many such animal and plant societies do descend from very close relatives, but others do not.

But sticking strictly with the possibility of protecting and aiding one's relatives, there is a rather special form of reproduction used by members of the order Hymenoptera to which ants, bees, and wasps belong. The males are produced by an unfertilized egg and have only one set of chromosomes, while females have the more normal two. Thus, if a single male mates with a single female, the female offspring all have genes corresponding to one of the mother's two sets of chromosomes, but all will have exactly the same chromosomes from their father. The degree of relationship between sisters is 75%; i.e., they all have the same set of genes on one of their chromosome sets, but a 50/50 chance of differences on the other.

Males, having only one chromosome set, of course have a 50/50 chance of being related, because it can be a duplicate of either one of the mother's. Note that the sisters are more closely related to each other than to their mother or father, since only 50% of their genes are the same as those of the individual parent, whereas 75% are the same as those of a sister.

This assumes that there is only a single queen in a nest and that the queen has mated with only one male. In our present case, this is true, but is by no means universal. Those hymenopterans which reproduce by having queens mate in the air and then come down to earth for their nest may well mate with somewhere between 10 to 20 males. In these circumstances, the relationship of the female workers is much less than 75%. This will be further discussed below.

All of this is quite different from the ordinary method of sexual reproduction in which you inherited half of your genes from your mother and half

---

8. See my "Economics of (Very) Primitive Societies," *Journal of Social and Biological Structures* 13, no. 2 (1990): 151–62.

from your father. Thus, in those ants, bees, etc., in which there is only one queen and it had mated with only one male, the mechanism I described before under which you would be willing to sacrifice yourself for anything more than a 50/50 chance of saving your sister is intensified. In the particular case of these hymenopterans, it would be more than a 25% chance. In other words, if you were a wasp, you might be willing to take greater risks or consume less food or something like that in order to keep a sister alive than if you were a human.

Many biologists feel that this means that the social system in which individuals do help their relatives is more likely among Hymenoptera than under other systems. They can point to confirmatory evidence. There are far more social groups in Hymenoptera than in any other similar group of animals or plants.[9] It should be kept in mind, of course, that there are far more solitary or nonsocial hymenopteran species than there are social. Still, the ants are such a dominant group that if you simply weighed all of the social hymenopterans, they would outweigh all the rest put together by a fairly high multiple.

This could explain why social habits would be more likely to originate among the hymenopterans. It does not explain why they continue to survive, particularly in those species in which there are multiple queens who have mated with several males. For that, we must turn to other explanations, and I think that the peculiar form of group selection that I have given above is a better explanation than the peculiar method of reproduction.

To repeat, this type of group selection is indeed peculiar. The individual member of one of these large communities really does not have much choice. In general, it is unlikely that they can even reproduce fertile offspring, and, if they can, without the social structure, they are more or less defenseless and are likely to be eliminated by the environment. Thus, an intelligent worker ant which was more interested in the 25% of its genes which were different from those of a neighboring worker than in the 75% which were identical might decide to be cooperative.

Even if it were possible for it to pass on its genes by some method other than working in the nest and passing them on indirectly through the queen, those genes would surely disappear because they would not have the powerful structure of the nest to protect them.

---

9. Note the emphasis on "similar." Colonial coelenterates and sponges (to be discussed later) are generated by cloning, with the result that parts of a jellyfish should be more willing than a worker ant to sacrifice for the survival of the rest.

There is also the fact that if we look at the more highly developed Hymenoptera, let us say the ants, we find that a good many of them are not particularly closely related to other workers in the same nest. Firstly, they may have quite a number of queens, up to hundreds. Secondly, the queens may have been fertilized by a number of different males.

This was simply theoretical until fairly recently, but now the possibility of comparing the DNA of different ants in a nest provides a direct method of measuring degree of relatedness. Hölldobler and Wilson, on pages 187–88 of their *Ants*,[10] have a table showing the degree of relationship shown by this new method for the members of a whole collection of different ant species. The measured relationship runs from 75% to 1%. Even the latter is greater than the relationship between two randomly selected ants, but not all that much.

In many ways, those ants in which the relationships are low are the most highly developed ones. It is hard for a single queen, which has been fertilized only once, to produce a very large number of offspring, so the more complex ant communities usually[11] have multiple queens. The mating, of course, takes place in the air, but there is no obvious reason to believe that the queens mate only once.[12]

The social habit seems to have originated more often in Hymenoptera than in other insects. Among the insects, the first and, to this day, still most highly developed type of social insect is probably the termite, which is many millions of years older than the social ants, bees, or wasps. They use ordinary sexual reproduction, with a king and a queen, and further, once again, there may be more of these royal pairs. In those species where there is normally only one royal pair, if something happens to it, they simply replace it by promoting workers. Thus, the maximum relationship would be the 50% which we observe among humans and other groups.

Humans, of course, have simple ordinary sexual reproduction and, as far as we know, have been social from earliest times. They are a recent, but very

---

10. Bert Hölldobler and Edward O. Wilson, *The Ants* (Cambridge: Belknap Press, 1990). The table occurs as part of an excellent discussion of the whole problem. Pages 184–95 make up a long section entitled "Testing the Kin Selection Theory," which will be very helpful for anyone interested in the question.

11. Usually, but not always. The giant army ant colonies usually have only one queen.

12. Most bees have only one queen. The degree of relatedness among the workers is low enough so that it is fairly certain that each queen mated with at least 10 or 20 males.

successful, social species. Looking the other way, I have mentioned cloned reproduction. If closeness of relationship is important in creating social habits, then cloned species would presumably be the most successful social group. Among the insects and vertebrates, termites do not seem to be particularly social, although soldiers have been observed among the aphids, which rather implies that some aphids are social.

A giant multi-individual jellyfish or coral produced by cloning, of course, is an extremely good example of integrated behavior. Once again, depending on their immediate environment in the jellyfish or coral structure, polyps have somewhat different duties and frequently are quite different in physical appearance, but they are all clones.

One would expect them to be even more integrated and the individuals more willing to sacrifice themselves for the genes of their relatives than hymenopterans. In fact, as far as we can tell from observation, this is true. Although it is a little difficult to see exactly what one would mean by sacrificing oneself if you were a polyp, which is a small part of a giant jellyfish.

There are other social animals which are not normally talked about, such as the slime molds or the sponges. They will all be discussed in some detail in a later chapter, but it should be said that sponges are an immensely ancient phylum, much older even than termites. Using the definitions of social, which we have given above, they are societies of single-celled amoeboid entities which engage in collaborative behavior.

Another and more astonishing group is the slime mold, again to be discussed later, in which individual amoeboid cells give up their individuality and become joined into a sort of plum pudding of nuclei and other cell parts which engages in integrated behavior.

There remain the plants, which I have only mentioned and not discussed in detail. I do not know very much about them, but it is clear that many plants could, using the definitions we have taken out of the dictionary above, be regarded as social. Most biologists do not use the term "social" in dealing with these groups, but that seems to be simply a technical usage of the term. Here again, at least in many cases, we have individuals which engage in "behavior" that is mutually beneficial. "Behavior," admittedly like everything that plants do, is extraordinarily slow and takes the form of growing in certain ways, but still they do cooperate and gain from that cooperation.

An even more extreme case, and one which will be discussed at greater length later is, of course, any large animal which is a cooperative collection of individual cells which have been cloned from an initial fertilized egg. That they cooperate is obvious. In an absolute literal sense, many of them sacrifice themselves, in that they die in order to provide protection, skin, or something of that sort for the remainder. This will be discussed later; once again, biologists have rarely referred to this as a society.

There is, however, another problem here. Suppose the cooperative entities are not related at all. They may be different societies. Above, I mentioned the lichens. These are tough pioneers which are likely to be the first occupants of a bare rock surface. They are, in fact, a cooperative arrangement between two different entities: a fungus and cyanobacteria, or blue-green algae. They are not only not closely related, they are not even members of the same kingdom. In high school, I was told that the fungi were members of the plant kingdom, and the bacteria, of the animal. This has since become more complicated, and there are now five kingdoms. It is still true, however, that they come from different kingdoms. But more of this below.

The biologists would call this symbiosis rather than society. There is no reason to quarrel about words; indeed, we will shortly turn to some other cases where the dictionary definition of "society" covers things that biologists call "commensalism" or even parasitism.

The first thing to be said about lichens is that biologists have, in some cases, succeeded in raising the two cooperating species separately. Mainly, they have not succeeded, but it is quite possible that this indicates simply that biologists have not devoted much energy to a boring and not particularly important task. Could we call this a society? Using the dictionary definition given above, the answer is yes, but most biologists do not use words that way. To repeat what we said earlier, biologists have dealt with this problem by making lichens a separate "form phylum." There are about 25,000 different species in this phylum.

This is not the only place in which we have different species which seem to be cooperating. Most of the termites—the Termitidae are an exception—are not able to digest wood, their principal source of food. In their gut, they carry protozoa, which digest wood for both themselves and the termite. Should the protozoa and its host, the termite, be regarded as part of the same society? Neither can live without the other.[13] To repeat, biologists would say it is not exactly the same society, but "commensalism" (a Latin word meaning "eating at the same table"). There is no point in quarreling about words, but it is obvious that the only difference between this and a society is that the termites are a different species than the protozoa.

---

13. The protozoa are a specially adapted species which cannot live outside the termite's gut.

Of course, there are many cases in which one of the two commensal species actually does not contribute anything much to the other. We have a lot of simple, mainly one-celled organisms living in our mouths or on our skin which, in most cases, do not do us any good. On the other hand, they do practically no harm. It is different with the protozoa and the termites. In fact, they cannot exist without each other.

There are many other species of this sort. The ruminants eat things like grass, which is rich in cellulose, and put it in a pouch where live a number of one-celled animals that can digest cellulose. After having gotten the food into their pouch, the ruminants partially regurgitate it and "chew their cud."

There are a series of stages here. Firstly, there are cases like the protozoa and the termites in which it is necessary for the different species to cooperate in order to keep each other alive. Secondly, there are cases in which they do live together, eating off the same table, but where they do each other very little good or very little harm.

Brer Rabbit of the Uncle Remus stories, you may recall, spent much of his time in the briar patch, which protected him. This could be regarded as a fictional example of a case where two species associate closely together and where, in any event, one of them gained considerably from it.[14] Either one could have gotten along reasonably well without the other. Many environmental communities have this characteristic of living together, but not having very much interaction. This is not thought of as either a society or commensalism.

There are, however, a good many cases in which species live closely together and one of them is parasitic on the other. This is a further step, and it is neither society nor commensalism.

There is the beetle, which is parasitic on ants. Although the beetle does not look in any way, to us, like either an ant or an ant larva, the ants appear to think that it is a larva. Once it gets to the outskirts of a nest, the ants will carry it down and deposit it with the grubs. It then proceeds to eat the grubs and lay eggs, which mature into grubs, which also eat the ant larvae. The ants do not seem to notice this behavior and treat it much as they do their own larvae.

Obviously, this is not an example of commensalism, and, equally obviously, if there are too many such beetles, the nest will perish. It is clear, however, that ants, like other social animals, can put up with a certain amount of this kind of thing. There are many species that live within ant nests and either

14. The briar patch may have gained fertilizer, too.

directly prey on ants or, much more commonly, succeed in getting food out of the ant food chain in one way or another. The same is true of the bees and, of course, the termites.

Since these intruders live peacefully inside the ant nest and, in most cases, do not cause destruction of the nest, their classification is hard to specify. In a way, it has some resemblance to the dogs and cats that human beings keep. In most cases, they contribute nothing positive to the production of the resources in the home, although they make the people who live there happier than they otherwise would be. Ants and termites are stupid enough animals so that referring to them as being happy does not seem to be terribly descriptive, but it may, nevertheless, be true that their nervous systems are somehow being soothed by the presence of these other animals. As I have mentioned, in some cases, the ants take care of them.

It is interesting that the ferocious army ants of the subtropics frequently have nonspecific guests, of the same sort as the ones I have been describing, marching along with them. They are fed by the army ants, which also refrain from eating them, although they eat almost everything else in the way of insect life they come upon.

In any event, there is a sort of gradation here. There is the society composed of closely related members of the same species. Then there is the society composed of members of the same species, but not particularly closely related. In both of these cases, as far as we can tell, their mutual association is generally beneficial. In other words, they engage in cooperative activity. We then proceed to a number of cases, of which lichens and termites are particularly good examples, where different species are engaged in closely cooperative activity and generate mutual benefit.

Beyond that, we have cases in which members of different species live very close together, perhaps sharing the same nest, but where there is little evidence of either benefit or injury to either species from this close living arrangement. In some cases, for example, some of the bacteria that live on your skin may be a benefit to one species with practically no cost to the other.

The final case is the parasitic one in which one of the two species in a community, which is otherwise social, inflicts damage on the other. Humans are victims of many diseases, of course, and recently we have learned how to inflict damage on the bacteria by the use of antibiotics.

The nonhuman social species, of course, also have bacterial and viral disease, but, in their case, there are many parasitic species which are as large and powerful as the hosts. The perfect expression of this is the slaving ants.

Obligate slaving ant communities cannot exist unless they are able to seize the eggs of one of their slave species. These they take home to their ant nest, where workers develop and proceed to take care of their masters. The masters are clearly parasitic on the ants, which are enslaved.

Lichens and slaving ants are extreme examples at the ends of a continuum. It is easy to distinguish the endpoints. In the intermediate stages, there may be difficulty classifying them. Fortunately, in this book, the problem can be skipped.

This has been a very brief introduction to the hereditary component of nonhuman societies. As the reader has no doubt already discovered, in my opinion, the important part of the heredity is the pattern of behavior which all these animals inherit. The fact that they are sometimes close relatives is, I feel, less important. What is required is a niche which can be exploited by a well-organized group of insects, single-celled animals, plants, or joint affairs like lichens, and which is relatively resistant to exploitation by individual entities.

The ants and a number of individual predators attack and consume somewhat the same kind of prey. The ants, however, are massively more efficient in doing so, to a considerable extent, simply because of large numbers. The food supply of one ant which has the right to, say, 1/1000 of the food collected by 1,000 ants is more stable than it would be if it simply had a complete right to all the food that it collected itself.

In addition, there are efficiency advantages of division of labor. Once again, the ants divide up construction and maintenance of the nest and specialized activity in connection with raising the young. All of this makes it possible for the ants, which, in terms of total actual weight, hold a wide margin over other insects, to maintain their elaborate and almost dominant nests in so much of nature.

The existence of this niche and of the organization, in essence, keeps the individual members on the straight and narrow path of cooperation. If any significant number of them failed to cooperate, the entire organization would die, and the genes which led to noncooperation would be selected out. It is somewhere between group selection and individual selection.

CHAPTER 3

COORDINATION AND THE
PRISONER'S DILEMMA

Human beings engage in elaborate coordinated activity of various sorts. This book is the product of such coordinated activity. The nonhuman social species also engage in elaborate coordinated activity, but their methods of coordination are radically different from those of human beings. It is sensible to emphasize the difference by beginning with human societies and then pointing out the radical differences which we observe.

Human beings presented with some complex problem, such as producing 25,000 Toyotas for export to the United States or building an interstate, use hierarchies with a central control engaging in making plans and giving orders, and then a large number of other human beings carrying out those orders. There is nothing like this in an ant society.

I do not want my fellow members of the Mont Pelerin Society to feel that I have forgotten the possibility of coordinating activity by market arrangements. We do, indeed, engage in market arrangements for many things. The hierarchies I have just mentioned obtain their resources, including the people who work for them and the planners and the chief executives, from the market; i.e., they hire them voluntarily. This will be dealt with shortly.

Of course, sometimes the human society does not depend on voluntary adhesion. I wasted a considerable period of time in the Army during World War II, and I can assure you that it was far from voluntary.

Nevertheless, such large hierarchies appear to be an intrinsic part of any significant human society. Consider an activity in which both humans and ants engage: building roads. Humans will design a road plan, acquire the resources, and set up a series of organizations to make the road. This is the hierarchical method. Ants, on the other hand, depend almost entirely on individual choice. There is no central road bureau; in fact, there is no central organization of any kind.

If an individual ant is going to some food source, it may stop from time to time to improve the path. With many repetitions of such actions, eventually it becomes a genuine road. Some of the ants, in fact, may cease looking for food completely and simply devote themselves to making minor improvements on the road. Once again, there is no central planning authority, and nobody tells these specific ants that this is what they should do.

As a rough rule of thumb, there is no central control in these large social insect communities at all. It is true that there are some rather feeble dominance relationships, but these relationships mainly have to do with the right to breed rather than anything else. Certain wasps and the mole rats fight for the right to be the breeding member of the nest. In the case of the wasps, it is simply the winner which becomes queen, and, in the case of the mole rats, the female queen is normally matched by one or several males which have exclusive rights for intercourse. These positions sometimes are obtained by fighting.

In many other species, fighting is not involved at all. The queen or other reproductives are selected by some means which does not involve fighting between them. At times, it is sort of a combination. The queen of a bee nest does not have to fight with the workers for her position, but it is quite possible she will have to fight a contending candidate for queen. Both of them will have been raised by the workers in such a way that they are prepared to be queen, but they fight to the death. No worker is involved in the fight, and no mature worker can become queen.

In many social species, there is more than one queen. In these cases, there normally is no fighting among the different queens; although sometimes, of course, there is.

Nevertheless, having said that this kind of semidominance does exist, I should point out that these queens or other reproductive units do not seem to have any very direct effect on the behavior of the remainder. It is thought that they release pheromones which keep some of the others from breeding in some species. In general, these hormones, which are transmitted among the members of the species by mutual grooming, or, in some cases, by eating each other's offal, do have certain effects on the nest.

Normally, however, the "message" transmitted is simply that the queen or royal pair are present and in good health. In some cases, it may also indicate the stage in the breeding cycle. Hormones released by the larvae may also affect the nest behavior. In all of these cases, however, the "message" is directed to all members of the nest. It may change the percentage of workers engaged in various tasks, but it does not single out individuals for the new tasks. Its closest analogy in human society, and the analogy is far from close, would be a call for volunteers for some task which can be undertaken without supervision. A drive to pick up litter in a park would be an example.

A number of ants and termites have a fairly radical specialization in which different types of feeding devoted to the larvae produce quite radically different appearing individuals. Sometimes soldier ants may be as much as a hundred times as big as the tiniest minim in the nest. There is no sign of anything which we would call dominance or control by the soldiers over the minims.

To take an extreme case: I mentioned previously the slaving ants in which the "master" ants seize the pupae of slave species and take them back to their nest. This category of enslaved workers is not, in any true sense, dominated by the slaver. Indeed, the workers will excavate a nest which is similar to the nest of their particular species, not the nest of the "masters." Thus, a particular species of slaving ants may live in several different kinds of nests, depending on what particular prey they use for slaves.

Since the slaving ants do not do a lick of work, live in nests which are constructed by their slaves, and are fed by their slaves, they might be regarded as an example of dominance. As a matter of fact, however, the slaves are no more likely to feed one of the big slaver ants than they are to feed another "slave" if they meet them in the tunnels.

All of this is radically different from human behavior. It immediately raises an important question: how do the ants do it? To turn to a mammal: the mole rats sometimes build tunnels of up to half a kilometer in length, which, for a mole rat, is roughly equivalent to 30 kilometers for us.[1] No one orders the individual mole rat to build a tunnel in that particular direction nor is there any evidence that there is a planning commission or politburo issuing orders. Nevertheless, the mole rat communities have a structure which is rather similar in different "nests," and hence one can regard it as being genetically coordinated activity. They have main highways and secondary roads. The main highways are equipped with turnaround spots.

To go further, no one tells the mole rat whether it should engage in digging tunnels, bringing food back to one of the rooms to feed the queen, or taking care of some other chore. We just observe that they do these things. The same is true of ants, termites, and, as you will see shortly, the single amoeboid cells which make up the sponge society.

The answer to this is, obviously, that they have an inherited pattern of behavior which leads them to live much the same way and to engage in cooperative activities. But this inheritance cannot possibly be a detailed set of instructions for exactly what to do, because different ant nests and different mole rat nests are not exactly the same shape.

---

1. This calculation is based on the longest dimension of a normal member of each species. If it were based on weight, the human tunnel would be over 1,000 kilometers in length.

Ants digging a tunnel may run into a stone, with the result being that they will have to deviate. Further, various emergencies may arise which require rapid changes in the amount and type of work in which the ants are engaging. As a more minor problem, which food is available may change, even without an emergency. This may also require a shift in labor inputs.

The microscopic brains we find in ants can hardly have a complete set of instructions for every conceivable contingency. They must have something in the way of a more general structure which provides for modifications. This raises the question, how is the nervous system of the ant designed so that the ants divide their labor in such an efficient way? The percentage of them that divides their labor efficiently will engage in nest repair and will hunt for food.[2] Whatever the system is, it must provide for these percentages changing from time to time according to conditions.

Perhaps it should be said here, parenthetically, that it has recently been discovered that among honeybees the descendants of different fathers (there is, of course, only one queen in these nests) have somewhat different behavior patterns inside the nest. Thus, when the queen flies out for fertilization and is fertilized by several drones, she produces a set of eggs with different fathers, and, to some extent, this nonidentity affects behavior. It is likely this is true of the other social insects.[3]

If the ants do not have the large command and control structures we observe in human society, what of the other principal way of coordinating human beings: the free market? This also seems to be almost completely missing in nonhuman societies. We do not observe, strictly speaking, exchanges of the market type occurring among them.

Exchanges do occur. I have already mentioned the fact that the protozoa in the termite's gut digest the wood which the termite eats. This could be regarded as an exchange between the termite, which provides the labor of getting the wood, and the protozoa, which digest it and excrete various food chemicals which the termite itself can consume.

Clearly this is an exchange, but it is far from a market exchange. Presumably, if the termite ate less food, the protozoa would digest less food and excrete less in the way of things which the termite can use as nutrition. Similarly,

2. Although the ant nest seems highly efficient, we have no real proof that it is optimal.

3. As mentioned in the last chapter, it is certainly true of many ants. Large ant super-colonies with many queens would appear to be particularly good places to look for such differences.

if the protozoa reduced the amount of chemicals that they excrete and which are digestible by the termite, this would no doubt reduce the efficiency of the termite in its wood-eating. But neither of these looks very much like a market exchange, even though there may be factors which lead both to operate at some kind of optimal level.

This is not, of course, the only case in which we observe different members of the cooperating species doing different things and the effects being, in essence, exported to other members of the species. The ant that repairs part of the nest is producing a good for other ants and, if it is an ordinary, healthy nest, will also be eating food which is brought into the nest from outside by other ants. Calling this a market exchange is, however, very difficult. In order to make this a market exchange, we would have to argue not that the individual ant is being paid by other ants collectively for this repair, but that something more direct is occurring between two particular ants. If the ants are observed under these circumstances, it will be found that the ant that has been engaging in nest repair will encounter an ant which is coming in from the outside with food, and there will be a brief sort of ceremony in which their antennae are tapped. At the end of this, the food-bearing ant will produce from its crop some food for the nest-repairing ant, and then both will continue on their way.

It could be argued that this is an exchange in which the food-bearing ant obtains the pleasure of having this particular set of antennae taps and pays for it with the food. I think this is a very strange interpretation, but, with our present knowledge, one cannot say for certain that it is untrue. In any event, granted the extremely simple nervous systems the ants have, it is not at all obvious that it "feels" anything which we would regard as closely analogous to pleasure or pain.

At a somewhat more realistic level, some species of wasps feed their larvae, and, at the time this is done, the larvae excrete a liquid which apparently the adult wasps find very attractive. Indeed, on some occasions when the adult wasp does not have food with it, it may engage in roughly mishandling the larvae in hopes of getting some of this liquid.

This does, indeed, look like an exchange, although it should be noted that none of the ordinary market characteristics in which the whole set of exchanges are brought into equilibrium by demand and supply occurs here. In any event, it is, as far as I know, the only case of anything that we can regard as even approximating market trade in the whole of the nonhuman social societies.

The normal case involves the different members of the society engaging in activity which is coordinated with no direct exchange between them. If we wish, we can say that the ant "pays" for its hard labor in repairing the nest through the acts of receiving food, protection, and assuring the reproductions of some genes that are at least related to it. This does have some slight, albeit extremely slight, resemblance to a market transaction.

If we look at human societies, we observe that there is a mix of hierarchies and markets. Some of the hierarchies—the governmental hierarchies—depend on coercion to get people to pay for their product. In many other cases, they are completely free transactions. Indeed, the governments normally have completely free transactions with their employees and their suppliers. It is only the taxpayers who are coerced.

Private hierarchies normally do not have much significant coercive power. The worst they can do to most people is to fire them. Employees, of course, can also be said to have some coercive power against the employer because they can also terminate the relationship.

Now all of this does not look at all like what we observe in the nonhuman species. It is a problem which we understand quite well with respect to human species, but in which it is clear that the nonhuman societies do not follow our techniques. In order to discuss this, I must begin by deviating a little bit and talking about something called the prisoner's dilemma. This is a very general phenomenon and does not necessarily have anything to do with prisoners, but it did actually start with a little tale about a district attorney and two prisoners. It is well known to most economists and many biologists, so the reader may want to skip it.

The district attorney suspected two prisoners, whom we shall call A and B, of having robbed a bank. He also knew for certain he could convict them of carrying concealed weapons. He put them in separate cells and then said to each of them that he would offer them a bargain. He pointed out that he could see to it that the individual prisoner he was talking to would get a year imprisonment on the concealed weapons charge. If the prisoner confessed to the bank robbery and implicated his confederate while the confederate did not confess, the district attorney would see to it that the prisoner he is speaking to got off scot-free while the confederate would get ten years. If both of them confessed, they would each get seven years. Of course, if the other confessed and the one he is talking to did not, he would get the ten years, and the other would get off scot-free.

The feature of interest is that regardless of what the other prisoner does, it is in the best interest of each to confess. We would predict that rational individuals, under these circumstances, would both confess and hence get seven years; although, if both of them stood fast, they would get one year apiece. If I do not confess and the other person does, I get ten years. If I do confess and the other does, I get seven years. If, on the other hand, I do not confess and the other man also does not confess, I get one year. But, if I confess and the other man does not confess, I get zero. In both cases, I am better off if I confess than if I do not.

Now I have said that the parties here are kept in separate cells. Strictly speaking, this is not necessary. The two parties can be permitted to communicate with each other, provided only that both of them realize that the other cannot be completely trusted. The noncommunication is put in for the reader's benefit and is not vital.

This does not seem to have very much relationship to the social insects, but let me go on a little bit further in talking about human society. It is not necessary that there be only two parties—there can be many parties. Consider the problem of air pollution by automobile exhaust which is, after all, the principal source.

I can put devices on my car which reduce the amount of air pollution it releases and thus reduce the amount of air pollution in the city of Tucson at a considerable expense to myself. If I do so, the reduction in air pollution for the city of Tucson would be obviously beneficial, and, let us assume, the total benefit would be considerably greater than the cost to me. On the other hand, the benefit to me would be very small, indeed, and I would pay the full cost. Suppose my air pollution devices reduce the total amount of pollution by 1×10^{-5}. Clearly, reducing the amount of pollution that I myself breathe by 1×10^{-5} is not worth its cost. If I am highly altruistic, I might put them in anyway, but most human beings are not that charitable.

Here we have a many-sided prisoner's dilemma. Whether other people put in an air pollution control device or not and regardless of how many, it is always better for me not to put in air pollution devices even though I would be better off if all or almost all of the people, including myself, put controls for air pollution on their cars.

Human beings, in this case, turn to coercion and the use of government. Voters in Tucson presumably are[4] in favor of compelling all the citizens of Tucson to put pollution control devices on their cars. To take a statement that is used a good deal in public choice, we all agree to coerce each other.

4. Or, at least, that is the way they vote.

Now note that in this case there is genuine coercion. If the rules said that everybody should put the pollution control devices on their cars but there was no punishment for not doing so, we would predict that there would be very few devices put on. Only if we have some formal system[5] do we accept the coercion and, in fact, are happy about it. We have dealt with the prisoner's dilemma problem by using a special government structure in which, to repeat, we all agree to coerce each other.

There is no such system of coercion in the insect societies and, in general, not in any nonhuman societies.[6] How then do they prevent the ant version of confessing? Perhaps I should stop here and say that we do not normally refer to confessing in economics. We call it free riding, a phrase which was used several times in the last chapter. This means taking the benefit of whatever collective good is being produced without paying for it.

The opportunities for this are endemic in all large societies that do not have coercion. The individual ant that just did not do anything except eat would be a free rider. Also, the ant that carried out whatever, from the ant's standpoint, are aesthetic preferences and, let us say, produced things in the nest that it liked, which were not useful for the nest, would be another. Of course, if some individual ant that is not the queen was able to reproduce, it would be an extreme case.

We do observe examples of something like this kind of free riding and, indeed, some examples of coercion to prevent it. The ants are subject to an immense number of parasites; indeed, almost as many as human beings. Many of these parasites are other insects, sometimes ants of other species, which obtain entry into the nest where they contribute, as far as we can tell, nothing to its economy but do draw on the resources of the nest for their own livelihood. Clearly, they are free riders.

However, it is by no means true that just any insect can enter an ant nest. The ants do guard the nest and not only will prevent other insects from entering, but will kill them if they find them inside. The parasitic species that I have been describing above have some method of fooling the ants so that the

---

5. In Tucson, the cars are regularly inspected for pollution control as part of the process of renewing registration.

6. It is possible that among some of the higher mammals the dominant member of the pack, if there is one, does engage in a certain amount of coercion of the others. This may involve a monopoly on sex and keeping order. It is unlikely to be seeing to it that they carry out any particular task. In any event, it is a very minor feature of life, even in a wolf pack.

ants do not realize what they are. In a way, it is like the AIDS virus, which is able to fool the immune system.

Obviously, since the ants and other social insects do not use coercion on their own members, whatever they may do to these parasites, they must have some other method of handling the problem, and this has something to do with their genetic structure. They must inherit genes that make them work. The way these genes operate, once again, will be dealt with much later.

This brief chapter has basically raised a number of questions without answering them. The answers are being put off until after the chapters describing several different nonhuman societies. The reason for this is partly for the benefit of economists who do not know much about these nonhuman societies; but, even for biologists, these chapters may be helpful. My objective is to emphasize both the remarkable degree of coordination and efficiency we observe in some nonhuman societies and the reasons why this requires an explanation, which is not based on anything we see in human societies. My theory, which is intended to solve the riddle, will be given after we have surveyed a set of nonhuman societies.

CHAPTER 4

CONSIDER THE ANT

It is obvious, however, that Pseudo-Aristotle did not understand how this division of labor is effected. He seems to have supposed that the worker bees are directed to join particular groups of bees employed on definite jobs as the need arises. Many earlier observers, and even some fairly recent ones, believed that the queen, or as they frequently miscalled her, the king bee, performs this function, directing the labours of the other bees of her colony who are her loyal servants.
—Colin G. Butler, *The World of the Honey Bee*
  (London: Collins, 1954), 76

If you look carefully on the floor of any American forest, you are apt to see the workers of a common wood ant moving about on their daily occasions. Note, I say *a* common wood ant. Apparently, the temperate woodland provides a niche for a particular type of ant social organization. In different parts of the world, different species have moved into this niche. Needless to say, their behaviors are not identical, but there is enough resemblance between wood ants of Hokkaido, England, and the northern part of the United States that the description that I am about to give more or less fits all of them.

This is interesting, because it would appear that evolution can adjust a number of different species to fit into the same niche. It is not, however, unique to ants. Australia has marsupials filling many of the environmental niches that are filled by mammals in the rest of the world. We should not be surprised to find behavioral similarity among wood ants in different parts of the temperate zone.

At first glance, these ants appear to be very ordinary small insects. In fact, they are most extraordinary. In the first place, they have what can only be called a rather high standard of living for an insect. Of course, the term "standard of living" does not really fit any insect very well. Further, all animals, except perhaps man, tend to press on their means of subsistence; that is, the population tends to expand until marginal members develop high death rates. This means that some of the ants must be suffering at least some "deprivation."

Nevertheless, our wood ant does eat regularly. Most wild animals which are not grazers eat rather irregularly, depending upon the availability of food. Our ant is more or less omnivorous, depending upon animal and vegetable food found in the forest. Further, the ant has a rather diversified diet, not only over time, but each day. It may spend its own time collecting, say, nectar, but it may eat meat and perhaps vegetable matter collected by other ants. If it has an unlucky day, or even week, this will have little or no effect on its food consumption.

In addition, the ant is remarkably safe, considering its small size and the prevalence of carnivores in the world. It spends much of its life in guarded and policed surroundings where it can rest in safety. When it is aboveground, it will more often than not be near its sister workers, and the formidable fighting power of a group of ants is such that most predators give it a wide berth.

It is not completely safe, of course (no wild animal is), but the ant is like the civilized human, in that old age and disease are its most likely causes of death. Predation and starvation are almost as unlikely causes of death as they would have been in, say, the late Roman Empire. In fact, the average wood ant lives two or more years,[1] which is remarkable for such a small insect.

The secret of the ant's relatively easy life is simple. The ant is civilized in the original sense of the term; i.e., it lives in a city. In a mature wood ant community, this city may be united with daughter cities into something closely analogous to the human nation. It may have 500,000 adult inhabitants. Of these, 50 to 100 may be functional females that are responsible for the production of the next generation. A considerable number of functional males may also be present, depending upon the season of the year. The remaining "citizens" are nonfunctional females which, in the case of the wood ant, are all rather similar workers. In other species, they may be divided into several types with rather different physical equipment. Further, this city is probably part of a "nation" containing several "cities" of varying size and a well-demarcated "national territory."[2] The borders will be well guarded, and, as with human nations, wars are not infrequent.[3]

---

1. Bert Hölldobler and Edward O. Wilson, *The Ants* (Cambridge: Belknap Press, 1990), 169–70. Queens live much longer. Hölldobler and Wilson dominate the literature. They are good writers, and the general reader can profit from most of the book, but some sections are highly technical. I recommend skimming some parts.

2. There is a partial map of one of these "national" territories on page 215 of Hölldobler and Wilson.

3. One unfortunate ant colony, the history of which is shown on a map on page 173 of Hölldobler and Wilson, lost a war and was forced to leave its nest. It then lost another war and was driven out of its new nest. The history rather resembles that of a number of unfortunate tribes in central Asia.

Internal dissidence leading to a "nation" splitting into two is also not particularly uncommon. One probable reason for the split is simply that as the community gets larger, the various odors that are normally passed around the colony gradually develop different concentrations in different parts of the area. Eventually, the ants in one segment do not recognize those in the other part of the nest. Thus, there is a break.

It should be said that two Japanese scholars (Higashi and Yamauchi)[4] allegedly found a giant super-nest of this sort with 307 million inhabitants spreading over many miles. Though I am obviously not an ant expert as they are, and their data have been repeated without any signs of skepticism by Hölldobler and Wilson, I doubt this.

The reader will remember that Jane Van Lawick–Goodall originally thought that chimpanzees were peaceful. She eventually found out they engage in vigorous wars with each other and, in fact, also had civil wars. The basic reason she thought they were peaceful was that her original study center happened to be in the middle of a tribal territory, and so she did not see the borders. It is rather like a Martian visiting the earth in 1916, finding very little fighting in the vicinity of the city of Bordeaux, where he landed, and coming to the conclusion that humans were peaceful beings.

In my opinion, somewhat the same effect influenced Higashi and Yamauchi. They made a number of observations of their ants from various places, and just by accident did not happen to hit the border between two colonies.

Wars are not particularly uncommon in any of the social species. Indeed, E. O. Wilson once said that species that have been observed for less than 1,000 hours will be thought to be peaceful and will be thought to be belligerent if they have been carefully observed for more than 1,000 hours. It is likely that human beings are the most peaceful of the large mammals.

It is not only ants that fight. The honeybee and, for that matter, the bumblebees that we observe in temperate zones never make any effort to protect territory and hence have no wars. The stingless bees of the tropics, however, sometimes have vigorous wars, with the result that a number of dead bees may be found on the forest floors.

The explanation for the difference apparently is that the dispersed nature of flowers in the temperate zone makes protection of territory too expensive.

---

4. S. Higashi and K. Yamauchi, "Influence of a Supercolonial Ant *Formica (Formica) Yessensis* Forel on the Distribution of Other Ants in Ishikari Coast," *Japanese Journal of Ecology* 29, no. 3 (1979): 257–64.

In the tropics, however, individual trees may come to brilliant bloom all at once. As a result, there is a very large concentrated store of nectar. That competing nests would fight over the tree nectar is not particularly surprising.

In any event, ants do sometimes fight, although not all species or all types. The larger the territory, the more food resources, and, hence, the larger number of ants that can be supported.

The size of the national territory and the number of workers always combing it for food are the fundamental reasons for the steadiness and diversity of the individual ant's food consumption. From the law of large numbers, it is obvious that stochastic variations in the food supply gathered by 500,000 or so ants will be relatively much less than the variation in the supply collected by a single ant. Since the food supply collected by those ants engaged in that activity (about a third of the whole population) is pretty equally shared by the whole citizenry, the individual ant gets a fairly stable diet. Further, in times of dearth, more workers will be shifted to food gathering, which tends to stabilize the food supply.

The division of labor among the ants has interested most people who have taken the trouble to think about the matter. Among the third of the ants engaged in food gathering, there is considerable internal specialization. Some will collect nectar, some hunt for insects which can be killed for meat, and still others search for other types of food. Of course, these specializations are not rigid; changes can occur if there is an opportunity. Still, a given ant is likely normally to return to the same area to forage day after day.

Once the food-gathering ants have filled their crops with whatever type of food they are gathering,[5] they turn toward the nest. More often than not, however, they meet porter ants before reaching the nest and transfer the food to them. This permits the foragers to return to their primary duties rather than wasting skilled labor in simple carrying.

In general, the principle of labor division and skill conservation is as important to the ant economy as it is to the human. Adam Smith began his famous book with a discussion of the division of labor, and, on pages 7–9,[6] he gives the three advantages gained from it. The first of these is that "the improvement of the dexterity of the workman necessarily increases the quantity of the work he can perform: and the division of labor, by reducing every man's business to some one simple operation, and by making this operation

5. Or picking up in their jaws if it is a solid, like a piece of an unfortunate insect.
6. *The Wealth of Nations* (New York: Modern Library, 1937).

the sole employment of his life necessarily increases very much the dexterity of the workman." The principle is equally important to the ants.

Since ants demonstrate the ability to inherit a large collection of behavior patterns, so much so that the nests of different species are readily distinguishable, it might be thought that they made little use of learned skills. The contrary is clearly the case, although the learned skills are, in a sense, derived from the hereditary behavior patterns. Ants fairly readily shift from foraging to nursing the young, or to repairing the nest when there is need for such a shift and, on the whole, do well in their new "occupation" right from the start.

Nevertheless, they clearly can learn. To return to the foragers, they can hardly carry hereditary instructions on how to find a given tree and limb upon which nectar is available. Presumably, they inherit a drive for foraging and a general program, including both search elements to find new foraging fields and exploitation elements to make use of them. In any event, however, individual ants do learn where food is to be found and then become specialists in collecting food from that particular area. They can shift to some other area if circumstances require it, but this requires a period of exploration and relearning.

It is fortunate for the ant community that this is the pattern of individual ant behavior. The ant has a very small brain, and it is inconceivable that any individual ant would be able to hold in its memory all of the foraging areas around its nest and the best routes to them. By dividing this memory in small pieces among different ants, the exploitation of a considerable territory is possible.

We humans, of course, make use of a similar technique. No human mind could hold all, or a considerable fraction, of the skills which are daily applied to our economic life; but specialization makes it unnecessary for any human to know very many of them. Like the ants, we each learn some special skill, increasing our facility with practice.

Also, like the ant, if some circumstance requires that we drop our acquired skill and learn another, we will have to devote time and energy to this task and will be rather inefficient at first. The difference lies simply in our more complex brains, which make it easy for us to hold much more in our memory than can an individual ant. This, however, is a difference of degree, albeit a very large and important one, not a difference in kind.

We can, perhaps, get a better idea of how the process works if we consider how an ant "learns" a new foraging area. Suppose, then, that a growing nest is gradually extending its foraging area, and further suppose that it has "open" frontiers; that is, it does not border on any other ant "nation" which will resist its expansion.

This would mean that at least some ants would be engaged in exploring the area beyond the frontier of exploitation. Presumably, the impulse to explore would arise from a combination of the food needs of the nest and "congestion" conditions in the area already in use. Since most of the ants would continue working on existing plots, and only a minority would engage in exploration, some mechanism for insuring that this type of division of labor exists must be provided.

Since one of the main purposes of this book is an elucidation of this coordinating mechanism, I will postpone its discussion until a later chapter. For the moment, let us merely note that the conditions lead some, but not many, ants to turn aside from the exploitation of existing resources to hunt for more.

Let us follow one of the ants which has been singled out by the still mysterious control forces of its city to push back the borders of darkness. If we follow it beyond the frontier, we will notice that it simply casts about at random, following a very irregular course which, however, very seldom crosses itself.

If it finds a food source, it will either pick up some of it in its mandibles or, if it is in liquid form, pack it into its crop. In any event, as soon as it has a full load, it will return to the nest. Its return route will be approximately the same as its outward route. Although it may straighten the route a little, it will basically follow back on its own tracks.

What happens next depends largely on whether the supply of food found by the ant is simply the small quantity which the ant has collected or whether there is still a supply left to be picked up on a future trip. Assuming the latter to be the case, the ant will transfer its burden of food either to another ant in the nest or to a porter ant on one of the well-traveled routes in the developed area near the nest and then return to the newly discovered food source.

If the food source is sizeable, it may bring a number of other ants back with it. The mechanism by which it brings these companions is still rather mysterious. The bees have a well-developed dancing language which they use to inform other members of the hive of the location of food supplies. So far, nothing similar has been discovered among the ants. Ants seem to be able to communicate only a feeling of excitement to one another. This may explain the ability of an ant which has found a food supply to bring some companions back to collect it.

If the new foraging area shows signs of being permanently productive, a regular system of exploiting it will grow up, with a number of ants specializing in gathering food there. The economy which the nest gains from this sort of specialization comes from the special skills and knowledge of the ants normally participating in this work.

Since this is obviously very simple, the advantage of specialized knowledge is not necessarily clear to humans. It must be remembered, however, that an ant has a very limited brain, even more limited than a college student's, impossible though that sometimes seems. Darwin, in a somewhat similar situation, pointed out that honeybees normally visit only one kind of flower in a given foraging expedition. He pointed out that this habit was beneficial, for once a bee has learned the structural intricacies of one kind of flower, it will be able to collect food from flowers of this kind more expeditiously than from many other kinds, each with its own peculiar structure. The same type of advantage can be gained by ants becoming familiar with certain regions.

The ants "working" the new region will gradually straighten out the route they follow to their foraging grounds until it approximates a straight line connecting the new area with the nest or one of the main avenues leading to the nest. This straightening process is a good example of the way an ant reaches rather efficient results without much thought. In fact, it resembles the method used by the Romans to lay out straight roads without the precise surveying instruments now available.

In addition to some ability to recognize landmarks, the ant marks its trail by periodically touching its abdomen to the ground and leaving a spot of scent. Since ants depend more on scent than sight anyway, this permits it to readily follow any marked trail. It also leads to a process of continual "corner-cutting," which will result in its trails gradually approximating a straight line.

Suppose an ant at A has regular business at C. The first trip was rather irregular, and two scent signs have been left at B and at C.

$$B$$
$$B^1$$
$$A$$
$$C$$

The ant is now at A, planning to repeat the trip. It receives scent from both points B and C, although with B closer, the odor from C will be fainter. The ant simply points itself at the "center of gravity" of the scent, which would be at an angle nearer to the straight line connecting A with B than to the straight line connecting A with C, but still this will cut off some of the "corner" at B.

If the ant now marks this new trail by a scent "blaze" at B^1, with the gradual weathering away of the original scent at B, the center of gravity of the scent, when observed from A, will gradually shift to the right, and hence the ant's course will also shift. Eventually, it will approximate a straight line from A to C.[7]

If the new forage area is sufficiently productive so that a very large number of ants regularly visit it, a regular road will be developed leading to it. Obstructions will be removed, and the ground will be smoothed so that trips to and from the nest will be as easy as possible. If the area is far out, small bivouacs will be constructed where ants can spend an occasional night in safety; thus they need not get back to the home nest. The whole thing looks very well organized. Some ants will be engaged in obtaining food; others will be engaged in "portering" it back to the nest. In addition, there may be a few ants engaged in "maintaining" the road.

Possibly, there will be a few ants gathering building material for use in the main nest. Certainly, there will be other ants hunting through the areas away from the main foraging areas for meat in the form of stray insects. Yet, this whole delicately balanced division of labor is achieved without any "planning board" or any orders or instructions of any sort transmitted from one ant to another. Although ants can "set examples" for each other and transmit a feeling of excitement, they have no language capable of transmitting even the simplest instructions.

But this efficient division of labor among the ants aboveground is only part—and the smaller part—of the total economic organization of the whole nest. About a third of the ants are engaged in foraging for food aboveground; the remaining two-thirds are engaged in complementary activities within the nest itself. The ratio of one-third food gatherers to two-thirds engaged in other activities is rather misleading. Until the industrial revolution, most human societies had about 80% of their population in the agricultural sector, and, therefore, it might appear that ant communities were more efficient than all but the most modern human societies. In fact, however, this is merely appearance.

The population of the agricultural sector of a human economy contains housewives and children. The housewives contribute basically nonagricultural

---

7. This must be considered an hypothesis, although a very likely one. There are innumerable "corner-cutting" procedures available which all would lead to approximating a straight line eventually. The choice of the correct one will be a problem for the experimentalist. Since it is a rather unimportant problem, its solution will probably be delayed.

services to the community. Since the analogous activities in ant communities occur within the nest,[8] the ants get an unfair advantage in the comparison.

Similarly, the younger ant generations—eggs, larvae, pupae, and callows (ants which have "hatched" from their pupae, have a relatively light skin, and are not yet fully mature in other ways)—are kept strictly within the nest. In a pre-industrial human society, it seems likely that the percentage of the total population actually engaged in agriculture is rather less than the percentage of ants engaged in food gathering.

Unfortunately, entomologists know less of what goes on belowground in a large ant nest than of what occurs on the surface. It is simple enough to observe ants on the surface, and you can, if you wish, follow one around all day.[9] Once they enter their nest, however, they become immune to systematic observation.

Glass-walled nests, of course, can be built and kept under observation, but, in practice, this technique is limited to fairly small installations, perhaps 5,000 ants as a limit. What goes on inside the giant nests of the civilized ants, therefore, is known more by deduction and analogy with small nests than by direct observation. Naturally, this means that our information is less full and reliable than our knowledge of the ants' surface activities.

The general structure of the work underground is, however, known. In the first place, there is a great deal of work on the nest itself. If the nest is growing, then it must be physically expanded, upon the basic plan which is characteristic for the particular species.[10] Even if no expansion is needed, there is a continual need for maintenance and repair. Keeping the nest clean by removing all debris is also a task which takes a good many workers. The really vital work of the nest, however, concerns the production of the next generation of ants.

The care of the queens, each of which is continually surrounded by her "court," and the careful collection of the eggs they lay is merely a first step.

8. So do they with human societies, of course.

9. Unless you have superhuman powers of discrimination, it is best to mark it in some way.

10. Specialists seem to frequently make the statement that all nests of a given species of ant are exactly alike. This is an exaggeration, although a pardonable exaggeration. It is frequently possible to distinguish the species of an ant merely from an inspection of the nest, but they do differ a good deal within the species. The situation is perhaps analogous to that of human dwellings in Northeast Asia. I can tell by very superficial inspection whether an aerial photograph shows a Japanese, Korean, or Chinese village, but this does not prove that all Korean villages are exactly alike.

The eggs must be carefully tended, being periodically cleaned and shifted around the nest so that they are always in an ideal environment in terms of temperature and humidity. When they hatch into larvae, they must be fed, and they still require cleaning and moving about. When the larvae pupate, they still require a good deal of care, and, finally, when the ant is ready to emerge from the pupal case, it must be helped, since ants are unable to get out by themselves. The newly hatched ant will be a "callow" and not yet fully mature. So, for a few days, it is unable to take full part in the operation of the nest and may require additional care.

In addition to these basic activities, some ant species go in for highly elaborate economic activities in the nest. They may raise livestock (root aphids, if they are kept permanently in the nest), engage in fungus farming, or simply build up large supplies of foodstuffs for the off-seasons of the year. Our wood ants do not go in for anything this elaborate. Ants also, however, have a lot of leisure. The legendary fame of the industrious ant appears to stem largely from the simple fact that they are normally seen only when at work. Most of their leisure hours are spent belowground away from casual observation.

Discussion of the ants' "leisure" does not seem possible without considerable anthropomorphizing. The words which seem best to describe certain ant activities were originally invented to describe human activities and necessarily carry certain overtones which are not really suitable for use with insects of which we know so little. Nevertheless, they are the only words we have. Using words in their normal sense, then, the ants appear to spend much of their time grooming themselves, grooming and licking other ants, in what appears to be socializing, and simply idling around.

Given the rather dim and highly routinized brain of the ant, there is no way of knowing if the mental processes which we would associate with social activity go on. All we can say is that the superficial appearance of ants moving about their nest, meeting and rubbing feelers with other ants, frequently with no obvious practical purpose, looks very much like social life.

The grooming and licking of other ants is normally explained in terms of the ants getting pleasure out of it, although here again we may be treating these insects too much like humans. Certainly, it has evolutionary value. The grooming serves some purpose in protecting the ant against disease. The mutual licking seems to play a major role in the coordination of the nest. It permits a slow interchange of hormones among the ants, which controls many of their actions.

In the first place, they apparently identify members of their own nest, or the ants from other nests which are federated into their "nation," by the odor, and the odor "badge" is apparently passed around among the ants by the mutual licking process. As I pointed out earlier, the civil wars which sometimes split a large ant nation seem to arise simply from the group becoming so large geographically that the process of mutual grooming develops a sort of gradient in the odor of the ants from one extreme of the nest to another.

Thus, ants from different parts of the nest will not necessarily recognize the mutual odor when they meet and, as a result, may treat each other as enemies. Under the circumstances, stochastic developments may lead to a genuine break in the continuity of odors at some point, which leads to fighting and a breaking of the mutual grooming relations. The odor difference becomes greater because of the stoppage, and the ant nation will be broken into two mutually hostile countries.

Even more important, a number of control hormones seem to be passed around the nest by the mutual licking process. The number of queens, for example, seems to be a function of the number of workers (or vice versa), and the mechanism seems to be based on the degree of dilution of certain hormones which the workers obtain by licking the queen and then interchange among themselves by mutual grooming. There are numerous other such relations. The ants, of course, do not know of the evolutionary and control aspects of the matter. They apparently engage in licking one another because they like the taste. Nevertheless, this simple hedonism serves a "social" purpose.

Returning, however, to the division of labor: the food supply distribution through the nest from the food collecting force is perhaps the most important single aspect of the internal economy of the ant "nation." The large feeding range of the whole colony of ants, and the fact that the food obtained is shared by all the ants, is the essential reason for the relative stability of the individual ant's diet. The law of large numbers insures against great daily changes in the "receipts" of each ant.

There is, however, no planned movement of food supplies. We could, perhaps, produce a completely random-walk model of the food transportation system of an ant community. Suppose there are 100,000 ants in an enclosure, and suppose that 33,000 of them regularly obtain food supplies. If we further suppose that each individual ant can carry about ten times its food requirements for a short period of time (which is realistic) and that when two ants meet, the one with the most food transfers enough to the other so that their supplies are equal (which is much simpler than whatever real rule the ants follow), then it seems likely that simple random walking and meetings would result in most of the ants getting an adequate diet.

In fact, the ants do not walk randomly. Ants that have obtained food in the forage areas immediately head for the nest. Similarly, hungry ants working in the nest go toward the nest entrances where they are more likely to meet returning food bearers. If there is a comparative dearth of food gathering, ants may have to go outside the nest for food, and, in serious shortage conditions, they may be led to visit the nests of other cities in the ant nation.

Thus, the food supplies are fairly evenly distributed without any central planning. The process is clearly stochastic, but, instead of random walks, the ants normally follow a pattern which brings the food suppliers and the food consumers into the same areas so that the food deliveries are carried out with great efficiency. Under the random-walk condition, there would be a finite possibility that at least one ant would receive no food. Given the real situation where increasing hunger motivates an ant to move toward the food supply points, this is not so.

There seems to be a vague feeling among ant experts that the ants receive about equal amounts of food. As far as I know, there has been no specific investigation of the matter. If all the ants have similar relative preferences for food, and if the total amount of food brought into the nest each day equalled or exceeded the amount which could be physically consumed by the entire population, then equal consumption would be highly probable.

Lacking these two conditions, and the second must be rare in a Malthusian world, it seems likely that some ants eat more than others. Thus, it is possible that ants are egalitarian on the consumption side, but there certainly is no proof of it. Possibly the degree of egalitarianism, however, is rather low. Certainly, there must be some proportion between the amount of activity of an ant and its food consumption, since it must obtain its energy somewhere, but the cause-and-effect relationship runs from restrictions on food consumption to a limitation on total activity. There is no natural mechanism which would insure that the hardest and most devoted workers received additional food for their trouble.

There is, in fact, no real evidence that *all* ants work hard, or even at all. The specialists in the study of the ant have, naturally, not followed large numbers of ants around for a day or so inside their nests in order to find out whether every ant engages in gainful activity. Certainly, some ants do work; equally certainly, some ants are sometimes engaged in sunning themselves, sleeping, or apparently at leisure.

Whether all of the ants have a well-balanced life with both work and leisure intermixed, whether some take much more leisure than others, or whether some ants never do a lick of work, depending upon the remainder for food, is a question which cannot be answered in the present state of our knowledge. In fact, investigators who have specialized in studying ants do not seem to have thought to ask it.

The problem lies in the fact that ants do little in the way of direct exchange. If one ant "paid" in food for some service performed by another, then we could feel some assurance that all were working, since those not working would not eat. This is not what happens, however; the food is delivered simply on "request" to the hungry ant. As mentioned in the last chapter, in some wasps, the workers bring the larvae a piece of meat to get a droplet of liquid. When food is scarce, the adults sometimes "rough up" the poor larvae in order to get the liquid without paying for it.

Some writers have tried to work out exchange relationships, but the effort is abortive. It may be pointed out, for example, that ants enjoy licking the queen and that they are highly interested in the eggs which she produces. Since it must be presumed that her production of both eggs and body exudates is a function of her food consumption, it is sometimes argued that an ant brings food to the queen in order to "exchange" it for the "products" of the queen.

In fact, however, the ant bringing in food is no more favored in licking the queen than is any other ant, while the eggs are most readily gathered at the other end of the queen from her mouth. Here we have an example of "the left hand of God," the activity which is in the social interest, but not in that of the individual. Surely the queen must be fed, but an individual ant wishing queenly exudates is not well advised if it starts out to gather food for the royal mistress.

That it would be possible for an ant, if so inclined, to avoid work and still continue to eat well seems clear. That this would not in and of itself destroy the nest is also reasonably certain. There are a number of dwellers in some ant nests which do, in fact, simply consume without producing. In the first place, there are the males, simply idling around until it is time for the mating flights. They appear to be more than adequately fed in spite of not doing a lick of work. Further, their presence is obviously not an insupportable burden on the nest.

In addition, there are a number of specialized parasites living in ant nests which, in various ways, get the ants to feed them. Some of these parasites, such as the *Lomechusa* beetles, may, if they become numerous enough, destroy the nest. Apparently, a considerable number of such parasites can be supported without much trouble.

The ant *Polyergus rufescens* can, perhaps, provide the clearest evidence of the possibility of idlers living in an ant nest in comfort. *Polyergus* is a slave-making ant, and the "workers" have become heavily specialized for fighting. They are unable to undertake any of the work of the nest. In fact, they must be fed by their slaves because their mouth parts have become specialized to the point where the workers cannot eat by themselves. Clearly, the slave ants must perform all the work of a *Polyergus rufescens* colony. The fact that the slaves are able to support, without apparent difficulty, a fairly large population of *Polyergus* is fairly good evidence that if they had been left to themselves they could have supported a good part of their own population in idleness.

While there seems to be no particular reason why an individual ant could not live quite well without work, it is by no means certain that any do. It is not even particularly likely, although it seems probable, that the ant republic is not particularly egalitarian in its distribution of workloads. Ant behavior is very heavily conditioned by inheritance. The inheritance of any given ant is through the queen, and the worker ant has no direct progeny. Thus, while the niche of an idler dependent upon the rest of the nest is evolutionarily open, and various parasites have exploited it, if an ant took this route, it would be unable to pass on its genes. The development of hereditary parasites within the species is impossible. In multi-queen nests, such as those of our wood ants, if the descendants of one of the queens had less hereditary drive to work than the others, this would in no way increase the likelihood that this queen would be the progenitor of other queens. In fact, it might slightly reduce it by reducing the total efficiency of the nest. On the other hand, of course, if one of the queens had more vigorous children, this also would slightly increase her share in future generations.

The second reason given by Adam Smith for the gains to be obtained from the division of labor is that "the advantage which is gained by saving the time commonly lost in passing from one sort of work to another is much greater than we should at first view be apt to imagine." For the ant, as for the human, this does not, at first view, seem very material a saving. In the absence of further research, we cannot even say for certain that it exists.

In the circumstances of an existing ant nest, the time spent in passing from one sort of work to another would, indeed, be quite considerable, since different jobs are normally carried on in quite different locations, with the result that an ant would have to travel a perceptible distance every time it changed its occupation. This, however, is more a result of the division of labor than a cause. If individual ants carried on all the work themselves, without division of labor, they would have no need for the elaborate nest and, hence, could undertake these various activities in a single area. Presumably, the saving would be more than counterbalanced by the inability of the solitary ant to fully exploit the resources available to a nest.

Adam Smith's third reason is rather confusingly presented in *The Wealth of Nations*. As anyone who has read him knows, he had a strong pro-labor bias, and this sometimes led him into errors. His third point, basically, concerns the advantage which division of labor gives through permitting development of specialized tools and equipment. Unfortunately, his extremely friendly attitude toward labor leads him to present the matter in the form of an allegation that such specialized equipment is largely the invention of the laborer. He does specifically mention (p. 10) that others also make such inventions, but it seems decidedly odd from the perspective of the present day. We can, however, abstract from his pro-laborism and merely discuss the advantage gained from the use of specialized capital equipment.

The ants do not, strictly speaking, make use of tools. There is a tropical tree ant which makes its nests by sewing leaves together. It obtains the thread from its larvae when they are in the pupating stage, preventing them from spinning cocoons, and uses the larva as a sort of live shuttlecock passed back and forth among the ants sewing the leaves together with the silk the larva is producing. This, however, is the closest to the strict use of tools in the whole social insect community, and it is not very close.

When one turns to other forms of labor-saving investment, however, the ants are very considerable capitalists. Some species go in for livestock raising on quite a scale. Their "stock"—aphids of one sort or another—require practically continuous attention. It would not be possible for the ants to undertake this form of enterprise on a part-time basis; therefore, it requires specialization and the division of labor. The agricultural ants, which are mainly fungus growers, also have a large amount of capital tied up in their crops. They normally collect leaves and grass, work this into a sort of mulch, and grow fungus upon it. The entire process is not well understood. Most of these ants are of the genus *Atta*, and they go in for nests of millions of workers, which makes them unsuitable for laboratory observation, but clearly they could not function without very considerable division of labor.

For most ants, however, the largest capital investment they own is clearly their nest. This is the result of vast amounts of labor and vastly increases the efficiency of the individual ant. Consider, for example, an ant road, which can be thought of as an aboveground extension of the nest. Given that a considerable amount of foodstuff is to be carried from some foraging area to the nest, it is likely that the task can be carried on by fewer total workers, with less total energy consumption, if some of the workers devote themselves to preparing a straight, level, and unobstructed road for the others.

Of course, a balance between labor expenditures in building the road and labor savings through its use must be maintained, but the ants do not seem to have any great difficulty with this. Altogether, the ant nest and the other results of the engineering activities of the ant can be regarded as dual-purpose construction. They are consumption goods, in the sense that they keep the ant warm, safe, and dry, but they are also gigantic pieces of capital equipment, in the sense that they greatly increase the efficiency of the ant's labor.

There is, however, another type of specialized "equipment" which the ant uses and which requires division of labor for its creation. Among our wood ants, which are among the least specialized of ants, there are three distinct types of ant, each performing a specialized task.

The workers—sterile females—are, by all odds, the commonest and the only ones that the casual observer is likely to see except at swarming time. They carry on all the work of building the nest, gathering the food, nursing the young, and policing the interior of the nest. They have nothing to do with reproduction, however. This function is entirely entrusted to two specialized types—male drones and queens—that make up only a tiny part of the total population of the nest. The net advantage which the ants obtain from this sort of specialization is too obvious to require extended comment.

One special aspect of this particular specialization should, however, be mentioned. New wood ant communities are created in two different ways. In one, the whole community "buds"—it sends off a group of workers, together with one or more queens, to establish a new nest which will, at least at first, be part of the original ant nation. This procedure is obviously the most safe and secure method of starting a new nest. However, it is used by only a relatively small number of species, and, in those species, as with the wood ant, it is only one of two methods.

The second method—and this is the only method for most ants and all termites[11]—consists of producing a very large number of queens and males

---

11. Dr. Snyder informs me that some termites have recently been found which apparently do not have winged queens. If this discovery is confirmed, and termite study is a very uncertain field, then this conclusion will have to be modified.

that, on a suitable day, fly away from their nests never to return. After mating in the air, the queen lands, sheds her wings, and starts a new nest.

Superficially, this second, but more common, method is highly inefficient. In the first place, the overwhelming majority of all swarming queens are lost. They die or are killed either before they are able to start a new colony or before the colony has more than a handful of members. In fact, these queens are almost unique in the ant dominion in having very short life expectancies.

The ant worker born in an established nest may expect to live two or more years. A queen in an established nest may well live ten years, but a queen participating in a swarming probably has a life expectancy measured in days, perhaps less than one. Such a radical difference in life expectancy, with the most important members of the species having the most dangerous lives, seems decidedly odd. Although a new nest established by a large group of workers and a few queens may fail to make a go of it, the odds are much more favorable than for a single queen attempting to establish a new colony.

The contrast is perhaps even stronger in the case of termites. These "dwellers in darkness" are soft-bodied creatures that can be killed by relatively short exposures to sunlight or even to normal outside air, which may be much less humid than that in a termite nest. The kings and queens must be radically different from the normal termite, in that they can stand both sunlight and dry air for protracted periods. Nevertheless, almost all of the termite royalty which is released to fly in the periodic swarming dies before establishing a successful nest.

This peculiar method of reproduction of the nest must have evolutionary advantages to compensate for the disadvantages outlined above, and these advantages pretty clearly come from the *flight* of the reproductives. An ant nest reproducing by sending out a party of workers and queens is limited by the fact that they must walk along the surface of the ground. If there is no suitable new nesting place within, say, 100 yards, or if there is a stream of any sort which must be crossed to find a new area, then the ants would be confined to their present area. The flight of the reproductives, however, is not even impeded by watercourses and may, in some wind conditions, extend up to ten miles or so. Obviously, a species which restricted itself to establishing new nests by ground travel, on the part of large groups of workers, would be handicapped evolutionarily by its very limited mobility.

That the flight characteristic of normal swarming accounts for its widespread use by ants and termites receives some confirmation from the nest reproduction method of the honeybees. All bees, of course, can fly, and it is possible for a group of workers to accompany the queen without, at the same time, drastically restricting her mobility. As a result, the bees use the dispatch of a large group of workers and one queen from a successful nest as their sole method of establishing new colonies. The advantage that this has in insuring the survival of the queen is obvious. In a Malthusian world, the total number of successful bee nests can hardly increase very much in any generation, but the bees do succeed in maintaining their species with a remarkably small production of new reproductives in each year.

Insects, in general, produce vast numbers of progeny, most of which die before reaching the reproductive stage. Ants and termites, with their thousands of reproductives produced by each nest every year, are examples of this tendency. The contrast between the long life expectancy of the normal worker and the extremely short life expectancy of the average queen merely emphasizes a phenomenon which characterizes most insects. With the bees, on the other hand, a healthy nest will produce only a few (normally fewer than ten) new queens in a year. Since these queens are sent out with the animate equipment for a complete new hive, they have a relatively high survival rate.

For almost any species of animal or plant, conditions will vary a good deal. Perfect adaptation to one set of conditions will normally be a handicap in a slightly different set of conditions. In particular, it would be desirable for the survival of the descendants of any given queen (or drone) to have some admixture of other genes in order to provide at least some variety.

Thus, in a few generations, the species will be able to adjust to a shift, and then adjust back, if the shift in environment is reversed. Over long periods, then, less-than-perfect genetic adaptation to any given environment is desirable. For each generation, however, the better the adaptation to the specific environment the better off that generation is. Thus, natural selection in each generation pulls toward perfect adaptation, while, over a period of time, the pull of natural selection is toward a less specialized gene pool.

For an individual insect which is not "social," this means that the width of the general gene pool of the species is limited by the elimination of individuals whose genes are not sufficiently well adapted to survive. With social insects, this is also true, but the permitted width of the gene pool is much wider, since the better-adapted individual workers can "carry along" their less well adapted sisters. Thus, the genes, which in a different environment might be useful, can be preserved as part of the gene pool. This particular type of "specialization" may not appear to fit traditional ideas of "division of labor," but it surely is an advantage to an ant.

The wood ant, which has been our example, carries functional specialization no further than this. Other ants, however, produce large numbers of specialized types of workers and sometimes soldiers. The so-called honey ants use individual workers as living storage jars, filling them with honey during good times, and then drawing on these supplies in times of dearth. The *Atta* ants of the tropics perhaps go furthest in this direction. One of their great nests, with perhaps 100,000 or more inhabitants, may have quite a number of specialized "designs" of worker ants. The *Atta* go in for fungus raising and produce tiny minims, whose principal duty is weeding and tending the fungus. These tiny specialists are less than a thousandth the size of the *Atta* queens.[12]

The regular workers, which come in several sizes, engage in the usual ant duties, one of the most important being collecting leaves for the fungus to grow upon. A caste of giant "soldiers," seeming to almost have supervisory functions as well as defensive duties, completes the economy. Clearly, this type of specialized development is only possible with a fairly radical division of labor. Equally clearly, it is highly efficient.

Efficiency, in fact, is the word for the ants. The giant colonies of civilized ants are dominant over all of the smaller forms of life in most of the world. Only humans have as much control over their environment as ants, and only humans are as relatively safe from predation as ants. One indication of the power and stability of the ant form of life may be found in the number of specialized parasites which have developed to exploit it. Here again, only humans are in the same league.

Perhaps the power of the civilized ant communities is best shown by their defensive strength. The army ants are, in many ways, the scourge of the tropics. Panthers, monkeys, and humans all move aside when a column of these voracious nomads approaches. The soldiers, however, turn aside from only one sort of animal life—the civilized ant communities. A column of warrior ants, which will march directly into and through a human village, will quickly change direction if it finds itself in contact with the outposts of a civilized ant community. Ants are like humans, in that their greatest enemies are specialized parasites and, in the case of ants, other ants.

---

12. This radical difference in size, in some cases, permits the *Atta* queen to take a small workforce along on her swarming flight. A few minims may cling to the queen and, in view of their small size, are of substantially no impedance to her flight. On arrival at a potential new nest site, of course, they are of very considerable use in setting up housekeeping.

CHAPTER 5

TERMITES AND BEES

Among the social insects, the termite is, in my opinion, the most highly developed. The termite and the social spiders are not closely related to most other social insects. The social wasps, the bees, and the ants are all members of the order Hymenoptera. The termites, on the other hand, are members of a more primitive group and are closely related to the cockroaches. Apparently the social way of life is much older among the termites than among hymenopterans.

Although there are numerous intermediate types of wasps, bees, and ants now living, which permits us to trace the evolutionary development of society among them, the termites are all members of fully developed societies.

The termites have other radical differences from the ants.[1] In the first place, many of them live in symbiotic conditions with certain protozoa. The termite "eats" wood, which is taken into its digestive tract where the protozoa live. The protozoa, which may make up as much as 35% of the termite's body weight, then digest the wood into a form which the termites use for food. Some groups of termites have no protozoa in their digestive tract but have, instead, symbiotic bacteria which perform the same function. For most termites, the symbiotic way of life is standard, and the foundation of a new nest requires both termite founders and protozoa or bacteria founders. The protozoa are heavy and contribute nothing to the flying ability of the royal pair; this raises problems, although not insoluble problems.

It will be seen that we have here a serious problem of coordination between two radically distinct species. Under the modern classification of biological entities, protozoa and termites are not even members of the same kingdom. Also, most termites have a diverse set of termite species, not just one. Further, the protozoa have a much shorter life cycle than the termite. The time from cell division to cell division is quite short compared with the life of a termite, even shorter if compared with the life of a termite colony. All this raises problems regarding the difference between group and individual selection.

---

1. Unfortunately, I have been unable to find any easy-to-read works on these two species. Long ago, a Nobel Prize winner in literature wrote *The Life of the White Ant*. It was apparently lifted from *The Soul of the White Ant*, by Eugene Marais. Although much progress has been made since then, they are still likely to be helpful to the general reader.

Suppose, for example, that one particular protozoan mutates, with the result that it takes more of the wood which it is able to digest and converts it into another protozoan and releases less into the termite's gut. As a result, the termite is not quite as well nourished as otherwise, but the protozoan multiplies much more rapidly than normal. It would, presumably, be quite a number of protozoan generations before the termite would begin having serious difficulties.

This is, however, not quite the total of this matter. The termites eat each other's waste, with the result that the protozoa get passed around a lot in the nest. There would be many protozoan generations before our "selfish" protozoan and its descendants began seriously affecting the efficiency of the nest. Eventually, of course, this might affect a number of daughter nests as well as the original nest. Eventually, this protozoan and all its descendants would cause the termites, which are a necessary part of their environment, to die of lost efficiency.

For all we know, this has happened to termites, and it may have happened frequently. We have no positive evidence of it, however. This would appear to indicate that the protozoa evolved in such a way that they are protected against this particular kind of mutation. This is almost, of necessity, group selection.

When we talked earlier about the difference between group and individual selection, we pointed out that an individual with a mutation which lowers the survival likelihood of the group may, in fact, be committing suicide over a long term. In the case of the protozoan, however, the "suicide" would be many generations in the future and would only occur if that particular mutated protozoan turned out to be superior in competing for livelihood within the termite's gut during the period before the termite dies.

To repeat, as far as we know, there are no "parasitic" protozoa of this sort in the gut of termites, but we must put great emphasis on that "as far as we know." We probably would not discover that this was happening, unless it was extremely frequent.

Another radical difference between the ants and the termites concerns sex. All the workers in an ant nest are female. In a termite colony, they will be about equally divided between the sexes. Instead of just queens, the termites have a royal pair consisting of both a king and a queen. Further, although most of the workers, both male and female, are infertile, there are in-between stages present which can, in emergencies, take the place of the king and queen. These "neotenic reproductives" are much less efficient producers of offspring than the full sexual types, perhaps taking 20 of them to replace a single royal pair. The colony can, in fact, continue to grow with only these replacement royalties. With the ants, the appearance of similar types—called pseudo-gynes—is a symptom of severe parasitism in the nest and normally only shortly precedes its collapse.

Further, the ants are hardy creatures, with armored bodies and considerable ability to take care of themselves in a fight. The termite is soft-bodied and only capable of living in a very carefully controlled environment.[2] Termites can only live in the tunnels of their nests, although they sometimes extend their tunnels for great distances in search of dead wood. They depend upon the carefully controlled environment of the interior of their nest, where the air is always near the saturation point in humidity, normally contains about 5% carbon dioxide, and is held to remarkable tolerances in temperature.

The ant spends much of its time above the surface of the ground, where it can be easily observed. The termite, on the other hand, lives inside its tunnels, free from observation. The construction of observation nests, which, in spite of limits on the practical size, has given us so much information on the ant, is the only recourse with the termite. Unfortunately, the necessarily small size of the nest means that the number of termites contained in it is normally too small to maintain the internal environment at its proper level.[3] Consequently, the laboratory nests have a strong tendency to die out. Altogether, although the economic importance of the termite is such that they probably are studied more than ants, we know less about their lives.

In part, this relative ignorance also proceeds from the simple fact that ant students are normally motivated by simple curiosity, which is perhaps the best background for pure science. Students of termites, on the other hand, almost universally are concerned with the very practical problem of how to kill them with the greatest efficiency. This leads the research onto somewhat different paths.

The different emotional tone of the investigators in the two fields is notable. The ant specialists normally like and, in a sense, admire the ants. The termitologists, although they may feel considerable respect for termite achievements,

2. Certain tropical termites have developed the ability to live outside their nests for short periods. They are pigmented, and their bodies have some surface armor. They even have rudimentary eyes. Altogether, they are most unlike the average termite.

3. Since all natural termite nests start out as simply a royal pair and then gradually grow, the laboratory experience with small nests would indicate that the natural mortality must be tremendous in the early stages.

normally are emotionally neutral or antipathetic toward them.[4] Consider an example of this difference in emotional tone: both termites and ants support specialized parasites in their nests, which succeed, normally, through having particularly attractive body exudates, in getting their hosts to feed and care for them without themselves doing any work. Ant experts tend to get quite emotional in their discussion of this phenomenon, referring to "subversion" and the parasites "tricking" the ants into supporting them when the food should go to the ants themselves. The termitologists, on the other hand, treat the matter with great equanimity, pointing out that the parasites have something—"body exudates"—which termites value, and so it is a fair exchange. Obviously, the principal difference lies in a different emotional outlook on the part of the observer, not in a difference in the nature of the parasites.

Regardless of the reason, however, we do know considerably less about termites than ants. What we do know shows that the two are radically different in everything except their social organization at its most basic level.

The great care with which the internal environment of the termite nest must be regulated is an example. The giant termite mounds of Africa, although normally fully exposed to the sun in the day and often located in arid areas where the nights are cold, show an internal temperature variation of less than one degree. Through the torrential rains of the wet season and the long arid period of the dry season, the internal humidity remains almost constant.

The method of control used in these nests, if not completely understood, is better understood than that of most termites and can serve as an example. The basis of the nest is an internal core. This is surrounded by a thick protective covering which is nearly as strong as cement. This covering is ar-ranged in rather unsightly bulges, which serve as diffusion vanes, increasing the outside area of the nest. The central core, in which the termites carry on most of their activity, is a center of heat, humidity, and carbon dioxide production.

Owing to the heat production, there is a continual upsurge of air through the center section, with the air returning downward through vertical channels near the outer surface of the vanes to the bottom chamber as it cools off. The temperature and humidity control is managed very simply by adjusting the flow of air through the return tunnels, which are constructed just under the outer surface of the nest.

4. The above remarks come from my personal observation. In the course of preparing this book, I talked to a number of ant specialists and termite specialists, and the difference in their emotional attitude toward their subject matter was quite notable.

Air passing through these tunnels absorbs or emits heat by radiation to the outer environment and absorbs oxygen and releases carbon dioxide by diffusion through the thin walls of the tunnels. The direction of water vapor flow also depends on conditions. The whole system is managed, apparently, by simply opening and closing the upper ends of the various vertical tunnels, and a small working crew of termites is continually occupied doing this job. Their efficiency is remarkable, although they would not be able to keep the temperature of the nest down if the outside environment were warmer than the normal interior temperature for long periods of time.

This is, however, characteristic of all animal heat-control systems. They only work because the internal temperature is characteristically higher than that of the outside environment. We generate enough internal heat to keep our bodies considerably warmer than the outside temperature on all but the very hottest day. Advanced animal types, such as humans,[5] do have evaporation cooling, so it is possible for them to survive external temperatures higher than their internal temperatures, but these mechanisms are much less well developed throughout the animal kingdom than the devices to protect against cold.

The careful control of the internal environment of the termite nest, the fact that termites never leave the nest but extend it toward food supplies so that it appears to "grow," and the inability of the individual termite to remain alive outside its nest have led some students to say that the basic organism is really the termite colony rather than the individual termite.

According to this view, the termite individual plays somewhat the same role in a termite colony as a cell does in a body. Any serious consideration of the termite's life does lead to the conclusion that the individual termite leads a much less independent existence than most other "individual" animals and, hence, raises questions as to what the proper "organism" is. Since this whole question will be discussed in a later chapter, it can be left undetermined here.

Returning to the differences between termites and ants, one of the most inconvenient, from the standpoint of the termitologists, is the fact that the termite grows by molting, while most ants stay in the larval stage until ready to pupate and will emerge from the pupa case as a full-fledged adult. The termite, on the contrary, emerges from its egg as a tiny but complete termite which, after a couple of molts, will begin to play its small part in the management of the nest. In the manner of cockroaches, the termite then grows

---

5. The bees, also, use evaporation cooling, bringing water to the nest and then fanning air over it to reduce temperatures on hot days.

by a series of molts,[6] in each of which it sheds its old skin and emerges as a slightly larger and, in most cases, somewhat changed version of its old self.

The importance which the immature stages of the termite play in the economy of the nest, where they may well be the bulk of the population, is most clearly illustrated in some of the most primitive termites. In these relatively backward insects, the final, fully mature stage is a soldier, able to defend the nest but unable to do any work or even feed itself. These "adult" termites are taken care of and fed by the "immature" termites that are, in these primitive species, the only ones able to engage in any sort of economic activity. This extreme reliance upon immature individuals has been abandoned by the more advanced species, but the "children" of the termites play an important role in the economy of all nests.

All of this causes considerable difficulty for the termitologists. The termites go in for quite extensive caste specialization, perhaps more so than the ants. The problem of determining whether a given type of termite found commonly in a nest is really a different caste, or merely a stage in the growth of a caste, is a difficult one. This is particularly so since the termites characteristically change form, to some extent, at each molt, and, in some cases, the change may be quite radical.

Thus, the literature on termites is replete with instances in which a student has classified the forms of some species of termite only to be set right later by further research which indicates that a stage was mistaken for a caste. A mistake of this sort, although to be avoided, is no indication of incompetence. The problem is difficult and not made easier by the fact that termites may spend very long periods in one stage and that different castes may have different numbers of molts, although they are members of the same species and nest.

In spite of these radical differences between the termites and the ants, they have very similar social systems. This has, perhaps, been recognized by the name "white ants," which is commonly applied to termites.

The fact that two such radically different insects, about as distantly related as insects can be, have developed such a similar social organization illustrates the advantages which that social order has. It is not only humans who can benefit from specialization and the division of labor, capital investment, and agriculture. The evolutionary niche for consumers of dead wood would not appear to be very wide. The gigantic social organizations which have been

6. The period between two molts is called an "instar" by the termitologists, but I shall follow common usage and refer to it as a "stage."

built in this narrow niche is a dramatic illustration of the efficiency of the social way of life.

In addition to ants and termites, bees and wasps, closely related to ants, are sometimes social. In most of these cases, the society is much more primitive than that of the civilized ants or the higher termites. The honeybees, however, although their nests seldom exceed 70,000 to 80,000 individuals, have a social order which deserves comparison with that of their terrestrial sisters.

We know more about the life of the honeybee than about any other social insects. This is partly because people have been closely associated, through bee raising, with honeybees for a long time and also because the bees are easily observed. In the first place, they are much larger than ants and termites, which is a great convenience to students. Secondly, the honeybee nest is laid out on strictly geometric lines, with the result that it is much easier to observe what goes on inside than within the curving passages of the anthill.

In fact, it is quite possible to design a glass-walled nest box within which the bees will build their comb in such a way as to provide good observation of a specific type of activity that the entomologist wishes to study.[7] Since a queen and her accompanying swarm of workers introduced into such a box will very quickly reach full production, this means that the experimental approach is relatively easy.

With European settlement of the Americas, bees were imported as well as other types of domestic[8] animals, and these imported bees have largely replaced the stingless bees as honey sources, except in the tropics. The continuance of beekeeping with the stingless bees in the tropics very likely reflects the fact that the bees imported from Europe were *Apis mellifer*, which is essentially adapted to temperate regions.[9]

Even if we consider only the eight species of the genus *Apis*, two of them — *indica* and *mellifera* — are more highly developed and make up the overwhelming majority of all bee colonies. The other two species are found only in India, are much more primitive in their social organization, and are of little

---

7. The South American stingless bees are harder to study, since they do not arrange the interior of their nest in such a geometrically regular way.

8. The term "domestic" is somewhat of a misnomer for the bees. Although they have been persuaded to build their nests in locations which are convenient for the beekeeper, they are not really domesticated in the way that, say, cattle and sheep are. The need for protective clothing for beekeepers illustrates this fact.

9. The "African" bees, which are currently so much in the news, are simply a different strain of the conventional honeybee.

economic importance. The fact that two species, one suited to the tropics and the other to the temperate zones, should dominate the whole Eurasian continent, to say nothing of the areas to which they have been transferred by human colonists, is most remarkable.

Presumably, this failure to develop specialized types can be put down to the mutualistic relationship between the bees and the flowers. The bees are obviously evolutionally selected to collect honey and pollen from the flowers, and the flowers are also obviously evolutionally designed to attract bees which transmit pollen from one flower to another. The fact that individual bees will normally "specialize" in one type of flower at any given time is thus of value to both the flower and the bee.

Nevertheless, the bees gain from being able to take honey from the widest possible range of flowers, and the flowers gain from attracting as large a percentage of the total bee population as possible. Although there are flowers which have specialized, so their pollen can only be carried by a few insects, and insects which have made the converse specialization, the bees and their flower partners are much more common.

The bees are simply a single example of one of the more remarkable evolutionary specializations we have in nature. A great many insects depend on honey or pollen from plants, and, at the same time, plants depend on these insects for pollination.[10] Once again, we have living entities from radically different biological kingdoms which engage in cooperative activity. How this joint development evolved is not easy to see.

In human life, we have a number of cases where this kind of thing can develop. In order to have color television, it was necessary both to have people broadcasting it and radically different people buying colored television receivers. Indeed, for many years, RCA lost immense amounts of money by broadcasting programs in color in hopes that people would buy RCA colored television receivers. When they eventually did begin buying colored television receivers, tragically, they were mainly not RCA.

There are other cases of this sort. Automobile exhaust is the most common, important, single source of air pollution. This could be sharply reduced, indeed, nearly eliminated, by the simple expedient of using natural gas as fuel instead of gasoline. It would require a fairly radical modification of existing automobiles, although it would not require actually replacing them.

10. Birds and bats also may engage in pollination. The beautiful night-blooming cereus in my yard is bat-pollinated.

The cost, under present circumstances, would be well over $1,000 per car. Mass production might bring that down, and, of course, if new cars were designed for natural gas, that would also be very helpful. At the moment, natural gas would be cheaper than gasoline although, if all the cars in the United States were driving on natural gas, it might be more expensive.

The problem here is that there are very few filling stations that carry natural gas, and so somebody who bought a car with a natural gas engine would have difficulty.[11] On the other hand, if you decide to put natural gas facilities into your filling station, you will find very few cars prepared. If we could somehow make the transition for the whole country at once, it would be easier.

Of course, this does not prove that we will not, eventually, make the transition. Color television did come in. As a matter of fact, there is a little bit of slow movement toward natural-gas–fueled cars now. I have brought this up primarily to indicate the difficulties that we observe in the case of insects and flowers. The honeybee is quite a generalist, and the flowers that provide honey and pollen for the honeybee normally are welcome to other insects, too.

There are, however, certain highly specialized cases. Darwin was an expert on orchids, and, in 1863, he predicted, from examining an orchid, that there would be a particular kind of moth, necessarily a rather large moth, with a tongue that could reach out five inches because that was the only way this particular flower could exchange its nectar for pollen carried by the insect. It should be noted that, from the standpoint of the flower, it is, of course, more efficient if you have an insect that is narrowly specialized for a particular type of flower. It does not waste its pollen on flowers of a totally different species which the bumblebee visits right after it picks up its pollen.

The moth that Darwin predicted was actually found 40 years later, but the story is further complicated. The only reason I know it is that recently an orchid was discovered that requires a seven-inch-long tongue, and the prediction that there must be a moth somewhere in Madagascar that can handle that kind of tongue was made and reported by the *New York Times*.

Once again, we have something that looks rather like evolution. The bee strain, for example, that is able to keep all the pollen it encounters on flowers and take it back to its nest, without wasting any of it on fertilizing the next flower that it met, would flourish, presumably, for many generations. Eventually, if it became the dominant form of bee and all other pollinating insects were somehow eliminated, it might be wiped out by its failure to act in a

---

11. Engines which run on both are possible, but somewhat more expensive.

generous way toward the flowers. In this particular case, I doubt the bee could be redesigned so that it did not accidentally transmit a certain amount of pollen from one plant to another. Still, at least theoretically, one could have a failure of coordination between these two radically different species.

Since all bees can fly, workers can accompany a queen setting up a new home, and so bees have been able to carry functional specialization of the queen farther than ants and termites. In ants, the queen must be an all-around individual, capable of founding a new nest and operating it for some time, either without assistance from workers or with very little. The bee queen has no such necessity and, hence, can be more of a pure egg-laying machine than can an ant or termite queen. The bee queens have anatomically less developed brains than the workers, and their sense organs are also fewer and less efficient than those of the workers.

This fact fairly thoroughly disposes of the myth that queens actually "rule" their hives. They are, of course, extremely important members of the hive — so important that their removal immediately sets the hive into a stage of tension recognized by beekeepers as "queenlessness," but they lack the brains to make even simple decisions that workers can make. The workers, in fact, will rapidly produce new queens, if necessary. Any female grub, less than two days old, can be made into a queen by enlarging her cell and giving her special food. This is fairly easy.

The ant and termite workers are, for insects, rather long-lived. The queen bee also may live many years, but the worker bees normally work themselves to death in a few weeks during the summer months. Owing, in part, to their relative inactivity during the winter months and, in part, to certain glandular changes, worker bees hatched in the fall normally live through the winter. They are, of course, only a small fraction of the number born during the spring (life in the hive goes on at a much reduced rate all winter) and summer. Perhaps, because of this relatively short life span, bees go in for age-grading of economic activities.

The newly hatched bee will specialize in "household" duties, going through a regular procession of them and eventually, when it reaches a certain degree of maturity, becoming a "foraging" bee interested in collecting nectar, pollen, and propolis for the hive. It should be emphasized, however, that this regular procession is a tendency, not a rigid rule. Individual bees may skip stages, different bees spend different amounts of time in different stages, and adjustments to changes in "need" for different economic activities lead to changes in the regular routine.

Bee specialists, for example, may remove all bees of some certain age from the nest. In general, the remaining bees quickly make the necessary adjustments so that the relative number of bees engaged in each activity will be much the same as before, although the age composition of the population is radically different. It is possible that this would not be so if all but the oldest bees were removed. The necessary flexibility may be largely confined to the younger bees. The difficulty of accurately age-grading older bees, however, has so far prevented the experiment from being made.

Leaving the honeybees, the remaining social insects are largely of lower and less highly evolved societies. The bumblebees and the many kinds of wasps produce simpler nests than the honeybees, normally maintain smaller colonies, and are unable to maintain their colonies from year to year. In all of these species, a few queens hiding in crannies are all that survive the winter, and the new colonies must be built from the ground up each year. These relatively primitive societies are of great interest to specialists interested in the evolutionary history of insect society, but of little interest to us.

CHAPTER 6

MOLE RATS, SPONGES, AND SLIME MOLDS

One of the extraordinary characteristics of biology as a field of study is the immense number of different species and types. This is such a gigantic number that mole rats are not even in the index of Wilson's monumental *Sociobiology*. The mole rat appeared in catalogs of African rodents well back into the 19th century, and its social nature was apparently known to at least some biologists. It was also a rather conspicuous denizen of the area because of its habit of engaging in "volcanoing" (to be explained later) in the middle of dirt tracks. Nevertheless, until very recently, the mole rat had almost completely escaped the knowledge of those people engaged in the study of animal societies.

In the past ten years, all of this has been reversed, and it has become a highly fashionable animal. Most readers will have probably seen this ugly little rodent on TV, and a great deal of research has been done on it. This research is continuing, and by the time a reader sees these words, our knowledge will probably be much greater than it is at the moment of my writing.[1] If readers are curious, they should do some of their own research and try and look up the most recent material.

What, then, is the mole rat? This small rodent is native to Africa and lives in underground tunnel systems in societies which may go up to 300 or 400 individuals. There is one functional female, two or three males that engage in impregnating the female, and a large number of workers of both sexes. The biologists coined the word "eusocial" for societies where there is this high specialization of reproduction. They were thinking of ants, termites, etc., and were highly surprised to discover a eusocial mammal.

With the discovery that the mole rat was an interesting species, it was also discovered that it has a number of relatives also living in Africa. Although nowhere near as fully social as the mole rat, nevertheless, they are more social than a wolf pack or a tribe of baboons. It is not at all unlikely that more rodents of this sort can be found in other parts of the world. Indeed, granted the fact that this particular social rodent escaped notice for such a long time,

---

1. I have drawn primarily on Paul W. Sherman, Jennifer U. M. Jarvis, and Richard D. Alexander, eds., *The Biology of the Naked Mole Rat* (Princeton: Princeton University Press, 1991), the best source on mole rats. It probably tells nonbiologists more than they want to know about this unpleasant mammal.

the prospect that a totally different species may be discovered to be highly social is by no means zero.

In order to understand the mole rat, we must begin by discussing its niche. Before it was discovered, a pure theorist thought that if there were any social mammals, they would have to live in a system of protected tunnels and eat some food that is available underground. The mole rat meets these specifications, and it is a rather good example of prediction, except for the fact that it was obvious that Alexander, who made the prediction, did not really think there were such species.

The mole rat flourishes in areas with intermittent rainfall. In these areas, plants develop stores of energy in the form of tubers on their roots. These tubers are the food source of the mole rat, which digs tunnels to the tuber and then takes pieces of it away, partly to eat and partly to feed to the queen and immature members of the nest. The tunnel systems may run a kilometer or more in a straight line. For some obscure reason, they tend to run along dirt tracks (or at least the ones that have been discovered tend to).

Construction of such tunnels means that there is a great deal of earth to be removed, and the way it is removed is the most conspicuous activity of the mole rat: volcanoing. Mole rats will push the dirt to near a hole which goes up to the surface and then one of them will stand with his back to the hole and kick the dirt up out of it. The appearance of this, at least according to the pictures I have seen, is rather like a small volcano with a cone-shaped "mountain" and dirt exploding out of the top, frequently for fairly long periods of time.

Apparently, the reason this attracted little attention until recently was that it was thought that some particular rodent was digging a hole and throwing the dirt out. That the activity was continued over long periods of time went unnoticed, and also that the tunnel system had to be extensive.

The tunnels divide roughly into two categories—the main highways and the secondary roads. The main highways are wide enough so that the mole rats can pass, sometimes by crawling over each other, and are equipped with short turnoff tunnels, apparently to make it easy for them to turn around. The mole rats are close to blind, and it may be that they navigate down these tunnels and, in particular, dig them straight by sensing the position of their rather long tails.

The main highways tend to be rather deep, are equipped with suitable drains, and there are arrangements for even deeper parts of the nest. This last point has annoyed people attempting to capture the entire nest, because the queen tends to retreat down to the bottom when you begin digging the top.

Near the surface are the smaller tunnels, which are essentially the roads followed by the mole rats attempting to get food.

The plant roots they eat tend to grow in semiclusters, i.e., more concentrated in some areas than others. Mole rats will run their smaller tunnels off
into such an area and then begin extensive branching in order to reach the
bulk of the tubers. It should be said that they do not necessarily take all the
tubers from a given plant, and, in fact, sometimes they run a tunnel right
through it. The plant will then build up the tuber again, which provides further food sources for the mole rats.

Biologists think that mole rats have no way of finding the tubers except to
simply run a tunnel out at random and hope it hits one. This may, indeed, be
true. However, with the tendency of all plants to excrete some chemicals, I
suspect that the mole rats do have some ability to hunt them down. In any
event, maps of mole rat burrowings I have seen seem to show a pattern,
which would be rather inefficient if they were simply engaging in random
searching.

In the mole rat nest, they have a well-established social system with the
queen and the males that impregnate her, the males apparently getting their
position largely by fighting. In this respect, they are rather like some species
of wasps. In one case of a mole rat which was under observation in a laboratory, the queen developed what appeared to be a weakness or illness and was
disposed of, and a new queen was developed. Whichever one is the queen,
however, has the distinct advantage of being fed better and generally taken
care of by other mole rats, in particular, the usually large, healthy males impregnating her. Thus, the fact that she is frequently pregnant does not terribly affect her ability to control the nest.

There is, then, the question of why the other females surrounded by other
males do not also breed. Occasionally, they apparently attempt it, but this is
prevented. Presumably, there is some kind of hormonal transfer within the
nest that makes this impossible. The mole rats have latrine areas. They also
have a habit of eating each other's offal, which would make transmission of
hormones through the nest very easy.

There is some evidence of age-grading, in which the mole rats, as soon as
they are big enough to engage in work in the nest, begin tunneling or volcanoing. As they get bigger, they apparently work less, and, if they are males,
they eventually end up as the functional males of the nest. If they are females,
they conceivably might become queen, although the odds in both of these
cases are against it. (I emphasize that this line immediately above and all I have

to say in this chapter are the result of recent and, as yet, highly incomplete research. In another ten years, we will know much more about mole rats than we do now.)

The volcanoing activity, which tends to be pushed off on smaller and immature members of the species, is the single most dangerous thing that the mole rats do. The mole rat engaging in this activity is, of necessity, conspicuous. Because of the volcano, the mole rat is close to the surface. Being blind and making quite a bit of noise, it would be unlikely to hear something quietly approaching the "volcano." Small snakes are probably the most dangerous predators of the mole rats, but they are not terribly dangerous, except for the volcanoists. Predators introduced into artificial habitats in the laboratory have been killed by the mole rats.

Mole rats do the actual digging with their teeth, which are long and tend to grow continuously, so the digging does not deprive them of teeth. These teeth are a rather dangerous weapon, and the fact that they are capable of killing snakes that get into the nest is not terribly surprising. In any event, the mole rats in the laboratory area very definitely undertook aggressive attacks on predators which had been introduced.

There is also the possibility of wars between different nests. In the laboratory, it is possible to arrange things so that two different mole rat nests, proceeding down two different pipes, which had been filled with dirt in order to make the mole rats feel at home, run into each other. These lead to combat among the mole rats and usually a blockage of the tunnel by putting more dirt in place.

It is possible that in the wild the larger mole rat community, instead of blocking the tunnel, would continue in and destroy the other mole rat community. Presumably, the defenders would attempt to fill the tunnel, but there is no reason to doubt that the larger, more aggressive nest could continue to excavate the tunnel and that eventually this would lead to the extermination of the smaller group. But all of this is pure speculation. As far as I know, no one has observed anything like it.

The same situation, incidentally, applies with respect to termites. As far as I know, no one has observed direct wars between termites when their tunnels intersect. It would be very difficult to observe this in the wild, and, in the laboratory, maintenance of termites is enough trouble without inciting wars. Nevertheless, there again, at least in theory, one termite nest could destroy another and occupy its tunnels and food sources. I repeat, as far as I know, no one has ever observed this.

The ants and, to a lesser extent, the termites are obviously highly effective and efficient occupiers of a wide diversity of niches. The mole rats seem to exist only in one rather narrow niche, one which, in many ways, is a particularly sheltered niche. It may be, therefore, that they are basically a less efficient society than those of the civilized social insects.

Eusociality is most surprising in a mammal. The very interest in them, I think, comes from that surprise. Still, there clearly is evidence that large-scale social organizations can be quite efficient and that eusociality is helpful in that area.

With respect to eusociology, however, let me emphasize that the most successful social species—human—does not have it. The social spiders also do not have it, as far as I can tell. To repeat what I mentioned earlier, it is hard to get information on these spiders. We will shortly turn to other species, which apparently do not have it, although it is a little hard to say.

The existence of the eusocial habits does not mean a centralized government among the ants or termites. In all these areas, communication facilities are poor, and there are no signs of anyone giving orders to anyone else. Each individual entity must decide for itself what it is going to do. The problem here is how they are arranged so that the ultimate outcome is a socially efficient cooperation rather than the kind of competition which is markedly more common in nature than this type of cooperation.

Human society, of course, has both cooperation and competition together with hierarchies, usually not covering the whole society but, nevertheless, hierarchies. These hierarchies, in turn, engage in cooperation or competition with other hierarchies and individuals. All of this is quite different from what we observe in the animal societies, but, as we shall see, there are certain overarching similarities in the functional structure.

So much for the mole rat. Let us now turn to some other species which are fully social and yet in which the individual entities are even less endowed with grey matter than ants and termites. The first of these will be the sponges.

Sponges are an immensely ancient group. There are actually sponges found in the Burgess Shale Beds that are fundamentally similar to present-day sponges. The basic sponge design is a simple cup. The body of the cup is pierced by numerous small holes through which water is driven into the interior. The "mouth" is the exit which lets the water out. The larger sponges are a pastiche of cups of this sort intercepting and feeding into each other, etc., and the larger holes are, in fact, the outlets for the individual cups.

For the rest of this discussion, I will talk about one of the simple sponges which has only one cup. I will only occasionally deal with the multiple-cup schemes or the possibility that different sponges from different origins mate much as two bushes located close together may mate or grow together. Most biologists think the possibility of such mating is near zero, but, since I do not agree, I will at least mention the possibility.

Many people tend to think that a sponge colony is this large collection of different cup-shaped arrangements. As a matter of fact, although these do exist, the colony itself is a very specialized collection of single cells, many of which are amoeboid in nature. The orthodox biologists believe that these cells are all clones. I am doubtful, but it makes little difference to the rest of this discussion.

Turning to our little single-cup area, the outer level of the sponge is a layer of cells which have converted themselves into a sort of epidermis, similar in function to our skin. As far as we know, there is no genetic difference between those cells and the others. Indeed, as far as we know, with the exception of some sex cells we will talk about later, all the different single-celled entities that I will be talking about have more or less the same genetic background.

The skin cells also cover part of the interior of the cup, but there are two other very important types of cells there. There are some which act as pumps to move water through the small holes in the outer edges of the cup and then out through the main opening. The other set of specialized cells seizes food particles that pass through and digests them, releasing energy for the organization as a whole. The Porifera, which have, after all, existed for a very long period of time, live entirely by taking small bits and pieces of things that they can convert into energy out of the flowing water stream which they create.

The interesting part of the sponge, however, lies between these two layers. In most sponges, in this area there is an interlocking matrix of silicon or carbonate spicules and an extracellular matrix of collagen. It is these interlocking matrices which make up the skeleton of the sponge.

In the living sponge, the space between the skeleton of spicules, collagen, and skin is a sort of jellylike substance. Through this jellylike substance, there is a large number of free-swimming or free-crawling (depending on what you think is the best way of moving through jelly) amoeboid cells which perform most of the basic work of the sponge.

The spicules, for example, are produced by a group of individual amoeboid cells. Several amoeboid cells will jointly secrete whatever is the particular type of spicule characteristic of that particular species.[2] Frequently, the classification of many sponges is primarily a matter of examining the spicules.

It should be emphasized that when amoeboid cells meet to form a spicule, there is no evidence that there is a leader, and followers obeying orders. They appear to behave quite spontaneously. Further, there is no obvious planning amoeba or planning commission of amoebas, which decides where the new spicule will be built. As far as we can tell, a group of amoeboid cells jointly "decide" that a new spicule is needed in this particular location and proceed to cooperatively produce it.

There are many other things that must be done inside the sponge. Food or energy sources must be taken from those specialized cells which take it out of the water and distributed to the other stationary cells. This is done by the amoeboid cells. Whether there is specialization here is not clear. It may be that all of the amoeboid cells, from time to time,[3] go to one of the food-harvesting cells, pick up food, and then either consume it themselves or transfer it to one of the immobile cells. On the other hand, they may transfer it to mobile cells just as ants may transfer food to other ants that move around doing various things.

I have been confining myself to the simple one-cup sponge, of which there are a number, but the larger sponges with many cups operate in the same way, and the amoeboid cells are not confined to the area around one particular cup. They can move freely through the jellylike interior of the whole structure.

The sponges have two methods of reproduction. Let me begin with sexual reproduction, which is a fairly easy process to explain because it is similar to other animal reproduction. Within the sponge, there are specialized sperm-producing cells, and this sperm is released into the water. On moving through the water, these sperm will occasionally encounter a sponge of the same type and be drawn into its interior. The individual sperm is then, by various mechanisms, put in contact with an egg, which it fertilizes.

The fertilized egg may then be expelled as simply a zygote, in which case it develops into a larva which swims around until it is destroyed or finds a suitable place to start a new sponge. Alternatively, the larva may begin

2. An illustration showing the whole process is on page 94 of Patricia R. Bergquist, *Sponges* (Berkeley: University of California Press, 1978), a simple introduction to sponges. It is also, perhaps, too long for someone not taking a course on the subject.

3. It should be said that the amoeboid cells do not seem to be all absolutely identical. The sponge experts can tell some types from others. This does not mean, of course, that they are genetically different.

development within the sponge and then be expelled. Once again, there is no sign of central control. This process is obviously risky and, like so many insect and plant reproduction procedures, involves immense waste, because only a few of these fertilized eggs actually will create sponges.

There is another reproductive procedure, which has some structural similarity to bees swarming. It is called gemmulation, and it is best explained by an example drawn from freshwater sponges which live in the temperate zone.

In gemmulation, a large number of the amoeboid cells form a special reproductive structure. This consists internally of a considerable number of active cells that will become inactive shortly and which have digested and absorbed various nutrients from a large number of the other amoeboid cells which stream to them for the purpose. This provides a large number of cells, each of which has a large energy supply, and, in many sponges, additional fats and other sources of energy are stacked around them. Outside this collection of cells, when it has reached the size typical of that species, a hard core will be formed by other amoeboid cells.

This whole structure is then expelled from the sponge and falls to the streambed. This normally takes place in the fall, and the gemmule, in essence, hibernates through the winter. Come spring and warmer water, it has enough cells and energy for it to produce a tiny sponge of ordinary form, and this sponge then sets to work. If its environment is suitable, it becomes a full-sized adult sponge which, in turn, come fall, will produce gemmules for reproduction. Note that if there are mutations in the amoeboid cells, then a mutated cell might be in the gemmule. Thus, such mutations might be carried on for many generations.

Once again, there is nothing instructing the individual amoeboid cell to participate in this practice. Indeed, since in the average sponge there will be several gemmules being produced at the same time in different parts of the sponge, it is a little difficult to see how any central control could cause it.

On discussing this subject with specialists, they are apt to say that the cause of all this is the development of gradients of various hormones or other chemicals. This is no doubt true, but the question arises of how these amoeboid cells decide to develop these gradients. If there was one central intelligent cell which issued orders to produce a gradient, this would be one thing. But that is not what we observe.

Looking at the matter in very general terms, what presumably happens is that as the temperature of the surrounding water falls, there is a tendency of the amoeboid cells to change their form a little bit. They begin excreting some hormone that they had not excreted before or, perhaps, increasing the quantity of it. This is done by a considerable number of them, and all of them respond to this hormone level increase in the jellylike mass by beginning to clump.

Of course, this hormone will be more dense in the areas where clumps have begun to form, and hence it will attract other amoeboids. They will be motivated by their internal chemistry to run up a gradient of this kind of chemical. Further details of this action can then simply follow from the existence of the group in the center with probably a rule that once the amount of whatever chemical concerned reaches a certain concentration (which would mean there is a considerable number of cells which have been clumped, etc.), the others will form a hard cover around them.

All this occurs quite automatically and obviously without any great thought on the part of the individual cell, but note that it involves a high level of cooperation and coordination. Hayek has done a good deal of writing about spontaneous order among human beings. There is no doubt that there are spontaneous orders among humans as well as planning and hierarchies. In the sponge, however, we find only spontaneous orders. Insofar as there is any planning at all, it has taken place many generations before in the construction of an appropriately shaped DNA molecule.

Confining ourselves to those sponges which reproduce by gemmulation, if there had been mutations in which the DNA molecules did not direct this kind of cooperation, those particular sponges have been destroyed by the normal evolutionary effects, and the ones left have these built-in behavior patterns. In general, although I think it has little effect on human beings, something like this undoubtedly has affected almost all of the nonhuman societies. In almost all of them, there is some release of hormones by various members of the society which affect the behavior of the others. In those which are eusocial, the breeders may be centers of a set of hormones which are different from the others and which have a considerable coordinating effect. Nevertheless, in all these cases, there is no central planning in any true sense. The planning took place long ago for the development of appropriate DNA sequences, not in the development of this particular group. All of this will be discussed in greater length in the next chapter, but it seems sensible to introduce the subject here.

Evolutionary selection, then, cannot take the form of individual selection of one entity when the entities are considered to be these amoeboid cells. It is true, of course, that within the sponge, some of the single cells might fail to survive because they somehow or other violated or were not fitted to the interior structure of the sponge. But that is not what is normally meant by evolution. In a larger sense, it probably should be included in evolution as we shall point out below.

In a real sense, the hereditary material of any species is carried in the whole of that species or subspecies. The sexual mating process means that it is rare for any individual to have exactly the same genes as its parents or, indeed, perhaps of any other single member of that species. What you have is a mix of genes. This is also true of the sponge.

Earlier, I discussed the general mathematical rule that individual selection dominates group selection unless the life expectancy of the group is of the same order of magnitude as the individual. I pointed out that there are some cases where this is not likely to be true, but, nevertheless, it is a good general rule.

Consider, however, the genes of any given cell—whether it is a cell in your body or a cell in a sponge. Firstly, they must keep the cell alive at least long enough so that it plays whatever role is required for that particular species. One of the amoeboid cells which, for some reason, could not stay alive in the interior of the sponge would obviously be eliminated. Secondly, it must be effective enough so that one way or another its genes are represented in the next generation. This representation could, of course, come not from it but from a relative. Thus, what biologists call inclusive fitness and what I would like to call nepotism[4] has meant that genes may not only try to reproduce, but also help facilitate reproduction of duplicates in another organism. Last, but by no means least, the genes must be such that the larger organism continues to exist. A spider can eat its young as long as it does not eat all of them.

Thus, we have, in this case, three (perhaps four) different evolutionary levels. The first is the evolutionary level that keeps the individual unit alive. It should be said that there is an even lower level, the chemical evolutionary level. The necessary hereditary apparatus has to be chemically stable enough so that it can be reproduced from generation to generation. This is probably the reason the DNA molecule evolved and persisted.

The second (or third) is that the individual entity produced must be functional. That it may be doomed to die by some hereditary defect before it reaches reproductive age is a violation of that particular rule, and it will be selected out individually. Lastly, it must not damage the group so much that the group fails to reproduce.

---

4. "Hamilton's altruism" is another name.

As an example of the latter: Jane Van Lawick–Goodall found that one pair of female chimpanzees were kidnapping, killing, and eating the babies of some of the others. This habit, if carried to extremes, would eliminate the species. Chimpanzees are not capable of living, or at least thriving, unless there is a fairly large group. If this infanticide gene developed good individual selective value, the chimpanzees would cease to exist.

Thus, evolution must select on all of these levels, and the resulting species must be a balance of evolution in each of these areas. It may well be that human beings would be massively more efficient if certain gene combinations existed, but these gene combinations are chemically unstable and hence cannot exist. On this subject, one cannot point to any examples, but it is best to keep an open mind. We certainly cannot say it is impossible.

The cells, whether they are the semi-independent cells of the sponge or the cells of your body, must also be functional, in the sense that there are no serious defects in their operation, if the individual and the society are to continue. The individual larger entity, if this entity is an ant or a human being living in a society, must be functional or it will be selected out.

Lastly, the group as a whole has to be functional also. This involves a careful balance. The individual cannot be expected to make sacrifices for the group, which would mean that particular genes would be selected out within the group even if it would help the group, but, at the same time, the individual cannot have genes which help its development but put too large a strain on the society of which it is part.

All of these different evolutionary levels must be balanced, and it must be true that the balance in all species is a pretty narrow one. We have millions of species, but, clearly, if we could avoid these balance requirements, we would have more.

But enough of theory. Let us turn to our final example of a society: the slime mold. This "society" is so peculiar that it is hard to believe that it exists. Wilson, who almost ignored the sponges,[5] devotes almost a full paragraph to slime molds.[6]

---

5. Edward O. Wilson, *Sociobiology* (Cambridge: Belknap Press, Harvard University Press, 1975). There is a passing reference in one sentence on page 156.

6. Ibid., 185. It is hard to find anything simple on slime molds, but pages 132–37 of Lynn Margulis and Karlene V. Schwartz, *Five Kingdoms* (Boston: W. H. Freeman, 1982–88), is a good introduction. As a general statement, anyone wanting to get a general resource in biology can do little better than this book.

The life cycle of the slime mold is peculiar. Let me begin at one point and then go through the rest of it. We begin, then, with a large number of single cells wandering around the floor of a temperate zone forest, each rather like an amoeba. At some signal, not fully understood, a large number of them begin to clump into a much larger entity. For reasons which will be explained later, it is not likely that these clumping cells are closely related.[7]

In any event, they form a solid body which looks rather like a cigar. Although the individual entities are small enough to require a microscope to see the "cigar," it is plainly visible and usually several inches long.[8] The individual amoebas do not join up to form a rigid structure, but flow within the cigar, which, from the standpoint of a microscopic amoeba, must be truly immense. As mentioned before, it may be several inches long.

The cigar-shaped object begins to move across the forest floor by a process rather like that of a Caterpillar tractor. The lower part, the part in contact with the ground, remains stable, but the rear end of this portion goes along the top to the front, comes down, and becomes the forward part of the tread. By this process, the cigar wanders across the forest floor for a period of time.

At some point, the cigar stops and shoots up a stalk at its front end. The cells in the stalk then form spores, and the spores are dispersed by wind action. On landing, if they find themselves in a favorable area, they form little amoebas and ingest food until they become large amoebas, and then the whole process is repeated.

It seems likely that the only reason for the combination of spore reproduction and the cigar is to provide a wider dispersal of the "descendants" of one of these entities than they would get if they simply split when the amoeba reached a large enough size. From our standpoint, the cigar moves very slowly, but compared with the amoeba itself, the distance it can travel is quite immense. Wind dispersal of spores leads to a massively wider spread of the next "generation" than would a simple splitting of an amoeba.

Nevertheless, the whole thing means that spores from a number of different cigars are apt to be intermixed on the ground. Indeed, the spore method

7. After I wrote this in my original draft, a biologist used DNA matching and found that the cells are not closely related. This shows that an outside theorist in any field can *sometimes* be right.

8. There is another group of slime molds which form a sort of pancake instead of moving into cigar-shaped entities. The basic evolutionary difference is that the cigar is mobile while the pancake is not. In other respects, their behavior is much the same. Interestingly, in the pancake slime mold, the cell boundaries dissolve, so it consists of sort of a porridge of cell parts.

of reproduction means almost of necessity that the spores of any one of these slime molds are far too widely distributed to ever get back together by amoeba motion. This is the reason it seems unlikely that the amoebas which joined to form one of the cigars are closely related.[9] There must be a mix of amoebas which have descended from spores of a number of different cigars. The problems that this poses for evolutionary selection are obviously great.

In particular, it would appear that this is a clear-cut case where a gene package, which was able to somehow cheat in the cigar so that it was more likely than the average to be one of the sporulating gene packages, would both improve its own survival possibility in the next generation and lower the survival probability of the species. It would be a clear-cut case in which individual selection and group selection are fighting in opposite directions.

One possible solution would be simply that those cells which are able to fight to maintain their position in the area of the cigar so that they will be reproduced will automatically kill off the cigar, which can no longer proceed in its caterpillar trip. Until we know more about the dynamics of the cigar interior, not much can be said about this, but I should say that it seems to me not terribly likely. If it were so, we would have the life expectancy group—i.e., the cigar—as short as that of the individual—i.e., the random cells.

From the standpoint of this book, the really intriguing feature here is cooperative behavior among a group of entities which cannot conceivably be regarded as having individual intelligence or as even being subject to any command and control apparatus.

Once again, when I talked to a biologist about this, he said that the reason for the formation of the stalk at the upper front with the spores on top was probably a hormone gradient. I would agree that this is probably true, but the question then becomes: how does the hormone gradient start?

Let us make up a little mechanism which seems plausible. Suppose that when amoebas join to form a large cigar-shaped body, they bring with them a fair amount of energy stores. The cigar, which is not capable of ingesting any significant amount of food, then moves forward, expending energy, of course, until such time as the total energy available falls below some threshold level. At that point, it moves on into the next stage because of the chemical change in its internal structure.

Note, however, that this does not say that any particular set of cells has issued a command to the rest. It is, once again, a cooperative measure in which

---

9. And, to repeat, they have been found to be unrelated.

each individual cell must "decide" what it is going to do. Some of them will join the stalk and eventually become clusters of spores which are dispersed. Others will die when the cigar dies. There is no evidence that any of them are selected in any particular way except randomly. Those which happen to be in the location of the potential stalk at the time the cigar stops moving and shoots up the stalk are apparently just lucky. The others sacrifice themselves on their behalf.

This is an extreme case. It is the clearest example I know of a "society" in which a group of apparently equal entities engage in elaborate cooperative behavior, the end product of which is that most of them sacrifice themselves in order to permit some of them to reproduce. There is no obvious central coordination of any sort.

By now, readers will have no doubt realized that I have what I think is an explanation for all of this. Indeed, if they have been paying careful attention, they will have a very good general idea of what I think. I am sure readers will have also come to the conclusion that, although the organization of slime molds does have some relationship to human society, the relationship is distant and certainly offers us no example which we should follow.

The next chapter is devoted to explaining how I think nonhuman cooperation works and how the human social analog to it works. My explanation is, of necessity, rather speculative because, as far as I know, no one has done anything in detail on this before. Indeed, biologists generally have not even raised the question of nonhuman cooperation. Nevertheless, it seems to me of moderate importance and, in a real sense, it is what I aim at in this book.

CHAPTER 7

A THEORY OF COOPERATION

I have emphasized several times that human society does not act in a completely cooperative manner, because individual entities decide "on their own." We have hierarchies. Even though, in some societies, people join or leave hierarchies voluntarily, this leads to a different pattern than we observe in nonhuman nature. We also have a market in which there is direct trading, and there is very little in nonhuman nature which is equivalent to this.

How, then, is cooperation obtained in nature? I suppose readers will not be surprised that my basic model here is drawn from the economics which has been studied since Adam Smith. I assume that the animals, plants, ameboid single-cells of the sponges, and the "individual" cells of the slime molds all have something which is functionally equivalent to the preference function that we find in human beings. Now note that I say only "functionally" equivalent. It must be immensely more primitive, and certainly it is not necessarily mediated by way of a nervous system. The slime mold cell surely does not have one. Nevertheless, the theoretical mechanics of the human preference function can be carried over to even the slime mold.

This book is concerned with social species, but solitaries must also have something similar as a guide to their behavior. Leopards are notably solitary in their lifestyle, but they all engage in somewhat the same efficient pattern of behavior. The mechanism to be elaborated below for social species would work for them, too. They simply would have different "preferences."

The clue here is what I call environmental coordination. Each entity, whatever it is, carries out its own pattern of behavior, and that changes the environment, possibly only to a tiny extent, for other entities. Each of these entities then "decides" what it should do in terms of the new environment. If these preference functions were properly arranged, this could lead to the high level of cooperation that we see in social species. Note, however, that they must be properly arranged. There is no obvious reason why this arrangement should be part of nature. It must be selected by the usual Darwinian process, and this, clearly, would be very difficult. This is probably the reason that social species are much rarer than nonsocial species.

As a simple example, consider a number of termites in their nest and assume that they have extremely simple preference functions; i.e., they are interested only in food and in keeping the nest in good order. Their preferences are subject to the usual declining marginal utility. Put simply, each "unit" of food consumed in a day reduces the individual termite's desire for the next one by some amount. Similarly, if there are only minor things wrong with the nest, the termite is less likely to turn to repair than if there are serious defects. Each "unit" of disrepair increases his desire to do something to improve the nest more than the last.

Suppose our termite, with this simple preference function, is engaged in his (or her) daily round when something damages the nest. The satisfaction that he (or she) can get from repairing it increases, and, hence, the termite is likely to shift to working on such repair. The opposite reaction would be expected if food supplies were short. Further, the individual termite's action changes the environment for the others. If it repairs the nest, the satisfaction that another termite could get from further work on the nest falls. Thus, this repair, by changing the environment for all the termites, changes their behavior.

Presumably, a solitary animal such as a leopard has its own preference function with similar declining marginal utility for each thing that it values.[1] The leopard's preferences, however, do not lead to cooperation. If it captures a gazelle, it improves its own satisfaction, but its only effect on other leopards is a slight reduction in the number of gazelles available for them. Its only contact with other leopards occurs in mating (outside the field of this book) and possible territorial defense. This is hardly cooperative behavior and unlikely to develop a society.

The situation with termites is radically different, but the difference is that the individual termite's preference function is such that its behavior significantly alters the environment of the other termites and, therefore, their behavior. For example, a termite providing food to the nest lowers the urgency of the food demand of others, with the result that individual termites turn to repairing the nest.

In practice, of course, each individual termite faces a somewhat different micro-environment. Exactly how hungry it is and its immediate surroundings are important in its decision as to what it will do. Its activity will affect only a very small part of the nest. Still, if it goes and gets food, the net effect is not only

---

1. So far, I have offered some simple reading for nonbiologists. Here I will offer some simple reading for biologists who are not economists. A good standard text is C. E. Ferguson and S. Charles Maurice, *Economic Analysis* (Homewood, Ill.: R. D. Irwin, 1970, 1974, 1978). Pages 75–215 give you all you need to know on this subject, probably more. Almost any economics text will have a section on the subject.

that it, and possibly other termites to whom it transmits the food, will be less hungry, but also that the need for nest repair will increase slightly.

Of course, the termite's preference function has many more "arguments" in it than the desire for food and the well-repaired nest of our simplified example. All of the "preferences," however, are subject to declining marginal utility, and so the mechanism, if the preferences are the right ones, will lead to the type of social coordination we see.

This structure is very obvious to economists, and we regularly talk about human beings behaving in this way. Frequently, economics texts will point out that it is one of the various reasons why human behavior is coordinated. The fundamental difference is that human beings are able to engage in foresight, can calculate, and have an immensely more complex preference function. These are all differences of degree rather than kind, but the net effect of them, taken all together, is that the resemblance between human behavior and that of a termite is only of the broadest and most general sort.

Earlier, I made the remark that all societies fall, in essence, under the same basic organizational structure, but that you can divide these societies into two great families: one is human society, and the other is all the rest. The fact that I have taken something out of the study of human society and applied it to termites does not prove that we are close to termites any more than the fact that we are both members of the animal kingdom proves it.

Obviously, the preference function is much more complicated than the one I have just given, even with termites. They do not have just two purposes. In addition to the need to repair the nest and gather food, they have many other things. They take care of the young and their royals, defend the nest against attacks, and build new additions to the nest according to whatever is the hereditary pattern of that particular kind of termite. At certain times of the year, they carry out breeding activities, with the result that winged termites fly away and spread the termite species.

All of these can be explained by the process I have outlined above, except that they require a more elaborate set of "preferences." When I refer to these preferences, note that I am not alleging that the termite feels the way we do. The whole thing may be completely automatic. I have a computer on my desk which responds to outside stimuli, sometimes in a most surprising way,[2] and

---

2. One of my former students, who became involved in computer research way back in the early pioneering days, said there were two problems with empirical research. The first was that the research assistants never did what you told them to, and the second was that the computer always did exactly what you told it to.

no one regards it as having any particular feelings. Nevertheless, you could say that it has a "preference function" by which, for example, it rejects certain commands.

Consider the termites at the top of one of those big termite mounds which stick up six or seven feet in parts of Africa. These nests are ventilated by thin channels that run down very close to the outer surface and can exchange gases, with carbon dioxide going out and oxygen coming in. Internal heat is also controlled by similar exchanges. The interior of these nests is kept remarkably stable in temperature in spite of very large fluctuations in outside temperature. Stabilization of the concentration of moisture, carbon dioxide, and oxygen inside is also the result of the termites' activities.

Those termites at the top of the thin channels have the "duty" of opening and closing them in order to adjust the internal nest heat at different times of the day. We can assume they have a "preference" for a particular level of carbon dioxide and a particular temperature. Presumably, it is some complex function of these two variables, because both of them are controlled by the same basic apparatus.

Note that they do not have to have any knowledge about the nest as a whole. They can simply consider the atmosphere which immediately surrounds them personally. If there is too much carbon dioxide, they can open some of the ventilation channels; if there is too little, they can close them. The individual termite need have no notion whatsoever of what is going on in the rest of the nest; indeed, it seems reasonable to say they have no notions of anything granted the size of their brain. Nevertheless, they act as a control just as the governor invented by Watt for steam engines opens or closes the throttle, depending on the speed of rotation.

Other routine behavior of the termite can be explained in the same way. In the literature, there are careful accounts of how termites extending their nest system build arches. There is no reason to believe that the individual termite has any knowledge of an arch at all. It simply has a preference function for placing small bits of stone or dirt in certain positions when its other preferences have been more or less fulfilled and the necessary external stimuli exist. The actions of other termites provide the necessary external stimuli.

Now, once again, all of this uses a preference function like that in human beings, but simpler, and assumes a really extraordinary degree of selectivity in the "preferences" of the nonhuman species. Anyone who has ever watched or thought of ant nests or termite nests or, for that matter, sponges or slime molds realizes that there is an immense amount of careful coordination. The mechanism must, of necessity, be something which is basically hereditary. An hereditary structure which functions in the same way as a human preference function is an obvious candidate.

I must confess here that I have not exhaustively analyzed all other conceivable alternative mechanisms. We do know that human beings have a preference function. We are related distantly, indeed very distantly, to the social species. It seems reasonable to believe that at this primitive level the two systems operate similarly.

I think I should once again pause, as I have from time to time throughout this book, to point out that this does not provide any particular guidance for the design of human society. It does not even particularly help us in studying human society except that it makes a certain amount of difference in how we think about it.

Earlier, I pointed out that the Roman legions practiced with weights on swords. Students of human society trying to apply their techniques to an ant hill are, in essence, doing something similar. Just as this drill meant that the Romans could fight better when they faced a real enemy without weights on their swords, so human social scientists can do a better job of analysis dealing with the human problem if they have first exercised their minds with the kind of problems dealt with in this book.

To return to animal species and sticking temporarily with the termites, from time to time, the entire routine of the nest is disturbed. This disturbance might take the form of a foreign invasion. If it does, and if the termite is one of the species that has soldiers, then the soldiers will take over the defense and, to repeat what I have said before, do not do terribly well.[3]

Other termites will undertake other activities, such as attempting to remove the eggs and shuttling the royal pair into a protected area. Whether they are successful in saving the nest is, of course, as dubious as the outcome of the human wars. Nevertheless, in this emergency, the "preference function" does give each individual something to do, and they adjust to this radical change in environment—perhaps not well—but they do adjust.

A more routine disturbance in the life of a termite colony is the breeding season, during which the nest is driven very strongly toward producing and

---

3. Dealing with both anteaters and chimpanzees, both of whom stick something into the nest—the tongue of the anteater and a stick from the chimpanzee—the soldiers are actually of negative utility. Their response is to bite down hard on it, and, therefore, they are drawn up into the mouth of the anteater or out of the nest and then licked off the stick by the chimpanzees.

then releasing a cloud of reproductives. Some biologists refer to the production of the next generation as the basic objective of almost any species, including the social insects. It is not clear to me that these things have brains enough to have a basic objective. In any event, I think what we should not say is that this is the only objective. The reproductive period is, indeed, something of a crisis, but we should not exaggerate its importance. It is true that if the reproductive operation fails, there will be no next generation, but the same is also true if the nest fails before it gets around to the reproduction crisis.

What we observe from the outside is that for a period of time the number of reproductives is rapidly increased. Then, at some particular point, all of these reproductives leave the nest and fly. In many species of termites, a number of different nests in the same general vicinity will release their reproductives at the same time, thus maximizing the likelihood of fertilization by non-relatives and minimizing the likelihood of predation, since the predators will tend to be swamped. Exactly what cues the various termite nests use to get this simultaneous release are not known, but, presumably, they have something to do with meteorological conditions or possibly sun angles.

This is a general change in the behavior of the nest and of most of its members. It seems almost certain that this is caused by a change in the nest environment, with a number of special pheromones being released and circulated through the nest, thus changing the reactions of each individual termite.

There is no doubt that the royal pair in termites, or the queen in ants, is a source of pheromones somewhat different from those of the other termites. Since they are hidden way inside the nest, and have practically no contact with the outside world, it is dubious that the royal pair or queen is responsible for this particular pheromone change which leads to initiating the breeding cycle.

It seems far more likely that those termites or ants which have contact with the outer world and which would, therefore, receive the cues of the time of year, etc., are the ones actually making the basic pheromone change. It would, presumably, be a situation in which a relatively small number of ants or termites initiate the production of the necessary pheromone change. This leads to the breeding cycle and then rapidly spreads through the nest and not only changes behavior in other ways but also changes the production of pheromones. Indeed, the royals might be stimulated by this to greater productivity rather than acting as the control.

In any event, the change in behavior around the breeding period is very substantial, and, once again, we have a large number of individual entities engaging in active cooperative behavior without either a market in which they exchange things or a direct hierarchy. Environmental coordination must exist here.

About the differences in behavior during the breeding cycle: the really extreme difference, of course, is in the reproductives themselves. Having been brought up in the dark and carefully controlled tunnels of the termite nests, they suddenly find themselves out in the open. They fly—something they have never done before, will never do again, and that no other termite does—and then attempt to start a new nest. All of this is radically different than the life of the ordinary termite or the life of the royal pair in the rest of the cycle.

Since there is no obvious reason to believe that the genes of the royal pair are particularly different from those of the workers, it must be that all of the termites have the built-in potential behavior patterns for both the royals and the workers. In the case of the workers, the royal part of the behavior is suppressed; in the case of the royals, the reverse is true.

This is not, of course, the only diversity. Termites tend to go in for elaborate castes; for example, soldiers are radically different from workers, and there are different kinds of workers. Further, as mentioned, they go through a series of molts as they grow. In the process, they become generally larger and change their behavior pattern in accordance with their size. Instructions for all these things must be contained in the DNA of all the termites.[4]

Looking at it from the standpoint of a single termite: when it comes out of the egg, its treatment will determine whether it is to be a reproductive and eventually fly away,[5] not do a lick of work but defend the nest when necessary, or be a worker of some particular caste which, over the course of its life, will engage in a considerable number of different activities, depending on what particular instar it is in. The basic reason it adopts one or the other of these courses of action is the immediate environment—the way it is fed and dealt with by the other termites.

However, this raises the question of what directs the nurse termites, and it seems almost certain that they are behaving according to the same kind of environmental coordination I have discussed above. When a successful[6] new termite nest is formed, it will produce only workers at first. After a relatively

---

4. Since there are both male and female termites in all of these roles, it is possible that there is some difference in the DNA of males and females other than that needed for those that become royals. As far as I know, no one has discovered whether this is true or not.

5. On some occasions, reproductives are used as replacements inside the nest.

6. The overwhelming majority of reproductives, of course, are subject to predation.

short time, however, it may begin producing one or two soldiers. Since the soldiers require more food, this is a luxury in a way.

The only basic explanation for it is simply that the number of workers and soldiers encountered by an individual termite engaged in nursing is taken into account by it in deciding how it shall allocate its nursing effort. I might even go further than that: the decision must be cooperative, since it is not true that an individual nurse termite will specialize in just a few eggs or nymphs.

Apparently, as the number of workers grows in this new nest, a situation arises in which the preference function of the termites engaged in nursing begins to show "desires" to produce soldiers. It would be more or less the same in all of the nurses, and the existence of a couple of pre-soldiers among their brood would reduce the urgency, with the result that only a few would be produced. It would again be cooperation induced by a preference function and environmental cooperation. Once again, the termite's action changes the environment so that other termites face a somewhat different environment, and, hence, their behavior is somewhat changed.

I have only rather generally referred to the circulation of pheromones in the nest, although it is surely of considerable importance. Much of the literature on social insects has adopted the communication theory developed essentially in the Bell Laboratories and talks about bits of information and direct communication. That there is integration is clear, and that individual termites affect the behavior of others is also clear. The question is whether it should be referred to as an information transfer. Now, I do not doubt that the mathematics developed by so many physical scientists worrying about telephone communication can also be applied to the termites. Normally, of course, the social insects and other social species transmit very little information compared with what is transmitted by a telephone system, but still the mathematics apply. What I am saying is that perhaps it should not really be referred to as communication.

Consider a bee nest in which the queen bee actually does undeniably release pheromones which affect the behavior of all the other bees. She also produces eggs which affect the behavior of all the other bees. In both cases, what she is doing is changing the environment, and the other individuals are responding to that change.

I realize that the difference between this and the human communication system is one of degree, but it is a very large one. Suppose I receive a telephone call inviting me to dinner and I accept. Firstly, the communication is directed actually to me and not just released into the environment for anybody who wishes to pick up. Secondly, there is a volitional act on the part of the person who transmits the communication as well as on the part of the person who receives it.

There are, of course, some cases in which, within the nonhuman social species, this is also true. The alarm given when an ant nest is being invaded is clearly a volitional act on the part of the ants, insofar as anything generated by such a primitive mental system can be regarded as volitional. Even here, however, the "communications" are automatic and are not "intended."

Once again, think of the bee queen affecting the behavior of other bees by releasing pheromones and also by laying eggs. In both cases, the environment is changed, and the worker bees respond to that changed environment by appropriate behavior. It is possible evolutionally that the function of the pheromone is entirely to control the behavior of the other bees, whereas the function of the egg is only partially to control. This provides us with a difference; nevertheless, the fact remains that both are changes to the environment so that the other bees will adjust to that environmental change and the nest will continue to survive.

Before going further with this theory, I should like to point out that in a strict sense heredity is not entirely determined by DNA. Once the cells begin to specialize in any way, cell division, which generates the growth of the larger entity, will provide not only duplicate sets of the DNA but also other parts of the differentiated cell.

For example, consider your skin cells. Generally, they have the same DNA as those cells which make up your brain. The rest of the cell protoplasm contains many differences, however. These cells are formed by division of similar cells, which have many differences from, say, a nerve cell. The DNA is the same, but the rest of the cell also divides, and, hence, the new cells "inherit" much more than the DNA. This "much more" is different in cells performing different functions. The protoplasm in the skin cell is not identical to that which would be provided in the event that one of your nerve cells began to divide. The inheritance of that cell is not entirely the same, regardless of where it comes from. We can say that its DNA components are pretty much identical,[7] but the remainder of the cell may be quite different in many ways.

This is important when we think about development of specialized castes in the social insects or, for that matter, among the amoeboid entities that

---

7. There are both errors in transcriptions and other mutations which may make the DNA of different cells nonidentical, even within the same entity.

wander around inside the sponge. Once the specialization has begun, let us say, after the bees have begun providing a larger cell and additional queen jelly to the larvae of the potential queen in a bee nest, it may affect the parts of the cell other than the DNA, with the result that the proceeding cell division produces somewhat different cells. Thus, in a true sense, they are not exactly like the workers' cells. The cells in the queen bee might be, on the whole, quite different from those in the workers, although, so far as I know, this is not true in that case. In the case of the amoeboid and other single-cell entities that operate in the sponge, they must be quite different, because the individual cells behave quite differently.

This does not change the environmental coordination I have been describing above, but, in some cases, it makes it a little more indirect. Each of the entities would adjust to its environment and, by its action, change the environment for others a little bit. If, however, the entities are different (not in their DNA, but in the rest of the cell components), the response would not be identical. Nevertheless, the development of these different cells would come from activity of the nurse ants or whatever it is in earlier life.

The obvious way to think of this is to think about cells within a large entity such as yourself. You started as a single fertilized egg cell, and this cell began dividing. Rather quickly, these cells began developing specializations. In the early days of embryo growth, removing the cell from one part of it and putting it in another part might well lead to its simply adapting itself to the new environment; i.e., it is still highly flexible. After a while, however, if it is brought across from one tissue to another, it will have enough "inherited" differences so that it is unable to adjust to the new environment. Its DNA will be the same as its new neighbors', but the rest of the cell components will differ.

This phenomenon, which I will turn to later when discussing cells in larger bodies, is also probably true in those social insects which have caste differentiation. As mentioned before, the amoeboid cells of the sponge have differentiation. Some of them, indeed, cease to be amoeboid and become skin or sexual mechanisms. Thus, the situation is not completely flexible. Not only is the termite mound, to some extent, committed once it has begun producing specialized types, the individual ant larva is, to some extent, committed once the nurses begin treating it in such a way that it will become, let us say, a queen. Of course, the sexual division is highly important here also. In that case, the DNA is not the same in the two sexes. Nevertheless, it seems likely that cells in a worker bee are not identical to those of the queen bee. When the queen bee is killed, it may be possible for the other bees to create new queens by the appropriate feeding of certain larvae that have already been produced. It is not always possible, however. It may be that cells have already adjusted to the more limited diet of the worker and, hence, cannot be made to adjust to the queen's diet. It would be the same as one of your skin cells being transplanted to a muscle area to which it cannot adapt.

So far, the discussion has been solely about things that are normally referred to as societies. Further, these societies are radically different than human societies. The first thing to be mentioned, as a way of difference, is that the human society cannot easily be regarded as genetically specified. The human race developed in the Old Stone Age under conditions which were very radically different from present-day conditions.

It seems likely that humans lived in hunter-gatherer bands which were nomadic and small. The bands might have friendly or unfriendly relations with neighboring bands, but essentially the society was that of the band itself. It is likely that the internal structure of these bands was rather like that of a baboon tribe. If it was not, some of their ancestors must have had that kind of structure, since the earliest pre-humans found seem to have lived in groups.

Beginning about 10,000 years ago, in favored parts of the world and later elsewhere, human beings progressed from the Old Stone Age to the New Stone Age. They became at least somewhat sedentary and began living in larger groups supported by agriculture.[8] They also had somewhat more permanent relations with neighboring groups. It is not known whether villages federated in some way. Evidence that they did is to be found in the rather elaborate grave goods in some burials. It is clear that there was considerable difference in the status of members of these societies. The ornateness of grave goods sometimes found gives rise to the theory that the person buried was of high status, not in a single village, but in a collection of them. Thus, small empires may have started very early.

It should be said that some human beings have progressed out of this status only recently. When Columbus reached the American continent, the native population was living in the New Stone Age, without wheels, with little metal,[9] and with only a few domesticated animals.[10] The blackfellows of

8. They continued to hunt and fish, of course. Indeed, we still do.

9. They had copper, silver, and gold.

10. Most of our present domesticated animals come from the Eurasian land mass. Failure to domesticate anything much except the turkey, llama, and guinea pig does not reflect on the ability of the Indians, but on their natural environment.

Australia were not even up to this level when they first came into contact with whites.

It should be emphasized that this technological backwardness does not indicate that they were inferior in other ways. Australian blackfellows, who, in physical equipment, were about as primitive as you can get, were able to live in such a harsh environment because of the high level of the skills they had developed. They had, for example, the ability to recognize human footprints, something which no one else could do. They also could engage in collective hunting without anyone giving orders—a most remarkable feat.

In the American continent, the so-called civilized tribes, roughly referred to as the Incas, the Mayas, and the Aztecs,[11] had large architectural structures (although no arch) and centralized government. The Mayas certainly could read and write, and the question of whether the Aztecs could is, to some extent, still open. The Incas could not.

The point of describing these radically different levels of civilization from the blackfellows through the Indians to the Mesopotamian pioneers of modern civilization is the clear-cut evidence that there is nothing genetic about it. The American Indian, the blackfellows, and various other groups have had not the slightest difficulty in adjusting. Those who have been brought up in contact with civilization immediately become mechanics, doctors, or even college professors. It is true that tribal people brought over as adults into modern culture frequently have difficulty adjusting, but this clearly is not a matter of genetic inheritance.

Therefore, it is clear that our society is not inherited in the same way that the other societies discussed in this book are. Nevertheless, it must be true that our inheritance at least permits development of a large civilization.

We also have inherited components in our preference function, although anybody who has had much contact with radically different civilizations[12] realizes it is not the whole story. Clearly, a great many of our preferences are learned, and, equally clearly, these preferences depend, to some extent, on how we have been brought up. There clearly is a large hereditary component. We walk upright, eat regularly, put pictures on our walls,[13] and have many other drives which are pretty uniform across the human race.

---

11. Because all three of these engaged in human sacrifice—the Aztecs on a large scale and the Mayas in ceremonial torture—there are people who would deny that they were civilized.

12. Chinese, in my case.

13. It is very hard to give a natural selection motive for this.

To postulate that we do have a set of hereditary preferences, and these preferences are at least helpful in the development of society, it is clear they do not directly lead to the development of society. Our societies are too diverse and, for that matter, too radically different from nonhuman societies for an hereditary component to be even remotely as closely and as sizeably determinant as it is with ants.

I said before that we use hierarchies, something we do not find in the animals, and the market. I have not discussed at any length why I think animals do not have the market, although I have talked a good deal about my conviction that they do not have hierarchies.

The first thing to be said about the market is that there is no direct trading in the nonhuman world. If there is something in the possession of one animal or plant that another wants, the stronger simply seizes it. Earlier I mentioned that some of the wasps seem to appreciate the liquid which is produced by their larvae when they feed them. This is not a clear-cut trait, however, because if a wasp does not have any food to give a larva, it is likely to assault the larva in an effort to get the liquid.

The closest thing to formal trade we have in the nonhuman societies involves radically different species. The flowers and the insects developed more or less at the same time, and they engage in what I suppose can be called a primitive trade. Flowering plants produce nectar and, for that matter, excess pollen which attract insects. Then the insects, by flying to other flowers with the pollen from the first, act as a fertilizing agent of the flowers.

In a number of cases, the flowers and the insects that deal with them are quite highly specialized; in others, it is a generalized rather than competitive business. The honeybees, for example, go from flower to flower, and many of these flowers are also visited by bumblebees and other insects. There is no sign of what might be called a property arrangement in which one bee's nest "owns" a particular set of flowers.[14] The flowers compete for the bees, and the bees compete for the flowers.

Although this can be referred to as some kind of a trade, note that there is no by-unit exchange, no way for them to come into equilibrium except by death through starvation in insects or failure to reproduce from nonpollination on the part of plants. This is, nevertheless, the closest approximation of market activities to be found in the nonhuman world. But, clearly, the phrase "closest" should be replaced by "least remote."

---

14. As described above, the tropical stingless bees sometimes fight "wars" over a given tree in bloom.

Thus, human society, with its hierarchies and markets, and nonhuman societies, without these two phenomena which, to a very large extent, control our lives, are radically different. I do think that studying the nonhuman societies is of help to the student of human societies. In recent years, biologists have been using many intellectual tools, taking from human economics for their own purposes. Cross stimulation is helpful, but in neither the human nor the nonhuman field is it more than a rather minor aspect. This book, I hope, will attract both biologists and students of human societies. I hope it will also be of help to them, but I would be very surprised if that help was really major.

CHAPTER 8

A SOCIETY OF CELLS

When I was in school, one of the popular theories of society was the "organic society." According to this view, society was not truly a freely contracting set of humans, but a more solid structure. This particular view has ceased to be common; indeed, I seldom see it even mentioned today. This is partly due to the fact that during World War II we were at war with the Nazis, who held this view. It can hardly be explained entirely that way, since the view was also held by a good many people on the left. In essence, it was a possible alternative to what you may call the libertarian view of society.

Obviously, I have no intent of reviving this organic theory, but the purpose of this short final chapter of this book is to suggest that its mirror image is correct. One should normally consider organisms as, to some extent, being societies, specifically, societies of individual cells.

This may seem a startling idea to most readers, although there are biologists and doctors who have already reached the same conclusion. Aside from its startling nature, it is hard to find any strong argument against it.

It is true, of course, that most of the cells of the human body are fixed in location; i.e., they are not mobile. But this is true only of most. Your body includes white blood cells,[1] which move around freely and somewhat resemble amoebas. There are other constituents in the blood, such as red cells or platelets, that also move freely. The platelets are, in fact, a sort of equivalent of the soldier ants, in that they go to places where structure has been damaged and begin the process of repair. They defend the body in the same sense—although not with the same tools, of course—as the soldiers among the ants and termites.

But mobility is not necessary to be a part of a society. In the sponges, for example, a considerable number of cells are fixed in location. They make up the skin and various other special functional parts and are served by the amoeboid cells, which are freely movable. There is no reason why a society could not be composed of relatively immobile cells or other entities. Ectoprocts, a bizarre social entity, are composed of smaller units which do not move about. The reference to the society of nonmoving entities is unusual, but not unheard of.

---

1. White cells is an old term. We now divide them into very large numbers of specialized cells. For our purposes, we need not go into that.

In every other respect, the cells of the human body or any other body have most of the requirements for a society. Like the amoeba of the sponge, or the individual cell of the slime mold, they do not seem to have any mentality, but they respond to their environment, and they change the environment and, hence, influence others.

In recent years, the interaction of neighboring cells has been a major field of study. This interaction, although rarely discussed in the terms we have used in this book, is an example of cooperative action. Each cell grows and releases certain chemicals and absorbs certain other chemicals and, in doing so, affects other cells in the body. It is also affected by them.

The clearest case of this, of course, is the specialization of our cells as we develop. It has been discussed before but can be profitably repeated here. The initial cells are literally identical, but as the single cell develops into an embryo, the cells rather quickly begin to specialize. Presumably, the specialization is guided by DNA, but, with time, the cell begins to be irreversibly different from cells in other organs.

Individual cells which will eventually become muscle begin to develop in selected parts of the embryo. Once they have begun to develop, they are self-perpetuating to a considerable extent. The individual cell, once it has acquired some of the characteristics of the muscle cell, then divides and transfers not only its DNA but the specialized cell characteristics. After a while, it becomes sufficiently specialized as a "muscle cell" so that if it is transplanted to some other part of the embryo it dies. At the same time, the existence of these muscle cells influences the production of further cells in the direction of being muscles or cells of the various things that are connected with, or close to, muscles.

All of this is, in essence, a cooperative activity of a very large number of entities. We can, if we wish, say that the entity is the collection of DNA molecules which are the same in each cell and that the cooperation leads to a larger entity which is, we hope, efficient.

I mentioned that this chapter would be short, and, short though it is, it is rather startling. It will startle biologists and doctors less than laymen, but, even to them, it is far from orthodox. There does not seem to be any argument against it except orthodoxy, however. We are not accustomed to using words in this way, but, if you think about it carefully, the statement that the human body is a society of cooperating cells makes sense.

As in the social insects, there is some control. The control of some cells over the others is just like the control of some social insects over the others.

There is the release of hormones from certain controlling organs, which affects the development of operations of other cells.

This, to some extent, is like the release of pheromones by the queen of an ant nest but is far more specialized. We have far more organs engaging in releasing specialized pheromones, and there are only a few ants that are releasing specialized pheromones. On the other hand, it is likely that almost all of them—ants, termites, etc.—release pheromones which affect the others to some extent. This is probably true with human beings, also.

We referred earlier to the alarm behavior which ants will undertake when the ant nest is invaded and the measures they take to protect it. The same, once again, happens in human society. If we are invaded, i.e., somebody sticks a knife in us or there are harmful bacteria, our alarm system alerts the defenses. The white corpuscles come to deal with the bacteria while the platelets and other repair facilities come to attempt to repair organic damage. This is, presumably, the result of the release of some kind of chemical into the general environment by the cells that are being damaged. This is alarm behavior just like the alarm behavior of the ants.

Humans do differ from other societies in that we have an internal nervous system. The individual ant, of course, has a nervous system, but there is no nervous system connecting one ant to the other. Humans have a centralized control system. This is different and gives us the ability to do things which we could not do if we depended entirely on chemical stimuli.

These nerve cells, however, develop in the same way as everything else in the human body and can be regarded as simply other members of the cooperative arrangement. They are specialized cells carrying out specialized functions, and, if we think these particular specialized functions are immensely important, we cannot deny that they are direct heirs of the initial fertilized egg by which we began. In the development of cooperation, they "chose" one line, and the muscle cells "chose" another.

Sociobiologists, in their first works, drew a lot of lessons on human behavior from the behavior of animals. I do not want to argue there are absolutely no such lessons, but surely they are rare, and we should inspect candidates with great care. That our cell structure has some resemblance to nonhuman societies, however, is, I think, true. Fortunately, it should raise no serious difficulties, because, speaking frankly, I can think of no implications for human social society which can be drawn from it. To say that the human body is a society of cells and has some resemblance, in this respect, to an ant nest is not to say that we should model our behavior on the ants.

We now come to the end of our survey. I hope the reader has enjoyed it and has learned. I think it is of some—not very great, but some—help to both biologists studying nonhuman societies and students studying human societies. Mainly, however, it has involved taking things we have learned from human societies and applying them to nonhuman societies.

In the process, we have improved our intellectual tools, but we did not learn anything of a revolutionary nature about human societies. The objective has not been to change our view of human society but to improve our understanding of nonhuman societies, taking techniques that we develop in human societies and using them to study animals. I hope that I have been successful and that readers now know more in these areas than they did when they started.

PART 4

PUBLIC FINANCE

SCIENCE FICTION AND THE DEBT

Suppose that a scientist has invented a remarkable machine. It will, on a strictly temporary basis, create gold bars. If it is set properly, gold bars in unlimited quantities will pour out. There is, however, a limitation: the gold must be returned to the machine within 20 years or certain conservation laws will be violated, and there will be an unimaginable catastrophe. If 100 gold bars are produced by the machine, 100 gold bars must be put back in. The bars returned to the machine simply disappear. The machine is already in existence in the scientist's laboratory and its operation is costless.

The scientist, being patriotic, offers the government exclusive use of this device for purposes of governmental finance. A bill is passed providing that a certain quantity of gold bars is to be temporarily produced and sold to the public, the proceeds to be used to cover various governmental expenditures. The bill also obligates the government 20 years in the future to buy back the gold and return it to the machine. Who bears the burden of the governmental expenditures?

Clearly, no one is in any way injured at the time the expenditure is made.[1] There is, then, no burden at the time. Twenty years later, however, it will be necessary to tax people for this purpose, and, hence, there will be a burden. What has happened is that the total wealth of the nation has been temporarily increased by the machine. Later, when the gold bars are returned to the machine, the national wealth will be reduced and the only burden felt by anyone is the result of this decrease.

Since the nation's wealth has increased at the time the gold bars appear, it is quite probable that both consumption and saving would also increase. Further, some individuals might decide that because their wealth has now increased, it would be sensible to invest money to offset the potential reduction in wealth which will occur 20 years in the future. Granted the uncertainty of all human affairs, it is not obvious that very many people would do this. Further, different people would choose different amounts. Certainly, the

Reprinted, with permission of Blackwell Publishing, from *Deficits*, ed. James M. Buchanan, Charles K. Rowley, and Robert D. Tollison (Oxford: Basil Blackwell, 1987), 75–78.

This article is a drastically modernized version of "Public Debt—Who Bears the Burden?" in *Rivista di dirrito finanziario e scienza delle finanze*, 22.

1. Any change in purchasing patterns does not affect some producers, but I follow the usual custom of ignoring both injuries and benefits from this source. Presumably, also, there would be some changes in investment patterns.

number of citizens who bought just exactly the right amount of assets (gold bars or otherwise) to meet what they thought was their likely cost in the future from the vanishing gold bars and who correctly anticipated that amount would be extremely unusual.

It would be inconvenient, however, for the gold-bar salesmen to carry around large stocks of heavy gold bars. Suppose then that when an individual purchases a gold bar from a government representative, he is given a receipt. The government undertakes, when the receipt is presented at the laboratory, to turn on the machine, produce a gold bar, and give it to the receiptholder. Different people, of course, would present their receipts at different times. It would be absurd, however, to assume that this changed things particularly. Mr A pays a salesman and receives his receipt. He promptly rushes to the laboratory and gets his gold bar. Lazy Mr B, on the other hand, pays a salesman on the same day as Mr A but puts off his visit to the laboratory until the following week, when he will be in that part of town on another errand. Suppose that the government spends the money that it has received from Mr A and Mr B during the interval. Does this make any difference? Surely, it would be absurd to say that a burden is imposed on the "present generation" when the government spends the money Mr B has paid in but not when it spends that paid in by Mr A. Further, this would require assuming that the burden somehow vanished when Mr B actually got his gold to reappear 20 years later.

Having a bar of gold around the house is, in some ways, inconvenient. It might be that some of the buyers of gold would decide to simply keep their receipt until such time as they actually needed the gold for some purpose. Clearly, since they consciously choose to hold the receipt instead of converting it into gold, they are in no way disadvantaged by the fact that they have no gold. To say that their choice in this matter somehow imposes a burden on their "generation" which would not have existed had they decided to exchange their receipts for gold seems ridiculous. Surely, the only person affected by the choice would be the chooser, and he cannot be assumed to be "burdened" by the results of his free choice.

The same conclusion would apply if some purchaser chose to keep his receipt for the full 20 years, with the consequence that the gold bar never even came into existence. It is still clear that no one suffers any burden when the government makes its sale and spends the proceeds. There is, however, a real burden on the taxpayers when the gold or certificates are repurchased.

Suppose the government produces the gold but keeps it in its own vaults, selling only warehouse receipts to the public. If it were necessary to return the identical gold bars to the machine this might well be a sensible precaution. If the government paid small amounts each year to the holders of the warehouse receipts, then they would hardly differ at all from bonds. The same thing would be true, of course, if the government contracted with a bank to store the gold instead of keeping it in its own vaults. Another alternative would be to sell the gold bars, but subject to the restriction that the purchaser, or his assigns, must preserve the individual bars and resell those specific bars to the government in 20 years. Since the purchaser would be providing storage for the gold, regular payments to him for this service would be sensible; thus the gold bars themselves would have a remarkable economic resemblance to bonds.

We can make a still further change. One of the advantages of an imaginary machine is that we can easily make changes in its design. Suppose, then, that the gold produced by the machine is rather peculiar in its nature. The process of making the gold has an aftereffect which leads the gold bars to expand at the rate of 4 per cent per year for the full 20 years. The government could sell these bars to the public and would then be completely free of any obligation for 20 years. The expansion of the bars, however, would give the holders a net return from the mere act of keeping them. At the end of the 20-year period, of course, the government would have to buy back all the gold, including that which had grown from the original bars, and this would be the equivalent of the discounted cost of paying 4 per cent interest over the period. This would appear a particularly clear case of shifting burdens to the future. Present taxpayers would pay nothing for the benefits they derive from the government expenditure, while the taxpayers of 20 years in the future, quite a different group of people, would pay an enormous fee for which they received nothing. Its economic effect on both individuals and the government, on the other hand, would be substantially identical with that of 20-year government bonds similar to the E Bonds which were so important in the financing of the American participation in the Second World War.

Following an example from Paul Samuelson: let us suppose that after the government has started this programme, the machine suddenly stops working, with the result that, as a matter of fact, no gold is produced. Would this make any difference? It is, of course, like the world store of gold on an island which sinks beneath the sea. As long as people think the gold is there, its nonexistence makes no difference.

All of this may seem simply playing with an unreal system, but it does serve to clarify the situation. None of the assumed sets of circumstances raises any problem for the economist who assumes that borrowing money rather than raising the same sum through taxation transfers the burden of the expenditure to the shoulders of future taxpayers. The economist who believes that such transfers do not take place, on the other hand, has great difficulty in dealing with these cases. Since some of the assumed sets of circumstances are economically identical with bond issues, this would seem to demonstrate that the "shifting" hypothesis is the correct one.

In order to make the point absolutely clear, let us introduce one final bit of science fiction. Suppose that 18 years after the original machine is put in operation another scientist discovers another machine. This machine makes it unnecessary to return the gold bars to the first scientist's machine. Thus, the burden of the original expenditures disappears. If the burden were transferred 20 years into the future, then it is still 2 years in the future at the time this machine is developed, and no problems are raised. If, however, the burden were borne by the economy when the gold bars were first produced, then it is eliminated retroactively, which is absurd.

The point of all this has been, essentially, that a government bond is, in a real sense, something that people want. Further, this item is available to anyone who wants, who in turn knows exactly how much of it he has. On the other side, we have at least potentially increased future taxes above what they would otherwise be. Those people who are expert at anticipating the future, and who happen to have a personal discount rate which is exactly the same as the market, and who do not have any superior investment opportunities buy our gold bars up to the amount of their future tax obligation. Truly such people will be a very small minority of the population.

There is one difference between our gold bar and a bond. The government may choose to pay off its bonded indebtedness by that specialized tax on money and bonds called inflation. Our science fiction model could be modified to parallel this situation, but for the time being let us simply point out that the very real potential of this happening means that buying government bonds or, indeed, any fixed return investment is a risky way of protecting yourself against future tax liabilities. Whether it is more or less risky than investing in real assets is not obvious. The world is a dangerous place, and exact anticipation of the future is unlikely.

SUBSIDIZED HOUSING IN
A COMPETITIVE MARKET

COMMENT

Edgar Olsen's recent article in this *Review* is a significant contribution to clarifying the economics of a complex and difficult area.[1] It is not the purpose of this comment to raise any questions as to his economic analysis, but to point out that, granted competition, it might be extremely difficult to subsidize low-income family consumption of superior housing by the method he suggests. In a sense, my objection is against interest, since I myself would much prefer that any subsidies on housing for lower-income families use the Olsen method rather than the method of direct government provision. As I shall suggest later, however, there is another possible procedure which I regard as superior to either the provision of public housing or the Olsen subsidy.

For simplicity, assume that some poor person receiving subsidies under the Olsen procedure would normally spend $60 a month on rent. He is permitted to purchase for $60 a $100 rent certificate which can then be used to rent superior housing. This amounts to giving him an income supplement of $40, but attempting to compel him to use it for one particular purpose. His utility would be higher if you simply gave him the $40 and permitted him to spend it on anything he chose. It seems reasonable that if you did so he would indeed improve his housing, but would also improve his consumption of other goods as well. To use a rough rule of thumb, let us assume that if he were given $40 in cash every month, he would choose to spend $10 of this in increasing his consumption of housing—renting an apartment at $70—and spend the other $30 on other matters. Clearly, from the standpoint of the poor person, the receipt of a direct subsidy would be superior.

Granted that this is so and that the market is highly competitive (even if not perfectly competitive), it seems likely that the individual would be able to find a landlord who is willing to rent him an apartment which is normally worth $70 for the $100 certificate, and then make an under-the-table rebate to him of $30. Olsen says that, "It would be illegal to exchange these certificates for

Reprinted, with permission of the American Economic Association, from *American Economic Review* 61 (March 1971): 218–19.

1. E. A. Olsen, "A Competitive Theory of the Housing Market," *American Economic Review* 59 (Sept. 1969): 612–22.

other than housing services," but it seems to me that this is a type of crime which is extremely hard to detect. The only people involved would be the landlord and the poor tenant, and both would benefit from the crime. The so-called crimes without victims, such as gambling, prostitution, and drug sale, all present problems in enforcing the law. In fact many people, including myself, feel that these laws should be repealed. Olsen, in effect, is creating a new "crime without victim," and we can assume similar problems in enforcement. Further, intensive police activity to limit rebates might create a risk, with the result that both the poor person and the landlord would be worse off than if the police activity did not exist, but most rebating would continue.

From the standpoint of the recipient, such a rent certificate is inferior to a direct cash payment. Surely there is some cash payment of slightly less cost to the state than the rent certificate which would be, from the standpoint of the recipient, superior to the certificate. Granting this, it seems to me that we should aim at direct cash payment. I presume that Olsen would agree. The reason he is advocating this particular mechanism is because he believes that subsidies aimed at increasing poor persons' consumption of housing services, rather than simply increasing their incomes, are a more or less permanent part of our economy, and he wishes to make them more efficient. I cannot quarrel with this desire on his part, but I doubt that his particular technique would work. It seems to me that we would be better advised to try to change government policy toward raising the incomes of the poor rather than trying to adjust their consumption toward the qualitative standards of those who are not poor.

OPTIMAL POLL TAXES

Most discussions of poll taxes have been either moral or linguistic. So far as I know, there has been no rigorous attempt to determine what is the efficient level of poll taxes, although most political scientists appear to think that the answer would be zero. There are, indeed, some students who favor a negative poll tax in the form of a fine or punishment for non-voting. But, to repeat, the arguments for these positions have characteristically been either moral or linguistic.

The moral arguments are essentially unanswerable. No doubt there are moral codes under which a zero or negative poll tax is morally correct and anything else morally wrong. Equally certain, there are moral codes which require a positive poll tax. Indeed, I think we may make the generalization that there is no conceivable human activity that is not proper by at least one set of morals and improper by at least one other.

The argument from the linguistic standpoint, i.e., determining what the word "democracy" means and then deducing whether some activity is or is not democratic in terms of that definition, is essentially a hangover from the ancient Greeks. In order to communicate with one another, we need to have a fairly clear idea of what the words we use mean. It does not follow, however, from the fact that some particular type of human behavior falls within the definition of the word "democracy" that the activity is either good or bad.

There are methods of discussing social issues which depend on neither morality nor linguistic analysis, and it is my proposal to subject the problem of the poll tax to such an analysis. I should like to begin with the negative poll tax, which, for simplicity, we shall assume is indistinguishable from compulsory voting. Whether this tax takes the form of a monetary fine for not voting, jailing, or some other punishment, need not concern us now.

Suppose, then, we have a country which has 105 people eligible to vote, of whom 100 regularly vote and 5 do not. It is proposed that legislation be enacted which would compel the 5 non-voters to vote. The first thing to note is that the 5 people who are now compelled to vote have surely had their level of satisfaction lowered, because their previous behavior indicated they pre-

Reprinted, with permission of the International Atlantic Economic Society, from *Atlantic Economic Journal* 3 (April 1975): 1–6.

ferred not to vote.[1] Those who were voting before the compulsory voting registration rule was put into effect also are injured, since they now individually have less political power than they had before. They now cast one vote out of 105 instead of one vote out of 100. Thus, all 105 people in this society find they are worse off after the change than before. It is an unambiguous case of inverse Paretian change, i.e., a situation in which everyone is injured and no one is benefited. Similarly, if such compulsory legislation already existed, removing it would injure no one and benefit everyone, as long as we consider only this rather bloodless political power variable.

Suppose, however, we look at this from the standpoint of some individual who has some specific preference for policy outcomes. Let us suppose that Mr. Smith is violently opposed to George Wallace and wishes to have his vote as low as possible. He is aware of the fact that Wallace's support among those who do not vote currently is higher than it is among those who do vote. He would, then, be opposed to compulsory voting, not for the reason I have given above, but because he feels he can predict the outcome from compulsory voting, and he regards it as inferior.

Mr. Jones, on the other hand, favors Wallace and would like to have him obtain as high a percentage of the vote as possible. Therefore, making exactly the same prediction as to the behavior of the non-voters, he might be in favor of compulsory voting because it makes it more likely that his preference will be realized.

From the standpoint of these two individuals, there is nothing irrational in their positions, although it should be pointed out that those elections which they can currently predict are only a very small part of the total elections they will see during the rest of their lives, and hence the political power calculation we gave before might be a wiser one for them to follow. Nevertheless, if they put enough weight on their favor or antagonism to George Wallace, they might decide to take their chances on all other elections in order to benefit themselves with regard to this issue.

In this situation, Mr. Jones is giving up part of his power to influence future events, because he believes that the general change will, in fact, lead to a decision that he favors. The situation can be most readily analyzed if we consider some individual who is, on the whole, unhappy with the outcomes produced by the democratic country in which he lives and votes. There is a

---

1. There is a very special circumstance in which this proposition might not be true. It will be discussed below.

potential dictator in this country whose preferences for policy are such that the individual feels that policy would be more in accord with his desires if that man were dictator. The individual, under these circumstances, might favor the dictatorship over democracy. In doing so, however, he would be expressing a desire for certain policy outcomes, even though it actually reduced his personal power to affect outcomes.

The distinction between my power to affect future decisions and my prediction as to the outcome under different possible institutional structures may be a bit subtle, but it is real. Even an individual who would be happier under some particular dictatorship than in a democracy would, nevertheless, have to admit that his personal power was lower in the dictatorship than in the democracy.

Here, however, let us leave our reference individuals and consider society as a whole. For simplicity, assume that of our current 100 voters, we know that 51 favor A and 49 $\overline{A}$, and it is known that of the 5 people not voting, 1 favors A and 4 favor $\overline{A}$. Thus, with compulsory voting, the outcome will be switched from A to $\overline{A}$. What can we say about this outcome? First, it is clear that the 51 voters who favor A are disadvantaged by the change. Second, the 5 voters who are compelled to vote are also disadvantaged because, although, presumably, they prefer the new outcome to the old, they were free to vote before, and their choice not to do so indicated that the tedium of voting is, for them, more significant than the change in the outcome. Thus, we know that 56 people have been injured by the change, and 49 have been benefited. A Paretian welfare economist would say that we could not tell for certain whether the change was an improvement or not; although, if the intensities of preference are reasonably evenly distributed, it would clearly be a bad move.

Political scientists, however, very commonly are in favor of majority voting, and it is hard to be in favor of majority voting and to argue that a change which would injure a clear majority of the population is desirable because it improves majority voting.[2] In most cases, of course, the effect of non-voters voting cannot be predicted with any high degree of accuracy, and it is, in any event, unlikely to change the outcome in this simple way. Where we have political problems which are essentially a continuum along some dimension (or dimensions), one could predict that the introduction of a group of new voters would move the median point—and hence the outcome of the political

2. In spite of the difficulty of this argument, I have no doubt that some of the readers of this paper will make it.

process—in one direction or another. The reasoning given above could be used to demonstrate that this also would injure more people than it benefited.

We may properly pause here to discuss briefly the costs and benefits involved in voting. An individual who votes expends a certain amount of resources in the act of voting, which is a cost to himself. At the same time, he presumably obtains some benefit from this vote, perhaps directly as a consumer good from the vote and perhaps through the possibility that his vote will have changed the outcome. This latter factor, however, is relatively minor, and the principal political effect of an individual vote falls upon other people, because the principal consequence of a change in political outcomes will be felt by other people. Thus, in addition to the individual, the rest of the population also has some interest in his decision whether or not to vote. To put it in Samuelsonian terms, he is making a decision in which the "publicness" is very great.

"Publicness," however, can be either a good or a bad thing. Putting potassium cyanide in the water supply is a "public" act. In this case, the individual—by deciding to vote—reduces the power of all the people who are already voting; i.e., he generates not a public good, but a public bad. If, however, his vote is predictable upon some given issue, then with respect to that particular issue, the situation is more complicated. First, his vote may make no change in the outcome. In that event, it has no public effect. Second, it may be that his vote will indeed change the outcome.

In order to discuss this, let us assume that we are talking of a pair of voters who will vote alike rather than a single voter, in order to avoid ties. Under these circumstances, if their vote will change the outcome, that means that the original majority of the voters must have been on the opposite side. Thus, their intervention in the voting process injures more of the old voters than it benefits. An individual, choosing to vote rather than to abstain, will always injure more people than he benefits, if his vote has any effect at all. It is a case where the public bad affects more people than the public good.

There is one special circumstance in which the introduction of compulsory voting might benefit more people than it injured. Once again, assume that 51 of our voters favor A and 49 favor $\overline{A}$, and, for simplicity, assume that all 5 of the remaining voters favor $\overline{A}$ strongly enough so that they would be willing to vote if it would change the outcome from A to $\overline{A}$. Each of the 5, however, feels that if he votes, it will simply change the vote from 51-49 to 51-50, and hence that A will still be adopted. He does not evaluate the return on voting under these circumstances as high as the cost to him of casting the vote.

An agreement among all the 5 non-voters to vote might well be, from the standpoint of all 5 of them, more desirable than none of them voting; although each one of them individually would prefer not to vote if that option is available to them. This would be a fairly characteristic example of the individual voter acting as a free rider on a public good and collectivization providing a gain for the "public," which in this case consists of the 5 non-voters.

Under these circumstances, if voting were made compulsory, the 49 people who favored $\overline{A}$ among the existing voters and the 5 non-voters would benefit, while the 51 voters favoring A would be injured. The net effect is a gain for the majority of the total population. This, again, does not prove that compulsory voting would be desirable in the Paretian sense, but it does raise a possibility that it could be.

There are two things to be said about this matter; the first is that non-voters, generally speaking, do not have a high degree of monolithicity in their opinions, and hence this kind of public good for the non-voters must occur only rarely.[3] Thus, this type of public-good generation is not terribly probable. Further, it is not exactly obvious why we should feel that it is incumbent upon the majority of the voting population to compel other people to vote in order to defeat the majority.

The second point to be made about this situation is that it is, in any event, very unlikely that the majority of voters in the existing system would accept compulsory voting for the non-voters if they thought it would lead to significant changes in the outcome. These changes could only disadvantage the majority. The minority of the voters might favor compulsion. We could predict that a democracy which directly voted on such an issue would introduce compulsory voting only if the voters were somehow confused. Granted the present state of the literature, one would not be surprised if they were so confused.

I am not familiar with very many cases in which compulsory voting has been adopted. It is not unknown, but I just do not know its history in those areas where it has been accepted. A somewhat similar issue in terms of the preferences of the majority of the voters, however, is involved when they consider the extension of the ballot to groups that have previously been prohibited from voting. The recent extension from 21 to 18 as the minimum age for voting in the United States is an example.

---

3. See, for example, the Harris poll on the effect of the non-voters voting on presidential candidates, *Washington Post*, 8 May 1972, p. A-2.

Let us assume, in a hypothetical example, that it is proposed to lower the voting age to 10. We would anticipate that the present voters would regard this as a reduction in their voting power and would vote against it. My impression is that, in general, that has been the outcome when proposals to expand the electorate were put to a vote.

Although the voters would feel this way, it is not clear that the political party in power would. At any given time, the group in power in a democracy is facing upcoming elections. One would anticipate that, through simple stochastic processes, periodically those in power would feel that some group which now cannot vote would vote for them in a higher percentage than the population as a whole and, hence, that their chance of winning the next election would be improved by extending the ballot. Under these circumstances, professional politicians would occasionally extend the ballot for substantially straightforward careerist reasons. It is my impression that the empirical evidence would support this hypothesis as to the way in which the ballot is characteristically extended.

So far we have been talking about negative poll taxes and have, in general, come to the conclusion that they are not desirable. Note that this argument has had substantially nothing to do with ethics or linguistics. Let us now turn to the question of whether a positive poll tax is desirable or whether a zero poll tax is the optimal level.

The actual process of voting takes resources, and, if we are interested in preventing people from voting many times and, hence, have a registration system designed to reduce the possibility of plural voting, this also takes resources. Let me assume, for the moment, that these resources work out to about $10 per head per year in those countries such as the United States where elections are fairly frequent. Although this is a guess, it is not drawn at random.

A recent study of the cost of gun registration contained data on a number of different methods of registering and checking guns from Illinois, where nothing much is done except to keep a list of the gun owners, to New York, where very elaborate procedures are utilized. An inspection of these costs led me to hypothesize that the full cost (counting overhead, capital cost, etc.) of voter registration and voting would tend to run about $10 a year. Nevertheless, this figure is very tentative and is introduced in this article simply for purposes of discussion and illustration.[4]

4. Ernest L. Staples and Richard T. Clayton, *A Preliminary Cost Analysis of Firearm Control Programs* (Silver Spring, Md.: Research Associates, 1960); see especially the table on page 14.

Under these circumstances, the taxpayer could pay individuals who refrained from voting $10 a head without increasing his cost. Those individuals who chose to take the $10 would be benefited because they have made a voluntary choice. Those individuals who chose not to take the $10 would also be benefited, because the value of their vote would increase. Each one could anticipate greater influence in political affairs as a result of some other people discontinuing their voting. Once again, we have a clear-cut Paretian change in which everyone is benefited and no one is injured.

In the above, I have assumed (probably accurately) that voting is not subject to either economies or diseconomies of scale in the likely range. If it is an increasing-cost activity, then the marginal cost should be substituted for the average cost in the paragraph above and in the calculations in the rest of this article. If it is a declining-cost industry, the usual problems of pricing for a public utility arise. Determining the actual optimal price might be very difficult, but paying people the current marginal cost would be an improvement over the status quo, even though not optimal.

This, of course, involves only political-power calculations. Once again, we may consider the situation in which we can predict how people will vote, and hence individuals might have preferences with respect to whether other people did or did not vote. Under these circumstances, the individuals who cease voting would still clearly benefit. Further, of the individuals who continued to vote, a majority would benefit if the withdrawal of this collection of voters changed the outcome; and if the withdrawal of these voters did not change the outcome, none of the remaining voters would be either benefited or injured. Here again, we have either a Pareto desirable situation—i.e., some people gain and no one loses—or one in which the gainers outnumber the losers.

We can, however, create the analogy of the situation in which the 5 voters would prefer voting as a bloc to not voting, but where each would prefer not to vote individually. It might be that this situation would exist here, also. Once again, however, it seems on the whole unlikely that we would find this degree of monolithicity among this bloc of citizens.

So far I have referred to a payment to the non-voters rather than the poll tax on those who vote. This payment would have to be financed by taxes, and these taxes would carry with them an excess burden. Thus, changing the situation by reducing the other taxes in our society in such a way that everyone's tax cost fell by $10, while putting a $10 tax on voting, would be a Pareto superior move. So far, then, we have demonstrated that a tax on voting, sufficient to cover the entire cost of the voting process, is superior to any other possible institution, unless the non-voters have a high degree of mono-lithicity and would actually prefer to be compelled to vote to being left free to make their choices themselves. This last modification would appear to re-fer mainly to an unlikely empirical case, but for theoretical completeness we must mention it.

Would, however, a higher poll tax be even better? Assume a $20 poll tax. This would involve $10 to cover the cost of operating the voting system and $10 for some other purpose. It is immediately obvious that such a tax would carry with it an excess burden and, hence, is not desirable in and of itself. The introduction of this tax would lower the satisfaction of at least some people, and no compensation scheme could be designed under which they would be repaid for the injury they suffered.[5] Thus, clearly, the movement to a higher poll tax could not be urged on arguments similar to those we have so far used.

A poll tax sufficient to cover the entire cost of the voting process, then, is optimal. Our present situation in which we do not have such taxes is clearly inferior. It is not, of course, obvious that the historic poll taxes were at the optimal level. Nevertheless, the arguments against poll taxes seem to have been basically misguided. They depended on moral or linguistic arguments and might appeal to the "nine old men" but not to social scientists.

5. It is, of course, necessary to raise public revenue, and the above argument does not prove that poll taxes are worse than other taxes as means of reaching that end.

OPTIMAL POLL TAXES

FURTHER ASPECTS

The subject of taxes on voting is one which has been very little discussed and which surely deserves further consideration. Unfortunately, it is an area where emotions and preconceptions are both strong, which makes objective reasoning difficult. No doubt this had some effects on my original article, and it seems to have also had some effect on Gärtner's comment.[1] For one example, he gives the impression that I was unaware of the existence of poll data on what nonvoters would do if they voted in the United States, although I refer to such information twice in my article.[2] Secondly, he does not seem to have noticed my discussion of "public bads."

Although in any individual vote the outcome is uncertain, when we change to the constitutional stage it seems dubious that this is so. First, as a matter of fact, the voters do pay the full cost of voting. Thus, if we have some person for whom the vote is not personally worth $10 and we compel him to pay the $10 and vote (or simply compel him to pay the $10 whether he votes or not), it surely makes him worse off unless he will gain from all nonvoters being compelled to vote. This point was made in my original article where I pointed out that it is on the whole unlikely that the similarity of preferences among the nonvoters will be strong enough so that they will gain from being compelled to vote.[3]

Gärtner raises the issue of the possible benefits for the people who would have been voting even if they had to pay the poll tax. This was also discussed in my article, but he suggests two institutional structures (which are not uncommon in the real world) and a theory by George Stigler which might indicate that the majority of such voters will be benefited by compelling the nonvoters to vote.

Before discussing these three situations, however, we should once again remember that a general decision on my part that I will vote in the future

Reprinted, with permission of the International Atlantic Economic Society, from *Atlantic Economic Journal* 4 (Fall 1976): 7–9.

1. Gordon Tullock, "Optimal Poll Taxes," *Atlantic Economic Journal* 3 (April 1975): 1–6; Manfred Gärtner, "Optimal Poll Taxes: Some Different Aspects," *Atlantic Economic Journal* 4 (Fall 1976).

2. Tullock, "Optimal Poll Taxes," 1–2, 4n3.

3. Ibid., 3.

certainly reduces the average power of all people who would vote even if I did not. There are some data, albeit of terribly poor quality, on the behavior of nonvoters in situations in the United States where there is no compulsory voting. We have no data at all on the behavior of those people who would stop voting if there were a poll tax.[4] Thus we are driven to discussions of poll tax effects entirely in theory. If, on the other hand, we are talking about compulsory voting, there is a small body of very bad data available. These data do seem to indicate that the nonvoters are not united among themselves, and, in consequence, they would rarely reverse the outcome of elections.

If current nonvoters were compelled to vote, Gärtner is perfectly correct in suggesting that, if they were compelled to vote, the parties would take the nonvoters into account in their decisions. Hence, the policies adopted would be somewhat different. This would mean that the uncompelled voters for the majority party would find the party policy not quite as much in accord with their desires. The nonvoters would prefer not to vote, and the remainder of the group winning the election would find that the policy actually adopted was less to their tastes than it would have been had their party won *without* these voters. Whether this is a good thing or a bad thing in such an individual election is rather an open question. In a long chain of elections, however, in most of which the outcome between the two parties is the same, but the parties changed their policies in order to attract the vote of the people who would rather not vote, surely the people who would vote without compulsion would find that they were less satisfied with the outcome. Thus, if we look at a long series of elections, it is likely that compulsory voting will injure substantially everyone.

All of the above has been applied to the simple-majority-voting context of the original article. Gärtner discusses two other circumstances, one in which a reinforced majority is required and one in which there is proportional voting. Finally he deals with Stigler's theory that the influence of a group depends on its size in a continuous manner rather than shifting abruptly at the 50 percent level. Let us discuss these one at a time.

To begin with the reinforced-majority situation: As a coauthor of *The Calculus of Consent*, I am rather in favor of calculating optimal voting majorities

---

4. During the period of the poll tax in the southern United States, voting fell to a very low level. However, this was the period of complete Democratic-party dominance in these states, and hence voting normally had no effect at all. Under the circumstances, it seems unlikely that we can draw much in the way of conclusions as to the actual effect of a poll tax from this experience.

for various proposals and using them.[5] This would only rarely lead to simple majority voting. If this procedure were followed, then the optimal majority needed for some particular category of vote would characteristically be different if there is a poll tax than if there is not. Generally speaking, it would be lower with the poll tax than without it, but, in any event, the optimum computed with the poll tax would be superior to the optimum computed without the poll tax.

In the real world, there is no reason to believe that the constitutional provisions requiring more than a majority have been properly calculated. Under the circumstances, it is quite impossible to say whether there would be a net gain from the introduction of the poll tax without a change in the voting rule. It is certainly true that if the two-thirds majority is required and a poll tax is instituted, this could injure in any one election the majority who favor the issue, if that majority is likely to be less than two-thirds with a poll tax and more than two-thirds without it. Over a long series of elections, however, the constitutional rules would indicate that the poll tax would work better because of the differential-intensity arguments put forth in *The Calculus of Consent*.

With respect to proportional representation, the Gärtner argument is a little hard to follow. If the individual parties each have less than a majority, which is the normal case, then the nonvoter who increased the voting weight of one party clearly injures the majority of the population in that particular election as well as over a long series of elections. If one party does already have a majority, then a nonvoter who voted on the side of the majority by increasing that vote would benefit a majority to some extent. However, it should once again be kept in mind that he will change the policy followed by the majority party; therefore, it is not obvious that the uncompelled voters will gain. If we look at the matter over a long series of votes, clearly those who would vote, normally have their power to affect matters reduced when other groups of people begin to vote. Thus, they are injured and the new voter is also injured by being compelled to vote.

Lastly we come to Stigler's discussion of the actual size of the vote.[6] Stigler argues that in a democracy the size of the majority or minority is very important. It is not clear whether he is right or wrong about this, but Gärtner clearly thinks he is right, and certainly Gärtner and Stigler could be right. Let

5. James M. Buchanan and Gordon Tullock, *The Calculus of Consent* (Ann Arbor: University of Michigan Press, 1962).

6. George J. Stigler, "Economic Competition and Political Competition," *Public Choice* 13 (Fall 1972): 91–111.

us, then, grant that increasing your majority from 51 percent to 60 percent increases the likelihood that you will be able to make changes in the government, pass desirable legislation, etc.

It should be pointed out, however, that if this is done by bringing into the voting process a set of voters who otherwise would not vote, they also, by this same argument, will have an effect on the policy of the party itself. Thus we can divide the population into three groups. Let us assume that originally there were 99 people voting, 50 of whom voted for the majority party and 49 who voted for the minority party, and 10 additional voters are forced to vote and chose the majority party. The 10 new voters themselves are injured by this change because they value the resources involved in voting at a higher level than the change in outcome.

The 49 are also injured by the Stigler-Gärtner line of reasoning because the majority party now enacts more of its legislation than it otherwise would have. Of our total population of 109, there remain the 50 who were the original majority. These 50 now find that their party is able to enact more legislation but that this legislation is less to their liking than it was before. Whether in net they gained or lost is ambiguous. If we look at this for a long chain of elections in the future in which we are not sure whether we will be in the majority, the minority, or the nonvoters in any given case, it is clear we would oppose compulsory voting.

Gärtner's comment compelled me to reconsider some of the arguments of my original paper, but it has not compelled me to change my basic conclusions. Still, the issue is an important one and should be discussed a good deal more than it has been. Let us hope that Gärtner and others are also led to reconsider matters and make further contributions.

BISMARCKISM

Introduction

The largest tax paid in a direct sense by the average American is the Social Security tax. When we add on (1) the money he pays for what amounts to a state medical insurance program (Medicare), which will benefit him only if he is under certain income levels or old enough to be pensionable, and (2) the money paid by his employer for unemployment insurance, the total is probably half or more of the total taxes he pays. Further, all of these taxes are used to provide him with a substitute for what traditionally would have been a strong motive for saving. As a result of paying these taxes, he is guaranteed an income when he is old; he is guaranteed his medical expenses now if he is in the lower income brackets and, in any event, when he becomes older; and lastly, he is provided with income for any period of unemployment. Thus he no longer has nearly as much need of savings as the traditional citizen had before these programs were introduced.

Consider that a citizen of the United States in the 1920s would be motivated to save money to provide for his old age, to take care of medical emergencies, and to act as a cushion in the event that he lost his job. He might do some of his savings by way of a private insurance company, but that insurance company would, of necessity, invest a large part of any premium he paid in order to have the funds available when he became pensionable or unemployed, as the case might be.

Thus, the general program of the welfare state directly reduces an individual's after-tax income, thus lowering the amount that he is likely to save, and eliminates or greatly reduces a number of the motives for saving. It does not, of course, *cancel out* the motives for saving, but it certainly makes them weaker than they would be without the welfare state.

Any economist looking at this would predict that in a society with this kind of welfare state there would be a lower level of saving, leading to a lower level of capital investment and, hence, to a lower level of growth and productivity than otherwise. This does not, of course, prove that it is a bad thing.

Reprinted, with permission of the Pacific Research Institute for Public Policy, from *Taxation and the Deficit Economy: Fiscal Policy and Capital Formation in the United States*, ed. Dwight R. Lee (San Francisco: Pacific Research Institute for Public Policy, 1986), 225–40.

If values are appropriate, one could prefer a slower rate of growth with "security" to a higher rate of growth without it.

It is frequently argued that the welfare state is necessary in order to help the poor. Prince Otto von Bismarck, the Prussian statesman, invented the welfare state, and there is no reason to believe that he was overly concerned about the well-being of the poor. To digress briefly into German history: Bismarck was concerned about winning elections and centralizing the newly founded German Empire. Ironically, he lost the election immediately after introducing the welfare state, but the centralization worked. A large centralized bureaucracy was set up at a time when the new German Empire was basically a federation of kingdoms.

But to return to our main theme: the development of the welfare state, first in Germany and then in the rest of the world. I suppose that politicians other than Bismarck found it politically attractive, because it was copied by nation after nation. The order in which nations adopted it tended to follow their proximity to Germany, both physically and culturally. Today the welfare state is more or less universal. It can, however, be studied by examining it on a country-by-country basis. I propose to discuss primarily the American system, mainly because that is the one that I know best. The discussion, although not completely applicable to other countries, would nevertheless fit most of them quite well. The reason is simply that Prince Bismarck's invention has been adopted in pretty much the same form almost everywhere. Prince Bismarck was a consummate politician, and other politicians found that his work met their needs almost perfectly.

Social Security

In talking about the American welfare system—or its impact on saving and capital formation—I propose to confine myself to its old-age pension provisions. Although there is much to learn from consideration of the medical and unemployment insurance portions of this Bismarckian program, in view of space constraints I have selected for discussion the old-age pension, since it is the largest segment of the system.

The Social Security system is set up as an independent fiscal entity. Instead of being part of the general budget, it is supported by a special tax on employees—one of the rare taxes that is genuinely regressive. The benefits come solely out of that tax arrangement.[1] In other words, it is our largest example of a rigorously earmarked tax system.

Economists have frequently argued for *use* taxes, that is, to have people taxed for the cost of some service more or less in proportion to the degree to which they take advantage of the service. The economic advantages of a use tax are obvious, but, of course, it cannot be used to redistribute money to the poor. The Social Security system to some extent is a use tax, in that if it ever reached its stable state (and one of the points of this chapter is that it will probably never do so), the individual would pay into it much the same amount that he got out, although the payment and receipt would be in different parts of his life. Note that I said "much the same." The system does permit transfers of funds from the well-off to the poor, and in fact there are some gestures in that direction albeit little real substance in the current act.[2] An earmarked tax has political advantages (first brought to public attention by James Buchanan[3]), in that it automatically creates two groups of people who are especially interested in this government action: those who pay the tax and those who receive the benefits. If the two groups are of about equal size, we can anticipate that since it will be equally easy for them to mobilize politically, the resulting pressure groups will tend to cancel each other out. We will see that the Social Security system is an example of this sort.

For the novice, let us simply analyze the way this joint system of tax and payment works. Let us begin by considering a state in which there is no rate of interest, no growth, and no change. Individuals live 80 years, the first 20 of which are spent going to school. They work from the age of 20 to the age of 65, then retire and live on their savings during their last 15 years. Each of them, we will assume, saves 20 percent of his income each year with a result that for the last 15 years they can live on 60 percent of their original income. It is not too much of a drop from the 80 percent of income that they had spent in the earlier part of their life.

1. I am ignoring here the arrangement under which some of the benefits are subject to income tax, with this tax then rebated to the Social Security Administration.

2. As will be shown below, there is a substantial transfer from the upper-income groups to the middle classes.

3. James M. Buchanan and Gordon Tullock, *The Calculus of Consent* (Ann Arbor: University of Michigan Press, 1965), p. 293. Although the book is jointly authored, this particular idea was Buchanan's.

Now suppose that a Prince Bismarck arrives and suggests changing this system. He suggests that all employed persons be taxed 20 percent and that the money derived be paid in the form of a pension of 60 percent of lifetime income to all people over the age of 65. The taxes and expenditures will be exactly balanced. At first it looks as if there is no change—and eventually that will be true. But consider the generation in existence at the time of the proposal. All of them except those just entering the labor market have existing savings. They are now free to spend those existing savings without affecting their eventual pension. They can, of course, if they wish, retain the savings and spend them when they are old. Clearly, they all benefit. The ones at the age of 65 benefit more than the ones at the age of 21, but all of them benefit.

This looks like magic. Nobody is injured and everybody benefits. Note that new people entering the system—18-year-olds, let us say, who are shortly going to become 20—will pay in taxes the same amount they would previously have saved and will upon retirement receive the same payment they would have obtained out of their savings, had this new system not come into existence. The problem, however, is that under this system the present generation of voters makes a promise that the next generation of voters will have to fulfill. If the pensions and tax were simultaneously canceled, by revolution, by foreign conquest, or perhaps by some kind of natural disaster, everybody over the age of 20 would lose because they would have no savings and they would lose their pension rights. Once again, people under the age of 20 would not be injured, because they could simply switch back to the savings mode. Thus we have a system that is beneficial to all voters when it is installed. When it is in a stable state, it neither benefits nor injures anyone. Terminating the system, however, would be injurious to everybody old enough to vote. Clearly, there would be suitable voting power to defend such a system. We would never need to worry about its termination.

Unfortunately, in the real world the credibility of the system is not that good, and indeed one can readily imagine the system gradually disappearing. To further explain this, however, we must complicate our model a bit. For this purpose we must introduce the rate of interest and a rate of growth of the economy. Suppose merely that the rate of interest is higher than the rate of growth of the economy, a situation that is more or less the world norm, although there have been, of course, periods when the reverse condition obtained. For these circumstances the system that I have described would have to have built into it some procedure for increasing the total pensions people received. The easiest way is to simply arrange that whatever is collected by the 20 percent tax on all income is then disbursed to older people. Under these circumstances the pensions granted to older people will increase at the same rate at which the economy grows.

Now compare this with savings as the alternative. It is immediately clear that even at the point at which the system is in a stable state, younger people lose because they would be better off if they invested their money at the rate of interest—which is higher than the rate of growth of the economy—than if they paid the tax. Thus it is no longer true that, looked at as a lifetime invest-ment, the system is essentially neutral. It now injures all the people who come into the system. It is still true, however, that if we start with a situation where people are investing to support themselves in their old age and a Prince Bis-marck comes along and suggests this system, many people could be made better off. It depends on the rate of interest as opposed to the rate of growth of the economy. Before the most recent changes in the Social Security pro-gram, it was generally thought that the break-even point was about 43—that is, that people under the age of 43 were losing on the deal and people over the age of 43 were gaining.[4] These calculations assume that the individual is concerned only with his own well-being—they ignore the prospect that he might find himself supporting his elderly parents. This rather complicated is-sue, however, will be deferred until later. For the time being I will use the number 43 as the break-even point and will make adjustments later in the chapter.

This situation is a little complicated. A new entrant into the labor force can look forward to a pension very materially smaller than the pension he could receive if he simply invested the tax money. As we take older and older people, this disadvantage shrinks. Someone at the age of 35, for example, as-suming that he regards his previous tax payments as a sunk cost, could look forward to a pension that would be less—but not very much less—than he would receive if he saved the money he is paying into the fund as taxes. At the age of 43 the two alternatives would be valued equally, and at the age of 50 he would prefer the Bismarck-state program. Once again, this assumes that these older citizens regarded their previous taxes as a sunk cost. This is, of course, the correct way of thinking about the matter if you are contemplat-ing a change of policy in the future.

4. The calculations are extremely difficult and uncertain.

In a famous article, Browning argued that this situation would lead to the Social Security payments always being higher than they should be.[5] He defined the desirable level of Social Security as that which would be chosen by a voter who was contemplating his whole lifetime of payments and receipts. Except for a small minority who are just entering the system, that is not the situation of any voters. For most voters, the taxes that they have already paid in are, in fact, a sunk cost in considering changes for the future. They therefore underestimate the total cost of the system. One would, however, expect people under the age of 43 to be in favor of cutting back the system, and those over the age of 43 to be in favor of enlarging it. The two groups are not radically different in size. Thus a functioning system of this sort might have much the same political support for an increase as for a decrease in program expenditures and, hence, remain stable. Obviously, however, the equilibrium would be an unstable one.

It seems likely that the observed tendency of these programs to expand depends more on another bit of Prince Bismarck–type genius than on the Browning effect. Prince Bismarck financed his program by a tax that, of course, fell on the laborers. Although our tax is nominally half on the laborer's salary and half on his employer, the employer, in fact, pays it and uses a single check for both halves of it. The wages of the laborer are reduced proportionately.[6] This particular bit of deception has had a long and very successful history. The Social Security Administration has never been willing to admit that employees pay the full cost of the system, and I think we can assume that they know their business. Economists, who do not have such a large material motive to mislead the workers, are unanimous in believing that the employer does not actually pay the "employer contribution."

It can be seen that every time the system is expanded, you have a small-scale version of the situation that has arisen for the system as a whole. Suppose, for example, the legislature raises the tax and the pension or imposes the tax on a new group and gives them a pension. There is here a gain for all members who are over 43 and a loss for those under 43.

5. Edgar K. Browning, "Why the Social Insurance Budget Is Too Large in a Democracy," *Economic Inquiry* 13 (Sept. 1975): 373–88.

6. It is sometimes argued that part of the cost, instead of being paid by the employee, is added to the price of the product. Since employees buy products, roughly in proportion to their income, this also means that the employee pays it—but by a different mechanism.

Continued success of the system requires that people now in the system believe that when they retire it will be retained intact. They are, in essence, "betting" that people will keep the bargain made by their parents. Consider, once again, our 43-year-old man. By the time he becomes 65, a little less than half of all voters will be people who were too young to vote at the time he was 43. Indeed there will be a substantial group of voters who were not even born at the time he passed his 43rd year. His prospects of a pension depend on these voters keeping, in essence, a promise made by their predecessors. And, of course, the situation is much more severe if we think of the pension he will receive when he is 75, at a time when a clear majority of the voters will be people who were too young to have voted when he was 43. His confidence that he will continue to receive the pension has to be based not on the faith that people will keep their promises but on the faith that certain voters will keep promises made by other voters.

Is It True?

This is the basic problem of credibility for the Social Security system. Suppose, theoretically, that an individual feels—when he decides to retire—that there is only a fifty-fifty chance the voters will decide to keep their "promises." Under these circumstances he would discount the future pensions by a very large risk premium. As a result, the turnover rate, the point at which he would begin regarding the net benefit to him from the system to be greater than the net cost, would be moved forward to somewhere around 56 or so. If the voters reach that conclusion, an overwhelming majority of them would have a selfish motive for terminating the system.

In the traditional literature on this point, the matter has hardly been discussed at all; when it has been discussed, it has simply been stated—very firmly—that there is no prospect of the scheme being canceled. Of course, if everyone believes that, the scheme is highly credible, and voters over the age of 43 have a selfish motive for favoring it. If the credibility of the system falls, the turnover point is moved, thus changing the probable vote in the future. This, in turn, affects the credibility still further. One can easily imagine a step process like the following:

1. Something happens that leads the voters to feel that everyone under the age of 45 will lose on the system.
2. The system is thus rendered politically less credible.

3. As a result, everyone under the age of 47 is led to believe that he will lose on the system.
4. The system is thus rendered still less credible.
5. As a result, and so forth . . .

Such an ongoing sequence of events will ultimately make the system literally vanish.

Here we have, simply, two theories. The implicit, unstated one of the conventional literature is that the system is completely credible, and, hence, people can depend on it; the other hypothesis, which I have been outlining here, is that if it is at all suspect, the loss of faith may gradually weaken the political support, thus making it more and more likely that the system will fail. So far we have generated no evidence against either hypothesis.

If we look at the history of these systems, we observe that until quite recently they steadily expanded. You could find examples in almost all of the systems, and certainly in the American system, in which some technical change made by Congress did in fact lower the pension receipts of some particular, usually narrowly defined, group. This was, however, quite exceptional. Further, most of the advocates of the system (and after all, at the moment, they are most of the people who have written about the system) concealed the existence of these minor downward adjustments and simply said that the system never was cut.

Recently, however, all over the world, countries have been cutting back on the system. I will be talking about the American adjustments in the most recent reform act, but similar steps were taken by such strong welfare states as West Germany, Denmark, and Sweden. The apparent reason for these cuts was simply that the system was becoming expensive enough to make younger voters object and threaten to "throw the rascals out."

Social Security Cuts

Cuts have taken two different forms. First, they have literally reduced the pensions, one way or another. And second, they have deferred eligibility for them. We will discuss these one at a time.

In the United States, the most recent reforms cut pensions in two ways. First, pensions above a certain level were made subject to regular income tax; this meant that upper-income people would, in fact, receive markedly smaller after-tax pensions than they had expected. Since the special tax on these particular pensions was not put into general receipts but rebated to the Social Security Administration, this involved a cutting of the benefits of these groups. However, the number of people counted as upper income for this purpose was by no means small, and, further, they were probably the most politically influential of the pensioners. And the people who are currently receiving pensions were cut quite significantly in real terms by deferring their cost-of-living adjustment. This was in fact the second such adjustment. The Congress had originally calculated the cost-of-living index in such a way that the pensions rose markedly faster than the cost of living. It then adjusted back to a new procedure in which they rose, as it turned out, somewhat faster than the growth of the wages of people who were paying the tax, but not faster than the cost-of-living index. The lowered expectations from the first cut were probably greater than those for the most recent cut, but in both cases they were sizable.

These cuts represented about half of the dollar value of the measures taken to bring the system back into potential solvency. The other half were accounted for by tax increases, and one of the tax increases clearly lowers the political credibility of the system. The payroll tax for Social Security has always been regressive, in that it is a tax only on some segment of income, let us say the first X of income a person earns. The value of X to be taxed was raised, while, as we have pointed out, the return received by upper-income people was cut back quite sharply. If we assume that upper-income people (and remember here we are talking of people with incomes above about $25,000) tend to be politically influential and that it is dangerous to cross them, this group probably now faces a situation where any of them under the age of 60 or so will actually lose from the continuation of this system.

There was, in addition, a general raising of taxes on everyone; in particular, arrangements were made to compel various people who had been opting out of the system—federal employees, employees of state and local governments, etc.—to come back in. The federal employees, a politically powerful group, were pretty much protected from the change, but the very junior members of the federal civil service and new employees, groups without much political power, were not protected.

The net effect of all of this has been to move the turnover point up. You now pay more for your pension, and the pension is worth less than it was before. The difference in pension value between upper-income people and lower-income people has been increased. It should be pointed out here, although we will elaborate on it later, that the poor did not gain from the change. The gainers were what we might call the lower middle class. The end result of this is that the turnover point is different for different income classes, with somebody who is paying the maximum or near the maximum amount of "contribution" probably having his turnover point somewhere around the age of 55 to 60, and someone in the $15,000 income bracket probably having the turnover point somewhere around 45. All of this assumes that the new arrangements are permanent and *thought* by the voters to be permanent, i.e., not likely to change.

The second change that was made was to move back the point for eligibility for a full pension. This was done in such a way that people over the age of 43 were unaffected; those below or at the age of 43, roughly speaking, got a one-year deferment of their eligibility.[7] Another category, those people under 25, got a two-year deferment. The fact that the break point was the age of 43 indicates, I think, that the Social Security actuaries had *calculated* that 43 was the turnover point, and I regard it as confirmation of my use of that number. They saw to it that the deferment applied only to people who are already provided with a material motive for being opposed to the system.

The cost of this kind of deferment is very great in present discounted terms. Roughly speaking, taken all by itself, it moves the turnover point back about eighteen months for people who have only the one-year deferment, and about three years for people who have the two-year deferment. Note, however, that at the time the bill was passed even the people who had the one-year deferment were already young enough so that the payment they would receive on the Social Security was less than the amount they put in. Looked at from the standpoint of the Social Security Administration, however, this last figure is not all that consoling. It is fairly obvious that further "reforms" will be necessary in the Social Security system in the near future. By the time these reforms get discussed in Congress, it will already be true that this deferment has moved the turnover point for voters in their forties back about eighteen months. Thus, the Social Security system will enter into the next reform drive in a worse condition than it is now politically. Further, the credibility of the view that no cuts will ever be made clearly is no longer high. Cuts have been made, not only here but in many other places in the world. The combination of the weakening political support and lowering credibility may mean that the cuts could be very severe indeed.

---

7. It was actually phased in over five years, but the details are unimportant.

Obviously I am not here making a prediction. The Gray Panthers are well organized and have a lot to fight for. Further, they have the bulk of the civil servants on their side, although with every year the number of civil servants ready to fight and die for their special pension rights under the Social Security Act declines.

Further, as we all know, the voters are not very well informed, and the rather abstract calculations I have been going through so far may be above them. Nevertheless, if they make random errors, the average would come out more or less where we have come out. This would be true no matter how large the random errors were.

Other Issues

I have deferred to this point two important issues. The first concerns the Social Security system as a way of transferring funds from upper-income people to lower-income people. The second concerns the role of Social Security in replacing other methods families would normally use to take care of their older members. These two matters must now be dealt with.

Let us begin with the issue of general-income transfers. The first thing to note here is that it has little or nothing to do with the genuine poverty population. If we go back to the 1920s, before the Social Security Administration was inaugurated and before the Great Depression (which, after all, was a highly abnormal circumstance), we find that only about 10 percent of all the people over 65 were thought to need state support.[8] These people were taken care of by various local programs, but not by social security.

Today if we look at the bottom of the income pyramid, particularly among older people, we find that a good many of them are indeed drawing Social Security pensions, but these pensions are too small to be thought adequate for their support. Our elderly citizens, therefore, receive a *supplementary* security payment that brings their income to the socially desired minimum. Those elderly who for one reason or another have not gotten into the Social Security system, and hence have not paid taxes, receive the same payment in their old age. Thus, the true poverty population depends not on Social Security, but on Supplemental Security Income (SSI), essentially a relief program,

8. Carolyn Weaver, *Crisis in Social Security* (Durham, N.C.: Duke University Press, 1982), 41–44.

just as they depended on relief in 1929. Further, as far as we can tell, in relative terms, the present scheme is not any more generous than its 1929 counterpart.[9]

There is, however, a difference between the treatment of the poor under Social Security and under the previous system. They now have to pay Social Security taxes. The average poor person is currently taxed on 12 percent of his earned income all of his life, and when he finally retires, he receives the same amount, roughly speaking, as he would if the Social Security system did not exist. Clearly, this makes the poor worse off.

Indeed, this is one of the arguments normally offered for the Social Security system. Again and again one can hear, "Lots of people wouldn't voluntarily save for their old age; if they weren't compelled to save for their old age by Social Security, we would have to support them." Regardless of whether this argument is true or false, it should be pointed out that, in any event, if we would have to support them *without* Social Security and now *tax* them significantly, clearly they are worse off. The nonpoor may be better off, but the poor are not.

There is, however, a substantial transfer away from upper-income groups, not as much as via the income tax (because of the regressive nature of the upper end of the Social Security tax), but there is nonetheless a substantial transfer. This transfer does not, however, go to the poor, defined as, let us say, the bottom 20 percent of the population. These people would be better off without the Social Security system (if we use as a basis their total lifetime income) because they would be saved the tax and would receive either the same income they now do—if their Social Security pension is smaller than the security minimum—or not very much less than they now do—if their Social Security payment was large enough to bar them from receiving SSI. Most of these people have their lifetime incomes reduced as a result of the existence of Social Security.

It does not, of course, follow that the elderly among them would positively gain from the abolition of the Social Security program. Some of them, indeed, might be hurt, but the difference would be small, and if we look not at the situation they face at present but at their lifetime earnings, they would

9. Here I must concede that the research is not very good. It seems to me that there is room for a good many doctoral dissertations looking into the question of whether the welfare state does or does not treat the poor better, in relative terms, than did the older, pre-Bismarckian system.

have been better off had the system never existed. Further, people who are now poor and young are paying taxes; they too would be better off if the system were abolished. The gainers from Social Security are also not the well-off who suffer considerable transfers away from themselves as a result of (1) the progressive nature of the repayment schedule and (2) the new provisions requiring them to pay income tax on one-half of their Social Security receipts. Roughly speaking, the bottom 20 percent and the top 30 percent of the population lose, and the 50 percent lying between them gains. The gain is probably largest at about the median of the population.

What all of this means is that the turnover point for the decision as to whether you are better off under the Social Security system varies a good deal according to your income. For the poor, abolishing it immediately would probably be a good deal, almost irrespective of their age. For the wealthy, unless they are very close to receiving their pension, abolishing it would probably be desirable. On the other hand, there surely are at least some people who are going to receive exceptionally large transfers and for whom the turnover point may be below 40.

Older Poor People

Let us now turn to the problem of taking care of older members of society without the Social Security system. Here I am not talking specifically about those who are poor and are taken care of by the state, but those who are better off and traditionally were taken care of by their families. I am old enough to remember the pre–Social Security situation. At different times we had two grandmothers living in our house. Indeed, both of them died there. Obviously, taking care of one's elderly parents puts some cost on the working generation.

In addition to the elderly people tending to live with their children — if they had them, of course — they normally made at least some contribution to the well-being of the family. Once again in 1929, 95 percent of people over 65 were working one way or another.[10] Generally, however, they were working at jobs where their productivity was low. After all, they tended not to be in the best of health; moreover, their pay was low. They were, however, making some contribution to the family income, and, of course, since they were

10. Weaver, n. 8.

living in an established household, the total cost of supporting them was not great. Contrast this with the present situation. Most elderly people are now living independently, either because the minimum income provided by the state is itself high enough so that they can do it or because they have Social Security and/or other income. Furthermore, not very many of them are working.

Here we must pause briefly to point out one rather peculiar characteristic of the Social Security payment. Those elderly people whose own income is good are nevertheless receiving transfers from the younger generation, rather indirectly from their children. This is something that would not have happened before. Moreover, because of the nature of the Social Security system, they normally actually receive larger absolute payments than do other elderly people without good private incomes. There seems to be no reason—other than the votes it affords aspiring politicians—for this particular feature to be considered desirable.

Let us return to the situation of those people who, in the absence of the Social Security system, would be living with their children and working at various low-productivity jobs to contribute to the family income but who are, instead, living on their own in Winter Park or Miami, Florida. The first thing to be said is that (since there is no law prohibiting them from continuing to work and living with their children) it is obvious that these seniors and their children prefer the present arrangement. It is true, of course, that the kinds of jobs formerly filled by this rather poor quality of labor[11] are no longer there, and elderly people might have some difficulty in finding jobs. Note that there is a separate labor market of this general sort in and around Winter Park, where a great many retired people live. It is organized in such a way that it does not cut very heavily into their Social Security pension, since work is done on a part-time basis. Of course, the minimum wage act might eliminate some of these specially contrived jobs. To repeat, such labor is not very productive.

If the elderly do prefer the present situation, the cost of the present pensions is not a good measure of the benefit they receive. The benefit received is the difference between the previous arrangement, in which they normally lived with their children and had various low productivity jobs, and the present situation, where they normally live in some place like Winter Park and do not have any employment at all. Clearly, the real improvement in welfare is considerably less than the full value of their pensions. Indeed, I would doubt

---

11. Retirees are frequently skilled, but rarely very strong.

in most cases that it is more than one-third of their pensions. I have included in this one-third the benefit their children receive from not having their parents live with them. As a matter of fact, however, if my recollection is correct, neither of my grandmothers was regarded as a significant cost to the family. They baby-sat, did odds and ends around the house, and participated in most household activities. This was generally thought to more or less compensate for their food and room.

In any event, the present scheme does have certain benefits which would be lost if it were canceled. However, to repeat, the benefits are clearly much smaller than the monetary value of the system.

Conclusion

All of this means, once again, that for different people the actual turnover point will be different. It is still true, however, that raising the tax, lowering the benefit, deferring the time when it will come into effect, and making the credibility of the promise of future pensions somewhat weak have all weakened the political support for the system. Whether the Gray Panthers will be able to mobilize well enough to more than compensate for that I cannot say. I can imagine a return to the previous situation in which Social Security programs increase steadily because of political pressure. However, I can also imagine a system in which, over time, the programs will shrink because each time it is cut, its credibility goes down, making the voters who pay the tax less and less sure of repayment in their old age. Altogether, it seems to be likely that the Bismarckian system has no steady state. It is either expanding or contracting.

So much for a survey of how the Social Security system actually works. I very much fear that many people who are now depending on the Social Security system will find that their confidence was misplaced. Note that I do not feel happy about this. I would prefer that the system had never been introduced to begin with. Once it is in, and once many people have planned their lives on the assumption that it will work, its cancellation or gradual shrinkage would be a true tragedy.

There is, of course, another tragic aspect of this program. As I had mentioned in the beginning, it reduces people's incomes, giving them less money to save, and it weakens their incentives for saving. The result surely is a fall in real savings, in real capital investment, and, hence, in income levels. If economic theory means anything, it means we have not been growing as fast as we would have grown had the Social Security system not existed. It may well be that without the Social Security system, our per capita incomes would be high enough to make the elderly, on the whole, markedly better off than they are now. Of course, that is mere speculation. What we *can* say is that the system certainly has not contributed to productivity but in all probability has sharply lowered it.

PART 5

MONETARY ECONOMICS

HYPERINFLATION IN CHINA, 1937–49[1]

Colin D. Campbell and Gordon C. Tullock

I

The unusual monetary developments that took place in China from 1937 to 1949 may prove instructive to Western economists. The period extends from the beginning of the Japanese invasion to the first year of Communist control of the mainland. This monetary experience generally supports our theories. However, events in China suggest a modification of the widely accepted principle that hyperinflation tends to drive currency out of use. Although rapid inflation lasted a long time, the various Chinese currencies served as media of exchange during the entire period.

II

Between 1937 and 1949 three governments—the Nationalists, the Japanese, and the Communists—occupied China, and each of them issued its own money. The National government issued Chinese Nationalist Currency until its monetary reforms in 1948–49, when the CNC was replaced first by the gold yuan and then by the silver yuan. The Japanese at first used both banknotes from Korea and from Japan and a script called "Military Yen." Later, notes were issued by their central banks in North China, Central China, and Inner Mongolia.[2] In North China the Japanese Federal Reserve Bank dollars remained in circulation almost two years after the surrender of the Japanese. However, since the Nationalists actively opposed the use of FRB notes, they eventually passed out of the picture. Between 1930 and 1948 the Communists issued approximately thirty local currencies, and ten

Reprinted, with permission of the University of Chicago, publisher, from *Journal of Political Economy* 62 (June 1954): 237–45. Copyright 1954 by The University of Chicago.

1. The personal observations of Mr. Tullock have provided the principal data for this study. He was in Tientsin as a Foreign Service Officer from 1948 to 1950.

2. U.S. Foreign Economic Administration, *The Japanese Occupation Technique in the Field of Money and Banking* (Washington, D.C., 1944), 1–3.

different paper currencies circulated in the border regions and "liberated" areas in 1948.[3] Soon after the People's Bank of China was established the Communists replaced almost all of their local issues with a unified paper money called "People's Currency." When the Communists took over North China, they converted the Nationalists' gold yuan into People's Currency at a realistic rate. On the other hand, in South China they did not honor the silver yuan which the Nationalists issued shortly before they lost the area.

To add to the confusion, the three governments in China engaged in monetary warfare. As early as March, 1938, the Japanese declared it illegal for anyone to carry or use Nationalist Currency. Similar policies were adopted by the Communists in the North and the National government in the South. These were accompanied by control of trade across borders in order to prevent the exchange of goods for the enemy's currency. The Nationalists claimed that after the Japanese puppet government recalled Chinese Nationalist Currency in the area they occupied, the Japanese leaders used it to purchase goods and foreign exchange from Free China—thus adding to inflation in Free China and draining away some of their supplies. The Communists accused the Nationalists of counterfeiting their poorly printed notes; however, this was seldom possible, because of the efficiency of the Communist police. Propaganda stating that the currency of their enemies was falling rapidly in value was issued on all sides.

In Free China rapid and continuous inflation resulted from extreme budgetary difficulties and the inability to sell bonds on terms acceptable to the government. Expenditures naturally increased to provide for expanded military outlays, and important prewar sources of revenue in the eastern cities were lost to the Japanese. Taxes also were usually in arrears because with inflation this was one way of getting them reduced. The Nationalists financed their deficits primarily by monetary expansion. They had abandoned the silver standard and established a managed currency in 1935. As Mr. K'ung, minister of finance, wrote: "When Japan invaded China in 1937, China's monetary system was prepared for the emergency. . . . The new system enabled the government to rely on the increase of bank credit as a means of emergency war finance."[4] Only a small percentage of the deficits were financed by selling

---

3. See Chao Kuo-chun, *Source Materials from Communist China*, vol. 3, *Fiscal, Monetary, and International Economic Policies of the Chinese Communist Government* (Center for International Studies, M.I.T., and Russian Research Center, Harvard University, 1952), 45, 75.

4. H. H. K'ung, "China's Financial Problems," *Foreign Affairs*, 23 (January, 1945), 222–23.

TABLE 1. *The Supply of Money and Wholesale Prices in Nationalist China, 1937–47*

YEAR	TOTAL MONEY SUPPLY*		WHOLESALE PRICES[†]	
	IN BILLIONS OF CNC DOLLARS	PERCENTAGE INCREASE[‡]	1937 = 100	PERCENTAGE INCREASE[‡]
1937	3.6		100	
1938	5.0	39	127	27
1939	7.4	48	214	68
1940	13.5	82	498	133
1941	25.0	85	1,258	153
1942	52.0	108	3,785	201
1943	104.0	100	12,556	232
1944	270.0	159	41,927	234
1945	1,472.0	445	158,362	277
1946	8,532.0	479	367,406	132
1947	55,000.0[§]	544	2,617,781	612

SOURCE: A. C. Huang, "Inflation in China," *Quarterly Journal of Economics*, 62 (August, 1948), 564, 569.
*Total note circulation of the four government banks before July, 1942, and of the Central Bank of China thereafter, plus total demand deposits of the four government banks.
[†]Average of monthly prices.
[‡]Percentage increase from previous year.
[§]December estimated.

bonds to individuals. The Nationalists were unable to sell many short-term securities, because they did not offer a positive real rate of return. In 1940, for example, when prices more than doubled, they offered rates of from 5 to 12 per cent a year.[5] Because of the long civil war and the precarious future of the Nationalist government, the salability of its long-term bonds would have been very low.

In 1938–39 the velocity of money in Free China shifted to a distinctly higher level. Table 1 shows that at this time prices rose faster than the quantity of money, whereas from 1937 to 1938 they had risen less rapidly than the money supply. In 1938–39 people evidently began to realize that prices would rise continuously. As soon as they tried to hold smaller cash balances because they expected inflation, velocity increased sharply.[6] The shift to a higher

5. F. M. Tamagna, *Banking and Finance in China* (New York: Institute of Pacific Relations, 1942), 266–67.

6. Although the public was trying to hold smaller cash balances, they actually were holding much larger cash balances because of the new issues by the government.

velocity must have been abrupt and undoubtedly caused considerable disturbance in the economy, but it was hidden by other catastrophes of the time.

Even after this initial shift to a higher rate of circulation, velocity continued to rise, but for a different reason. Table 1 shows that in 1938–44 and in 1946–47 wholesale prices rose more rapidly than the money supply.[7] The rate of circulation continuously increased because holding money became more and more costly. During inflation the cost of holding money depends largely on the rapidity of the rise in prices. For example, if prices rise at a constant rate, the cost of holding money will tend to be constant. However, from 1937 to 1947 the quantity of money and prices in Free China generally increased at an increasing rate. Since the cost of holding money rose continuously, people tried to hold less currency, and velocity became more rapid.

Both a deteriorating military situation and an anticipated monetary reform caused runaway inflation in 1948. The Communists claim that in Nationalist China prices in August, 1948, were over sixty-three times the monthly average in 1947. In the fall of 1948 the Nationalists exchanged the CNC for the gold yuan at 3,000,000 to 1. The reform failed to stabilize prices mainly because the Nationalists did not stop printing money. Both the enactment of price controls and the announced limit on currency that could be issued legally had little effect. The limit was so much above the amount in circulation that it was irrelevant. A simultaneous program to buy United States currency, silver, and gold accelerated the issuance of notes. After approximately three weeks of comparative stability, the new currency depreciated faster than the old.

Many small fluctuations in the rate of inflation occurred, but they lasted such a short time that they are not shown in Table 1. To some extent, these correlated with the volume of new notes put in circulation. The rate of printing was so high that persons frequently received neat packets of one hundred brand new notes from banks or in change from merchants. The appearance of many new bills or of new and larger denominations almost always coincided with a sharp fall in the value of money. On the other hand, when new notes became rare, prices were comparatively stable. These periods lasted only a week or ten days. Many Chinese believed that high officials manipulated the rate of inflation by varying the release of new currency.

The Nationalists and later the Communists made several bizarre attempts to stop inflation by refusing to supply currency to banks. When this happened,

---

7. In 1945–46 velocity dropped sharply probably because people believed that inflation would cease or, at least, slow up when World War II ended.

although one could not cash checks, banks were not considered bankrupt. Since everyone understood that the banks could not pay, a sort of moratorium on obligations occurred until the government issued more notes. The only effect was a disruption of business. If the government had cut off the supply and at the same time required prompt payment of all debts, presumably the value of currency would have shot upward.

The reported use of wheelbarrows for carrying money is a case of seizing upon a conspicuous, but unimportant, detail. This was usually unnecessary because, as inflation progressed, the government issued notes in larger denominations. Ordinarily, the largest bill widely used was worth between three and fifteen cents in American money. This was small, but, by using bundles of ten and one hundred notes, they were adequate for normal usage. Occasionally, the Nationalists attempted to control inflation by collecting old small-denomination bills and insisting that payments be made with them for about a week. At such times, carrying money was a problem, and carts were of considerable assistance. This policy created several other problems. It hurt wage earners, since merchants usually accepted this paper only at a discount, and firms had great difficulty meeting pay rolls with small-denomination bills.

During inflation in China interest rates rose to allow for depreciation. The computation of future transactions at interest rates that took depreciation into account was difficult and was a social waste compared with computations with a stable currency, but it was a minor one.[8] Because interest rates discounted the depreciation in the value of currency, markets for short-term loans operated as usual, even though political instability precluded long-term lending. The continuous operation of the short-term money markets was extremely significant. It meant that numerous transactions depending on deferred payment were unimpeded. Of course, interest rates were phenomenally high, but, because they primarily discounted anticipated inflation, they did not constitute the almost insuperable barrier to investment claimed by some observers.

Depreciation of Japanese puppet currencies was nearly as severe as that of CNC, for the Japanese also financed the bulk of their expenditures by

8. The close relationship between interest rates and inflation is illustrated by their sharp decline when the Communists eventually stabilized the price level. The official commercial rates charged by the People's Bank of Shanghai dropped from 100 per cent per month in November, 1949, to 2.3 per cent in March, 1952. The decline in black-market rates was probably more rapid than this (Chao, op. cit., 62).

continuously expanding bank credit. Just before the end of hostilities, prices in Occupied China rose faster than in Free China because of the anticipated defeat of the Japanese. However, after the war, one dollar FRB was worth more than one dollar CNC probably because the Japanese puppet government had received large amounts of aid from Japan.

The numerous Communist currencies undoubtedly depreciated at least as rapidly as the CNC. This is indicated by the following announcement of their new monetary policy in 1950–51:

> Instead of issuing huge quantities of paper money, as we were forced to do previously, we are now collecting taxes in a planned way and the finances of our country thus have a comparatively stable foundation. Since March of this year, we have almost achieved a balanced budget and stability of prices.[9]

Although estimates of the rise in prices in Communist China before 1949 are not available, Communist statisticians admit that in 1949 prices rose more than 7,000 per cent.[10] Twice during this year the People's Currency dropped to one-third its value in a period of one week. This was faster than the decline in the value of the CNC at any time from 1937 to 1949. The Communists claim that the rise in prices was reduced to 93.2 per cent in 1950 and to 13.8 per cent in 1951.

The extreme depreciation in the value of the People's Currency in 1949 was related paradoxically to attempts by the Communist government to stabilize its currency by discontinuing increases in the money supply. They had learned from experience (and partly by reading their own propaganda about the Nationalists) that price stability required limiting the quantity of money. They were unaware of the difficulty of administering a smooth transition from an economy adjusted to continuous inflation to one based on price stability. The Communists at first stopped increasing the money supply. This caused the velocity of circulation to fall, because the populace no longer anticipated rapid inflation. Very soon the government gave in to pressure from its various departments for more money and also relaxed its restrictions on private credit. The combination of a fall in velocity and an increase in the quantity of money kept prices stable. However, this could last only as long as velocity was adjusting to its new, lower level. Since the Communists kept on

9. Ibid., 16.
10. Ibid., 71.

issuing large amounts of currency, an explosive inflation occurred as soon as the populace realized that prices were not going to be stabilized. Once the fall in the value of their money began, the Communists undertook severe, and occasionally cruel, methods of reducing the money supply. These methods probably prevented the value of currency from falling further than it did and led to new stabilization efforts.

These unsuccessful attempts to stabilize prices and the explosive inflations that followed were more upsetting to the business community than the steady depreciation to which the Chinese had become accustomed. The future level of prices became completely unpredictable, and many firms were forced out of business. Imagine the plight of business firms that had borrowed at rates of 1 or 2 per cent per day when the government decided to stop printing more money. A scramble for currency followed, borrowers were unable to pay their debts, bankruptcies flourished, and lenders probably found their promissory notes worthless. When the government failed to control the money supply, the shift back to continuously rising prices also resulted in serious market disturbances and ruined lenders who had invested money at interest rates based on expected price stability. The two unsuccessful attempts by the Communists to stabilize prices resulted in such extreme uncertainty that they were a major factor in breaking the power of the business groups.

There is little basis for the belief that in monetary affairs the record of the Nationalists was worse than that of the Communists. Historians have probably exaggerated the role of inflation in the rise of Chinese communism. The following quotation is an example:

The themes of latter-day Nationalist corruption, strategic stupidity, administrative ineptitude, and general incompetence have been sufficiently elaborated in our press and official records; what needs to be more fully understood is the Nanking government's gradual bankruptcy of morale, which in turn sapped the morale of its erstwhile supporters and produced a general rout and debacle. Loss of morale cannot justly be attributed to Chiang Kai-shek as an individual, but perhaps it may be traced to the power structure which he headed, and which had become conservative and anti-revolutionary. This sessile spirit affected the lower and higher echelons of the KMT party organization, the minor officials in the sprawling government agencies, and even the clerks, shopkeepers, and students in the cities. As the war-time and post-war inflation endlessly progressed, all these people were consumed by it in substance and finally in spirit.

Spiralling prices made life increasingly precarious and hard, month after month and year after year. Malnutrition, disease, and depression followed. The government in power offered no way out, and Free China lost its feeling of support for, or tacit acquiescence in, the Generalissimo's regime.[11]

Of course, both the Sino-Japanese War and the Chinese civil war imposed extreme hardships on the Chinese people. However, the usual conclusion that the middle class—students, teachers, shopkeepers, office workers, and government employees—were impoverished assumes incorrectly that these groups received fixed nominal incomes. When inflation is anticipated, as it was in China, persons with fixed nominal incomes become extremely rare. The wages of office workers and other employees almost always rose as fast as prices and even discounted anticipated inflation. Government employees in Nationalist China actually lost a little, since their wages were computed by multiplying their 1937 wage rates by a cost-of-living index that was usually a few days behind the market. This was approximately equivalent to a reduction of 10–20 per cent in their wages, which was not uncommon during this period. The fortunes of shopkeepers were extremely uncertain. Some merchants became wealthy, and others failed. However, as a group they probably did not bear an especially heavy burden. City landlords suffered, since effective price controls existed only on urban real estate. In the country, rents and taxes were usually paid in kind; so landlords and farmers neither gained nor lost.

III

Continuous inflation in China caused the official currencies to be discarded both as units of account and as stores of value. During these years money could not serve as a store of value, because it did not keep its real value. Nonetheless, business firms and individuals needed some relatively liquid funds and quickly replaced Chinese currency as a store of value with other assets. Wealthy persons usually retained United States currency. This type of asset was not available to ordinary persons, since the activities of counterfeiters had made small bills suspect, and the smallest note that was salable without a discount was the five-dollar bill. The Chinese silver dollar was occasionally used, but for the poorer classes even this was too large. In the South, Hong Kong

11. C. Brandt, B. Schwartz, and J. K. Fairbank, *A Documentary History of Chinese Communism* (London: Allen & Unwin, 1952), 19–20.

currency was available in small denominations, and in the last days of the Nationalists it was probably more widely used as a store of value than any other foreign currency. However, the poorer Chinese usually saved by buying consumer's goods in larger quantities than they expected to use. Business firms customarily held reserves in United States dollars, Chinese silver dollars, gold, short-term notes, or readily disposable commodities such as rice and flour.

The social costs of using commodities as stores of value undoubtedly were higher than those of using a stable currency. Capital goods were held in reserves instead of being used for production. But this was not the only undesirable effect. Since the basic technique of adjusting to inflation was to retain currency as briefly as possible, businessmen planned to put funds back into their firms immediately. When they sold anything, they rushed out to lay in more stock. This made careful buying difficult and increased the markup. It also resulted in various businesses having all sorts of commodities on hand, depending on what happened to be available. When a loan was repaid unexpectedly, even a bank would purchase commodities to avoid holding an excessive amount of currency.

An institutional change that helped to provide liquid reserves was the expansion of the stock markets in Chinese cities. Securities markets obviously were used to avoid the effects of inflation. On the Shanghai Stock Exchange the monthly turnover increased from about 1.5 million shares in 1937 to 10 million in 1940.[12] Even though corporation stocks were safer stores of value than currency, after World War II the prices of stocks did not keep up with the fall in the value of currency. The Chinese probably understood the political situation well enough to withdraw their money from permanent, capitalistic investments. When the Communists took over in Tientsin, the market value of all stocks outstanding was less than 5 per cent of the book value of the corporations' property. Even so, it was a wonder that stocks at this time had any value at all.

Banks provided another organized method of retaining the value of one's liquid assets. They offered extraordinarily high interest rates on deposits. In Tientsin, 2 per cent a day compounded daily was not unusual following World War II. The bank rate did not fluctuate exactly with the rate of inflation, but at least it was similar. Nonetheless, deposits were not used as much as one would expect. Since a Communist victory was possible, few persons desired to have their money recorded on the books of a bank.

---

12. Tamagna, op. cit., 233.

The unusually large holdings of commodities by persons and business firms were very obvious during these years in China. Both Western observers and Chinese writers thought that the purpose of the "hoarding" was to make profits, and they condemned it as a waste of resources. Few of them realized that commodities were replacing currency as a store of value and that the purpose of holding commodities in place of cash was to maintain the real value of one's assets. Instead of diverting businessmen from productive activity, the holding of commodities provided firms with the liquid assets that they needed at all times.

Writers have exaggerated the profitability of hoarding goods in China at this time. Actually, when inflation is anticipated, although the value of goods increases, normally one cannot make real profits by hoarding. This is because buyers who expect inflation immediately bid prices of goods up so high that the opportunity to make real gains by holding commodities disappears. Since hoarders profit only when the rise in prices is greater than generally anticipated, success or failure becomes a matter of chance or exceptional judgment.

The prevalent belief that businessmen were better off under conditions of inflation is questionable. Uncertainties were increased significantly, and many fortunes must have been lost almost overnight. Because the securities and commodities held as reserves were not perfectly liquid, they were not reliable stores of value. In addition, the small size of the markets for many reserve items frequently made it difficult for large firms to secure or sell the quantity of liquid assets desired.

Another effect of inflation was that the Chinese Nationalist dollar and the other currencies were no longer used as units of account. Modern money usually serves both as a medium of exchange and as an accounting unit. This has not always been true. In the days of metallic currency, for example, the unit of account was often a theoretical coin, while the medium of exchange was a real coin. A division in the functions of money also occurred at this time in China.

The Chinese theoretically might have kept their accounts in the deteriorating monetary unit by the use of advanced mathematics and the compound-interest formula. In practice, this would be extremely complex. As a result, and despite the law, small shops in Free China usually kept their accounts in United States dollars. The shopkeepers bought and sold with Chinese currency, but they computed prices by applying the daily exchange rate to a price on their books in United States dollars. Larger businesses ordinarily used elaborate commodity indexes and computed prices by multiplying the price of the product in a base year by their current index number. Long-term loans were occasionally drawn up in terms of commodities or United States dollars; however, because of political uncertainties, few Chinese were willing to enter into long-term contracts. The National government used 1937 prices in its accounts and then multiplied this value by its cost-of-living index to get actual payments. The Communists required all businesses to keep their accounts in terms of corn flour or some other commodity. The *Tientsin Daily News* published the current price of corn flour; and all wages, debts, taxes, and other costs were then paid in currency at this standard rate. If the price of corn flour doubled between the time one borrowed money and the time he repaid it, he would repay twice as much. While the use of the corn flour index was an improvement over the numerous different accounting units prevalent under the Nationalists, it was subject to seasonal fluctuations and other disadvantages of a one-commodity base. Later, for bank deposits, the Communists introduced the "parity unit" based on several commodities. In Shanghai the parity unit was the sum of the price of 1.72 pounds of medium-grade rice, one foot of twelve-pound "Dragon Head" cloth, one ounce of peanut oil, and 1.33 pounds of coal briquettes. These "deposits in kind" were kept in terms of the parity unit of account, and, since their monetary value varied with the prices of the four commodities, depositors were protected, at least partially, against loss due to inflation. However, since bank accounts often were blocked, the parity unit never was given an adequate trial.

The most significant characteristic of inflation in China from 1937 to 1949 is that Chinese Nationalist Currency and the various Japanese and Communist issues stayed in circulation as media of exchange. There was neither a significant shift to barter nor the use of unofficial means of payment. Westerners in China realized that this was unusual. A reporter wrote: "Ordinarily inflation of the sort that China is undergoing would have brought about collapse several years ago. In fact, orthodox economists predicted it." Some persons have assumed that because both United States and Hong Kong currencies were used as stores of value during this period, they were also substituted for Chinese currencies as media of exchange. Actually, transactions in foreign money were the exception rather than the rule. The agricultural property tax payable in kind which was adopted by the Nationalists was a type of barter, but the enactment of such a tax does not indicate a public preference for barter or the unacceptability of the circulating medium.

There is some evidence that in rural areas the use of barter became more prevalent just before the monetary reforms in Free China and in Communist China in 1949. In February, 1951, the Communists announced that their currency was being used by increasing numbers of peasants and was "replacing steadily the silver coin and the barter system."[13] However, monetary collapse was not the cause either of the monetary reforms in Free China or of the stabilization attempts in Communist China. The purpose of these programs was to stabilize the value of their currencies and especially to reduce the rate of velocity. No evidence exists that commodities took the place of money as a medium of exchange in the cities of China, and even in the rural areas it was never claimed that currency exchange was entirely displaced by barter.

There are several reasons for this extraordinary acceptability of Chinese currencies as media of exchange. Regulations requiring the use of official currencies were strictly enforced, and the Chinese are by nature law-abiding. Even though these laws were related to the monetary wars and primarily sought to prevent circulation of the enemy's money, they also contributed to the acceptability of their own issues. The governments also controlled the terms of many transactions. Taxes in Free China, except for the agricultural property tax, were paid in legal tender, and goods and services distributed by the government were sold for the official medium. Since foreign trade was negotiated through government exchange banking facilities, the official medium also was required for such transactions.

The almost complete lack of effective price controls in China contributed to the use of currency as a means of payment. This is probably the principal reason for the different experiences in postwar Germany and China. In Germany after World War II extensive price controls made barter attractive, even though normally barter exchange is extremely disadvantageous. Since controlled prices were still at their prewar level, individuals insisted on being paid in kind, and business firms also acquired most of the commodities they wanted through barter, even though barter was illegal. The government forced some commodities through legitimate trade channels, and people used money to buy their meager rations, but generally money did not serve as a means of payment. In China, under the Nationalists and later under the Communists, no effective price ceilings existed except on rents and a few goods that were rationed and distributed by government agencies in large cities. The rental ceilings were frequently circumvented by the institution of key

13. A survey in one of the provinces concluded that before August, 1950, 55 per cent of the trade was conducted in silver dollars, 20 per cent by barter, and 25 per cent in People's Currency. In the spring of 1951, 81 per cent of the trade was conducted in People's Currency, 17 per cent in silver dollars, and 2 per cent in barter trade (Chao, op. cit., 74).

money. Since prices could rise freely, monetary transactions were not penalized, and the Nationalists' cost-of-living index even helped merchants compute higher prices.

Finally, by anticipating inflation, the Chinese were able to eliminate many of the disadvantages of a depreciating currency. Because the Chinese expected depreciation, they discarded the official currencies both as stores of value and as units of account and developed their own occasionally ingenious substitutes for these functions of money. In addition, since interest rates rose to allow for depreciation, borrowing and lending of money for short periods were relatively unimpeded. This ability to adjust to inflation required a steady rise in prices, which depended on careful control of new issues and on the absence of monetary reforms and stabilization programs.

IV

The Chinese experience from 1937 to 1949 shows that under conditions of hyperinflation people may retain currency as a medium of exchange but discard it as a store of value and as a unit of account. Many economists have thought that under such conditions the use of currency would have been given up completely. Cannan has stated:

> A continuance of rapid change in either direction will cause a currency to go out of use. This is perfectly reasonable, stability of value being one of the most important requisites of useful currency, and Gresham's law that bad money drives out good being fortunately quite untrue of the long run.
>
> The explanation seems to lie in the fact that human intelligence anticipates what is coming. When it is seen that the value of currency is steadily falling, people see that it is more profitable to hold goods than currency, the demand for currency fails to extend in proportion to the enlargement of the supply, and its value consequently falls more rapidly. The issuer very likely redoubles his efforts to keep up with the fall by issuing new currency at a still more rapidly increasing rate, but all to no purpose—he is bound to lose the race.[14]

14. Edwin Cannan, "The Application of the Theoretical Apparatus of Supply and Demand to Units of Currency," *Economic Journal*, 31 (December, 1921), 460–61; reprinted in American Economic Association, *Readings in Monetary Theory* (New York: Blakiston, 1951), 12.

In China, anticipation of inflation had just the opposite effect from that expected by Cannan. Instead of contributing to collapse, it resulted in adjustments that cushioned the impact of inflation. Depreciation significantly increased the cost of using money, but the Chinese apparently were willing to pay a high price to avoid the disadvantages of barter, and price controls which might have made barter more profitable than monetary exchange were not established.

PAPER MONEY—A CYCLE IN CATHAY

In the twelfth and thirteenth centuries the Mongols overran most of the then known world. As a result, a firm and efficient government was established across the breadth of Asia, and it became possible for European merchants and missionaries to travel to Peking. Nothing seems to have impressed the numerous travellers who took advantage of this opportunity more than the fact that the inhabitants of "Cathay" (the Chinese portion of the domains of the Great Khan) used paper money.[1]

Marco Polo included a chapter on the use of paper money in "Cathay" in his book:

In this city of Kanbalu [Cambulac-Peking] is the mint of the Great Khan who may truly be said to possess the secret of the alchemists, as he has the art of producing money by the following process.

He causes the bark to be stripped from those mulberry trees the leaves of which are used for feeding silk-worms, and takes from it that thin inner rind which lies between the coarser bark and the wood of the tree. This being steeped, and afterwards pounded in a mortar, until reduced to a pulp, is made into paper, resembling in substance, that which is manufactured

Reprinted, with permission of Blackwell Publishing, publisher, from *Economic History Review* 9 (June 1957): 393–407.

1. The bulk of these travellers, of course, left no written record, but, of those who did, almost all mention this peculiar custom. Friar Odoric of Portenone, William of Rubriquis, Hayton the Armenian, Josepha Barbaro, Ibn Battuta (who started his travels in Morocco rather than Europe), the Archbishop of Soltania (tentatively identified as John de Cora of the Dominican Order), and Hajji Mohammed, the rhubarb merchant whom M. Giov. Battista Ramusio, Ambassador of the Serene Republic of Venice, met at dinner in Constantinople, all mention the matter. Francis Peglotti, an agent of the great Florentine house of Bardi, discussed the use of paper money in China in the China trade section of a sort of commercial geography he wrote. John of Montecorvino, first Archbishop of Cambulac, however, does not mention the subject. Whether this is due to his generally saintly character and disdain for earthly goods or to the fact that we have only a few pages from his pen is an open question. See W. W. Rockhill (tr. and ed.), *The Journey of William of Rubriquis in the Eastern Parts of the World* (1900), p. 329; annotated translations of the accounts of the other travellers mentioned above will be found in Sir Henry Yule, *Cathay and the Way Thither* as revised by Henri Cordier (1913–16). Their references to paper money occur on the following pages: vol. 1, Hayton, p. 259; Hajji Mohammed, p. 296; vol. 2, Odoric, p. 240; vol. 3, the Archbishop of Soltania, p. 91; Peglotti, pp. 97 and 154–55; John of Montecorvino, pp. 1–28; vol. 4, Ibn Battuta, p. 112.

from cotton, but quite black.[2] When ready for use, he has it cut into pieces of money of different sizes, nearly square, but somewhat longer than they are wide. Of these, the smallest pass for a half tournois; the next size for a Venetian silver groat; others for two, five, and ten groats; others for one, two, three, and as far as ten bezants of gold. The coinage of this paper money is authenticated with as much form and ceremony as if it were actually of pure gold or silver; for to each note a number of officers, specially appointed, not only subscribe their names, but affix their seals also. When this has been regularly done by the whole of them, the principal officer, appointed by his Majesty, having dipped into vermillion the royal seal committed to his custody, stamps with it the piece of paper, so that the form of the seal tinged with the vermillion remains impressed upon it. In this way it receives full authenticity as current money, and the act of counterfeiting is punished as a capital offense.

When thus coined in large quantities, this paper currency is circulated in every part of the Great Khan's dominions; nor dares any person, at the peril of his life, refuse to accept it in payment. All his subjects receive it without hesitation because, wherever their business may call them, they can dispose of it again in the purchase of merchandise they may require; such as pearls, jewels, gold, or silver. With it, in short, every article may be procured.

Several times in the course of the year, large caravans of merchants arrive with such articles as have just been mentioned together with gold tissues, which they lay before the Great Khan. He thereupon calls together twelve experienced and skillful persons, selected for this purpose, whom he commands to examine the articles with great care, and to fix the value at which they should be purchased. Upon the sum at which they have been thus conscientiously appraised he allows a reasonable profit, and immediately pays for them with this paper. To this the owners can have no objection, because, as has been observed, it answers the purposes of their own disbursements; and even though they should be inhabitants of a country

---

2. The surviving specimens of paper money from this period are varying shades of dirty grey. It is not possible to determine their exact original colour, but they cannot have been black since they are printed in black ink. As a general rule, Polo was remarkably accurate, but even Homer nods. A. M. Davis, *Certain Old Chinese Notes* (Boston, 1915), contains an excellent collection of reproductions of Chinese notes from the period of this study. Morse also reproduces several notes, and Vissering one.

where this kind of money is not current, they invest the amount in other articles of merchandise suited to their own markets.

When any persons happen to be possessed of paper money which from long use has become damaged, they carry it to the mint, where, upon the payment of only 3%, they receive fresh notes in exchange. Should any be desirous of procuring gold or silver for the purposes of manufacture, such as of drinking-cups, girdles, or other articles wrought of these metals, they in like manner apply to the mint, and for their paper obtain the bullion they require.

All his Majesty's armies are paid with this currency, which is to them of the same value as if it were gold or silver. Upon these grounds, it may certainly be affirmed that the Great Khan has a more extensive command of treasure than any other sovereign in the Universe.[3]

It will be noted that Po-lo, the Assessor (as he appears in the Chinese histories), thinks of the printing of paper money simply as an efficient way of getting money for the government; he is unaware of the other problems raised by a continuous inflation. Indeed, he does not even mention the year-by-year decline in the value of the paper currency during the period he spent in the service of the Great Khan. Probably Polo thought of this as a minor matter to be met by expansion of the printing department.

The Chinese have tended to be less impressed with paper currency than were the foreigners from what was then a backward part of the world. Since paper, ink, and printing were all invented in China, it is not surprising that paper currency also first appeared there. The history of paper money in old China stretches over a millennium, from the ninth to the nineteenth century.[4] Its greatest development, however, was during the period between A.D. 1000 and 1500. The few economists who have discussed the history of paper

3. Manuel Komroff (ed.), *The Travels of Marco Polo* (New York, 1926), pp. 156–58.

4. For reasons which are unclear to me, most Chinese historians begin their historical account of paper money in China almost 1000 years earlier with the "deerskin money" of the Han. The Han "deerskin money" system, which lasted only a short time and had no effect on the later development of real paper money, was a peculiar form of taxation invented by one of the least distinguished emperors of the Han dynasty. Pieces of deerskin upon which had been inscribed phrases reminiscent of those usually found on currency were distributed by what amounted to a compulsory sale to various wealthy persons. There is no evidence that they ever circulated (most of the "notes" were in extremely large denominations) or performed any of the functions of money.

money in China have treated it as a single story of the rise and fall of this institution.[5] There is a sense in which one can speak of the developments in China as a single cycle, but in fact, the history of paper money in China covers seven dynasties, each with its own monetary institutions. In addition, the province of Szechuan had its own currency system. Unfortunately, our information on these eight currency systems is sadly lacking in many respects.[6] Information is so scarce, in fact, that this article contains practically everything that is known on its subject and is still only a rather bare outline of developments.

Before discussing the history in detail, however, something in the nature of a road map is desirable.[7] The first step in the development of paper money in China was a long period during which the people and government gradually became accustomed to the use of paper money. By the eleventh century this process had proceeded to the point where it was possible for the succeeding governments to establish inconvertible currencies and use inflation for budgetary purposes.[8] All of the governments in China between 1100 and 1500 succumbed to this temptation, and their monetary histories have a

---

5. W. S. Jevons, *Money and the Mechanism of Exchange* (1875), p. 198; H. D. Macleod, *Dictionary of Political Economy* (1863), pp. 667–71. Jevons's account is not only oversimplified, it is inaccurate. He commits the gaffe of using Sir John Mandeville to expand on Polo's account. In the late Middle Ages, Mandeville's book was the most widely read account of the east. Long before Jevons's time, however, scholars had realized that Sir John was a liar. See Hugh Murray, *Historical Account of Discoveries and Travels in Asia* (Edinburgh, 1820), 1, 193–97.

6. A number of historians, both western and Chinese, have worked on the history of money in China. The most recent and most comprehensive study of Chinese paper money is contained in Lien-sheng Yang (subsequently referred to as Yang), *Money and Credit in China* (Cambridge, Mass., 1952). Most of these historians, however, have had little or no knowledge of economic theory and have confined themselves to the bare assemblage of data. Dr. Yang is an economist, but devotes most of his attention to the fascinating (to a Chinese historian) and fantastically difficult philological problems of determining what the Chinese historical texts really mean. This article attempts to place the facts assembled with such diligence by the historians in their proper economic context and to point out certain implications for general monetary theory suggested by the Chinese experience.

7. Since this article is written for economists, I have confined myself to the strictly monetary history, giving only such background information as is absolutely necessary for the understanding of monetary developments.

8. The necessity of a lengthy indoctrination in the use of paper money before an inflationary policy becomes possible can be illustrated by an incident which occurred during the Mongol dynasty. The Mongol Il-Khans in Persia, impressed by the use of paper money by their suzerain in China, decided to use the same device themselves. Technical advisers were sent from Peking, and an elaborate organization was set up. The Persians, however, had not been accustomed to

strong family resemblance. In each case there was a period of inflation, usually quite a long one. Except in the case of the Southern Sung dynasty, which was conquered by the Mongols before the evolution was completed, the use of paper money was, in each case, eventually abandoned. This abandonment of the use of paper currency is the most interesting feature of the history of paper money in China and will be discussed at some length after the historical evidence has been presented. After 1500, the governments of China no longer issued paper money on any significant scale. It is interesting to note, however, that private banknotes were issued on a considerable scale in the centuries after the government ceased printing currency. Eventually, of course, paper money was brought back to China as part of the westernization process in the nineteenth and twentieth centuries.

By A.D. 700–800 there were shops in China which would accept valuables and, for a fee, keep them safe. They would honour drafts drawn on the items in deposit, and, as with the goldsmith's shops in Europe, their deposit receipts gradually began to circulate as money. It is not known how rapidly this process developed, but by A.D. 1000 there were apparently a number of firms in China which issued regular printed notes and which had discovered that they could circulate more notes than the amount of valuables they had on deposit.

At about the same time, the Chinese government was developing another type of pre-money. In order to maintain the court and army, large amounts of tax receipts had to be remitted from the provinces to the capital. To avoid physically transporting the money, the provincial governments set up offices in the capital which sold drafts payable in the provincial capitals. Apparently some private firms were also involved in this business, which closely resembles the type of banking which made the Fuggers wealthy in Europe. In 811 the government prohibited private operators, and in 812 the central government established its own system. The drafts on the provincial governments which were sold in the capital (called "flying money") are considered by the Chinese historians to be the origin of paper money in China. In Europe also, central government treasuries, at the time when paper money was developing, frequently issued drafts on local tax collection agencies.[9] Thus, when paper money was beginning to develop, there were both public and private drafts in

---

the use of paper currency by several hundred years of gradual developments. They simply refused to believe that these nicely printed pieces of paper were worth anything, and the experiment was a failure.

9. For an account of the system in England, see Sir John Craig, *A History of Red Tape* (1955), p. 26.

circulation in both Europe and China. It is interesting that money developed out of the private drafts in Europe and out of government drafts in China.

The Tang dynasty, which had ruled China since the seventh century, fell in 907. In most of China it was replaced by the Northern Sung which was established (after the customary period of confusion) in 960. Within ten years of its establishment, the Northern Sung had founded a "bureau of credit cash" which issued drafts totalling one to three million "strings"[10] per year. There were also private drafts to an unknown amount circulating during this period, and the various local and provincial governments issued considerable numbers of commodity certificates based on salt, tea, and other commodities.[11] The importance of money, both paper and metallic, was growing rapidly during the Sung, a period in which commerce rapidly expanded. Government taxes, for example, were collected over 80 per cent in kind in A.D. 1000, but by 1050 the share collected in kind had shrunk to less than 50 per cent.

A tabloid history of China for the next few centuries is necessary as a background for the history of paper money there. Northern Sung was ended by a barbarian invasion. The barbarians established the Chin dynasty in the north, and a cadet of the Sung imperial house established the Southern Sung in the south. In the latter half of the thirteenth century still another group of barbarians, the Mongols, destroyed both the Chin and the Southern Sung. In the mid-fourteenth century they were driven out, and a native dynasty, the Ming, was established. Ming, in its turn, was replaced by Ch'ing in the seventeenth century.

The great province of Szechuan has always been somewhat of a law unto itself, and, during the Northern Sung period, it developed a paper currency of its own which lasted almost to the end of Southern Sung. Iron currency had earlier come into use in Szechuan. Since this currency circulated at approximately its metallic value, it was excessively cumbersome. As a result, private banknotes seem to have developed more rapidly there. About A.D. 1000 a provincial government decree restricted the issue of such notes to a group of

---

10. The "string" was literally a string upon which, theoretically, 1000 copper cash had been threaded. (This custom is the reason for the hole in the middle of Chinese coins.) The actual number of copper cash on the string was fixed by custom and law and varied from time to time and from place to place. The size of the standard copper coin was also occasionally changed, and the value of copper varied significantly from time to time.

11. W. Vissering, *On Chinese Currency* (Leiden, 1877), p. 212 (subsequently referred to as Vissering).

sixteen merchant houses, which were permitted to charge a fee of 3 per cent for this service. The merchants did not always redeem the notes promptly. Any reasonably cynical observer would suspect that the "squeezing" of the officials was a major factor in the merchants' difficulties. The officials, however, did not take this view, and in the early part of the eleventh century, the government took over the issue itself.

The system under which the Szechuan currency was issued was rather different from any European system. Each year a fixed quota of currency was issued. This quota had to be redeemed in new notes in the third year. As long as the quota was not increased, the issuing authority profited only to the extent of "seignorage" and of those notes which were accidentally destroyed and therefore not presented for redemption. There does not seem to be any available information on the origins of this system. Possibly it was first established as a governmental regulation for private bankers and then continued when the government took over the issuing privilege. At any event, this system became the Chinese equivalent of the gold standard; by putting a limit on the number of notes which could be printed, it prevented the government from indulging in inflation.

In 1072 the Szechuan provincial government "went off the gold standard" by running off a second series of 1071 notes to repay the 1069 notes which were up for redemption, thus reserving the 1072 issue for other, more immediately useful purposes. This seems to have inaugurated a period of inflation in which yearly issues were enlarged and redemption dates frequently missed. In 1098 a decree set the yearly quota about 50 per cent higher than the 1072 quota, but actual printings seem to have been considerably higher. In 1107 the total of outstanding notes was equivalent to fourteen years' issue at the legal quota. By 1200 the note issue had again doubled. By that date the Szechuan provincial currency was passing out of use. Circulation appears to have ceased completely some time before the Mongol conquest.

It is interesting to note that during the Szechuan inflation unredeemed earlier issues were sometimes worth only one-fourth of the new issues. Speaking generally, the great advantage of a paper currency inflation over the more primitive debasement of a metallic currency lies in the fact that the newly printed paper notes are the same as the ones already in circulation. A new coin containing less metal (or less valuable metal) is obviously worth less than the older coinage, and legal efforts to make the two equivalent will merely bring on the effect discovered by Gresham. If, however, there are ten units of paper currency in existence and the government prints an eleventh, all eleven are worth 0.9 of the value of the original notes. All the currency, the old and new, is equally debased. Since the government holds the new note and the people the other ten, this is obviously an advantage to the government. In Szechuan, however, the government succeeded in doing even better than this. The newly printed notes which it issued were valued more highly than the old notes already in private hands. This was presumably the result of the system of periodic redemption. The Szechuanese may have felt that a government promise which had already been broken was worth less than one which would probably be broken in the future.[12]

Outside of Szechuan, however, the development of paper money was less rapid. Turning first to Southern Sung, in 1136 the government made an unsuccessful effort to circulate notes in the capital city. By the middle of the century, private agencies were issuing notes which circulated in the neighbourhood of the capital. In 1160 the government forbade their further circulation and began issuing its own paper currency (successfully, this time). In 1166 an effort was made to circulate paper notes in the frontier region of the Huai valley, and in 1168 a formal system for issuing paper money was established. The period of circulation was fixed at three years, and a quota of 10,000,000 strings per year was established. This would mean that a total of about 30,000,000 strings would be in circulation at one time. In practice, of course, the government soon turned to meeting fiscal deficits by expanding the currency issue. In 1176 certain issues were "permitted" to circulate for six to nine years. In 1195 the yearly quota was raised to 30,000,000 strings. Even this limit was shortly exceeded, however, and in 1209 there were 117,600,000 strings from three years in circulation.

This increase in the number of paper notes in circulation does not appear to have affected their value. Until well into the first decade of the thirteenth

12. The Chinese, however, take a somewhat irrational attitude toward the valuation of different types of money. When I was in Tientsin in 1948–50, only U.S. five-, ten-, and twenty-dollar notes circulated at par with each other. You could get six one-dollar notes for one five, and two twenties would buy a fifty. The reasons given were that singles were bulky and hard to conceal at the same time there were counterfeit fifties in circulation. Similarly, the "big head" and "little head" dollars, the two types of silver dollar in normal circulation, were sold at a fixed percentage difference in price which had no relation with the real difference in silver content. Since all these transactions were illegal, government regulations cannot be the explanation. While all of this is irrational from the standpoint of the whole society, the individual traders, of course, behaved rationally in exchanging the various types of money at the values given by society rather than in terms of "real value." Where possible, they engaged in arbitrage.

century, the paper money remained fairly stable at a value about 10 per cent less than copper in the capital and discounted another 15 per cent in the provinces. The explanation of this phenomenon seems simple. The Chinese historians tell us that during this period the circulation of these notes, at first confined to the immediate environs of the capital, gradually spread until they were used throughout the empire.[13] The government was setting a trap for itself, however, by covering a portion of its regular expenditures by expansion of the currency supply. Although this expansion might temporarily be matched by the expansion in the use of paper currency, eventually the point would be reached where paper money circulated throughout the empire, and any further expansion would cause a decline in the value of money. This dangerous point appears to have been reached in the first decade of the thirteenth century. The Southern Sung chose this delicate moment to launch a war intended to drive the Chin out of north China. The war failed, and the value of the Sung paper money went into a decline. By 1232 the notes in circulation had more than tripled, and in 1247 notes of unlimited periods of circulation were issued. The continued printing of currency pressed the value of the paper notes down, and the gradually deepening shadow of the Mongols along the northern frontier had a further depressing effect. After the Mongols had conquered Sung, they converted the Sung notes into their own paper currency at 50 to one. It is not possible to say whether this conversion rate corresponded with the market value of the two currencies at the time.

Meanwhile, in the north the barbarian dynasty of Chin was also issuing paper currency. In 1153, immediately after moving their capital from Manchuria, they printed their first notes. The Chin currency was remarkable in that there were separate issues for the various geographical areas of the empire. The period of circulation was fixed at seven years, and, until 1190, the notes were regularly retired when they came due, and the fixed quota of notes was strictly adhered to. As a result, the value of the paper currency remained stable. In 1190 a new Emperor abolished the period of circulation, and the expansion of the currency issue with a concomitant fall in value began. The

---

13. The stability of the paper notes at this time may be partially an illusion. The Chinese historians tell us that it remained stable in terms of copper; they do not tell us whether both currencies changed in value with respect to other commodities, however. Logically, if paper currency was replacing a metallic currency, the value of the currency metal would fall because of the reduced demand. If the value of copper was falling during this period, then the paper money, which kept a constant value with respect to copper, must have fallen proportionately.

inflation does not appear to have been very great at first. Provided the printing quota was retained, as it probably was for the first few years, the increase in currency each year would have been one-seventh or less of the amount in circulation.

Various measures were taken to prevent too rapid depreciation of the currency. In 1192 the Emperor decreed that the amount of paper in circulation was not to exceed that of copper cash. In 1193 certain taxes previously paid in copper were ordered to be paid in paper. In 1197 the government began an obscurely motivated experiment in silver coinage. Silver ingots were cast and circulated along with the paper notes. One ounce[14] of silver was decreed to be worth two strings of copper cash. Apparently both the silver money and the paper currency were over-valued as against copper,[15] and Gresham's law began to operate; the government found it necessary to prohibit hoarding or export of copper coins. Other, more realistic, measures were taken. Certain taxes were made payable in notes and silver, and, in Manchuria, a law was passed requiring all transactions involving more than one string to be made in silver and notes. From this time forward we will encounter more and more administrative measures designed to eliminate types of money which compete with the official currency. In 1200 the issue of silver currency was discontinued, allegedly because of counterfeiting, but probably because the supply of silver was more limited than that of paper. In 1203 local note issues, put out by city governments, which had apparently gained considerable popularity were abolished.

All of the above measures, except the initial issuance of silver currency, were obviously aimed at increasing the demand for paper currency. Any effect they may have had, however, was more than cancelled out by the activities of the government mint. The government, nevertheless, continued its attempts to keep the value of money up while steadily expanding the note issue for revenue purposes. In 1206 efforts were made to withdraw the largest denomination bills; in 1207 it was ordered that certain taxes be paid one-third in large notes, and this was later raised to two-thirds.[16] Business transactions of more value than one string were ordered to be made in paper throughout

14. The Chinese measure translated "ounce" is actually a little heavier than our ounce.

15. In 1201, silver sold against copper at 20 per cent under its official value.

16. The belief that large denomination bills are somehow more inflationary than small bills totalling the same amount seems to be endemic in China. It was observable in the post–World War Two inflation in China.

the empire, and further regulations were issued to restrict the hoarding and export of coins. Token conversion of small denomination notes into copper was undertaken by the treasury, and the small denomination notes of the various geographical areas were permitted to circulate nationally.

None of these measures, however, was enough seriously to counterbalance the steady printing of money. It will be recalled that the currency of the Southern Sung had, at about this time, been seriously affected by the expenses of a military effort to drive the Chin out of China. Defence against this effort was also a blow to the Chin currency. It was at this time, too, that the Mongols began to be a serious menace along the northern border. The Chin, being located between the Southern Sung and Mongolia, were the first to feel the weight of Mongol arms. Under the impact of high military expenditures, Chin paper currency went into a rapid inflation. In 1210 eighty-four cartloads of paper currency were distributed among the troops just before a major defeat by the Mongols. By 1214 the old currency was practically worthless, and 20- and 100-string notes were issued. Shortly thereafter, 200- and 1,000-string notes came into circulation. In 1215 a new issue of notes was printed, and circulation of copper coins was prohibited. There was also a brief, unsuccessful experiment in price controls. The new issue of notes depreciated so rapidly that by 1216 they were worth less than 1 per cent of their face value. In 1217 these notes were converted into a new issue at the rate of 1,000 to 1. In 1222 this issue was again converted at the rate of 800 to 1,[17] which was its current "black market" value. By the following year the new note had fallen to less than 1 per cent of its face value. Various other efforts were made to issue new notes in the ten years remaining to the dynasty, but they do not appear to have been successful.

By 1220 silver had replaced copper as the dominant currency metal. And, although there does not seem to be any evidence on the point, it is probable that this shift, in about twenty years, from copper to silver was directly connected with the government's monetary policy. The various legal prohibitions on the use of copper coins combined with the steady depreciation of the paper notes would naturally lead to the use of any available substitute. Legalistically, it could be argued that transactions involving silver were barter rather than currency transactions; realistically, an ounce of silver is easier to conceal than is the string of 1,000 cash, which is its copper equivalent.

---

17. Actually the rate of conversion was 400 to 1, but the legal value of the new notes was only half of the old.

When the Mongols first entered north China and overthrew the Chin, they seem to have given little attention to the possibilities of paper currency. By 1260 there were a number of currencies in circulation which had been issued by various governmental units, but the total value was probably small. These notes were silver notes rather than copper notes as previous issues had been and usually had a period of circulation of three years. In 1260, Khubilai Khan ascended the throne, making his former tutor his principal adviser. This man came from a family of Chin dynasty officials, and it was probably on his advice that Khubilai began the systematic use of the printing press that was to characterize Mongol governmental finance. In any event, in 1260 the various local currencies were called in and redeemed at fair values and a national currency issued. No period of redemption was established; the new notes were to remain in circulation indefinitely. This currency was, I think, historically unique in that its value was legally fixed at one-half its face value. Two one-ounce silver notes were legally worth one ounce of metallic silver.

For the first few years the value of the new currency was well maintained. As in the early days of the Southern Sung currency, apparently the steadily growing volume of money in circulation was matched by the steadily growing demand for the currency as its use spread through the empire. The government also had very large reserves of gold and silver, and, although they seem to have made no use of these reserves to stabilize their currency, the knowledge that they existed may have had a stabilizing effect. In 1262 the use of gold and silver as media of exchange was prohibited. Whether this indicates that the new currency had already begun to slip is not known, but the regulation probably had more practical effect than such rules usually do. The Mongol polity made a modern totalitarian state seem liberal and tolerant. Intermittently throughout the dynasty the project of killing all the Chinese and converting China to pasture land was discussed by the government. The project was never adopted, but a government which could consider it would feel few compunctions about the methods used to enforce its decrees.

Table 1 shows that the rate of issuance of currency rises sharply in the middle 1270's. The very high figure in 1276 is probably accounted for in part by the conversion of Southern Sung currency which was effected that year. It seems likely, however, that the period when the expansion of the currency issue was matched by the expansion of the demand for currency ended about this time, and the currency began to fall in value. With the value of the currency falling, it was necessary to increase the printing rate to cover that

TABLE 1. *Mongol note issue, 1260–1330* (100,000 ounces)*

YEAR	FIRST ISSUE	SECOND ISSUE[†]	THIRD ISSUE[‡]	CUMULATIVE TOTAL[§]
1260	36	–	–	36
1261	19	–	–	55
1262	40	–	–	95
1263	23	–	–	118
1264	44	–	–	162
1265	58	–	–	220
1266	38	–	–	258
1267	54	–	–	312
1268	19	–	–	331
1269	11	–	–	342
1270	48	–	–	390
1271	23	–	–	413
1272	43	–	–	456
1273	55	–	–	511
1274	123	–	–	634
1275	199	–	–	833
1276	709	–	–	1,542
1277	510	–	–	2,052
1278	No data	–	–	–
1279	394	–	–	2,446
1280	567	–	–	3,013
1281	No data	–	–	–
1282	No data	–	–	–
1283	305	–	–	3,318
1284	315	–	–	3,633
1285	1,000	–	–	4,633
1286	1,000	–	–	5,633
1287	41	500	–	8,174
1288	–	460	–	10,400
1289	–	890	–	14,400
1290	No data	–	–	–
1291	–	250	–	16,100
1292	–	250	–	17,400
1293	–	250	–	18,600
1294	–	96	–	19,100
1295	–	155	–	19,900
1296	–	200	–	20,900
1297	–	200	–	21,900
1298	–	150	–	22,600
1299	–	450	–	24,900

(continued)

TABLE 1. (*continued*)

YEAR	FIRST ISSUE	SECOND ISSUE[†]	THIRD ISSUE[‡]	CUMULATIVE TOTAL[§]
1300	–	300	–	26,400
1301	–	250	–	27,600
1302	–	1,000	–	32,600
1303	–	750	–	36,400
1304	–	250	–	37,600
1305	–	250	–	38,900
1306	–	500	–	41,400
1307	–	500	–	43,900
1308	–	500	–	46,400
1309	–	500	–	48,900
1310	–	–	725	67,000
1311	75	1,000	–	72,500
1312	50	1,111	–	78,100
1313	100	1,000	–	83,200
1314	50	1,000	–	88,300
1315	50	500	–	90,800
1316	50	200	–	91,900
1317	50	240	–	93,100
1318	50	200	–	94,200
1319	50	740	–	97,900
1320	50	740	–	101,700
1321	25	500	–	104,200
1322	25	400	–	106,200
1323	25	350	–	108,000
1324	75	300	–	109,600
1325	50	200	–	110,600
1326	50	200	–	111,700
1327	50	200	–	112,700
1328	No data	–	–	–
1329	15	155	–	113,500
1330	20	596	–	116,400

*Based on a table on p. 23, H. B. Morse, *Currency in China* (Shanghai, 1906). Figures for 1285–86 from Yang, p. 64.

†Valued at five times the first issue.

‡Valued at five times the second issue.

§In order to make the figures comparable, second-issue notes are counted as five, and third-issue notes as 25. Since there are a number of years for which we have no data, and since we have no way of knowing how many notes were accidentally destroyed, these figures should be considered only as indicating the general trend of the volume of currency in circulation. From 1288 the last two digits are rounded off.

portion of the budget which was not covered by more conventional methods of taxation. In 1273 fractional notes had been issued; in 1278 they were abandoned, presumably because the falling value of the currency made them too small to be useful. Various measures were taken to improve the demand for the currency. In 1280 its use was extended into the Uighur areas, in what is now west China, and in the same year silver and gold coins were abolished in the former domains of the Southern Sung. At this time it was possible, as in the present-day United States, to obtain gold or silver from the treasury in exchange for paper currency provided it was to be used for manufacture, not circulation. In 1283 private trade in gold and silver for any purpose was prohibited. In 1285 this restriction was relaxed.

In 1287 a new currency was issued, which was legally valued at five times the older issue. The old currency continued in circulation, however. Under the system explained by Marco Polo, old notes were replaced with new ones by the treasury so that, except for accidental loss or destruction, notes remained in circulation indefinitely. It seems likely that the new currency was given a value five times that of the old currency because the old currency had fallen to 20 per cent of its original value, but it is not possible in this case to make any accurate comparisons between the decline in value of the currency and the increase in the supply. It would appear, however, that the expansion of the currency area to include the former Southern Sung empire and the Uighur areas at least cancelled out the inflationary effect of the increase in velocity of circulation which would have occurred when the value of the currency began to decline.

In order to promote the circulation of the new notes, private trade in gold and silver was once again prohibited. Since the new notes were worth five times the old, the first year's printing was equivalent to two and one-half times the highest yearly issue of the old notes. Thereafter the chart shows, first, a fall in the amount of yearly issue and then a rise. The rate at which the currency was depreciated by the government declined, however. The 50,000,000 ounces printed in 1287 increased the total number of notes outstanding by about 40 per cent; in 1309 the same absolute amount of new notes increased the total only a trifle more than 5 per cent.

In 1294 an imperial decree was issued prohibiting the circulation of "wooden or bamboo money." It is fairly easy to guess what this "money" was. We are all familiar with street-car tokens and restaurant coupon books. In China this type of token has had very great popularity, and small wooden or bamboo tokens entitling the bearer to various things from a pound of salt to a pail of hot water circulated in most Chinese cities in imperial times. In a period of currency depreciation, such tokens, issued by a reputable commercial establishment and redeemable in some commodity of general usefulness, might well begin to replace the national currency in local areas.

In 1310 a new note was issued, legally valued at five times the worth of the second issue and twenty-five times the worth of the first. Table 1 shows that the amount of currency issued had increased to almost 900 per cent of the amount outstanding when the second issue was first issued. We have no data on the "black market" value of either the new or the old currency, but it seems likely that even the new note was valued at considerably less than par. In any event, the new note was almost immediately given up, and the issue of the two older issues was resumed on a large scale. While the absolute amount of new notes was increased, however, the rate of expansion of the currency supply was much lower than it had been in the first thirty-five years of large-scale use of paper money by the Mongols (see Fig. 1). Since the Mongol empire, which was beginning to run into difficulties on both the international and internal fronts, was not in a position to give up voluntarily any major source of income, it must be assumed that their very minor use of the printing press during the latter part of their reign was the result of factors beyond their control. What these factors were will be discussed below.

Our statistical data on Mongol note issues terminate in 1330, but there is no evidence that the situation changed much between then and 1350. Probably the currency issue was increased a few per cent each year. With the gradually increasing disorder as Mongol control slipped, however, the currency probably fell in value more than could be accounted for by the increase in the currency volume. Rules against the use of hard currency became harder and harder to enforce, and the depreciation of the paper currency was accelerated as more and more of the demand for currency was filled by metals. In 1350 a new note was issued, valued at twice the 1287 issue. Interestingly, its value was stated not in silver, but in copper. It will be recalled that in 1949, when the gold yuan had collapsed, the National Government of China replaced it with the silver yuan. Perhaps in both cases the government hoped, by returning to an older currency metal in the name of their new paper, to disassociate it from the previous currency disaster. If this was their motive, it was unsuccessful in both cases. In 1350 "people valued only hard cash." By 1356 all Mongol paper money had become practically worthless. The dynasty ended in 1368.

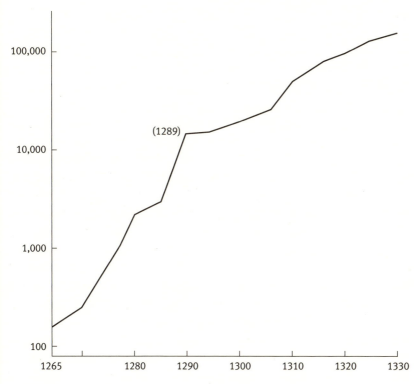

FIGURE 1

Graph of total Mongol income note issue 1260–1330 (in 100,000 ounces, at five-year intervals)[18]

It is customary to allege that the reckless printing of paper currency was one of the prime causes of the downfall of the Mongol dynasty in China.[19] This may be so, but the Mings who overthrew the Mongols were equally reckless in their monetary policy during and after their successful uprising. Various issues printed during the revolutionary period were consolidated in 1375, and a new note was issued. Although this note was not convertible, it

18. Since this graph is simply a graphic representation of the fourth column of the chart of Mongol note issues, it is subject to the same limitations on accuracy mentioned in n. $, Table 1.

19. The same statement is sometimes made about the Southern Sung. Vissering, pp. 215–20.

was officially worth one string of copper or one ounce of silver. In an effort to give the note value, it was ordered that commercial taxes were to be paid 30 per cent in cash (copper) and 70 per cent in notes. Trading in gold and silver was also forbidden, but no effort was made to enforce this prohibition. In 1385 the officials' salaries, previously paid in rice, were converted to notes, and, in 1389, fractional notes were issued. It would seem that, once again, we are encountering a situation where the expansion of the currency issue by the government approximately matches the expansion of the use of the paper notes, with the result that their value remains stable. As we have seen, the time inevitably comes when no further expansion of the area of circulation is possible.[20] The Ming apparently reached this stage in the early 1390's. In 1393 the circulation of metallic copper was "temporarily prohibited," presumably because the paper notes were beginning to depreciate. By 1400 the paper currency notes had fallen to 3 per cent of their face value. In 1404 the salt tax was ordered to be paid in notes in hopes of drawing off the "excess" currency. In 1429 a special tax organization was set up specifically to draw in the paper currency. None of these measures was successful, however. In 1425 the note issue was valued at only slightly more than 1 per cent of its face value; by 1450 it had fallen to less than one-tenth of 1 per cent of face value. Circulation of paper currency seems to have practically ceased by 1500, and the notes were becoming collector's items.

The collapse of the Ming currency was not, however, due to a runaway printing press. In the early years of the fifteenth century, the Ming gradually stopped printing currency. At the same time, it gradually relaxed its efforts to support the currency. Since the currency was already badly depreciated, and, of course, inconvertible, it was rapidly replaced by metal coins when government support was withdrawn.

From 1500 to the breakdown of the old Chinese system under western influence, we hear little of paper currency. Printing of paper currency was discussed by the Ming government just before the dynasty fell, but none was issued. The newly established Ch'ing dynasty issued a few notes from 1650 to 1661, but the issue, which totalled less than 1,000,000 ounces at face value, was abolished in 1661. In 1853, during the Taiping rebellion, the Ch'ings once again issued a few notes to help pay for their military operations, but their value dropped very rapidly, and they ceased to circulate after 1861.

---

20. I am not discussing the modern world, where a perpetually expanding economy appears to be possible.

In 1853 the Ch'ing also tried another type of token money. Iron coins were issued, but they also depreciated to their metallic value very quickly. For some reason, however, these iron coins remained the common circulating medium of the imperial capital of Peking until almost the end of the dynasty.[21]

But, while the Chinese government, as long as it remained Chinese, eschewed the printing of paper currency, private banknotes once again became an important part of the Chinese monetary system. At least as early as the seventeenth century, banks and goldsmiths were issuing credit instruments. In the eighteenth and nineteenth centuries, they issued regular private banknotes. There are no statistics available, but the circulation of such notes in the nineteenth century was very great. Not only banks but other commercial companies sometimes issued notes. It is interesting that in the north, where the trade in brick tea was important, these notes frequently were based on tea bricks rather than on metal.

On the whole, Chinese monetary experience seems more or less in accord with modern monetary theory. Only once, and then only for a short period under the Chin, did any Chinese government try to combine inflation with price control.[22] The rate of inflation was also normally low. In the latter part of the Chin dynasty, rates of inflation which would do credit to a modern European country were obtained, but this was the exception. Normally it would appear that the amount added to the money supply ran well under 20 per cent per year. This is particularly remarkable when it is remembered that the various dynasties were engaged in active warfare for much of the period studied.

From the standpoint of the economist, however, the most interesting feature of the history recounted above is the fact that, after some 500 years' experience, the Chinese eventually abandoned the use of state-sponsored paper money and returned to a combination of hard currency and private banknotes.[23] There were four separate occasions when the use of governmentally

21. S. W. Bushell, "Coins of the Present Dynasty of China," *Journal, North China Branch, Royal Asiatic Society*, vol. 15 (1880).

22. That is, general price stabilization by use of the police power. The Chinese have always believed in "interventionism," and during the period of our study there were doubtless thousands of government orders, mostly by local governments, fixing specific prices. It seems likely that the experience obtained in attempting to enforce such orders may have been a factor in the decision not to institute an O.P.A.

23. Both Jevons and Macleod seem primarily interested in this point in brief accounts they give of the Chinese experiment in paper money. From the perspective of the 1950's, however,

issued paper money was abandoned. The paper currency of the Southern Sung was still circulating when the dynasty fell. In the cases of Chin, the Mongols, Ming, and, probably, the provincial currency of Szechuan, however, the paper notes simply ceased to circulate. Chin and the Mongols stopped issuing paper currency when they were on their last legs, when one would expect the printing presses to be working overtime. Ming, however, gave up at the height of its power.

Unfortunately our historical records are weak on this issue. We must turn to theoretical analysis to explain the actions of the various Chinese governments which gave up the use of the printing press as a source of revenue. Any explanation of the abandonment of paper currency must explain both why the people abandoned its use and why the government let them. After the populace has established the habit of using paper currency, its abandonment must take the form of either a return to barter or a development of a substitute currency. Barter is an extremely inefficient system, and a currency would have to depreciate at an extreme rate to make barter an attractive alternative.[24] An alternative currency presents less of a problem, however. The most diverse commodities have been used as currency. The use of cigarettes in postwar Germany harks back to the use of tobacco in colonial Virginia. In our survey of Chinese monetary history we have seen "warehouse receipts" for brick tea and tickets for various other commodities partially taking the place of money. Historically, however, gold and/or silver have been the primary "commodity" moneys.

The inconvenience of direct use of the precious metals as currency lies not so much in their weight as in the fact that they must be assayed at each transaction. In a time of inflation, people are confronted with the necessity of deciding whether they find the gradual shrinking of their money more or less inconvenient than the inconveniences which necessarily surround the use of the precious metals. The higher the rate of depreciation of the paper currency, the more the cases in which it would be replaced by precious metals. Since each replacement of paper by metal restricts the sphere in which the paper circulates, this replacement, in and of itself, accelerates the inflation. Presumably,

---

the explanation that inflation led to loss of confidence, loss of confidence led to abandonment of paper currency seems a trifle over-simplified (op. cit.).

24. This assumes free markets. A system of price controls in a period of inflation can make barter attractive by making monetary transactions practically impossible.

at a fairly low rate of expansion of the money supply, the use of paper money would, in time, be abandoned if the people were left to make their own decisions.

In a period of mild inflation, however, the replacement of a paper currency, to which the people have become accustomed, by some commodity would take some time. As people begin to realize that the paper currency is gradually shrinking in value, different people will turn to different expedients to keep up the value of their liquid reserves. Only when one or a few commodities begin to be accepted by everyone as a store of value will paper begin to be displaced as a circulating medium. The speed with which paper passed out of circulation would be influenced by the rate of inflation, the relative availability of commodities suitable for use as currency,[25] and the temperament of the population.

The successive Chinese governments covered in this study had not the advantage of officials trained in economics,[26] but they early realized that they must prevent the use of competing forms of money if their paper money was to continue in use. The slow rate of inflation maintained in the latter half of the Mongol dynasty would appear to indicate that by the early part of the fourteenth century they had realized that a high rate of expansion of the money supply might rapidly drive paper money out of circulation. We have seen a large number of measures taken against the use of commodity moneys by the various Chinese governments. Undoubtedly a government can, by use of its police powers, markedly reduce the speed with which paper currency is replaced by something else, even in a period of inflation. It is, however, an area where enforcement becomes progressively more difficult. The difficulty of enforcement is accentuated by the fact that the enforcement officials themselves have as much motive to violate the legal restriction as have private citizens. All of the Chinese governments eventually gave up the fight. It would appear that they found inflation of the currency a wasting asset. At first the raising of government funds by printing currency seemed miraculously easy.

25. Too many commodities suitable for use as money would slow down the standardization on one which is necessary for development of a substitute money.

26. Vissering is largely an annotated translation of a work by a thirteenth-century Chinese historian which, in turn, is largely a collection of contemporary documents on monetary problems. These materials clearly demonstrate that the Chinese of the thirteenth century knew little more about monetary theory than their contemporaries in Europe.

As time went on, however, the administrative measures necessary to prevent the development of a competing currency became administratively more and more difficult and/or less and less effective. The value to the treasury of new currency issues shrank as the share which paper had of the total currency "market" shrank. Eventually, it became administratively more difficult to raise a given amount of funds via the printing press than by taxation.

SOME LITTLE-UNDERSTOOD ASPECTS OF
KOREA'S MONETARY AND FISCAL SYSTEMS

Colin D. Campbell and Gordon Tullock

In recent years many Americans have learned that the task of giving advice to foreign countries is not easy. The principal difficulty is that foreign countries have economic and political systems that are different from our own. Not knowing the real situation in foreign countries, Americans sometimes assume incorrectly the existence of their own institutions. We propose to illustrate the difficulty with a few examples based on American experience with the problem of inflation in South Korea from 1945 to 1954. Although many of these examples are unique, they may suggest similar situations in other countries and add to our general understanding of the problem of giving economic advice to other countries.

I. Adjustments to Continuous Inflation

From the beginning of the American occupation in 1945 to the present, the Korean people appear to have anticipated a very rapid rate of inflation. Although it is well known by Western economists that general anticipation of inflation will profoundly change the way in which a country's money system operates, few American economists have had any acquaintance with a monetary system in which rapid inflation was anticipated. The strangeness of such a system has been the principal difficulty confronting American advisors in South Korea.

It is not known exactly when during the Second World War the Korean populace first began to anticipate some inflation. Immediately before and after the surrender of Japan in August 1945, the Japanese system of price controls collapsed and prices rose from 20 to 25 times.[1] Following this change from suppressed to open inflation, most prices either remained stable or rose

Reprinted, with permission of the American Economic Association, from *American Economic Review* 47 (June 1957): 336–49.

1. A. I. Bloomfield and J. P. Jensen, *Banking Reform in South Korea* (Federal Reserve Bank of New York, March 1951), p. 27.

a little in the final quarter of 1945.[2] Prices of major grain commodities actually fell, probably because the Koreans suddenly stopped exporting 40 per cent of their annual rice crop.[3] In the first nine months of 1946, however, the people apparently came to expect a much more rapid rate of inflation than previously. At this time there was a remarkable increase in the rate of velocity of money. Wholesale prices increased 666 per cent, while the money supply rose only 58 per cent. A reaction then set in, and the velocity declined so that the index of wholesale prices actually fell during the last three months of the year in spite of a continued increase in the money supply. Since 1946, changes in the rate of velocity have been small compared with the changes in that year.

One result of the general expectation of rapid inflation was that the Korean people discarded the use of Korean money as a store of value. This was noted by Bloomfield and Jensen, who were advisors to the Korean Ministry of Finance in 1950.[4] Most Koreans shifted from the use of Korean money as a store of value to the use of hoarded goods or dollar notes. This hoarding has been viewed with alarm by many Americans. They have thought that the purpose of the hoarding was to speculate.[5] Actually, when inflation is anticipated, there are few alternatives to hoarding. Both persons and business firms must have some relatively liquid assets, and when prices are expected to rise, a depreciating money will no longer serve this purpose.

Bloomfield and Jensen also noted the unusually high rates of interest in the free market. Interest rates in the open market have ranged from 5 to 20 per cent per month. As Bloomfield and Jensen explained, this also was primarily the result of anticipated inflation. In determining rates of interest, borrowers and lenders were discounting the anticipated rise in prices. Again, some Americans have not understood the reason for these high interest rates.[6] They have blamed the money lenders and have thought that the high interest rates were impediments to needed investment.

2. National Economic Board, H.Q., U.S. Army Military Government in Korea, *Price Developments in South Korea* (Seoul, Sept. 1947), p. 2.

3. G. M. McCune, *Korea Today* (Cambridge, 1950), p. 119.

4. Bloomfield and Jensen, op. cit., pp. 31–32.

5. For example, see United Nations, *An Economic Programme for Korean Reconstruction*, prepared by R. R. Nathan Associates for the U.N. Korean Reconstruction Agency (Washington, March 1954), p. 10.

6. For example, see the informative news article by W. L. Worden, "We Can't Ignore Korea," *Saturday Evening Post*, Oct. 15, 1955, 228, 182. See also J. P. Lewis, *Reconstruction and Development in South Korea* (Washington, 1955), p. 27.

Although Korean money was discarded as a store of value, it has been used during this entire period as a medium of exchange. The widely accepted belief that rapid inflation must eventually result in complete monetary collapse received careful formulation in the works of such a distinguished economist as Cannan and is still held by many economists.[7] In 1950 Bloomfield and Jensen wrote: "The basic economic problem that overshadows all others in South Korea today is to stop further inflation before it develops into a full-scale flight from the currency with inevitable monetary and financial collapse."[8]

Yet, after Bloomfield and Jensen made this prediction, even though inflation became much more rapid during the Korean War from 1950 to 1953 and has continued up to the present, Koreans still have used their money as a means of payment. Western economists have probably underestimated the usefulness of money as a medium of exchange in an inflationary economy. In spite of the greater theoretical interest in the speculative and precautionary motives for holding money, the principal function of money is to make transactions. In a period of inflation people will, of course, try to hold money for transactions for shorter periods of time. This has been true in South Korea. But they may still find the depreciating money more desirable than barter as a means of exchange. There has been a remarkably small increase in barter trade in South Korea during this period. Effective price controls during suppressed inflation could undoubtedly make barter more attractive than the use of money, as was the case in Germany after the Second World War. But in South Korea, there have been no effective general controls over prices since the Japanese controls broke down in 1945. The Korean government has fixed the prices of aid goods, grains collected by the government, and numerous items produced by government enterprises, but the government itself sells these items for cash, so there has been no chance for a shift to bartering for these items. Finally, government enforcement of the use of its money as a medium of exchange is an important factor keeping it in circulation.

The Republic of Korea unsuccessfully attempted to stabilize prices by means of a monetary reform in February 1953. Because of the rapidity of the rise in prices, the advisability of a reform had been under consideration for several years. The old won currency was converted into a new currency called

7. E. Cannan, "The Application of the Theoretical Apparatus of Supply and Demand to Units of Currency," *Economic Journal*, Dec. 1921, 31, 460–61; reprinted in American Economic Association, *Readings in Monetary Theory* (New York, 1951), p. 12.

8. Bloomfield and Jensen, op. cit., p. 57.

the "hwan" at a ratio of 100 won to 1 hwan. People were required to surrender won notes and payment orders and to declare and register won bank deposits and other monetary obligations within nine days after the announcement. The initial exchange that was permitted was limited to 500 hwan per person, and a portion of the surrendered money was blocked for a period up to three years. Good reasons for thinking that the conversion would help the inflationary situation are hard to find. Monetary conversions are usually recommended to prevent a sharp rise in prices when rationing and price controls are withdrawn, but in 1953 there was no need for reducing the monetary supply for this purpose. Between 1945 and 1954 only a few articles were rationed—mostly commodities sold by the government in the cities. The reform could have been part of an overall program to return to conditions of monetary stability, but there was no reason to believe that the government would be able to balance its budget and avoid an expansion of bank loans. The reform, however, did afford the police an opportunity to check on some cases of tax evasion. Also, although there was some redistribution of wealth held in the form of currency and deposits because large holdings were blocked, at this time most wealthy persons undoubtedly held the bulk of their assets in hoarded commodities or dollar notes.

A common error among those who are unfamiliar with rapid inflation is the belief that inflation necessarily results in an excessive bulkiness of the money supply. When the currency conversion in 1953 was announced, the *New York Times* reported that the Korean government believed that the new issue of currency would cut printing costs and eliminate "mountains of paper" in any major money transaction.[9] Actually, although the quantity of money increased almost 130 times from 1945 to 1952, the number of paper notes in circulation only tripled.[10] In most countries, because the government is willing to exchange notes of different denominations at par with each other, the denominations outstanding—and thus the number of paper notes in circulation—depend primarily on what the public wants. This was apparently the situation in South Korea. To avoid problems of bulkiness, however, a government must occasionally issue larger denomination notes as inflation progresses. This was done in South Korea in 1950 when the new 1,000 won note replaced the 100 won note as the largest note in circulation. Although the monetary reform initially reduced the number of paper notes outstanding by

9. "South Korea Acts to Bolster Forces," *New York Times*, Feb. 15, 1953, p. 3.

10. The number of paper notes in circulation can be computed from data on note issue by denomination in the *Monthly Statistical Review* published by the Bank of Korea.

approximately 10 to 1, their number was almost restored in the two years after the reform.

Koreans have also continued to use their money as a unit of account even though inflation has caused the money unit of account to have little meaning. They kept their bookkeeping accounts in terms of won prior to the monetary reform and then in terms of hwan. This continued use of their money as a unit of account would be surprising except for their primitive accounting practices. During the Chinese inflation from 1937 to 1949, even though the Chinese used their currency as a medium of exchange, they quickly resorted to several alternative units of account such as U.S. dollars, various commodity indexes, and 1937 prices.[11]

An unusual characteristic of the Korean inflation is that from 1947 to 1949 and from 1953 to 1954 the velocity of circulation apparently declined. As shown in Table 1, in these years the percentage increase in the wholesale price index from the end of one year to the end of the next lagged behind the large expansion in the money supply.[12] It is widely accepted by Western economists that rapid inflations normally accelerate prior to their collapse, and in many cases this has been true.[13] Bloomfield and Jensen state that the decline in velocity in South Korea from 1947 to 1949 can be "accounted for

11. See the authors' "Hyperinflation in China, 1937–49," *Journal of Political Economy*, June 1954, 62, 242–43.

12. The lag in the rise in prices behind the increase in the money supply in 1953 is probably smaller than the wholesale price index in Table 1 shows. The small increase in wholesale prices in that year resulted from the drop in the index for grain, which has a weight of 39 and is the largest component of the wholesale price index. In 1953 the wholesale index excluding grain rose 81 per cent. The variation in the components of the index resulted in a downward bias because there was no change in the weight given to grain even though the percentage of income spent for grain must have dropped sharply.

Another reason that the rise in prices following the Korean War was smaller than might be expected was the rapid economic recovery at this time. In 1953–54 the rice crop was larger than in the two previous years. Electric power generation and industrial and mining production also increased significantly. After the armistice in July 1953 about 1,500,000 persons — 7 per cent of the population — moved back to Seoul, and many more persons returned to other evacuated areas. The reopening of these areas restored the market for housing and utilities for these persons and for regular transportation facilities between these areas and the rest of the country. Many refugees had been uninterested in building up business facilities until the war ended and they were permanently located.

13. See League of Nations, *Memorandum on Currency 1913–1923* (Geneva, 1924), pp. 16–17, for numerous examples of accelerated inflation following the First World War. Two exceptions, however, are the inflations in Portugal and Greece from 1921 to 1923.

TABLE 1. *The Supply of Money and Wholesale Prices in South Korea, 1945–1954*

END OF YEAR	MONEY SUPPLY[a]		INDEX OF WHOLESALE PRICES IN SEOUL[b]	
	AMOUNT[c]	PERCENTAGE INCREASE[d]	ANNUAL AVERAGE IN 1947 = 100	PERCENTAGE INCREASE[d]
1945	11,828	–	11.8	–
1946	27,194	129.9	74.4	530.5
1947	53,647	97.3	142.4	91.4
1948	73,671	37.3	185.0	29.9
1949	130,617	77.3	289.9	56.7
1950	290,462	122.4	831.1	186.7
1951	784,806	170.2	2,599.2	212.7
1952	1,564,117	99.3	5,256.8	102.2
1953	3,489,600	123.1	6,466.1	24.9
1954	6,687,100	91.6	10,036.7	55.2

SOURCES: A. I. Bloomfield and J. P. Jensen, *Banking Reform in South Korea* (Federal Reserve Bank of New York, March 1951), p. 29; Bank of Korea, *Monthly Statistical Review*, various issues, 1952–55.

[a] Includes Bank of Korea notes held outside banking institutions, all private and commercial checking or other deposits in all banks, financial associations, and the Bank of Korea, and a small amount of treasury deposits from 1947 to 1953. These figures were revised in the *Monthly Statistical Review*, July 1955. The old figures are used here because new data for the factors affecting the money supply in Table II are not available and because the old and new figures differ very little in the percentage increase from the end of one year to the end of the next.

[b] In Pusan from 1950 to 1952.

[c] Prior to 1953 in millions of won. In 1953 and 1954 in 10,000 hwan. In February 1953 won currency was converted into hwan at 100 to 1 hwan.

[d] Percentage increase from end of previous year.

only in terms of a failure on the part of the bulk of the population fully to grasp what was happening to the purchasing power of their money, or of a belief that the rise in prices would soon come to an end."[14] This explanation, however, seems incorrect because the continuance of high interest rates and the use of commodities as a store of value show that the populace did anticipate inflation. These declines in the velocity of circulation may have resulted from the slowing up of the rate of increase in the money supply from 1946

14. Bloomfield and Jensen, op. cit., p. 33.

to 1948 and from 1951 to 1954. Slowing up the rate of new issues would tend to reduce the rate of inflation and, by reducing the amount of depreciation over a given period, the cost of holding money. As people became accustomed to the new rate, this might have caused them to economize less in the use of money. Just the opposite situation may have occurred during the Korean War, when the rate of expansion in the money supply was increasing, and prices rose more rapidly than the quantity of money. The receipt of larger and larger amounts of aid goods both before and after the Korean War probably contributed to the decline in the annual percentage increase in the money supply in these periods. United States government grants and credits to Korea, not including military grants, rose from $32 million up to the end of 1946 to $134 million in 1948. They also rose from $118 million in 1951 to $192 million in 1953.[15] Although the annual amounts of these grants seem small to Americans, from the point of view of the Korean national income, they are important.

II. Nonbudgetary Sources of Revenue

Lack of knowledge of Korean fiscal institutions has been another obstacle to giving useful advice. A specific example of a policy that was based on a misunderstanding of their fiscal institutions is the proposal to raise the prices of foreign-aid goods. It was believed by officials of the United Nations and by many others that this would contribute significantly toward economic stability. Although Table 2 shows that beginning in 1947 sales of aid goods have yielded significant amounts of revenue even though they have been priced far below market levels, they would have yielded much higher revenues if their prices had been raised. The Combined Economic Board Agreement between the United Nations and the Republic of Korea, which was signed December 14, 1953, provided that "Aid goods from all sources which are offered for

15. U.S. Bureau of the Census, *Statistical Abstract of the United States, 1954* (Washington, 1954), p. 902. In 1954 grants and credits for nonmilitary aid dropped temporarily to $123 million because a new program which was undertaken immediately after the Korean armistice by the Foreign Operations Administration did not expand until late in the year. E. S. Kerber, "Foreign Grants and Credits—U.S. Government, Fiscal 1954," *Surv. Curr. Bus.*, Oct. 1954, 34, 11. Military aid furnished under the mutual security program cannot be shown by country, but only by areas as designated in the authorizing legislation. Military grants to Asia and the Pacific rose from $189 million in fiscal 1951 to $721 million in fiscal 1954; ibid., 20.

TABLE 2. *Major Factors Affecting the South Korean Money Supply, 1945–1954*

(Prior to 1953 in millions of won; in 1953 and 1954 in 10,000 hwan.)

END OF YEAR	MONEY SUPPLY[a]	NET GOVERNMENT BORROWING AT BANK OF KOREA[b]	PROCEEDS FROM SALE OF AID GOODS[c]	BANK LOANS[d]	OTHER FACTORS[e]
1945	11,828	81	–	4,008	7,739
1946	27,194	6,048	–	12,026	9,120
1947	53,647	21,301	−4,391	27,536	9,201
1948	73,671	37,234	−8,602	36,499	8,540
1949	130,617	83,110	−44,176	78,336	13,347
1950	290,462	202,466	−53,893	87,699	54,190
1951	784,806	202,023	−197,911	307,017	473,677
1952	1,564,117	132,614	−495,331	809,961	1,116,873
1953	3,489,600	1,721,900	−783,500	2,066,900	484,300
1954	6,687,100	5,653,000	−2,062,400	3,095,500	1,000

SOURCES: Bank of Korea, *Monthly Statistical Review*, various issues, 1953–55.

[a] See Table 1.

[b] Borrowings by the government minus government deposits, except for deposits representing proceeds from the sales of aid supplies.

[c] Prior to September 30, 1948, covers proceeds from Government and Relief in Occupied Areas supplies. Includes Economic Cooperation Administration goods from October 1948, goods supplied under the Korean Civil Relief Program from March 1951, and goods financed by the Foreign Operations Administration and United Nations Korean Rehabilitation Administration imports from January 1954.

[d] Includes loans by the Bank of Korea and other banks to private borrowers and government agencies. It includes loans by the Federation of Financial Associations and the financial associations, but excludes interbank loans (chiefly from the FFA to the FA's).

[e] Chiefly consists of the interbranch accounts of individual banking institutions, uncleared checks and drafts, and Bank of Korea purchases of foreign exchange. Beginning in 1950, also includes net UN Forces borrowings at the Bank of Korea less proceeds from the sales of government foreign exchange holdings. The main source of government foreign exchange holdings is the repayment of advances to UN Forces. In 1951–52, UN borrowings far exceeded proceeds from the sales of foreign exchange because of the delay by the UN in making these payments.

sale in Korea shall be sold at prices approximating those of similar items in the free market. . . ."[16] In spite of this agreement, the Republic of Korea has not raised prices of aid goods. Although selling them at higher prices would appear to help balance the budget, actually because of the peculiar fiscal system in South Korea, the government has been getting full value for aid goods even though it has not charged the highest prices it could get for them. This is because most governmental agencies and other organizations receiving aid goods have been reselling part of them at a profit in order to supplement their money receipts from the budget. These profits are used to finance their regular activities. If low-priced aid goods were not available, these governmental agencies would require larger budget allocations to maintain the same activities. The larger revenues that the central government would receive from selling aid goods at higher prices would merely offset larger expenditures, and the budget would come no closer to being balanced. In addition, some organizations have been able to sell their services cheaper because the receipt of aid goods at low prices has reduced their cost of production, but the government would not necessarily decide to stop subsidizing the activities of these organizations.

The distribution of gasoline, which is one of the most important aid products, is a good example of the way in which the Korean government distributes aid goods. Gasoline is imported and sold wholesale by an organization that represents a group of American oil companies, but it is controlled almost completely by the Korean government. The bulk of the gasoline goes to government bureaus, the army, and various companies that the government wishes to favor. The organizations use some of the gasoline themselves and sell the remainder at market prices. The profits from the sales of gasoline provide operating funds that do not appear in the budget. Through this means the government also subsidizes users of various services such as low-priced bus transportation.

The distribution of fertilizer, which is another important aid product, has frequently been criticized by Americans. A reporter recently wrote that fertilizer sales in 1954 produced only 3 billion hwan instead of 40 billion hwan because the government fixed the price of fertilizer with little regard to economic realities in order to make itself popular with farmers. Actually, only a

---

16. U.S. Committee on Government Operations, 83rd Cong., 2nd Sess., *Relief and Rehabilitation in Korea*, House Rept. No. 2574, Union Calendar No. 882 (Washington, 1954), p. 70.

part of this difference represents a subsidy to farmers. Although the Korean Federation of Financial Associations, which distributes fertilizer, officially charges farmers prices for fertilizer not far above those paid for it, farmers usually must make additional payments in order to insure the prompt delivery of their fertilizer. The Financial Associations are a major source of funds for local government expenditures, and they also use the profits of their fertilizer business to finance some of their business activities that operate at a loss. Although Westerners should not be surprised to discover that countries in the Far East also have agricultural subsidies, the same reporter severely criticizes the Republic of Korea for "outright theft, for political purposes, of most of the fertilizer money." [17]

Another United Nations proposal that was based on a misunderstanding of the Korean fiscal system was the suggestion to lessen inflationary pressures by curtailing the expansion of bank loans. The Combined Economic Board Agreement of December 14, 1953, requires that the Republic of Korea set a limit on the annual expansion of credit granted by the Bank of Korea and the commercial banks. [18] Although Table 2 shows that from 1945 to 1954 the expansion of bank loans accounted for approximately one-third of the expansion in the money supply, it is necessary to examine the nature of these loans before knowing whether curtailing them would actually reduce inflationary pressures. If bank loans in Korea were granted for investment in plant and equipment, the United Nations proposal to set a limit on the annual expansion of bank credit would undoubtedly help check the rise in prices. But in South Korea the bulk of the bank loans are used to make up losses incurred by government and other important enterprises that sell their goods and services at prices less than cost. Recently a Seoul newspaper frankly announced that the Bank of Korea had fixed at 13.5 billion hwan the funds to be supplied financial institutions for the second quarter of the fiscal year. [19] It is a general policy in South Korea for the government to subsidize the consumers of many goods and services through its lending program. As long as the Republic of Korea maintains these subsidies, if bank loans were not available, the government would be forced to find some other source of revenue such as budgetary allocations. Politically, eliminating subsidies by setting prices that cover costs of production would probably be impossible.

17. Worden, op. cit., 181.
18. U.S. Committee on Government Operations, op. cit., p. 69.
19. *Seoul Shinmun*, Oct. 4, 1955.

Not only would Koreans oppose paying higher prices for subsidized goods and services, but political leaders would probably not be able to explain to the Korean populace how inflation could be prevented by raising the prices of many important goods and services.

Westerners frequently have not realized that Korean banks are significantly different from commercial banks in the United States. In Korea the principal function of these banks is to provide revenue for the government. The Taehan Coal Company, for example, covers its yearly deficits by obtaining "loans" from various banks. Normally, these "loans" involve issues of new money, but on those rare occasions when the banking system has funds available to make real loans, they are treated in the same way. Needless to say, the Taehan Coal Company would be badly shocked if anyone suggested that it repay its "loans." Although Korean banks charge interest, and official rates of interest in Korea seem normal to Westerners, considering inflation, they "lend" money at substantially negative rates of interest. Money shops called "kye," rather than the big government banks, are the equivalent of Western commercial banks as far as loans are concerned. These money shops are illegal, although not strenuously suppressed. They pay depositor members 15 to 20 per cent interest per month and charge their borrowing members comparable rates. They are an important source of capital for investment in Korea today and have provided the resources for the rapid recovery of retail trade since the Korean War. In one respect the big banks are similar to commercial banks in the United States. They perform the service of transferring funds via check, which is important to the government and the larger industries because of the hazard of carrying large amounts of currency.

Both of the major nonbudgetary sources of revenue in South Korea—bank loans at negative rates of interest and receipts from the resale of aid goods—are extremely cumbersome, and cause great confusion in the statistics on government finance. These nonbudgetary revenues, however, may be transferred from one organization to another as need requires. The government may determine the allocation of additional funds by deciding which enterprises are to be permitted to buy aid goods at less than market prices. Also, further subsidies may be granted in the form of bank loans at low interest rates to the various government organizations.

It is occasionally claimed that some civil servants become rich from the unofficial income attached to their positions while others are forced to neglect their official duties by accepting outside employment. Actually, a well-organized government bureau in Korea will have regular procedures whereby those members of the staff who can obtain funds from nonbudgetary sources transmit their take to other members of the staff performing essential services which do not bring in large amounts of extra income. From the Korean point of view, an advantage of using nonbudgetary funds is that Korean officials can politely agree with their foreign advisors when changes in spending are suggested, but can deprive organizations of nonbudgetary sources of revenue necessary for their effective operation.

Most Westerners have not realized that the Korean policies of pricing consumer goods and services below market levels and using bank loans and aid goods as sources of government revenue are important to the political stability of the Republic of Korea. Eliminating these policies would abolish important sources of political power. By requiring important enterprises to provide services to the public at less than cost, the central government can keep the lower echelons of government in line through its control over their sources of funds. Such a pricing policy also makes the government appear as a benefactor of the public. Although the Republic of Korea is frequently criticized for the way it has used its economic powers, some method of minimizing social tensions and maintaining a stable government is undoubtedly desirable. If the Republic of Korea were deprived of these economic powers, it might be forced to resort to less acceptable means of control. It should be added that although the government of South Korea is not a democracy in the sense in which this form of government is understood in the United States, the Korean assembly is not controlled by President Rhee. The assembly often passes laws that are not approved by him, and there are frequent examples of compromise and agreement between the executive and the legislature.

III. The Ideological Environment

A major increase in the productivity of the Korean economy would, of course, solve most of its fiscal problems. Many Westerners have suggested that the productivity of the Korean economy could be improved by transferring public enterprises to private ownership and management. This suggestion is also based on a lack of understanding of Korean attitudes and institutions. As a result of its vesting of all Japanese property in South Korea, the Republic of Korea owns practically all industrial enterprises of any size and a large amount of residential real estate. However, even if the Republic of Korea sold large amounts of this property, it probably would not cease granting the new owners bank loans at negative real rates of interest, allocating low-priced aid goods to them, or setting the prices of their services or products below market levels. The small amount of property already sold appears to have been purchased by supporters of the present government, and the funds with which to buy them have been obtained from bank loans. Koreans do not distinguish sharply between government and nongovernment, and insofar as such a distinction is drawn, it is largely a matter of size. To Koreans, the government should not be concerned with small matters, but anything that is large, whether it is a business, a sports organization, or a church, is a legitimate concern of the government. It is traditional in the Far East for the government to operate or closely control all significant economic activity. Also from the time the Westernization of oriental societies was begun, almost all Asiatic intellectuals have been devoted to socialism. They have typically believed that Marxism was the "most advanced" economic theory of the West.

When the land reform bonds were issued in payment for lands that were taken from Korean landowners, it was suggested that the holders of these bonds be permitted to use them to buy former Japanese plants. However, this policy will probably not be followed generally, because bondholders are frequently members of the opposition. Also, because of their intense nationalistic feelings, Korean leaders would never permit foreigners to purchase this property.

Another obstacle to establishing free private enterprise in South Korea is that the necessary legal conditions do not exist. Although there is a code of laws, a Korean lawsuit is not even in theory an effort to establish an impersonal concept of justice, but an effort to find an acceptable compromise between the parties. Viewed from the standpoint of limiting social tensions, there is much to be said for the Korean system. Economically, however, it has the unfortunate result that no contract is really binding, and a further element of risk is added to all business operations. Under present conditions wealthy Koreans would not want to purchase large enterprises except at extremely low prices. Funds invested in a large plant are simply exposed to the exactions of the bureaucracy.

IV. Fiscal Inadequacy

Western advice was probably not needed to inform the Koreans that the way to prevent inflation was to balance their revenues and expenditures so as to avoid expanding the quantity of money. However, some of their difficult fiscal problems should be mentioned. Even though taxes have been far from adequate, they have taken a large part of the national income. Per capita income is less than $100 per annum, of which the government either for domestic investment or government expenditures takes almost one-third.[20] Raising tax rates also has a serious disadvantage. Although most South Koreans are hostile to the Communist government in North Korea, their hostility is not based on Western ideas of freedom and democracy, but on, among other things, the fact that taxes are considerably lower, and most consumer goods are cheaper in South Korea.

On the expenditure side, although a large part of the cost of maintaining the armed forces is borne by the United States, the remainder is still a heavy burden. Koreans usually claim that military expenditures are too small, and because of the present precarious situation of South Korea, Westerners cannot argue with any degree of assurance that they are wrong. Eventually the Republic of Korea might be able to reduce its expenditures on defense without undermining its security by developing an active military reserve on the Swiss model, but this would have little effect on their fiscal problems in the next few years. Most civilian agencies appear to be heavily overmanned, and many subsidies seem unnecessary. Politically, however, reducing these expenditures would be very unpopular.

As in many other countries that have recently obtained their national independence, there are in South Korea great pressures to expand expenditures for developmental projects. The United Nations has participated in the formation of ambitious developmental programs in spite of the fact that such programs would undoubtedly stimulate further inflation. A recent five-year program prepared by the UN for South Korea provides that total investment increase from $198 million in 1953–54 to $468 million in 1955–56 and then decline to $300 million in 1958–59, when self-sufficiency is expected to be achieved.[21] It also provides for a 37 per cent increase in nonmilitary government expenditures from 1953–54 to 1958–59.

Another pressure tending to expand government expenditures which is unfamiliar to most Westerners is the need to raise the salaries of government employees so as to make it unnecessary for civil servants to rely on bribes or solicited contributions as a source of income. In recent years the government has raised the pay of civil servants; however, the services of bureaucrats are

20. See United Nations, op. cit., p. 41.
21. Ibid., pp. 88, 106.

still usually unobtainable without countenancing acceptance of some kind of contributions, and the armed forces and police solicit contributions by force. Although such contributions would be considered immoral in most Western countries, in Korea they are usually accepted without any feeling of impropriety. These contributions create an unfavorable environment for business by subjecting it, if successful, to heavy exactions from bureaucrats. They cause private enterprise to be directed to activities that do not attract attention and cannot easily be expropriated. Such contributions are also slightly inflationary because borrowers must usually make additional bank loans to cover their cost.

The Republic of Korea has attempted to sell government bonds to the public since 1950, but it probably cannot reduce inflationary pressures significantly in this way. Because free market rates of interest have fluctuated by 60 to 240 per cent per year, private investors will not voluntarily purchase five-year 5 per cent National Bonds. About two-thirds of these securities have been sold to the Bank of Korea and other government banks and appear to be no more than a means of credit-creation through the banking system. The rest of the bonds have been sold to private owners (including government enterprises which in some cases probably have to borrow to buy the bonds) primarily by some type of compulsory allotment. It is curious that compulsory sales of government bonds have been used to narrow the gap between low official exchange rates and the much higher black market rates for foreign exchange. Persons buying foreign exchange at the low official rates—including Korean students who come to the United States—are compelled to purchase a certain amount of bonds. Out of bonds worth 3,300 million hwan issued in 1954, 1,475 million hwan were sold chiefly by tying them in with sales of foreign exchange.[22] The amount of bond purchases required has varied, but the total amount of bonds plus the official rate paid for exchange tends to approach the various black market rates. Because of the rapidity of inflation, the bonds soon lose almost all value.

V. Conclusions

There are no easy solutions to the problem of inflation in South Korea. Although numerous efforts have been made to end inflation, price stability has not been achieved. Something could be done if it were possible to change their

22. Bank of Korea, *Monthly Statistical Review*, Jan. 1955, No. 74, p. 48.

legal institutions and their traditional conceptions of the proper relationship between government and both persons and business firms. This would take time and undoubtedly would require establishing much more Western control than exists at present. Such a program is out of the question because of the intense nationalistic feelings in South Korea and probably also because it would conflict with conceptions in the West of their relationship with other countries of the world. This study does suggest that Western advisors might be more useful if they accepted inflation as inevitable, at least for the present, and attempted to make the inflationary monetary system in South Korea work as well as possible. For example, in order to improve business and government accounting, a significant contribution could be made by discarding Korean money as a unit of account and developing an alternative unit of account as was done in China from 1937 to 1949. Also, the social cost of using hoarded goods as stores of value could be reduced if it were possible to provide a sufficient quantity of an alternative store of value such as foreign currency or "precious metals." Finally, careful attention should be given to the rate of increase in the money supply. If acceleration can be avoided, the system may prove sufficiently stable. In this respect, the economic aid program of the United States, in addition to its other benefits, has probably contributed much toward the achievement of a workable monetary system in South Korea.

COMPETING MONIES

Situations in which there is more than one money in existence at the same time are by no means uncommon. Before the development of paper money, a number of kinds of metallic currency normally would be circulating simultaneously, and they might have varying rates of exchange with each other if they did not happen all to be in the same metal. In a real sense, gold or silver or, in China, copper was the money, and the coins in circulation were merely convenient forms of it. In modern times, however, there is frequently competition among paper currencies.

To draw from my own experience, in China in 1948–50, the U.S. dollar, two different kinds of silver dollars, small gold bars (which were nominally one ounce but might vary a bit from that weight), and the Chinese Nationalist paper currency—or, later, the Chinese Communist paper currency—all circulated at the same time. In Korea in 1952–53 there were, once again, three currencies. In addition to the Korean currency and U.S. dollars, there were Military Payment Certificates. Gresham's Law, of course, enshrines into the corpus of economic theory one proposition about competing currencies. Further, it is clear that the initial development of money, or, more precisely, a money metal, must have occurred in a competitive situation. Originally there were many products that were being bartered against each other. One of them was eventually socially selected as the money. Money in and of itself is an almost perfect expression of a large externality. The reason I want money is because I realize that many other people want it, and hence, it is readily exchangeable for other things I want. Its wide acceptability, paradoxically, depends upon its wide acceptability.

Under modern circumstances, there is usually only one money in a country that has this wide acceptability. A politician whose expected period of control of the government is fairly short may find it profitable to inflate this currency. This may set in motion a process under which the dominant currency no longer has a monopoly. Assume that there are two possible monies circulating in some country, one of which is controlled by the local government and one of which is not. Let us assume that the one controlled by the local government starts with almost the entire market. This would mean that

Reprinted, with permission of The Ohio State University Press, from *Journal of Money, Credit and Banking* 7 (November 1975): 491–97.

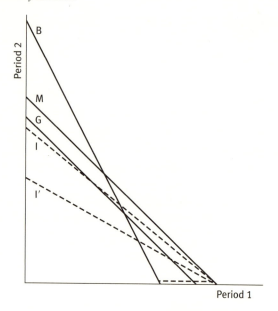

FIGURE 1

it would have wide acceptability and the low transactions costs we normally expect with money.

The other money, being less widely used, would have larger transactions costs and less acceptability. Anyone who has been in a foreign country where the tourist business is large has discovered that he can quite readily use dollar instruments in some shops, but the exchange rate is not very good in those shops. The foreign currency provides little competition to the domestic currency. Suppose, however, that the government is engaging in inflation for some reason. Under these circumstances, individuals would find that the native money was a rather poor store of value for longer term transactions. Figure 1 shows the situation.[1] The individual is assumed to hold in period 1 paper money equivalent to the intersection of the *M* line with the horizontal axis. He proposes to hold these assets until period 2, and, of course, if he

---

1. The figure is a simplified version of the figure introduced by Peter Bernholz ("Erwerbskosten, Laufzeit und Charakter zinstragender Forderrungen," *Zeitschrift für die gesamte Straatswissenschaft* 123 [1967]: 9–24). Bernholz uses a much more general form of the diagram, but my simplified version will do for our present purposes.

keeps them in the form of stable money, it means that line M should have an inclination of 45°.

He has other alternatives, however. He could choose to convert the money into some other non-interest-bearing asset which can then be reconverted in period 2. There will be a transactions cost for the two conversions, and, for convenience, I have put that entirely in the form of a transactions cost in period 1. In essence, he buys the sale price of the commodity, not its purchase price. The transactions cost is the dotted line along the horizontal axis, and line G shows the projection of this investment on the future period. It is obviously dominated by the money alternative. Another possibility is purchasing a bond that will pay interest. Again there is a transactions cost, and it will be higher than the transactions cost of the nonmoney fixed asset, because the present value of the bond must be computed every time it changes hands. In the long period, of course, these additional transactions costs are offset by the interest. Line B, then, starts farther left on the horizontal axis, but is more steeply slanted than lines M and G. Assuming that the individual has normal indifference curves, his choice is entirely between M and B, and most people in fact choose some of each.

Inflation changes the situation, however. A mild inflation's effect on money is shown by the dashed line I. Individuals will find themselves on a lower indifference curve and will hold more bonds and less money. They would still hold none of the fixed-value asset G, because it is strictly dominated.

With a higher rate of inflation, shown by the dashed line I', the possibility of holding G arises. Once again, individuals will be forced to a lower level of satisfaction; but now they might hold either B, G, or I' (the inflating currency) and would probably hold some combination of them. An individual contemplating the choice from among the depreciating currency, a bond or gold or a foreign currency, would make an estimate of the price at which he could sell each of these assets at the time in the future he expected to use his liquid reserve. If the anticipated depreciation of money for the period during which he expected to hold his reserve was greater than the transactions costs in either of the other two forms of holding reserves, he would choose one of the other two forms.

The fact that this individual has chosen to hold some of his assets in either bonds or foreign currency means that the demand for the existing currency declines. This in and of itself has some effect in lowering the value of that currency, i.e., increases the rate of inflation; but more important, it lowers the total value of the national currency, since this value, in essence, is the sum of effective demands for the currency.[2] Thus, the return to the government from the next round of inflation will be less than it was when this individual was keeping more of his reserves in currency.

Further, in choosing to hold more of these other assets, the individual increases the demand for such assets and, hence, increases their value. If we assume that they are being kept at constant value (in the case of the bond by an appropriate interest rate and by supply elasticity, and in the case of gold or other currencies simply by supply control), this means that the supply of these items must be increased.[3] Further, the greater demand lowers transactions costs because they become easier to sell. In essence, the intersection of line G—and to a lesser extent, line B—with the horizontal axis is moved to the right. This should in itself increase the demand for these other assets, which, in turn, will further lower transactions costs. The amount of the other fixed asset and bonds held in the society should increase, and the amount of the national currency should fall, as a result of the process. One can imagine that this would, over time, lead to one or the other of these assets completely replacing the standard currency.

Unfortunately, or perhaps fortunately, this is not inevitable. If there is more than one possible asset to substitute for the currency (and in the real world there are many), then the fact that different people prefer different substitutes might mean that the transactions costs will always remain higher for the substitutes than for the basic currency. Under the circumstances, there would always be at least some demand for the basic currency. Needless to say, the more rapidly the basic currency is inflated, the smaller the demand for the basic currency, and the higher the demand for the substitutes. However, this does not necessarily lead to the emergence of one substitute.

2. This is the reason that the government attempting to maximize its revenue from inflation will not simply choose the largest possible rate. The revenue-maximizing rates of inflation for several governments with different historic experiences and different domestic conditions were computed by Martin Bailey ("The Welfare Costs of Inflationary Finance," *Journal of Political Economy* 64 [April, 1956]: 93–110, esp. 107–9). Phillip Cagan's monumental work, *Determinants and Effects of Changes in the Stock of Money, 1875–1960* (New York: Columbia University Press for the National Bureau of Economic Research, 1965), provides much additional data on the point, but they are dispersed through the book rather than concentrated at one point.

3. The contrary assumption that they increase in value causes no difficulty, but we will leave it aside for now.

Note that this use of inflation for revenue automatically generates revenue opportunities for others. The issuers of bonds, gold miners, and foreign governments producing possibly competitive currencies find they have an opportunity for expanding their output without depreciating its unit value. If rapid inflation in France increases the French demand for Swiss banknotes, the printing of these notes is a source of revenue to the Swiss government, and there is no offsetting decline in the value of their own currency. Virtue very conspicuously pays. The possibility that one substitute for the base currency will become dominant is, of course, never zero. Any tendency on the part of the population to specialize one asset as their store of value tends to reduce the transactions costs for that particular asset; hence, it is self-reinforcing.

With time, one would anticipate that the use of the foreign currency, gold, and/or the bond would tend to replace the regular currency in even short-term uses. Assume that we have two people, both of whom keep their long-term assets in the form of bonds. One is proposing to buy a house from the other. In the early years of the inflation, the purchaser would change his bonds into the current currency and pay the owner of the house, who would then convert the cash to bonds again. Eventually these conversion and reconversion steps would tend to be eliminated. In this form, the phenomenon depends on both parties having the same noncurrency store of value. However, even if they have differing stores of value, they may nevertheless skip the national currency stage. For example, the purchaser may keep his money in bonds, and the seller keep his in a foreign currency. Either the purchaser pays in bonds, which the seller immediately changes into foreign currency, or the purchaser makes the change into foreign currency and delivers that to the seller.

All of these changes depend on the gradual development of habits. In general, it is not sensible to reexamine all of your economic transactions every day in order to see if they are optimal. The tremendous savings we can obtain for ourselves by following habitual courses of action as opposed to recalculating are a special kind of savings on transactions costs. With time, however, habits do change. The gradual movement to some other currency, then, could be slow if the rate of inflation is slow, but might proceed quite rapidly if the rate of inflation is high. It is likely that the existing currency will remain in circulation longest for small, casual transactions.

So far we have assumed that the currency is depreciating at a stable rate. In the real world it does not, and, indeed, if we assume that the government is attempting to maximize its returns from inflation, then a varying rate is optimal. Gains from inflation involve an element of fraud, and this can be maximized if the details of the government's policy are concealed.[4] If the rate of inflation is not stable, then our bond, of necessity, becomes an index bond. This makes the transactions costs in converting into regular currency automatically rather high, even if you do have a pocket computer. Indeed, unless the index is genuinely continuous, you can never make a perfect calculation of the present value of the bond. Under the circumstances, the bond has a competitive disadvantage as opposed to the foreign currency or gold. In other respects, however, our analysis is not affected.

Let us, however, turn to the final and most realistic assumption we will make, which is that the other assets are not stable either. Assume that the bonds that are available have a finite credit risk attached to them and that gold or foreign currency is not truly stable. Under these circumstances, the individual must once again make calculations as to the future value of possible liquid assets. Clearly, the foreign assets and the bonds are less attractive under these circumstances. Equally clearly, if the rate of inflation is high enough, they may still be more attractive than the regular money.

The basic point, of course, is that the inflation of the national currency means not only that its future value has a high variance, but that the predicted mean of that variance is falling. The variance of possible money substitutes is high, perhaps higher, but the mean is not predictably falling.[5] Thus, there is no safety from short-term fluctuations, and the expected value of the bond, gold, or foreign currency at any specific point in the moderately distant future will be higher than the expected value of the currency. Where the difference is greater than the transactions costs, individuals will choose to hold the alternate assets.

This is true even if the currency is depreciating in a highly predictable manner. If the currency is depreciating in a highly predictable manner, then there is no risk associated in holding it. Since there would be risk on the gold or foreign asset, then the rate of depreciation would have to be somewhat higher in order to lead to the use of the foreign asset. Under these circumstances, presumably the bond would be the dominant store of value. In any event, if the rate of inflation is reasonably rapid, one would anticipate that the national currency would gradually go out of existence. The speed with which

---

4. Bailey, "The Welfare Costs of Inflationary Finance."

5. In the case of foreign currencies, it might be predictably falling, but at a lower rate than for the domestic currency.

it would go out would depend on the availability of substitutes, the strength of the habits, and so forth.

Clearly the government attempting to obtain revenue through inflation would prefer that no substitutes develop. Let us temporarily turn to competitive techniques. First we will consider the problem from the standpoint of a government that is attempting to depreciate its currency but still keep it in circulation. Since the problem of alternative currencies is one of transactions costs, the government would be well advised to make transactions costs in competing currencies high. Simply making them illegal is the obvious way of doing this. In "Paper Money—A Cycle in Cathay" I argued that in a sense it was always sensible for the government to enforce such rules weakly to allow only a slow tendency (and by slow I mean a tendency that might take 50 to 100 years to reach completion) for the alternative currency to grow.[6] I am no longer confident of this, and it might be that the profit-maximizing course of action of a government is to enforce its rules against the alternative currencies strongly enough to keep the transactions costs quite high. It would always be true, however, that people wishing to hold very long-term stores of liquidity would find something other than money a superior alternative.

Think of the matter now from the standpoint of some potential competitor, a foreign country or perhaps a bank or gold mining company, which is attempting to provide an alternative currency for an area. The problem they face is that of giving credibility to their currency. The reason this is difficult is, of course, that the demand for this currency will be growing in an unstable way, with periods in which it falls off sharply, perhaps because of an increase in enforcement activities on the part of the inflating government. This means, for credibility, either that convertibility into one commodity or a bundle of commodities will be guaranteed or that some index will be stabilized.

Both of these clearly involve the use of large resources in the form of reserves, and the prospect of having too few reserves and being unable to guarantee the stability of the currency is very great. Still, it is not impossible, and, in any event, profits of a considerable magnitude for a period of, let us say, 10 years could be gained even if at the end of that time there was a devaluation as a result of a run on reserves. If we consider the alternative currency as being some metal, then of course the miners are the people who expand its

---

6. Gordon Tullock, "Paper Money—A Cycle in Cathay," *Economic History Review* 9 (June, 1957): 393–407. See also Gordon Tullock, "Inflazione Prolongata," *Revista Internazionale di Scienze Economiche e Commerciali* 13 (1966): 632–45.

supply. Historically, metals have been subject to a good deal of fluctuation in price, and there is no reason to believe that they will not continue to be.

The possibilities of profit opportunities from maintaining a stable currency are real, however. It seems likely that the basic reason we do not observe such profit-motivated stability is that governments are characteristically in the control of people who have no great security of tenure. Under the circumstances, maximizing the present value of income over the next few years, rather than over the entire income stream, is their objective. In general, inflation is a better way of achieving this objective than is an effort to give a good reputation to your currency and then use that good reputation as an asset in expanding the circulation of the currency. Thus, in a way, what competition now exists is competition between a number of national currencies, all of which are inflating, and gold and silver, which are highly unstable.

COMPETING MONIES

A REPLY

Benjamin Klein does not appear to have read my article very carefully. His second sentence, for example, says that I

> fail[ed] to make important distinctions between the average level of the inflation rate and its predictability, between non-interest-bearing or high-powered money and interest-bearing money, and between the store of value and medium of exchange roles of money.[1]

The distinction between the average level of inflation rate and its predictability will be found on page 495 of my original article, and between the store of value and medium of exchange (called "short-term") roles of money, on page 494.[2] The latter is perhaps not as clear as it could be. It is true that I have only one kind of money in my model, and *that* money is not interest-bearing, but I do have an interest-bearing bond, and I do not think substituting interest-paying checking accounts for the bond would make any significant difference in my reasoning.

I could go on finding places in which Klein's statements about my article are not in accord with the article itself. Indeed, he does not discuss the bulk of the article. The article is mainly devoted to presenting and discussing a theoretical model which he almost entirely ignores. Thus, his very long comment (slightly longer than the original article) is mainly devoted to a rather small part of my article. It does not seem worthwhile, however, to catalog in full the cases in which he has misdescribed the article.

More important is what I can only refer to as Klein's odd attitude toward "empirical methodology." Even this could be let go as a harmless eccentricity, except that I believe that Klein is, in this area, accurately representing a great many scholars in the field of money. Since I think they are wrong, it is worthwhile to explain why. Although in what follows I will talk mainly about Klein's comment, I am treating it merely as an illustration.

Reprinted, with permission of The Ohio State University Press, from *Journal of Money, Credit and Banking* 8 (November 1976): 521–25.

1. Benjamin Klein, "Competing Monies: Comment," *Journal of Money, Credit and Banking* 8 (November 1976), 513.

2. Gordon Tullock, "Competing Monies," *Journal of Money, Credit and Banking* 7 (November 1975), 491–97.

The progress of science in general involves two strands, the elaboration of improved theory and empirical work, which in part tests that theory and in part turns up new information about the world—which in turn becomes raw material for the development of further theory.[3] There is no reason to believe that theory is more important than empirical investigation or that empirical investigation is more important than theory. The two strands are interwoven. However, it is a valid empirical observation that in all branches of science, except mathematics, there is a great deal more empirical work than theoretical.

If we look at the literature in any science, we will find that there are some purely theoretical articles, mainly very abstract, and some purely empirical articles. Most of the articles, however, are basically empirical but start with some theoretical work. So far as I can see, Klein's objection fundamentally amounts to the statement that my article does not fall in this mainstream of mixed theory and empirical investigation. It is possible, however, that what he is really objecting to is that it is not absolutely pure theory. It is basically a theoretical article, but there are some rather casual empirical observations contained in it. Perhaps he feels that theoretical articles should have no casual empirical statements, or perhaps even that no casual empirical statements are permitted in any article.

In any event, however, it seems to me this is basically a perverse point of view. Division of labor is one of the fundamental principles of economics, and there is no reason why I cannot specialize in theory,[4] while others specialize in empirical work. The existence of people, like Klein himself, who do both empirical and theoretical work is desirable, but there is no reason why they should have a monopoly.

There is another problem with Klein's empirical methodology, which is that he has chosen the wrong empirical tests. He objects to my statement that "Situations in which there is more than one money in existence at the same time are by no means uncommon" (p. 491). He does not note the first sentence of my third paragraph, "Under modern circumstances, there is usually only one money in a country that has this wide acceptability" (p. 491). It must be admitted that my article is rather vague on the subject of frequency.

---

3. Some economists seem to think that the word "theory" should be reserved for very abstract mathematical investigation. I do not like to quarrel about the definition of words, but if "theory" is reserved for *that* meaning, then another word would have to be created to cover the kind of theory found in Adam Smith, Ricardo, Marshall, etc.

4. The basic reason I specialize in theory is that I am naturally lazy.

I was not attempting to make a quantitative statement about the relative frequency of competitive situations. I was simply trying to indicate that the subject matter, which I propose to discuss in theory, was one that had some real-world counterparts. I did not then, and do not now, have any clear idea as to whether, over the history of the human race, competitive monetary systems would have made up 95 percent or 1 percent of the total examples.

Certainly it is true that direct competition within a country is unusual today. The Maria Theresa dollar in East Africa, the peculiar situation with several privately produced monies in Hong Kong, and the West Bank where two national currencies circulate side by side are the only examples that spring to mind. Nevertheless, if we look at the long sweep of history, it is clear that there have been many cases of monetary competition. The assignats are a famous case, and colonial American history has a number of examples. The early history of the establishment of paper money almost everywhere involved competition between monetary systems.[5] Indeed, the present laws that restrict the circulation of competing monies were normally initially enacted by various governments as a competitive device; i.e., they were attempting to give the newly established paper monies a competitive edge over the older coinages.

All of this will no doubt convince Klein that I am continuing my habit of making "many 'reasonable' but undocumented assertions about the true state of the world."[6] The point here, however, is that I am not trying to prove anything very much about the real world. To borrow a famous example from the philosophy of science, I am saying that black swans exist, and such a statement requires only very slight evidence. Statements as to the frequency of black swans or their distribution require a great deal more.

Klein himself introduces a certain amount of evidence which is supposed to indicate that competing monies are "uncommon." This is a very difficult thing to do. A disproof of the statement "there are black swans" or black swans "are not uncommon" involves an immense amount of data. The proof that there are no black swans in England or Argentina or the United States does not disprove the original statement.

Regardless of this logical problem, however, Klein's empirical evidence is simply that in certain areas—for example, American history between 1880

5. See, for example, Gordon Tullock, "Paper Money—A Cycle in Cathay," *Economic History Review* 9 (June 1957), 393–407, and Tullock, "Inflazione Prolongata," *Revista Internazionale di Science Economiche e Commerciali*, 13 (1966), 632–45.

6. Klein, "Competing Monies: Comment," 513.

and 1972—there was only one currency in circulation. Since during a large part of this period gold coins circulated, as well as paper money, it is not obvious that even in this case he is right, although I would incline to the view that he is. In any event, however, the listing of cases in which only one money was circulating cannot be taken as proof that there are no or only a few cases where more than one money circulates. Certainly, the extremely limited set of cases examined by Klein would not prove it.

Indeed, in some cases, Klein quotes empirical evidence that is simply irrelevant from any standpoint. For example, his only equation deals with the effect of "price uncertainty" on the demand for money. He finds that this uncertainty increases the demand for money over the period 1880–1972. Theoretically, we would expect that deflations would tend to increase the demand for money, and inflation would tend to reduce the demand. Mild inflations or deflations, however, might have very little effect,[7] and it is not obvious what the direction of that effect would be. If long continued, fairly rapid inflation would tend to reduce the demand for money, a fact with which, I take it, Klein does not disagree. Indeed, he cites evidence from the German inflation of the 1920s indicating that foreign monies had taken over almost the entire store-of-value function of money, leaving the existing mark with only the transactions portion of the money function. The estimates he cites indicate that something between 80 percent and 93 percent of the total demand for money was being filled by foreign currency. Theoretically, one would assume that an inflating currency would be replaced in the store-of-value function before—indeed, long before—it is replaced in transactions.

It is notable that when he gets out of formal monetary theory, Klein does not follow his own prescriptions for empirical studies but depends on "reasonable but undocumented assertions about the true state of the world."[8] For example,

> Much of the domestic competitive pressure is felt not in the narrowly defined economic marketplace, as Tullock asserts [sic], but in the political marketplace. Rather than demanding a new competing dominant money the public simply produces a change in the government and a "currency reform," which creates a new monopoly supplier.[9]

7. Particularly since the interest rate is also included as an independent variable in his equation.

8. Klein, "Competing Monies: Comment," 514.

9. Ibid.

This would appear to be contrary to his "empirical" standards. Although I do not object to this *kind* of statement in an article, I am by no means convinced this particular one is in accord with the real world.[10]

Altogether, there seems to be a clear methodological difference between Klein and me, but as far as I can see, the difference is simply that Klein objects to theoretical discussions of money that do not have detailed statistical backing. In addition, he does not realize that the citing of one instance is enough to prove existence, whereas the proof of nonexistence is extremely difficult or even impossible empirically. Similarly, a few instances may be sufficient to prove a phenomenon "not uncommon." Disproof requires looking at the entire sample universe and measuring the frequency.

There is one theoretical point in my original article that I feel escaped Klein, perhaps because it was given very little emphasis. Since it may well have escaped other readers, I should like to take this opportunity to present it a bit more strongly. Klein, in a number of places, remarks that it is surprising how hard it is for competing monies to replace the existing paper currency in circulation, albeit not in the store-of-value function.[11] It seems to me the explanation for this is fairly simple, although I have to turn to public finance for my explanation.

Almost anything that an individual values and that he believes he can eventually sell can serve as a store of value. In order for something to be suitable for circulation, however, it is necessary that a large number of other people

10. There is a very large volume of empirical evidence here which, generally speaking, does not lead to any very strong conclusion. A debate in the December 1975 *American Political Science Review* presents the most recent work in this area and cites substantially all of the earlier work: Francisco Arcelus and Allan H. Meltzer, "The Effect of Aggregate Economic Variables on Congressional Elections," *American Political Science Review* 69 (December 1975): 1232–39; Arcelus and Meltzer, "Aggregate Economic Variables and Votes for Congress: A Rejoinder," *American Political Science Review* 69 (December 1975), 1266–69; Howard S. Bloom and H. Douglas Price, "Voter Response to Short-Run Economic Conditions: The Asymmetric Effect of Prosperity and Recession," *American Political Science Review* 69 (December 1975), 1240–54; and Saul Goodman and Gerald H. Kramer, "Comment on Arcelus and Meltzer, 'The Effect of Aggregate Economic Conditions on Congressional Elections,'" *American Political Science Review* 69 (December 1975), 1255–65.

11. Klein also seems to think that the government monopoly power on money is stronger than I think it is. Since at no point did I make a statement as to how strong I thought it was, and he also presents no measure, it is a little difficult to tell whether he is right or wrong about this. Certainly government monopoly powers are very great, but competition does tend to overcome most monopolists in the long run.

also be interested in holding it, either as a store of value or as a circulating medium. In other words, a sort of social agreement is necessary, and this is a characteristic externality. The development of a general social agreement that the same commodity, piece of paper, or large ring of stone shall be this store of value is a good example of the kind of extreme externality we tend to refer to as a public good.

The development of such social agreements is apt to be slow, and it is particularly apt to be slow if the government is actually trying to prevent it. Thus, one would anticipate that in periods of inflation that are both long enough and severe enough to break through the cake of customs surrounding an existing currency, people will turn to quite a number of different things for stores of value rather promptly. Replacement of the existing money as a circulating medium is, however, much harder and may take quite a long period of time. This is not particularly surprising, and it is not obvious that the government could not permanently keep such a social agreement from arising by adequate use of its police power.

Last but not least, Klein points to the possibility that political competition will lead to stabilizing currency. My own inclination is to feel that political competition is likely to lead to *de*stabilizing the currency, but the possibility of developing institutions that would, even in a democracy, stabilize the currency seems to me worth further thought. I hope that Klein will think about the matter, and I intend to myself.

WHEN IS INFLATION NOT INFLATION?

Discoveries of valuable minerals in undeveloped parts of the world frequently lead to a very sharp rise in prices of daily necessities. Examples are the diamond and gold mine rushes and, perhaps, the situation in Saudi Arabia and a number of other Arab states. Discussing the matter with a number of economists, I find that they take the view that these situations are inflationary because prices have gone up. This is, I believe, erroneous. The prices of daily necessities are going up very sharply, but other prices, concealed within the internal accounting system of producing units, have fallen even more.

Let us suppose that diamonds are discovered in some rural area. People pour in from all over the world for the purpose of mining diamonds, and prices of housing, food, and the like shoot up. Whereas before, the very occasional visitors found it possible to get the use of some farmer's spare room for little or nothing, now the right to sleep on the ground in half of a pup tent may cost $10 per night. The currency in which this payment is made, however, is still stable currency elsewhere. Is there then an inflation?

In Figure 1 the quantity of something—let us say housing—is shown on the horizontal axis, and the supply curve and demand curve before the discovery of diamonds are shown, respectively, by line S and line D. This leads to quantity Q_0 being consumed at price P_0. With the discovery of diamonds, the demand shifted up to line D'. At the same time, however, there was a fairly rapid influx of capital in the form of such things as tents, with the result that the supply curve fell to S'. Nevertheless, the intersection of the new demand curve and the new supply curve leads to quantity Q_1 being purchased at price P_1. P_1 is very much higher than P_0. Is this an inflation? Note that the marginal cost of each unit is now lower than it was previously. What has happened is that there has been a very large shift in demand, with the result that much more is being demanded. The thousandth unit of housing would have had, effectively, an infinite price under the old regime, and now it has a finite new price. Nevertheless, the fact remains that prices are much higher than they were before.

Computing a theoretically correct price index for our little diamond mining town is quite difficult. Let us consider two special cases. One is a company that is mining diamonds in a town, and the other is one of its employees.

Reprinted, with permission of The Ohio State University Press, from *Journal of Money, Credit and Banking* 11 (May 1979): 219–21.

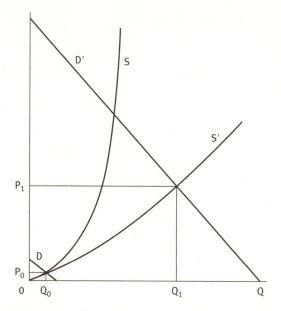

FIGURE 1
Supply and demand curves before and after the discovery of diamonds

Beginning with the company, it is paying in the diamond area four times as much per unit for the resources used in its mine as it would pay in the nearest port city. In spite of these prices for factors, it is able to sell diamonds profitably.

If we build up a set of accounts for our diamond mining company, we would find that it is paying a great deal for all the resources but that the implicit price it pays for diamonds in the ground is very low, and this more than compensates it for the high prices it is paying elsewhere. (For a similar, but not identical, criticism of existing price indices, see Alchian and Klein.)[1] It is a little hard to see how its internal cost would be built into a price index, but the theoretically perfect price index should include it.

The laborer is an even more interesting problem. Let us suppose that he is being paid in nominal terms four times what he would earn elsewhere but that the cost of everything he buys in daily life is five times as high. He may nevertheless be better off than he was before. The reason is that one particular "cost," the amount of labor he must put in to save a dollar, has gone down.

---

1. Armen A. Alchian and Benjamin Klein, "On a Correct Measure of Inflation," *Journal of Money, Credit and Banking* 5 (February 1973, part 1): 173–81.

Suppose that before he had earned $10 a day. If he had restricted his consumption to 50 percent of his earnings, he would have saved only $5. Now that he is being paid $40 a day, he can purchase the same living standard that he would have purchased with half of his previous salary for $25. Thus, he can save $15 with the same "abstinence" as would have provided him with $5 savings before. He may well regard himself as better off, although the apparent price schedule he faces is much higher. Once again it will be hard to adjust to this in terms of a price index, but in theory we would like to do it.

Note the paradoxical nature of the situation. The community that is totally dominated by its export trade appears to have higher prices on substantially everything traded in the community. Nevertheless, resources pour in for the purpose of going into the export trade. This can only be true if there is something in the community that in real terms is very inexpensive indeed, and this something in our example is diamonds in the ground. In equilibrium the cost of diamonds in the ground plus the expense of getting them out will be about the same as the cost of diamonds elsewhere. A "properly" computed price index would include diamonds in the ground with an immense weight to offset the other prices.

This situation applies not only in cases of a mineral rush, but in any case in which economic opportunities attract a great deal of labor and resources at very high speeds; for example, the decision of the Saudi Arabian government to rebuild its capital. Everything in Riyadh appears to be that much more expensive than anywhere else in the world, even though the Saudi Arabian currency is, in fact, completely and freely interchangeable with the dollar. The cheap factor here is, in fact, oil, even though little of the oil gets to Riyadh.

Part of this essay has been to suggest that the common symptom of inflation, i.e., a sharp rise in prices of daily necessities, can occur under a situation that in truth is not inflationary. This is essentially a short-run phenomenon, but even so, using conventional indexes, the symptoms of inflation may appear just as inflationary as a South American country with a runaway printing press.

PART 6

SIZE AND GROWTH
OF GOVERNMENT

AN EMPIRICAL ANALYSIS OF CROSS-NATIONAL ECONOMIC GROWTH, 1951–80

Kevin B. Grier and Gordon Tullock

1. Introduction

Recent perceptions of relatively poor U.S. economic performance have led to a renewed interest in the causes of secular economic growth. Existing empirical research has tended towards specialized topics, mainly the size or growth of government and the importance of initial conditions for subsequent growth. While these are important considerations, they are far from the sole causal factors of economic growth.[1] A welcome exception to this pattern is the more general empirical model provided by Kormendi and Mequire, who examine a wide range of interesting macroeconomic hypotheses about growth.[2] In this paper we further generalize Kormendi and Mequire by considering a larger country sample and using an experimental design that allows testing of both the temporal and cross-country stability of the model coefficients.

Specifically, we use annual data on 113 countries to construct a pooled cross-section/time-series data set and examine the effects of seven variables on economic growth. These variables are (1) initial per-capita real GDP, (2) the growth of government's share of GDP, (3) the standard deviation of GDP growth, (4) population growth, (5) inflation, (6) the change in inflation, and (7) the standard deviation of inflation.

Reprinted from *Journal of Monetary Economics* 24 (September 1989): 259–76, copyright 1989, with permission from Elsevier.

We thank R. C. Kormendi, M. C. Munger, and an anonymous referee for helpful comments and acknowledge financial support from the Center for Study of Public Choice.

1. There is also a large-growth accounting literature that attributes economic growth to various factor inputs. See Angus Maddison, "Growth and Slowdown in Advanced Capitalist Economics: Techniques of Qualitative Assessment," *Journal of Economic Literature* 25 (1987): 649–98, for a recent survey.

2. R. C. Kormendi and P. G. Mequire, "Macroeconomic Determinants of Growth: Cross-Country Evidence," *Journal of Monetary Economics* 16 (1985): 141–63.

We do not present or test a comprehensive theory of secular economic growth. The econometric results reported below cannot be interpreted as structural estimates of a well-defined model. Rather, we are investigating empirical regularities in these data, with emphasis on the stability of coefficients over time and across countries.

This empirical exercise is especially relevant now, given the recent development of endogenous growth models. Romer, Lucas, and Barro work with growth models that, in various ways, remove the standard assumption of diminishing returns and allow the possibility of persistently different growth patterns across countries.[3] Our results can give evidence on the empirical support for the standard model and point out regularities that may aid in the further refinement of endogenous growth models. We find that the effects of the macro variables listed above differ greatly across countries in the sample, providing a relatively good fit for developed Organisation for Economic Co-operation and Development (OECD) countries, but working less well for developing nations. In fact, several standard stylized facts about the neoclassical growth process cannot be confirmed by the data from African or Asian countries. Our results imply that social and political institutions may be important factors in the growth process, at least over a 20- to 30-year horizon. Two results in this paper illustrate the importance of institutional factors: we find significant negative correlation between the growth of government consumption and GDP growth in three of the four groups of countries in the sample, and a similar effect from a measure of political repression in the African and non-OECD western hemisphere samples.

---

3. Paul M. Romer, "Increasing Returns and Long-Run Growth," *Journal of Political Economy* 94 (1986): 1002–37; R. E. Lucas, "On the Mechanics of Economic Development," *Journal of Monetary Economics* 22 (1987): 43–70; Robert J. Barro, "Government Spending in a Simple Model of Endogenous Growth" (Cambridge: Harvard University, 1988, mimeographed). In standard growth models with diminishing returns, permanent economic growth comes from population growth or exogenous technological change. The papers cited allow for endogenously determined permanent growth by assuming constant or increasing returns to some reproducible factor. Romer works with increasing social returns to knowledge, Lucas mainly with human capital. Barro's model relates to government as is discussed in footnote 16 below. Besides allowing for nonconvergence, endogenous growth models allow institutional factors that affect investment incentives to help determine long-run growth.

2. Data and Empirical Design

The data used here come from Summers and Heston, who have compiled internationally comparable annual figures on output and its composition, prices, and exchange rates for 115 market economies from 1950 to 1981.[4] There are several ways to organize this data, ranging from estimating individual time-series equations for each country to averaging each country's experience into one data point and estimating a single cross-section.

Since we are interested in secular growth patterns, some amount of averaging is required to net out cyclical fluctuations. Here we use five-year average data. Further averaging is avoided because it can destroy information contained in the sample. Averaging over the entire sample period eliminates the information contained in the sample about the effect of changing conditions on growth in individual countries and allows only cross-country variation to inform the estimates. Given repeated observations on a wide range of countries, it is important to test the validity of pooling all the data into a single equation. In the estimations that follow, we test for temporal coefficient stability and the appropriateness of pooling a wide variety of countries into a single sample. Specifically, we first divide the sample into the OECD countries and the rest of the world (ROW), then further divide the ROW by continent to test the validity of a pooled sample.[5]

In contrast to this approach, Kormendi and Mequire have 28 years of data on 47 countries. They average each country's time-series experience into a single data point and estimate a cross-section of 47 observations using no information about the variance in any one country's performance over time and providing no evidence about the advisability of equating coefficients across their sample countries. Kormendi and Mequire do recognize that "moving to decade, five-year, or even annual data, one could exploit a pooled

4. Robert Summers and Alan Heston, "Improved International Estimates of Real Product and Its Composition," *Review of Income and Wealth* 30 (1984): 207–62. In our work, we exclude Malta and Cyprus from the sample (see footnote 5). Summers and Heston also provide some data on centrally planned economies.

5. The OECD is the Organisation for Economic Co-operation and Development. The appendix lists the OECD countries and the other countries in our sample by continent. Malta and Cyprus were deleted because they are the only European countries in the sample that are not OECD members.

structure in which more refined and potentially more powerful tests may be possible."[6] With 30 years of data on all the 24 OECD countries and 20 years on the 89 ROW countries, five-year averaging produces 500 total observations for analysis.

3. Hypotheses and Variables

In this section we outline the hypotheses motivating our regressors, noting previous results where applicable.

(1) *Initial conditions.* Simply stated, there is a widely held belief that, from any starting point, countries that are behind in technology will grow faster relative to more advanced countries owing to diminishing returns to investment in a given technology. Baumol summarizes this convergence phenomenon for 16 industrialized nations since 1890. In a related paper Abramowitz points out that convergence should not be considered a mechanistic inevitability, arguing that the physical or social infrastructure necessary to absorb technology may not exist in all countries.[7] Endogenous growth models generally do not predict convergence, because they allow for permanent nondiminishing returns. While Baumol and Abramowitz mainly look at the convergence of productivity levels, we examine convergence of per-capita income by including initial per-capita GDP as a variable explaining subsequent GDP growth. Here convergence means that higher initial wealth implies lower future growth compared with other countries, owing to diminished returns to additional investment in any given technology.

(2) *Population growth.* As Kormendi and Mequire note, neoclassical growth theory implies that labor force growth has a one-to-one effect on income growth. Here we only have data on population growth, which should have a positive effect on growth but may be different from one-to-one because of trends in labor-force participation or lagging capital accumulation.

(3, 4) *Inflation.* Older Phillips curve models that imply a permanent, or long-lasting, trade-off between inflation and output predict a positive coefficient on inflation. The Tobin-Mundell hypotheses that anticipated

6. Kormendi and Mequire, "Macroeconomic Determinants of Growth," 143.

7. William Baumol, "Productivity Growth, Convergence, and Welfare," *American Economic Review* 76 (1986): 1072–85; Moses Abramowitz, "Catching Up, Forging Ahead, and Falling Behind," *Journal of Economic History* 66 (1985): 385–406.

inflation causes portfolio adjustments that lower the real rate of interest and raise investment also imply a positive coefficient. Conversely, in economies with "cash-in-advance" constraints,[8] anticipated inflation reduces capital accumulation and growth, implying a negative coefficient. Finally, in developing countries, inflation is often caused by political crises that depress growth. We use both the level and first difference of inflation as regressors in our analysis.

(5) *Standard deviation of inflation.* Hayek and Friedman argue that variable inflation interferes with the information content of market prices, reducing economic activity.[9] Time-series studies of the U.S. have found the variability of inflation negatively correlated with GNP growth.[10]

(6) *Standard deviation of income growth.* As Kormendi and Mequire point out, the theory of saving under income uncertainty[11] implies that more variable income streams lead to higher savings, and therefore to a positive association between this variance and average income growth. Alternatively, there may be an aggregate risk-return trade-off in technology,[12] which also implies a positive effect for income growth variability on average growth rates.

(7) *Government.* As noted above, there is a large and controversial literature on the effects of government on economic growth. Several studies have focused exclusively on this issue, and Barth, Keleher, and Russek provide an exhaustive survey of these studies.[13] The problem here is defining the relevant type of government activity to put in the equation. Government production of basic valuable public goods (e.g., roads, property rights) clearly will be

8. Alan Stockman, "Anticipated Inflation and the Capital Stock in a Cash-in-Advance Economy," *Journal of Monetary Economics* 8 (1981): 387–93.

9. F. A. Hayek, *The Road to Serfdom* (Chicago: University of Chicago Press, 1944), and Milton Friedman, "Inflation and Unemployment," *Journal of Political Economy* 85 (1977): 451–72.

10. Maurice Levi and John Makin, "Inflation Uncertainty and the Phillips Curve: Some Empirical Evidence," *American Economic Review* 70 (1980): 1022–27; Donald Mullineaux, "Unemployment, Industrial Production and Inflation Uncertainty," *Review of Economics and Statistics* 62 (1980): 163–68.

11. Agnar Sandmo, "The Effect of Uncertainty on Saving," *Review of Economic Studies* 37 (1970): 353–60.

12. Fisher Black, "Business Cycles in General Equilibrium," working paper, MIT, Cambridge, Mass., 1979.

13. James Barth, Robert Keleher, and Frank Russek, "The Scale of Government and Economic Activity," 1987, mimeographed.

growth-enhancing. Government regulation of economic activity (e.g., mandating performance standards, forcing new procedures on entrepreneurs, environmental regulation) will probably slow down economic growth.[14] For example, Denison provides some evidence on the negative effect of U.S. government regulation on economic growth.[15]

Our data are limited to the share of government consumption of GDP. This variable nets out government investment and transfers. Since these are among the obvious government activities that may enhance growth, we expect the consumption variable to have a negative coefficient. We use the growth rate of this government share as our variable representing the effect of government size on economic growth. Using the growth rate rather than the level of government reflects our belief that increased government activity will temporarily affect growth as production patterns or transaction requirements or investment procedures are altered. Using the level of government activity implies that a one-time change in government intervention will permanently change economic growth and create, *ceteris paribus*, increasing wealth differences across countries.[16]

We can claim no innovations in this list of variables. Convergence and the effect of government have been widely examined, and our other regressors are used by Kormendi and Mequire (except they use the standard deviation of money surprises rather than inflation). We are refining and extending the Kormendi-Mequire analysis by using a data set with considerably more countries and by using multiple observations on each country.

---

14. Of course, regulatory activities can provide significant benefits and we are not equating GDP growth with social welfare.

15. E. F. Denison, *Trends in American Economic Growth: 1929–82* (Washington, D.C.: The Brookings Institution, 1985).

16. This point is not considered in most studies of the effect of government on growth. Empirically, Barth et al. note that the level of government is both used more often and is more significant than the growth rate.

Barro ("Government Spending") derives a nonlinear relationship between the size of government and economic growth in a growth model where production exhibits constant returns to scale in private capital and public-sector inputs taken together, but diminishing returns to private capital alone. Government is financed by a flat-rate income tax, and, at low levels of tax rates, increasing government spending raises the growth rate. Eventually, the corresponding higher tax rates cause increased spending to start lowering the equilibrium growth rate. Assuming all governments maximize citizen utility, the only sources of cross-country variations in the size of government would be differing preferences or technology.

4. Econometric Results

4.1. SUMMARY

We have six five-year average observations for each of the 24 OECD countries and four on each of the 89 other countries. Table 1 contains the results of estimating our model for the OECD, while the ROW results are presented in table 2. When these two data sets are concatenated and constrained to have the same slope coefficients, the F-statistic testing the appropriateness of combining the data is 4.25, which is significant at the 0.01 level and strongly rejects pooling the two groups of countries in a single sample.

A comparison of the two tables reveals the following major differences: (1) In the OECD, initial per-capita income has a negative and significant coefficient, confirming the convergence hypotheses. In the ROW, the coefficient is positive and significant, indicating that here richer countries grow faster. (2) Population growth is positive and significant in both samples. However, the OECD coefficient is within one standard deviation of 1.00, while the ROW coefficient is two standard deviations below 1.00. (3) Average inflation has no effect on the growth rates of OECD countries but is negative and significant in the ROW.

Government growth is negative and significant in both samples, as is the standard deviation of inflation, while the standard deviation of GDP growth is positive and significant in both equations. The OECD regression explains 63 percent of the variation in the dependent variable, while the ROW regression explains only 13 percent. The two major differences between these results and Kormendi and Mequire's are the finding that the OECD differs significantly from the other countries (with 47 observations Kormendi and Mequire did not test for this possibility) and that government growth is a significant negative factor in determining GDP growth. We now examine the results for the OECD in more detail, then further subdivide the ROW sample by continent.

4.2. OECD RESULTS

To test the temporal stability of the OECD coefficients in table 1, we split the sample into halves (1951–1965 and 1966–1980), estimate separate equations, and compare the fit of this unrestricted model with table 1, which constrains the slope coefficients to be constant over time. The F-statistic testing the null hypothesis of stable coefficients is 0.24, which does not reject the null at any meaningful level.

TABLE 1. *Pooled Regressions on Five-Year Averaged Data for 24 OECD Countries, 1951–1980*[a]

VARIABLE	COEFFICIENT	*t*-STATISTIC
Intercept	5.903	13.46
Initial per-capita real GDP	−0.00083	8.61
Mean growth of government share of GDP	−0.320	6.88
Mean population growth	0.870	5.53
Std. deviation of real GDP growth	0.170	2.48
Mean inflation rate	0.014	0.21
Mean change in inflation	−0.042	0.90
Std. deviation of inflation	−0.114	4.00
Dummy for 1956–1960	−0.896	2.25
Dummy for 1961–1965	0.978	2.65
Dummy for 1966–1970	1.435	3.42
Dummy for 1971–1975	1.069	1.91
Dummy for 1976–1980	1.562	3.25

[a] $N = 144$, $R^2 = 0.635$, $F_{13.131} = 19.04$.

These countries display a significant convergence effect over this sample period. A one standard deviation increase in per-capita GDP (around \$1000 in 1950) implies a 0.83 percentage point decline in average growth. Population growth has a significant coefficient of 0.883. Actual population growth varies widely in this sample, from Turkey (2.63%) to Austria (0.26%), and a one standard deviation increase in population growth is estimated to increase growth by 0.59 percentage points. The variability of GDP growth is also positive and significant, indicating there is a modest historical aggregate trade-off between risk and return. A one standard deviation increase in the standard deviation of GDP growth is associated with an additional 0.17 percentage point of average growth. These results are similar to those reported by Kormendi and Mequire.

The other regressors provide information about the effect of government on economic growth. Both the average level and first difference of inflation are completely neutral in the OECD over this period, but the variability of inflation does have a negative and significant effect.[17] A one

17. Kormendi and Mequire use the average change in the rate of inflation and find that variable negative and significant. They also use the variance of unanticipated money growth instead of the variance of inflation.

TABLE 2. *Pooled Regression on Five-Year Averaged Data for 89 ROW Countries, 1961–1980*[a]

VARIABLE	COEFFICIENT	*t*-STATISTIC
Intercept	4.156	4.22
Initial per-capital real GDP	0.00057	1.89
Mean growth of government share of GDP	−0.064	1.91
Mean population growth	0.669	2.56
Std. deviation of real GDP growth	0.097	2.06
Mean inflation rate	−0.159	3.42
Mean change in inflation	0.041	0.82
Std. deviation of inflation	−0.081	2.49
Dummy for 1966–1970	−0.099	0.19
Dummy for 1971–1975	0.595	1.10
Dummy for 1976–1980	−0.349	0.66
Dummy for Africa	−1.373	2.98
Dummy for the Americas	−1.312	2.50

[a]$N = 356$, $R^2 = 0.130$, $F_{13.343} = 4.37$.

standard deviation increase in inflation variability is associated with a 0.35 percentage point decline in average growth. These results provide no support for Mundell-Tobin notions of the benefits of inflation for growth, but do support Friedman's argument about the harmful effect of erratic inflation.

We also find a strong negative effect of the growth of government consumption as a fraction of GDP. The coefficient of −0.32 is highly significant, and, taken literally, it implies that a one standard deviation increase in government growth reduces average GDP growth by 0.39 percentage points. This result is not found by Kormendi and Mequire, who use the same variable definition but a different country sample and data source. Kormendi and Mequire also only use one average observation per country. While our testing indicates that it is inappropriate to pool OECD and ROW countries, we can average our data over the full sample and allow only cross-country differences to determine the model coefficients.

The result of this exercise is reported below in eq. (1), where the variables are the same as those in table 2 but are averaged over 30 years (*t*-statistics in parentheses),

Real GDP % = 5.16 − 0.0099 Initial Real GDP
    (6.16)   (3.52)

    − 0.348 Government % + 1.047 Population %
       (2.42)   (3.52)

    + 0.290 σ Real GDP % + 0.114 Inflation
       (1.60)   (0.58)

    − 0.061 Δ Inflation − 0.107 σ Inflation,   (1)
       (0.97)   (1.33)

$$N = 24, \qquad R^2 = 0.82, \qquad F_{8,16} = 10.90.$$

The coefficients in this fully averaged regression have the same sign and general magnitudes as those in table 1, along with the smaller t-statistics to be expected when the variances of the explanatory variables are reduced. Specifically, the coefficient on government growth changes by −0.028 to −0.348, and its significance level falls to 0.05 (t-statistic = 2.42). The result that changes the most when time is eliminated is the effect of variable inflation. The t-statistic falls from 4.0 in table 1 to 1.3 in eq. (1).

While the slope coefficients are stable over the full 30-year sample, there are substantial changes in the intercept as shown by the time-period dummy variables in table 1. Except for the 1956–1960 period, the average OECD growth rate, holding our other variables constant, is significantly higher in all cases than the 1951–1955 level, with some indication of an upward trend. Replacing the dummy variables with a trend variable produces the following result (t-statistics in parentheses):

Real GDP % =   5.44 − 0.00087 Initial Real GDP
      (12.82)   (8.72)

    − 0.279 Government % + 0.886 Population %
       (5.77)   (5.39)

    + 0.135 σ Real GDP % + 0.009 Inflation
       (1.91)   (0.24)

    − 0.035 Δ Inflation − 0.132 σ Inflation
       (0.87)   (4.54)

    + 0.428 Trend,   (2)
       (4.49)

$$N = 144, \qquad R^2 = 0.58, \qquad F_{9,135} = 21.86.$$

TABLE 3. *GDP Growth in Canada, Australia, U.K., Ireland, and Turkey*

	CANADA	AUSTRALIA	U.K.	IRELAND	TURKEY
Deviation of growth from convergence prediction	+1.13	+0.58	−1.67	−1.88	+0.79
Due to:					
Population growth	+0.80	+0.83	−0.56	−0.54	+1.47
Government growth	−0.11	−0.26	+0.16	−0.06	−0.73
Std. deviation of GDP growth	0.00	+0.07	+0.17	−0.12	+0.44
Std. deviation of inflation	+0.22	+0.38	+0.03	−0.04	−1.13
Residual	+0.22	−0.44	−1.47	−1.12	+0.75

This model can shed some light on the statistical sources of growth differentials across OECD countries. Besides the U.S. and Japan (considered in detail below), Canada, Australia, the U.K., Ireland, and Turkey are the countries whose growth rates diverge the most from what might be predicted from initial conditions. Table 3 details the estimated effects the other independent variables have on these countries' growth patterns. The higher-than-expected growth in Canada and Australia is due to higher-than-average population growth and more stable inflation. The lower-than-expected growth in the U.K. and Ireland is partly due to low population growth but is mostly unexplained by our model. Turkey displays extreme values of all the independent variables. Its higher-than-expected growth comes from high population growth and variable income growth. However, in our model this prediction is offset by high government growth and unstable inflation. A structural interpretation of our coefficients implies that Turkey would have surpassed Japan as the fastest growing country in the sample except for these governmental factors.

4.3. THE U.S. AND JAPAN

Over this 1951–1980 sample, the average U.S. growth rate is 3.27, which is 1.17 points below the average of the OECD countries. The single largest factor explaining this below-average U.S. showing is convergence. In 1950 the U.S. per-capita output was about twice the OECD mean level. Combining this difference with the negative coefficient on initial wealth from table 1 gives the prediction that U.S. growth will be 1.9 percentage points below the

OECD mean. The U.S. growth rate on average is 0.73 percentage points larger than what is predicted by initial conditions. This is attributed partly to higher-than-average population growth (+0.26) and lower-than-average inflation variability (+0.38). The other 0.10 percentage point of "extra" growth is unexplained by the model.

Now consider the change in U.S. growth from the 1960's to the 1970's. From 1961 to 1970, U.S. growth averaged 3.79 percent. In the next decade, average growth fell to 2.88 percent, a decline of 0.91 percentage points. In our model this decline is attributed to convergence (−1.19 points) and lower population growth (−0.40 points), along with an increase in inflation variability (−0.14 points). However, this is partly offset by a fall in the growth of government consumption (+0.32 points) and a rise in the variability of output growth (+0.19 points). On the whole, U.S. growth fell less than what is predicted by convergence and 0.30 less than what is predicted by our full model. It appears that America is not going down without a fight.

We can also examine the Japan-U.S. growth gap with the model. The $3700 larger 1950 per-capita income in the U.S. implies that Japan should grow, on average, 3.07 percentage points faster than the U.S. The actual average difference is 4.88 points. In our model the extra 1.9 points of Japanese growth is attributed to slower government growth in Japan (+2.3 percentage points). Over the sample, our measure of the share of government consumption in Japan's GDP falls dramatically from 0.20 to about 0.07. The fact that Japan is a large positive outlier in GDP growth and a large negative outlier in government growth made us wonder if the significant negative association between these two variables is driven mainly by the six observations on Japan. However, this is not the case. We dropped Japan from the sample and re-estimated eq. (1), finding that while the coefficient on government growth dropped from −0.32 to −0.25, it was still significant at the 0.01 level (t-statistic = 5.45). None of the other coefficients was affected.

We are not arguing that slashing government growth in the U.S. would close the U.S.-Japan growth gap. As noted above, our model is not structural; it is not derived from any basis that can be used to make predictions about the effect of policy shifts on growth rates. Such simulations would run aground on Lucas's classic warning about predicting the effects of policy changes from nonstructural models when the behavior of the public is not invariant to policymakers' actions. Strictly, it is no more correct to argue that reductions in government growth will raise output than it is to argue that erratic fiscal policies that increase the variability of output or a government-enforced doubling of the birth rate would raise average growth rates. The most we can say is that controlling for initial wealth, population growth, and the variability of GDP and inflation, there is a strong, significant negative association between government growth and output growth in these data.

4.4. SUBDIVIDING THE ROW

To investigate the appropriateness of pooling the 89 ROW countries in a single sample, we estimate separate equations for Africa, the Americas, and Asia.[18] These regressions are reported in table 4. The F-statistic testing the null hypothesis that our slope coefficients are constant across continents is 4.25, which strongly rejects the aggregate model in table 2 in favor of the separate regressions in table 4. We then split each continent data set in half (1961–1970 and 1971–1980), testing the temporal stability of the continent-specific slope coefficients. The F-statistics are 1.32, 1.43, and 0.83, and the null hypothesis that the model coefficients are stable over time is not rejected, even at the 0.10 level, in any case.

The model coefficients vary dramatically across the three subsamples. Population growth is positive and significant in the Americas but insignificant in Africa and Asia. The coefficient on initial per-capita wealth is positive and significant in Africa and Asia (0.10 level) and insignificant in the Americas. Average inflation is negative and significant in Africa and insignificant elsewhere, while the change in inflation is always insignificant. Government growth is negative and significant in Africa and the Americas but positive and significant in Asia. The standard deviation of GDP growth is positive and significant only in Africa, and the standard deviation of inflation is negative and significant in the Americas and Asia.

The most interesting findings here are the lack of convergence effects on growth and the one case (Asia) of a positive government growth coefficient. The coefficients on initial per-capita income in Africa and Asia are consistent with the proposition that there are increasing returns to technology at low initial conditions and that the relatively rich countries get even relatively richer. In Africa and Asia, average per-capita income in 1960 was about

---

18. The countries in each subsample are listed in the appendix. The Americas sample is North, Central, and South America minus OECD members. The Asia sample includes Fiji, Indonesia, and New Guinea.

TABLE 4. *Pooled Regression on Five-Year Averaged Data for 43 African Countries, 24 Central and South American Countries, and 22 Asian and Far Eastern Countries, 1961–1980*[a]

VARIABLE	AFRICA	AMERICAS	ASIA
Intercept	2.030	4.047	6.396
	(1.46)	(3.26)	(2.74)
Initial per-capita real GDP	0.00099	−0.00019	0.00098
	(1.74)	(0.53)	(1.79)
Mean growth of government share of GDP	−0.207	−0.126	0.113
	(3.57)	(2.08)	(1.99)
Mean population growth	0.502	0.849	0.252
	(1.19)	(2.91)	(0.32)
Std. deviation of real GDP growth	0.152	−0.051	−0.133
	(2.38)	(0.59)	(1.15)
Mean inflation rate	−0.276	0.135	−0.107
	(4.17)	(1.59)	(0.97)
Mean change in inflation	0.087	−0.095	−0.006
	(1.18)	(0.86)	(0.06)
Std. deviation of inflation	0.016	−0.095	−0.148
	(0.28)	(1.89)	(2.58)
Dummy for 1966–1970	0.160	0.520	−0.903
	(0.19)	(0.77)	(0.82)
Dummy for 1971–1975	1.173	−0.395	0.748
	(1.43)	(0.60)	(0.60)
Dummy for 1976–1980	−0.222	−0.361	−0.892
	(0.25)	(0.53)	(0.74)
N	172	96	88
R^2	0.223	0.292	0.213
F	4.65	3.61	2.40

[a] Numbers in parentheses are *t*-statistics.

one-third the average 1950 level in the OECD. The coefficients imply that a one standard deviation increase in initial income produces a 0.32 percentage point increase in growth for African countries and a 0.93 increase for Asian countries. Though the regression coefficient for the Americas is insignificant, the cross-correlation coefficient between initial wealth and growth is −0.38, which is significant at the 0.10 level. This should serve as a warning about looking at simple correlations to draw inferences about the strength of convergence patterns across countries. Also in contrast with the OECD results, none of the time-period dummy variables is significant in these ROW regressions. There is no evidence of a rising average growth rate, holding other factors constant. There are significant cross-continent differences in the intercept, with Asia's growth rate estimated to be three times larger than Africa's, holding our macro variables constant.

In Africa and the Americas, government growth is significantly negatively correlated with GDP growth, and though the coefficients are smaller than what we observe for the OECD, government growth is more variable in these countries, so a one standard deviation increase in government growth reduces GDP growth by 0.58 points in Africa and 0.25 points in the Americas. In Asia, a one standard deviation increase in government growth corresponds to a 0.38 percentage point increase in the real GDP growth.[19]

These three equations have no coefficients that have the same sign and are significant in each case, nor are all coefficients significant in any one equation. The equations explain between 20 and 30 percent of the variation in real GDP growth, compared with the 0.63 R^2 in the OECD equation. Our findings for these 89 countries are mainly negative. Coefficients do not pool across continents; variables often do not retain significance from equation to equation; the specification that explains a large part of the OECD growth experience does not work nearly as well in the rest of the world.

One thing the ROW data do clearly show is that economic convergence is not a ubiquitous phenomenon. Rather, we find a pattern of *divergence*, where the "rich" grow relatively richer. When combined with the result that in Africa and Asia population growth has no effect on economic growth, a bleak picture of growth prospects in these poorest countries emerges.

4.5. OPEC, "FREEDOM," AND THE ROW

We can investigate, at least on a crude level, some factors that may influence these results. The first possibility is oil wealth. There are eight OPEC members in the sample, and it is possible that either the divergence or noneffect of population results is produced by superior economic growth in these oil-exporting countries. The other factor is a proxy for the political infrastructure of these countries. Freedom House provides a ranking of civil liberties around the world that is explained by Gastil, investigated by Bilson, and used by

---

19. Just as Japan had a very high growth rate and low government consumption growth in the OECD sample, Hong Kong has a very high growth rate for both GDP and government consumption. Deleting Hong Kong from the sample slightly lowers the government growth coefficient and lowers the significance level to 0.10.

TABLE 5. *Controlling for Civil Liberties and OPEC in the ROW Regressions, 1961–1980*[a]

VARIABLE	AFRICA	AMERICAS	ASIA
Intercept	3.570	4.849	6.383
	(2.47)	(3.55)	(2.65)
Initial per-capita real GDP	0.00006	−0.00039	0.00095
	(0.10)	(0.95)	(1.67)
Mean growth of government share of GDP	−0.225	−0.118	0.110
	(4.08)	(1.97)	(1.90)
Mean population growth	0.394	0.661	0.254
	(0.95)	(2.03)	(0.31)
Std. deviation of real GDP growth	0.100	−0.069	−0.125
	(1.64)	(0.81)	(0.98)
Mean inflation rate	−0.287	0.135	−0.114
	(4.53)	(1.61)	(1.00)
Mean change in inflation	0.090	−0.077	−0.005
	(1.28)	(0.70)	(0.05)
Std. deviation of inflation	0.029	−0.074	−0.125
	(0.53)	(1.39)	(2.55)
Dummy for OPEC membership	4.156	0.205	0.383
	(3.58)	(0.77)	(0.33)
Dummy for lack of civil liberties	−1.480	−1.668	−0.213
	(2.83)	(1.88)	(0.20)
N	172	96	88
R^2	0.307	0.321	0.214
F	5.87	3.47	2.10

[a]Numbers in parentheses are t-statistics. Time-period dummies were estimated in these regressions but not reported above.

Kormendi and Mequire.[20] Kormendi and Mequire use a dummy variable defining countries in the two highest civil liberty classes of the seven categories given by Freedom House. Here we use a dummy variable that includes countries in the two most repressive categories.

In table 5 we add these dummy variables to the regressions for Africa, the Americas, and Asia. The effects are most dramatic in Africa. *Ceteris paribus,*

20. R. D. Gastil, *Freedom in the World: Political Rights and Civil Liberties* (New York: Freedom House, 1978); J. F. Bilson, "Civil Liberty—An Econometric Investigation," *Kyklos* 35 (1982): 94–114.

the OPEC countries (Algeria, Gabon, and Nigeria) grew 4 percentage points faster and severely repressive countries 1.5 points slower. These variables increase the fit of the equation by 50 percent and knock out the significant divergence effect on the African continent, though population growth remains completely insignificant.

In the Americas, the OPEC countries are not significantly different, but the repressive countries have, on average, a growth rate 1.7 percentage points lower than the other countries. In the Asia sample, neither variable is significant, the coefficient on population is still insignificant, and the coefficient on initial wealth is still positive and significant. However, five OPEC countries that belong in this sample are not in the Summers-Heston data.

As with all the ROW results, the effects of OPEC and political repression vary significantly across continents. Neither of these variables applies to the OECD, which contains no members of OPEC and no countries below the third rank of civil liberty in the Freedom House index.

4.6. POPULATION WEIGHTED REGRESSIONS

The above results give each country equal weight in determining coefficients regardless of their relative size. For example, Belgium and the U.S. in the OECD and Sri Lanka and India in Asia have an equal opportunity to influence the results despite their staggering population differentials. As a check on the stability of our results, table 6 reports population-weighted regressions for the four subsamples. This will show whether the results are driven by small countries.

Table 6 shows that the basic flavor of our results carries through to the population-weighted regressions. In the OECD and the Americas, the convergence effect is slightly stronger, population growth has a bigger coefficient, and the first difference of inflation is now negative and significant. In Africa, population growth becomes positive and significant for the first time. In the Asia sample, the standard deviation of GDP growth becomes negative and significant. Otherwise the results are largely the same.

5. Summary and Conclusions

We use the Summers and Heston data to extend Kormendi and Mequire's empirical model of cross-country growth. For OECD countries, we find a strong convergence effect and a persistent negative correlation between the

TABLE 6. *Population-Weighted Regressions for the OECD, Africa, Americas, and Asia Subsamples* [a]

VARIABLE	OECD	AFRICA	AMERICAS	ASIA
Intercept	7.225	2.621	2.587	3.950
	(14.08)	(1.87)	(1.44)	(1.67)
Initial per-capita real GDP	−0.0010	−0.00042	−0.00060	0.0016
	(11.26)	(0.89)	(1.48)	(2.08)
Mean growth of government	−0.310	−0.113	−0.296	0.164
share of GDP	(7.36)	(2.37)	(4.11)	(2.39)
Mean population growth	1.261	0.943	1.334	0.250
	(5.83)	(2.08)	(3.12)	(0.28)
Std. deviation of real GDP growth	0.155	−0.065	−0.044	−0.399
	(1.78)	(1.13)	(0.36)	(3.35)
Mean inflation rate	0.060	−0.216	0.228	−0.009
	(0.89)	(4.19)	(1.91)	(0.11)
Mean change in inflation	−0.080	0.098	−0.306	−0.100
	(1.68)	(1.34)	(2.58)	(0.84)
Std. deviation of inflation	−0.189	−0.008	−0.098	0.015
	(5.42)	(0.20)	(2.24)	(0.37)
Dummy for OPEC membership	−	2.746	−0.819	1.351
		(4.39)	(0.91)	(1.74)
Dummy for lack of civil liberties	−	−1.515	−1.637	0.228
		(3.40)	(1.92)	(0.21)
N	144	172	96	88
R^2	0.747	0.306	0.538	0.336
F	32.24	5.85	8.05	3.26

[a] Numbers in parentheses are *t*-statistics. Time-period dummies were estimated in these regressions but not reported above.

growth of government's share in GDP and economic growth. We find no positive association between inflation and growth, and a significant negative relationship between inflation variability and growth. In the specific case of the U.S., our results indicate that, while U.S. growth is lower than the OECD average and declining from the 1960's to the 1970's, these effects are less than what simple convergence or our complete model predict.[21]

Since we cannot pool the countries in the ROW and the OECD or even across continents in the ROW, we estimate separate equations for Africa, the

21. E. F. Denison, *Accounting for Slower Economic Growth: The United States in the 1970's* (Washington, D.C.: The Brookings Institution, 1979).

Americas, and Asia. Here we find no evidence for the convergence hypotheses. In fact, for Africa and Asia, the relatively advanced countries grow faster. There is still no positive association between inflation and growth (for Africa, inflation is a negative and significant influence), but the negative effect of inflation variability shows up (at the 0.10 level) only in the Americas. Government growth is negative and significant in Africa and the Americas but has a positive coefficient in Asia. Finally, we note the Malthusian result that population growth has no positive effect on output growth in either Africa or Asia (except for the population-weighted coefficient for Africa).

These results demonstrate that we do not have a single empirical model of secular growth that applies around the world. Idiosyncratic variations, what Abramowitz calls social capabilities, are much more important than can be inferred from the highly aggregated results presented by Kormendi and Mequire. Much more research is needed on the causes of economic growth in less advanced countries.

Appendix: Division of Countries in the Sample

A.1. OECD (24)

Australia	Greece	New Zealand
Austria	Iceland	Portugal
Belgium	Ireland	Spain
Canada	Italy	Sweden
Denmark	Japan	Switzerland
Finland	Luxembourg	Turkey
France	Netherlands	United Kingdom
Germany (F.R.G.)	Norway	United States

A.2. ROW

A.2.1. Africa (43)

Algeria [22,23]	Benin [23]	Burundi [23]
Angola [23]	Botswana	Cameroon

22. OPEC member; note that the Arab OPEC countries of Kuwait, Libya, Qatar, Saudi Arabia, and the United Arab Emirates are not in the Summers-Heston data set.

23. Country with low civil liberties (Freedom House index of 6 or greater).

Central African Republic[23]   Madagascar   South Africa[23]
Chad[23]   Malawi[23]   Sudan
Congo[23]   Mali[23]   Swaziland
Egypt   Mauritania[23]   Tanzania[23]
Ethiopia[23]   Mauritius   Togo[23]
Gabon[22, 23]   Morocco   Tunisia
Gambia   Mozambique[23]   Uganda[23]
Ghana   Niger[23]   Upper Volta
Guinea[23]   Nigeria[22]   Zaire[23]
Ivory Coast   Rwanda   Zambia
Kenya   Senegal   Zimbabwe
Lesotho   Sierra Leone
Liberia   Somalia[23]

A.2.2. Americas (24)
Argentina   Ecuador[22]   Nicaragua
Barbados   El Salvador   Panama
Bolivia   Guatemala   Paraguay
Brazil   Guyana   Peru
Chile   Haiti[23]   Surinam
Columbia   Honduras   Trinidad & Tobago
Costa Rica   Jamaica   Uruguay
Dom. Republic   Mexico   Venezuela[22]

A.2.3. Asia (22)
Afghanistan[23]   Israel   Philippines
Bangladesh   Jordan[23]   Singapore
Burma[23]   Hong Kong   South Korea
Fiji   Malaysia   Sri Lanka
India   Nepal   Syria[23]
Indonesia[22]   New Guinea   Taiwan
Iran[22]   Pakistan   Thailand
Iraq[22,23]

PROVISION OF PUBLIC GOODS
THROUGH PRIVATIZATION

A special example is presented in which government provision is apt to produce less in the way of public goods than private provision. The reason is that the government is normally only interested in what goes on within its frontiers, whereas private producers of patented pharmaceuticals will be interested in the world market. Thus, for patentable pharmaceuticals a public-spirited government would provide less in the way of research funds than would a private company even if the private company is headed by a group of selfish and greedy individuals.

The basic justification for government in public choice and conventional public finance is the existence of large externalities or public goods. This article will discuss a special (perhaps unique) case in which privatization will lead to better internalization of externalities than will government provision. This still depends on the government protecting private property rights, but even most libertarians approve of that.

The particular case we will deal with is pharmaceutical research. I propose to demonstrate that the government provision of pharmaceutical research fails to internalize sizeable externalities. This may, of course, also be true with respect to other kinds of research, but I know of no other examples. Note that throughout I will assume, unrealistically, a very high level of intelligence and virtue in governments. More realistic assumptions would strengthen my case.

There are two ways of providing research on new drugs: firstly, the government can raise taxes and spend the money on maintaining laboratories or, for that matter, hiring private companies to maintain laboratories to search for new and improved pharmaceuticals. As a normal rule, the government, when it does this, simply makes the new medical knowledge freely available. Occasionally, it may charge a fee, and in some cases, for example vaccinations, it may actually compel its citizens to consume them.

The alternative is to have private companies put their own money into research with the intent of getting their money back by way of returns on their patents. In both cases, what we want is to have the margins match; that is, the last dollar spent in research should produce a benefit of a dollar in terms of curing diseases. Of course, we don't expect perfection, particularly not since

Reprinted, with permission of Blackwell Publishing, publisher, from *Kyklos* 49 (1996): 221–24.

we are talking about a particularly chancy type of research. Nevertheless, that is the goal, and I shall assume, temporarily, that it is what we want and that we can reasonably hope for an approximation with no systematic deviations.[1]

A private corporation will invest money out to the point where it thinks the returns on its patents are maximized. An ideal government will invest in research to the point where it thinks the benefit to its citizens of the last dollar will just match the cost to the taxpayers of that same last dollar.[2]

The externality to which this paper is directed, however, is an international one. An ideal government would take into account the benefit to its citizens and the cost to its citizens. The American government would not be much concerned, except for possible charitable reasons, with what happens in Liberia. A private company, on the other hand, which is proposing to sell the drug for profit, will automatically think of the world market.

In other words, there is a sizeable potential externality, which you can call a public good, which is the well-being of people outside the originating country. This will be taken into account by a company attempting to develop its own patent structure and will not be taken into account by a government which is interested in its own voter-taxpayers.[3]

Note that this is no criticism of our ideal government. It is attempting to maximize the well-being of its citizens and will do so if it follows this rule, but there is the externality of the health of foreigners, which the government of the United States pays little attention to, and a private pharmaceutical company will pay a great deal of attention to. In both cases, we have a simple attempt to maximize. Even though the pharmaceutical company may be run by a group of extremely selfish and greedy persons, it still will engage in research which would not be regarded as paying by a national government devoted to the well-being of its citizens.

In the real world, national governments seem to be almost antagonistic to medical research. Maximum prices on drugs are imposed in many places, including now the United States. Regulations making the introduction of new drugs very expensive also retard research.

---

1. The reader will note that I am giving the government the benefit of every doubt. This is not my usual practice.

2. This article applies only to patentable research. Medical research sometimes produces unpatentable improvements; a new surgical procedure would be an example.

3. Occasionally a government organization patents the result of its research and then charges for its use. It is then acting like a private company.

The reason for this I think is obvious, even though it is perverse. The great improvement in medicine over the period of my lifetime has been pretty much, not entirely, but very largely, a development of new pharmaceuticals. Germ diseases, for example, are no longer very dangerous in most cases, whereas they were big killers when I was a boy. This is the result of the development of highly specialized poisons which will kill germs but not their hosts.

Despite the importance of these drugs, they are actually an inexpensive part of medical treatment. They normally make up less than 5% of the total medical expenditure. The time of specialized personnel, including doctors, and hospital care are the large items in medical expenditures. Savings from forcing down the price of drugs are not very great, and, in the long run, they may even be perverse because of the increase in the need for custodial care.

On the other hand, drug companies, because of the need to insure against very large risk for any given piece of research, need to maintain laboratories that are engaging in many different kinds of research, and hence tend to be very big. The organizations which provide direct medical attention, custodial care, etc., are usually quite small. Further, they include many people—doctors, nurses, etc. These people not only can vote, they are apt to be influential members of their communities.

Politically, we would expect the local providers to be more successful than the distant pharmaceutical giant corporation. Hence there are many more restrictions on the companies than on the local practitioners. A citizen worried about the cost of medical care will tend to think it is a bunch of big capitalists who are raising the price, not the friendly neighborhood practitioners.[4] In fact, that is what we see. Regulations intended to cut the profits of the drug companies are politically popular all over the world. As a result, fewer new drugs are produced, and the world death rate will be worse, not today, but 10 years from now.

The above applies only, of course, to patentable research. There is a great deal of pure research which is of use medically, and there is nothing here about the desirability or undesirability of government doing the research. It should be noted, however, that following the arguments given above, governments probably underprovide, because they engage in it only up to the point where they think the net long-run payoff to their citizens will meet their tax payments.

---

4. I owe this point to an anonymous referee for this journal.

Turning to patentable types of medical types of research, however, government research may actually slow total progress. This is because they will invest less in resources per given bit of research than a private company would, because the government takes into account only a fraction of the return, while the private company takes the entire return into account.

Pharmaceutical research is risky. Suppose that there is a private company which feels that it could possibly put $250 million into work on a particular drug, realizing there is a real possibility some other private company will beat them out or that they won't discover the drug. If they then hear that the government is beginning to work on the same area, the government having less resources and only proposing to put in $150 million, they may regard this as increasing their risk enough so that they drop out and work on something else. This is speculation, but it is not impossible that this might happen. Government should, in general, stick to pure research, where there is little in the way of private competition.

The intriguing feature of this is that we have what appears to be a public good, and government provision is, in theory, inferior to private provision. The reason is simply that the government in the international field does not generate public goods. Indeed armies generate public bads for foreigners. In this case, we should privatize as a way of improving the production of what is close to a pure public good.

PART 7

THE THEORY OF GAMES

AN ECONOMIC THEORY
OF MILITARY TACTICS

METHODOLOGICAL INDIVIDUALISM AT WAR

Geoffrey Brennan and Gordon Tullock

*Nothing can wisely be prescribed in an army . . . without exact knowledge of
the fundamental instrument, man, and his state of mind, his morals, at the
instant of combat.*
—Ardant du Picq, *Battle Studies* (1946, p. 39)

1. Introduction

The theory of military tactics that is presented here is not economic in any
obvious sense. We are not concerned with the role of the productive economy as a strategic element in the conduct of total warfare. Nor are we concerned with what might be termed "economic" aspects of logistics. Our discussion is, rather, economic in terms of the method of analysis.

Two aspects of economic method are relevant here. The first is the individualistic perspective. Although in modern economics, collections of individuals are sometimes treated as "entities" for analytic purposes (examples
of "the household," "the firm," and even occasionally "the state" spring to
mind), the *ultimate* unit of analysis is always the individual; more aggregative
analysis must be regarded as only provisionally legitimate. In other words, the
economist is always sensitive to the possibility that the holistic treatment of
groups of individuals may mislead greatly or involve overlooking dimensions
of reality that are extremely important. This paper reflects such a sensitivity.

The second aspect of economic method relevant here is that much of economics deals with the problem of how to structure the institutional order
that governs the ways in which individual agents interact with one another to
achieve certain well-defined objectives. The prime example of such an institutional order is the freely operating market: the market is widely recognized
among professional economists to possess the attractive property that under

Reprinted from *Journal of Economic Behavior and Organization* 3, no. 3 (1982): 225–42,
copyright 1982, with permission from Elsevier.

certain circumstances all the scope for mutual benefits is exhausted. The operation of the market in such settings is often contrasted with the operation of other social co-ordinating/decision-making mechanisms such as majoritarian politics which do not have this property. More generally, the properties of alternative institutional structures represent a major line of enquiry in modern economic analysis.

That these aspects of economics bear particularly on the question of military tactics is perhaps not entirely obvious and certainly does not appear to have been explicitly recognized in much of the relevant literature. More conventional analysis of military tactics seems to involve an approach in which opposing *armies* are conceived of as the units of analysis. Battle can then be analyzed in much the same way as a game of chess may be. The role of the general is seen to be the deployment of his forces in the most effective way: discussion of good "generalship" focuses naturally on such matters as intelligent use of terrain, rapid mobility, concentration of strength at crucial points, and so on. Disaggregation to the level of the individual soldier is seen as an unnecessary refinement and presents only the danger of losing sight of the forest for the trees.

However, as the initial quotation from du Picq cogently reminds us, the forces available to the general are not chess pieces, but men—men whose actions are governed by their individual states of mind and not necessarily by the wills of their generals. We must at least allow the logical possibility that at times the interests of any one individual may be at odds with the interests of the general or of the army "as a whole." Indeed, the central element of our thesis in this paper is that this is characteristically the case, and that an essential ingredient in the analysis of military engagements is missed if this fact is not recognized. Armies must be analyzed as collections of independent individuals who are, in some senses, as much at war with one another and their own leaders as they are with enemy forces.

There are, of course, some aspects of the problem here that have been widely discussed in orthodox military literature. The importance of "morale" in unifying the perceived interests of individual soldiers has, for example, been emphasized as a crucial ingredient in ensuring success in battle. "Morale is to the physical," remarks Napoleon "as three is to one." And it is not for nothing that much of our referenced material comes from the (largely ignored) writings of du Picq, for whom morale is the sine qua non of tactical strength. Where our treatment differs from du Picq's, and, a fortiori, from other writers in the area is that the economist's perspective encourages an examination of technical, or "institutional," rather than purely psychological aspects of what might broadly be termed the "morale problem."

Our argument develops as follows. In section 2 we lay out the theory in terms of some simple examples. In section 3, we discuss the relevance of this general theory for military contexts. Section 4 discusses incentives and monitoring as aspects of a theory of military science, and section 5 spells out some implications of the argument. Section 6 draws the relevant conclusions.

2

The central analytic element in our discussion is a variant of the familiar prisoners' dilemma problem. This particular form of interaction in its many guises underlies a large part of the more interesting areas of economics—the theory of market failure in the provision of public goods, the modern theory of the firm, much of the economic theory of politics, and the theory of labor unions, to mention some of the more conspicuous examples. In one sense, the prisoners' dilemma is so familiar a tool of modern social analysis that to rehearse it yet again may seem entirely unnecessary. On the other hand, the military application is probably of sufficient intrinsic interest to justify spelling out the details. Moreover, there are some major wrinkles in this application that merit its being viewed as an analytically distinct and independently interesting case.

We shall begin our discussion with the simplest possible example and complicate the analysis where necessary as we proceed. Accordingly, let us consider the following example.

Two individuals, A and B, are walking a deserted street. Suddenly they see a man, C, running towards them. The man is waving a meat cleaver about his head and has a wild eye; he yells abuse at them and shouts out his intent to kill them both. What is rational for A and B to do?

It is clear that if A and B jointly tackle C, the probability that they will overcome him is quite large; the probability that either A or B will be seriously hurt is not zero but is fairly small (say, one in five). Hence, the expectation that either A or B will be seriously hurt *if both stay* is low, in this case, one in ten.

Suppose, however, that A runs away and B stays. Then A will be perfectly safe, but B will face a significant chance, say one in two, of being seriously hurt—likewise, if A stays to fight while B runs. There are, then, in this example, significant "economics of scale" in fighting: the chance of C killing either is much smaller when both remain than when only one does. In other words, there are strong *technical* advantages to numerical superiority.

But what if both run away? In this case, it is fairly likely that C will catch up with one of them—a probability of two in three, say. But since there is no way of knowing ex ante who will be the unlucky one, the probability that each faces of being hurt if both run is only one in three.

We can depict this situation as a non-zero-sum-game matrix as in table 1. The first entry in each payoff pair is the probability that A will be seriously hurt—the second entry, the probability that B will be seriously hurt. If we can presume that A and B are indifferent to one another's fate and that being seriously hurt is something each would prefer to avoid, then we can depict this matrix in more familiar payoff terms, as illustrated in table 2. The payoff pair (a, b) for each outcome indicates the payoff a to A and the payoff b to B, respectively.

The characteristic feature of this interaction is that the rational course of action for each individual is to *run*; that is, the strategy "run" maximizes the payoff (minimizes the loss) to each individual irrespective of what the other does. Consider B's calculus, for example. If A chooses to stay and fight, B will endure an expected cost of 10 if he also stays, but zero if he runs—it is therefore

TABLE 1

		B'S ACTIONS	
		STAY AND FIGHT	RUN
A's actions	Stay and fight	$[\frac{1}{10}, \frac{1}{10}]$	$[\frac{1}{2}, 0]$
	Run	$[0, \frac{1}{2}]$	$[\frac{1}{3}, \frac{1}{3}]$

TABLE 2

		B'S ACTIONS	
		STAY AND FIGHT	RUN
A's actions	Stay and fight	$[-10, -10]$	$[-50, 0]$
	Run	$[0, -50]$	$[-33, -33]$

rational to run. If A runs, however, B faces an expected cost of 50 if he stays to fight, but faces an expected cost of only 33 if he runs—it is again rational to run. In toto, B finds that it is rational to run whatever A does. And since the interaction is totally symmetric, A will find it rational to run whatever B does. Yet clearly, for the two of them, considered as a group, the worst possible outcome is for both to run; what is collectively rational is individually irrational and vice versa.

This simple example is an entirely standard version of the prisoners' dilemma problem. It captures, in our view, the essential element in the relation between members of an army under attack; the *collectively* rational thing to do is to stay and fight; the individually rational thing to do is to run (or attempt to avoid conflict in some other manner). It also exposes the *essential* tactical problem—how to organize one's forces in such a way as to induce each individual to behave in the collective interest. It fails, however, to capture one crucial feature of the strategic element in military engagement because it assumes that the attacking force, C, is going to attack independent of what A and B do.

To depict the essential nature of military confrontation, we need to be able to reflect in our analytics, simultaneously, the prisoners' dilemma interaction that connects each individual with his fellow soldiers on his own side *and* the overall strategic interaction between the opposing "collectivities." We expand our example modestly. We suppose the "attacker" to be not one determined madman, C, but two ordinary "soldiers," C and D. We thus have two armies, each composed of two persons[1]—and for simplicity of treatment, we shall suppose that each individual is exactly like all the others. This total symmetry assumption means that the payoff matrix and the consequent calculus can be set out simply for a single representative individual. This matrix is, however, complicated by the fact that, in deciding his course of action, the individual must consider not just the possible actions of his comrades but also the possible actions of his enemies. And we must be careful to motivate the

---

1. It may be complained that the two-person case is too small a scale to represent any interesting model of military reality. Two responses are possible. First, that military units are typically composed of sub-units and that the incentive structure here outlined is applicable to the decision makers for those sub-units as well as for individuals *within* those sub-units. Second, that the relevant dimensions of the problem are *under*stated not overstated by focusing on the small-numbers case. With larger numbers, the influence that any one individual soldier exercises on the outcome of battle tends to correspondingly lower, and hence, the incentives to "free ride" correspondingly greater.

TABLE 3. *Probability of Victory*

Army I	2	2	2	1	1	1	0	0	0
Army II	2	1	0	2	1	0	2	1	0
Probability that I beats II	50%	80%	100%	20%	50%	100%	0	0	no outcome

individuals in such a way that it is in some manner "rational" for them to be involved in the military confrontation at all.

In setting out our example, several pieces of background data are necessary. In particular, we need to specify the payoff to each if his army is victorious, the probability of victory, the probability of being injured, and the costs of being injured. Where applicable, we shall follow the terms of the earlier, simpler case.

Accordingly, suppose that two armies, I and II, are disputing the ownership of some territory, which has a value to each army of 20 units (10 units to each soldier) if the army proves victorious.[2] The probability of victory is, of course, a function of the relative actual fighting strengths, and is assumed to be as indicated in table 3.

The probability of being seriously injured in the course of battle depends crucially on what other individuals choose to do. We show the relevant probabilities for the typical soldier in table 4. They correspond as far as possible to the earlier example—specifically, the structure of probabilities in the third and fourth rows exactly mirrors that in table 1. As before, we suppose that cost of injury to be 100 to each.

Finally, we include, as an additional potentially relevant consideration, the psychic cost of running away: "cowardice" may be personally demeaning. We therefore indicate a cost of, say, two units sustained by anyone who adopts that strategy. On this basis, we can collect the information in tables 3 and 4 and the various values of injury and victory to the individual soldier and depict it all in the form of a payoff matrix, shown as table 5. The structure of the matrix is identical to that of table 4, but here we show the *returns* to the soldier from running and from fighting, for all the relevant possible actions by others.

---

2. The territory can be assumed to be currently owned by other parties who cannot or will not defend themselves.

TABLE 4. *Probability of Serious Injury*

ENEMY'S ACTIONS	OWN ACTIONS FIGHT	OWN ACTIONS RUN	COMRADE'S ACTIONS
Both run	$\frac{1}{100}$	0	fights
	$\frac{1}{50}$	0	runs
One runs,	$\frac{1}{10}$	0	fights
One fights	$\frac{1}{2}$	$\frac{1}{3}$	runs
Both fight	$\frac{1}{2}$	$\frac{1}{20}$	fights
	$\frac{4}{5}$	$\frac{2}{3}$	runs

TABLE 5

ENEMY'S ACTIONS	OWN ACTIONS FIGHT	OWN ACTIONS RUN	COMRADE'S ACTIONS
Both run	9	8	fights
	8	-2	runs
One runs,	-2	3	fights
One fights	-45	-36	runs
Both fight	-45	-5	fights
	-78	-68	runs

Several aspects of this interaction are worth emphasizing. First and most important for our purposes is that the "rational" strategy for the individual is *always* to run unless both enemies run away first. If the enemies both run away, then it is rational for the individual to "stay and fight" *whatever* his comrade does. If there is to be battle, however, then it is rational for the individual to run, and to do so whatever his comrade does. It follows that the soldier's behavior is independent of the behavior of his *comrade*: it depends solely on the behavior of the *enemy*. For this reason, each individual soldier has to predict what the enemy will do before he can choose the action that is best for himself. In this sense, the individual soldier is engaged in a complex multi-person game of "chicken" which has the structure indicated in table 6. Clearly, the best outcome for each soldier is that where the enemy runs. However, since this is also true for opposing soldiers, the essential feature of this game becomes one of *bluff*, because if the opposing army chooses to fight, it is individually rational to run away. If the soldier believes the opposing army will indeed engage in actual combat, then the prisoners' dilemma

TABLE 6

		OPPOSING ARMY	
		FIGHT	RUN
Individual soldier	Fight	(−40, −40)	(9, 9)
	Run	(−30, −30)	(−2, −2)

interaction depicted in table 2 will apply, and it is rational for him to break ranks and flee. If, on the other hand, he believes that the opposing army will break ranks before his own does, it is rational for him to stand.

Suppose, however, that we collapse the interaction in table 5 into an aggregate interaction between opposing *armies*. To do so, we note that:

(i) since if the opposing army flees, it is rational for each soldier to stay, the return to each is 9 units in the top left-hand corner of the payoff matrix,

(ii) since if the opposing army fights, it is rational for every individual to flee, the return to each is −68 units in the bottom right-hand corner of the payoff matrix.

The return to each *army* becomes the simple sum of the returns to the individual soldiers who compose that army; accordingly we can represent the interaction between opposing armies as in table 7.

This aggregative interaction clearly has an "equilibrium" outcome: that in which both armies *fight*.[3] This interaction, too, is of the prisoners' dilemma form—the outcome generates a payoff (or −90 units) to each army, which is less than the payoff (of −4) to each that might have emerged if both had agreed not to fight. This fact simply reflects our belief that battle is not in toto a positive-sum activity. The object of conflict is simply the distribution of a given prize between warring parties; the prize is not *created* by the conflict itself. And since conflict uses up resources, the result is necessarily negative sum.[4]

---

3. The case in which all soldiers on both sides run away is set aside. Presumably if this happened, the battle game would be replayed until some outcome emerged.

4. There is a clear analogy here between battle and the general problem of "rent-seeking." See James M. Buchanan, Robert D. Tollison, and Gordon Tullock, eds., *Toward a Theory of the Rent-Seeking Society* (College Station: Texas A&M University Press, 1980), and Gordon Tullock, *Trials on Trial* (New York: Columbia University Press, 1980).

TABLE 7

		ARMY II	
		FIGHT	RUN
Army I	Fight	(−90, −90)	(18, −136)
	Run	(−136, 18)	(−4, −4)

Our interest here is not, however, in whether warfare is a globally rational activity. It is rather in the proper understanding of warfare for purposes of developing a theory of military tactics. What we have tried to expose by our simple example here is the following set of propositions:

(1) that, considering the payoffs to the *collection* of individuals who make up an army, it will, in general, be *collectively* rational to stand and fight (rather than run),

(2) that, notwithstanding this fact, it will typically be in the interests of individual soldiers *not* to stand and fight, unless the enemy runs,

(3) that, therefore, there is a divergence between the individual and collective interests of those who make up an army, which is a crucial ingredient in successful conduct of war to overcome.

On this reckoning, the central element in the conduct of battle is *not* an actual engagement of opposing forces, but rather a confrontation of two opposing *networks* of agents, in which it is that *network* rather than the agents themselves which is the object of destruction. In other words, victory is not so much a matter of killing one's opponents as it is of breaking apart the intrinsically delicate basis for co-operation among the separate elements that compose the opposing force.

3

This account may well appear totally obvious as a theoretical construct and yet have virtually nothing to do with the actual conduct of battle. In order to establish at least a presumptive connection between our simple theory and what actually occurs in the field, it may be useful to offer a few appropriate quotations from Ardant du Picq's *Battle Studies*.

Consider, for example, in the light of our claim of the relevance of the general prisoners' dilemma interaction, du Picq's description of "the advance":[5]

> We rush forward, but . . . generally we rush with prudence, with a tendency to let the most urgent ones, the most intrepid ones, pass on. It is strange but true that the nearer we approach the enemy, the less we are closed up. (p. 145)

Shirking on a minor scale perhaps? We get a feel for du Picq's assessment of the magnitude of the problem in his account of Napoléon's attack on Wagram:

> Out of the twenty-two thousand men (that made up Napoleon's mass) three thousand to fifteen hundred reached the position. Clearly the position was not carried by them, but by the material and moral effect of a battery of one-hundred pieces, cavalry, etc. etc. Were the other nineteen thousand men disabled? No! Seven out of twenty-two, a third—an enormous proportion—may have been hit. What became of the twelve thousand unaccounted for? They had lain down on the road, had played dummy in order not to go on to the end. In the confused mass of a column of deployed battalions, surveillance—difficult enough in a column at normal distances—is impossible. Nothing is easier than dropping out through inertia; nothing more common. (p. 150)

Du Picq also clearly recognized the implications of all this for incentives to cut and run:

> He who calm and strong of heart awaits his enemy has all the advantages of fire. But the moral impulse of the assailant demoralizes the assailed. He is frightened; he sets his sight no longer; he does not even aim his piece. His lines are broken without defense, unless indeed his cavalry waiting halted, horsemen a meter apart and in two ranks, does not break first and destroy all formation. (p. 127)

On this basis, he further saw that the chief element in victory was to convince the opponent of one's determination to fight. Once so convinced, the opposition would flee. As du Picq saw it, this gave a considerable intrinsic

5. Charles Jean Jacques Joseph Ardant du Picq, *Battle Studies: Ancient and Modern Battle* (Harrisburg, Pa.: Military Service Publishing Co., 1946).

advantage to offense—but whether or not he was correct in this, he clearly interpreted battle as a "moral" rather than "physical" engagement.

> Indeed, the physical impulse is nothing. The moral impulse is everything. The moral impulse lies in the perception by the enemy of the resolution that animates you. They say that the battle of Amstetten was the *only one* in which a line actually waited for the shock of another line charging with the bayonets. Even then the Russians gave way before the moral and not before the physical impulse . . . They waited long enough to receive bayonet thrusts, even blows with the rifle (in the back . . .). This done, they fled. (p. 126)

Or again, on the psychological dimensions of aggression:

> but the enemy does not stand; the moral pressure of the danger that precedes you is too strong for him. Otherwise, those who stood and aimed even with empty rifles, would never see a charge come up to them. The first line of the assailant would be sensible of death and no one would wish to be in the first rank. Therefore, the enemy never merely stands; because if he does, it is you that flee. This always does away with the shock. The enemy entertains no smaller anxiety than yours. When he sees you near, the question for him also is whether to flee or to advance. Two moral impulses are in conflict. (p. 146)

4

In this view of things, a crucial ingredient in the whole military enterprise is to circumvent the natural predilection towards breaking formation and fleeing or towards not engaging the enemy in the first place—a predilection which is endemic to the basic nature of collective conflict. There are, in fact, three distinct ways in which this might be done:

(i) we might seek to change the individual's valuation of alternative actions *directly* by psychological means,

(ii) we might adopt a system of "side payments" (rewards and/or punishments) which alter the relative costs and benefits so as to redirect self-interest to the desired ends,

(iii) we might adopt an "institutional arrangement"—in this case some means of deploying men, organizing forces, or some such—which changes the costs and benefits of alternative courses of action, without any direct "side payments" within the group.

The distinction between (ii) and (iii) can possibly be clarified by examples as the discussion proceeds. What should at this point be emphasized is that the three options are not in any sense mutually exclusive. In general, we should expect all three to be used—that optimization would occur at all (three) margins, to use the economist's jargon.

Let us briefly examine the options in turn.

4.1. PSYCHOLOGICAL "MORALE BUILDING"

The means of morale-building through changing individuals' preferences directly has been widely discussed in military contexts and requires no additional commentary from us. Building affection among comrades, developing hatred for the enemy, establishing and augmenting a sense of military honor are all part of what is at stake here. Likewise, presumably, uniforms and military music and parades—indeed, all the panoply of chocolate-box soldiery—can be accounted for along such lines.[6] The point to be made here is the simple one that changing individuals' preferences—overcoming the natural predilection towards self-concern—is not a costless operation by any means. One would therefore not expect it to be the only, or necessarily the most important, instrument used to solve the prisoners' dilemma problem in its military variant.

4.2. POSITIVE INCENTIVES

Economists typically focus on "side payments" or "bribes" as the primary means of changing individuals' behavior. The market is, after all, the prime institution through which this is done in social life. In the military context, positive incentives (such as profits and incomes in markets) are an important element in structuring individual behavior, though such effects are not widely discussed in the military literature (at least to our knowledge).

Some examples are obvious. Military decoration for acts of "bravery" is one such.[7] A system of promotion, based on acts of bravery, is another,

---

6. Interestingly enough, these psychological techniques of minimizing "shirking" seem relatively less significant in most market contexts—although international experience differs somewhat in this respect. In Japan, for example, there seems to be more attention to "morale" in this sense than in the U.S. or Europe.

7. Military decoration clearly has an intrinsic prestige value. It probably also has some financial value in addition (improvement of future employment prospects, for example).

particularly when promotion involves being shifted out of the "firing line." At one level, it might seem that moving a courageous and effective soldier out of the direct line of battle and into some "safe" behind-lines job for which he may be relatively ill-equipped is a mammoth violation of the principle of comparative advantage. It does, however, have the virtue of establishing incentives for courageous behavior among persons whose natural instincts are not towards bravery at all and can in principle be entirely justified on such grounds.

In some ways the most conspicuous example of positive incentives in military history has been the "spoils" system. To take a specific case, consider the British navy in the days of sail. Any enemy merchant ship captured by a British ship was auctioned with its cargo, and resultant proceeds divided: one quarter to the admiral of the relevant British fleet, one quarter to the captain, one quarter shared among the officers, and one quarter among the enlisted men of the successful British vessel. If an enemy naval vessel was captured, the British Admiralty would pay its assessed value to be divided in the same proportions. Interestingly enough, the Admiralty would also do this for enemy naval vessels *sunk*. This structure of incentives obviously provided the admiral with some cash incentive to dispose his ships in such a way that they were more likely to make captures, and the captain and men of each ship to be anxious to engage. Free-rider problems were not necessarily entirely overcome, but were substantially moderated by this means.

4.3. NEGATIVE INCENTIVES

Negative incentive structures have always been extensively used in military settings. Traditionally, anyone who was detected displaying cowardice in battle—anything from running away to shirking—became the victim of the stringent system of military discipline, enforced by execution and/or torture (flogging was the standard form). Indeed, in some cases, offenders would be dispatched instantly by an officer's pistol.

Again the example of the British navy is instructive. All non-commissioned officers carried truncheons which they were free to use in dealing with men who were too slow, clumsy, or reluctant in battle. The hatches of a naval vessel during engagement were guarded by marines whose orders were to prevent anyone going below deck who had no business there. Marine guards enforced these positions rigorously: superior officers were perfectly capable of enforcing orders and would have, no doubt, executed an entire ship's crew if necessary (or clapped them in irons for future attention). In fact, this marine assignment was, as warship assignments go, somewhat less dangerous than most: on a wooden ship being fired at by cannon at close range, no location was safe, but the hatch guard was less dangerous than most.

For the record, the navy was by no means alone in extensive use of negative incentives. The British army of the day also had a strict disciplinary system, and punishment was hardly less severe than in the navy.[8] And such systems long predate the period of British ascendancy. Frederick the Great, for example, is reported to have remarked that a soldier should be more frightened of his officers than of the enemy!

Since, from the point of view of the military establishment, negative incentives are cheaper than positive ones, one would perhaps expect them to be used more extensively. There are, however, obvious natural limits: enforcement of negative incentives requires some agent whose actions are enforced by some other agent higher up the hierarchy. Not all of these agents can be motivated by negative incentives. A system that applies negative incentives at the lower end and moves gradually to positive incentives at the top seems like a natural equilibrium arrangement. Likewise, in the use of positive incentives, one would expect the structure of rewards to be strongly regressive: higher officers must be given a strong incentive to enforce negative incentives imposed more extensively at lower levels of the institutional hierarchy. In this connection, recall the characteristically regressive structure of the British navy's distribution of spoils.

Now one might suppose that limits are also placed on the use of negative incentives by the requirement to obtain recruits for the rank and file. Beyond some point, this is clearly a valid conjecture. But it must be emphasized that the incentive structure itself—even if implemented by severe punishment—is in the positive interests of potential recruits. Within the prisoners' dilemma interaction that connects individual members of the army, each individual has a preference for an institutional structure in which *no one* runs away: strong enforcement procedures ensure the *collectively preferred* outcome where everyone stays to fight, as opposed to the individually rational equilibrium where both run. Consider again the interaction depicted in table 2. The effective choice is between the $[-10, -10]$ outcome under effective enforcement, and the $[-33, -33]$ outcome in its absence. Clearly, the former is to be preferred. In that sense, recruitment is *easier*, not more difficult, in a context where the expected costs associated with "free riding" on one's comrades-in-arms are

---

8. The British army was entirely a volunteer force: the lower ranks of the navy at this time were filled by conscription.

larger rather than smaller. It was not for nothing that England maintained an entirely volunteer army throughout a period in which discipline was strict and punishment for violation extremely severe: this is *precisely* what the theory predicts.

4.4. STRATEGIC SOLUTIONS

There is a further form of solution to the free-rider problem in the military context—one that depends not on internally arranged side payments, but on purely strategic considerations. The characteristic feature of these solutions is that forces are so organized that the *enemy* effectively enforces the appropriate incentive structure. Essentially, the group is able to precommit itself in such a way that it is no longer individually rational for any soldier to cut and run.

A simple example may illustrate. The British square was, on the face of it, a slightly absurd military formation. It exposed the British force to attack from all sides at once, was relatively immobile, and relinquished all possible protection that the terrain might have afforded. Yet from Fontenoy to Abu Clea in the Sudan, no British square was ever broken. Why? Given the focus on "incentive" questions, the answer seems simple. No soldier could effectively break ranks without running towards the enemy. This fact entirely altered the strategic interaction between individual British soldiers: it was now in each soldier's self-interest to stay and fight, and hence, the collectively desired outcome required virtually no enforcement. The situation facing each individual soldier in the square formation can be depicted in table 8. The equilibrium outcome in this interaction is to stay and fight: this is the best course of action for A *whatever* B does and vice versa.[9] Presumably, highly mobile heavy artillery rendered the square entirely obsolete as a strategic device—but its success for over a century illustrates the central analytic point nicely.

A somewhat similar example seems to be provided by late-nineteenth- and twentieth-century trench warfare. One of the strategic advantages of "digging in" was that the individual soldier in many cases took greater risks by "running" than by staying to fight, since in order to run away he had to leap out of his trench and expose himself to enemy fire. No such analogous incentive structure was relevant for *attacking* forces, who necessarily had to

---

9. Du Picq's diagnosis of this is beautifully to the point: "Moral reasons and no others make the soldier in a square feel himself stronger than when in a line. He feels himself watched from behind and has nowhere to go" (*Battle Studies*, p. 169).

TABLE 8

		B'S ACTION	
		STAY AND FIGHT	RUN
A's action	Stay and fight	[−10, −10]	[−20, −30]
	Run	[−30, −20]	[−30, −30]

expose themselves in "going over the top"—a fact which in itself substantially altered the relative advantages of attack and defense.

The basic point here is that there may exist means of deploying forces, using terrain, and so on—all standard parts of military strategy as conventionally conceived—that serve not so much to increase *physical* strength vis-à-vis one's enemy as they do to circumvent the "free-rider" incentives within one's own forces.

4.5. MONITORING AND STRATEGY

Even where this is not so, and one must rely on the various forms of incentives earlier discussed, strategic considerations remain relevant to the "morale" problems we are dealing with here. This is so because *any* form of incentives requires a strict monitoring system: individual soldiers who are encouraged to undertake acts of bravery because of the prospects of reward must believe that those acts will be observed; those who are discouraged from shirking (in its various forms) because of the prospects of punishment must believe that such shirking is likely to be detected.

It seems clear that the ease with which behavior can be monitored is partly dependent on such considerations as the deployment of forces, the use of terrain, the width of the front, the formation of units, and so on. Napoléon, it is said, always kept his crack troops in reserve—doubtless to maintain flexibility in his battle strategy. But the monitoring advantages are also not negligible. Crack troops are much less likely to drift quietly away from the scene of battle when unobserved. And front lines will be much more reluctant to break ranks if they suspect that they will be observed in doing so and possibly run directly into the line of fire of their own rear lines.

Of course, the precise monitoring arrangements that are optimal cannot be specified in abstraction from the nature of the weaponry, the magnitude of the forces involved, the range of "visibility," and so on. What seems clear, however, is that while wars continue to be fought by man (and not machines) "morale" will remain a major element of military theory, and the implications of alternative military tactics for the feasibility of monitoring will remain central to the whole strategic question.

5

It may be useful at this point to spell out some implications of the foregoing discussion for some particular issues in military theory. We do so briefly and suggestively in what follows for a couple of matters on which our approach sheds, we believe, interesting light.

5.1. THE ROLE OF RELATIVE NUMBERS

One interesting question in military theory is why numerical superiority has not generally proven a better predictor of success than it appears to have been. Examples abound in war history of cases in which forces have overcome opposing armies that had *overwhelming* numerical superiority. To mention some specific famous cases: at the battle of Arbela in 331 B.C., Alexander overcame a Persian army *five* times larger than his own; Hannibal, at the famous battle of Cannae, totally destroyed a Roman army of 85,000 men with a force scarcely more than half that; in the American Civil War, Lee consistently defeated Union forces in spite of their significant numerical superiority.

Or, to put what is the same question a slightly different way, why is it that it is usually necessary to inflict only modest losses on one's enemy to secure victory? Losses of say 30 percent killed or wounded are exceptionally large—normally too large for an army to sustain, *even when despite its losses it remains numerically superior to its foe.*

This is perhaps difficult to explain if war is conceived as a battle to the death by opposing generals: but once the prisoners' dilemma interaction among members of each army is recognized and elevated to its proper place in the understanding of actual warfare, there is little to explain. In fact, there is considerable literature on the effects of increased numbers of "players" on likely outcomes under the prisoners' dilemma interaction. As the number of players increases, the incentives for each player to free ride increase—the "collectively rational" outcome becomes less and less likely. The role that any single individual plays in whether his army wins or loses becomes increasingly insignificant. To be sure, there are important threshold effects here: being one of an army of one hundred thousand is not, perhaps, so different from being one in an army of three hundred thousand, in terms of perceived contribution. On the other hand, being one of ten colonels in command of ten thousand men may be rather different in incentive implications from being one of thirty. In any case, we do not claim that numerical superiority is a military *disadvantage*—only that the advantages of numbers are rather less striking than a holistic approach would indicate.

5.2. ON GUERILLA WARFARE

The cases in which guerilla tractics have proven successful as the major means of conducting a war are surprisingly few. It could no doubt be argued that the Boers did much better (given their resources) by pursuing guerilla tactics than they would have done in open battle against the British, though the record is not entirely clear. And in the other often-cited case of the Vietnam War, it is by no means obvious that, absent political crisis at home, the U.S. forces could not have ultimately secured victory in the field relatively easily.

The rarity of successful guerilla tactics is "surprising" because one would have thought that with the advantages of consistent surprise and rapid mobility that guerilla operations make possible, a force might over the long haul be able to inflict much greater losses on its opponent than in direct conflict between entire armies.

But guerilla operations clearly greatly increase monitoring costs. Scope for shirking on the part of entire units, lying low unobserved by individual soldiers, and leaving everything to the "intrepid few" is much greater than in conventional warfare. Accordingly, the theory here would predict that guerilla operations would inflict much less damage on the enemy than its apparent tactical advantages would suggest.[10]

The case of guerilla tactics that seems to have come closest to success is that of German submarine operations in the two world wars. We have not seen any relevant figures on this, but we conjecture that the extent of shirking was considerable—that many U-boats more or less quietly sat out the war on the ocean floor, participating minimally in naval conflict.

---

10. We should note in this connection that in modern times the night attack has rarely been used, although it apparently represents an easy method of avoiding the aimed fire from rifles and machine guns. It is likely that the reason it has rarely been used is the impossibility of enforcing the advance by a dispersed body of men at night. In the nineteenth century when night attacks were more common, the formations were very dense and depended on very straight lines, frequently made straight by carrying a rope stretched between the two ends.

5.3. THE ROLE OF INDIVIDUAL HEROISM

Can a single act of heroism by a single individual or small group exercise any sort of influence on the course of a battle in which the number of participants is enormous? Certainly, the romantic mythology of military history would have us believe so. But are such possibilities purely mythical? It is surely tempting to think so; we would predict that conventional "morale-building" would involve assuring individual soldiers that they exercise a major influence on the course of battle even when in fact they only do so *collectively*. But there seem to be many examples where small numbers of individuals (sometimes a single person) have had a major effect on battle outcomes. The attack by American torpedo planes, for example, at Midway was spectacularly dangerous and led to a much higher casualty rate than, say, the famous charge of the Light Brigade. But because it distracted Japanese fighter planes from the approaching dive-bombers, it made the U.S. victory at Midway decisive and, thereby, ultimate victory in the Pacific war possible. A somewhat similar circumstance arose at the battle of Chancellorsville when Stonewall Jackson was rolling up the flank of the Union army. The commander of the troop of cavalry who was guarding the Union headquarters suddenly observed Jackson's army corps coming down the road towards him. He instantly charged directly into the front of Jackson's corps. This was a totally suicidal act. But it threw Jackson into sufficient confusion that he stopped the advance to straighten things out. By the time he was reorganized, sufficient Union forces were available to stop him. Without this suicidal charge the Confederate forces might have wiped out the Union army at Chancellorsville.

In the account of military engagement that we have given, the possibility that a single "suicidal" act may turn the course of battle is not too remote. In the initial example depicted in table 2 above, A and B will individually have an incentive to flee if they are convinced that C will in fact attack. As the number of individuals subject to attack increases, the strength of the incentive to run increases—again, given the conviction that C will attack. If an apparently suicidal feat is undertaken by C (or by C and a relatively small number of his comrades), and if A, B, and comrades see this as evidence that C's force *will* attack *whatever* the cost, the tide of battle can be decisively turned in C's favor—the *moral* strength (in du Picq's terms) passes to C. In this sense, "impossible" feats of daring, victory against "insuperable" odds, become entirely possible.

Our account acknowledges room for the hero. It is difficult to see how a more holistic account can coherently do so.

6

In this paper, we have attempted to provide a perspective on military engagement that focuses attention on the relation between individuals who *compose* an army, rather than on the relation between opposing armies. That former relation can be characterized as a "prisoners' dilemma." That is, each individual soldier has an incentive to act in a way that is disastrous for the army as a whole. Accordingly, a central problem in military tactics is to establish a set of private incentives that will induce each individual soldier to act in the collective interest. Such an incentive structure requires enforcement, and such enforcement requires monitoring. For this reason, differential monitoring costs become a crucial ingredient in such tactical decisions as how to deploy forces, what military technology to use, what use to make of terrain—indeed, how to conduct the entire war. We do not claim, of course, that monitoring costs are the *only* issues in tactical choices. We do claim that they are much more important than most military literature allows. We also claim that recognition of the intrinsic prisoners' dilemma problem in the military context is central to a proper military theory.

The economist may, of course, reply that all this is obvious—that anyone familiar with the modern theory of the firm is entirely aware of the importance of monitoring "worker performance" and that the incentive to shirk is no different in the military setting than it is in other sorts of labor markets. It seems to us, however, that this claim ignores the peculiar role that free-riding plays in the context of military theory. When firm competes against firm, the central object in that competition is to outsell one's competitor: it is *not*, specifically, to "prise apart" the individuals who compose the competing firms. But that "prising apart" is precisely the central object in military confrontation. An army is not a single mass but is, rather, a collection of individuals connected to one another and their common purpose by an inherently fragile web. The aim of battle is not to annihilate the opposing mass, but to sever that web within it. This particular understanding is not, we think, a conventional one in military literature, where holistic methods of analysis are common. Nor, perhaps, is it entirely obvious. Yet it is an understanding that springs naturally from an individualistic approach to military science. And in our view, that individualistic approach is, here as elsewhere, the uniquely appropriate one for the study of human conduct.

JACKSON AND THE PRISONER'S DILEMMA

Jackson's discussion of Marshall raised a strong feeling of déjà vu in me.[1] I was in Korea (in the Embassy, not in the army) when a group of sociologists appeared to advise the army. Knowing Marshall's work, they suggested that the army could sharply reduce training musketry, because the troops rarely fired their guns at the enemy. The army, I'm happy to say, looked over their training schedule and discovered that the standard infantry training did not indoctrinate the troops on the point. The army had assumed it was unnecessary. They simply added such indoctrination to basic training. I have no idea of the outcome. From the general inefficiency of the Pentagon, I would not have high expectations, but it certainly was better than the sociologist's recommendation.

Actually, the problem of rifle fire in battle is a very good example of the prisoner's dilemma, but before discussing that, I would like to make a brief digression. Jackson accuses Brennan and me of assuming, in "An Economic Theory of Military Tactics," "ethical egoism."[2] As far as I know, neither Brennan nor I have ever expressed the view that egoism is particularly ethical. We think most people, most of the time, are relatively egoistic. But this is an observation, not an expression of an ethical desideratum.

If we look at human behavior, we observe occasional people, St. Francis for example, who seem to have very little egoistic drive, but they are exceptional. Almost all of us will, at least occasionally, make sacrifices for other people, sometimes quite extreme sacrifices. Still, the generalization that we are 95% selfish and only 5% altruistic is reasonably accurate.[3]

Reprinted from *Journal of Economic Behavior and Organization* 8 (December 1987): 637–40, copyright 1987, with permission from Elsevier.

1. M. W. Jackson, "Chocolate-Box Soldiers: A Critique of 'An Economic Theory of Military Tactics,'" *Journal of Economic Behavior and Organization* 8 (1987): 1–11; Samuel L. A. Marshall, *Men against Fire* (Gloucester: Smith, 1947).

2. Geoffrey Brennan and Gordon Tullock, "An Economic Theory of Military Tactics: Methodological Individualism at War," *Journal of Economic Behavior and Organization* 3 (1982): 225–42.

3. The infantryman cited by Jackson, who, finding that a hand grenade attached to his flack jacket was going to go off and being unable to detach it, ran away from his fellow soldiers, was engaging in only quite modest altruism. He was going to die anyway, and the decision to die without killing other people, although no doubt admirable, was not an example of serious self-sacrifice.

To return to the infantry not firing their rifles: Firstly, there is a problem of arithmetic. Marshall found that no more than 15% of the troops, when asked after combat whether they had fired their rifles, said they had. He also investigated the rifles of casualties and must have found a very much higher rate of firing with their rifles, because he "came to the conclusion that the ratio of fire was no more than 25%."[4] If all of the casualties had fired their weapons, the casualty rate would have to be 13.33% in order to get 25% of total weapons fired. No doubt there were days in which casualty rates of this sort were run, but they would have been exceptional. It seems dubious that every single one of the casualties would have fired his weapon, although for reasons given below, casualties were far more likely to have fired their weapons than people who were not casualties.

Leaving the arithmetic aside, firing raises the basic prisoner's dilemma problem rather neatly. Jackson emphasizes the feeling of fear and danger which is prominent on the battlefield. If you are on the battlefield, your basic impulse is to hide. Firing your weapon attracts attention and, hence, is not helpful in hiding. On the other hand, a soldier who does fire his weapon generates a public good for his unit by somewhat suppressing enemy fire. Unless he has the good fortune to shoot somebody who is in the act of shooting him, his private benefit will be no greater than that of any other member of his unit.

Thus, the theory that we were presenting in our article offers an explanation for the rather low level of fire. A person is far more likely to become a casualty if he fires his weapon than if he doesn't. Since firing attracts enemy attention, the higher casualty rate of people who had fired is understandable.

Indeed, the problem here is why anybody fires his weapon at all. There are perfectly good reasons why groups of soldiers would tend to feel less inhibited about firing than individuals. Such a group is a more conspicuous object and, hence, is likely to draw enemy fire even if it doesn't return the fire. Further, of course, a group of that sort is reasonably likely to have a noncom or an officer present. Individual soldiers sometimes find themselves in exposed positions where they will attract fire whether they shoot or not. Of course, there is the fact that they are only 95% egoistic to explain the rest of the firing. Altogether these figures fit the prisoner's dilemma model rather well.

Marshall, of course, knew nothing about these matters; indeed, the first article on the prisoner's dilemma was not published until after he had

4. Marshall, *Men against Fire*, 40.

completed his research. If the research is ever repeated, the prisoner's dilemma model would suggest a profitable line of inquiry.

In addition to these fairly cold-blooded calculations, military officers, like leaders of any sort, including teachers and business managers, are well advised to devote some energy to trying to build up morale and group cohesion within their force. It is possible to some extent to change people's preferences, and these changes may have positive benefits for any organization. Military units have always given more attention to this matter than other organizations. Whether this reflects some special characteristic of group cohesion in the military or simply the fact that the military in all states of society spend a good deal of time training and drilling before they get into battle is an open question. Further, for most members of any military machine, the tasks actually performed in battle are fairly simple and could be learned in a fairly short period of time. Under the circumstances, there is a lot of available time for indoctrination and efforts to change the preference function.

It is, however, dangerous to rely solely on morale. Traditionally, the Roman army is thought to be the best that history has ever seen. After the defeat which led to the burning of Rome by the Gauls, the new commander "Camillus's first act was to punish in accordance with martial law the men who had deserted during the panic at Veii—an act which taught troops to know something worse than the enemy to fear. . . ."[5] To give the reader some idea of what "military law" meant, we can turn to another part of Livy. After an earlier defeat, Appius "gave orders that every soldier who had lost his equipment, every standard-bearer who had lost his standard, every centurion, too, and distinguished-service man who abandoned his post, should be first flogged and then beheaded. The remainder were decimated."[6] The army of the Roman Republic was not a terribly pleasant one to serve in. They usually won, however.

Another matter should be mentioned here, since it is an important difference between economists and sociologists. Economists have had a very large experience with people who say they are doing something which is in fact different from what they are doing. Businessmen will, for example, normally deny they are maximizing profits, although if you put the question in such a sufficiently devious way, you can get them to make statements which clearly do imply that they are doing so. They also frequently will tell you that they

5. Livy, *The Early History of Rome* (Middlesex: Penguin Classics, 1971), 362.
6. Ibid., 175.

use markup pricing and are genuinely surprised when you prove from their accounts that they don't.

The reasons for this are several. Firstly, people have strong motives for thinking carefully over what they are doing. They rarely have strong motives to think carefully about the explanation which they give to other people about what they are doing. Further, most people are not trained in verbalizing their own emotions and motives. Further, the real reason they are doing something may appear to them to be somewhat immoral. This latter appears to be the reason that businessmen reject the hypothesis that they are maximizing profits.

For all of these reasons, it seems dubious that the testimony of the soldiers as to why they did not fire should be given much weight. I have great difficulty believing that any soldier would explain that he did not fire because he thought that although firing would tend to suppress enemy fire and, hence, reduce total casualties of the unit, it would tend to raise his own prospect of being killed. In any event, I must confess, I am a little surprised at the explanation offered that he didn't want to kill someone else. Indeed, I rather suspect that this was the contribution of the investigating sociologist. There are a number of ways in which the opinion of an interviewer may indirectly influence the interviewee, and this kind of opinion seems to me far more likely for an intellectually trained sociologist than for infantry riflemen. Regardless of that, Jackson has provided a very neat example of the prisoner's dilemma functioning in the real world. That he mistakenly thinks that he has disproved it is striking.

ADAM SMITH AND THE
PRISONERS' DILEMMA

In ordinary life, we engage in many transactions with other people in which there is potential profit for both parties from some kind of cheating. Normally, we do not see much of this cheating. I have no doubt that the merchant will put in the package the merchandise which I buy, or which I ordered, even though if he put in something else cheaper it is quite dubious that I would be able to win a lawsuit. On my part, if I decide I do not like the product and return it with the remark that it is defective, having first damaged it so that it is indeed defective, I could get a gain. Neither I nor the merchant worries particularly about this kind of behavior, although the merchant worries more than I do for reasons that will become plain below. If we worried about it, we would both take precautions, with the result that socially we would be worse off by the cost of these precautions. We have here what appears to be a prisoners' dilemma matrix, but the two parties are behaving cooperatively.

What Adam Smith called "the discipline of continuous dealings" takes care of the matter. The point of this article is to work out Adam Smith's insight in the terminology of a modern game theory. We shall see that Smith was right, and there are some cases, indeed, in practice, very important cases, where what appears to be a prisoners' dilemma in fact leads to cooperative behavior.

Consider the prisoners' dilemma game shown in Figure 1. It is orthodox that if A and B are playing a single turn of this particular game, they will end up in the lower right-hand corner with a net loss of one dollar each. If we go from a single game to a long series of games played by the same players, however, there is no agreed-upon solution.[1] Experimental evidence seems to indicate that the players play a mixed strategy, with some cooperative plays and some noncooperative plays, and the mixture can be modified by changing the payoffs.[2] All of these situations are simplifications of the real world, and it is

Reprinted, with permission of MIT Press Journals, publisher, from *Quarterly Journal of Economics* 100 (1985): 1073–81. Copyright 1985 by the President and Fellows of Harvard College.

1. The author of this article is one of the people who have attempted to solve the problem. See H. Edwin Overcast and Gordon Tullock, "A Different Approach to the Repeated Prisoner's Dilemma," *Theory and Decision* 1 (1971): 350–58.

2. The *Journal of Conflict Resolution* has run an immense number of articles with varying payoffs.

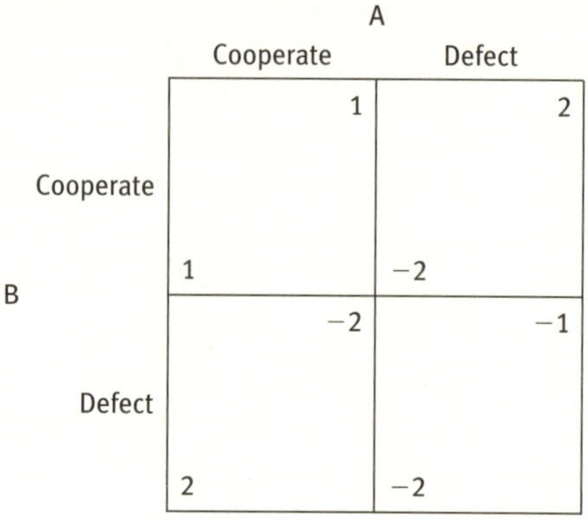

A

	Cooperate	Defect

FIGURE 1

a point of this article to suggest that if we make the game more like many real-world games, then there will be a very high tendency for play to concentrate in the upper left-hand corner.

If we compare a prisoners' dilemma game and an ordinary competitive market, there is an immediate, obvious difference. The partners in the prisoners' dilemma game are pre-selected and cannot change. The partners in the competitive market select their opposite numbers.[3]

To illustrate, let us follow the physicists and perform a thought experiment. Suppose that we have a large room, and along one wall, a series of isolation booths. There are about 30 experimental subjects in the room. They are free to communicate with each other in any way they want, and if they wish to make side payments, they are also free to do that, but it does not seem likely that they will. It is, however, possible for any two of them who wish, to play the game shown in Figure 1. They simply go into two adjacent isolation booths and make their strategy choices on a game matrix on a computer terminal. They are immediately paid the amount that they win, or are charged the amount that they lose. They are free, of course, to communicate the

---

3. Robert Rosenthal and Henry J. Landau have looked into the situation in which prisoners' dilemma games are played by pairs of people who are changed randomly but who know the reputations of the previous players. This mathematically fascinating situation turns out to have a reasonably well specified equilibrium See R. W. Rosenthal, "Sequences of Games and Varying Opponents," *Econometrica* 47 (1979): 1353–66, and R. W. Rosenthal and Henry J. Landau, "A Game-Theoretic Analysis of Bargaining with Reputations," *Journal of Mathematical Psychology* 20 (1979): 233–55.

outcome of the game to anyone else they wish, and they are free to play more games if they wish or to change partners. All that is required is that the people who play the games do so in voluntarily chosen pairs.

I take it that all of my readers will agree that under these circumstances all plays would be in the upper left-hand corner except possibly by mistake or possibly in the "endgame" if the time at which the experiment was to be ended was announced in advance. In the real world, of course, the game—or, to be more precise, the series of games—never ends, although individual players are removed by death or other circumstances. If some individual player did for some reason, possibly mental pathology, make a mistake and play a noncooperative strategy, he would find it very difficult to get people to play with him in the future. Almost certainly, he would have to offer some side payments until he had established something in the way of a reputation.

We can complicate the game yet further by, for example, assuming that the experimenters charge a small fee for playing the game. This fee could be high enough so that the two parties make only a modest profit if they play the cooperative strategy, but the person who double-crosses his cooperative partner will do quite well—for example, a 50-cent fee or even a 75-cent fee.

This is one type of ownership price; another type would be to assume that some of the people in our room are landlords and some peasants. The landlords each own the right to one pair of isolation booths, and the games played there. The peasants own only themselves. Assuming that the peasants are numerous, we would presumably reach an equilibrium solution in which the peasants received only the value of their services. If the peasants were less numerous than the landlords, there would be nothing to prevent landlords from playing with each other, so the peasants' bargaining situation would not be perfect, but nevertheless, they should be able to do well.

Games are not necessarily two-party. Figure 2 represents the payoff to one player in a five-sided prisoners' dilemma game. He has the choices represented by the columns of either cooperating or defecting, and the rows show the payoff to him, granted that the other four players cooperated or defected in the numbers shown. It will be seen that the defect column always dominates the cooperating column, but if we repeat our experiment—i.e., permit people voluntarily to make up little groups of five in which each individual is free to enter or leave as he wishes and permit public communication so that the reputation of the individual is well-known—all of them would play the cooperative strategy, and the payoff to each would be nine in each game played. Anyone who chose to defect in any given game would, in essence, put

	Cooperate	Defect
4 Cooperate	9	10
3 Cooperate 1 Defect	7	8
2 Cooperate 2 Defect	5	6
1 Cooperate 3 Defect	3	4
0 Cooperate 4 Defect	1	2

FIGURE 2

himself in a situation where it would be extremely difficult for him to get partners for any future game.[4]

In all of these cases, the prisoners' dilemma vanishes because the individual players have a strong desire to establish credibility so that they can play in future games. The basic reason is simply that people voluntarily choose their own partners. As far as I know, this aspect of the prisoners' dilemma has never been discussed before. It has pretty clearly, however, been in at least the subconscious mind of almost everybody who has written in this field. All of the previous articles that I have seen are situations in which the individual does not have a choice of partners. Either he is stuck with his colleague, like the two prisoners in the initial story, or the state of nature is such that he cannot change partners. Consider, for example, an industry in which there are five firms. They get together and form a cartel. Any individual member of this cartel has a motive to cheat, and it is not possible for the other partners to exclude him from the cartel, because that, in essence, would give him the best

---

4. He could perhaps get back into the game by elaborate promises of good behavior and side payments, but certainly a second defection would finish that.

of all possible worlds. He would be under no obligation whatsoever to restrict production, and the other four companies would be attempting to raise prices. The only threat that the other four companies have against a possible cheater is that they shall all stop cooperating, and that threat has limitations which are known to all economists. Similarly, in international relations problems, countries cannot choose their neighbors.

Although this is true of existing games, in the real world something can be done to make credibility valuable. The two prisoners in the prisoners' dilemma could have originally formed their partnership in crime because each had a well-established reputation for keeping his mouth shut. Each could think that talking under these circumstances would reduce his prospects for future profitable criminal activity jointly with any partner, not just with this particular partner and, hence, remain silent. With the flexibility of modern economic production, the possibility of companies choosing industries to enter in terms of the cooperativeness of other members is real, and establishing a reputation of being a good cartel partner might be quite valuable to a company that produced products in a number of different lines. Only in those particular industries where all members had a reputation for keeping their cartel agreements would any cartel agreements be entered into. As far as I know, this is not a conscious part of the strategy of any American conglomerate, but it is at least possible.

There are, of course, other techniques for establishing credibility. The businessman who regularly goes to church and regularly makes contributions to all kinds of worthy causes may be attempting to convince people that he is a safe partner. It is, after all, true that in a very large number of economic dealings it is possible for either, and in most cases both, parties to cheat. We do not usually tie our transactions so tightly in legal strings that there is not some room for uncooperative behavior on the part of either or both parties. Parties presumably refrain from this because of Adam Smith's discipline of continuous dealings or, in my more modern terminology, because they want to be partners in further prisoners' dilemma games.

Novelists and other critics have frequently made fun of the conformists' attitude that we frequently see in American business communities. As a matter of fact, conformism is found in all sorts of communities, including those of letters and social critics, although they, of course, conform to a different set of standards. This conformism is, in a way, an effort to convince people that you are the standard individual; i.e., the individual who, in the prisoners' dilemma situation, will not choose the noncooperative play. Similarly, if you have considerable hostages (you are, for example, a member of a fairly tight social group, and you and your family would be severely injured if you were, in essence, removed from the social group for bad behavior), you are more trustworthy.

The same rule applies to politicians, and for that matter to a somewhat limited extent in international dealings. Dishonesty is, of course, so common in international dealings that it would take a long time for anyone to produce a reputation for honesty.[5] A reputation for being "sound" is a valuable asset, and we should expect people to make every effort to get it. In many cases these efforts seem to an outsider prosaic, or even foolish, but there is every reason to believe that most of us would, in fact, prefer to enter into deals with the prosaic, conventional businessman with a well-established business than with a long-haired radical poet if there was something we could lose if the person we were dealing with decided to take advantage of us.[6]

We can see here also why I can be much more trusting in dealing with a merchant than he can in dealing with me. His reputation spreads over far more people, and it is harder for him to change partners readily. Blacksburg is a small town, but I am about to move to Washington. In Washington I presumably could spend a long time regularly returning products because I decided I did not want them, damaging them and claiming that they were damaged when I received them, without running out of new merchants to deal with. Merchants knowing this do take rather more precautions than the customer needs to. They are particularly concerned, of course, about the credit-worthiness of their customers.

Of course, the game does not have to be symmetric. I referred earlier to the fact that I do not worry very much about stores cheating me, but they may worry about my credit card. The explanation here is simple: they are heavily dependent on their reputation, but probably they do not know me. It is, of course, true that credit card companies do their best to make holders of bogus or stolen credit cards known, i.e., to create a negative reputation for them, and checking that list is probably the only thing the store will do. Still, the situation is, with respect to reputation, asymmetric in the sense that the store has to do research to find out the reputation of its customers.

5. See Laurence W. Beilenson, *The Treaty Trap* (Washington, D.C.: Public Affairs Press, 1969).

6. Of course, the long-haired radical poet might simply behave erratically without any calculation.

It is likely that almost all interactions between human beings can be drawn as prisoners' dilemmas, because it is possible for one party, or all parties, to make a one-time gain by cheating. In practice, almost no one even thinks of this opportunity in a competitive market in which he intends to remain for a while, because the cost of getting a reputation for cheating is too high. In essence, the two-strategy prisoners' dilemma matrix is extended by a third strategy—refuse to play with some specified person as shown in Figure 3. Under these circumstances, the cooperative solution is usually an optimum.

There is another application of this analysis. If an individual has lost reputation, there is little or no reason why he should play cooperative strategies in the future. If anyone agrees to play with him, which is not terribly likely, it would take a large number of plays before his reputation for reliability was as good as that of the person who had not already blotted his copybook even if he played cooperatively each time. Under the circumstances, he should attempt to con people into games, and when he gets them in, the decision to play noncooperatively may well be perfectly rational.

All of this would provide one more explanation for the tendency of people who once slipped to continue on that course of action. Thus, the habitual criminal or the "shady" businessman who continues to be "shady" are both responding rationally to their situation. Once they have a bad reputation, the cost of building up a reputation for reliability is extremely high.

	Cooperate	Defect	Don't Play
Cooperate	1 1	2 −2	0 0
Defect	−2 2	−1 −1	0 0
Don't Play	0 0	0 0	0 0

FIGURE 3

There are many other examples. When individuals can freely change the jurisdiction in which they live, then governmental "cheating" has only short-run payoffs. Note that there usually are at least some barriers to changing one's residence, and the height of these barriers in a way provides a threshold. With respect to a small suburban town outside a major city, this threshold is apt to be very low, indeed. For a major nation, on the other hand, it can be quite large.

It is notable that this kind of threshold can be increased. The United States has elaborate and not very effective procedures along its borders that are supposed to prevent outsiders from coming in. The Soviet Union has much more elaborate and much more effective barriers around its borders, the purpose of which is to prevent its own citizens from going out. The direction of the American barriers indicates that the American polity must be rather attractive by world standards. The need to have such extremely high barriers around the Soviet Union indicates that its internal practices are much more objectionable to the average Russian than the practices of most countries.

Hirschman, in a famous book *Exit Voice and Loyalty*, argued that if people, for one reason or another, do not want to change their bargaining partners, the railroads they use, etc., then they will exert pressure to improve the quality of the services they receive.[7] This may, indeed, be so, but if it is, we are dealing there with a quite different phenomenon. It is certainly true that the individual who can readily change from the railroad in Nigeria, with which Hirschman starts, to trucks is better off than he would be if he were compelled to use the railroads. Perhaps, of course, Hirschman is correct that railway service would be markedly better if this alternative did not exist.

But this is more an exercise in general political philosophy than a discussion of the market. It is, indeed, true that the freedom to change what government you serve under will make it easier for you to better your lot. It is also true that this privilege will mean that governments, regardless of their formal structure, will find it necessary to pay considerable attention to the wishes of their citizenry. Individuals in a democracy must consider to at least some extent when they vote not only the effect of that vote on themselves but its effect on their neighbors who might conceivably decide to move to the next suburb, thus lowering real estate values in this suburb if they are sufficiently offended.

7. Albert O. Hirschman, *Exit Voice and Loyalty* (Cambridge: Harvard University Press, 1970).

But the main theme of this discussion has been that the prisoners' dilemma, strictly speaking, occurs only in a rather narrow area. Where there are a number of potential players available, the dilemma is proportionately weakened. Indeed, here we have what amounts to a mapping of the usual economic distinction between monopoly on the one side and competition on the other. If there is only one person with whom I can play the game, both he and I very likely will decide not to cooperate. As the number of people playing increases, the prospect that either he or I can get another partner, if we find our current partner objectionable, exerts steadily increasing pressure to always play cooperatively. In the limit, as in the limit of perfect competition, behavior is always mutually advantageous, with the individual not taking a course of action which with respect to a particular play of the game seems desirable.

It is not only numbers here; it is also improved information. Brokers are specialists in this kind of thing. I have just finished selling a house in Blacksburg and buying an apartment in Washington. Brokers who assisted me were, among other things, very knowledgeable not only on what was on the market and the legal precautions necessary to see to it that I was not cheated, but also on the reputation of various parties. Additional precautions were sometimes suggested. Brokers themselves, of course, live and die with a reputation for efficiency and fairness.

All of this, however, was known to Adam Smith and has probably been known to successful merchants from time immemorial. Where the market is broad and there are many alternatives, you had better cooperate. If you choose the noncooperative solution, you may find you have no one to noncooperate with.

GAMES AND PREFERENCE

Not since Ellsberg's[1] "Reluctant Duelist" has any general attack on game theory come to my attention. I am not a specialist in this field, and I may have missed something, but surely my memory is that of the average economist, political scientist, and so on. My intent is to fill the gap by arguing that in general it is not particularly wise to follow von Neumann and Morgenstern's advice.

All of this represents a considerable change in opinion on my part. I was originally a strong proponent of the game theory and inflicted it on my students. I also used some of the simpler aspects of the theory in my work. It may seem odd that at a time when game theory is undergoing a marked revival I began to have doubts. But I have always had a tendency to be out of step.

I should probably also confess that I continue to make some use of certain aspects of game theory. Prisoner's Dilemma, for example, can be found scattered through my writings. In all of the cases where I use it, however, it is simply a convenience—something that makes it easier to think about the problem. My objection to game theory is as a formal body of mathematics allegedly applying to human action, not as a heuristic which makes it easier to think about certain problems.

Let us begin with the clearest case, a zero-sum game, which has an easy-to-compute strategy. Matrix 1 is a game between Mr. Row and Mr. Column. The numbers are objective, as they were in the early work on game theory. We will turn to utility numbers later. The strategy is easy. Column, if he has followed von Neumann and Morgenstern, will flip a coin, hence getting a 50-50 weighting for each of his columns, and Row will use a single die playing row C when it turns up six and row D when it turns up anything else.

Let us assume that, like most of us, Row is risk averse. This is, of course, not a particularly difficult assumption; indeed, an assumption of general risk aversion is fundamental to the part of game theory that Ellsberg mainly criticized.

Suppose, then, that Row rolls his die and finds six. Should he play row C or row D? It seems rather obvious that if he is risk averse, he should play

Reprinted, by permission of Sage Publications Ltd., from *Rationality and Society* 41 (January 1992): 24–32. Copyright 1992 by Sage Publications.

1. Daniel Ellsberg, "Theory of the Reluctant Duelist," *American Economic Review* 46, no. 5 (1956): 909–23; John von Neumann and Oskar Morgenstern, *Theory of Games and Economic Behavior* (Princeton: Princeton University Press, 1944).

MATRIX 1

row D unless he thinks that Column would anticipate his doing so. Let us temporarily assume that he is convinced that Column is a true-blue game theory player. Therefore, he is certain that Column will flip a coin and will take whichever choice comes up. Then, clearly, he not only should play row D even if he rolled the die, he should not have bothered to roll the die at all.

Now let us consider Column. Suppose that he is convinced that Row is a devout believer in game theory (hence will play row C if he gets six on his die and otherwise row D). Column is like most people who engage in gambling, in that he prefers a large chance of a small loss and a small chance of a large gain to the reverse. We can tell that most people feel this way from the fact that most professional gambling games are set up so that the customer gets that kind of a chance.

Granted he has these preferences, he should play column B. He should do this regardless of how his coin turns up, and, in fact, there is no real point in flipping a coin unless, perhaps, he wants to do so conspicuously to deceive Row. In this case, however, if Row were able to figure out what Column was doing, he would have an even stronger motive for playing row D. On the other hand, if Column figures out what Row is doing, he should, of course, play column A.

The basic problem here is best summed up in an oral comment by Jack Hirshleifer: "Mixed strategy simply is not robust." The play of a mixed strategy on the part of one party means that the other party has no motive to do so.

When I discussed the first of these propositions (that is, what Row should do) with a game theorist, he asked if I meant that Row should violate his contract. I pointed out there was no contract, but if he did choose to violate a contract, so what? The theorist's reply was that he would like to think the matter over and give me his response later. Since he had just finished a transatlantic flight, I could hardly object, but, as a matter of fact, he has never given me his response.

It is easier to discuss the matter if we turn to a very ingenious article by Hillman and Samet.[2] They consider a game in which a fixed prize, let us say $100, is to be sold to the highest bidder. The "bid," however, is made in the form of cash which is not returned. They produced a solution to this, which is a mixed strategy that is both highly ingenious and very simple. To make the discussion easier, I will assume there are only two players.

Each of these two players each time the game is played (and it is not intended as a single-play game but a series) chooses at random a number between 1 and 100 and plays that. It will be observed that this procedure turns the game into a zero-sum game in which each party, over a long series of plays, will break even.[3]

The problem with this is that if I know that I am playing Hillman and Samet, I simply bid $90 each time. If they continue playing their strategy, I will break even, but they will have disastrous losses. I will have converted the game back into a non-zero-sum game with the intent of driving them out. At this point, they have to make decisions in another game. If they attempt to compete in high bids, both of us will have a pronouncedly negative prospect for the future. If they continue playing with their strategy, they face disaster. If they withdraw, I am presented with a very strongly positive-sum game.

Obviously, their decision in this case would depend predominantly on efforts to guess what I would do, and, in fact, the fundamental aspect is guessing what the opponent's psychology is. Ingenious as their solution is, it only changes the infinite regression of the original game into a new infinite regression in which their strategy is one of the set. In this game, the important point is my determination and my guess as to the other person's determination. The winner will be the best actor.

---

2. A. L. Hillman and D. Samet, "Dissipation of Contestable Rents by Small Numbers of Contenders," *Public Choice* 54 (1987): 63–82. See also Gordon Tullock, "Another Part of the Swamp," *Public Choice* 54 (1987): 83–84, and A. L. Hillman and D. Samet, "Characterizing Equilibrium Rent-Seeking Behavior: A Reply to Tullock," *Public Choice* 54 (1987): 85–87.

3. If there are more than two players, the strategies are more complicated, but they still create a zero-sum game for all of them.

Use of objective numbers in game theory is rather old-fashioned. Presently, most game theorists use utility measures in their matrices.[4] This is a change from von Neumann and Morgenstern or, for that matter, Luce and Raiffa.[5] If the theory could be saved by this change, of course we should make the change. There are two problems here, one of which is simply a matter of definition. Return to the game of Matrix 1. Suppose that the parties have a declining marginal utility for money. With this assumption, the game immediately ceases to be zero sum. The value of an increase in wealth by $5.00 is less than the cost of a similar reduction. But with almost any utility values, the game also is no longer zero sum. Further, each party must now make an estimate of the utility value of the other, and there is not the slightest reason to believe that these estimates would be highly accurate.

But there is a more difficult problem. Suppose that, as a matter of fact, the 1s and 5s do represent the utility which these parties would obtain from either receiving the prize or being penalized by that amount. On the other hand, assume that the Row player is indeed risk averse. It is not that he puts different values on the outcome than the Column player does; rather, it is the actual act of playing row 1 that is to some extent painful to him.

This is a different meaning of "utility," and I have great difficulty in seeing how it could be entered into the matrix. Note that risk aversion affects the play of Row player, but it has no effect on Column except insofar as Column anticipates its effect on Row. We seem, once again, to be in an infinite regress. My mathematical friends seem to think that this is not a problem which should cause difficulty, albeit they have not revealed to me their solution.

This other problem is particularly severe, however, if we turn to the Hillman and Samet solution of their game. Even if I think that I should put a new set of values in my own personal matrix, depending on my desire or lack of desire to play particular types of strategy, I cannot do it unless I have a good estimate of what the other party will do. The feeling of risk that I get in a given play depends on my estimate of my opponent's strategy. If I adjust my play to that risk, then if he can anticipate that, he should adjust his play to my new level of risk aversion; hence, his risk changes, and he should play something else. Once again, we have an infinite regress.

4. Or at least claim that they do. A job candidate here told me firmly that he only used utility numbers. When he read his paper, however, each party had the same values, which is unlikely if they are utilities.

5. R. Duncan Luce and Howard Raiffa, *Games and Decisions: Introduction and Critical Survey* (New York: Wiley, 1957).

This game has the interesting characteristic that the optimist will always beat the pessimist. But if they are both optimists, believing that their opponent will shortly withdraw, both suffer disastrous losses. My view of the odds I face changes those odds. Once again, we have a paradox closely resembling the paradox of the liar which so puzzled St. Paul.

Game theorists have pointed out to me that if you do not play your properly calculated mixed strategy in the preceding games, then you are in an infinite regress. This, of course, is Pascal's argument for games of strategy being actually incalculable. The conclusion he drew from it was that we should not calculate them, and it seems to me that is also the appropriate judgment for game theory.

Harsanyi produced a justification for the mixed strategy in game theory which I am not at all positive that I understand.[6] If I do understand it, however, it, in essence, says that everyone plays a pure strategy. Since everyone is at least to some extent uncertain about the strategy that his opponent will play, however, he calculates the mixed strategy in deciding which pure strategy to play. The mixed strategy that you compute is an aid in guessing the parameters of your opponent's play.

But note that even for this defensive use of the mixed strategy, one has to know what the opponent's utility numbers are if you are using utility numbers in your matrix. Since his estimate of your choice of strategy, among other things, changes his utility numbers if we use the second definition of utility given earlier, it is very difficult to see how this could be done.

But let us go back to the origin of the matter, particularly the work of Pascal. He was, of course, the first great probabilist and worked out the foundations of pure gambling games. If you consider a pair of fair dice, for example, the probability of various combinations turning up is not susceptible to human control; hence, it is calculable.[7]

On the other hand, if one has human beings making decisions, as, for example, in poker, then this kind of calculation is impossible. You do not know what my two hole cards are and I do. What you should do after I raise is dependent both on your hole cards and on your estimate of my strategy. Whether you should meet my raise or perhaps raise again depends on what you think my strategy is. Further, my decision as to my strategy depends on my estimate of your strategy. A number of people—Mr. Hunt, for example—have

---

6. John C. Harsanyi, "Games with Randomly Distributed Payoffs: A New Rationale for Mixed-Strategy Equilibrium Points," *International Journal of Game Theory* 2 (1973): 1–23.

7. This, of course, assumes that the man who throws them does not have unusual abilities.

won very large sums of money by making this kind of judgment correctly. It is clear that skill is involved here as well as luck.

Nevertheless, the infinite regress that led Pascal to feel that there was no true solution is, in fact, a correct description of the game. If there is a correct strategy for your play, then I can calculate it too.[8] If I can calculate it and make my best reply, then your strategy was wrong. You should thus do something else, and so on.

Von Neumann and Morgenstern purported to get out of this problem by producing a mixed strategy for such games.[9] As an intellectual accomplishment, it is hard to overpraise this work. They demonstrated that all zero-sum games of strategy can be converted into games with various probabilities played by each party on the various pure strategies. They further demonstrated that these new games have saddle points and gave the method of calculating that saddle point. The mixed strategy that I have given earlier is, of course, the joint set of probabilistic saddle points, assuming that the numbers are objective.

To repeat, this was a massive intellectual accomplishment. The question is whether or not it actually solves the problem. Look once again at Matrix 1 and assume we are considering it before von Neumann and Morgenstern. Column may feel that playing B gives him a good chance of making more money than he may lose. But, on the other hand, it looks obvious, so probably Row would play row D. On the other hand, if Column plays A which guarantees him a gain when Row plays D. . . . Once again, one can go on forever with this line of reasoning.

But it is my point here that von Neumann and Morgenstern did not get out of the infinite regress but only changed its structure. Column can legitimately say that if he plays the properly calculated mixed strategy, then Row will be motivated to play row D because, like all of us, he is risk averse. Hence, Column should play column A. But, if that is the correct line of reasoning and Row also can follow it, he would either go back to the mixed strategy and actually play it or, alternatively, he would simply play row C. Once again, you have infinite regress. The only difference between this infinite regress and the others is that playing the properly calculated mixed strategy is one of the elements in the regress.

---

8. Since the hole cards are still covered, such calculations would have a stochastic character.

9. Actually, for less complex games. Calculating it for poker, even assuming that the parties are prevented from looking at each other's faces—hence, cannot make judgments that way—is extraordinarily complicated, and as far as I know, no one has actually done it.

Here also, there is something closely akin to the paradox of the liar. If my opponent has been convinced by von Neumann and Morgenstern that he should play the properly calculated mixed strategy, then, from my standpoint, the present discounted numerical value of either of the two plays is exactly the same. However, like most people, I have some preferences other than to pure numbers; hence, I have an opportunity to choose a strategy which is better than my mixed strategy. On the other hand, if I do choose this strategy, then he has a good response, and so on. We are back in the infinite regress.

The problem here, of course, is that the zero-sum requirement is an impossible one if the numbers are utility numbers. If they are not, then the parties should not play as if they were. The two parties practically never have exactly reversed utilities for a given objective outcome. Risk-averse Row really could convert the matrix to fit his own preference function by, say, subtracting one from each of the values in row C. We now no longer have a zero-sum game. Further, the two parties are now playing different matrices. Suppose that I can accurately estimate the matrix which my opponent is using and calculate an appropriate mixed strategy for that.[10] Note that I can select a pure strategy in terms of my own personal matrix values. Presumably, his estimate of these is not as good as mine, and hence, his play of the mixed strategy has benefited me.

There is, for some reason, in the game theory literature an apparent feeling that playing a mixed strategy and actually throwing the dice somehow or other reduces your risk. This is, of course, true if you consider your expectancy before you throw the dice. At that point, you have a generalized strategy with various weights on different pure strategies. The net effect of the probabilities is to minimize the expectancy of losses.

Once you have thrown the dice, however, this ceases to be true. We now have an instruction to play one particular pure strategy, but it is by no means obvious that that particular pure strategy is a risk-avoiding one. The top row in Matrix 1 would be an example where it is not.

There is another possible justification here, which is that it is a procedure to prevent your opponent from guessing exactly what you will do. This is, of course, perfectly true. Preventing your opponent from anticipating your moves has been important in most strategic contests. At the time of this writing, I think Saddam Hussein is very curious indeed as to what the allied powers plan.

---

10. This assumes that I am also making some kind of estimate of what he thinks is the matrix that I am using.

Unfortunately, concealing your intent by use of this particular randomizing device has no very obvious advantage over concealing it by any one of a number of other randomizing devices. Further, traditionally—both in poker and in war—successful players make decisions by nonrandom means. They simply attempt to conceal those decisions from their partners.

As a final problem here, it is not at all obvious that there is such a thing as a set of mixed strategies for this realistic approach to games. With utility numbers, the two parties are playing on different matrices, each one attempting to estimate what the other person's matrix looks like. It is dubious that a proper mixed strategy can be calculated under these circumstances.

Let us abandon mixed strategies and consider the simpler aspects of von Neumann and Morgenstern's approach to games. If there is simple dominance, then obviously the parties should play that. Once again, the use of utility numbers rather than objective numbers might make it hard to tell whether there was simple dominance or whether the other party thought there was. In some cases, this can be solved by going back to objective numbers without much difficulty. In the case of simple dominance, it is extremely likely that the objectively dominant play is also utility dominant. Of course, the objective numbers may not be known with any accuracy, and then the two players must still make guesses as to the value given by their opponent.

A saddle point with pure strategies also raises no difficulty if you use objective numbers and they are known to both parties. Once we begin introducing utility numbers or "the fog of war," however, the prospect that the two parties will think that the saddle point is in two different locations becomes real.

Once again, we are back to the game of guessing what the other party thinks and then responding to it. The problem is that parties with no knowledge of formal game theory are likely to go through the same process as the trained game theorist. Consider Villeneuve on that morning off Trafalgar. We know that he and his officers rapidly canvassed Nelson's possible strategies. Would a modern game theorist have been able to improve on their method of approaching the problem?

Nelson was also attempting to guess what Villeneuve would do. In his case, he knew what he was going to do, and he had a fairly good idea of what the French would do in response. His estimate turned out to be wrong, but it is, once again, hard to see what a game theorist could have done to improve Nelson's decision process.

But what could a game theorist have recommended them to do that they did not do? Their thought processes were correct; the basic difference was they did not have the modern vocabulary. The question is whether the use of that vocabulary really makes a great deal of difference.

If we look at most games of strategy, whether they are wars or bargaining sessions, the basic effort by the two parties is devoted to something which is really outside of game theory. When I am, let us say, buying a house, I attempt to give my opponent a false impression as to the value that I put on the house. He is attempting to similarly mislead me. Both of us are attempting to guess the actual situation and strategy of our opponent. Mr. Hunt and Napoléon, for example, were extremely skilled in this activity. It is, however, outside formal game theory, except insofar as the game theorist would point out the desirability of investing resources here. Once again, this does not seem to be new.

We are thus left with three things in game theory. The first is a vocabulary which is clearly improved and easier to use than the previous vocabulary when talking about games of strategy. Indeed, even realizing that such things as bargaining were games of strategy is an important step forward.

As an important subsection of this improvement in vocabulary, the use of the von Neumann and Morgenstern matrix showing payoffs to various strategies is frequently extremely helpful in clarifying one's thoughts. So is their tree diagram, which today is frequently referred to as either "backward induction" or "subgame-perfect equilibriums," but that has not in any way reduced its utility. Once again, these things are improvements in our vocabulary and ways of thinking about the problems, not an actual solution to them.

The end result is not that the effort in game theory was totally wasted, because it clearly has improved our understanding of a lot of problems even if it has solved few. There actually are a number of what you may call technical problems for which the game theory solution is completely correct. As an obvious example, differential games are a great help in designing fighter aircraft. There are other cases in which specific technical devices can be optimized by a differential game approach.

Note that in all of these cases there is an objective and well-specified payoff. There is no reason to believe that all pursuit pilots receive the same disutility from being shot down, but counting a plane loss as one, no matter who was in it, is surely legitimate.

The end product, however, is that game theory has been important in that it has affected our vocabulary and our methods of thinking about certain problems. In general, this effect has been for the good. We find it easier to deal with these problems now than we did before. It has not, however, provided genuine solutions for more than a very small collection of special cases.

INDEX

References to bibliographic information appear in italics.

Abramowitz, Moses, 382
abstractions, 5–6
academia: division of labor in, 368; efficiency in, 111
academics, discrimination against, 111–12
Africa: countries in cross-national sample, 397–98; economic growth, 391–92, 396–97
agreements, cheating on, 148. *See also* cartels
agricultural ants, 219, 224
agricultural subsidies via foreign aid, 352
Alchian, Armen A., *13n. 6, 374n. 1*
Alexander, Richard D., *236n. 1*
Allen, William R., *13n. 6*
Allyon, T., *104nn. 12, 13*
altruism: in animal societies, 145–47; Becker's view, 133–38; evolution of self-sacrificing behavior, 159–61; genetic theory of self-sacrifice, 160–69; of social insects, 130–31. *See also* nepotism
Americas: countries in cross-national sample, 398; economic growth, 391–92, 396–97; OPEC countries in, 395
animals: rational behavior, 96; studies about rational behavior of, 105–10; variable behavior, 125–26. *See also* cellular animals
animal societies: conflict in, 121–23; contrasted with human societies, 115–17, 142–54; dominance in, 116, 123–24; lessons for human society, 124–25. *See also* human societies; plant societies; societies, primitive
anthropomorphizing, 184
ants: and beetles, 194–95; civil wars among, 208–9; difference from termites, 226–28, 229–30; division of labor, 209, 216–24; food supply, 206–7, 209, 216–18; free riding, 218–19; hives, 207–8; learned skills, 210–15; life cycles, 206–7; reproduction, 189–91; similarities with termite societies, 230–31; social life, 215–16; social organization, 128–29, 143–44. *See also* agricultural ants; army ants; bees; slaving ants; termites
Arcelus, Francisco, *371n. 10*
army ants, 224
Asia: countries in cross-national sample, 398; economic growth, 391–92, 396–97; OPEC countries in, 395
Australian economic growth, 389
Azrin, N. H., *104nn. 12, 13*

Bailey, Martin, *362n. 2, 364n. 4*
banks in South Korea, 352–53
bargaining, 446
Barro, Robert J., 380
barter vs. use of depreciating currency, 317–20, 345
Barth, James, *383n. 13, 384n. 16*
Battalio, R. C., *104n. 10, 105, 107*
Battle Studies (du Picq), 405, 413–15
Baumol, William, 382

Bean, Frank D., *81n. 13*
Becker, Gary S., *25n. 1, 36nn. 7, 8, 37n. 10, 39n. 1, 79n. 9, 95nn. 1, 2*; "Altruism, Egoism, and Genetic Fitness," 133–38; hypothesis about punishment, 76
Bedau, Hugo Adam, *77n. 6*
bees: division of labor, 206, 234–35; environmental coordination, 257; genetic inheritance, 200; joint development with flowers, 232–34; lack of specialized types, 231–32; nests, 229n. 5, 231; reproduction, 189–91; self-sacrifice, 160–61; social organization, 143–44. See also ants; termites
beetles and ants, 194–95
Beilenson, Laurence W., *434n. 5*
Berger, Jacques, *109n. 24*
Bergquist, Patricia R., *242n. 2*
Bernholz, Peter, 360n. 1
Bilson, J. F., *394n. 20*
biology: and economics, 117–18, 139, 142; language of, 184
birds, 108–9. See also chickens; sea gulls
Bismarck, Otto von, 290
Black, Fisher, *383n. 12*
Block, Michael, 81
Bloom, Howard S., *371n. 10*
Bloomfield, A. I., *343n. 1, 344n. 4, 345n. 8, 348n. 14*
bonobos, 165
Boulding, Kenneth, 6
Brandt, C., *314n. 11*
Brennan, Geoffrey, *425n. 2*
bribery: to change individual behavior, 416; of civil servants, 356–57. See also incentives
Browning, Edgar K., *294n. 5*
Buchanan, James M., *412n. 4*; on advantages of earmarked taxes, 291; *The Calculus of Consent*, 287

Burger, J., *155n. 1*
Burgess, J. W., *186n. 4*
Bushell, S. W., *339n. 21*
Butler, Colin G., 206

Cagan, Phillip, *362n. 2*
Calculus of Consent, The (Buchanan and Tullock), 287, 291n. 3
Campbell, Colin D., *347n. 11*
Canadian economic growth, 389
Cannan, Edwin, *319n. 14, 345n. 7*
Carr-Hill, R. A., 82
cartels, 18–19; reputation of members, 432–33
cells of human beings, 129, 259, 264
cellular animals: protozoa, 225–26; rational behavior, 109–10; social organization, 144–45; as societies of individual cells, 264–67; within sponges, 241–42. See also societies, primitive
Central America: countries in cross-national sample, 398; economic growth, 391–93, 396–97
Chao, Kuo-chun, *308n. 3, 311n. 8, 312nn. 9, 10, 318n. 13*
charitable giving, 161–62
cheating: on agreements, 148; in the market, 429–37
chickens, 123
children: cost of creating, 52–53; as economic goods, 39–43, 46; quality, 49, 51; supply and demand, 43–50. See also fertility rates
chimpanzees, 122, 164, 166, 246
China: Chin dynasty currency, 329–31; Ch'ing dynasty currency, 338–39; Communist currencies, 312; currency 1937–1949, 317–18, 319–20; early monetary history, 324–26; hyperinflation, 1937–1949, 307–20; Ming dynasty currency, 337–38; Mongol dynasty currency, 332–37;

origin of paper money, 325; paper money in ancient, 321–24; Sung dynasty currency, 328–29; Szechuan dynasty currency, 326–28

Chinese coins, 326n. 10

civilization: early human, 166–67; as hereditary behavior, 261–63

civil liberties in OPEC countries, 393–95

civil servants: bribes of South Korean, 356–67; sharing of unofficial income among, 353–54

civil war in nonhuman societies, 208–9

Clayton, Richard T., *282n. 4*

cloning, 187–88; and social success, 192–93

coal tits, 108–9

Cobb, William E., *83n. 21*

coercion: by government, 203–4; mutual agreements to use, 92; in private hierarchies, 202

collective action, 407–13. *See also* cooperation

communication vs. information exchange, 257–58

Communist currencies in China, 312

computers, preferences of, 252–53

conflict: geographical location of, 156–57; origin of group, 164–65; payoff from, 412–13. *See also* fighting; war

contagious diseases example, 89

contracts. *See* marriage contract

cooperation: within animal societies, 147–50; in prisoners' dilemma games, 429–37; by termites, 257; theory of, 250–63. *See also* collective action; environmental coordination

costs: child rearing, 41–43; cowardice, 410; crime avoidance, 62–65; crime prevention, 67; to criminal for crime, 56–57, 60; definition, 10–11; divorce, 28, 36; as explanatory factors, 11–12; of fighting, 121–22,

157; gun control, 282; marginal, 12–14; marriage, 28–31; monitoring individuals, 424; producing children, 52–53; Social Security, 294; to society from crime, 57–58; to victims of crime, 57. *See also* decision costs

costs and benefits: of crime, 56–58; of crime avoidance, 62–65; involved in voting, 280–81

courts, role in divorce process, 27

Craig, John, *325n. 9*

credit limits in Korea, 352–53

crime: costs to society from, 57–58; costs to victims of, 57; economic vs. sociological view, 73–77; punishment as deterrent, 76, 77–83; as rational behavior, 58–60; total community level of, 59. *See also* violent crime

crime avoidance, costs and benefits, 62–65

crime prevention, 60; costs, 67

crime rates, 60, 61, 62, 69–72

crimes against property, 68, 71

criminals: benefits of crime to, 56; cost of crime to, 56–57, 60; irrational or "sick," 60–62, 77; public opinion about, 77; rational, 58–60; rehabilitation, 74, 77; risk of being caught, 72

cross-national economic growth, 1951–1980: design of study, 381–82; hypotheses about, 382–84; results of study, 385–95; variables used in study, 379, 384

currencies: ancient Chinese paper money, 321–24; vs. barter in China, 317–20, 345; in China, 1937–1949, 307–8; Chin dynasty in China, 329–31; Chinese communist, 312; Ch'ing dynasty in China, 338–39; competing forms of, 359–66;

currencies (*continued*)
depreciation of, in China, 311–12; difficulty of replacing existing, 371–72; frequency of competing forms of, 368–70; functions of, 319, 367; Ming dynasty in China, 337–38; Mongol dynasty in China, 332–37; South Korean, 1945–1954, 350; Sung dynasty in China, 328–29; Szechuan dynasty in China, 326–28; use as media of exchange in China, 1937–1949, 317–18; use of precious metals as, 339. *See also* Chinese coins; paper money
Cushing, Robert G., *81n. 13*

Darwin, Charles, 117
Davidson, Diane W., *140n. 1*
Davis, A. M., *322n. 2*
Dawkins, R., *188n. 7*
death penalty, 77, 78, 83
decision costs, 29
decision making: within families, 29–30; whether to have children, 43
demand, 14–19
Denison, E. F., *384n. 15*, *396n. 21*
DeTray, Dennis, *49nn. 10, 11*
developing countries: in cross-national sample, 397–98; vs. developed country empirical studies, 380; economic growth, 391–93, 396–97; population explosion, 50
de Waal, Frans, *165n. 7*
discrimination: against assistant professors, 111–12; against women, 34
division of labor: Adam Smith's view, 209–10, 219–20; ants, 209, 216–24; bees, 206, 234–35; in scholarly work, 368; as survival mechanism, 223; termites, 230–31, 257–58
divorce, 26–28; costs, 36; relation to spouse selection, 36

dominance, 123–24; male, 116. *See also* fighting; hierarchies
du Picq, Armand, 405, 406, 413–15, 419

earmarked taxes, 291
ecology. *See* environmental coordination
economic growth: Africa, 396–97; Africa, Americas, and Asia, 391–92; Australia, 389; Canada, 389; effect on government, 386–87; impact of government on, 380; impact of inflation on, 390; Ireland, 389; Japan, 390–91; OECD countries, 385–89; and population growth, 386, 391; Turkey, 389; United Kingdom, 389; United States, 389–91. *See also* cross-national economic growth, 1951–1980
economic growth variables, 379
economic models, 6
economics: and biology, 117–18, 139–41, 142; changes in field of, 3; defining, 4–5; difference from other fields, 22; emphasis on individuals, 3–4, 7–8, 405; emphasis on structuring of institutions, 405–6; experimental evidence of rationality, 95–102; importance of abstractions to, 5–6; lack of concern about moral values, 7; and sociobiology, 133–38, 139–54; view of crime, 73–77
economists: contrasted with sociologists, 427–28; definition, 5n. 2
education and fertility, 50–52
efficiency in families, 32–34
Ehrlich, Isaac, *82n. 18*, 83
Ellsberg, Daniel, *438n. 1*
environmental coordination, 250–52; bees, 257; termites, 255–56
Erickson, Maynard L., *83n. 19*
eusociality, 236, 240

evolution, 130, 140; of human beings,
150–53
exchange rates in China 1948–1950,
328n. 12
Exit Voice and Loyalty (Hirschman),
436
externalities: market vs. government
dilemma, 91–94; when privatization
better internalizes, 399. *See also*
public goods

Fairbank, J. K., *314n. 11*
families, 85; roles, 33–34
FBI (Federal Bureau of Investigation),
69
Ferguson, C. E., *246n. 6*
fertility rates: future, 53–54; impact
of education on, 50–52; impact of
government policy on, 48; impact
of income on, 49–50; and overpopulation, 52–53
fetus transplants, 53
Field, Alexander, *159n. 1*
fighting: costs of, 121–22; in human
vs. nonhuman societies, 198–99; as
rational choice, 156. *See also* conflict;
dominance
fines, 76–77
foreign aid programs: goods to South
Korea, 351–52, 353–54; United
Nations developmental projects in
South Korea, 356
Fouraker, L., *99n. 5*
free riding: definition, 204; in the military, 409n. 1, 418–19, 420, 421–
22, 424; in nonhuman societies,
183–85, 204–5, 218–19
Freiden, Alan, *36n. 9*
Friedman, Milton, 383, 387
full income, 14

games of strategy, 438; gambling
games, 439; mixed strategy, 442–

45; prisoners' dilemma, 429–37;
usefulness, 446
Gardner, Bruce, *49n. 10, 50n. 12*
Gärtner, Manfred, 285–86
Gastil, R. D., *394n. 20*
GDP growth in Africa, Americas, and
Asia, 391
gemmulation, 243
genetic egoism, 186–87
Genghis Khan, 321
Ghiselin, Michael T., *159n. 2*
Gibbs, Jack P., 80–81, *83n. 19*
globalization, 399–400
Goodall, Jane, 122, *165n. 6*, 246
Goodman, Saul, *371n. 10*
goods, definition, 10
gorillas, 164–65
government bonds, 357
government debt, 271–74
government policy and fertility rates,
48
governments: in animal societies, 147–
48; definition, 147; effect on economic growth, 380; Far Eastern,
355; impact of economic growth on,
386–87; institutions other than
markets or, 85–86; and pharmaceutical research, 400; promotion of
inflation, 359–62; restriction of
competitive currencies, 365–66;
South Korea, 354
government share of GDP (variable),
384; in Africa, Americas, and Asia,
391
government vs. market problem: externalities, 91–93; Pigou's example,
87–91; police services, 65–66;
and the public good, 86–87; and
redistribution, 86
Gray, Louis N., *81n. 12*
Gresham's Law of money, 359
group vs. individual selection, 182–86,
225–26, 244–46. *See also* nepotism

guerilla warfare, 422
gun control, 282

Hamiltonian altruism, 188
haploidy theory of society, 143–44
Hardin, Garrett, 118, 142
Harsanyi, John C., 442
Hashimoto, Masanori, *50n. 13*, *51n. 14*
Hayek, Friedrich A., 244, 383
hereditary behavior, 181; and DNA,
    258–59; and human civilization,
    261–63; reproduction, 187–96
heroism: effect on military battles,
    423; self-sacrifice for genetic sur-
    vival, 188; as survival mechanism,
    181
Heston, Alan, *381n. 4*
hierarchies: human vs. nonhuman,
    179–80; importance of, in human
    society, 197; private, 202. *See also*
    dominance
Higashi, S., *208n. 4*
Hillman, A. L., 440, 441
Hirschman, Albert O., 436
Hirshleifer, Jack, *115n. 1*, 439
Hochman, Harold M., *138n. 8*
Hölldobler, Bert, *191n. 10*, *207nn. 1–3*
Horton, P. B., *75n. 3*
households: decisions of, 30; public
    goods provided by, 31–32. *See also*
    families
Howell, John, *82n. 16*
human behavior: applied to animals,
    120, 130, 146; importance of to
    economics, 2–3; learned skills, 210
human cells, 129, 130, 259, 264–67
human societies: contrasted with ani-
    mal societies, 142–54; development
    of, 260–61; lessons of animal soci-
    ety for, 124–25; organic society
    theory of, 264; studying animals
    to learn about, 115–17; using, to
    understand nonhuman societies,

175. *See also* civilization; nonhuman
    societies
Hutcheson, Francis, *146n. 8*
Hutt, William, 85
hyenas, 123, 126, 152

imprisonment, 77
incentives: negative, 417–19; posi-
    tive, 416–17. *See also* bribery;
    punishment
incest, 162–63
inclusive fitness, 188
income: effect on fertility, 49–50;
    effect on Social Security payments,
    301; full, 14; upper income groups
    under Social Security, 296–97,
    300–301
income redistribution: and government
    vs. market problem, 86; via Social
    Security, 300–301
income tax in United States: negative,
    135; personal exemptions, 48
individuals: costs of monitoring, 424;
    and group selection, 225–26;
    importance of, in military, 406–7;
    importance of, to economics, 3–4,
    7–8, 405
individual vs. collective action, 407–
    13; soldiers firing weapons, 425–28
individual vs. group selection, 182–86,
    225–36, 244–46. *See also* nepotism
inflation: in Africa, 391; in China,
    1100–1500 A.D., 324–26; in Chin
    dynasty in China, 331; Chinese ad-
    justment to, 314–16, 319; Chinese
    attempts to stop, 310–11, 312–14,
    339; defining, 373–75; and denomi-
    nations of paper money, 330n. 16,
    346–47; effect on economic growth
    of United States, 390; effects of,
    in China, 316–17; in free China,
    1937–1949, 308–10; government
    use of, 359–62; monetary collapse

from, 345; in Mongol dynasty in China, 341–42; possible remedies for South Korea, 358; South Korean adjustment to continuous, 343–49; South Korean attempts to control, 345–46; South Korean difficulties with, 355–57; as spur to competitive currencies, 363–65; in Szechuan dynasty in China, 326

information transfer among termites, 257

insane people, rational behavior by, 102–5

institutions, structuring of, 405–6

interest rates during inflation in China, 311

Ireland, economic growth, 389

Ireland, Thomas R., *53n. 18*

Jackson, M. W., *425n. 1*

Japan, economic growth, 390–91

Jarvis, Jennifer U. M., *236n. 1*

Jensen, J. P., *343n. 1, 344n. 4, 345n. 8, 348n. 14*

Jevons, W. S., *324n. 5, 339n. 22*

Kagel, John H., *105n. 16, 107n. 19*

Kasarda, John D., *46n. 8*

Keating, Barry, 100

Keleher, Robert, *383n. 13, 384n. 16*

Kerber, E. S., *349n. 15*

Kirzner, Israel M., *95n. 2*

Klein, Benjamin, 367–72, *374n. 1*

knowledge, how we gain, 6

Komroff, Manuel, *322n. 2*

Korea. *See* South Korea

Kormendi, R. C., 379, 381–82, 383, 384, 385, 386n. 17, 395–96

Kramer, Gerald H., *371n. 10*

Krohm, Gregory C., *83nn. 19, 21*

Kruuk, Hans, *123n. 5, 152n. 13*

K'ung, H. H., *308n. 4*

Kupinsky, Stanley, *46n. 8*

Landa, Janet T., *160n. 2*

Landau, Henry J., *430n. 3*

Lanting, Frans, *165n. 7*

law of demand, 16–17

legal system of South Korea, 355

Leibenstein, Harvey, *39n. 1*

Leibowitz, Arleen, 79–80

Lerner, Abba, 85

Leslie, G. R., *75n. 3*

Levi, Maurice, *383n. 10*

Lewis, J. P., *344n. 6*

lichens, 193

lions, 122, 126, 151

Livy (Titus Livius), *427nn. 5, 6*

Lucas, R. E., 380

Luce, R. Duncan, *441n. 5*

lying and genetic survival, 163–64

Macleod, H. D., *324n. 5, 339n. 22*

Maddison, Angus, *379n. 1*

Magaddino, Joseph P., *83n. 19*

Makin, John, *383n. 10*

Malthus, Thomas, 117

Marais, Jan, 116

marginal cost (MC), 12–14

marginal utility (MU), 14

Margulis, Lynn, *246n. 6*

markets: absence of, in nonhuman societies, 200–202, 262–63; buyer/seller relationship, 429, 434; and central planning, 197; cheating in, 429–37; supply and demand curves, 20, 21

market vs. government problem: externalities, 91–94; Pigou's example, 87–91; police services, 65–66; and the public good, 86–87; and redistribution, 86

marriage contract, 25–26; benefits, 31–35; costs, 28–31; efficient, 37–38. *See also* monogamy; spouse selection

Marshall, Samuel L. A., *425n. 1, 426n. 4*

Martin, J. David, *81n. 12*

Martinson, Robert, *74n. 2*

mate selection. *See* spouse selection

Maurice, S. Charles, *246n. 6*

maximization of utility, 16, 20

Maxwell, Donald, *83n. 19*

MC (marginal cost), 14

McConnell, Campbell R., *13–14n. 6*

McCune, G. M., *344n. 3*

McIntosh, Susan, *41n. 2*

Meltzer, Allan H., *371n. 10*

Mequire, P. G., 379, 381–82, 383, 384, 385, 386n. 17, 395–96

Michael, Robert T., *51nn. 15, 16, 52n. 17*

military: economic model of tactics, 405; free riding in, 409n. 1, 418–19, 420, 421–22, 424; individual as basic unit of, 405–7; motivation of individual combatants, 409–13; numerical superiority of forces, 421–22; prisoners' dilemma, 407–9, 425–28; as a public good, 92

Mises, Ludwig von, *8n. 4*

mole rats, 199–200, 236–40; reproduction, 236; social system in nests, 238–40; tunnels, 237–38; volcanoing, 237, 239

monetary policy: in ancient China, 339–42; fraudulent, 364; Mongol dynasty in China, 335; Sung dynasty in China, 329

money: as public good, 372; as store of value, 360–61; two roles of, 367. *See also* Chinese coins; currencies

money supply: government control over, 365–66; in Nationalist China, 1937–1947, 309; relation with inflation, 346–47; in South Korea, 1945–1954, 352

monogamy, 168–69

monopoly markets, 21

Morgenstern, Oskar, 438, 443–44, 445, 446

motives: for collective action, 415–16; of individuals in combat, 407–9

MU (marginal utility), 14

Mullineaux, Donald, *383n. 10*

murderers, 70, 71, 72

Murray, Hugh, *324n. 5*

Nationalist China: impact of inflation on currency, 316–17; monetary policy, 313–14; money supply and wholesale prices, 1937–1947, 309

naturalistic fallacy, 116

negative incentives, 417–19. *See also* punishment

negative income taxes, 135

negative poll taxes, 277–80

nepotism, 188–96, 245. *See also* altruism

nonhuman societies: absence of markets in, 200–202, 262; differences from human societies, 197–200; free riding in, 204–5; hereditary behavior, 181–96; wars, 239. *See also* animal societies; plant societies

nonhuman species, preferences, 250–54

OECD countries: in cross-national sample, 397; economic growth, 385–89, 395–96

older poor people, 301–3

Olsen, E. A., *275n. 1*

Olsen subsidy, 275–76

OPEC countries, 393–95

organic society theory, 264

organizations, non-government and non-private, 86

Overcast, H. Edwin, *429n. 1*

paper money: in ancient China, 321–25; Chinese government abandon-

ment of, 339–42; competition among forms of, 359. *See also* Chinese coins
parasitic species, 194–96, 204–5
Pascal, Blaise, 442, 443
pensions: children as, 40; taxation of, 296–97. *See also* Social Security System
pharmaceutical research example, 399
Phillips, Llad, *82n. 16, 83n. 19*
pigeons, 108–9
Pigou, Arthur, 88–91
plant societies, 192; cloning within, 187; territories, 119. *See also* lichens
Plott, Charles, 100, 101–2
police services, protection from crime, 65–68
poll taxes, 285–88; negative, 277–80; to raise government revenue, 284
pollution abatement: economic experiments, 101–2; optimum amount of, 88–89; prisoners' dilemma, 203
poor people, 301–3
population explosion: and fertility rates, 52–53; in lesser developed countries, 50
population growth: and economic growth in Africa, Americas, and Asia, 391; and economic growth in OECD countries, 386; effect on economic growth of United States, 390; and size of country, 395
preferences: of computers, 252–53; of married partners, 38; for more over less of something, 9; of nonhuman species, 250–54
prescription drugs. *See* pharmaceutical research example
Price, H. Douglas, *371n. 10*
price controls: in China, 318–19, 320, 339; Chin dynasty in China, 331; effect on barter, 318

price elasticity and rational behavior, 103
price equilibrium, speed of approach to, 99
price indices, 373–75
primates: conflict among, 164–65; territoriality, 165–66. *See also* chimpanzees
prisoners' dilemma, 202–3
prisoners' dilemma games, 429–37; played with changing partners, 430n. 3; with chosen partner, 431–32
prison system effectiveness, 60
private enterprise in South Korea, 355
privately produced money: in ancient China, 325–26; bank notes in ancient China, 339–42; on Mongol dynasty in China, 336–37
private property: animals vs. humans, 119–20; plants vs. humans, 119; in South Korea, 354–55. *See also* crimes against property
privatization, provision of public goods through, 399–402
proportional representation, 287
protozoa, 225–26
Pryor, Frederic L., *164n. 5*
public good, 86–87
public goods: household, 31–32; inefficiency in provision of, 92; military as, 92; money as, 372; provision of, through privatization, 399–402
public goods problem, 90
public housing subsidies, 275–76
public opinion about criminals, 77
punishment: as crime deterrent, 76, 77–83; of criminals, 76–77; effect of certainty vs. severity of, 80, 81; effect of severity of, 60. *See also* negative incentives; negative poll taxes

quotas vs. taxes, 101

Raiffa, Howard, *441n. 5*
Rapport, David J., *109nn. 24, 25,*
    110n. 26
rational behavior, 8–10; of criminals,
    58–60; experimental evidence in
    economics of, 95–102; by insane
    people, 102–5; of rats, 105–8
redistribution, 86
Reed, Ritchie H., *41n. 2*
regulation: of drug companies, 400,
    401; effectiveness, 101
Reid, D. B. W., *109n. 24*
reinforced majorities, 286–87
reproduction of species: ants, 189–91;
    bees, 189–91; hereditary behavior,
    187–96; social insects, 186–87,
    223; sponges, 242–44; termites,
    254–57. *See also* cloning; eusociality;
    gemmulation
reputation, 432–34, 435
research, theoretical and empirical,
    368. *See also* pharmaceutical research
    example
Reynolds, Morgan, *82n. 17*
rich people, defined, 11
risk: of being victim of crime, 63;
    of criminals being caught, 72
risk cost, 12
road building by ants, 220–21
Rockhill, W. W., *321n. 1*
Rodgers, James D., *138n. 8*
Romer, Paul M., 380
Rosen, R. R., *110n. 26*
Rosenthal, Robert, *430n. 3*
rotifers, 109–10
Russek, Frank, *383n. 13, 384n. 16*

Samet, D., 440, 441
Samuelson, Paul, 92, *115n. 1*
Sandmo, Agnar, *383n. 11*

saving: definition, 14; impact of Social
    Security on, 303–4; and taxes, 289
Schumpeter, Joseph, 160
Schwartz, B., *314n. 11*
Schwartz, Karlene V., *246n. 6*
scientific progress, 368
scientific research example, 399
sea gulls, 125
sexual behavior among humans, 168–
    69
Shaftsbury, Earl of, *146n. 8*
Sherman, Paul W., *236n. 1*
side payments, 416
Siegel, S., *99n. 5*
Sjoquist, David L., *83n. 19*
Skinner, B. F., 108
slaving ants, 195–96, 199, 219
slime molds, 144–45, 192, 246–49
Smith, Adam: discipline of continuous
    dealings, 429; on division of labor,
    209–10; view of human nature,
    181n. 1; *The Wealth of Nations*, 3n. 1,
    209, 220
Smith, Vernon, 95, *96n. 3, 97n. 4*, 99–
    100
snails, 108–9
Sober, Elliott, *159n. 2*
social group behavior, 8
social insects, 225; cells, compared
    with human cells, 265–66; haploidy
    theory of, 143–44; reproduction,
    186–87, 223; social organization,
    143–44; variable behavior, 125–26.
    See also ants; bees; termites
Social Security System, 290–95; cuts
    to, 296–99; deferment of payout
    age, 298; effect on saving, 303–4;
    effect on upper-income groups,
    296–97, 300–301; employer con-
    tribution, 294; older poor people
    with and without, 301–3; prob-
    lem of credibility, 295–96. *See also*

pensions; Supplemental Security Income (SSI)

societies: characteristics of, 174–76; definition, 173; general theory of, 145, 174, 175–79; of unrelated species, 174, 193–95. *See also* human societies; nonhuman societies

societies, primitive: of cells, 264–67; self-sacrifice within, 249; slime molds, 144–45, 192, 246–49. *See also* cellular animals; social insects

sociobiology, 115–17, 131–32; definition, 142; and economics, 133–38, 139–54; findings, 118–20; general theory, 143, 145; reason to practice, 254

Sociobiology (Wilson), 147

sociologists: contrasted with economists, 427–28; view of crime, 73–77

South America: countries in cross-national sample, 398; economic growth, 391–93, 396–97

South Korea: adjustment to continuous inflation, 343–49; bank loans with negative rates, 352–54; Combined Economic Board Agreement with U.N., 349, 352; compulsory sales of government bonds, 357; fiscal problems, 355–57; government, 354; ideological environment, 354–55; legal system, 355; money supply, 1945–1954, 352; nonbudgetary sources of revenue, 349–54; possible remedies for inflation, 358; private enterprise, 355; resale of foreign aid goods in, 351–52; United Nations developmental programs, 356

specialization. *See* division of labor

sponges, 192, 240–46; amoeboid cells, 241–42; colonies, 241; repro-

duction, 242–44; social organization, 144–45

spouse selection, 35–36

squirrels, 119–20

SSI (Supplemental Security Income), 299–300

Staples, Ernest L., *282n. 4*

Stern, N. H., 82

Stigler, George J., 287, 288

Stockman, Alan, *383n. 8*

strategies: military, 405–24; mixed, 442–45. *See also* games of strategy

subsidies: agricultural subsidies via foreign aid, 352; for housing, 275–76

Summers, Robert, *381n. 4*

Summers-Heston data, 381, 395

superorganisms, 130

Supplemental Security Income (SSI), 299–300

supply and demand, 19–22. *See also* demand; markets; supply curves

supply curves, 13–14

surrogate mothers, 54

symbiosis, 193

Tamagna, F. M., *309n. 5, 315n. 12*

Tarr, David G., *105n. 15*

Tax, Sol, *147n. 9*

taxes: earmarked, 291; on pensions, 296–97; on people opting out of Social Security, 297; for police services, 66–67; vs. quotas, 101; relation with savings, 289. *See also* income tax in United States; poll taxes; use taxes

taxes on voting. *See* poll taxes

tenure, 111

termites, 225–31; colonies, 229; differences from ants, 226–28, 229–30; division of labor, 230–31, 256–57; environmental coordination, 256; information transfer among,

termites (*continued*)
257; nests, 228–29; preferences,
250–52, 253; reaction to attacks,
254; reproduction, 254–57; responses to environmental factors,
129–31; similarities with ant social
structure, 230–31; social organization, 126–28; swarming, 222–23;
symbiosis with other species, 193.
See also ants; bees
territories: defense of, 120–23; economic model of, 155–58; of insects,
120; migrating, 126; of plants and
animals, 119; shape of, 157; territoriality among species, 165–66
Tittle, Charles R., *81n. 14*
Tobin-Mundell hypotheses, 382–83,
387
Tollison, Robert D., *412n. 4*
trade in nonhuman societies, 262
tribal societies, 166, 167–68
Tullock, Gordon: "Altruism, Malice,
and Public Goods," *115n. 1, 134n. 4,
145n. 6*; "Altruism, Malice, and
Public Goods: A Reply to Frech,"
115n. 1, 145n. 6; "Altruism, Malice,
and Public Goods: Does Altruism
Pay?" *145n. 6*; "Another Part of the
Swamp," *440n. 2*; articles on biology, 141n. 2; "Biological Externalities," *115n. 1, 133n. 1; The Calculus
of Consent*, 287, 291n. 3; career,
307n. 1; "The Coal Tit as a Careful
Shopper," *108n. 21, 115n. 1, 133n.
1*; "Comment on 'The Physiological
Causes of the Evolution of Man
from Apes,'" *115n. 1*; "Competing
Monies," *367n. 2; Coordination without Command, 130n. 8, 145n. 7*; "A
Different Approach to the Repeated
Prisoner's Dilemma," *429n. 1*;
"Economics of Primitive Societies,"
189n. 8; "An Economic Theory of

Military Tactics," *425n. 2*; "Hyperinflation in China, 1937–49,"
347n. 11; "Inflazione Prolongata,"
365n. 6, 369n. 5; model of competing currencies, 360; "On the Adaptive Significance of Territoriality,"
115n. 1, 155n. 2; "Optimal Poll
Taxes," *285nn. 1–3; The Organization of Inquiry, 111n. 1*; "Paper
Money—A Cycle in Cathay,"
365n. 6, 369n. 5; "Switching in
General Predators," *109n. 23,
115n. 1, 133n. 1; Toward a Theory
of the Rent-Seeking Society, 412n. 4;
Trials on Trial, 412n. 4*; "The Welfare
Costs of Tariffs, Monopolies, and
Theft," *79n. 9*
Turkey, economic growth, 389
Turner, J. D., *109n. 24*

United Kingdom, economic growth,
389
United Nations: developmental programs in South Korea, 356; misunderstanding of South Korean
fiscal system, 352
United States, economic growth, 389–
91
U.S. foreign policy toward South
Korea, 343, 349, 351
use taxes, 291
utility: marginal, 14; maximization of,
16, 20

Van Lawick–Goodall, Jane. *See*
Goodall, Jane
violent crime, 68, 69, 70, 71, 72
Vissering, W., *326n. 11, 337n. 19,
341n. 26*
von Neumann, John, 438, 443–44,
445, 446
Votey, Harold L., Jr., *82n. 16, 83n. 19*
voting: actual size of total vote, 287–

88; compulsory, 277–80, 285–88; costs and benefits, 280–81; easing restrictions on, 281–83; reinforced majority, 286–87. *See also* negative poll taxes

wage-price controls, 67
war: in animal societies, 164, 208–9, 239; relevance of game theory to, 446. *See also* conflict
wasps. *See* bees
Wealth of Nations, The (Smith), 3n. 1, 209, 220
Weaver, Carolyn, *301n. 10*
Westoff, Leslie and Charles, *44n. 5*
white corpuscles, 129, 264
wholesale prices in Nationalist China, 1937–1947, 309
Williams, G. C., *188n. 7*

Wilson, David Sloan, *159n. 2*
Wilson, Edward O., *133n. 3, 191n. 10, 207nn. 1–3, 246nn. 5, 6*; on ants, 128–29; area of ignorance, 143; on conflict among animals, 122; impact on sociobiology, 175n. 5; on male dominance, 116; *Sociobiology*, 147
Winch, R. F., *35n. 6*
Winkler, R. C., *104n. 14*
wolves, 122, 124, 125
women, discrimination against, 34
wood ants. *See* ants
Worden, W. L., *344n. 6, 352n. 17*

Yamauchi, K., *208n. 4*
Yang, Lien-sheng, *324n. 6*
Yule, Henry, *321n. 1*

zero-sum games, 438–40

TITLES OF WORKS INCLUDED IN THE SERIES

"Adam Smith and the Prisoners' Dilemma," **10**:429
"Administrative Transfers," **7**:319
"Agreement and Cheating," **8**:334
"Aid in Kind," **7**:133
"Another Part of the Swamp," **5**:93
"Approach to Empirical Measures of Voting Paradoxes, An" (John L. Dobra and
    Gordon Tullock), **4**:297
"Are Rents Fully Dissipated?" **5**:236
"Avoiding the Voter's Paradox Democratically: Comment," **4**:295

"Back to the Bog," **5**:88
"Bargaining," **4**:86
"Becoming a Dictator," **8**:63
"Biological Applications of Economics," **1**:553
"Biological Externalities," **1**:541
"Bismarckism," **10**:289
"Bouquet of Governments, A," **4**:401
"Bouquet of Voting Methods, A," **4**:437

Calculus of Consent: Logical Foundations of Constitutional Democracy, The (James M.
    Buchanan and Gordon Tullock), **2**
Case Against the Common Law, The, **9**:397
"Casual Recollections of an Editor," **1**:36
"Charitable Gifts," **7**:89
"Charity of the Uncharitable, The," **1**:262
"Child Production" (Richard B. McKenzie and Gordon Tullock), **10**:39
"Coalitions under Demand Revealing" (T. Nicolaus Tideman and Gordon
    Tullock), **4**:366
"Coal Tit as a Careful Shopper, The," **1**:537
"Competing for Aid," **1**:199
"Competing Monies," **10**:359
"Competing Monies: A Reply," **10**:367
"Computer Simulation of a Small Voting System" (Gordon Tullock and Colin D.
    Campbell), **4**:283
"Cooperative State, The," **8**:13
"Corruption and Anarchy," **1**:323

"Cost of Transfers, The," **1**:180
"Costs of a Legal System, The" (Warren F. Schwartz and Gordon Tullock), **1**:456
"Costs of Government, The," **4**:114
"Costs of Rent Seeking: A Metaphysical Problem, The," **5**:203
"Coup d'Etat: Structural Factors," **8**:261
"Coups and Their Prevention," **8**:292
"Court Errors," **1**:495

"'Dead Hand' of Monopoly, The" (James M. Buchanan and Gordon Tullock), **9**:241
"Defending the Napoleonic Code over the Common Law," **9**:339
"Demand Revealing, Transfers, and Rent Seeking," **7**:142
"Demand-Revealing Process, Coalitions, and Public Goods," **1**:164
"Demand-Revealing Process as a Welfare Indicator, The," **1**:149
"Democracy and Despotism," **8**:107
"Democracy as It Really Is," **4**:395
"Does Punishment Deter Crime?" **9**:252
"Duncan Black: The Founding Father, 23 May 1908–14 January 1991," **4**:301
"Dynamic Hypothesis on Bureaucracy," **1**:297

"Economic Analysis of Political Choice, An," **4**:3
"Economic Approach to Crime, An," **1**:441
"Economic Approach to Human Behavior, The" (Richard B. McKenzie and Gordon Tullock), **10**:3
"Economic Aspects of Crime, The" (Richard B. McKenzie and Gordon Tullock), **10**:56
Economic Hierarchies, Organization and the Structure of Production, **6**:239
"Economic Imperialism," **1**:3
"Economics and Sociobiology: A Comment," **10**:133
"Economics of Lying, The," **4**:259
Economics of Nonhuman Societies, The, **10**:171
"Economics of Repression, The," **8**:186
"Economics of (Very) Primitive Societies, The," **1**:558
"Economic Theory of Military Tactics: Methodological Individualism at War, An" (Geoffrey Brennan and Gordon Tullock), **10**:405
"Economic versus the Sociological Views of Crime, The" (Richard B. McKenzie and Gordon Tullock), **10**:73
"Edge of the Jungle, The," **1**:309
"Education and Medicine," **7**:294
"Efficiency in Log-rolling," **4**:346
"Efficient Rent Seeking," **1**:222

"Efficient Rent Seeking, Diseconomies of Scale, Public Goods, and Morality,"
     5:231
"Efficient Rent-Seeking Revisited," **5**:85
"Empirical Analysis of Cross-National Economic Growth, 1951–80, An"
     (Kevin B. Grier and Gordon Tullock), **10**:379
"Entry Barriers in Politics," **1**:69
"Epilogue—The Grating People," **7**:149
"Epilogue to *The Social Dilemma: The Economics of War and Revolution*," **8**:368
"Evolution and Human Behavior," **10**:159
"Exchanges and Contracts," **5**:261
"Excise Taxation in the Rent-Seeking Society," **5**:196
"Expanding Public Sector: Wagner Squared, The" (James M. Buchanan and
     Gordon Tullock), **1**:302
"Exploitive State, The," **8**:22
"Externalities and All That," **4**:97

"Federalism: Problems of Scale," **1**:78
"Future Directions for Rent-Seeking Research," **5**:295

"Games and Preference," **10**:438
"General Irrelevance of the General Impossibility Theorem, The," **1**:90
"General Welfare or Welfare for the Poor Only," **7**:245
"Giving Life," **7**:339

"Hawks, Doves, and Free Riders," **1**:427
"Helping the Poor," **7**:11
"Helping the Poor vs. Helping the Well-Organized," **7**:171
"Horizontal Transfers," **7**:179
"Hotelling and Downs in Two Dimensions," **4**:305
"How to Do Well While Doing Good!" **1**:589
"Hyperinflation in China, 1937–49" (Colin D. Campbell and Gordon Tullock),
     10:307

"Income Redistribution," **7**:3
"Industrial Organization and Rent Seeking in Dictatorships," **5**:122
"Information and Logrolling," **7**:198
"Information without Profit," **1**:394
"Inheritance Justified," **1**:247
"Inheritance Rejustified," **1**:258
"International Conflict: Two Parties," **8**:311
"Introduction to Gordon Tullock's *Autocracy*," **8**:33

"Irrationality of Intransitivity, The," **1**:62
"Is There a Paradox of Voting?" **1**:124

"Jackson and the Prisoner's Dilemma," **10**:425
"Judicial Errors and a Proposal for Reform" (I. J. Good and Gordon Tullock),
 1:484
"Juries," **1**:521

"Legal Heresy: Presidential Address to the Western Economic Association Annual
 Meeting—1995," **1**:509
"Legitimacy and Ethics," **8**:225
"Local Redistribution," **7**:117
Logic of the Law, The, **9**:3

"Machiavellians and the Well-Intentioned, The," **7**:155
"Marriage, Divorce, and the Family" (Richard B. McKenzie and Gordon Tullock),
 10:25
"Measure of the Importance of Cyclical Majorities, A" (Colin D. Campbell and
 Gordon Tullock), **4**:275
"Mixed Case, The," **7**:217
"Monarchies, Hereditary and Nonhereditary," **8**:141
"More Complicated Log-rolling," **4**:331
"More on the Welfare Costs of Transfers," **1**:194
"More Thought about Demand Revealing," **4**:373
"Mosquito Abatement," **4**:49
"Motivation of Judges, The," **9**:324

"Negligence Again," **9**:364
"New and Superior Process for Making Social Choices, A" (T. Nicolaus Tideman
 and Gordon Tullock), **1**:133

"Objectives of Income Redistribution," **7**:71
"Old Age Pensions," **7**:263
"On the Efficient Organization of Trials," **1**:465
"On the Efficient Organization of Trials: Reply to McChesney, and Ordover and
 Weitzman," **1**:480
"Optimal Poll Taxes," **10**:277
"Optimal Poll Taxes: Further Aspects," **10**:285
"Optimal Procedure," **9**:274
Organization of Inquiry, The, **3**
"Origins of Public Choice," **4**:11

"Paper Money—A Cycle in Cathay," **10**:321
"Paradox of Not Voting for Oneself, The," **4**:293
"Paradox of Revolution, The" (1971), **1**:329
"Paradox of Revolution, The" (1974), **8**:174
"Paradox of Voting—A Possible Method of Calculation, The," **4**:280
"(Partial) Rehabilitation of the Public Interest Theory, A," **1**:577
"People Are People: The Elements of Public Choice," **4**:32
"Political Ignorance," **4**:225
Politics of Bureaucracy, The, **6**:1
"Politics of Persuasion, The," **4**:241
"Polluters' Profits and Political Response: Direct Controls versus Taxes (James M.
        Buchanan and Gordon Tullock)," **1**:412
"Polluters' Profits and Political Response: Direct Controls versus Taxes: Reply"
        (James M. Buchanan and Gordon Tullock), **1**:425
"'Popular' Risings," **8**:201
"Problem of Succession, The," **8**:82
"Problems of Majority Voting," **1**:51
"Property, Contract, and the State," **4**:68
"Proportional Representation," **4**:381
"Provision of Public Goods through Privatization," **10**:399
"Public and Private Interaction under Reciprocal Externality" (James M.
        Buchanan and Gordon Tullock), **1**:349
"Public Choice," **1**:16
"Public Choice: What I Hope for the Next Twenty-five Years," **1**:27
"Public Decisions as Public Goods," **1**:388

"Rationality and Revolution," **1**:341
"Rationality in Human and Nonhuman Societies (Gordon Tullock and Richard B.
        McKenzie)
"Reasons for Redistribution [1983]," **7**:23
"Reasons for Redistribution [1986]," **7**:42
"Remedies," **4**:137
"Rents, Ignorance, and Ideology," **5**:214
"Rents and Rent-Seeking," **5**:148
"Rent Seeking" (1987), **1**:237
"Rent Seeking" (1993), **5**:11
"Rent Seeking: The Problem of Definition," **5**:3
"Rent Seeking and Tax Reform," **5**:171
"Rent-Seeking and the Law," **5**:184
"Rent Seeking as a Negative-Sum Game," **5**:103
"Revolution and Welfare Economics," **8**:163

"Rhetoric and Reality of Redistribution, The," **1**:276
"Risk, Charity, and Miscellaneous Aspects of Social Security," **7**:278
"Roots of Conflict, The," **8**:3

"Science Fiction and the Debt," **10**:271
"Simple Algebraic Logrolling Model, A," **4**:319
"Social Cost and Government Action," **1**:378
"Social Costs of Reducing Social Cost, The," **4**:156
"Sociobiology" (Gordon Tullock and Richard B. McKenzie), **10**:115
"Sociobiology and Economics," **10**:139
"Some Further Thoughts on Voting," **4**:270
"Some Limitations of Demand-Revealing Processes: Comment" (T. Nicolaus
    Tideman and Gordon Tullock), **4**:361
"Some Little-Understood Aspects of Korea's Monetary and Fiscal Systems"
    (Colin D. Campbell and Gordon Tullock), **10**:343
"Still Somewhat Muddy: A Comment," **5**:95
"Subsidized Housing in a Competitive Market: Comment," **10**:275

"Technology: The Anglo-Saxons versus the Rest of the World," **9**:291
"Territorial Boundaries: An Economic View," **10**:155
"Theory of the Coup, The," **8**:273
"Thoughts about Representative Government," **4**:413
"Three or More Countries and the Balance of Power," **8**:354
"Transitional Gains and Transfers," **5**:136
"Transitional Gains Trap, The," **1**:212
"Two Kinds of Legal Efficiency," **9**:263

"Universities Should Discriminate against Assistant Professors," **10**:111
"Uses of Dictatorship, The," **8**:48

"Various Ways of Dealing with the Cost of Litigation," **9**:309
Vote Motive: An Essay in the Economics of Politics, The, **4**:167
"Voting, Different Methods and General Considerations," **4**:427

"Welfare and the Law," **9**:380
"Welfare Costs of Tariffs, Monopolies, and Theft, The," **1**:169
"What to Do—What to Do," **7**:355
"When Is Inflation Not Inflation?" **10**:373
"Where Is the Rectangle?" **5**:241
"Which Rectangle?" **5**:253
"Why Did the Industrial Revolution Occur in England?" **5**:160
"Why Government" (Gordon Tullock and Richard B. McKenzie), **10**:85
"Why So Much Stability," **1**:105

CUMULATIVE INDEX

References to bibliographic information appear in italics.

AAA (Agricultural Adjustment Act),
   5:212
AAA (American Automobile Association), **5**:50; **7**:213
ABA (American Bar Association), **5**:51
Abelson, Philip H., **3**:*37n. 9*
Abraham, Henry J., **8**:*85n. 6*
Abramowitz, Moses, **10**:382
abstractions, **10**:5–6
abstracts, **3**:81
academia
   division of labor in, **10**:368
   efficiency in, **10**:111
   as example of environmental coordi-
      nation, **6**:337–38
   social mobility in, **6**:21–23
   See also higher education institutions
academic disciplines
   cross-disciplinary training and re-
      search, **3**:64, 70–71, 179
   definitions of, **3**:81
   framework for promoting coopera-
      tion among, **1**:7–10
   law school, **9**:179–80
   overlapping of economics and biol-
      ogy, **1**:555–57
   spread of economics among, **1**:3–7
   that study ethics, **9**:9
   See also interdisciplinarity; public
      choice theory; scientific fields;
      social sciences
academic freedom, **3**:175–76
academic journals
   classification of, **3**:68, 69–70
   economics journals, **1**:589
   edited by Tullock, **1**:36, 42
   motives of editors of, **5**:20–21

printed comments on papers in,
   1:41–42
publication in, **1**:598–601
with public choice articles, **4**:16–17
referees **1**:39–41; **5**:21
See also economics journals; scientific
   journals
academic research
   cooperative interdisciplinary,
      1:555–56
   impact of government funding on,
      1:208
   money allocation for, **1**:37–38
   See also cross-disciplinary training
      and research
academic researchers in science
   fellowships for, **3**:177–78
   impact of grant proposals on careers,
      3:177
   induced research by, **3**:30
   pressures on, **3**:47
   tenure, **3**:171, 172–77
   See also interdisciplinary scientists
academics
   characteristics of successful,
      6:21–23
   discrimination against, **10**:111–12
   educational freedom, **9**:124
   motives, **4**:39
   political advocacy by, **4**:251–52
   promotion and tenure, **6**:122–23,
      220n. 3
   self-interest, **4**:173–74; **7**:280, 281
   tenure, **6**:122–23, 220n. 3; **9**:394–
      95; **10**:111
   See also higher education institutions;
      intellectuals

accessibility for handicapped persons, **7**:211

accidental injury
  choice of court to deal with, **9**:122–23
  compensation, **9**:118–22
  insurance, **9**:378
  laws, **9**:111
  liability, **9**:117–18
  to self vs. others, **9**:116–18
  See also automobile injury; personal injury

accident prevention, **9**:112–16
  costs, **9**:366–74, 388–90

accidents
  categories, **9**:376
  costs, **9**:370–79, 388–90
  definition, **9**:98, 121
  fault, **9**:101
  risk aversion and, **9**:31
  risk of, **9**:111
  two problems raised by, **9**:117
  where both parties negligent, **9**:369–70
  See also negligence–contributory negligence rule

accidents in scientific research, **3**:123–24, 125–26
  discoveries from, **3**:86–87

accounting as supervision technique, **6**:210–16, 227
  in corporations, **6**:358–59
  in government agencies, **6**:362–64
  limitations to, **6**:289, 300
  pseudo-accounting systems, **6**:217
  Russian government's difficulties with, **6**:335
  in U.S. federal government, **6**:281
  See also corporate auditing

accuracy of scientific research, **3**:5
  impact of discussion on, **3**:129
  impact of social environment of science on, **3**:107–11
  use of approximation in applied research, **3**:42
  See also faking of research results; "truth" of scientific theories

accusatory system of law. *See* adversary system of law

Ace Hardware, organizational structure, **6**:254

Acheson, Dean, **6**:122–23

Acton, Lord, **2**:253; **8**:36

Adam, G. Mercer, **8**:*112n. 11, 118nn. 32, 35, 133n. 84, 137–38n. 97*

Adams, J. B., **3**:*135n. 1, 169n. 8*

administrative hypocrisy, **6**:193–94

administrative theory, **6**:4–6

administrative transfers, **7**:366–68.
  See also horizontal transfers; transfers within middle class

administrators. *See* managers

adversary system of law
  arguments in favor of, **9**:301–2
  compared with inquisitorial system, **1**:465–66, 473–79, 510; **5**:186, 188–89; **9**:85–96, 291–95, 303–8, 344, 351–56
  disadvantage, **1**:482
  erroneous interpretations under, **5**:192–93
  inferiority to Napoleonic legal system, **9**:339, 363
  inquisitorial aspects, **9**:311–13, 319
  judges and juries in, **1**:477–78
  relative inefficiency, **1**:475
  rent seeking in, **9**:422
  use of judges and juries, **9**:80–85
  weaknesses, **9**:430
  where resources are expended in, **9**:299–301
  See also inquisitorial system of law

adverse selection (insurance term), **7**:105–6

advertising
  calculating effective, **5**:299

lying in, **4**:266
political, **4**:248
rent seeking and, **5**:171–72
restrictions on, **5**:4–6
that defrauds, **9**:208–10
advisory boards, **6**:225
AEC (Atomic Energy Commission),
    4:158–59; **6**:329
Africa
  countries in cross-national sample,
    10:397–98
  economic growth, **10**:391–92,
    396–97
African one-party states, **8**:111
Agassi, J., **3**:*34n. 3, 38n. 12*
agenda control, **4**:435–36
aggregate preferences
  Arrow's impossibility theorem,
    1:90, 104
  optima, **1**:101–4
  problems of aggregating, **1**:73
agreement equilibrium, **1**:199
agreements
  cheating on, **10**:148
  cost of reaching, **4**:6
  costs of, **2**:94
  as criterion for improvement, **2**:6–7
  See also bargaining; cartels; treaties
Agricultural Adjustment Act (AAA),
    5:212
agricultural ants, **10**:219, 224
agricultural economics, **1**:556
agricultural inventions, **3**:20
agricultural subsidies
  allocative costs of, **5**:236–37
  Chicago doctrine on, **5**:301–6
  demand-revealing example,
    7:142–45
  direct cash payments vs., **5**:222
  effects of, **7**:326–29
  elimination of, **4**:353–54
  externalities, **4**:338
  via foreign aid, **10**:352

"iron triangle," as examples of, **5**:58
land use restrictions and, **5**:219
logrolling and, **4**:396–97
motives for, **7**:29
national vs. local, **7**:127
as a public good, **1**:583
public good and, **7**:319–20
as rent seeking, **5**:29
tobacco taxes and, **5**:198
as transfers, **1**:269
transitional gains from, **1**:218
types of foods subsidized, **7**:173
See also farm lobbies
Ahlbrandt, Roger, **4**:*204n. 28*
Ahrens, E. H., Jr., **3**:*74n. 24*
aid. *See* charitable giving; foreign-aid
    programs; in-kind aid; transfers
Aiken, Henry D., **2**:300n. 6
aircraft industry lobbying, **5**:306
airline flight insurance, **9**:112–16
airline industry, **7**:324–26
airline industry cartel, **1**:589–90
Alaska oil revenues, **5**:136–38, 139,
    140, 141–42, 145
Albanian government, **8**:213
Alchian, Armen A., **1**:553; **3**:*173n. 11*;
    6:*273n. 12*, 274; **7**:112–13;
    10:*13n. 6, 374n. 1*
Alchian-Demsetz transactions costs
    theory, **6**:245
alcoholic beverage taxes, **5**:196
Alexander, Richard D., **10**:*236n. 1*
Alexander the Great, **7**:179
Alexandrian science, **3**:84
Alfven, H., **3**:*178n. 16*
Algerians in France, **7**:82, 83
Ali, Abdiweli M., **8**:*152n. 17*
Allee, W. C., **3**:*110n. 11*
Allen, Ernest M., **3**:*166n. 5*
Allen, Richard C., **8**:*86n. 10*
Allen, William R., **10**:*13n. 6*
allies, **6**:54–56
  within corporations, **6**:287, 311

allies (*continued*)
    definition, **6**:54
    superior and inferior vs. equal, **6**:56
allocation of resources. *See* resource
    allocation
Allyon, T., **10**:*104nn. 12, 13*
Althusius, Johannes, **2**:238, 302
altruism
    in animal societies, **10**:145–47
    Becker's view, **10**:133–38
    degree of, **1**:337, 342, 345
    evolution of self-sacrificing behavior,
        10:159–61
    family and, **8**:240
    genetic theory of self-sacrifice,
        10:160–69
    in larger groups, **8**:241–42
    of social insects, **10**:130–31
    See also nepotism; self-sacrifice
amateur scientists, **3**:178, 184
American Automobile Association
    (AAA), **5**:50; **7**:213
American Bar Association (ABA), **5**:51
American Economic Review, **5**:19, 24, 25
American Public Choice Society, **4**:16
    academic backgrounds of members,
        4:171
    presidents, **4**:14n. 4, 19–20
American Revolution, **8**:208–9, 295
Americas
    countries in cross-national sample,
        10:398
    economic growth, **10**:391–92,
        396–97
    OPEC countries in, **10**:395
Ames, Richard, **9**:433
amnesty, **8**:288
Amos, Orely M., Jr., **7**:*26n. 5*
anarchists, **9**:189, 232–33
anarchy, **1**:324–25
    despotism vs., **4**:82
Anderson, Gary, **5**:*218nn. 11, 12,*
        221n. 15, 226n. 24
Anderson, P. W., **3**:*129n. 31*

anger, rationality of, **1**:310–11
Anglo-Saxon legal procedure. *See*
    adversary system of law;
    common law
animals
    dominance behavior, **1**:309, 310–
        11, 313, 557
    rational behavior, **10**:96
    social activities, **1**:557
    studies about rational behavior of,
        10:105–10
    variable behavior, **10**:125–26
    welfare of, **1**:428–29, 548
    See also cellular animals; societies,
        primitive
animal societies
    conflict in, **10**:121–23
    contrasted with human societies,
        10:115–17, 142–54
    dominance in, **10**:116, 123–24
    lessons for human society,
        10:124–25
    See also human societies; plant socie-
        ties; societies, primitive
annuities, **1**:253n. 6, 255n. 8
anthropology, **3**:81
    reason for rapid advance of, **3**:148
anthropomorphizing, **10**:184
antitrust cases, **9**:318
antitrust policies, **1**:178
Antonov-Ovseyenko, Anton, **8**:*127–*
        28n. 71
ants
    beetles and, **10**:194–95
    civil wars among, **10**:208–9
    difference from human beings,
        6:328
    difference from termites, **10**:226–
        28, 229–30
    division of labor, **10**:209, 216–24
    economic theory about, **6**:327–28
    food supply, **10**:206–7, 209, 216–
        18
    free riding, **10**:218–19

hives, **10**:207–8
learned skills, **10**:210–15
life cycles, **10**:206–7
reproduction, **10**:189–91
social life, **10**:215–16
social organization, **10**:128–29,
143–44
trade by, **6**:334n. 14
See also agricultural ants; army ants;
bees; slaving ants; termites
ant societies, **1**:558, 560, 571
similarities with termite societies,
10:230–31
apartheid, **1**:278
apartment house governance, **4**:141
appearance vs. reality, **3**:33–35, 49.
See also recognizing human
individuals
appellate courts
appeals process in, **9**:181–84,
185–86
basis for appeals to, **9**:180
errors by, **9**:55–56
judges' motives, **9**:417–18
process, **6**:395, 397
applied research, **3**:10
deductive reasoning in, **3**:89–90
difference from pure research,
3:62–63
dissemination of results from,
3:112–15
distribution of rewards and costs,
3:17
as an economic investment, **3**:16–17
funding, **3**:15
importance to pure research, **3**:11–
12, 150–51
in industrial laboratories, **3**:22–23
inferiority to pure research, **3**:10–
12, 14–15
interrelationship with pure research,
3:43
marginal productivity of effort in,
3:15–16

prizes for, **3**:167–68
role of patents in promoting,
3:18–21
in the social sciences, **3**:150–51
use of teamwork vs. literature searching for, **3**:79
See also induced research; inventions; laboratories; scientific
discoveries
applied science journals, **3**:121
applied scientists
cheating by, **3**:109–10
comparative disadvantage of, **3**:26
effect on scientific communities,
3:131
malingering by, **3**:21
self-education, **3**:75
unity sought by, **3**:63
use of approximation, **3**:42
applied social science research
application of new ideas from,
3:154–55
beginnings, **3**:151n. 24
lack of, **3**:150–51
appropriations. *See* funding
approval voting, **4**:441–42
approximation, use in applied research,
3:42
Aquinas, St. Thomas, **8**:*256n. 53*
Arab countries, oil revenues, **5**:137,
138, 139, 140, 141, 142
Arab governments, logrolling, **4**:342
arbitration, **9**:304–8, 454–55
commercial, **9**:353
contracts, **9**:82
international, **9**:56
of litigation, **1**:480–81, 520
arbitrators
accuracy, **9**:332
bias on part of, **9**:332–36
choosing, **9**:337–38
compensation for, **9**:336–37
motives, **9**:324, 327, 338
role, **9**:73

Arcelus, Francisco, **10**:*371n. 10*
archaeology as a science, **3**:49, 53
Ardrey, Robert, **1**:*310n. 1*; **8**:*236n. 19*
Arendt, Hannah, **2**:*106–7n. 4*
Argentinian government, **5**:128, 129;
    8:124
arguments in higher education,
    3:175–76
  in the sciences, **3**:129–31
  in the social sciences, **3**:157–58
aristocratic coalitions, **1**:111
Aristotelian theory of overthrow of
    democracy, **8**:127–28
Aristotle, **4**:33
  theory of politics, **4**:122
Arizona, government in, **6**:368
Armed Services Committee, **5**:158
Armey, Richard, **1**:125n. 2
armies. *See* military
arms industry, **6**:253. *See also* weapons
    development
arms race, **1**:469; **8**:318, 321–23
  alliances between countries and,
    8:359
Armstrong, Edward, **8**:*102n. 59*
Armstrong, John A., **8**:*109–10n. 6*
Armstrong, W. E., **1**:*66n. 11*
army ants, **10**:224
Arnold, Thurmond, **7**:*280n. 6*
Arrow, Kenneth J., **1**:102n. 18, *391n.*
    4; **2**:8, *31n. 1*; **7**:*32n. 18*
  influence of Duncan Black on,
    4:301
  politics, **4**:18
  relation with Public Choice field,
    4:14
  Social Choice and Individual Values,
    1:90, 91, 103, 104, 124–25;
    3:154; **4**:275–76, 283
  "Tullock and an Existence Theorem,"
    4:*320n. 3*
  on voting, **1**:391–92
  See also impossibility theorem

Arrow's paradox of voting, as applied
    to dictatorships, **5**:131–32
art experts, **3**:97
artificial intelligence, **3**:94n. 7
Ashby, W. Ross, **3**:*41n. 15*
Ashley, Maurice, **8**:*42nn. 44, 46, 43n.*
    47, 205n. 20
Ashton, T. S., **8**:*135n. 90*
Asia
  countries in cross-national sample,
    10:398
  economic growth, **10**:391–92,
    396–97
  OPEC countries in, **10**:395
Asian countries, buying of government
    jobs in, **5**:111
assessors (legal), **9**:345, 352
Association of Trial Lawyers of
    America, **9**:431
assumption of transitivity. *See*
    transitivity
astronomy, practical importance of
    research in, **3**:13
asymmetric contract, **9**:65
Athenian Empire, **6**:350
Athenian government, **8**:39, 144
Athenian juries, **1**:521–22
atomic energy
  debate over, **3**:108
  history of the bomb, **3**:162
Atomic Energy Commission (AEC),
    4:158–59; **6**:329
attorneys. *See* lawyers
Aubyn, Giles St., **8**:*42nn. 40, 41,*
    250nn. 38, 39, 40, 253n. 47
auditing. *See* corporate auditing
Audubon Foundation, **7**:210, 212
Auster, R. D., **1**:*213n. 4*
Austin, C. J., **3**:*86n. 29*
Australian economic growth, **10**:389
Austrian school of economics, **9**:204
autocracy
  assuming power in, **8**:144–45

definition, **8**:33–35
dominant form of, **8**:41
hereditary succession in, **8**:90–92,
99–101
maintaining power, **8**:146–49
"stationary bandit" model, **8**:154
types of popular overthrow of,
8:217–19
See also dictatorships; limited autocracy; monarchies
Autocracy (Tullock), **5**:132n. 11
automobile accident costs, **1**:444–47;
9:142–43
automobile design, social costs of,
4:158
automobile injury, **9**:117–18. *See also*
motor vehicle offenses
automobile insurance, **9**:377
reform, **9**:98–100
automobile manufacturers, **5**:247
competition among, **5**:241–42
import restrictions on foreign,
5:228, 263; **7**:18–19
new automobile development,
5:282
organizational structures, **6**:215–16
shifting of research and development
to suppliers, **6**:414
See also gasoline price controls;
General Motors
"Avoiding Difficult Decisions"
(Tullock), **7**:97n. 10
"Avoiding the Voter's Paradox Democratically" (Davis), comment by
Tullock, **4**:295–96
awards for scientific discoveries.
See prizes for scientific
discoveries
Azrin, N. H., **10**:*104nn. 12, 13*

Baden, J., **1**:*555n. 5*
Baer, Gabriel, **8**:*102n. 60*
bail, **9**:174–75

Bailey, Martin, **9**:13; **10**:*362n. 2,*
364n. 4
Bain, Joe S., **1**:*71n. 2*
Baird, Charles W., **1**:425
Baker, John R., **3**:*67n. 14*
Bakhash, Shaul, **8**:*59nn. 24, 25*
Balageur, G., **1**:*23n. 8*
Balaguer, Joaquín, **8**:70
balance of power among countries,
8:354–57, 364
with nuclear capacity, **8**:361–67
balance of power in U.S. government.
See checks and balances in U.S.
government
Baldwin, John, **1**:*511n. 3, 528n. 4*;
9:*347n. 20, 350n. 30, 444n. 8*
"band of brothers" in British civil service, **6**:404
Banfield, Edward C., **6**:*347n. 13*
banking industry, **4**:245
deregulation, **5**:310
regulation, **1**:590
in South Korea, **10**:352–53
See also currencies
bankruptcy
as cost for efficient economy, **5**:107
demand-revealing process and,
4:363–64
due to government decisions,
4:362–63
bankruptcy laws, **9**:53–54
banks. *See* banking industry
Barber, Bernard, **3**:*122n. 21*
bar examinations, **9**:421
bargaining, **10**:446
activities involved in, **8**:4–5
asymmetrical information in, **9**:391
bargaining power of poor people,
7:17
conflict and cooperation within, **8**:8
efficiency and, **2**:104
between employees, **6**:380
externalities during, **4**:86–91

bargaining (*continued*)
impact of courts on, **9**:447
impact of lying on, **4**:99
loss of temper while, **1**:311–12
lying while, **9**:396
markets and, **2**:99–100
model, **2**:96–99
modern theory of, **4**:*323n. 5*
as negative sum game, **1**:184
in pretrial settlements, **1**:503–4
range, **2**:94–96
to reduce externalities, **4**:79–81
without transactions costs, **9**:381
transactions costs from, **9**:396
unanimity rule and, **2**:65–67, 103
uncertainty and, **2**:*36n. 4*
wealth maximization and, **9**:396
welfare costs, **1**:180–85
See also agreements; contracts; labor
unions; logrolling; political
negotiation
bargaining costs
as basis for existence of government,
4:81–82
curve, **4**:7–8
demand revealing and, **1**:152–53
government-created externalities
and, **5**:269–70
importance in government action,
4:96
need for study, **4**:6
use of government to lower,
4:37–38
bargain theory of contracts, **9**:408
Barland, Gordon, **9**:*361n. 50*
Barnes, D. W., **9**:*446n. 13, 447n. 16,*
448n. 19
Barnes, Thomas G., **8**:*33–34n. 4,*
65n. 6, 75n. 34, 88n. 15, 95n.
32, 100n. 54, 102n. 59, 104n.
64, 105nn. 69, 70, 114n. 17,
116n. 25, 118n. 31, 119–20n.
39, 123n. 52, 130–31n. 78,

132nn. 81, 82, 132–33n. 83,
133n. 85
Barnett, Correlli, **8**:*305n. 25*
barons, **6**:121, 122–24
barratry, **9**:313
barristers, **9**:178
fees, **9**:314
See also trial lawyers
Barro, Robert J., **7**:*269n. 10*; **10**:380
barter, **1**:308–13
in politics, **5**:283
use of depreciating currency vs.,
10:317–20, 345
Barth, James, **10**:*383n. 13, 384n. 16*
Barzel, Yoram, **4**:*58n. 7, 116n. 2*;
5:*43n. 46*; **6**:*412n. 11*
Batchelder, Robert C., **8**:*72n. 31*
Bates, Robert H., **7**:*180n. 2*
Batson, Gladys, **2**:xxv
Battalio, R. C., **10**:*104n. 10, 105, 107*
Battle Studies (du Picq), **10**:405,
413–15
Baumol, William J., **1**:*414n. 5*;
2:*41n. 1*, 306; **10**:382
Baumol's law, **4**:420n. 17
Bavelas, Alex, **3**:*140n. 9*
Bay, Stephen, **8**:*39n. 29, 44nn. 50, 51,*
66n. 13, 107n. 1, 293n. 4,
303n. 16
Bean, Frank D., **9**:*258n. 16*; **10**:*81n. 13*
Beard, Charles, **2**:*14n. 3*, 24–25
Beck, Morris, **1**:302–4
Becker, Gary S., **1**:*174n. 10, 323n. 1,*
441n. 1, 461n. 6; **5**:*66n. 85*;
9:*189n. 1, 254n. 2, 433n. 6*;
10:*25n. 1, 36nn. 7, 8, 37n. 10,*
39n.1, 79n. 9, 95nn. 1, 2
on agricultural subsidies, **5**:301
"Altruism, Egoism, and Genetic
Fitness," **10**:133–38
on collective action, **5**:51–52
hypothesis about punishment,
10:76

on interest group competition,
5:36, 46–47
on rent seeking, 5:246
on rent-seeking costs, 5:52–53
on subsidies, 5:226–27
"Theory of Competition among
Pressure Groups for Political
Influence, A," 5:*145n.12*
Bedau, Hugo Adam, 10:*77n. 6*
bees
division of labor, 10:206, 234–35
environmental coordination,
10:257
genetic inheritance, 10:200
joint development with flowers,
10:232–34
lack of specialized types, 10:231–32
nests, 10:229n. 5, 231
reproduction, 10:189–91
self-sacrifice, 10:160–61
social organization, 10:143–44
See also ants; termites
bee societies, 1:558–59, 560
Beeson, Irene, 8:*70n. 25*
beetles and ants, 10:194–95
Begam, Robert G., 9:354n. 35
begging, 1:186
in China, 5:22, 25
beginners' mind, 3:103–4
behavior analysis, 3:36, 37
Beilenson, Laurence W., 8:*347n. 7*;
10:*434n. 5*
Beitz, Charles R., 1:*280n. 7*; 7:*47n. 6*
Bélanger, G., 5:*59n. 71*
Bellarmine, St. Robert, 3:35
Bell Telephone Laboratories, 3:23
Ben-Ami, Shlomo, 8:*88n. 15, 110–
11n. 7*
benchmark, 2:193
bench trials, 9:347–50
argument for, 9:437
superiority of, 9:444
benefit principle in taxation, 2:277–80

benevolent despot model of political
order, 4:170
Bennett, James T., 1:*23nn. 9, 10,
113n. 19*; 6:*346n. 11, 385n. 12*
Benson, B. L., 9:*412n. 5, 413n. 1,
414n. 2, 419n. 14, 420nn. 15, 16*
Bentham, Jeremy, 5:208–9, 212;
7:112–13, 120; 9:3, 10, 131,
221
Bentley, Arthur, 2:xvi, 9, *11n.1, 18n. 2,
21n. 9,* 119n. 4, 270
Berger, Jacques, 10:*109n. 24*
Berger, M., 9:*435n. 12*
Bergquist, Patricia R., 10:*242n. 2*
Bergson, Abram, 8:*166n. 1*
Berkeley, Bishop, 3:33, 34, 35
Berkson, Joseph, 3:*35n. 6*
Berlin, Isaiah, 2:*4n. 1, 12n. 2, 294n. 2*
Berman, H., 5:*81n. 106*
Bernholz, Peter, 4:15, 16; 10:360n. 1
Bernstein, Richard, 8:*157n. 27*
better-informed voters, 5:210. *See also*
ill-informed voters; well-
informed voters
Beveridge, W. I. B., 3:*17n. 12*
beyond-reasonable-doubt criteria,
9:201, 287–90, 410, 443
judges' interpretation of, 9:438
See also preponderance of evidence
criteria
Bhagwati, Jagdish, 5:27
compared with Anne Krueger,
5:30–31
Biaggi, Mario, scandal, 5:214, 219,
225n. 21
bias
as desirable, 1:233–34
in scientific research, 3:123–24,
124–25
in social science research, 3:157
Bibby, Geoffrey, 3:*165–66n. 4*
bibliographies, 3:81
bicameralism, 2:xxii, xxiv–xxv, 222–36

bicameral legislatures with different
constituencies, **5**:291
bills
combining several projects in one,
7:196–97
lying to voters about intent of,
7:331–32
that are slipped through U.S. Congress, **6**:237
See also laws; legislation
Bilson, J. F., **10**:*394n. 20*
Bingham, Woodbridge, **8**:*89–90n. 19*
biological applications of economics,
1:553–57. *See also* societies,
primitive
biological externalities, **1**:541–52
biology
economics and, **10**:117–18, 139, 142
language of, **10**:184
birds, **10**:108–9. *See also* chickens;
sea gulls
Bismarck, Otto von, **5**:310; **7**:16, 63,
169; **8**:55; **10**:290
effect of his health care program,
7:311n. 22
Bjorklund, Oddvar, **8**·*64n. 5*
Black, Duncan, **1**:*16n. 1, 51nn. 2, 3,*
90n. 5, 381n. 2; **2**:*324n. 19*;
3:*154–55n. 27*; **4**:*54n. 5,*
276nn. 4, 5, 279n. 10, 284n. 3,
319n. 1
Committee Decisions with Complemen-
tary Valuation, **1**:*95n. 12*;
4:*284n. 3*, 285
cyclical majorities and, **1**:101n. 16
importance, **1**:16, 606
logrolling model, **4**:319
"majority motion," **1**:98
move to United States, **4**:14
"On the Rationale of Group Decision
Making," **4**:275
opinion about explicit logrolling,
4:331

politics, **4**:18
role in public choice field, **4**:301–4
single-peaked preference curves,
1:90–91
spatial models for voting systems,
4:284
Theory of Committees and Elections,
The, **1**:105; **2**:8, 127, 314–15,
318n. 9, 319–20; **4**:220
Black, Fisher, **10**:*383n. 12*
Black, Hugo, **9**:417
black box (Cantillon), **6**:270, 271
blackmail, legal, by politicians,
5:72–73
Blackstone, W., **9**:339, *404n. 2*
black (underground) economy, **5**:295,
296; **7**:171
Blau, Peter M., *The Dynamics of Bu-*
reaucracy, **6**:193–94, 217–20
Blennerhassett, Lady, **8**:*223n. 68*
Block, Michael, **9**:*256n. 8*; **10**:81
Bloom, Howard S., **10**:*371n. 10*
Bloomfield, A. I., **10**:*343n. 1, 344n. 4,*
345n. 8, 348n. 14
blue laws, **1**:215–16
Blum, Jerome, **8**:*33–34n. 4, 37n. 19,*
65n. 6, 75n. 34, 88n. 15,
95n. 32, 100n. 54, 102n. 59,
105nn. 69, 70, 114n. 17,
116n. 25, 118n. 31, 119–20n.
39, 123n. 52, 130–31n. 78,
132nn. 81, 82, 132–33n. 83,
133n. 85
Blum, Walter, **9**:*98n. 1, 99n. 3,*
116n. 21
Boak, Arthur E., **8**:*91nn. 21, 23,*
92n. 24, 113nn. 12, 13, 15, 16,
125n. 59, 126n. 63
board of judges, **9**:84–85, 180–81
in European courts, **9**:325
boards
advisory, **6**:225
in government vs. business, **6**:308–9

that are ultimate sovereigns, **6**:302
See also commissions; committees
boards of directors
  dealing with, **6**:302–3
  mutual insurance companies, **6**:274
  nonprofit organizations, **6**:346, 347
  type of sovereignty, **6**:70n. 1
Bobbitt, Philip, *Tragic Choices*, **7**:97–
  99, 100–101, 339, 340–42,
  346–51
Boddle, Dirk, **8**:*225n. 1*
Bombaugh, Robert L., **9**:*98n. 1*,
  100n. 5
bonobos, **10**:165
bonuses for executives, **6**:408
book reviews, **3**:73
books about science, **3**:72–74
Borcherding, Thomas E., **1**:*218n. 7*,
  593n. 4; **4**:*202n. 25*
Borda, Jean Charles de, **2**:315
Borda voting method, **1**:126–27
Bork, Robert, **9**:415
Bornet, Vaughn Davis, **8**:*86n. 9*
Borts, George H., **5**:24, *24n. 25*
Boskin, Michael J., **7**:*282n. 8*
Boston Tea Party, **5**:162n. 3
Boulding, Kenneth, **1**:*3n. 1*, 337n. 6;
  8:182n. 7; **10**:6
Bourgeois, Emile, **8**:*132–33n. 83*,
  219n. 56
Bowen, H. R., **1**:*134n. 6*
Bower, Blair T., **1**:*413n. 3*
Bowra, C. M., **8**:107n. 2, 116n. 23,
  119n. 36
Brady, G., **5**:*19n. 13*
Brain, Lord, **3**:*3n. 1*
Brams, Steven J., **1**:*115n. 26*;
  8:*284n. 11*
Brams, W. E., **4**:347
Brandeis, Louis, **9**:417
Brandt, C., **10**:*314n. 11*
Brandt, Willy, **1**:280–81
Brandy, Lillian, **1**:*395n. 6*

Braudel, Gernand, **8**:*129n. 73*
Brazilian economy, **9**:265
Brazilian government, **5**:128; **8**:92–
  94, 137, 138–39
breach of contract, **9**:57–60, 340–41
breach of duty, **9**:409
Brecher, R. A., **5**:*27n. 28*
Breit, William H., **1**:*461n. 6*; **7**:*29n. 13*
Brennan, H. Geoffrey, **1**:232;
  5:*54n. 67*, *226n. 24*;
  8:*154nn. 19, 22*; **10**:*425n. 2*
Brennan, Walter, **9**:417
Breton, A., **9**:*263n. 1*
Brewer, John, **8**:*136n. 93*
bribery
  to change individual behavior,
    10:416
  of civil servants, **10**:356–57
  of government officials, **1**:240–41,
    323–24; **5**:112–13, 115, 247–
    48; **7**:208–9
  of judges, **6**:394n. 5
  of jurors vs. judges, **9**:81, 345
  of police, **9**:221
  of politicians, **5**:214, 295
  relation to collectivization, **1**:355
  of voters, **5**:262
  in voting, and demand revealing,
    4:367
  See also incentives
Bridgman, Percy Williams, **2**:*137n. 11*;
  3:*34n. 3*
Britain
  electoral government, **8**:121–23
  Elizabethan-era poor laws, **7**:120
  government transfers to poor,
    1:263–64
  immigrants in, **1**:279–80
  industrial revolution in, **5**:160–70
  National Health Service, **1**:356
  parliamentary system, **1**:76–77
  period of limited autocracy, **8**:42
  social welfare programs, **7**:257

Britain (*continued*)
  succession of monarchs, **8**:100,
    201–5, 250–51
  voting peculiarities, **1**:32
  See also British Parliament
British civil service, **6**:404
British Columbia Egg Control Board,
    1:592–93
British Empire, **6**:185; **7**:45–46
British legal system
  arbitration, **9**:305, 308
  common law in, **9**:441–42
  compared with U.S. system,
    9:85–86, 178–79, 356
  criminal justice system, **9**:318
  history of legal profession,
    9:419–20
  history of trial by jury, **9**:424–25
  paying for lawsuit costs, **9**:313–14
  payments of money for evidence,
    9:177
  See also adversary system of law;
    common law
British National Health Service,
    7:155–60, 166, 311
  care for incurably ill under,
    7:249
British Parliament
  common law and, **9**:404
  history, **5**:164–65
  Houses, **4**:340–41
  logrolling, **4**:206–7, 212, 213–14
  relation with military, **8**:218
  seventeenth century, **5**:161
  system for debate, **4**:393
  See also House of Commons
Broad, C. D., **3**:*88n. 1*
broadcasting. *See* cable television
    industry
broad liability, **9**:375–76. *See also*
    strict liability
Brock, W. A., **5**:*65n. 83, 74n. 95*
Broderick, J., **3**:*35n. 5*

Brooke, John, **8**:*206nn. 24, 26,*
    207n. 27
Brough, W., **5**:*128n. 6*; **9**:*420n. 17,*
    421n. 20
Brown, Archie, **8**:*95n. 36*
Brown, J. P., **9**:364, 365
Brown, Robert E., **2**:*14n. 3*, 25;
    3:*157n. 30*
Browning, Edgar K., **1**:*194n. 1,*
    195n. 5; **5**:23, *24n. 23*;
    7:*240n. 17, 241n. 20, 269n. 9,*
    277n. 20; **10**:*294n. 5*
Brown v. Board of Education, **9**:348
Brunner, Elizabeth, **1**:*71n. 2*
brute force. *See* coercion
Bryce, James, **8**:*144n. 6, 156n. 25*
Buchanan, James M.
  on advantages of earmarked taxes,
    10:291
  Calculus of Consent, The, **1**:25, 108–
    12, 264; **4**:220, 230–31;
    5:299–300; **6**:89–90; **7**:38,
    67n. 23, 231; **9**:13; **10**:287
  Calculus of Consent, The, cited,
    1:*125n. 3, 129n. 6, 288n. 21,*
    354n. 5, 388n. 1; **3**:*73n. 22*;
    4:*3n. 1, 10n. 8, 13n. 3, 56n. 6,*
    65n. 11, 115n. 1, 119n. 5,
    183n. 15, 210n. 31, 249n. 5,
    276n. 3, 347n. 1, 367n. 3,
    392n. 6; **5**:*33n. 37, 46n. 48,*
    78n. 102, 176n. 2, 238n. 6;
    7:*78n. 2, 191n. 12, 197n. 19,*
    236n. 13; **9**:*11n. 1, 17n. 2*
  career, **4**:13
  "Coase Theorem and the Theory of
    the State, The," **1**:*423n. 9*
  "'Dead Hand' of Monopoly, The,"
    1:*212n. 2*
  Deficits, **5**:*77n. 101*
  Demand and Supply of Public Goods,
    The, **4**:220
  "Externality," **1**:*349n. 1*

"Gasoline Rationing and Market Pricing," **1**:*424n. 10*

"Inconsistencies of the National Health Service, The," **7**:*308n. 20*; **9**:*110n. 10*

Journal of Conflict Resolution, **1**:*66n. 12*

"Marginal Notes on Reading Political Philosophy," **6**:*140n. 1*

"Note on Public Goods Supply, A," **1**:*350n. 2*

on pattern recognition, **3**:*98n. 10*

"Political Economy of Franchise in the Welfare State, The" **1**:*160n. 9*

"Polluters' Profits and Political Response," **1**:*425n. 1*

"Positive Economics, Welfare Economics, and Political Economy," **1**:*418n. 8*; **2**:*87–88n. 3, 89n. 4*

Power to Tax, The, **5**:*54n. 67*; **8**:*154n. 22*

"Public and Private Interaction under Reciprocal Externality," **1**:*177n. 13*; **4**:107

Public Principles of Public Debt, **5**:*79n. 103*; **9**:*246n. 3*

"Rent Seeking and Profit Seeking," **5**:*53n. 64*

role in *The Calculus of Consent*, **2**:xxiii, 8

"Samaritan's Dilemma, The," **7**:*102n. 16*

"Social Choice, Democracy, and Free Markets," **2**:*xiin. 5, 31n. 1, 320n. 13*

solution to rent seeking, **5**:181

support of Tullock's career, **1**:*541n. 2*, 607, 608; **2**:xix; **3**:xx

on theory of constitutions, **2**:329–30, 331

Toward a Theory of the Rent-Seeking Society, **5**:28, *95n. 2, 189n. 13*; **6**:*375n. 1*; **7**:*174n. 4, 214n. 13, 319n. 1*; **10**:*412n. 4*

on Tullock's work, **6**:3–10

"Voter Choice," **5**:*226n. 24*

"What Kind of Redistribution Do We Want?" **7**:*96n. 8*

"Who Should Distribute What in a Federal System?" **7**:*117n. 2*

Buchanan, Percy, **8**:*64–65n. 5*

Buchholz, Bernard, **9**:*185n. 6*

Buckley, William F., **7**:334

budget deficits, **4**:232, 233–34

budgets

  balanced federal government, **5**:79

  discretionary, **5**:59

Buer, M. C., **8**:*135n. 90*

building industry example, **6**:264–68, 318–19

Bullock, Alan, **8**:*87n. 13, 110n. 7*

Bunce, V., **8**:*95n. 36*

bureaucracies

  in centralized vs. decentralized democracies, **6**:278

  Chinese, **5**:104–8

  cliques within, **6**:43

  of common law system, **9**:450

  communications within, **6**:149–52

  continuing expansion of, **1**:297, 305

  control in multilevel, **6**:203–4

  control over vs. influence through, **6**:369

  cost, **1**:84

  definition, **6**:280

  effect on government spending, **4**:45

  efficiency, **4**:132–33

  equilibrium size, **1**:300

  external vs. internal view of, **6**:176–78

  failures, **6**:204

  government vs. private, **4**:133–34

bureaucracies (*continued*)
  growth of, **6**:145–47, 185–88
  imperfection of, **6**:326
  imperial bureaucratic systems,
      6:178, 181–85
  improving, **4**:196–97
  information flow in, **6**:76–77
  introducing competition into,
      4:203–5
  limit on tasks able to perform,
      6:134, 136
  line vs. staff structures, **6**:158–59
  loss of control in, **6**:263–64
  merit systems, **6**:19–21
  monopoly, **4**:197–99
  morality within, **6**:33–35
  Napoleon's use of, **6**:369
  need for research on, **1**:28
  pay scales in, **5**:118
  politics, **6**:13
  power, **4**:199–200
  power within, **6**:143–44
  purposes, **6**:136–38
  reducing monopoly within, **4**:201–3
  scientists and, **3**:176
  self-survival tactics, **4**:200–201
  South American, **1**:300–301
  at their worst, **6**:24
  theory, **6**:4–6
  Tullock's experiences with, **4**:11–12
  using for making life-and-death deci-
      sions, **7**:350
  using to achieve income redistribu-
      tion, **7**:77–78
  See also bureaucratic free enterprise;
      control within organizations;
      hierarchies; organizations; the-
      ory of bureaucracy
*Bureaucracy and Representative Govern-
    ment* (Niskanen), **4**:156–57,
    201, 202, 220
bureaucracy theory, **2**:xxiii
bureaucratic free enterprise, **6**:178–81
  growth of, **6**:185

  inefficiency of, **6**:187–88
  U.S. government, **6**:237–38
bureaucratic imperialism, **6**:145
bureaucratic opposition to change,
    8:271
bureaucrats
  absence of external norms,
      6:140–41
  accountability to elected representa-
      tives, **4**:193
  characteristics of successful, **6**:21–23
  commonality with corporate execu-
      tives, **6**:279
  compared with businessmen,
      4:192–93
  compared with entrepreneurs,
      1:406, 407
  controlling of, **6**:329
  coups against, **8**:71
  curiosity of, **6**:77
  dealings with inferiors, **6**:313–26
  definition, **5**:55; **6**:280
  under dictatorships, **5**:127–29
  difference from businessmen, **6**:280
  dilemmas when following orders,
      6:295–96
  disagreements with superiors,
      6:70–71
  growth of wages, **1**:298–300,
      303–4
  information flow to and from subor-
      dinates, **6**:149–52
  intellectual capital, **8**:271
  leaving decisions to, **4**:61
  lobbying by, **1**:194–95
  maximization of bureaucracy by,
      4:195–96
  misinformed, **5**:309
  moral level of top, **6**:25–26
  motives, **1**:16, 23; **4**:194; **6**:296,
      328
  preferences, **4**:133
  role in rent seeking, **5**:54–60
  self-interest, **7**:280, 281

tactics to preserve bureaucracy,
4:200–201
Tullock's analysis, 6:5
upward and downward mobility,
6:19–21
uses for media, 6:224–25
voting by, 1:23–24, 218
See also civil servants; government
officials; political appointees;
reference politicians
Burg, Steven, 8:*97n. 42*
Burger, J., 10:*155n. 1*
Burger, Warren, 9:413
Burgess, J. W., 10:*186n. 4*
burglary, 9:256. *See also* theft
Burke, Edmund, 2:303
Burn, A. R., 8:*38nn. 23, 24, 305n. 23*
Burns, James M., 4:*388n. 3*
Burrows, Paul, 9:272
Burt, Al, 8:*101n. 56*
Bury, J. B., 8:*120nn. 40–43*
Bushell, S. W., 10:*339n. 21*
Bush model of natural distribution,
1:309
advantages to moving out of,
1:319
business, self-interest in, 4:174. *See
also* businessmen
business administration, 2:293n. 1
businessmen
agreements, 8:349
behavior of, 3:36, 37
difference from bureaucrats, 6:280
honesty of, 4:260–61
lying by, 9:210–11
morality, 6:26
rent avoidance by, 5:114–17,
118–20
rent seeking by, 5:120
who become government officials,
5:133
who preferred nonprofitable goals,
6:410
See also salesmen

Butler, Colin G., 10:206
Butler, H., 1:*113n. 18, 118n. 28*
buyers. *See* consumers
Byers, Edward, 5:*141n. 9*

CAB (Civil Aeronautics Board),
1:589–90; 5:224, 229, 310;
7:324–26
cabinet governments, logrolling,
4:342–43
cable television industry, 5:157–58.
See also television broadcasting
regulation
Caesar, Augustus, 8:127, 159
Caetano, Marcelo, 8:75
Cagan, Phillip, 10:*362n. 2*
Calabresi, Guido, 1:*456n. 1;* 9:*98n. 1*
Tragic Choices, 7:97–99, 100–101,
339, 340–42, 346–51
Calculus of Consent, The (Buchanan and
Tullock), 1:25, 108–12, 264;
4:220, 230–31; 5:275, 299–
300; 6:89–90; 7:38, 67n. 23,
231; 9:13; 10:287, 291n. 3
Charles Rowley on, 5:299–300
origins of, 4:13
California, 1:31
government, 5:78; 6:385
transfers to poor outside of,
7:359–60
Cameron, Rondo, 8:*33–34n. 4,
65n. 6, 75n. 34, 88n. 15,
95n. 32, 100n. 54, 102n. 59,
104n. 64, 105nn. 69, 70,
114n. 17, 116n. 25, 118n. 31,
119–20n. 39, 123n. 52, 130–
31n. 78, 132nn. 81, 82, 132–
33n. 83, 133n. 85*
Camp, Roderic A., 8:*92n. 25*
campaign contributions, 5:41–42
restrictions, 1:228, 235
small size of, relative to returns,
5:214–15
Campbell, Angus, 7:*343n. 5*

Campbell, Colin D., **1**:*90n. 2*;
    4:*280n. 1, 284nn. 3, 4,*
    291n. 10, 320n. 2; **7**:281n. 7;
    10:*347n. 11*
campus protests. *See* student protests
Canadian economic growth, **10**:389
Canadian government, **4**:396
    contracting out by, **4**:404–5
Canadian health plan, **7**:258
cancer research, **3**:90
Cannan, Edwin, **10**:*319n. 14, 345n. 7*
Cantillon's black box, **6**:270, 271
Cantor, Norman F., **8**:*34n. 6,*
    42nn. 42, 43, 43n. 48, 75n. 37
Cao Garcia, R. J., **5**:*134n. 14*
CAP (Central Arizona Project), **5**:250,
    254–55, 277
capital accumulation
    inheritance tax to promote,
        1:256–57
    preconditions for, **1**:314, 316
capital investment
    impact of "perpetual gale" on, **5**:153
    impact of Social Security system on,
        7:62–63, 269
    riskiness of, **5**:150–51
    through U.S. foreign aid, **7**:100
Capitalism and Freedom (Friedman),
    2:x; **7**:13, 90, 118
"capitalist" dictatorships, **5**:123–24
    rent seeking in, **5**:122–23
capital providers, **6**:342
capital punishment. *See* death penalty
Caplovitz, D., **4**:*242–43n. 2*
Caplow, Theodore, **3**:*30nn. 31, 32*
Caracas, Venezuela, black (under-
    ground) economy, **5**:296
Cardozo, Benjamin, **9**:417
career advancement
    choice of superior to give allegiance,
        6:111–12
    conformity, **6**:47–48
    dealing with boards of directors,
        6:302–3

dealing with committees, **6**:305–8,
    309–11
ethics within organizations, **6**:45
flattery, **6**:84–86
by government bureaucrats, **6**:177
under group sovereign, **6**:119
individual choice of action and,
    6:70–71
intelligence level and, **6**:23, 80–82
through keeping superiors informed,
    6:304
key to, **6**:72–74
loyalty, **6**:46–47
over peers in single sovereign situa-
    tion, **6**:116–18
personal characteristics needed for
    success, **6**:21–23
self-interest, **6**:32–33
of self vs. advancement of organiza-
    tional goals, **6**:23–25
skills needed for promotion,
    6:48–50
through study of superiors, **6**:57–58
See also job hierarchies; performance
    evaluation; promotions within
    organizations
carelessness by scientists, **3**:5
Carneiro, Robert L., **8**:*134n. 88*
Caro, Robert A., **8**:*86n. 9*
Carr-Hill, R. A., **9**:*256n. 9*; **10**:82
Carroll, Lewis, **2**:315–16, 317n. 7;
    4:301, 302, 383, 430;
    9:*382n. 9*
    voting method, **4**:444–45
Carroll, Stephen J., **9**:*343n. 13,*
    350n. 29
carrot-stick metaphor. *See* rewards
Carson, R. T., **7**:56
cartels
    British Columbia Egg Control
        Board, **1**:592–94
    combining with subsidies, **5**:258
    of doctors, **7**:311–12
    entry restrictions, **1**:594–95

as form of rent seeking, **5**:6
OPEC, **5**:138, 141, 142; **7**:35–36, 172
publishing about, **1**:599
reputation of members, **10**:432–33
resulting from government taxation, **5**:5
as result of government regulation, **1**:212, 416; **5**:220
taxi medallion, **1**:213–15; **5**:67
transfers of oil revenues from, **5**:138–42
U.S. airline industry, **1**:589–90
of women, **10**:18–19
See also government-created monopolies
Carter, April, **8**:*97n. 42*
Carter, R. L., **4**:*179n. 10*
Carthaginian government, **8**:113, 117–18
cartography and navigation, **3**:150–51
case law, **1**:513; **9**:318
   in criminal justice system, **9**:433
cases. *See* lawsuits; trials
Casinelli, C. W., **2**:*19n. 3*
Casstevens, Thomas, **4**:*293n. 1*
Castiglione, Baldassare, *Courtier*, **6**:304
casually informed voters
   definition, **5**:44
   lying to, **5**:44–45, 46
cataloging of knowledge, **3**:84. *See also* classification systems; indexing methods
Catholic Church
   governance, **8**:120–21
   succession of power, **8**:94–95, 156
cattle-grazing example, **1**:543–46; **5**:249
cells of human beings, **10**:129, 259, 264
cellular animals
   protozoa, **10**:225–26
   rational behavior, **10**:109–10

social organization, **10**:144–45
   as societies of individual cells, **10**:264–67
   within sponges, **10**:241–42
   See also societies, primitive
cement factory in small country example, **1**:71–75
Center for Study of Public Choice, **1**:608
Central America
   countries in cross-national sample, **10**:398
   economic growth, **10**:391–93, 396–97
Central Arizona Project (CAP), **5**:250, 254–55, 277
centralized control of organizations, **6**:337
   large organizations, **6**:417–18
   without use of cost accounting, **6**:367–68
   See also control within organizations
centralized planning, **4**:82
centrally planned economies, **6**:238
   Eastern Europe, **6**:388–91
   impossibility of, **6**:135, 366
   Russia, under Lenin, **6**:271, 371–72
CEOs. *See* chief executive officers (CEOs)
certification examinations, **1**:595, 596
   in China, **5**:104–7
   civil service, **1**:228
   higher education as, **5**:143
   See also licenses
Chadwick, Henry, **8**:*94n. 29*
chain of command
   functional, **6**:228, 230
   what can go wrong, **6**:353–54
   See also crisscross system of supervision
"Chairman's Problem, The" (Jouvenel), **4**:392–93
Chancery, **9**:85
Chandler, Alfred, **6**:241

Chang, David W., **8**:*97n. 41*

change, managing, **9**:11–13

Chao, Kuo-chun, **10**:*308n. 3, 311n. 8, 312nn. 9, 10, 318n. 13*

Chapman, David, **7**:*80n. 4*

charitable donors

  difference from consumers, **1**:399, 400–402

  lack of incentive to be well informed, **1**:403

charitable giving

  actions that can be taken, **1**:274–75

  cognitive dissonance about, **1**:270–71, 273

  costs and benefits, **7**:8

  definition, **7**:4, 11

  degree of, **4**:173

  effect on recipient organizations, **5**:22–23

  efficiency, **7**:105–10

  through government, **1**:262, 272–73, 285–86, 407–8, 409

  government assistance vs., **4**:134–35

  hidden limits on, **7**:98, 99, 101

  to higher education, **7**:299, 300

  impact of geographic contiguity on, **7**:118

  impact of religion on, **7**:57–58

  in-kind aid, **7**:95–99, 133–41, 348

  internationally, **7**:8–9, 226

  as maximization of total utility, **7**:29–31

  to nonprofit organizations, **7**:90

  paternalism in, **7**:95–96

  as percentage of personal income, **7**:26

  political activism as a form of, **1**:601

  to political organizations, **7**:26

  to the poor, **1**:270–72, 273

  preferences, **7**:10

  private vs. public, **7**:101–5, 122, 357

  problems, **7**:3–4

  relationship between giver and recipient, **10**:161–62

  relation with transfers, **8**:8–9

  to rich people, **7**:3n. 1, 26

  Samaritan's dilemma, **7**:102–3

  similarity to revolution, **1**:337

  sources of finance for, **7**:358

  strength of individual impulse toward, **4**:70–71

  superoptimality of, **7**:89

  transfers vs., **7**:12–19, 65–66, 90–95

  using demand-revealing process for, **7**:89

  using Lindahl tax for, **7**:95

  utility of, **5**:208–9

  via voluntary gifts, **7**:362

  welfare costs of, **1**:182, 185–87

  See also charities; matching grants; organ donation; transfers

charitable motives

  altruistic, **7**:11

  are not enough, **1**:411

  avoiding distress from, **7**:345

  for criminalizing behavior, **7**:139–41

  toward criminals, **9**:200

  of doctors, **7**:313

  effect on income redistribution, **1**:285–86

  externalities from, **7**:7–8

  hypocrisy around, **7**:58–59

  for income redistribution, **7**:65–66, 355–56

  in-kind aid and, **7**:95–99

  irrational element in, **1**:394–95

  for military pensions, **7**:34

  mixed with other motives, **7**:243

  paternalistic, **5**:210

  of recipients, **7**:6

  toward the rich, **7**:337–38

  for transfers for public education, **7**:296, 298, 299

transfers made from dubious,
7:156–58
See also gift motive
charities
advertising, 1:399, 402n. 9, 404
fraud, 1:397–98, 403
fund-raising, 1:396
inefficiency, 1:402–4
lobbying by, 5:179
management, 1:403n. 11, 406,
407
marketing, 1:402, 404–7
maximization of payments to,
1:405–6
subsidies for, 5:174
suggested reforms, 1:408–11
"Charity of the Uncharitable, The"
(Tullock), 7:360
Charnov, Eric L., 1:427n. 1
Chase, Salmon P., 6:95
cheating
on agreements, 10:148
in the market, 10:429–37
checks and balances in U.S. government, 1:32; 4:388; 5:60
intention behind, 5:81
chemistry, pattern recognition in,
3:99–100
Chew, Geoffrey, 3:99n. 11
Cheyney, Edward P., 8:100n. 51,
123n. 51
Chicago School of Economics
Keynesians vs., 4:18
policy recommendations, 4:229
relationship with public choice,
7:334
transfer models, 5:66
view of agricultural subsidies,
5:301–6
view of subsidies, 5:227
chickens, 10:123
chief executive officers (CEOs),
6:155–57
stock bonuses to, 6:408

children
cost of creating, 10:52–53
as economic goods, 10:39–43, 46
legal competency, 9:126–27
moral education for, 4:263–64
quality, 10:49, 51
supply and demand, 10:43–50
See also fertility rates
chimney-smoke example, 4:97–101,
106–7
chimpanzees, 10:122, 164, 166, 246
China
beggars' tactics, 5:22, 25
bureaucracies in, 5:104–8; 6:43
Chin dynasty currency, 10:329–31
Ch'ing dynasty currency, 10:338–39
Chou dynasty, 8:37
Communist currencies, 10:312
currencies, 1937–1949, 10:317–18,
319–20
early monetary history, 10:324–26
empire, 6:331–32
Gang of Four, 8:303
government employment in classical,
6:16n. 2
great leap forward, 8:26
hyperinflation, 1937–1949,
10:307–20
Imperial Censorate (civil service),
6:157, 226–27, 319–20,
359–60
legal system, 8:225–26; 9:225
Manchu dynasty, 8:145
Ming dynasty, 8:249
Ming dynasty currency, 10:337–38
Mongol dynasty currency,
10:332–37
origin of paper money, 10:325
paper money in ancient, 10:321–24
policies of leaders, 8:55
public education about law, 9:340
self-governing local governments,
4:142–43
succession of power in, 8:99

China (*continued*)
Sung dynasty currency, **10**:328–29
supervision of Hsien magistrates,
   6:323–26
Szechuan dynasty currency,
   10:326–28
U.S. foreign policy toward, **5**:207
warlords, **8**:64
See also Nationalist China
Chinese coins, **10**:326n. 10
Chipman, Robert A., **3**:*8n. 10*
choices
avoiding hard, **7**:342
constitutional, **2**:90–91, 105
economic freedom of vs. political
   freedom of, **6**:250–51
efficiency as criteria for, **9**:378–79
externalities and, **5**:273–74
external restrictions on, **9**:22–23
free vs. coerced, **6**:8–9
future, **9**:53–54
between future events, **9**:25–30
individual preference for, **9**:19
involving discounted value of income stream, **9**:24
life-and-death, **7**:97–99, 345, 351
lying about distressing consequences
   of, **7**:346
most efficient, **9**:306–7
payment to attain favorite, **9**:25
preferred number of alternatives,
   9:20–21
range open to reference politicians,
   6:42
real world, **1**:12–14
relation with wealth, **9**:23
responsibility in collective, **2**:36–37
within rules, **2**:105
science of, **1**:10
using lotteries for, **7**:349
See also decision making; preferences
Chorley, Katherine C., **8**:*45n. 52*
Chrisophilos, Nicholas, **3**:179–80

Chrysler Corporation, **5**:214
organizational structure, **6**:414
Churchill, Winston, **6**:142
Cifuentes, Lucy, **4**:*72n. 5*
cigarette taxes, **5**:196–200
citation counting of articles, **3**:*27n. 26*,
   31. *See also* new ideas
cities
building codes and restrictions,
   4:147–48
collective action within, **4**:144
See also urban renewal projects
Civil Aeronautics Board (CAB),
   1:589–90; **5**:224, 229, 310;
   7:324–26
civilization
early human, **10**:166–67
as hereditary behavior, **10**:261–63
civil liberties, **9**:361
in OPEC countries, **10**:393–95
civil servants
bribes of South Korean, **10**:356–67
compared with corporate managers,
   6:15
compensation, **1**:218–19, 303–5;
   7:209
examinations, **1**:228
excess number of classes of, **6**:124
firing of, **6**:383–84
government efficiency and, **4**:405–7
motives, **4**:163
as "new class," **7**:333
pensions, **7**:33–34
power over political appointees,
   1:23–24
public good vs. self-interest, **6**:27
as representatives of voters,
   4:425–26
self-interest, **4**:174–75; **7**:280, 281
sharing of unofficial income among,
   10:353–54
social security payments to, **7**:34
as special-interest group, **4**:406–7

theory of decision making by,
  4:161–62
See also bureaucrats; government
  officials
civil service systems, **1**:74
  British, **6**:404
  Chinese, **6**:16n. 2, 157, 226, 227,
    319–20, 359–60
  pay scales in U.S., **4**:406
  U.S. Civil Service Commission,
    6:384
  See also theory of bureaucracy
civil wars, **8**:288–89
  following partial coups, **8**:76–77
  in nonhuman societies, **10**:208–9
Clark, G. N., **8**:*100n. 52*
Clarke, Edward H., **1**:134, 141;
  4:447; **5**:289
Clarke, Roger A., **8**:*109n. 5*
Clarke tax, **1**:135–36
  demand-revealing process and, **4**:363
  effect on demand-revealing process,
    7:142–47, 148
  formula for, **1**:145
  mechanism for determining,
    7:146–47
class action lawsuits, **9**:210
classical theory of contract, **9**:408
  Adam Smith's defense of, **9**:446–48
  See also law of torts
classification systems
  engineering vs. science, **3**:63, 69
  history of science and, **3**:81
  Linnaean, **3**:84
  necessity of, **3**:82
  problems of inclusion/exclusion,
    3:79–81
  rectification of, by indexing systems,
    3:82–83
  in scientific and engineering jour-
    nals, **3**:68, 69–70
  See also cataloging of knowledge;
    indexing methods

class interest in politics, **2**:25–26.
  See also ruling class theory of
    state
Clayton, Richard T., **10**:*282n. 4*
Clifford, Clark, **5**:116
Clifford, Esther Rowland, *A Knight of
  Great Renown*, **6**:277
Clinton, William (Bill), **5**:262
cloning, **1**:560–62, 570; **10**:187–88
  social success and, **10**:192–93
coalition governments, **4**:387, 388
  relation to proportional representa-
    tive democracies, **4**:390–91
coalitions
  of equals, **7**:188–89
  externalities from, **5**:274–75
  instability of, **7**:239–40
  involved in transfers, **7**:189–91
  Keynes's point about, **5**:77–78
  logrolling advantage over, **7**:192–93
  to overthrow governments,
    8:269–70
  permanent, **5**:273–74
  relation with rent seeking, **5**:239
  Riker-Brams study, **8**:284
  that can remove dictators, **5**:131
  See also logrolling
coalitions of voters
  bargaining problems in establishing,
    1:165–66
  under demand revealing, **4**:366–72
  in demand-revealing process,
    1:146–47
  efficiency of logrolling by, **4**:357
  examples, **1**:53–57
  genuinely superior, **4**:329
  income redistribution and,
    1:265–66
  minority, **4**:326
  reducing power of small, **4**:344–45
  of two political parties, **4**:387
  See also formal logrolling coalitions;
    logrolling models

coal tits, **10**:108–9
  "shopping" by, **1**:537–40
Coase, Ronald H., **1**:*355n. 6*, *423n. 9*,
    458n. 2; **2**:*51n. 6*, *87n. 2*;
    4:*109n. 10*; **6**:*258n. 10*;
    9:*407n. 12*
  compensation of capital owners and,
    5:150
  on externalities, **9**:380
  influence on organizational theory,
    6:252
  "Nature of the Firm, The," **6**:244,
    252, 258
  "Problem of Social Cost, The,"
    9:383
  transactions costs model, **6**:244
  Tullock's career and, **1**:37–38, 608
  views on subsidies vs. taxes, **4**:109
Coase theorem, **9**:407
  applied to corruption, **1**:324–25
  consumption externality control
    analogue, **1**:423
Coate, S., **5**:*245n. 6*
Cobb, William E., **9**:*257n. 12*;
    10:*83n. 21*
cockroach societies, **1**:560
Coelho, Philip, **1**:425
coercion
  in choices, **6**:8
  connotation, **8**:7
  definition, **8**:11–12
  desirable or undesirable, **8**:10–11
  by different levels of government,
    6:251, 351
  drawbacks, **1**:308–12
  effect of removal, **1**:343–45
  by government, **5**:75–76; **7**:179–
    81; **8**:8; **10**:203–4
  mutual agreements to use, **10**:92
  in private hierarchies, **10**:202
  public charitable giving and,
    7:101–2
  takings power and eminent domain,
    9:407–8

through threat of future violence,
    8:18
  transfers and, **9**:411–12
  using for transfers, **7**:82
  using to control consumers' behav-
    ior, **7**:139–41
  See also police
cognitive dissonance, **8**:247–48
Cohen, Michael Marks, **9**:*306n. 15*
Cohen, Seymour S., **3**:*66n. 11*
cold war, **8**:318–23
Cole, W. A., **8**:*135n. 90*
Coleman, James S., **4**:19, *283n. 1*,
    324n. 8; **8**:*284n. 11*
collections costs of tariffs, **1**:171
collective action, **10**:407–13
  asymmetric impact on free riding,
    5:48–49
  combined with individual action,
    4:65–66
  decision rule and, **2**:198–99
  external costs of, **2**:60–65
  to finance scientific research, **3**:20
  individual action vs., **4**:62–64
  for mosquito abatement, **4**:52
  in neighborhoods, **4**:140–41, 144
  "net gain" from, **4**:65
  by private means, **4**:105–6
  range, **2**:192–201
  selective incentive toward, **5**:49
  See also cooperation
collective choice theory, **2**:3
collective decision-making
  costs, **2**:65–67; **4**:55, 81
  cumulative effects of, to voters, **4**:65
  effect of technology on, **4**:56,
    59–60
  individual rationality and, **2**:230–32
  Olson's work on, **2**:*260n. 2*
  relation to bargaining costs, **4**:81
  rules, **2**:60–80, 294–95
  those most likely injured by, **4**:56
  voting as a means of, **4**:181–92
collectivity as organism, **2**:30–31

collectivization
adjustment under, **1**:352–55
arguments for, **1**:361, 379
chiseling and, **1**:366–67
effect on individual, **1**:367–69
externalities imposed by, **1**:383–84
geographic contiguity as basis,
1:387
growth and, **1**:370–73
impact of equitable solutions on,
1:355–56
optimal, **1**:376–77
rationing under, **1**:366
without relevant externality,
1:356–58
responsibility in, **2**:36–37
tax collection effects on, **1**:364–65
college professors. *See* academics
colleges. *See* higher education; higher
education institutions
Collier, David, **7**:*255n. 7*
colonial coelenterate societies, **1**:560
colonialism, **8**:114–15, 124
Colt, Samuel, **7**:36, 129–30n. 16
commensals, **1**:570–71
commissions
definition, **6**:91
"God Committee," **7**:350
independent, **6**:66, 67
inefficiency of, **6**:93
as mere councils, **6**:95
uses for, **6**:94
See also boards; committees
Committee Decisions with Complemen-
tary Valuation (Black and
Newing), **4**:285
committees
Armed Services Committee, **5**:158
being subordinate to, **6**:305
Congressional, **4**:335; **5**:59
in corporations, **6**:309–11, 379
decision making, **4**:433–34
effect on rent seeking, **6**:382
government vs. corporate, **8**:80–81

reasons for organizing, **6**:305–8,
309–11
voting, **4**:284–89, 292
See also boards; commissions
common law
arbitration, **9**:308
aspects of criminal justice system,
9:409–10
compared with civil law, **9**:399
courts, **9**:413–14
court system under, **1**:481–82
efficiency, **9**:270–72, 419
in England and Wales, **9**:441–42
expert witnesses, **9**:429–30
history of, **9**:402–10
history of, in England, **9**:444–45
history of, in United States,
9:445–46
inefficiencies, **9**:431–32
judges, **9**:406, 414–19
juries, **9**:423–29
lawyers, **9**:401, 419–23
legal precedent and, **9**:185–86
Napoleonic civil law system vs.,
9:451–55
Posner's view, **9**:449–51
public choice perspective on,
9:411–12
roots in standards, **9**:400
as socialistic bureaucracy, **9**:450
tort and civil suits, **9**:193–98
in United States, **9**:441
wealth maximizing efficiency,
9:431–32
See also criminal justice system;
law of contracts; law of property; law of torts
commons, **2**:55
communication
information exchange vs.,
10:257–58
within organizations, **6**:191–96
among scientists (*see* discussion
among scientists)

communism
  collapse of, **1**:344–45
  public choice and, **4**:15, 17
  See also Marxism
Communist countries
  China, **6**:360
  control of citizens, **6**:271, 330–31
  in Eastern Europe, **6**:388–90
  elections, **6**:330n. 8
  government concern about specific
    crimes, **8**:226–27
  lying by government, **8**:243–44
  mass murders by leaders, **8**:148
  poverty in, **5**:124–25
  profit motive in, **6**:398n. 11
  reliance on punishments, **6**:401
  succession of power in, **8**:78–79,
    95–98, 156
  tendency toward torture, **8**:215
  totalitarianism, **8**:40–41
  unpopular governments, **8**:213–14
  See also centrally planned economies;
    Soviet Union
Communist currencies in China,
  10:312
Communists
  care of lunatics in Russia, **9**:127
  court system in Russia, **9**:182
  Tullock's test for, **8**:88
  use of death sentence, **9**:197n. 12,
    198
Communist view on income redistribution, **7**:52–53
community of scientists. *See* scientific
  community
Company of Merchant Adventurers to
  the East, **6**:248–49
comparison shopping, **1**:430–32,
  538–39. *See also* discount clubs
compensation
  for accidental injuries, **9**:118–22
  to accident victims, **9**:98
  of injured voters, **4**:64

for injury due to legal reforms,
  9:267–68
of innocent persons charged with
  crimes, **9**:174–75
for losses from competition, **5**:150
as measure of injury, **9**:12
for police searches, **9**:175–76
to stockholders of monopolies,
  9:250–51
unanimity and, **2**:86–87
in welfare economics, **2**:86–87
for wire tapping, searches, seizures,
  9:177
for witnesses at trials, **9**:77–78
compensation mechanism
  in bargaining, **1**:180
  for collective actions by government,
    1:386–87
  quotas as, **1**:426
compensation mechanism in voting,
  1:134
  compensating voters who lose,
    1:137–38
  in demand-revealing process voting,
    1:159–60, 161
  per unit, **1**:142
compensatory damages, **9**:407, 448,
  451. *See also* pain and suffering
  (legal damages)
"Competing for Aid" (Tullock), **5**:25
competition
  bargaining and, **2**:99–100
  in business, **6**:345
  compensation for losses from, **5**:150
  constructive and destructive, **6**:418
  costs vs. gains from, **5**:6–8
  duplication of efforts in, **5**:3–10
  as duplication of services, **4**:203
  effect on management of firms, **5**:15
  in government, **4**:202–3, 391
  government need of, **1**:25, 75–77
  for government transfers, **1**:204,
    206, 208–11

"handicapped," **5**:220
Marxist view of, **6**:275
in nonbusiness sectors, **6**:345–48
not always a good thing, **5**:117
by peers subject to single sovereigns,
   6:115–18
by political parties, **5**:80
among special-interest groups,
   5:246
for territory, **1**:556
that leads to lower welfare, **1**:206
between U.S. and foreign manufacturers, **5**:241–42
*Complete Book concerning Happiness and
   Benevolence, A* (Huang), **6**:331
Comptroller General of United States,
   6:321n. 7
computers
   hypothetically perfect utility-
      maximizing, **5**:207–10
   indexing and, **3**:84–85
   preferences of, **10**:252–53
   programming to "think," **3**:94n. 7
   using for managing political debate,
      4:393–94
   using for voting, **4**:382
condemnation of property, **9**:408
condominium associations, **4**:42–43;
   8:158
   constitutions, **5**:270
Condorcet, Marquis de (Marie-Jean
   Caritat), **2**:315; **4**:21, 301,
   302
conference committees in Congress,
   4:335
conferences for scientists, **3**:74–75.
   See also discussion among
   scientists
confiscatory actions of government
   inheritance taxes, **1**:252
   seizure of property, **1**:426; **9**:408
conflict
   connotation, **8**:7

cost of, **8**:165
definition, **8**:7–8
geographic location of, **10**:156–57
origin of group, **10**:164–65
payoff from, **10**:412–13
welfare costs, **1**:192–93
See also coups d'état; fighting;
   revolutions; war
conflicts of interest, **4**:267
of judges, **9**:328–30
conflict studies and prisoners' dilemma,
   8:4
conformity in organizations, **6**:287–89
Congleton, Roger D., **6**:*382n. 10*
conglomerates
   diversity and number of, **6**:416–18
   efficiency of, **6**:253–54
congressional committees, **5**:59
   Armed Services Committee, **5**:158
   conference committees, **4**:335
   investigations, **9**:352
congressmen
   constituency work by, **4**:424–25
   costs of constituency work, **7**:216
   costs of intervention by, **5**:41
   failure to read bills, **5**:37
   influence of political donations on,
      5:41–42
   lame duck, **4**:418
   letters from constituents to,
      6:225–26
   logrolling by, **7**:336–37
   motives behind votes of, **4**:421–23
   motives for brokering rent seeking,
      5:36
   requiring to read bills passed, **5**:80
   theories of what they do, **4**:415–16
   voters' attitudes toward, **5**:38
   See also congressional committees;
      elected officials; politicians;
      United States Congress
Connard, Alfred E., **9**:*98n. 1, 100n. 5*
conscience, and survival, **4**:263–64

consensus, **9**:11–13. *See also* unanimity
"consensus of the informed," **3**:40,
    43–45
conspiracies
    carefully laid, **8**:73
    difficulty of keeping secret,
        8:214–16
    effectiveness of short-term, **8**:285
    payoff to members, **8**:193
    rewards for betrayal, **8**:276
    suppression, **8**:300–306
    See also informers
Constant, Benjamin, **2**:*246n. 2*
constitutional choice, **2**:105
    self-interest and, **2**:90–91
constitutional monarchy, **8**:122–23,
    135–36, 205–7
Constitution of United States, **1**:35;
    4:427
    dual majority voting provision,
        5:291
    freeing of violent criminals and,
        9:435–36
    need for changes, **7**:367
    relation of federal judges to,
        9:416–18
    relation of Supreme Court to, **9**:10
    relation with three branches of gov-
        ernment, **5**:81
    right to jury trial, **9**:425–26
    vulnerability to special interests,
        5:52
    See also checks and balances in U.S.
        government; Fifth Amendment
        protection
constitutions, **1**:34
    for individual, **2**:93
    Pareto criterion and, **2**:89–90
    rationality and, **2**:77
    as rules, **2**:6
    See also theory of constitutions
constraint, problem of moving to,
    1:150–52

construction industry example,
    6:264–68, 318–19
consumer protection laws for politics,
    4:129–30
consumers
    assumption of perfectly informed,
        4:35
    coal tit as careful shopper,
        1:537–40
    compared with voters, **4**:36–37;
        7:177
    comparison shopping, **1**:430–32,
        538–39
    compulsory regulation by govern-
        ment of, **7**:36–37
    controlling their behavior by coer-
        cion, **7**:139–41
    corporate, **6**:398
    cost-saving vs. convenience, **1**:216
    difference from charitable donors,
        1:399, 400–402
    difference from voters, **6**:283–84
    geographic proximity of, **4**:66–67
    of government activity, **6**:272
    government vs. private goods, **4**:73
    impact of lies on, **4**:269
    information levels, **4**:126–28
    as ultimate sovereigns of businesses,
        6:211n. 1
    as voters, **4**:173
    well-being of, **5**:153–54
    See also customers; discount clubs;
        preferences
consumption externalities, **7**:7
contagious diseases example, **10**:89
contempt of court, **9**:348
contiguity problems, **4**:91–92
    economies of scale vs., **4**:66–67,
        144–45
    from unwise laws, **4**:112–13
    See also geographic contiguity
Continental system of law. *See* inquisi-
        torial system of law

contingency cases, **1**:504
contingency fees, **9**:309–11
  in England and Wales, **9**:442
contract enforcement, **8**:348–49
contracting out, **4**:44–45; **6**:266–67
  by government, **4**:153–54, 404–5;
    6:368, 409–10
  of government services, **4**:203–4
  by service organizations and associa-
    tions, **4**:153
  See also privatization
contracts
  arbitration of commercial, **9**:332–35
  assumptions made about, **5**:261
  asymmetric, **9**:57–65
  contingencies, **9**:42–46
  corporations and, **4**:84n. 11
  court costs, **9**:61
  difference from government, **4**:84
  drawing up of, **5**:191–93
  efficiency vs. costs, **9**:394
  employment contracts, **9**:54
  enforceable, **5**:188–89
  enforcement, **9**:57, 58
  externalities from, **5**:262–63
  insurance contracts, **9**:102, 104
  international contracts, **9**:305–6
  judicial errors when enforcing,
    9:40–41
  justifications for, **9**:9
  labor contracts, **6**:14–17
  law pertaining to, **9**:390–96
  market vs. government, **6**:283
  method of enforcement, **9**:55–56
  optimal degree of detail, **9**:46
  optimum restrictions, **9**:37–38
  "resolution by analogy," **9**:44
  social costs, **9**:423
  standardization, **9**:211–12
  status system of law vs., **9**:124
  symmetric, **9**:57–65
  that should be denied enforcement,
    9:51–54

Tullock's assumptions, **9**:16, 18–19
  unenforceable, **9**:37
  as way of reducing externalities,
    4:79
  See also breach of contract; law of
    contracts; marriage contract
contract theory, **2**:xxii, 6–7, 238–41,
    295, 304–6
control within organizations,
    6:189–96
  deterioration, **6**:314–16
  difficulties with, **6**:264–67
  impact of market stages on,
    6:268–70
  incentives to subordinates and,
    6:407–15
  with little in way of supervision,
    6:395
  methods of increasing, **6**:399
  need to relax, **6**:353–59
  through selection of subordinates,
    6:391–99
  techniques to help relax, **6**:365–67,
    369–74
  See also centralized control of organi-
    zations; supervision
controversies. *See* arguments; discussion
    among scientists
conventions. *See* conferences for
    scientists
Converse, Philip E., **7**:*343n. 5*
conviction of offenders
  cost of erroneous, **9**:199–200
  court bias against, **9**:201
  deciding on evidence needed for,
    9:285–86
  false convictions of innocent people,
    9:191–92
  innocence/guilt tradeoff in court
    proceedings, **9**:201–3
  likelihood of, **9**:159–60, 161, 192,
    226
  of professional criminals, **9**:156–57

cooperation
in politics, **2**:254
in prisoners' dilemma games,
10:429–37
theory of, **10**:250–63
See also collective action; environmental coordination
cooperative behavior of animals, **1**:557
within animal societies, **10**:147–50
survival of societies and, **1**:566–69
by termites, **10**:257
cooperative organizations, **1**:369
reducing externalities with,
4:152–54
coordination of science. *See* social organization of science
coordination of tasks, **6**:162–67,
172–75
by decentralization of decision making, **6**:327–28
under functional chain of command,
6:230
organizational structures and, **6**:136
See also supervision; tasks in
hierarchies
Cooter, R., **9**:407*nn. 10, 13, 409n. 14,*
432n. 4, 441nn. 1–3
Corcoran, Thomas (Tommy the Cork),
5:111–12, 116
Corcoran, W. J., **5**:*64n. 82,* 88–92
Cornford, Francis M., **8**:*56n. 16*
Cornuelle, Richard, **1**:*395n. 5, 408n. 17*
corporate auditing, **6**:320–21, 397
corporate executives
characteristics of successful, **6**:21–23
commonality with bureaucrats,
6:279
decision making, **6**:353
performance evaluation, **6**:282
politics, **6**:14–15
relationships with subordinates,
6:56
rotation of junior, **6**:381–82
stock bonuses to, **6**:408

See also chief executive officers
(CEOs); supervision
corporate lawyers, **6**:324, 365
corporate reorganizations, **6**:415
corporate takeovers, **1**:166; **4**:92,
440; **6**:246
proxy fights vs., **6**:344–45
See also leveraged buyouts
corporation law, **9**:128–29
corporations
alliances of managers within, **6**:311
areas where supervision relatively
easy, **6**:397–99
backgrounds of CEOs, **5**:118
board voting methods, **4**:440–41
categories of players connected with,
6:341–45
closed, **6**:253
committees in, **6**:309–11, 379
company prospectuses, **6**:262*n. 16*
compared with government, **4**:84
compared with monarchies, **8**:149
debate over existence of, **9**:265
decentralized, **6**:253–54
decision making by, **5**:282
dishonesty and, **4**:261
diversified, **6**:272–73
employee-owned, **6**:341–42
European, **6**:345*n. 8,* 349
franchises, **4**:151
franchising by, **6**:254, 414
incentive systems, **6**:408–9
internal function of, **6**:241
law enforcement within, **6**:397–98
levels of bureaucracy in, **4**:133
mergers, **6**:416
motives of boards of, **4**:174
need for some disorganization in,
6:385–86
organizational structures of large,
6:215–16
as persons, **9**:128–29
relation with associated lobbying
organizations, **5**:50

rent seeking by, **5**:120
rent seeking within, **6**:376–82
representation within, **4**:423–24
rotation of managerial personnel
    within, **6**:381–82
scandals, **6**:347, 348, 349
size and shareholders, **6**:262
that are governments, **6**:248–49
as way of limiting liability, **9**:129
See also conglomerates; cooperative
    organizations
corruption. *See* government corruption
cost accounting. *See* accounting as su-
    pervision technique
cost-benefit analysis, **1**:358;
    6:302n. 10
cost of conscience, **9**:191, 225–26
costs
    of accident prevention, **9**:366–74,
        388–90
    of accidents, **9**:370–79, 388–90
    of automobile accidents, **9**:142–43
    bargaining, **1**:152–53; **5**:269–70
    bureaucracy, **1**:84
    charitable giving, **7**:93
    child rearing, **10**:41–43
    of collective decision-making, **2**:65–
        67; **4**:55, 81
    of collective organization, **2**:42
    of conflict, **8**:165
    of congressional intervention, **5**:41
    constituency work by congressmen,
        7:216
    contracts, **5**:262–63
    cowardice, **10**:410
    crime avoidance, **10**:62–65
    crime prevention, **9**:197, 207–8;
        10:67
    to criminal for crime, **10**:56–57, 60
    deadweight, **5**:255
    definition, **10**:10–11
    divorce, **10**:28, 36
    of effort invested in persuasion,
        4:250

to eradicate poverty in India, **7**:343
as explanatory factors, **10**:11–12
external, **2**:42–43, 60–65; **4**:4–6
of fighting, **10**:121–22, 157
government-created monopoly,
    5:126–30
of government for any given voter,
    4:115–17
gun control, **10**:282
from ill-informed voters, **5**:203
of inaction, **8**:264–65
for individual of voting, **5**:43
individual recordkeeping, **1**:453–54
interdependence, **2**:46, 49
of inventions, **5**:158–59
involved in negligence, **9**:384–86
of law enforcement, **9**:226, 265,
    341–42
of legal reforms, **9**:344
lobbying, **1**:174, 188–91; **7**:201
lobbying for protective tariffs, **5**:309
logrolling, **1**:119; **5**:288
in lowering vehicle speeds,
    1:444–47
of lying, **4**:263
marginal, **10**:12–14
marriage, **10**:28–31
monitoring individuals, **10**:424
monopoly, **5**:19, 286
of negative and positive incentives,
    6:406–7
in obtaining information, **4**:230,
    239–40, 253–54; **7**:206–7
of organization, **9**:241–42
from poor information about politi-
    cal process, **4**:129–31
pork-barreling, **1**:194
from possibility of transfers,
    1:191–93
of prevention of violent crimes,
    9:217–22
from private vs. public externalities,
    4:85
in producing children, **10**:52–53

costs (*continued*)
  protective tariff, **1**:172
  of and from public goods, **4**:73–74
  of regulation, **7**:211
  related to insurance, **9**:117
  road repair or nonrepair, **1**:201
  scientific research, **3**:163–65,
    182–84
  from shift from private to public
    sectors, **4**:5n. 3
  social, from rent seeking, **6**:376
  social science research, **3**:141–43
  Social Security system, **7**:291–92;
    10:294
  to society from crime, **10**:57–58
  of specific policy output, **5**:36
  from targeted transfers, **7**:160–62
  of theft, **9**:190, 191–92
  transaction, **6**:244–45, 258–60,
    269
  transaction, and externalities, **2**:85
  of transfers, **1**:173–79; **7**:211, 338
  of transfers for universal-aid pro-
    grams, **7**:162–65
  of unanimity, **2**:65–66
  U-shaped curve, **5**.231, 297
  to victims of crime, **10**:57
  of vote specialization, **5**:299
  of voting, **4**:235, 270; **7**:205–6
  See also bargaining costs; court costs;
    decision-making costs; legal
    costs; legal fees; lobbying costs;
    monopoly costs; rent-seeking
    costs; social costs; transactions
    costs; welfare costs
costs and benefits
  charitable giving, **7**:8
  of court system, **9**:282
  of crime, **10**:56–58
  of crime avoidance, **10**:62–65
  of fraud, **9**:207
  income redistribution, **7**:73
  of institutional change, **9**:268
  involved in voting, **10**:280–81
  of monopolies, **9**:247
  proposed use by U.S. government,
    9:13–14
Costs of Economic Growth, The (Mishan),
  4:110
Cottrell, Leonard, **8**:*99n. 48*
Coulborn, Rushton, **8**:*38n. 22*
councils, advisory, **6**:225
countries
  logrolling by, **1**:117–18
  peacetime deficits, **1**:29–30
  taxation of the wealthy, **1**:268
coups d'état
  against bureaucrats, **8**:71
  counter coups, **8**:76
  decision to join, **8**:71–74
  difference from external overthrow,
    8:261
  difference from revolution,
    8:267–72
  false alarms, **8**:147
  final act in, **8**:75–76
  how organized, **8**:277–78
  killing of officials during, **8**:283
  neutrality during, **8**:263–67
  obstacles to prevention of, **8**.268–70
  officials' decision to join, **8**:284–85
  overthrow of sovereigns by, **6**:59–60
  payoffs in event of, **8**:262
  prediction of, **8**:232
  pronunciamientos, **8**:281–82
  random walk hypothesis, **8**:77
  revolutions following partial,
    8:287–88
  in Soviet Union, **8**:267–68
  success of, and legitimacy, **8**:232–33
  as usual way dictators overthrown,
    8:69
  why people "entrepreneur,"
    8:285–87
  See also military coups; revolutions
couriers, **6**:121–22
court costs
  accuracy vs., **9**:274–82

high levels of, **5**:186–87
likelihood of judicial error and, **9**:61
making losers pay, **9**:430, 442
in theft equation, **9**:192
for witnesses, **9**:77–78
See also legal costs
court decisions
accuracy, **9**:330–38
accuracy and cost, **9**:322–23
"correct," **1**:484–89, 511–12
errors of fact, **1**:495–508
probability of "correct," **1**:488,
493–94
role in making law, **1**:481–82, 491–
92
"Court Errors" (Tullock), **5**:186
Courtier (Castiglione), **6**:304
Court of the Star Chamber, **5**:164,
166, 170
court proceedings
historical reconstructions in, **9**:62
improving efficiency of, **9**:79–96
optimal investment of resources in,
9:62–65
role of facts in, **9**:62
courts
appellate, **6**:395, 397
as bureaucracies, **5**:118
chief functions of, in United States,
9:399–400
choosing type of, **9**:122–23
common law, **9**:413–14
control of law enforcement via,
6:393–97
costless improvements to, **9**:201–3
disagreements between, **1**:515
distrust of juries, **1**:530; **9**:434–37
duties, **5**:38
effect on bargaining, **9**:447
efficiency, **9**:60, 201–3, 274, 312
efficiency in judging evidence,
9:63–64
ethical system of, **9**:198
European, **1**:516

four foundational principles,
9:400–402
function, **1**:309–10
in historical England, **5**:164
improving efficiency of, **9**:41
within insurance companies, **9**:70
without lawyers, **5**:193
military courts, **9**:185
proposed reforms, **1**:489–93,
516–20
relation with legislatures, **9**:186
role in divorce process, **10**:27
role in promoting rent seeking, **5**:61
technology of, **9**:291
types of bias of, **9**:287–89
unrealistic notions about, **9**:39
See also contempt of court; court
costs; court decisions; judges;
judicial errors; juries; legal proceedings; out-of-court settlements; probate; tax courts;
traffic courts; trials; United
States Supreme Court
covenants to deeds to property, **4**:147
Craig, John, **10**:*325n. 9*
Crain, W. Mark, **4**:*172n. 3*; **5**:*33n. 38,
62n. 76*
Crassweller, Robert D., **8**:*70nn. 26,
28, 29, 102n. 58*
credit, **1**:314
credit limits in Korea, **10**:352–53
Crew, M. A., **5**:*15n. 7, 16n. 9, 52n. 59,
64n. 80, 69n. 87, 71n. 90*
crime
Communist concern about specific
types, **8**:226–27
costs to society from, **10**:57–58
costs to victims of, **10**:57
economic analyses, **9**:433
economic vs. sociological view,
9:257–59; **10**:73–77
factors affecting rate of, **9**:253
likelihood of, **9**:152–56
penalties for, **8**:19, 21

crime (*continued*)
  profit from, **9**:256–57
  punishment as deterrent, **10**:76,
    77–83
  as rational behavior, **10**:58–60
  requiring citizens to report, **8**:192
  total community level of, **10**:59
  See also organized crime; sex crimes;
    violent crime
crime avoidance, costs and benefits,
  10:62–65
crime control. *See* law enforcement
crime prevention, **9**:193–98; **10**:60
  costs, **10**:67
  of fraud, **9**:207–8
  as justification for particular punish-
    ment, **9**:259
  propaganda in, **9**:225–26
  sentencing and, **9**:163
  of violent crime, **9**:222
crime rates, **10**:60, 61, 62, 69–72
  reducing, **9**:192, 193
crimes against person. *See* violent crime
crimes against property, **9**:215;
  10:68, 71
crimes of impulse, **9**:218–20
  impact of punishment on, **9**:260
  prevention, **9**:222
  See also violent crime
criminal act, **9**:410
criminal informants, **9**:177–78
criminal intent, **9**:139
  automobile accident penalties and,
    9:144
criminal justice system, **1**:177
  bias in proceedings, **9**:202, 287–90
  civil suits vs., **9**:193–98
  common law provisions in,
    9:409–10
  inefficiencies, **9**:432–39
  law enforcement for, **9**:186–88
  motor vehicle offenses, **9**:137
  myths, **9**:152, 171–72

tax evasion, **9**:146–51
  in United States vs. England, **9**:318
  See also defendants; evidence of
    crime; illegal activities; plea
    bargaining
criminals
  benefits of crime to, **10**:56
  bribing, to not commit crimes,
    8:17n. 4
  charitable motives toward, **9**:200
  cost of crime to, **10**:56–57, 60
  curing vs. punishing, **9**:187–88
  economic transactions of, **8**:12
  impact of likelihood of capture on,
    9:258–59
  irrational or "sick," **10**:60–62, 77
  knowledge about likelihood of own
    punishment, **9**:260–61
  parole process, **9**:171
  professional criminals, **9**:156–57
  profit from crime, **9**:256–57
  public opinion about, **10**:77
  rational, **10**:58–60
  rehabilitation, **10**:74, 77
  rehabilitation through punishment,
    9:252, 261–62
  risk of being caught, **10**:72
  stupidity of, **9**:156
  things that deter, **9**:193
  See also offenders; punishment
criminological research, **9**:174,
  252–54
crisscross system of supervision,
  6:228–31, 316–20. *See also*
    chain of command
Crofts, Alfred, **8**:*64–65n. 5*
Cromwell, Oliver, **5**:165; **8**:204
cross-disciplinary training and research,
  3:64, 70–71, 179. *See also*
    interdisciplinary scientists
cross-national economic growth,
  1951–1980
  design of study, **10**:381–82

hypotheses about, **10**:382–84
results of study, **10**:385–95
variables used in study, **10**:379, 384
Croyle, J. L., **9**:*365n. 6*
Crozier, Bernard, **8**:*297n. 11*
Cuba, **5**:307n. 11
Culbertson, W. P., **7**:*29n. 13*
cultural differences in organizations,
    6:42–44
Cummings, M. M., **3**:*86n. 29*
cumulative indexes, **3**:81
curiosity
    definition, **3**:33
    social sciences vs. sciences, **3**:151–53
    types, **3**:23–26
    See also induced curiosity
currencies
    ancient Chinese paper money,
        10:321–24
    barter in China vs., **10**:317–20, 345
    in China, 1937–1949, **10**:307–8
    Chin dynasty in China, **10**:329–31
    Chinese Communist, **10**:312
    Ch'ing dynasty in China, **10**:338–39
    competing forms of, **10**:359–66
    depreciation of, in China,
        10:311–12
    difficulty of replacing existing,
        10:371–72
    frequency of competing forms of,
        10:368–70
    functions of, **10**:319, 367
    Ming dynasty in China, **10**:337–38
    Mongol dynasty in China,
        10:332–37
    South Korean, 1945–1954, **10**:350
    Sung dynasty in China, **10**:328–29
    Szechuan dynasty in China,
        10:326–28
    use as media of exchange in China,
        1937–1949, **10**:317–18
    use of precious metals as, **10**:339
    See also Chinese coins; paper money

curve of external economies. *See* external economies curve
Cushing, Robert G., **9**:*258n. 16*;
    10:*81n. 13*
customers, **6**:341, 342
    nonprofit organizations, **6**:347
    See also consumers; salesmen
cycle, majoritarian, **2**:316–18
cyclical majority, **1**:91, 92–93;
    5:270–71
    as applied to dictatorships, **5**:270–71
    Duncan Black's discovery, **4**:304
    frequency, **4**:276, 280–82, 297–98
    importance, **4**:275, 278
    origin of problem, **4**:275
cycling
    absence of, in real world, **4**:357
    assumption of transitivity and,
        1:62–63
    Black's expectation of, **1**:105
    in demand-revealing process, **4**:364
    detecting, in real world, **1**:98–100
    among discrete groups, **1**:102–3
    in small voting bodies, **4**:284,
        288–91
    things that stop, **4**:333–34
    in voting, **1**:19–20, 95–98
    when using demand-revealing
        process, **1**:140–41

Dacey, Norman F., **9**:*130n. 7*
Dahl, Robert A., **2**:*8, 20n. 8, 22n. 10,*
    23, 31n. 2, 148–49n. 7;
    8:*33n. 1, 39n. 27*
dairy industry, **7**:184–86
Daland, Robert T., **8**:*92–93n. 28,*
    137n. 95
Dales, J. H., **5**:*180n. 5*
damages in lawsuits
    compensatory damages, **9**:407, 451
    expectation damages, **9**:408
    fixing of, **9**:309–10
    too many, **9**:448

Damaska, Mirjan, **9**:*309n. 1*

Danziger, Sheldon, **7**:*27n. 6, 241n. 19*

Darby, Michael R., **7**:*269n. 10*

Darman, Richard, **4**:27

Darwin, Charles, **1**:555; **10**:117

data
  patterns in, **3**:95–102
  relation with hypotheses, **3**:53–54
  See also experimental data

data collection
  for its own sake, **3**:85, 86
  relation to data dissemination, **3**:111
  relation to hypothesis development, **3**:55–56, 101
  relation to hypothesis testing, **3**:101
  in verification of scientific theories, **3**:112

data dissemination
  relation to data collection, **3**:111
  See also dissemination of scientific discoveries

Dates, J. H., **1**:*426n. 2*

Davidson, Diane W., **10**:*140n. 1*

Davies, Norman, **8**:*65n. 10*

Davis, A. M., **10**:*322n. 2*

Davis, Angela, **9**:315

Davis, Michael, "Avoiding the Voter's Paradox Democratically," **4**:295–96

Davis, Otto A., **1**:*349n. 1, 413n. 2*; **2**:xxv, 6n. 3, *54n. 8*; **4**:*283n. 1*, 319, 327

Dawkins, R., **10**:*188n. 7*

deadweight costs, **5**:255

deadweight public debt, **9**:250

De Alessi, Louis, **4**:*172n. 3*

Deane, Phyllis, **8**:*135n. 90*

death duty, **1**:253

death penalty, **9**:259; **10**:77, 78, 83
  for economic crimes, **9**:197, 198
  for minor crimes, **9**:198–200

death squads, **8**:198

debates, allocation of time during, **4**:392–93

debtors' prisons, **9**:53–54

debt repayment, **1**:314

deceased persons, legal status, **9**:130–34

decentralization, **2**:109–10
  decision-making, **6**:328
  in government, **6**:276, 359–61, 370, 413–14
  without loss of central control, **6**:276
  See also federalism

decentralized economic enterprises, **6**:253

deception, **1**:313, 314
  by charities, **1**:402
  exposing, **1**:600
  "honest deception" by politicians, **4**:260
  about transfers, **1**:289–90, 293

decision making
  changes of mind, **1**:64, 67–68
  about charitable giving, **1**:394–95
  about cheating on a treaty, **8**:338–43
  of civil servants, **4**:161–62
  within committees, **4**:433–34
  of consumers compared with voters, **1**:72–73
  corporate, **4**:84; **5**:282
  correct decisions followed by poor results, **6**:75–76
  of courts, **1**:484–93, 511–14, 518
  decentralized, **6**:328
  demand-revealing process, **1**:135–38
  in democracies, **1**:104
  erroneous, **1**:484–85
  about evading payment of income taxes, **9**:148–49

within families, **10**:29–30
frequency of lawsuit involvement
    and, **9**:65
in games of strategy, **1**:229–30
about going to war, **8**:327–29
by government, **7**:350; **9**:13–14
by high-level officials, **6**:353
by ill-informed superiors, **6**:199
impossibility of centralized, **6**:152
individual, **5**:208–9
in inquisitorial proceedings,
    1:473–75
intelligence in hierarchies and, **6**:23
involving bundles of alternatives,
    1:83–84
of juries, **1**:514–15
by legal authorities, **9**:324–38
of legislatures, **1**:25; **4**:417–23
life-and-death decisions, **7**:339–42
by low-ranking personnel, **6**:192
about participating in revolution,
    8:167–68
political, **5**:302–6
private vs. public sector, **1**:388–92
about public vs. private problems,
    4:225
rationality of, **6**:31
reaching consensus, **9**:11–13
relation with externalities, **5**:268
rights of poor people, **7**:347
risk aversion and, **9**:30–31
of sovereign's subordinates, **6**:72–
    74, 79
about starting a war, **8**:323–26
techniques for making life-and-death
    choices, **7**:346–51
about transfers, **7**:78
by ultimate sovereigns, **6**:159
of voters, **4**:247
when voters are self-interested,
    1:162
whether to have children, **10**:43

about whether to sue, **9**:57–61
as to who makes first decision,
    4:80n. 9
about whom to help, **7**:342–46
worthiness-of-recipient criteria,
    7:350
See also choices; collective decision-
    making; court decisions; judi-
    cial decisions; preferences
decision-making costs, **2**:93–111
agreement and, **2**:94
collective action and, **2**:198–99
decision-making rules and, **2**:43,
    63–67
family, **10**:29
group size and, **2**:107–8
information costs, **1**:401
majority rule and, **2**:103–4
deduced hypothesis, **3**:89
deduction, **3**:89–92
possible, **3**:90–91
probable, **3**:90–91
relation with induction, **3**:92–94,
    98–99
See also hypothesis testing
defendants
duty of care, **9**:409
falsely charged, **1**:461–62, 517
odds of losing cases, **1**:501
relation between guilt and evidence,
    1:497–99
See also trials
defense industries and lobbying, **5**:158
deficits. *See* budget deficits; national
    deficits
DeForest, Lee, **3**:8
de Gaulle, Charles, **6**:*222n. 4*; **8**:297
de Jasay, A., **9**:*448n. 20*
de Jouvenel, Bertrand, **8**:*91n. 21*
Dekmejian, R. Hrair, **8**:*89n. 16*
de la Vallee Poisson, D., **1**:*135n. 8*
Delli Carpini, M. X., **5**:*239n. 7*

demand, **10**:14–19
Demand and Supply of Public Goods, The
(Buchanan), **4**:220
demand-revealing process, **5**:289–90
advantages, **1**:153–54
coalitions under, **1**:146–47, 164–
66; **4**:366–72
compared with majority voting,
7:145–48
compensation mechanism for,
1:133–34
confiscatory characteristics, **1**:138
costs, **1**:152–53
demand curves generated by,
4:373–75; **7**:182, 183
difference from other voting processes, **1**:134–35, 153
effect on motives for income redistribution, **7**:76–77
equilibrium, **1**:145–46
examples, **1**:135–48, 164–65
examples of transfers using, **7**:81–85
limitations, **1**:154–57, 159–60;
4:361–66
Milton Friedman's opinion, **4**:25
origin of, **4**:447
similarity to market process, **1**:158
Tullock's preference for, **1**:110
uses, **1**:156, 157–58; **7**:195n. 16
using for charitable giving, **7**:89
using for income redistribution,
7:71–77
using for voting by poor, **7**:147–48
using for voting on transfers,
7:224–25
virtue of, **4**:362
voter regard for others in own demand curve, **4**:375–77
wealth and income distribution
problem, **1**:160–63
wealth effect in, **1**:140–41
as welfare criterion, **1**:158–59

when minorities have intense feelings, **4**:428–31
See also Clarke tax; Lindahl tax
"Demand-Revealing Process, Coalitions, and Public Goods"
(Tullock), **4**:366
democracies, **4**:37
actual help given to poor people, **7**:9
advantages relative to dictatorships,
8:152–53
Aristotelian theory of overthrow of,
8:127–28
better form of government than,
4:165
centralized vs. decentralized, **6**:278
compared with dictatorships, **1**:33;
8:55, 61–62
compared with monarchical governments, **5**:278
control of corruption in, **1**:325–26,
327
crucial weakness, **5**:44
definition, **5**:265; **8**:39–40,
143–44
despotism vs., **6**:92–93
development, **7**:180
dictatorships developed out of,
8:108
differences from dictatorships,
5:132–34
direct, **2**:116
ease of overthrowing, **8**:172–73
efficiency of, **5**:230
as an electoral system, **8**:38–39
ethics, **2**:253–68
externalities in, **5**:266
government reorganizations, **6**:247
government spending, **1**:302, 305
group sovereigns, **6**:133–34
as illusion or fraud, **1**:19–20
income redistribution in, **1**:264–65
individualist, **2**:4, 95–96

inefficiency in reducing social costs, **4**:162

as least imperfect system, **4**:395

legislative role in, **6**:361–62

limitations, **5**:278–81

military extension of, **8**:112–15

military roots of development, **8**:125–27

as model of cooperative government, **8**:25

modern vs. ancient, **4**:413

nonrevolutionary development of, **8**:171–72

overthrow of, **6**:62–64, 308

as permanent systems, **6**:386

without political parties, **6**:101

popular uprisings against, **8**:220–21

presidential succession in, **8**:84–87

relationship to electoral systems, **8**:107–8

representative, **1**:52; **2**:203–13; **8**:143

rise and decline of, **8**:221–24

role of intellectuals, **8**:131–32

stability, **1**:105

stability vs. efficiency, **1**:120

strength of bureaucrats in, **5**:54–55

successful functioning, **1**:104

that replace dictatorships, **8**:130–33

theory of economic externalities, **1**:78

three major periods, **8**:173

transfers actually observed in, **7**:6

twentieth century, **8**:123–24

universal suffrage, **6**:3

use of torture in, **8**:215–16

variations of, **1**:31

voting processes used in, **7**:80, 82–85

See also electoral systems of government; limited autocracy; nondemocratic systems; voting

democratic groups, **6**:90

demonstrations, **1**:342. *See also* revolutions; student protests

Dempster, J. P., **1**:*542n. 4*

Demsetz, Harold, **1**:*174n. 10*; **4**:*106n. 6, 112n. 14*; **6**:*273n. 12,* 274. *See also* Alchian-Demsetz transactions costs theory

D'Encausse, Hélène Carrére, **8**:*65n. 10, 109–10n. 6, 127–28n. 71, 132n. 80*

Denison, E. F., **10**:*384n. 15, 396n. 21*

density dependent consumption, **1**:538

Department of State, U.S. *See under* United States government agencies

department store example, **4**:122, 124–25

dependence on irrelevant alternatives, **1**:139–40

deregulation of industries, **1**:590; **4**:41–42; **7**:326

banking industry, **5**:310

transitional-gains trap and, **5**:67–69

Derthick, Martha, **5**:*216n. 8, 229n. 31*

de Santillana, Giorgio, **3**:*35n. 5, 147n. 20*

Design of Experiments, The (Fisher), **3**:126

despotism

anarchy vs., **4**:82

corruption and bribery under, **1**:326–27

democracies vs., **6**:92–93

earliest, **8**:116–17

hierarchies in, **6**:276

historical prevalence of, **7**:179–80

inefficiency, **8**:274, 276–77

juries under, **1**:522–23

loyalty of officials, **8**:285

despotism (*continued*)
  popular uprisings against, **8**:289–91
  prevalence, **8**:30
  prisoners' dilemma of rulers, **8**:287
  relationship to electoral systems,
      8:134–35
  rise of, in twentieth century, **8**:124
  supervision under, **6**:322
  See also exploitative government;
      totalitarian governments
detection of crime, likelihood of,
    9:226
DeTray, Dennis, **10**:*49nn. 10, 11*
Deutsch, Karl, **2**:*143n. 1*
developing countries
  in cross-national sample, **10**:397–98
  developed country empirical studies
      vs., **10**:380
  economic growth, **10**:391–93,
      396–97
  population explosion, **10**:50
  transfers from rich countries to,
      7:8–9
developmental research. *See* applied
    research
de Waal, Frans, **10**:*165n. 7*
Dewey, John, **2**:*19n. 4*
Dexter, Ralph W., **3**:*167n. 7*
Dicey, Albert Venn, **1**:*304n. 8*;
    7:*148n. 8*; **9**:*405n. 5*
dictators
  abilities, **8**:144–45
  advantages of war to, **8**:312
  assassination of, **8**:82–83
  attention to public opinion,
      8:151–52
  command of military by, **8**:304–5
  committees who appoint successors
      to, **8**:94–97
  concessions by, **8**:199–200
  danger of appointing a successor,
      8:84–85
  danger of criticism to, **8**:287

  decision to start war, **8**:323–26
  differences from monarchs,
      8:52–53
  emerging from a junta, **8**:78, 79–81
  end of tenure in office, **8**:151,
      156–57
  government vs. market problem, **8**:57
  importance of legitimacy to, **8**:257
  investments abroad, **8**:51–52
  maintaining power, **8**:146–49, 293–
      95, 296, 300–306
  mass murders by, **8**:147–48
  means used to prevent overthrow,
      8:274–76
  motives, **8**:48–49, 56, 60–62
  need for legitimacy, **8**:254–55
  with no legitimate heir, **8**:150–51
  overthrow of, **8**:71, 273, 297–99
  paths to power, **8**:63–69
  personal expenditures, **8**:49–52
  plots against, **8**:69
  policies of, **8**:53–61
  power against coups, **8**:269
  strategies used to become, **8**:74
  succession after death of, **8**:82, 89
  things that indicate strength in,
      8:300, 302
  traits of highly successful, **8**:68–69
  why duration of tenure secures
      power, **8**:281
  See also monarchs
dictatorships
  advantages of democracies over,
      8:152–53
  basic features, **6**:274–75
  "capitalist," **5**:122–24
  changes in structure, **6**:247
  choices about control in, **6**:372–74
  compared with democracies, **8**:55,
      61–62
  compared with monarchical govern-
      ments, **5**:122
  demand-revealing process in, **1**:157

developed out of democracies,
8:108
difference from democracies, 5:279
difference from monarchies,
8:154–55
ethics in, 8:46
junior officials, 8:254
juntas, 6:91
keeping secrets in, 8:336
law enforcement by, 6:395
with legislatures, 8:136
motives of dictators, 5:127–29, 130
negative characterization of, 1:29,
32–33
officials, 8:71–73
overthrow of, 6:59–64
petition system in, 6:225–26
political freedoms under, 8:157
relationship to monopoly, 8:33
relationship to totalitarian government, 8:40–41
replaced by democracies, 8:130–33
replaced by hereditary monarchs,
8:101–3
as subject of study, 1:46
switch to hereditary control,
8:292–93
that change into electoral systems,
8:112–14
three ways to overthrow, 8:43–46
See also autocracy; despotism; juntas;
monarchies
Diederich, Bernard, 8:*101n. 56*
Dietz, Henry A., 1:*342n. 7*
DiLorenzo, Thomas J., 6:*346n. 11*,
385n. 12
diminishing returns. *See* law of diminishing returns
DiPerma, P., 9:*424nn. 31, 32, 426n. 36*
diplomatic service, 5:120
diplomats. *See* Foreign Service of
United States
direct democracy, voting rule, 4:1–10

directed research
government vs. private, 3:20–21
investments in, 3:17–18
See also induced research; laboratories; research and development
direct investigation, methods of, 3:85
directly unproductive profit seeking
(DUP), 5:30–31
direct popular voting. *See* referendum
on government policies
direct regulation
of consumption, 1:419–24
of output, 1:412, 413, 414–17
See also quotas on consumption;
rationing
direct transfers. *See* taxes
disability special-interest groups,
7:211
disagreement
in higher education, 3:175–76
in the sciences, 3:129–31
in the social sciences, 3:157–58
disarmament
agreements, 8:334, 335–36
impacts of, 8:332
model of, 8:366–67
mutual, 8:326–27, 335
prisoners' dilemma, 8:338
reasons for not cheating, 8:336
secrecy, 8:249–50, 353
unilateral, 8:323
See also treaties
discipline of continuous dealings,
1:314, 317, 318, 320
role in civilization, 1:321
disciplines of study. *See* academic
disciplines
discount clubs, 9:243–44. *See also*
comparison shopping
discounting of future events,
9:26–30
contracts and, 9:51–54
of income stream, 9:24

discoveries, **3**:148
  rapid circulation of, **3**:27
  See also new ideas; scientific
    discoveries
discovery (legal), **1**:463; **9**:74–75
discrimination
  against assistant professors,
    10:111–12
  relative poverty and, **7**:229–30
  in tax-prices, **1**:375–77
  Tullock's definition, **7**:230
  against women, **10**:34
discriminatory pricing, **1**:374–75
discussion among scientists, **3**:129–
    31, 133
  effect on accuracy of scientific re-
    search, **3**:129
  effect on scientific observation,
    3:129
  importance of gossip, **3**:66–67
  relation to publication of scientific
    discoveries, **3**:131, 133
  See also arguments in higher
    education
disease. *See* ill and injured people
disease treatment vs. immunization
    example, **1**:356–58
diseconomies of scale, **5**:231–32
dishonesty
  in government, **4**:43
  by politicians, **6**:27
  See also lying
dissemination of scientific discoveries
  from applied research, **3**:112–15
  by gossip, **3**:66–67
  relation with verification process,
    3:133–34
  See also publication of scientific
    discoveries
distribution, **8**:9
  under majority rule, **2**:144
distributional gains, **8**:5

distribution problem applied to ecol-
    ogy, **1**:547, 548
division of labor
  Adam Smith's view, **10**:209–10,
    219–20
  ants, **10**:209, 216–24
  bees, **10**:206, 234–35
  disadvantages of, **3**:79
  in scholarly work, **10**:368
  as survival mechanism, **10**:223
  termites, **10**:230–31, 257–58
divorce, **10**:26–28
  costs, **10**:36
  relation to spouse selection, **10**:36
Dmytryshyn, Basil, **8**:*78n. 40, 78–
    79n. 41*
doctors
  income effects from universalization
    of health care, **7**:311–12, 313
  motives, **4**:40
  special-interest groups, **7**:311–12,
    364–65
  variations in expertise among,
    7:314–16
Dodgson, C. L. *See* Carroll, Lewis
Dohaney Amendment, **9**:283
Dolbear, F. T., **4**:*90n. 3, 98n. 1,
    109n. 10*
Domes, Jurgen, **8**:*74n. 32, 79n. 43*
dominance, **10**:123–24
  majoritarian, **2**:170
  male, **10**:116
  territoriality, **1**:556
  See also fighting; hierarchies
Dominican Republic, **5**:127–28
Donahue, John D., **5**:*214n. 3*
donations. *See* charitable giving
Dorosh, Gary W., **1**:*593n. 4*
Dougan, W. R., **5**:236–37
Downs, Anthony, **1**:*17n. 2, 51n. 2,
    137n. 10, 262n. 2, 392n. 5,
    394n. 2;* **2**:*213n. 5;* **4**:*6n. 4,*

127n. 12; **5**:*39n. 43, 42n. 45,*
54n. 68; **8**:*39n. 30*
defense of two-party system,
4:388–90
economic approach to democratic
process, **2**:116n. 1
Economic Theory of Democracy, An,
1:5–6; **2**:8; **4**:220, 225, 305;
5:226; **6**:90; **7**:5–6
on importance of individual vote,
5:276
income redistribution in democracies, **1**:262, 264–65
"In Defense of Majority Voting,"
2:246n. 3
logrolling model, **4**:319
on majority voting, **7**:80
politics, **4**:18
relation with public choice field,
4:14
on right amount of income redistribution, **7**:222
rule of ill-informed voters, **1**:137
theory of candidates and elections,
2:325–29
theory of voting, **2**:127
on transfers, **7**:5–6
on universalization of services,
7:255
views about political information,
7:207
voting process, **4**:236n. 14
work on political parties, **2**:9
See also Hotelling-Downs model
Downs paradox, **1**:145
Drew, Ann Barthelmes, **9**:*356n. 41*
Dreze, J. H., **1**:*135n. 8*
driver's licenses
restrictions, **9**:145n. 11
revocation vs. restriction, **1**:449
Drucker, Peter, **6**:241
Drury, Allen, **2**:*119n. 3*

due process, **8**:198; **9**:405–6
Dugatkin, Lee, **8**:*146n. 10*
Duguit, Leon, **2**:303
Dulles, John Foster, **6**:123
Dunningan, James, **8**:*39n. 29,*
44nn. 50, 51, 66n. 13, 107n. 1,
293n. 4, 303n. 16
Dunn-Pattison, R. P., **8**:*125n. 61*
DUP (directly unproductive profit
seeking), **5**:30–31
du Picq, Armand, **10**:405, 406, 413–
15, 419
DuPont Corporation, **5**:118
Dupuy, R. Ernest, **8**:*34n. 5, 35n. 10,*
42n. 45, 43n. 48, 64n. 5,
68nn. 20, 21, 89–90n. 19,
100n. 51, 112n. 11, 115n. 19,
119n. 39, 124n. 54, 125nn. 60,
61, 126nn. 62, 66, 126–27n. 67,
203n. 13, 218n. 54, 249–
50n. 37, 252n. 46, 305n. 24
Dupuy, Trevor N., **8**:*34n. 5, 35n. 10,*
42n. 45, 43n. 48, 64n. 5,
68nn. 20, 21, 89–90n. 19,
100n. 51, 112n. 11, 115n. 19,
119n. 39, 124n. 54, 125nn. 60,
61, 126nn. 62, 65, 66, 126–
27n. 67, 203n. 13, 218n. 54,
249–50n. 37, 252n. 46,
305n. 24
Durden, G. C., **5**:*19n. 12*
Dynamics of Bureaucracy, The (Blau),
6:193–94, 217–20
Dziewanowski, M. K., **8**:*65n. 10*

Eadie, John W., **8**:*126n. 63*
earmarked taxes, **10**:291
Eastern Europe, **1**:344–45
Eastern European governments,
6:388–90
ecology, **1**:541, 550. *See also* environmental coordination

economic approach to politics,
4:170–71
ethical issues raised by, 4:172–73
readings for, 4:220–21
See also public choice theory
economic development, 8:357
economic growth, 5:153–54
Africa, 10:396–97
Africa, Americas, and Asia,
10:391–92
Australia, 10:389
Canada, 10:389
effect on governments, 10:386–87
impact of government on, 10:380
impact of inflation on, 10:390
Ireland, 10:389
Japan, 10:390–91
OECD countries, 10:385–89
population growth and, 10:386, 391
Turkey, 10:389
United Kingdom, 10:389
United States, 10:389–91
variables, 10:379
See also cross-national economic
growth, 1951–1980
economic man, 2.16
economic models, 10:6
economic privileges, 9:17
economic relationships compared with
political relationships, 6:6–9,
250–51
economics
assumptions of, 1:14
biology and, 1:553; 10:117–18,
139–41, 142
changes in field of, 10:3
compared with politics, 4:32–34;
6:6, 9, 14
compared with science, 3:52
defining, 10:4–5
development of the field, 1:4–5
difference from other fields, 10:22
effect on policy, 1:589–91
emphasis on individuals, 10:3–4,
7–8, 405
emphasis on structuring of institutions, 10:405–6
experimental evidence of rationality,
10:95–102
foundation of, 8:3
importance of abstractions to,
10:5–6
of information, 7:176
lack of concern about moral values,
10:7
link with political science, 1:5–6,
7–8, 16
methodological differences from
biology, 1:554–55
methodology, 2:xxi
neoclassical, view of social cost of
monopoly, 5:14
predictive aspects of, 6:9
problem ignored by, 8:4
public sector, 4:169
public utility, 5:297
relation to public choice theory, 1:9,
16–17; 4:16–20
relation to science, 3:10
relation with other social sciences,
1:10–11
role of reason and the passions in,
1:8
scarcity in, 1:13–14
small-scale models, 7:198
sociobiology and, 10:133–38,
139–54
study of preferences, 1:9–10
of theft, 1:174–77, 178
Tullock's role in, 1:606–8
two-good universe, 7:133
view of crime, 10:73–77
See also economists; publication in
economics
economics imperialism, 1:3–7
definition, 1:4n. 1

economics journals
  rejection of Tullock rectangle,
    5:19–20
  rejection of Tullock rent-seeking
    article, **5**:25
Economics of Income Redistribution, The
    (Tullock), **7**:61n. 16, 63n. 18,
    118, 160, 161
*Economics of Special Privilege and Rent
    Seeking, The* (Tullock), **4**:24;
    5:75, 236
Economics of Welfare, The (Pigou),
    4:68
economic theories, **2**:4; **3**:36. *See also*
    theory of constitutions
Economic Theory of Democracy, An
    (Downs), **1**:5–6; **4**:220, 225,
    305; **5**:226; **6**:90; **7**:5–6
economies of scale
  centralization of government and,
    4:401
  contiguity problems vs., **4**:144–45
  from division of labor, **4**:73
  existence of smaller companies and,
    6:216
  geographic contiguity and, **4**:66–
    67, 144–45
  in higher management, **6**:273
  size of organizations and, **6**:411–12
economists
  contrasted with sociologists,
    10:427–28
  definition, **10**:5n. 2
  difference from political scientists,
    4:124
  educational influence, **1**:293
  efforts to stop rent seeking, **1**:594
  as experts for the public, **1**:597–601
  importance of, **5**:310–11
  influence on policy, **6**:305n. 16
  perception of utility, **7**:95–96
  sociologists' view of crime and pun-
    ishment vs., **9**:257–59

See also academic research; publica-
    tion in economics
editors of academic journals, motives,
    5:20–21
editors of scientific journals, **3**:67–68
  attributes needed, **3**:116
  improving the quality of, **3**:117
  motivations, **3**:120, 121
  prestige, **3**:121–22
  role in preserving information, **3**:80
  rules for selecting papers, **3**:119–20
education
  educating children for the future,
    3:159–60
  fertility and, **10**:50–52
  See also higher education; public
    education
education of scientists, **3**:56–64
  amateur scientists, **3**:179–82
  most important aspect, **3**:65–66
  See also higher education institutions;
    self-education of scientists
Edwards, Thomas Joseph, **8**:*38n. 26*
efficiency, **2**:165
  bankruptcy as cost of, **5**:107
  bargaining and, **2**:100
  in biological systems, **1**:428
  bureaucracies, **4**:132–33
  business vs. government, **6**:281
  of charities, **1**:398–99
  of compensating for externalities,
    4:351–53
  court procedures, **9**:79–96
  of courts, **9**:60–61, 201–3, 274,
    312
  of courts in judging evidence,
    9:63–64
  as criteria for choice, **9**:378–79
  definition, **4**:346
  of democracies, in reducing social
    costs, **4**:162
  of democracies vs. dictatorships,
    5:135

efficiency (*continued*)
  effect on survival of societies,
    1:564–65, 572–73
  of effects from logrolling, 4:347,
    357–58
  as explanation for society, 1:558
  "false," 7:360–62
  in families, 10:32–34
  of government, 1:75, 291–92,
    366–67; 6:411–12; 7:74–76
  of government transfers, 5:147
  income redistribution, 7:40–41
  individuals vs. groups, 6:307, 310
  issues in charitable giving, 7:89,
    105–10
  of large enterprises, 6:411
  of law enforcement, 9:263–73
  of legal systems, 1:462–64
  of logrolling by coalitions of voters,
    4:357
  measuring, by government agencies,
    6:348
  of nonprofit organizations, 6:346
  of police, 9:174
  preference for less than optimal,
    6:110–11
  "process efficiency," 5:116n. 9
  quantity of public good needed for,
    1:141
  of rent seeking, 5:63–66
  required for nepotism to work,
    1:560
  of special-interest groups, 5:47
  in supervision, 6:387–88
  of transfers, 7:184, 194–97
  of transfers motivated by self-
    interest, 7:184–87
  types of, 7:181
  types of, at workplace, 6:132
  wealth equalization vs., 7:50
  See also government efficiency;
    judicial inefficiency; utility

"Efficient Rent Seeking" (Tullock),
    5:221, 231, 250–51, 297
  mathematical problem solutions,
    5:95–100
  revisited, 5:85–87
egalitarian coalitions, 1:111
egalitarian governments, 1:321–22
egalitarianism (Mises), 5:114
egalitarian systems of voting, 1:157–58
Egyptian government succession of
    power, 8:99
Ehrlich, Isaac, 9:255, 259;
    10:*82n. 18*, 83
80 percent majority rule, 5:270
Einstein, Albert, 3:35, 176, 178;
    9:233n. 6
Einsteinian vs. Newtonian systems,
    3:36, 37–38, 42
Eisenberg, M. A., 9:*399n. 2, 400nn. 4,
    5, 401n. 6, 415n. 3*
Eisenberg, Theodore, 1:*500nn. 4, 5*
Eisenhower, Dwight David, 6:97–98,
    296n. 4
Eisenstadt, S. N., 8:*112n. 10*
Eisner, Robert, 9:*114n. 16*
Einsfeldt, Otto, 8:*201n. 19*
Ekelund, Robert B., Jr., 8:*57n. 19,
    154n. 21*
  *Economic Regulation in Mercantile
    England*, 5:*162n. 4, 164nn. 6,
    7, 165n. 8*
  *Institutions and Political Economy of
    Mercantilism, The*, 5:*241n. 2*
  *Mercantilism as a Rent-Seeking
    Society*, 5:*122n. 1, 126n. 5,
    237n. 3*
"Elaborations on a Theme by Fried-
    man" (Tullock), 7:91n. 5
elected officials
  compensation, 1:76
  difference from others, 1:391–92
  fixed fee system for, 1:73–74

logrolling by, **1**:112–16, 119–20,
585–86
losers as auditors of winners,
1:88–89
nonelected officials vs., **4**:407
selling out by, **1**:111–12
timesaving devices, **1**:119–20
voting by, **1**:580
See also legislatures; politicians
election procedures. *See* voting process
elections
in Communist countries, **6**:330n. 8
level of government involved,
4:130–31
with more than two candidates,
6:101–3
party differential, **4**:236
predominance of issues over candidates, **6**:104
single-candidate, **6**:100–101
See also political candidates; primary
elections; voting
electoral systems of government
definition, **8**:38–39, 107–8, 124
emergence in Middle Ages,
8:121–24
foreign conquest of, **8**:116–19
longevity, **8**:128–29
overthrow, **8**:129–30
relation with despotism, **8**:134–35
that change into dictatorships,
8:112
See also constitutional monarchy;
democracies; limited autocracy;
voting process
electric power production, **4**:112
elements, weights of, **3**:99–100
Elgin, R. S., **5**:*59n. 70*
Ellis, L. V., **5**:*19n. 12*
Ellsberg, Daniel, **1**:*56n. 6*; **2**:135n. 9;
10:*438n. 1*
Elzinga, Kenneth G., **1**:*461n. 6*

embezzlement, **9**:204, 205
eminent domain, **1**:426; **9**:408
empires
Athenian, **6**:350
British, **6**:185; **7**:45–46
Chinese, **6**:331–32
largest ever, **6**:249
organization of, **6**:183
Persian, **6**:275
Roman, **6**:184
Spanish, **6**:276, 370
See also British Empire
empirical research. *See* applied
research
empirical vs. theoretical science,
3:49
in mapmaking in Middle Ages,
3:150–51
empiricism, **3**:33–35
employee-owned firms, **6**:341–42
employees, **6**:341–42
bargaining among, **6**:380
firing, **6**:378, 383–84, 401
firing, relative to other punishments, **6**:407
nonprofit organizations, **6**:347
rotation of, **6**:381–82, 385
See also subordinates; supervisors
employers. *See* residual claimants;
sovereigns
employment
government, **6**:15–16
waste of resources in obtaining,
5:110–12
See also civil service systems
employment contracts, **9**:54
employment market, **6**:14–17. *See
also* labor
encomienda, **7**:39–40
enforcement of legal activities. *See* law
enforcement
Engels, Friedrich, **8**:*45n. 52*

engineering fields, **3**:62, 63
engineering publications, classification
  systems, **3**:69
England. *See* Britain
"English" system of voting, **4**:441;
  6:99–100
Enke, Stephen, **8**:*168n. 3*
Enker, Arnold, **9**:*164n. 9*
Enlightenment, **1**:8; **2**:289
entertainment value
  of investing, **1**:434–35, 437
  of revolutions, **1**:332, 339
Entrepreneurial Politics (Tullock), **6**:90
entry barriers, **1**:71
  economics of monopolies and,
    1:74–75
  efficiency of government services
    and, **1**:75–76
environmental coordination,
    10:250–52
  bees, **10**:257
  of organizational structures,
    6:334–37
  outcomes from, **6**:338–39
  in regard to markets, **6**:333–34,
    335
  termites, **10**:255–56
  universities as example of, **6**:337–38
  See also ecology
environmentalists, **1**:429, 547–48
envy, **7**:27–28, 55, 66–67, 69–70
  income redistribution and,
    1:286–88
Epstein, R. C., **5**:*12n. 2*
Epstein, Richard A., **9**:*375n. 16*
equality
  in choice of rules, **2**:76
  myth of social, **6**:10
  among participants in game, **2**:76
  in wealth, **1**:252–53
equality in law, **9**:181
equalization of income. *See* wealth
  equalization

equerry, **6**:84
equilibrium
  agreement vs. independent adjust-
    ment, **1**:199
  Lindahl, **1**:145–46
  Nash, **1**:230
  natural vs. man-made, **1**:542–46
  political, **1**:376
  pseudo, **1**:241–42
  rent seeking, **1**:222–23
  See also hawk/dove equilibrium
equitable relief, **9**:407, 408
Erickson, Maynard L., **10**:*83n. 19*
erroneous scientific discoveries,
    3:123–28
errors by courts. *See* judicial errors
errors of professionals vs. amateurs,
    9:324–25, 439
Ertel, Hans, **3**:109n. 7
Espenschied, Lloyd, **3**:*8n. 10*
estate taxes. *See* inheritance taxes
ethical imperialism, **5**:206, 207
ethics
  definition, **8**:225–27
  of democracy, **2**:253–68
  of dictatorships, **8**:46
  efficiency and, **2**:253–68
  internal systems of, **6**:44–46
  justification of, **9**:11
  law without, **9**:9–14
  in organizations, **6**:201
  origin, **8**:229
  philosophers' approach to,
    8:230–31
  pressure groups and, **2**:279–80
  reason for, **8**:246–47
  relation with law, **9**:225–28, 340,
    346
  relation with legitimacy, **8**:227–28
  trade and, **2**:255–57
  worldwide code, **9**:227
  See also cost of conscience; morals
Ethiopian famine, **7**:118–19

Ethiopian government, **8**:123
Euclid, **3**:13-14
European Common Market, **5**:121
European corporations, **6**:345n. 8, 349
European dominance of the world,
    1:30
European electoral governments,
    8:114-15
European political parties, **4**:420-21
European Public Choice Society,
    4:15-16
European system of law. *See* inquisitorial
    system of law
European vs. U.S. legislatures, **1**:118
eusociality, **10**:236, 240
Evans, Peter, **1**:*477n. 2*
Evans, Rowland, Jr., **8**:*85n. 7*
evidence
    illegally obtained, **9**:358-59
    needed for conviction, **9**:285-86
    payments of money for, **9**:177
    strength of, **9**:62-63
    See also facts in lawsuits and trials;
        preponderance of evidence cri-
        teria; rules of evidence
evidence of crime, **1**:495
    effect on litigation, **1**:503
    exclusionary rules of, **1**:517-18,
        530
    as recent methodology, **1**:525-26
evolution, **10**:130, 140
    of human beings, **8**:236-41;
        10:150-53
evolutionary theory, **1**:427-28, 553-
    54; **3**:100. *See also* natural
    selection
"Exact Consumption-Loan Model of
    Interest, An" (Samuelson),
    7:264-65
    Tullock's variations on, **7**:284-85,
        294-96, 304-5
exchange
    ethics and, **2**:255-57

mechanism in politics, **6**:164n. 2
    in politics, **2**:17-22, 238-41
    relationship of, **6**:7
    in votes, **2**:257-61
exchange rates in China 1948-1950,
    10:328n. 12
excise taxes, and rent seeking,
    5:196-97
executive branch of government,
    4:403-4, 407
    power over judiciary, **9**:416
executive officers. *See* chief executive
    officers (CEOs)
executives. *See* corporate executives
Executive Suite (Hawley), **6**:114
Exit Voice and Loyalty (Hirschman),
    10:436
expectation damages, **9**:408
expenditures. *See* funding; military ex-
    penditures; personal expendi-
    tures by dictators
experimental data, and deductive/
    inductive reasoning, **3**:90-91.
    See also scientific experiments
experiments on human subjects,
    3:137-39
    deception of subjects, **3**:139-41
    reasons for lack of stellar results,
        3:141-43
expertise, **3**:103-4
    about art works, **3**:97
    of economists, **1**:597-601
    in legal matters, **9**:45, 48
    stock market, **1**:436-37
experts
    intellectual, **7**:334
    self-interest of, **7**:254, 280, 281
expert witnesses, **9**:77, 429-30.
    See also testimony
explicit logrolling, **1**:119, 120-22,
    586; **4**:207-10; **7**:191
    stability of, **4**:323-24, 328
exploitation, **8**:168-71

exploitative government, **8**:22–26.
    See also despotism
external costs, **4**:4–6
external diseconomies
    in consumption, **1**:419–24
    in production, **1**:413–18
    ways of controlling, **1**:412
external economies curve, **1**:352,
    353n. 4
    under collectivization, **1**:354
external economies equilibrium solu-
    tions, **1**:371
externalities
    in adversary system of law, **9**:355
    alternative ways of internalizing,
        1:204
    argument for public education based
        on, **7**:296–97
    as arguments for large governments,
        6:413
    associated with adversary proceed-
        ings, **1**:472–73
    during bargaining, **4**:86–91
    in charitable giving, **7**:4
    in charitable giving to poor people,
        7.118
    from choice of collectivization,
        1:383
    from coalitions, **5**:274–75
    in collective action, **2**:60–65,
        84–85
    from common law, **9**:414
    in commons, **2**:55
    compensation for, **4**:349–55
    from contracts, **5**:262–63
    David Hume's discussion, **4**:176–77
    decision rules and, **2**:59
    definition, **1**:349n. 1
    ecology and, **1**:541, 550
    economic definition of, **4**:97
    in education system, **7**:366
    effect of changing technology on,
        4:180–81

effect on vs. cost to individuals,
    5:204
eliminating, by technology, **4**:113
eliminating, by use of small govern-
    mental units, **4**:143–46
from externalities, **5**:268
from failure to transact, **5**:263–64
foreign aid as, **5**:267
generated by plants and animals,
    1:549–50
geographic impact, **4**:343
geographic nature of typical, **4**:92
government and, **4**:177–78
within government bureaus,
    4:151–52
government grants and, **1**:211
government role concerning, **9**:380
from government subsidies,
    4:107–8
in helping the poor, **7**:7–8
in higher education, **7**:300–301
impact of changing technology on,
    4:179
impact of logrolling on, **4**:101
imposed on nonvoters, **5**:266–67
income distribution effect, **4**:110
    among individual lobbies from each
        other, **5**:232
inheritance of wealth and, **1**:258–60
insurance and, **9**:111–12
internalization of, **4**:137–41
from law enforcement by govern-
    ment, **6**:351
majority rule and, **2**:84–85
in majority voting, **2**:139–40,
    192–93
market for, **1**:355
market vs. government dilemma,
    10:91–94
"mere pecuniary," **4**:338; **5**:155–56
optimal government size and, **1**:78,
    80–81
Pareto optimality and, **2**:182–91

Pareto relevance problem, **4**:109–11
political organization and, **2**:275–77
in politics, **2**:41–44
positive, **4**:77–78
positive and negative, **1**:550–52
principle for dealing with, **5**:264
as reason for government, **6**:350
reducing
    through bargaining contract,
      4:79–81
    through government, **4**:84
    through setting up service organi-
      zations, **4**:152–54
    through subsidies, **4**:154–55
    through taxation, **4**:109, 154–155
    through use of reinforced majori-
      ties, **4**:352–53, 356
    within businesses, **4**:151
relation with natural monopolies,
    4:111–13
research on, **4**:108
roots of, **4**:97
self-inflicted, **5**:274
social order and, **2**:57–58
solutions for government-created,
    7:195
synergism with poor information,
    5:211–12
from tariffs, **5**:267
taxes and, **4**:99, 103–4
technical methods of reducing,
    4:146–55
from transactions, **5**:262–63
in transfers, **7**:5
in transfers within middle class, **7**:7
Tullock's model of organizations
    and, **6**:164nn. 1, 2, 166n. 4
urban renewal and, **4**:141–42
from voting, **5**:265–66, 273–74
when privatization better internal-
    izes, **10**:399
See also consumption externalities;
    contiguity problems;

    government-created externali-
    ties; negative externalities;
    production externalities; public
    goods; reciprocal externalities
"Externalities and Government"
    (Tullock), **5**:262
extinction of species, **1**:566–69

facts in lawsuits and trials, **9**:180,
    330–31
    errors in, **9**:442–43
    See also evidence
faculty. *See* academics
Fainsod, Merle, **8**:*50n. 8*
Fairbank, J. K., **10**:*314n. 11*
Fairfield examples, **6**:264–68, 318–
    19, 320
fairness in legal proceedings, **9**:329–30
    public opinion about, **9**:344
faking of research results
    and keeping them secret, **3**:113
    in science, **3**:5, 47, 107–11
    in the social sciences, **3**:156–57
    See also accuracy of scientific
    research
falcons and pigeons, **1**:429
"false" efficiency, **7**:360–62
families, **8**:240; **10**:85
    as hierarchies, **6**:419
    roles, **10**:33–34
family law, **9**:128
Far East Public Choice Society, **4**:16
farmers. *See* agricultural subsidies
farm lobbies, **5**:49. *See also* agricultural
    subsidies
farm program subsidies. *See* agricul-
    tural subsidies
fault, legal, **9**:410
FBI (Federal Bureau of Investigation),
    10:69
FCC (Federal Communications Com-
    mission), **1**:293; **4**:180–81;
    5:34–35

FDA (Food and Drug Administration), 6:419–20; 9:283
federal appellate courts, 1:490–91
federalism, 6:414
  advantages of, 4:399; 6:235–38
  definition, 6:250
  problems of scale, 1:78–89
  See also decentralization
Federalist No. 10, The, 2:24, 25
federal judges, 6:65–69; 9:415–18
  salaries, 9:418
Federal Reserve System, public image, 4:254
fellowships for scientists, 3:177–78
Felstiner, William L. F., 9:*341n. 5*
feminism, 8:157–58
Ferejohn, John A., 1:*114n. 23*; 4:293
Ferguson, C. E., 10:*246n. 6*
Ferguson, James, 9:*246n. 3*
Ferrara, Peter J., 7:*266n. 5*
Ferry, W. H., 6:10
fertility rates
  future, 10:53–54
  impact of education on, 10:50–52
  impact of government policy on, 10.40
  impact of income on, 10:49–50
  overpopulation and, 10:52–53
fetus transplants, 10:53
feudalism
  difference from modern hierarchies, 6:110–13
  local control and, 6:371
  rarity of, 6:277; 8:35–38, 153, 204
  wage slavery and, 6:7
fiction, political impact of, 4:253
Fiechter, Georges-André, 8:*92n. 27*
Field, Alexander, 10:*159n. 1*
Fieldhouse, D. K., 8:*114n. 18, 115n. 22, 132–33n. 83, 237n. 20*
fields of study. *See* academic disciplines; scientific fields
Fifth Amendment protection, 1:518–

19; 9:356–57, 435–36, 445. *See also* witnesses in trials
fighting
  costs of, 10:121–22
  in human vs. nonhuman societies, 10:198–99
  as rational choice, 10:156
  See also conflict; dominance
Fijalkowski-Bereday, G. Z., 1:*253n. 5*
financial standards for charities, 1:409–10
Finer, Samuel E., 8:*144n. 5*
fines, 10:76–77
  upon individuals, 1:325–26
  parking, 1:442–43
Finger, J. M., 1:*290n. 23*
Finkel, Steven E., 1:*342n. 7*
Finlay, Robert, 4:*438n. 1, 439n. 2*
Fiorina, Morris, 4:293
fire and police services
  historical origin in United States, 4:204
  private, 4:204
  voting on, 4:187–89
fire insurance example, 9:102–9
fireside equities, 9:422
Firey, Walter, 9:*137n. 1*
firing of employees, 6:378, 401
  civil servants, 6:383–84
  relative to other punishments, 6:407
firms
  cause of X-inefficiency in, 5:15
  See also corporations
Fisher, F. M., 5:*74n. 94*
Fisher, Herbert A. L., 8:*100nn. 51, 52, 121n. 48, 210n. 41*
Fisher, R. A., *The Design of Experiments*, 3:126, *127n. 28*
FitzGibbon, Constantine, 8:*76n. 35, 302n. 14*
Fitzpatrick, Sheila, 8:*59n. 24, 78n. 39, 109n. 5, 127–28n. 71, 138n. 98, 211n. 42, 221n. 64*
Fitzpatrick, Thomas B., 5:*141n. 9*

flattery of the sovereign, **6**:73, 84–86
Fleming, Alexander, **3**:9
Flexner, James T., **8**:*208n. 30*
flight insurance, **9**:112–16
fluoridation of water, **4**:163–64
followers of reference politicians,
  6:125–26. *See also* subordinates
Foote, Paul D., **3**:*147n. 21*
Foppa, Klaus, **5**:*302n. 6*
Foraker, Alvan G., **3**:*179n. 17*
force. *See* coercion
Ford, Gerald, **4**:184n. 18
Ford Motor Company, **5**:282;
  6:309n. 19, 336–37, 408, 410
foreign affairs, **6**:179
foreign-aid programs, **4**:71–72;
  5:267–68
  capital investments via, **7**:100
  charitable giving via, **7**:12–15
  of goods to South Korea, **10**:351–
    52, 353–54
  matching grants, **7**:120
  private alternatives to, **7**:99
  United Nations developmental proj-
    ects in South Korea, **10**:356
  U.S. program, **7**:54
foreigners, attitudes toward, **1**:278–80
foreign investment by dictators,
  8:51–52
Foreign Service of United States
  diplomatic dilemma for, **6**:77–78
  expectations about, **6**:181
  junior officials in, **6**:403
  regulations, **6**:280n. 4, 323n. 9
  skills needed to be in, **6**:48–49
  See also diplomatic service; United
    States government: foreign
    policy
formal hearings, **6**:395
formal logrolling coalitions, **1**:109,
  110–11
  absence in real world, **1**:112–13,
    115
  building, **1**:115–16

instability, **1**:116–18
  with stable outcomes, **1**:120
  two types, **1**:111
Forrest, William G., **8**:*35n. 9,
  38nn. 23, 24, 39nn. 28, 29,
  42n. 39, 107n. 2, 112n. 10,
  116n. 23, 118n. 34, 119n. 37,
  125n. 58, 127n. 70, 137–
  38n. 97*
Forscher, Bernard K., **3**:*86n. 32*
Fortas, Abe, **5**:116
Fouillée, Alfred, **2**:302, 303
foundations
  effect on social science research,
    3:155–56
  indirect vs. direct funding of scien-
    tific research, **3**:166
  support for indexing and cataloging,
    3:84
Founding Fathers, **2**:24, 284
Fouraker, Lawrence E., **2**:*100n. 1*;
  3:*137n. 3*; **10**:*99n. 5*
France
  government of, **5**:123–24
  tax farmers, **5**:127
franchises, **4**:151; **6**:254, 414; **9**:211
Franco, Francisco, **8**:54, 110–11,
  295–96
Frank, Jerome, **3**:*66n. 10*
Frank, Peter, **8**:*95n. 31, 96–97n. 39,
  109n. 5*
Frankfurter, Felix, **9**:417
Franz, R., **5**:*30n. 33*
Fraser Institute, **1**:593
fraud, **1**:313, 314; **9**:204–8
  cases, **9**:350n. 27
  by charities, **1**:397–98, 399, 402,
    403
  gold mine example, **1**:505–6
  prevention, **9**:208–14
  by scientists, **3**:5, 6, 123–24
  theft prevention and, **8**:15
  See also deception; faking of research
    results; lying

fraudulent research results. *See* faking of research results
free choice, **6**:8–9
freedom. *See* political freedom
Freedom and the Law (Leoni), **9**:444
freedom hypothesis, **9**:24
free licensing of patent rights, **9**:251
Freeman, Roger, **1**:*287n. 18*
free riding, **1**:428, 430, 437–38; **4**:159–60
  asymmetric effect on collective action, **5**:48
  in coalitions, **4**:371
  definition, **10**:204
  Mancur Olson proposition, **5**:49
  in the military, **10**:409n. 1, 418–19, 420, 421–22, 424
  in nonhuman societies, **10**:183–85, 204–5, 218–19
  within private vs. public charitable giving, **7**:101
  by special-interest groups, **5**:47, 48–52
  within special-interest groups, **7**:214
free trade, **1**:178
  effect on rent seeking, **5**:168–69
  restrictions, **3**:157–58
Freiden, Alan, **10**:*36n. 9*
French elections, **7**:82, 83
French government
  coup by de Gaulle, **8**:297
  monarchy, **8**:145
  republics, **8**:132
French Revolution, **8**:209–10
Frey, Bruno S., **1**:*24n. 11, 262n. 3, 268n. 13*; **4**:15, 16; **5**:*302n. 6*
Friedgust, Theodore H., **8**:*109n. 5*
Friedlander, Ann F., **4**:*209n. 30*
Friedman, David, **5**:66; **7**:32–33n. 20
Friedman, Milton, **1**:*271n. 16, 277n. 3*; **9**:*31n. 11, 125n. 2*

argument for government charity, **7**:13–15
Capitalism and Freedom, **2**:x; **7**:13, 65n. 21, 90
  on certification and licensing, **1**:595
  on demand revealing, **4**:25
  on externalities, **7**:118
  on government regulation, **7**:330n. 8
  on inflation and prices, **10**:383, 387
  suggestion for student loans, **7**:303
  on use of coercion for income transfer, **7**:82
  views on Federal Reserve System, **4**:254
  views on gold standard, **4**:244–45
Friedman's Second Law, **1**:212n. 1
Friedrich, Carl Joachim, **2**:*302n. 8*
Frontiers in Economics, **1**:36
Frost, Robert, **2**:xxix
"fruit of the poison tree" doctrine, **9**:357–58, 435–36
Fry, B. R., **1**:*262n. 3*
Fukuyama, F., **5**:*76n. 97*
full income, **10**:14
full-text searching, **3**:85
functional chain of command, **6**:228, 230
functional organization of hierarchies, **6**:166–67, 228
  governments, **6**:275–76
funding
  economic impact of local government spending, **7**:9
  effect of annual renewal, **1**:220
  favoring limited group of people, **1**:195–96
  formula allocation, **1**:119–20
  government aid to localities, **1**:202–3, 204–5, 207–11
  of highways, **1**:203–4
  impact of tobacco taxes on, **5**:200

intergovernmental fiscal relationships, 1:369-70
of judicial system, 1:463
for lawsuits, 9:316-22
line-item vetos, 4:408
military, 5:58
of poor by U.S. government, 7:16-17
procurement industry, 4:44-45
of public education by individuals, 7:294-96
relation with tax measures, 4:230
of Social Security system by individuals, 7:279
with strings attached, 1:210-11
subsidies and externalities, 4:107-8
that benefits specific groups, 4:118
between two alternatives, 1:127-28
of U.S. military, 5:58
on welfare, 4:71-72
See also personal expenditures by dictators; subsidies; transfers
funding for scientific research
direct vs. indirect, 3:165-66
government vs. private, 3:20-21
of indexing and cataloging projects, 3:83-84
in large scientific organizations, 3:165
as motivation for specific research, 3:28-30
pure vs. applied, 3:15
riskiness, 3:6
shifting, from natural to social sciences, 3:161, 163
for social sciences research, 3:155-56
fund-raising by nonprofits, 1:396
future impact of government debt, 9:246-50

Galileo, 3:35
Gallman, Robert E., 5:20

Galton, Francis, 2:315
gambling, 1:229
on stocks, 1:434-35
gambling game. *See* lottery game model
games of strategy
attack on, 10:438
degrees of cooperation, 1:569
development of, 1:229
differential weighting of players, 1:233-34
discussion of, in *The Calculus of Consent*, 2:xxiv
as forerunner, 2:310-14
gambling games, 10:439
logrolling and, 2:151-53
majority rule and, 2:143-64
mixed strategies, 1:229, 312, 448-49; 10:442-45
norms and, 2:293n. 1
precommitment games, 1:231-32
prisoners' dilemma, 10:429-37
rationality in, 2:154-56
rent seeking as, 1:230-31
usefulness, 10:446
Gardner, Bruce, 10:*49n. 10, 50n. 12*
Garfield, Eugene, 3:*77n. 26*
garment industry in New York, 6:253
Gärtner, Manfred, 10:285-86
gasoline price controls, 7:330-31
in 1973, 7:171-73
See also oil price controls
Gasset, José Ortega, 8:*132n. 80*
gas shortages in United States, 5:141n. 9
Gastil, R. D., 10:*394n. 20*
Gates, Gary Paul, 8:*85n. 7*
Gay, Peter, 8:*6n. 1*
GDP growth in Africa, Americas, and Asia, 10:391
Gell-Mann, Murray, 3:*99n. 11*
gemmulation, 10:243
general curiosity, 3:25-26

General Electric organizational structure, **6**:216

General Impossibility Theorem. *See* impossibility theorem

"General Irrelevance of the General Impossibility Theorem, The" (Tullock), **1**:106

applied to small voting groups, **4**:284

generality

in legislation, **2**:277–80

in rules, **2**:20–21, 74

General Motors, **4**:112–13, 133; **5**:241, 242, 245, 252

organizational structure, **6**:215–16, 252

general theory of relativity, testability of, **3**:144. *See also* Einsteinian vs. Newtonian systems

general will, **2**:12

in Rousseau, **2**:303

genetic egoism, **10**:186–87

Genghis Khan, **10**:321

geographic contiguity

collectivization and, **1**:387

economies of scale and, **4**:66–67

effect on charitable giving, **7**:118

legal uniformity and, **9**:184

See also contiguity problems

geographic mapmaking, **3**:150–51

geographic organization of hierarchies, **6**:228

empires, **6**:183

governments, **6**:275–76, 325–26

geometrical model of voting, **1**:93

George, M. Dorothy, **8**:*135n. 90*

Germany

government, **8**:119

judicial promotion system, **9**:331

social welfare programs, **7**:256

voting system, **4**:446–47

See also Bismarck, Otto von

gerontocracy, **8**:96

Gershoy, Leo, **8**:*114n. 17*

Ghana, government officials, **5**:111, 112

Ghiselin, Michael T., **1**:*554n. 1*, 557, *561n. 5*; **10**:*159n. 2*

Gibb, J., **1**:*537n. 4*, *539n. 5*

Gibbon, Edward, **8**:*113n. 16*

Gibbs, Jack P., **9**:258; **10**:80–81, *83n. 19*

gift motive, **7**:38

Gilbert, W. S., **9**:*265n. 7*

Gilder, George, **7**:*33n. 23*

Giliberg, T., **8**:*97n. 44*

Gilio, Maria Esther, **8**:*197n. 6*

Gilison, Jerome M., **8**:*109n. 5*

Gillespie, Robert, **1**:*478n. 12*

Gipson, Lawrence Henry, **8**:*66n. 11*

Gittings, John, **8**:*304n. 21*

Glasser, Donald, **3**:182n. 23

Glasser v. United States, **9**:427

globalization, **10**:399–400

"God Committee," **7**:350–51

Godwin, Melville. See *Melville Godwin* (Marquand)

Godwin, R. Kenneth, **5**:*215n. 4*

Goetz, Charles J., **1**:*412n. 1*, 608

Goldfarb, Robert S., **8**:*9n. 4*

gold standard, **4**:244–45

Good, R. J., **1**:*495n. 1*

Goodall, Jane, **8**:*238n. 23*; **10**:122, *165n. 6*, 246

Goodman, Saul, **10**:*371n. 10*

goods, definition, **10**:10

Gorbachev, Mikhail, **1**:344–45

gorillas, **10**:164–65

gossip, importance to scientists, **4**:267

Goubert, Pierre, **8**:*34n. 6*

Gough, John Wiedhofft, **2**:*302nn. 9, 10*

government actions

argument for, **4**:53

benefit to society as a whole, **4**:65

charitable giving vs., **4**:134–35

compensation for externalities from, 4:349–52
differential impact of, 4:208–9
external costs imposed by, 4:332
externalities generated by, 4:102
externality reduction through, 4:84
imperfect outcomes from, 4:99–101
importance of bargaining costs in, 4:96
individual bankruptcy resulting from, 4:362–63
involving items sold at less than cost, 5:256
with mixed motives, 7:34
motivation of, 5:9
operation of natural monopolies, 4:111–12
profit to citizens from, 7:194
in public interest, 4:177–78
as solution to problems, 4:40–41
See also government services
government agencies
advantages of having multiple, 4:145
"aresponsible" or "para-aresponsible," 7:350
attempts to eliminate, 6:186
budgets, 5:56–58
capital intensive nature, 1:304
competition among, 4:204–5
competition within, 4:203–4
contiguity problems, 4:91–92
contracting out by, 6:368, 409–10
costs of expansion, 1:81–84
determining maximum size, 1:383
discretionary budgets, 5:59
duplication of output among, 4:44
economies of scale, 1:78–79, 80
external effects of one on another, 1:85
externalities within, 4:151–52
impact of history on, 6:413
jurisdictional area of, and externalities, 4:100–101, 102

justifying existence of, 6:204
law enforcement, 6:392–97
length of time efficiency lasts in, 6:188
location and optimal size, 4:42
with no real output, 5:60
optimum size, 4:57–59
performance evaluation, 6:324–25, 362–64
for planning the government, 5:9
with private sector competition, 4:153, 202
rent seeking in, 6:383–86
rent-seeking potential of, 5:55–60
special purpose, 4:117, 120
use of external checks for supervision, 6:225–27
use of violence by, 8:11
See also government structure
government-aid programs, 1:212
government bonds, 10:357
government charity. *See* transfers
government corruption, 1:323–28
bribery of government officials, 1:240–41, 323
government-created externalities, 5:261–62
external, 5:265–68
internal, 5:268–71
government-created monopolies
Civil Aeronautics Board, 7:324–26
costs of, 5:126–30
in democracy vs. dictatorships, 5:134–35
in dictatorships, 5:122, 123–24
in historical England, 5:164–65
Interstate Commerce Commission, 7:74–76
natural monopolies, 1:69–70, 74–75
protective tariffs and, 5:125
riskiness of investment in, 5:153
taxation, for collecting revenue vs., 5:126–27

government debt, **10**:271–74
  advantages over taxation, **9**:251
  future generations and, **9**:246–50
government efficiency, **7**:74–76
  competition and, **4**:233
  job security and, **4**:405–7
  possibility of improving, **4**:74
  reasons for, **4**:96, 121–22
  studies of, **4**:203
  ways to attain, **4**:114
government employment, **6**:15–16.
    See also civil service systems
government expenditures. *See* funding
government income transfers. *See*
    transfers
government monopolies, **1**:213–15
government officials
  behavior, **4**:43–44
  bribery of, **1**:240–41; **5**:112–13,
    115, 247–48; **7**:208–9
  chiefs of staff, **6**:322–23
  in Communist countries, **8**:50
  comparing abilities of, **6**:364
  decision making, **6**:353
  decision to join coups, **8**:284–85
  in democracy vs. dictatorships,
    5:134
  denial about own privileges,
    5:125–26
  depriving, of the vote, **4**:135
  in dictatorships, **8**:44, 71–73, 254
  elected vs. nonelected, **4**:407
  following of orders by, **8**:265–66
  imperfect knowledge, **1**:22
  jeopardy of jobs after coup,
    8:280–81
  killing of, during coups, **8**:283
  lifestyles, compared with expendi-
    tures by, **5**:248
  loyalty of, in despotism, **8**:285
  payoffs in event of a coup, **8**:262–67
  public choice theory view of, **1**:16
  public-goods problem created by,
    1:390
  purchasing of own positions,
    5:108–12
  during revolutions, **1**:338, 344
  role in revolutions, **8**:183–84
  stake in coups, **8**:271–72
  supervision of, **6**:323–26
  unpaid vs. paid, **4**:402–3
  who were businessmen, **5**:133
  See also bureaucrats; politicians
government policy
  cost of specific policy output, **5**:36
  costs from fragmentation of, **5**:37
  fertility rates and, **10**:48
  See also referendum on government
    policies
government reform. *See* theory of
    constitutions
government regulation. *See* regulation
governments
  activities of, **1**:291–92
  aid to localities, **1**:202–3, 204–5
  amount of coercion needed by, **9**:56
  in animal societies, **10**:147–48
  areas where supervision relatively
    easy, **6**:397–99
  best way to run, **4**:402–4
  cabinet, **4**:342–43
  capital accumulation policies,
    1:251–52
  charitable giving through, **1**:262,
    271–73, 285–86, 407–8, 409
  choice of competing, **4**:131–32
  of civil servants, **8**:153
  coercion by, **5**:75–76
  coercion on behalf of profit-making
    organizations by, **7**:179–81
  compared with corporations, **4**:84
  connection with church, **6**:248, 275
  contracting out of services, **1**:71–
    74, 292
  corrupt, **8**:196, 215
  costs and benefits, **4**:38–39
  dealings with citizens/subjects,
    1:318

decision making by, 7:350
defects, 4:178–79
deficit finance by, 5:79
definition, 10:147
effect on economic growth, 10:380
effect on wealth equalization, 7:174
efficiency, 6:411–12
efficiency vs. orderliness, 1:89
egalitarian, 1:321–22
ethics and power within, 6:44
Far Eastern, 10:355
federalism, advantages of, 4:399
first ones, 7:180
funding for lawsuits, 9:316–22
giving individuals more say in,
    4:132
impact of economic growth on,
    10:386–87
impact of transfers on, 7:202
incentives to employees, 6:409, 413
income redistribution as function of,
    7:23
inefficiency in, due to rent seeking,
    5:113–14, 115
inheritance of wealth and, 1:249–
    50, 253–57
international comparisons, 1:33–34
justifications for, 4:37–38, 81–82,
    95, 175–81; 5:76; 7:117;
    9:382
legitimacy of, 8:225
Marxist vision of, 2:12
measuring of efficiency of, 6:348
methods used to overthrow,
    8:278–85
minimizing influence on, 1:228,
    235
models of, 8:24
necessary conditions for, 1:325
need for competition, 1:25, 75–77
nonexploitative, 8:171
organic theory of, 2:11–12, 30–31
origin, 1:290–91
outstanding characteristic, 4:81–82

Pareto-optimal outcome, 4:345
pharmaceutical research and,
    10:400
popular overthrow, 8:201
promotion of inflation, 10:359–62
protection of individual wealth by,
    8:170
public choice view of, 4:18, 45
"public interest" and, 4:70, 122–23
purpose of, 5:212
pursuit of private interests and,
    4:39–40
reasons for existence, 6:260
reforms of, 4:345
relationships between, 4:408–11
relation with legal systems,
    6:251–52
resource allocation by, 4:9
restriction of competitive currencies,
    10:365–66
revenue from parking fines,
    9:139–40
role, 5:54
role in internalizing externalities,
    9:380
role in social change, 3:155
role in transfers, 7:243–44; 8:9–10
as rules, 2:292
ruling class theory of, 2:12
signs of legitimacy, 8:251
social contract with, 9:407–8
social costs imposed by, 4:156–59
as "stationary bandit," 8:154
that are corporations, 6:248–49
traditional opinions about, 4:20–
    21, 50
transfers among different levels of,
    5:25
transfers by local vs. national,
    7:126–28
Tullock's opinion of, 7:202
Tullock's recommendations,
    6:235–38
undermining of public faith in, 6:10

governments (*continued*)
  uniform performance measures,
    6:355–57, 359–60
  use for transfers, **1**:277
  use of, to break up monopoly,
    9:241n. 1
  use of, to reduce transactions costs,
    9:114–16
  use of accounting controls, **6**:321
  use of assassination, **6**:42
  vague public image of, **5**:304–6,
    307
  Wagner's law of increasing activity,
    1:367–69
  waste caused by, **7**:5
  why have, **4**:37; **6**:350
  why people support, **8**:233–34
  See also autocracy; bureaucracies;
    democracies; electoral systems
    of government; funding; legisla-
    tures; military governments;
    nondemocratic systems; policy
    making; political negotiation;
    public choice theory; small local
    governments; state govern-
    ments; United States govern-
    ment; welfare state
government services
  collective action vs., **1**:379–81
  contracting out of, **1**:25
  free, **1**:361–62, 365–68
  how voters choose, **1**:85–86
  optimal scale, **1**:78–80, 86–88
  rental of parking spaces, **1**:443
  roughly equal to private, **1**:384–87
  See also government actions; govern-
    ment vs. market problem
government share of GDP (variable),
  10:384
  in Africa, Americas, and Asia,
    10:391
government-sponsored insurance,
  9:110

government-sponsored scientific
  research
  indexing and cataloging, **3**:84–85
  indirect funding, **3**:166
  private research vs., **3**:20–21
government structure
  changes in size of, **6**:254–55
  coalition, **4**:387, 388
  commonest form in world, **8**:34–35
  contracting out, **4**:153–54, 404–5
    of services, **1**:25
  decentralized, **4**:399–400, 401;
    6:359–61, 370
  degree of federalization, **1**:88
  direct limits on size and growth of,
    5:79–80
  divisions between levels of, **4**:121,
    130–31
  ever-increasing dimensions, **6**:3
  functional vs. geographic organiza-
    tion, **6**:275–76
  highly centralized, **1**:89
  historical overview of sizes of, **6**:249
  impact of size
    on power of individual voter,
      7:360–62
    on transfers, **7**:6, 8–10
  largest one, **6**:249
  methods of control within,
    6:274–78
  need for some disorganization in,
    6:385–86
  nonoptimal size of U.S., **6**:237
  one-party, **8**:108–11
  optimal size, **1**:78, 80–81;
    6:412–13
  organizational alternatives within,
    1:365–66
  profit-making enterprises within,
    6:281
  rule by small committee, **8**:79–81
  size, **2**:108; **4**:195–96; **6**:413
  size, relative to GNP, **1**:28–29

superior form, **8**:139
three branches, **1**:327
war, impact on size of, **6**:412
See also checks and balances in U.S.
    government; government
    agencies
government vs. market problem
    additional areas outside of, **4**:69
    changeability of, **4**:179–81
    commonality of both sectors, **2**:18
    coordination of tasks, **6**:172–75
    of dictatorships, **8**:57
    differences between the sectors,
        4:174–75
    externalities, **10**:91–93
    in history, **6**:260–61
    imperfection of both sectors, **4**:41–
        42; **5**:282–83
    income redistribution and, **7**:67–68
    institutions other than these two
        types, **10**:85–86
    market alternatives, **4**:42–43
    Pigou's example, **10**:87–91
    police services, **10**:65–66
    the public good and, **10**:86–87
    redistribution and, **10**:86
    reduction of externalities and, **4**:146
    resolving, **4**:85, 95–96; **6**:350
Grampp, William Dyer, **6**:*347n. 13*;
    8:*56n. 16*
grand juries, **9**:179, 425–26
Grant, A. J., **8**:*205n. 21*
Grant, Ulysses S., **6**:322n. 8
grants
    effect on careers of academic re-
        searchers, **3**:177
    scientific research proposals for,
        3:166–67
Gray, Dwight E., **3**:*115n. 14*
Gray, Louis N., **9**:*258n. 16*;
    10:*81n. 12*
gray economy. *See* black (under-
    ground) economy

Great Britain. *See* Britain
Great Depression of 1930s
    effect on following generations, **7**:9
    possible causes, **7**:278
Grebe, John, **3**:23
Greek government, **8**:38, 118–19
Greek juries, **9**:424
Green, Christopher, **7**:*107n. 19*
Green, John C., **3**:*77n. 26*
Green, V. H. H., **8**:*254nn. 49, 50*
Greene, Kenneth V., **1**:258–60,
    287n. 18
Greenfield, Meg, **3**:*109n. 8*
Greenstein, Fred, **8**:*86n. 8*
Gresham's Law of money, **10**:359
Griffin, Martin J., **8**:*122–23n. 50*
Griswold, Dean, **9**:*357n. 43*
Griswold, E. H., **9**:*435n. 12*
Grossman, Joel B., **9**:*341n. 5*
Grossman, Sanford J., **4**:*361n. 1*
group selection, **1**:561
group size and decision costs, **2**:107–8
group sovereigns, **6**:89–114
    characteristics, **6**:91–92
    definition, **6**:89
    in democracies, **6**:133–34
    peers subject to, **6**:118–19
    size of, **6**:91
    types of, **6**:90–91
group vs. individual selection,
    10:182–86, 225–26, 244–46.
    See also nepotism
Groves, Theodore, **1**:134, *148n. 15*;
    4:361
growth and collectivization, **1**:370–73
growth paradox, **1**:28
growth rate of grass, **1**:542–43
Gruenwald, Peter, **3**:*73n. 20*
Grum, Bernard, **8**:*108n. 4*
Grünbaum, A., **3**:*26n. 24*
guerrilla warfare, **10**:422
guest workers, **7**:44, 82–83
Guilbaud, Georges T., **4**:280–82

guilds, legislation on behalf of,
9:124–25
guilt, 8:235
guilty pleas in court, 9:158, 164, 166.
See also plea bargaining
gun control, 10:282
Gungwu, Wang, 8:*89–90n. 19*
Gunning, J. P., Jr., 9:*257n. 12*
Gurley, John, 5:19
Guttridge, G. H., 8:*208n. 31*

Haddock, David D., 8:*154n. 19*
Hæfele, E. T., 7:*195n. 18*
Hagood, Johnson, 6:126n. 1
halfway houses, 9:127
Hall, H. K., 1:*290n. 23*
Hallet, George H., 2:315
Hamilton, Alexander, 2:262n. 4
Hamiltonian altruism, 1:558, 559;
10:188. *See also* nepotism
Hammitt, James K., 9:*343n. 13,
350n. 29*
Hand, Learned, 9:364, 365, 386,
417
handicapped people, 7:211
Hansmann, Henry, 6:273
Hanson, C. J., 9:*453n. 3*
Hanson, N. R., 3:*95n. 9*
haploidy theory of society, 10:143–44
Harasymiw, Bohdan, 8:*95nn. 31, 32,
97n. 40, 109n. 6*
Harberger, A. C., 1:*169n. 4*; 5:*11n. 1,
20n. 15*; 9:*247n. 4*
interpretation of Tullock rectangle,
5:18–19
Harberger triangle, 5:12
equivalent, 5:255
Leibenstein's challenge to, 5:14–17
Hardin, Garrett, 1:*537n. 1, 541n. 1,
555n. 5*; 10:118, 142
Hardy, Charles Oscar, 2:137n. 13
Hardy, G. H., 3:*13n. 7*
Hare, Paul, 8:*55n. 14*

Haring, Clarence H., 8:*92–93n. 28*
Harington, Sir John, 4:*130n. 16*;
9:*213n. 4*
Harlem, 4:143–44
Harris, J. R., 8:*101n. 55*
Harrison, G. B., 8:*100n. 54*
Harsanyi, John C., 1:*12*; 7:31;
10:442
Hart, Liddell, 8:*125n. 61, 126n. 63*
Harvard Law School graduates, careers,
5:111–12
Hashimoto, Masanori, 10:*50n. 13,
51n. 14*
Haskins, Charles Homer, 8:*121n. 46*
Hastie, Reid, 1:*507n. 17, 512, 529n. 5*;
9:*342nn. 8–11, 345n. 18,
439n. 17*
Haveman, Robert, 7:*27n. 6, 241n. 19*
hawk/dove equilibrium, 1:427;
5:88n. 2
applied to rent seeking, 5:99–100
investing as, 1:437
Hawley, Cameron, *Executive Suite*,
6:114
Hay, George, 1:*414n. 6*
Hayek, Friedrich A., 1:*279n. 6*,
2:7n. 5, *57n. 8*, 74n. 6;
4:*5n. 3*; 6:135; 8:*132n. 80*;
9:*400n. 3, 406n. 7*; 10:244,
383
health care
life-and-death decisions, 7:339–45
in United States, 7:364–65
See also universal health care
health insurance, 9:109–10
government-funded, 7:304–5
for poor people, 7:364
hearsay evidence, 9:88–89, 359–60,
436–37
hearsay rule, 1:518
Hellman, J. A., 8:*92–93n. 28, 137n. 95*
Henry, Merton G., 8:*125n. 60*
Henry VII, 8:250

hereditary behavior, **10**:181
DNA and, **10**:258–59
human civilization and, **10**:261–63
reproduction, **10**:187–96
hereditary dictatorships, **8**:141
contrasted with other forms of government, **8**:152–53
sons of dictators, **8**:130–31
hereditary monarchies, **1**:227–28; **8**:105–6, 141–42
hereditary succession into power, **8**:90–92, 99–101
when not previously existed, **8**:103–4
heroism
effect on military battles, **10**:423
self-sacrifice for genetic survival, **10**:188
as survival mechanism, **10**:181
Herold, J. Christopher, **2**:*200n. 5*
Herring, Pendleton, **2**:*9n. 15, 18n. 2,* 270
Hershey, Robert L., **3**:*19n. 15*
Heston, Alan, **10**:*381n. 4*
Hibbert, Christopher, **8**:*54nn. 10, 11, 206n. 23, 210n. 39*
Hieder, F., **5**:*129n. 7*
hierarchical organizations
decisions within, **6**:23
difference from feudalism, **6**:110–13
efficiency within, **6**:24–25
ethics within, **6**:44–46
government vs. market, **6**:419
immense numbers and variety of, **6**:421–22
individual's relation with goals of, **6**:23–24
merit systems in political, **6**:19–21
morality within, **6**:25–29, 33–35
with no sovereign, **6**:58–59
political behavior within, **6**:29–33
relationships in, **6**:82–84
reputation in, **6**:53
single-sovereign situation in, **6**:82–84
structure, **6**:39–42
success within, **6**:21–23
time devoted to supervision in, **6**:263–64, 268, 357–65, 387–88
types, **6**:418–19
view from within, **6**:279, 284–94
why they exist, **6**:350
See also chain of command; large hierarchical organizations
hierarchies
definition, **6**:193
descriptive accounts about, **6**:243–44
diversified activities by, **6**:272
diversity of human, **6**:243
extension in size of, **6**:187
family, **6**:419
geographic vs. functional divisions, **6**:228
human vs. nonhuman, **10**:179–80
importance of, in human society, **10**:197
justifications for, **6**:135–37
markets vs., **6**:266–68
mixed, **6**:248
power of individuals in, **6**:308
private, **10**:202
question of ultimate control of, **6**:273
relationships with market organizations, **6**:261
similarities among, **6**:244, 351–52
specialization, **6**:385–86
theory of individual behavior in, **6**:3–10
Tullock's definition, **6**:256
why they exist, **6**:255–62
See also dominance; hierarchical organizations; tasks in hierarchies
Higashi, S., **10**:*208n. 4*

Higgins, R. S., **5**:*64n. 82*; **9**:*418n. 11*
  on efficient rent seeking, **5**:88,
    91–92
higher education, **9**:124
  academic freedom in, **9**:124
  charitable giving to, **7**:299–300
  externalities in, **7**:300–301
  law school programs, **9**:179–80
  subsidies, **1**:327–28
  transfers for, **7**:299, 301
  transitional gains from, **5**:142–44
  See also education of scientists
higher education institutions
  effect on scientific research, **3**:29–31
  faculty organization, **3**:64
  hypothesis development and,
    3:61–62
  tenure for scientific researchers,
    3:171–78
  using, to maximize theorizing,
    3:58–62
  See also academia; arguments in
    higher education; education
    of scientists
highway funding, **1**:203, 204
  costs for safety, **1**:115–17
  See also road repair
Hill, Ronald J., **8**:*95n. 31, 96–97n. 39,*
    109n. 5
Hillman, A. L., **5**:*64n. 82, 65n. 84*;
    10:440, 441
Hillman's equilibrium, **5**:93–94
Himmelfarb, Gertrude, **7**:*120n. 7*;
    8:*36n. 16*
Hinich, Melvin J., **4**:*283n. 1*
  career, **4**:19–20
  influence of his work, **4**:303
  logrolling model, **4**:319, 327
Hirschman, Albert O., **8**:*35n. 8*;
    10:436
Hirshleifer, Jack, **10**:*115n. 1*, 439
Hirst, David, **8**:*70n. 25*
historians' bias regarding revolutions,
    8:177–78

historical data in social sciences,
    3:143–46
history
  as a science, **3**:49
  as a social science, **3**:151–52
history of science, **3**:xx, 37
  methods of classifying knowledge
    and, **3**:81
Hitti, Phillip K., **6**:*42n. 1*
Hittle, J. D., **4**:*196n. 22*
Hobbes, Thomas, **1**:309, 322; **2**:238,
    297–98; **4**:33; **8**:13
Hochman, Harold M., **1**:*262n. 1,*
    276n. 2; **5**:*22n. 21*; **7**:*29n. 10*;
    8:*9n. 4*; **10**:*138n. 8*
Hoffman, Fred, **8**:*322n. 8*
Hofheinz, Roy, Jr., **8**:*37n. 21*
Hogue, A., **9**:*402n. 1, 404nn. 3, 4,*
    406nn. 8, 9
Holborn, Hajo, **8**:*55n. 12*
Hölldobler, Bert, **10**:*191n. 10,*
    207nn. 1–3
Hollywood movie producers, **5**:99–
    100
Holmboe, Haakon, **8**:*64n. 5*
Holmes, Oliver Wendell, **3**:*121n. 21,*
    9:*191n. 3*, 417
homeless people, **7**:121–22, 149–51
honorariums, **3**:29
Hoover, G. E., **1**:*247n. 1*
Hoover, J. Edgar, **6**:287–88
horizontal transfers
  definition, **7**:181
  models, **7**:182–84, 187–92
  See also administrative transfers;
    transfers within middle class
Horton, P. B., **10**:*75n. 3*
Hostetler, John A., **8**:*95n. 31*
Hotelling, Harold, **2**:325; **4**:302
Hotelling-Downs model, **4**:305, 319
  generalization to two dimensions,
    4:312–15
  Tullock's version, **4**:311–12
Hough, Jerry F., **8**:*96n. 36, 109–10n. 6*

households
decisions of, **10**:30
public goods provided by, **10**:31–32
See also families
House of Commons, **8**:205–7
American Revolution against, **8**:208
origin, **8**:202
voting in, **4**:439; **5**:290–91
housing examples
Belvedere Park, **4**:138–40
condominium governments,
4:42–43
construction that cuts off view,
4:146–49
hut location example, **4**:74–80, 82
paint colors, **4**:109–11
real estate development, **4**:92–95
See also neighborhood governments;
rosebushes example
Hoveyda, Frereydain, **8**:*212n. 44*
Howard Johnson Company, **9**:211
Howell, John, **9**:255, *256n. 11,*
257n. 13; **10**:*82n. 16*
How to Succeed in Business Without Re-
ally Trying (Mead), **6**:293, 303,
307
Huang Liu Hung, *A Complete Book con-*
cerning Happiness and Benevo-
lence, **6**:331
Hubbert, M. King, **3**:*74n. 23*
Huber, P. W., **9**:*447n. 18*
Huddle, Donald L., **5**:*111n. 8*
Hull, Raymond, *The Peter Principle*,
6:303
Human Action (Mises), **4**:12
human behavior
applied to animals, **10**:120, 130, 146
importance of to economics, **10**:2–3
learned skills, **10**:210
human/bird analogy, **1**:540
human cells, **10**:129, 130, 259,
264–67
human limitations, **6**:170–71. *See also*
rationality

human mind, economy of, **8**:242–46.
See also intelligence; reasoning
human nature
cognitive dissonance, **8**:247–48
indoctrinability, **8**:234–35, 241,
247, 251–52
in politics, **2**:254
self-interest and, **2**:26
human social groups, structure of,
3:140–41
human societies
contrasted with animal societies,
10:142–54
development of, **10**:260–61
lessons of animal society for,
10:124–25
organic society theory of, **10**:264
studying animals to learn about,
10:115–17
using, to understand nonhuman
societies, **10**:175
See also civilization; nonhuman
societies
human subjects
experiments on, **3**:137–39
theories about, **3**:151
Humboldt, Wilhelm von, **2**:307, 308
Hume, David, **3**:*106*
on balance of power, **8**:354
discussion of externalities, **4**:176–77
interdisciplinary approach, **1**:7
political obligation and, **2**:299–300,
306
on power of rules, **8**:296
problem with induction, **3**:88
on reason and the passions, **1**:8
Spinoza as precursor, **2**:298
views on bargaining, **4**:336n. 2
views on dictatorship, **5**:131
views on government, **4**:37
views on human nature, **4**:33
Hundred Years' War, **8**:100
Huntington, Edward Vermilye,
2:322n. 16

Hutcheson, Francis, **10**:*146n. 8*
Hutt, William, **10**:85
hyenas, **10**:123, 126, 152
hypotheses
   deduced, **3**:89
   infinity of possible, **3**:95–96
   investigative, **3**:76
   possible/probable, **3**:94–95
   relation with data, **3**:53–54
hypothesis development
   data collection and, **3**:55–56
   deductive reasoning in, **3**:89–92
   by induction, **3**:101
   principal source for, **3**:90–91
   relation to pattern recognition,
      3:99–100
   See also investigation of reality
hypothesis testing, **3**:54
   in field of history, **3**:152
   procedure for, **3**:95–96
   through scientific experiments,
      3:144–45
   of scientific theories, **3**:88
hypothesis verification
   in science, **3**:111–12, 126–28
   in the social sciences, **3**:115–16
   statistical methods, **3**:126–28,
      145–46

"I, Pencil" (Read), **6**:268
ICC (Interstate Commerce Commission), **1**:293; **4**:111; **5**:229,
   310; **7**:331
   rent seeking and, **5**:167, 169
idealism in political theory, **2**:xxii
identification of patterns. *See* pattern
   recognition
ideology
   importance in voting, **5**:226
   in political voting, **4**:421–23
   related to legitimacy, **8**:255–56
ill and injured people
   care for ones with catastrophic prob-
      lems, **7**:306

income redistribution to, **7**:56–57
resource allocation for, **7**:346–51
universal health care programs and,
   7:249
wealth equalization for terminally,
   7:347–49
See also disease treatment vs. immunization example
illegal activities, **1**:174n. 10, 314
   deterrence, **1**:496–97
   economic approach to, **1**:441–55
   relation between evidence and guilt,
      1:497–98
   See also bribery; fraud; theft
illegal parking, **1**:442–43
ill-informed voters
   benefits to society from, **5**:210
   biased ignorance of, **5**:39–40
   consequences from, **5**:42
   contradictory ideas held by,
      5:303
   costs from, **5**:203
   under demand revealing, **1**:137
   disadvantages due to, **5**:210–11
   example of, **5**:276–77
   impact of rent seeking on, **5**:307–10
   as inefficient rent seekers, **5**:249
   intellectuals as, **7**:333
   price controls and, **7**:176–77
   public choice discovery of, **1**:17
   public opinion pollsters' experiences
      with, **5**:38–39
   reasons for, **1**:392, 586–87
   role in rent seeking, **5**:237, 239–40
   in simple logrolling models,
      4:329–30
   transfers and, **7**:69–70
   vote trading by politicians and,
      4:396, 398
   who vote on social costs, **4**:159–62
   See also better-informed voters; well-
      informed voters
illth, **5**:218n. 13
illumination. *See* insights

illusion vs. reality, **3**:33–35, 49.
See also recognizing human
individuals
immigrants, **1**:278–79, 282
denying welfare to, **7**:130
illegal U.S., **7**:82–83
Mexicans in United States, **7**:44–
45, 46–47
worldwide restrictions against,
7:48
See also guest workers
immunization example, **1**:352–55,
359–64
impacted information, **6**:260
imperial bureaucratic systems, **6**:178,
181–85
implicit logrolling, **1**:52, 120–22;
4:207, 210–11, 315
in Britain, **4**:212
definition, **1**:585
instability of, **4**:324, 328
relation with median voter theorem,
4:211–12
in United States, **4**:212–13
import quota and tariffs, **1**:414n. 6
import restrictions
on Japanese cars, **5**:263; **7**:18–19
voluntary quotas on American imports, **7**:322–24
impossibility theorem, **1**:90, 104;
2:320–24; **4**:21, 283–84, 292
avoiding, **4**:295
demand-revealing process and,
1:140, 148
hidden assumption in, **1**:124–25,
129
imprisonment, **10**:77
improvement, Pareto definition,
1:548–49
incentives
for being well informed, **1**:399, 402
negative, **10**:417–19
positive, **10**:416–17
See also bribery; punishment

incentives to subordinates, **6**:400–415
to corporate executives, **6**:408
costs to employers, **6**:407
formal systems of, **6**:409
positive vs. negative, **6**:404–7
pursuit of superior's own goals and,
6:401–4
relation with information and control within organizations,
6:407–15
incest, **10**:162–63
inclusive fitness, **10**:188
income
charitable giving as percentage of,
7:26
compensation of scientists, **3**:170
effect on fertility, **10**:49–50
effect on Social Security payments,
10:301
estimation in demand-revealing
process, **1**:143
full, **10**:14
impact of universalization of health
care on doctors', **7**:311–12,
313
of judges, **9**:416
maximization of present discounted
value of future, **9**:24
minimum universal, **7**:356–57
psychic, **1**:343
from publication of scientific discoveries, **3**:67
relation to need for collectivization,
1:370–73
of retired vs. working Americans,
7:275–76
upper income groups under Social
Security, **10**:296–97, 300–301
See also income redistribution; means
tests; wealth equalization
income distribution effect of externalities, **4**:110
income equalization. *See* wealth
equalization

income inequalities and reciprocal ex-
    ternality, 1:373–77
income insurance motive, 7:67–68, 70
income redistribution
    barriers, 7:189
    after breakup of British Empire,
        7:45–46
    to citizens vs. noncitizens, 7:43–47
    Communist view on, 7:52–53
    confiscatory inheritance taxes and,
        1:252
    confusion and ignorance about,
        7:42, 68–70
    costs and benefits, 7:73
    definition, 7:38–39
    in democracies, 1:262, 264–65, 291
    designing bureaucracy to achieve,
        7:77–78
    economic literature on, 1:276–77
    efficiency, 7:40–41
    as function of government, 7:23
    via government regulation, 7:19
    government vs. market problem and,
        10:86
    to ill and injured people, 7:56–57
    through in kind aid, 7:133
    justifications for, 7:3, 29–33
    Lerner justification for, 1:280
    through lobbying for monopolies,
        1:239
    by local governments, 7:117, 132
    logrolling and, 7:175
    motives for, 1:284–89; 7:25–26,
        27–29, 59–64
    motives not admitted to, 7:57–58
    motives other than self-interest for,
        7:64–68, 355–56
    nationalism and, 7:48
    need for honesty about, 1:293–94
    objectives, 7:255
    optimal amount of, 7:220–27
    Pareto optimality and, 2:182–91
    to poor people, 7:29–33

    from poor to better-off people,
        7:301–2
    public education and, 7:365–66
    as reason for government, 1:291
    relation to other government poli-
        cies, 1:250–51
    rent seeking and, 7:174–78
    via Social Security, 10:300–301
    in South Africa, 7:43–45
    in United States vs. abroad, 7:51–
        56, 67
    universal health care and, 7:309–18
    using demand-revealing process for,
        7:71–77, 225
    through voting, 1:160–63
    See also charitable giving; intrafamily
        gifts; resource allocation; trans-
        fers; wealth equalization
income subsidies for working poor,
    7:112–16, 257
income tax in United States, 1:195–96
    alternative to, 5:173
    evasion, 1:450–55
    income effect of, 7:50–51
    negative, 10:135
    personal exemptions, 10:48
    progressive, 7:123–25
    See also negative income taxes
income tax law, 9:146–51. *See also* tax
    courts
income transfers. *See* transfers
indecent exposure, 9:221
independent adjustment equilibrium,
    1:199. *See also* bargaining
independent preferences
    cyclical majority phenomenon and,
        4:275, 278
    situation where invalid assumption,
        4:434
indexing methods, 3:82–83
    citation counting of articles,
        3:27n. 26, 31
    computer-aided, 3:84–85

subject specialization, **3**:81
See also classification systems
India, **1**:282–83
cost to eradicate poverty in, **7**:343
social welfare programs, **7**:257
Indians, Spanish slavery of, **7**:39–40
indifference in transitive nature of
preference orderings, **1**:64n. 8,
65–67
indirect taxes
to control externalities, **4**:106–7
visibility, **4**:232n. 8
individual action
collective action vs., **4**:52, 62–64
combined with collective action,
4:65–66
political options, **4**:254
to protect own reputation, **9**:213
regulation of, to eliminate externalities, **4**:149–51
See also bankruptcy; collective action
individual bargain logrolling,
1:109–10
persistence of, **1**:114–18
small groups left out, **1**:113–14
individualism
democracy and, **2**:95–96
methodological, **2**:xxii, 3, 11–15,
301–2
normative, **2**:xxii
individualism of scientists, **3**:4–5
from self-education, **3**:65
See also planned science
individual preferences. *See* preferences
individuals
costs of monitoring, **10**:424
group selection and, **10**:225–26
impact vs. cost of externalities on,
5:204
importance of, in military, **10**:406–7
importance of, to economics, **10**:3–
4, 7–8, 405
knowledge of others' utility, **5**:210

individual vs. collective action,
10:407–13
soldiers firing weapons, **10**:425–28
individual vs. group selection, **10**:182–
86, 225–36, 244–46. *See also*
nepotism
indoctrinability, **8**:234–35, 241, 247,
251–52
induced curiosity, **3**:24, 28–29
denial of inducement, **3**:29–30
effect on research results, **3**:110–11
in social sciences, **3**:153–54
induced research, **3**:24–25
by academic scientists, **3**:30
monetary rewards for, **3**:28–30
quality of, **3**:46–48
See also directed research; pure
research
induced researchers
dissemination of discoveries,
3:115–22
motivations, **3**:46
self-education, **3**:65n. 9
induction, **3**:54
definition, **3**:92–93, 95, 98
how it works, **3**:94–95
hypothesis development by, **3**:101
logical basis for, **3**:88
pattern recognition and, **3**:96–101
relation with deduction, **3**:92–94,
98–99
unplannable nature of, **3**:105
See also hypothesis testing
industrial accidents codes, **9**:389
industrial espionage, **3**:113
Industrial Revolution, **5**:160–70
inefficiency
in charities, **1**:399, 402–4
definition, **1**:402n. 10
in government, due to rent seeking,
5:113–14, 115
of policies created by rent seeking,
5:226–30

inefficiency (*continued*)
  rationale for inefficient transfers,
    5:144–48
  rent-seeking costs from, 5:222
  of rent transfers, 5:215–18
  in scientific research, due to patents,
    5:3–4
  of socialism, 5:124
  See also X-inefficiency
inefficient transfers, 7:184–87,
    194–97
inegalitarian societies, 1:315–19
inertia effect, 4:110
inferiors. *See* subordinates
inflation
  in Africa, 10:391
  in China, 1100–1500 A.D.,
    10:324–26
  in Chin dynasty in China, 10:331
  Chinese adjustment to, 10:314–16,
    319
  Chinese attempts to stop, 10:310–
    11, 312–14, 339
  defining, 10:373–75
  denominations of paper money and,
    10:330n. 16, 346–47
  effect on economic growth of United
    States, 10:390
  effects of, in China, 10:316–17
  in free China, 1937–1949,
    10:308–10
  government use of, 10:359–62
  monetary collapse from, 10:345
  in Mongol dynasty in China,
    10:341–42
  possible remedies for South Korea,
    10:358
  Social Security system and, 7:287
  South Korean adjustment to contin-
    uous, 10:343–49
  South Korean attempts to control,
    10:345–46

  South Korean difficulties with,
    10:355–57
  as spur to competitive currencies,
    10:363–65
  in Szechuan dynasty in China,
    10:326
  unemployment and, 7:279
information
  access to, 1:432–33
  assumption of more or less perfect,
    1:112
  assumption of perfect, 1:341–42
  in bargaining process, 9:391
  causes of poor, 5:210
  about charities, 1:398–99, 408–10
  consumers' levels of, 4:128
  control over, 9:208–14
  costs, 1:401
  costs of obtaining, 7:206–7
  costs to voters, of obtaining, 4:230,
    239–40, 253–54
  degradation during transmission,
    6:148
  difficulties of poor people in obtain-
    ing, 7:254
  economics of, 7:176
  effect on public interest, 1:578
  effects of imperfect, 4:398–99
  in enforcing legal contracts,
    9:44–45
  flow in bureaucracy, 6:76–77, 404
  flow in organizations, 6:379–80
  impacted, 5:308n. 14
  incentives to subordinates and,
    6:407–15
  limited vs. full models of, 4:249
  loss of control over, 6:263
  for making preferences, 4:89, 91–92
  motivating voters to acquire,
    4:131–32
  in multiparty political systems,
    4:391

payment for, by law enforcement
officials, **9**:177
perfect information models of,
4:231
possessed by voters vs. consumers,
4:126–28
problems for voters, **7**:204–8
proprietary, **5**:298
relation of fraud with, **9**:205, 207
relation to externalities, **5**:211–12
results of asymmetric, **5**:277
rewards for, **8**:188–89, 197, 276
about special interests, **1**:597
about transfers, **7**:69
used in trials, **9**:73–79
voters' levels of, **4**:129
See also knowledge; mass media;
political information; rational-
ignorance model of voting
information accumulation, **3**:56–58
facts, **3**:75
information clusters, **3**:103
See also data collection
information overload, **3**:80
information retrieval, **3**:77;
6:294n. 17
impact of terminological change on,
3:82
literature about, **3**:133n. 33
See also classification systems; literature searches
information transfer among termites,
10:257
"Information without Profit" (Tullock),
1:36; **7**:4n. 2, 101n. 15
informers, **8**:190–96. *See also* conspiracies; coups d'état
Ingram, J. K., **8**:35n. 9
inheritance of wealth
absence of, **1**:258
arguments against, **1**:258–64
arguments for, **1**:247–48
permitting or not permitting, **1**:248
See also law of inheritance; probate
inheritance taxes
argument against, **1**:254
avoidance of, **1**:260–61
Pareto-optimal, **1**:255
probate and, **9**:131–32
wealth equalization and, **1**:252,
253–57
In His Image (Rorvik), **8**:246
injury. *See* personal injury
in-kind aid
charitable giving that uses, **7**:348
motives for giving, **7**:95–99
to poor people, **7**:133–41
transfers via, **7**:99–100, 193, 209,
348
to welfare recipients, **7**:136, 138–39
innocent offenders, erroneous conviction of, **9**:174–75, 202
innovations. *See* new ideas
inoculation example, **4**:107
inquiry
difference from science, **3**:48,
49–51
subjects of, **3**:33
inquisitorial system of law, **1**:466
advantages, **1**:516
appeals under, **1**:506
arguments against, **1**:476–77
compared with adversary system,
1:473–79, 510; **5**:186, 188–
89; **9**:85–96, 291, 303–8,
344, 358
history, **1**:527–28
juge d'instruction, **9**:173
resource expenditures, **9**:299–301
role of precedent within, **9**:186
use of judges and juries, **9**:80–85
See also adversary system of law;
arbitration; Napoleonic legal
system

insane people
  legal competency, **9**:126–28
  rational behavior by, **10**:102–5
insider trading, **1**:432–33, 437n. 11
insights, **3**:73, 95, 103–4
insoluble problems, **3**:104
institutions, structuring of, **10**:405–6
instrumental actions, **6**:31
insurance
  ability to reject, **9**:99
  abolishing, **9**:111–16
  collective redistribution and,
    2:185–91
  contracts, **9**:102, 104
  costs, **9**:108–10
  government vs. private, **7**:364
  law of torts applied to, **9**:99
  legal costs, **9**:117
  medical insurance by government,
    7:304–5
  premiums, **1**:498
  as proxy for rent seeking, **5**:74
  risk and, **9**:102–8
  as a transfer, **7**:36–38
  See also automobile insurance; health
    insurance; liability insurance;
    Social Security system
insurance companies
  internal court system, **9**:70
  motives, **9**:378
  premium structures, **9**:106–7
  standardization of policies, **9**:212
insurance industry view of aid to poor
    people, **7**:105–6
insurance motive. *See* income insurance
    motive
intellectual capital as disputed turf of
    scholars, **1**:6, 7
intellectuals
  bias about government, **8**:233
  chance for public service by, **7**:367
  charitable giving and, **1**:273–74
  democracy and, **8**:131–32

  as ill-informed voters, **7**:333
  image of revolution painted by,
    8:177–79
  impact of New Deal on, **1**:267n. 12
  law and, **9**:48–51
  relation with special-interest groups,
    7:333–37
  South American, **8**:251
intelligence
  position in hierarchies and, **6**:23
  of sovereigns, **6**:80–82
  See also knowledge; reasoning
interdependence
  costs and, **2**:46, 49
  between rules and organization,
    2:78–79
  of utility functions, **7**:29
interdisciplinarity
  caused by protective tariffs, **4**:18
  of early economics, **1**:7–8
  in modern economics, **1**:3–7
interdisciplinary scientists, **3**:63–64.
    See also cross-disciplinary train-
    ing and research
interest groups, **2**:269–90
  equilibrium, **2**:274–75
  in politics, **2**:9
  See also special-interest groups
interest rates during inflation in China,
    10:311
Internal Revenue Act, **5**:37
Internal Revenue Service (IRS),
    1:452; **8**:11
internal transfers, **7**:181
Interstate Commerce Commission
    (ICC), **4**:111; **5**:229, 310;
    7:74–76, 331
  rent seeking and, **5**:167, 169
intrafamily gifts, **7**:11, 26
intransitivity, **4**:284–85
  experimental errors that cause,
    1:63
  May's hypothesis, **1**:63, 64–65, 67

*Introduction to Positive Political Theory,
An* (Riker and Ordeshook),
4:220
inventions
competition for, 5:7–8
costs, 5:158–59
from directed research and development, 3:17–18
government support for, 5:159
labor-saving, 3:18
legal stimuli for, 3:164–65
lobbying for and against, 5:154–55
measuring social value of, 5:298
under monopoly, 5:156–67
national secrecy about, 8:352
scientific method and, 3:8
See also patent system; scientific discoveries; social inventions
inventors, compared with lobbyists,
5:152
investigation of reality
direct, 3:85
particular or specific, 3:75–85
point of cessation, 3:85
types, 3:75–76
See also hypothesis development;
hypothesis testing; literature
searches
investigative hypothesis, 3:76
investigative research. *See* investigation
of reality
investments
advice, 1:433–34
tax-sheltered, 7:124–25
See also capital investment; stock
exchange rules; stockholders
"invisible college," 3:66–67
"invisible hand," 6:333
in scientific research, 3:4–5
undermining of public faith in, 6:10
involuntary transactions, 1:187
Iran, 1:32
government, 6:331

overthrow of Shah, 8:62n. 28,
211–13
Ireland, economic growth, 10:389
Ireland, Thomas R., 1:*185n. 1*, 258–
60, *287n. 20*; 4:*71n. 4, 84n. 12*;
7:*26n. 5*; 8:*167n. 2, 174n. 2*;
10:*53n. 18*
Iron Chancellor. *See* Bismarck, Otto
von
"iron triangle" in Washington politics,
5:58
IRS (Internal Revenue Service),
1:452; 8:11
Islamic countries, government, 6:276
Islamic legal system, 5:194; 9:173,
182, 356
Israel, government, 5:130, 132, 291
Issacharoff, Samuel, 4:*442n. 5*
Italy
government, 8:133
voting system, 4:446

Jackson, M. W., 10:*425n. 1*
Jackson, Raymond, 8:*169n. 4*
Jackson, Robert, 9:417
Jacobs, Everett M., 8:*109n. 5*
Jagannadham, Vedula, 7:*257nn. 12, 13*
Japan
economic growth, 10:390–91
voting method, 4:442–43
Japanese cars, 5:228, 241–42, 263
Japanese government, 7:334–36;
8:290
feudal system, 8:37
legislature, 6:106–7
Japanese Public Choice Study Group,
4:16
Jarman, T. L., 8:*87n. 13, 110n. 7*
Jarvis, Jennifer U. M., 10:*236n. 1*
Jaszi, Oscar, 8:*103n. 61, 127n. 68*
Jefferson, Thomas, 1:586n. 7
Jeffersonian ideal of free society, 6:10
jellyfish societies, 1:561

Jennings, George H., **8**:*202n. 9*

Jensen, J. P., **10**:*343n. 1*, *344n. 4*,
  345n. 8, *348n. 14*

Jensen, Michael, **6**:*273n. 12*, 274

Jevons, Marshall, **1**:*430n. 6*

Jevons, W. S., **10**:*324n. 5*, *339n. 22*

Jewkes, John, **3**:*181n. 22*

Jews
  compensating others not to perse-
    cute, **4**:351, 353
  discrimination against, **4**:427–28
  in pre-Davidic times, **8**:204

job descriptions, **6**:311

job hierarchies, **6**:21–23. *See also*
  career advancement

job security, **6**:122–23

Johnson, Alvin H., **1**:*247n. 1*

Johnson, Chalmers, **8**:*45n. 53*

Johnson, David B., **1**:*185n. 1*; **4**:*71n. 4*;
  7:*26n. 5*

Johnson, Earl, Jr., **9**:*356n. 41*

Johnson, Harry G., **3**:*164n. 3*; **5**:*13n. 3*

Johnson, Kenneth F., **8**:*92n. 27*, *92–
  93n. 28*, *137n. 95*

Johnson, Lyndon, **4**:255n. 11

Johnson, Paul, **8**:*11nn. 35, 36, 44n. 40*,
  54n. 11, *55n. 13*, *60n. 26*,
  66nn. 14, 15, *75n. 36*, *109n. 5*,
  110–11n. 7, *115n. 21*, *117n. 29*,
  124n. 55, *127–28n. 71*, *130–
  31n. 78*, *132–33n. 83*, *138n. 98*,
  211n. 42, *216n. 51*, *221nn. 62*,
  63, *256n. 59*, *296n. 8*

Johnson, Ronald N., **6**:*383n. 11*

Johnson, William R., **7**:*240n. 17*,
  241n. 20

Jones-Lee, M., **5**:*15n. 7*

Joravsky, David, **3**:*107n. 1*

journalism, lying in, **4**:266

Journal of Economic Criticism, The, **1**:36

Jouvenel, Bertrand de, "The Chairman's Problem," **4**:392–93

judges
  advantage over juries, **9**:83–85
  allowing parties to choose, **9**:83
  amount of work done by, **1**:478–79
  attempt to select unbiased, **1**:579
  bribery, **6**:394n. 5
  British, **9**:85
  as bureaucrats, **5**:118
  buying the best, **9**:298–99
  common law, **9**:414–19
  difference from juries, **9**:346
  disagreement with juries, **1**:507
  economic consequence of good,
    1:474
  effect on adversarial system, **1**:475
  errors, **1**:484–94, 513, 515, 518;
    4:267
  evaluation and promotion,
    9:330–32
  expertise, **9**:73
  "faithful agent" notion of, **9**:417
  federal U.S., **6**:65–69; **9**:415–18
  how hard they work, **9**:302–3
  impact of appeals on, **9**:183
  impartiality, **4**:267
  instructions to juries, **9**:345
  judicial experts other than, **9**:73–74,
    328
  lawsuits against, **9**:313
  legal backgrounds, **6**:394
  motives, **1**:479; **4**:39–40;
    9:328–38
  necessary qualifications, **6**:395
  number of, at trial, **9**:180–81
  performance evaluation of, **6**:397
  powers, relative to jury's powers,
    5:169–70
  preference for complex rules, **9**:49
  public-goods problems created by,
    1:388–90
  relation to average citizen, **1**:524
  research about, **1**:477–78

role in common law, **9**:406
salaries, **9**:416
sample population of, **1**:486–87
selection of, **6**:396
tenure for, **9**:325
traffic court, **1**:449–50
training of, **9**:179–80
See also arbitrators; board of judges;
    courts; judicial errors; sanctions
judicial decisions
biased, **9**:315n. 5
jury verdicts vs., **9**:438
truth vs., **9**:39
when circumstances change,
    9:42–46
judicial errors, **9**:38–41, 388, 442–44
appeals due to, **9**:182
from bias of judges, **9**:328–30
court costs and likelihood of, **9**:61
criminal vs. civil cases, **9**:343
effect of reducing, **9**:61
in enforcement of contracts, **9**:55–
    56, 61–62
in inquisitorial and adversary legal
    systems, **9**:342–43
by judges, **9**:38–41
reduction of, **9**:79–96
side favored by, **9**:41
judicial inefficiency
effect on contracts, **9**:67–70
exception where desirable, **9**:264
judicial precedent. *See* legal precedent
judicial reform, **9**:174
judicial review, **2**:xxii
juntas, **6**:91; **8**:78, 79–81. *See also*
    military governments
juries
accuracy, **1**:524, 528–29; **9**:332
under adversary and inquisitorial
    systems, **9**:80–85
alternatives to, **9**:343–44
attempt to select unbiased, **1**:579

avoiding use of, **9**:347–50
bias in favor of accused, **9**:350–51
"blindfolding" of, **9**:439–40
control of law enforcement via,
    6:396
court distrust of, **1**:517–18, 530
decision-making, **1**:514–15
distrust of, **9**:434–37
in fraud and embezzlement cases,
    9:205
historical development, **1**:526–27
history of common law, **9**:423–29
how hard they work, **9**:302–3
ignorance, **9**:74
under inquisitorial system of law,
    9:344–45, 352, 454
jury selection process, **9**:427–28
legal instructions to, **9**:439
making life-and-death medical deci-
    sions with, **7**:349
motivation, **1**:479
number of jurors on, **1**:527;
    9:426–27
"of one's peers," **9**:428
origin, **1**:521–22, 525–26
powers, relative to judges' powers,
    5:169–70
qualifications, **9**:326–27
rationales for, **1**:522–24, 524–25,
    531; **9**:345–47, 350
rent seeking and, **5**:166–68, 169–70
research about, **1**:477–78, 507–8,
    511–13, 529–30
research needed, **1**:533
selection, **1**:532–33
See also grand juries
justices-of-the-peace, **9**:328
juvenile offenders, **9**:128

Kaempffert, Waldemar, **3**:*38n. 10*,
    39n. 13
Kafka, Alexandre, **1**:*442n. 3*; **9**:139n. 3

Kafoglis, M. Z., **1**:*350n. 2*
Kagel, John H., **10**:*105n. 16, 107n. 19*
Kaiser, Joseph H., **2**:*270n. 1*
Kakalika, James S., **9**:*341n. 5*
Kaldor, Nicholas, **1**:*253n. 5*
Kalven, Harry, Jr., **1**:*477n. 9, 511n. 2,
    528n. 3*; **9**:*98n. 1, 99n. 3,
    116n. 21, 157n. 6, 185n. 6,
    347n. 20, 350n. 30, 437n. 15*
Kamien, M. I., **4**:*90n. 3, 98n. 1,
    109n. 10*
Kammerer, Paul, **3**:107
Kant, Immanuel, **2**:132, 301
"Kantian" median voting, **1**:54–55, 59
Kapitsa, Pyotr L., **3**:*172n. 10*
Kaplan, Morton A., **2**:239n. 1; **8**:354
Kapuscinski, Ryszard, **8**:*123n. 53*
Karel, L., **3**:*86n. 29*
Karels, G. V., **5**:*64n. 82*
    on efficient rent seeking, **5**:88–90
Karnew, Stanley, **8**:*304n. 21*
Kasarda, John D., **10**:*46n. 8*
Katz, E., **5**:*64n. 82, 65n. 84*
Katz, Jerold J., **3**:*88n. 2*
Kay, Hugh, **8**:*75n. 33*
Keating, Barry P., **7**:*90n. 1*; **10**:100
Keating, Maryann O., **7**:*90n. 1*
Keegan, John, **8**:*227n. 5*
Keeley, Michael C., **1**:*284n. 13*
Keeter, S., **5**:*239n. 7*
Keleher, Robert, **10**:*383n. 13, 384n. 16*
Kelidar, A. R., **8**:*83n. 2*
Kelley, Walt, **2**:*129n. 3*
Kendall, Willmoore, **2**:*246–47n. 3*
Kennedy, John F.
    assassination, **8**:141n. 1
    election vs. Nixon, **4**:217n. 3
Kennedy, Ted, **5**:306
Kennedy Center (Washington, D.C.),
    1:578
Kenya, government in, **5**:127–28
Kepler, Johannes, **3**:27
Kerber, E. S., **10**:*349n. 15*
Kessler, Lawrence D., **8**:*99n. 46*

Keynes, John Maynard, **1**:436; **2**:x
    point about coalitions, **5**:77–78
Keynesianism as cause of government
    growth, **1**:29
Keynesians vs. Chicago School of
    Economics, **4**:18
Khomeini, Ayatollah, **8**:212;
    9:*344n. 16*
Khrushchev, Nikita, **8**:268
Kimenyi, Mwangi S., **8**:*146n. 10*;
    9:*418n. 12, 420n. 17,
    421n. 20*
Kingsley, J. Donald, **4**:*196n. 22*
Kinross, Lord, **8**:*48n. 1*
Kirby, Maurice, **8**:*55n. 14*
Kirzner, Israel M., **10**:*95n. 2*
Klahr, David, **4**:280–82
Klein, Benjamin, **1**:*500nn. 4, 6*;
    10:367–72, *374n. 1*
Kleinmuntz, Benjamin, **9**:*361n. 50*
Kline, Morris, **3**:*41n. 16, 92*
Klingaman, David., **1**:*114n. 22*
Knapton, Ernest J., **8**:*220n. 60*
Kneese, Allen V., **1**:*413n. 3*;
    4:*154n. 6*
Knight, Frank H., **2**:*19n. 6, 93, 99,*
    106n. 4, 195; **3**:*16n. 10*;
    4:13, 18
Knight of Great Renown, A (Clifford),
    6:277
Knollenberg, Bernard, **8**:*209n. 35,
    295n. 6*
knowledge
    graphic representation of, **3**:68, 78
    how we gain, **10**:6
    relationship to scientific method,
        3:7–8
    sought by early scientists, **3**:9
    about subordinates' actions,
        6:205–9
    subordinates' superiority in, **6**:313
    about superiors' desires, **6**:362
    three ways of finding things out,
        6:17

See also classification systems; information; information accumulation; intelligence; investigation of reality
knowledge levels and efficiency of courts, 9:63–64
Koller, Roland H., II, 1:258–60, 287*n. 20*
Komroff, Manuel, 10:*322n. 2*
Kormendi, R. C., 10:379, 381–82, 383, 384, 385, 386n. 17, 395–96
Kornhauser, L., 9:*432n. 4*
Korvik, David, 8:*246n. 35*
Kramer, Gerald H., 10:*371n. 10*
Kreidberg, Marvin A., 8:*125n. 60*
Kristol, Irving, 7:334
Kritzer, Herbert M., 9:*341n. 5*
Kroeber, A. L., 3:*145n. 16*
Krohm, Gregory C., 9:*256n. 10, 257nn. 12, 14*; 10:*83nn. 19, 21*
Kronenberger, Louis, 8:*102n. 59, 108n. 3*
Krueger, Anne O., 1:*237n. 1, 240n. 4*; 6:*376n. 3*
    article on rent seeking, 5:25–26
    compared with Jagdish Bhagwati, 5:30–31
    "Political Economy of the Rent-Seeking Society, The," 5:*74n. 93, 110n. 7, 285n. 8, 287n. 9*
Kruuk, Hans, 10:*123n. 5, 152n. 13*
Kuhn, Thomas, *The Structure of Scientific Revolutions*, 3:xix
K'ung, H. H., 10:*308n. 4*
Kung, Hans, 8:*228n. 8*
Kupinsky, Stanley, 10:*46n. 8*
Kurrild-Klitgaard, Peter, 8:*155n. 23*

Laband, David N., 5:*74–75n. 95, 246n. 7*
labor
    evaluation of physical, 6:402
    maximizing return to, 1:537–40
    uncompensated, 6:271
    See also employment market; occupational monopolies
laboratories, 3:50, 136–37
    costs of, 3:183
    industrial, 3:21–23
laboratory research
    compared with historical research, 3:144–46
    compared with literature searches, 3:12–13
    for its own sake, 3:86
    privately funded, 3:23–25
    See also directed research
labor contracts, 6:14–17. *See also* job security
labor-saving inventions, 3:18
labor unions
    support for Social Security system, 7:285
    unionization, 1:217–18
Lack, David, 1:*537nn. 2, 3*
LaCourture, Jean, 8:*89n. 16*
Laird, John, 2:*19n. 6*
Lakewood Plan, 4:404
Lampman, R. J., 1:*263n. 4*
Land, Edwin Herbert, 3:180
Landa, Janet T., 10:*160n. 2*
Landau, Henry J., 10:*430n. 3*
Landes, William M., 5:*61n. 74, 62n. 76*; 9:306, 307*n. 17*, 308
Langer, William L., 8:*89n. 18, 89–90n. 19, 94–95n. 30, 99n. 47, 103n. 61, 105nn. 69, 70, 112n. 11, 115nn. 20, 21, 116nn. 24, 25, 117n. 30, 118n. 34, 119n. 38, 119–20n. 39, 123n. 53, 124n. 56, 126n. 67, 129nn. 73, 74, 130n. 76, 130–31n. 78, 131–32n. 79, 132n. 82, 132–33n. 83, 133n. 86, 219nn. 56, 57, 220nn. 58, 61, 256n. 54*

language, evolution of, and information retrieval, 3:81–82
Lanick, Hugo, 8:*238n. 23*
Lanting, Frans, 10:*165n. 7*
Laplace, Jean, 2:316
large hierarchical organizations
centralization in, 6:417–18
efficiency, 6:411
social mobility in, 6:19
theory, 6:260
Tullock's view of, 6:9–10
types, 6:248–49
See also conglomerates; government
agencies; military
Larsen, Roy, 2:271
Larson, Arthur, 8:*85n. 7*
Laski, Frida, 2:*303n. 11*
Laski, Harold, 2:*303n. 11*
law enforcement, 1:314–16
applied to ruling class, 1:319–20
civil vs. criminal offenders,
9:186–88
within companies, 6:397–98
costs, 1:458–62, 463; 9:226,
341–42
courts and police, 9:173–74
efficiency of, 9:263–73
externalities from, 6:351
government organizations that
engage in, 6:392–97
through paying for information,
9:177–78
purpose of, 9:340–41
social cost, 9:341
speed limits, 1:447–49; 9:143–44
against theft, 9:189–90
transition from the jungle and,
1:315
of treaties, 8:344–48
two parts to, 1:465
See also fines; penalties; police force;
sanctions; trials
Law Enforcement Assistance Administration, 9:252

law of contracts
bargain theory, 9:408
classical theory, 9:408
distinction from law of torts, 9:447
will or autonomy theory of, 9:446
See also contracts
law of demand, 10:16–17
law of diminishing returns
in research, 3:105–6
scientist's view of, 3:53
law of evidence. *See* rules of evidence
law of inheritance, 9:130–34
law of intestacy, 9:131–32
law of large numbers in supervision,
6:221–22
task allocation and, 6:402
law of property, 9:406–7. *See also*
property rights
law of torts, 9:99
culpability and, 9:101–2
distinction from law of contracts,
9:447
economic efficiency discussions concerning, 9:378–79
justification of, 9:264n. 4
physical injuries under, 9:372
tort lawsuits, 9:376
laws
efficiency of, 9:263
ethics subordinated to, 9:225–28
government of, 9:346
uniformity of, 9:181, 184–85
See also bills; legal systems;
legislation
law school education, 9:179–80
laws of nature, 3:34–35, 53
laws of science, 3:9
lawsuit damages. *See* damages in
lawsuits
lawsuits
accuracy and costs, 9:354–56
bias in proceedings, 9:287–90
class action, 9:210
costs, 9:277–78, 280, 309–23, 341

court enforcement of penalties,
9:186
criminal law vs., 9:193–98
decisions to engage in, 9:57–61, 65
expenses vs. likelihood of success,
9:292–95
frequency of involvement in, 9:65,
68–70
about inheritance, 9:133
against judges, 9:183, 313
lottery model of, 9:295–99
over new drugs, 6:420
use of government funds for,
9:316–22
See also arbitration; courts; legal
proceedings; out-of-court
settlements; trials
lawyers
choice of taking contingency cases,
9:311–13
common distrust of, 9:49
corporate, 6:324, 365
fees, 9:309–11
licensing of, 9:421
motives of trial attorneys, 1:502
number of, in United States,
9:421–23
as proxy for rent-seeking waste, 5:74
role in adversary legal systems,
9:85–87
role in common law, 9:401, 419–23
role in drawing up contracts,
5:191–93
social costs of, 5:194–95
special-interest groups of, 1:475–
76, 531–32
training of, 3:66n. 10
types, 9:422–23
learned journals. *See* academic journals;
scientific journals
Leathes, Stanley, 8:*33n. 3, 65n. 6,
222n. 66*
Lebanese government, 8:117
Lebergott, Stanley, 1:*286n. 17;*

5:*179n. 4;* 7:*65n. 20, 121n. 9,
240n. 18*
Ledyard, John, 1:*148n. 15;* 4:361
Lee, Dwight R., 5:*147n. 14*
left-wing political parties, 6:106
legal activities. *See* illegal activities;
law enforcement
legal competency, 9:126–28
legal costs, 1:456–64; 9:389
from erroneous convictions,
9:199–200
in inquisitorial vs. adversary systems
of law, 9:299–303
of insurance, 9:108–10
of lawsuits, 9:277–78, 280, 309–
23, 341
of plaintiffs, 9:310–13
research, 9:392
See also court costs; legal fees
legal errors. *See* judicial errors
legal fees
paid by third parties, 9:315
payment of, in England, 9:313–14
See also contingency fees
legal institutions, 9:266
legalization
fraud, 9:204, 205
prostitution, 9:221
theft, 9:268–69
legal or equitable remedies, 9:407
legal positivists, 9:9–10
legal precedent, 9:406
from case law, 9:318
effect on common law, 9:400–401
within inquisitorial system of law,
9:186
rule by single, 9:185–86
legal principles not based on ethics,
9:10–11
legal proceedings
bias in, 9:282–87
fairness, 9:329–30
how to evaluate, 9:339
optimal, 9:275–90

legal proceedings (*continued*)
  people's view of fair, **9**:344
  for prosecuting thieves, **9**:193–98
  resemblance to lobbying, **5**:295–96
  similarity to rent seeking, **5**:184,
    186–90
  See also courts; lawsuits; trials
legal process, compared with market
    economy, **9**:450
legal reforms, **9**:266–68
  costs of, **9**:344
  subsidization of expenses, **9**:281
  time needed to implement, **9**:3
legal rules
  general standards vs., **9**:16–18
  knowledge of, **9**:44–45
legal systems
  case law, **1**:513
  China, **8**:225–26
  costs, **1**:457–58
  economic value of, **1**:456
  efficiency, **1**:456
  ideal, **9**:184–85
  imperfection, **1**:516
  influence on monopolies, **4**:112n. 14
  Islamic, **5**:194
  medieval England, **8**:202
  more than one, within one govern-
    ment, **6**:251–52
  other hierarchical organizations vs.,
    6:192
  pre-Napoleonic, **9**:356
  relation with politics, **5**:81–82
  South Korea, **10**:355
  suggested reforms, **1**:462–64,
    516–20
  three stages, **1**:509–10
  Tullock's views about jury system,
    5:170
  two bodies of law in United States,
    6:68
  using positive incentives in, **9**:338
  Western, **5**:81–82, 186

  See also adversary system of law; case
    law; common law; courts; crim-
    inal justice system; inquisitorial
    system of law; Napoleonic legal
    system
legislation
  on behalf of guilds, **9**:124–25
  about billboards, **5**:4
  complexity of, **5**:277–78
  congressmen's failure to read,
    5:37, 80
  deception about, **9**:50–51
  effective special interest, **5**:304–5
  European vs. Anglo-Saxon, **9**:454
  impact of lobbying on content of,
    5:301
  "milker bills," **5**:73
  pork-type, **5**:285–89
  requiring congressmen to read,
    5:80
  See also bills; laws
legislators, term limits, **6**:385
legislatures
  bicameral, with different constitu-
    encies, **5**:291
  decision making by, **4**:417–23
  decision-making procedures, **1**:25
  under dictators and monarchs,
    8:217–18
  in dictatorships, **8**:136
  difference from executive branch,
    4:403–4, 407
  efficient rent seeking from,
    5:63–66
  European vs. American, **1**:118
  influence of bureaucrats on, **5**:55
  influence of lawyers on, **1**:531–32
  logrolling, **1**:107–8
  opposition parties in, **1**:76–77
  process of, **5**:37
  proportional representation,
    1:31, 34
  relation with courts, **9**:186

sale of seats in, **8**:137
single-member constituency voting,
   1:31–32
that are "mirror of the voters,"
   4:382–85, 445
time in session, **4**:417
two-chamber, **1**:31, 32
unicameral, **1**:32
voting method for obtaining majority party, **4**:432
voting methods within, **4**:433–36
widespread benefit-sharing within,
   1:113–14
See also British Parliament; proportional representation; United
   States Congress
legitimacy
   definition, **8**:225, 228
   dictators' need for, **8**:252–53, 254–
     55, 257
   erroneous calculations about,
     8:231–32
   of monarchs, **8**:253–54
   relation with ethics, **8**:227–28
   relation with ideology, **8**:255–56
   roots of, **8**:249
   of socialist governments, **8**:252
   in South America, **8**:251, 252
   success of coups and, **8**:232–33
Le Grand, Julian, **7**:33, *249n. 1*,
   250n. 3, 257n. 14, 308n. 19
Leibenstein, Harvey, **1**:*169nn. 1, 3*;
   5:14–17, 21; **10**:*39n. 1*
   "Allocative Efficiency vs. X-
     Efficiency," **5**:*13n. 4*
Leibenstein theory of transactions
   costs, **6**:245
Leibowitz, Arleen Smigel, **9**:234–35;
   10:79–80
Leites, Nathan, **8**:*174n. 2*
Lenin, Vladimir, **1**:339; **6**:271, 371–
   72; **8**:127
Leoni, Bruno, **1**:*492n. 12*; **2**:xxv, 8,

   23n. 12; **3**:*157n. 31*; **9**:*405n. 6*,
   444
Lerner, Abba P., **2**:x; **7**:29–30; **10**:85
Leslie, G. R., **10**:*75n. 3*
lesser developed countries
   impact of rent seeking on, **5**:120–21
   rent seeking applied to, **5**:27
   socialism in, **5**:29
Letwin, William, **3**:*52n. 26*
leveraged buyouts, **6**:246, 253–54,
   376–80. *See also* corporate
   takeovers
Levi, Maurice, **10**:*383n. 10*
Levy, Ferdinand, **9**:244
Lewis, Bernard, **8**:*102n. 60, 117n. 28*
Lewis, J. P., **10**:*344n. 6*
Lewis, John D., **8**:*103n. 61, 127n. 68*
liability
   for accidental injuries, **9**:117–18
   broad, **9**:375–76
   limited, in corporation law, **9**:129
   pairing with risk, **9**:115
   strict, **9**:364, 370–79
   waiver of, **9**:54
liability insurance, **9**:387–88
Libecap, Gary D., **5**:*215n. 6, 216n. 7*;
   6:*383n. 11*
libel, **9**:213
libertarianism, **6**:10
library filing systems, **3**:79. *See also*
   classification systems
licenses
   driver's, **1**:449
   to pollute, **1**:426
   See also certification examinations
licensing of lawyers, **9**:421
lichens, **10**:193
Lie, Berit, **8**:*64n. 5*
lie detectors, **9**:93–97, 168, 178,
   361–62, 430
life insurance, **9**:112–16
Lima, Peru, black (underground)
   economy, **5**:296

limited autocracy, **8**:41–43, 206–7, 222

Lindahl equilibrium in demand-revealing process, **1**:145–46

Lindahl tax
applicability, **7**:200
demand revealing and, **1**:159, 161
negative, **7**:72–73
using for charitable giving, **7**:95
using for transfers, **7**:71–76, 82

Lindblom, Charles E., **1**:*395n. 5*; **2**:8, *31n. 2*

Lindsay, Cotton M., **7**:*258n. 15*, *311n. 24*

line-item veto power, **4**:408

Linnaean system, **3**:84

lions, **10**:122, 126, 151

lion societies, **1**:309, 310–11

Lippmann, Walter, **2**:237

literature, effect on social sciences, **3**:151

literature searches, **3**:76–77
citation counting of articles, **3**:*27n. 26*, 31
compared with laboratory research, **3**:12–13
computer-assisted, **3**:84–85
point of cessation, **3**:85
teamwork in applied research vs., **3**:79
See also classification systems; information retrieval; self-education of scientists

litigation, **1**:463
arbitration, **1**:520
contingency cases, **1**:504–5
impact of evidence on, **1**:503
probability of success in, **1**:466
resource commitments in adversarial proceedings, **1**:466–68, 473
See also pretrial settlements

Livy (Titus Livius), **10**:*427nn. 5, 6*

loans. *See* unsecured loans

lobbying, **4**:163
aircraft industry, **5**:306
on behalf of special-interest groups, **7**:175
by bureaucrats, **1**:194–95
for charities, **5**:179
compared with related government outlays, **5**:75
decision to engage in, **1**:197
diseconomies of scale, **5**:231–32
effect on industries/products lobbied for, **5**:158
effect on technology, **5**:220–21, 222–25, 228–30
effects of, **4**:421
gains to individuals not involved in, **1**:197–98
for and against inventions, **5**:154–55
limitations to, **5**:90
as major social cost, **1**:243
maximum investment in, **5**:249
optimal size and number of lobbies, **5**:232–33
as productive activity, **5**:184–85
for protective tariffs, **5**:307–10
against regulation, **5**:154–55, 157–59
relation with associated businesses, **5**:50, 51
relation with transfers, **5**:23
resemblance of lawsuits to, **5**:295–96
size of payments for, **5**:214
tax reform and, **5**:174–76
Wagner-type, **1**:194
in Washington, D.C., **4**:163
See also farm lobbies; lobbyists; rent seeking; special-interest groups

lobbying costs, **1**:188–91; **5**:23; **7**:201
gains vs., **5**:300
of special-interest groups, **1**:220

lobbyists
  compared with inventors, **5**:152
  in different forms of government,
    8:58
  lying by, **5**:308
  pressures on, **5**:96–100
  See also lobbying
local governments. *See* small local gov-
    ernments; state governments
local politics, **1**:75–76
  Arrow's impossibility theorem and,
    4:283
  logrolling, **5**:33
  party differential in elections, **4**:236
  perfect information model and,
    4:231
  See also road repair; small local
    governments
Locke, John, **2**:238, 299; **8**:139–40;
    9:*407n. 11*
Lockhard, Leonard, **3**:*18n. 14*
Loeb, M., **1**:*134n. 5*
Loewenstein, Karl, **8**:*33n. 2*
Logic of Collective Action, The (Olson),
    4:220; **5**:233; **7**:212, 213
Logic of the Law, The (Tullock),
    9:268n. 13, 343n. 14, 389,
    393, 394
logrolling, **2**:xxiv
  advantage over coalitions, **7**:192–93
  alternatives to, **4**:352
  Arrow's omission of, **1**:125
  benefits, **4**:119, 214–15
  benefits, to politicians from, **4**:248
  in Britain, **4**:206–7, 213–14
  byproducts, **4**:228n. 6
  coalitions and, **5**:271–75
  "complete diversity" and, **2**:225
  by congressmen, **7**:336–37
  costs, **1**:119; **5**:288
  currency for, **5**:283–84, 289–90
  with cycling, **1**:105
  defects, **4**:215–16

definition, **4**:205
in demand-revealing process, **4**:371
under different forms of govern-
    ment, **4**:340–45
effect on poor people, **7**:233–38
efficiency of, in government, **4**:346–
    47, 355–58
efficiency of effects from, **4**:347,
    357–58
empirical tests, **4**:339
externalities from, **4**:348–52
externalities from government vs.
    market and, **4**:99
about funding, **1**:119–20
impact of cost of information on,
    4:231
impact of limited information on,
    4:249
implicit vs. explicit, **1**:52, 120–22,
    585–86
importance to public choice theory,
    4:20
by individual voters, **4**:121
individual vs. coalition, **1**:108–10
by majorities, **5**:273
majority rule and, **1**:51–61
under majority voting, **4**:344, 352–
    53; **7**:200–202
minorities and, **4**:353
need for, **5**:284
need for study, **2**:21, 119
non–Pareto optimal outcomes,
    1:112
optimum distribution of resources
    and, **1**:59
original Tullock analysis of, **5**:249
with quota arrangement, **4**:338
reducing, **5**:79
relation with income redistribution,
    7:175
relation with rent seeking, **5**:33,
    238, 239
restrictions on, **5**:305

logrolling (*continued*)
   social benefits and losses from,
      7:196–97
   Tullock's opinion of, **7**:202
   types, **2**:130–31
   in United States vs. abroad, **7**:231
   voting rules and, **2**:202, 211–12
   See also bargaining; coalitions;
      explicit logrolling; formal
      logrolling coalitions; implicit
      logrolling; individual bargain
      logrolling; vote trading
logrolling models
   applications, **4**:328–30
   appropriate use, **4**:232–33
   with five voters, **4**:325–27
   game theory and, **2**:151–53
   higher-dimensional, **4**:305
   many-dimensional, **4**:327–28
   with multiple voters and options,
      4:336–45
   simple model, **1**:53–54
   simple model results, generalized,
      1:59–61
   with three voters, **4**:320–25, 331–
      33, 336
   two-dimensional, **4**:315–17
Loguet-Higgens, H. C., **3**:*50n. 24*
Loomis, William Farnsworth,
      3:*145n. 17*
loopholes. *See* tax loopholes
Losch, A., **1**:556
lose-lose outcomes, **1**:183–84
loss of companionship (legal damages),
      9:448
lotteries, **7**:349
lottery example, **1**:469–73
lottery game model, **9**:295–98
lottery metaphor for rent seeking,
      5:85–94
   ticket price equilibrium, **5**:95–96
Louis Harris & Associates, **5**:38
Louis XVI, **8**:54

loyalty and career advancement,
      6:46–47
Lucas, R. E., **10**:380
Luce, R. Duncan, **2**:*143n. 1, 155n. 10,
      168n. 2, 170n. 3*, 173; **3**:*128–
      29n. 30*; **10**:*441n. 5*
Luddism, **5**:218
lunacy. *See* insane people
Luttwak, Edward N., **8**:*125n. 59,
      283n. 10, 285n. 12*
luxury taxes, **5**:196–97
lying, **1**:184–85
   through advertising, **9**:208–10
   while bargaining, **9**:396
   by businessmen, **4**:260–61;
      9:210–11
   in business vs. politics, **6**:100
   to casually informed voters, **5**:44–
      45, 46
   costs of, **4**:263
   in the course of business, **4**:262–69
   in court, **9**:429–30
   about distressing consequences of
      choices, **7**:346
   effect on bargaining, **4**:87–89, 98
   equations, **4**:261, 263
   genetic survival and, **10**:163–64
   information dissemination and,
      8:243–46
   in large hierarchical organizations,
      6:260
   during legal proceedings, **9**:76–77
   about legislation, **9**:50–51
   likelihood of, in various professions,
      4:265–69
   by lobbyists, **5**:308
   about peers, **6**:292–93
   by politicians, **7**:168–69; **9**:212–13
   prevalence of, **4**:259–62
   problems involved in, **4**:262
   public demand for, **7**:169
   publicly, **6**:119
   rationality of, **4**:261

reduction of, **4**:264
about self to superiors, **6**:291-92
by special-interest groups, **5**:212-13
by subordinates, **6**:403-4
unsuccessfully, **4**:264-65
to voters about intent of bills,
    7:331-32
to voters about reasons for transfers,
    7:156-60
to well-informed voters, **5**:44-45
by witnesses in trials, **9**:90-96
See also deception; dishonesty; fraud
Lynskey, Elizabeth, **8**:*94n. 29*

Maas, P., **9**:*433n. 7*
Macassey, Lynden, **9**:*306n. 15*
Mach, Ernst, **3**:34-35, 37
Machiavelli, Niccolò, **2**:41; **4**:33;
    6:304; **8**:*147n. 11*, 301, 306
Machlup, Fritz, **3**:*18n. 14*
Mackay, Carolyn Weaver. *See* Weaver,
    Carolyn L.
Mackenzie, J. M., **4**:*284n. 2*
Mackie, J. D., **8**:*100n. 52, 121n. 48*
Macleod, H. D., **10**:*324n. 5, 339n. 22*
Macridis, Roy C., **8**:*126n. 67*
macroeconomics, **4**:169
Maddison, Angus, **10**:*379n. 1*
Madison, James, **2**:23-24, *205n. 2*
Madisonian theory of democracy,
    2:23-24
Mafia. *See* organized crime
Magaddino, Joseph P., **9**:*256n. 10*;
    10:*83n. 19*
Magee, S. P., **5**:*65n. 83, 74n. 95*
Mahan, Linda, **9**:*283n. 3*
Main, Jackson T., **8**:*208nn. 32, 33,*
    209n. 34
Main, Robert S., **1**:425
Maine, Henry, **2**:*262n. 4*; **9**:124
Mair, Lucy, **8**:*63n. 2, 90n. 20*
majority influence in science vs. social
    sciences, **3**:147, 154-55

"majority motion" (Black), **1**:98
majority rule, **2**:143-64
decision costs and, **2**:103-4
expected costs and, **2**:84-85
game theory and, **2**:165-81
logrolling and, **1**:51-61
orthodox model and, **2**:237-50
Pareto optimality and, **2**:165-71
qualified, **2**:202-21
redistribution and, **2**:183-85
unanimity and, **2**:243-44
See also majority voting
"Majority Rule and Allocation"
    (Ward), **6**:89
majority voting, **2**:7, 127-42, 143-64
compared with demand-revealing
    process, **7**:145-48
cycle, **2**:316-18
difference from demand-revealing
    process, **1**:134, 138-39
disadvantage, **4**:119
effect of, **5**:77-78
explanations of stable outcomes
    from, **1**:105
external costs and, **2**:192-93
externalities and, **2**:139-40
imperfect outcomes, **1**:91
involving large numbers, **1**:103-4
juries as representative of, **1**:522-24
with and without logrolling,
    1:106-12
logrolling under, **4**:352-53;
    7:200-202
with more than two alternatives,
    4:430-35
on mosquito abatement, **4**:54
as most efficient way to decide, **4**:56
Pareto optimality and, **2**:89-90
Pennock's argument for, **1**:81
problems of, **1**:51-61
qualified, **2**:202-21
in real world, **4**:361-62
relation with logrolling, **4**:344

majority voting (*continued*)
  side payments in, **2**:148–51
  above simple majority, **1**:31, 59
  social waste and, **2**:156–59
  tendency toward cycling, **1**:94–98
  on transfers, **7**:80
  with two nonidentical majorities, **5**:291
  by U.S. Supreme Court, **1**:487–89
  See also coalitions of voters; cyclical majority; demand-revealing process; reinforced majorities
Makin, John, **10**:*383n. 10*
malevolence, **8**:182n. 7
Malthus, Thomas, **1**:553; **10**:117
managers, **6**:341, 343–44
  decision to fire subordinates, **6**:378
  incentive plans for, **6**:348
  See also administrative theory; bureaucrats; corporate executives; supervisors
Mango, Cyril, **8**:*101n. 55, 116n. 25, 132n. 81*
Manne, Henry G., **4**:440; **9**:129n. 5, *211n. 3*
Mantoux, Paul, **8**:*135n. 90*
Mao, Chairman, **9**:439
Maplethorpe, Robert, **4**:346
mapmaking, in Middle Ages, **3**:150–51
Marais, Jan, **10**:116
marginal cost (MC), **10**:12–14
marginal utility (MU), **10**:14
Margolis, Howard, **4**:373–77
Margolis, Julius, **1**:*51n. 1, 52n. 4*; **2**:130n. 4
Margulis, Lynn, **10**:*246n. 6*
Marighela, Carlos, **8**:*194n. 5*
market economies
  adjustment under, **1**:350–52
  inheritance of wealth and, **1**:250, 253
  three different cases of, **1**:359–64

"market failure," **4**:178
market organizations, **6**:256–57, 261
markets
  absence of, in nonhuman societies, **10**:200–202, 262–63
  application to analysis of bureaucracy, **6**:17
  areas where they don't work, **5**:282
  assumption of perfect, **1**:355
  assumptions about government and, **4**:20–21
  attrition of control and, **6**:268–70
  buyer/seller relationship, **6**:8; **10**:429, 434
  central planning and, **10**:197
  as charitable institutions, **6**:3
  cheapest, **1**:538
  cheating in, **10**:429–37
  compared with government, **4**:174–75
  compared with legal process, **9**:450
  compared with scientific community, **3**:52
  comparing with collectivization, **1**:350
  environmental coordination, **6**:333–34, 335
  externalities from choices in, **5**:274
  government and, **2**:18
  government intervention in, **6**:333
  hierarchies vs., **6**:266–68
  imperfection in, **4**:41–42, 347–48
  information in, **4**:128
  legal counterpart to, **9**:446
  making life-and-death medical decisions via, **7**:346–49
  nonoptimal bargaining problem, **4**:91–92
  political methods in, **6**:16, 113–14
  relation with government, **4**:37–38
  role of standards in, **9**:212
  supply and demand curves, **10**:20, 21

as technique for coordination of
   tasks, **6**:172–75
where equilibrium does not clear,
   5:231
See also customers; employment
   market; market vs. government
   problem
market vs. government problem
   additional areas outside of, **4**:69
   changeability of, **4**:179–81
   commonality of both sectors, **2**:18
   coordination of tasks, **6**:172–75
   differences between the sectors,
      4:174–75
   externalities, **10**:91–94
   in history, **6**:260–61
   imperfection of both sectors, **4**:41–
      42; **5**:282–83
   income redistribution and, **7**:67–68
   Pigou's example, **10**:87–91
   police services, **10**:65–66
   public good and, **10**:86–87
   redistribution and, **10**:86
   reduction of externalities and,
      4:146
   resolving, **4**:85, 95–96; **6**:350
Markl, Hubert, **8**:234n. 12
Marquand, John P., **6**:114
Marques, A. H. de Olivera, **8**:*75n. 33*
marriage contract, **10**:25–26
   benefits, **10**:31–35
   costs, **10**:28–31
   efficient, **10**:37–38
   See also monogamy; spouse selection
marriage laws, **9**:128
Marshak, Jacob, **2**:*10n. 16*
Marshall, Alfred, **4**:193n. 21
Marshall, George, **6**:126n. 1
Marshall, John, **9**:417
Marshall, Samuel L. A., **10**:*425n. 1,
   426n. 4*
Marsot, Afaf Lutfi al-Sayyid,
   8:*102n. 60*

Mart, Phebe, **8**:*60n. 27*
Martin, J. David, **9**:*258n. 16;*
   10:*81n. 12*
Martin, John Bartlow, **8**:*102n. 58*
Martin, William H., **1**:*71n. 2*
Martinson, Robert, **10**:*74n. 2*
Martinus Nijhoff, **1**:45
Marx, Karl, **8**:*45n. 52*
Marxism
   compared with religion, **8**:244–56
   vision of government, **2**:12
   See also communism
Marxists, **6**:275; **7**:334
   in public choice, **4**:15, 17
   scientists, **3**:6n. 5, 11
mass media
   accuracy, **8**:245
   cable television industry, **5**:157–58
   coverage of socialist countries,
      5:124–25
   effect on transfers, **7**:209
   effect on voters, **4**:250, 252
   high class, **4**:251
   impact of ad revenues on, **5**:5
   political content, **4**:241
   political impact of non-news pro-
      grams, **4**:253–54
   politicians and, **4**:248
   rent-seeking role of, **5**:44–46
   use for supervision of subordinates,
      6:224–25
   working with, **1**:597, 600
   See also television broadcasting
      regulation
mass production, **4**:73
Master, John, **6**:*157n. 2*
matching grants
   charitable giving, **7**:13–14, 118
   foreign aid, **7**:120
   transfers to poor people, **7**:217
mate selection. *See* spouse selection
mathematical models of voting, **1**:16,
   19–21

mathematical problems of rent seeking, **5**:85–87, 95–100
mathematics
of political scientists, **4**:19
practical importance of research, **3**:13–14
truth of propositions in, **3**:39
Mattheissen, Peter, **8**:*237n. 22*
Matthias, B. T., **3**:*129n. 31*
Maurice, S. Charles, **10**:*246n. 6*
Maurizi, A., **9**:*421n. 19*
maximization
of beef production, **1**:545
in biology and economics, **1**:553
See also utility maximization
"maximizers," **1**:55
Maxwell, Donald, **9**:*256n. 11*; **10**:*83n. 19*
May, Kenneth O., **2**:*148–49n. 7*
intransitivity hypothesis, **1**:63, 64–65, 67
Mayberry, E. R., **1**:*113n. 19*
Mayer, Martin, **9**:*160n. 8, 168n. 16*
MC (marginal cost), **10**:14
McCabe, Sarah, **1**:*477n. 2*
McChesney, Fred S., **1**:*480–83*; **4**:*32n. 1, 39–40n. 12*; **9**:*303–6*
model of rent extraction, **5**:71–73
McConnell, Campbell R., **10**:*13–14n. 6*
McConville, Michael, **1**:*511n. 3, 528n. 4*; **9**:*347n. 20, 350n. 30, 444n. 8*
McCormick, Robert E., **5**:*33n. 38*; **8**:*57n. 19*; **9**:*411n. 1*
McCune, G. M., **10**:*344n. 3*
McDonald, Forrest, **3**:*157n. 30*
McDonald's organizational structure, **6**:254
McGee, John S., **9**:*241n. 1*
McGee, Reece J., **3**:*30nn. 31, 32*
McGovern, Eugene, **4**:431n. 7
McGovern, George, **7**:114
McGuire, Martin C., **8**:*154n. 20*

McIntosh, Susan, **10**:*41n. 2*
McIntyre, Donald M., Jr., **9**:*176n. 4*
McKean, Roland N., **4**:*239n. 18*, 270; **6**:378
McKelvey, R., **1**:106
McNeill, William H., **8**:*114n. 18*
McWatt, Jack, **3**:*115n. 14*
Mead, Lawrence M., **7**:*20nn. 2, 3*
Mead, Shepherd, *How to Succeed in Business Without Really Trying*, **6**:293, 303, 307
means tests
for benefit eligibility, **7**:155
groups who pay costs from, **7**:162
to protect poor people, **7**:167, 245–47
types of, **7**:247
meat inspection, **9**:115–16
mechanism-design studies, **6**:245
Meckling, William
"Theory of the Firm," **6**:*273n. 12*
view of corporations, **6**:274
media. *See* mass media
median "consensus," **4**:186–87
median consumer, **5**:273
median line, **1**:95
median preference theorem (Black), **4**:303–4
median voter theorem, **4**:182–86
relation with implicit logrolling, **4**:211–12
Medicaid, **7**:159, 256, 307, 314
medical experiments, **3**:137–39
medical insurance. *See* health insurance
medical systems. *See* universal health care
Medicare, **5**:33; **7**:159, 256, 307, 314
medieval governments, **8**:120–21
meetings of scientists, **3**:74–75. *See also* discussion among scientists
Meltzer, Allan H., **10**:*371n. 10*
Melville Godwin (Marquand), **6**:49, 114
Mencius, **7**:*85n. 8*
Mendel, Gregor, **3**:27–28, 42

Mendeleev, **3**:100
Mequire, P. G., **10**:379, 381–82, 383, 384, 385, 386n. 17, 395–96
mercantilism, **5**:122–23, 310
mergers of companies, **6**:416
merit systems in bureaucracies, **6**:19–21
Messick, Richard E., **7**:*255n. 7*
methodological individualism, **2**:xxii, 3, 11–15, 301–2
Metzger, Walter P., **9**:*395n. 27*
Mexicans in United States, **7**:44–45, 46–47
Mexico, **5**:307n. 11
  government, **8**:92–93, 137, 138–39
Mexico City, lobbying costs vs. gains, **5**:300
Meyer, Paul A., **8**:*9n. 4*
Michael, Robert T., **10**:*51nn. 15, 16,* 52n. 17
Michelman, Frank I., **1**:*418n. 7*
middle class
  gains from universalization of programs, **7**:251–53
  superiority in obtaining transfers, **7**:156
  transfers from poor to, **7**:159–60, 165–67
  transfers within, **1**:268–71; **5**:24, 145–46; **7**:7, 60, 125
Migué, Jean-Luc, **1**:*23n. 8*; **5**:*59n. 71*
military
  civilian commanders, **6**:280
  command of, by dictators, **8**:304–6
  curtailing power of, **8**:304–5
  decisions at Gettysburg, **6**:354
  economic model of tactics, **10**:405
  elections in, **4**:423
  in England, **8**:202, 218
  examples of control in, **6**:189–91
  free riding in, **10**:409n. 1, 418–19, 420, 421–22, 424
  funding, **5**:58
  growth of staff functions in, **6**:230

individual as basic unit of, **10**:405–7
  inspections, **6**:198–99
  motivation of individual combatants, **10**:409–13
  numerical superiority of forces, **10**:421–22
  pay scales, **4**:72
  performance evaluations, **6**:324–25
  prisoners' dilemma, **10**:407–9, 425–28
  procurement problems, **6**:172–75
  promotions within, **6**:49–50, 222–23
  as a public good, **10**:92
  purchasing of officers' commissions, **5**:108
  relationships among officers, **6**:284–85
  role in democracy, **8**:222–23
  role in revolution, **8**:213
  rotation of personnel within, **6**:381
  secrecy, **8**:349–53
  in small countries, **8**:359–60
  as special-interest group, **5**:178–79
  supervision within, **6**:321–23, 355
  taxing rich people to support, **5**:181–82
military coups, **8**:73–74, 273
  as executive branch coups, **8**:129
  in Roman republics, **8**:207–8
military courts, **9**:185
military draft, **8**:223
military expenditures, **1**:577, 581–82
military governments, **5**:128, 129; **8**:78
  legitimacy of rule by, **8**:251n. 42
  See also juntas
military pensions, **7**:33–34
Mill, John Stuart, **5**:218n. 13; **9**:10
Miller, D. T., **5**:*129n. 7*
Miller, James C., III, **4**:26–27, *60n. 9, 125n. 11*; **5**:*215n. 5*
Miller, John H., **8**:*109–10n. 6*
Miller, Norman N., **8**:*89n. 17*

Miller, Warren E., 7:*343n. 5*
Millsaps, S. W., 5:*19n. 12*
mind. *See* human mind, economy of
minorities
    compensating others not to perse-
        cute, 4:351, 353
    representation of, in democracies,
        4:381
minority influence in science vs. social
    sciences, 3:147, 154–55
minority of voters. *See* representative
    democracy; voters with strong
    preferences
minority rule, 2:243–47
Mises, Ludwig von, 2:*44n. 2, 294n. 3,*
    301n. 7; 5:114, 153;
    8:*132n. 80;* 10:*8n. 4*
    Human Action, 4:12
Mishan, Edward J., 4:110, *142n. 3,*
    148n. 5
Mitchell, William C. (Bill), 1:46;
    5:*52n. 60, 54n. 66*
Mitterand, François, 5:123
Modigliani, Franco, 1:*71n. 2*
Moes, John, 2:xxv; 4:13n. 2
Mohammedan law. *See* Islamic legal
    system
mole rats, 10:199–200, 236–40
    reproduction, 10:236
    social system in nests, 10:238–40
    tunnels, 10:237–38
    volcanoing, 10:237, 239
mole rat societies, 1:559
Mommsen, Theodor, 8:*104n. 66,*
    113nn. 12, 15, 127n. 71,
    137n. 97
monarchies, 1:227–28
    basic features, 6:274–75
    compared with democracies, 5:278
    compared with dictatorships, 5:122;
        8:154–55
    hereditary, 1:227–28; 8:105–6,
        141–42
    historical English, 5:163–64

legitimacy, 8:253–54
    order of succession, 8:155–56
    overthrow of, 6:59–64
    power struggles within, 6:122
    problems of, 5:276
    relationship to dictatorship, 8:33
    relation with feudalism, 6:277
    right of petition, 6:225–26
    royal councils, 6:94–95
    tendency toward, 8:142
    See also autocracy; constitutional
        monarchy; dictatorships
monarchs
    assassination of, 8:83
    attention to public opinion,
        8:151–52
    differences from dictators, 8:52–53
    maintaining power, 8:146–49
    precaution against assassination,
        8:104
    removing reigning, 8:142
    successors, 8:101–4, 105–6
    use of lese majesty, 8:159–60
    See also dictators
monetary policy
    in ancient China, 10:339–42
    fraudulent, 10:364
    Mongol dynasty in China, 10:335
    Sung dynasty in China, 10:329
money
    absence of political, 5:283
    as public good, 10:372
    as store of value, 10:360–61
    two roles of, 10:367
    See also Chinese coins; currencies
money supply
    government control over,
        10:365–66
    in Nationalist China, 1937–1947,
        10:309
    relation with inflation, 10:346–47
    in South Korea, 1945–1954,
        10:352
monogamy, 10:168–69

monographs about science, **3**:72–73
monopolies
"burden" of, **9**:246–47
costs and benefits, **9**:247
Harberger triangle omission of costs
of, **5**:19
inventions under, **5**:156–57
justifications used by, **5**:224
main effects, **5**:11
models of creation, **9**:247–48
occupational, **9**:124–25
from patents, **3**:18
patents as, **5**:3
prevention, **9**:250–51
relation with rent seeking, **5**:6
riskiness of investment in, **5**:153
on scientific discoveries, **5**:8
taxi company, **5**:67
use of government to break up,
9:241n. 1
welfare costs of, **1**:169, 174–79
See also government-created monopolies; monopoly costs; natural
monopolies; welfare losses to
monopoly; welfare triangle
monopoly costs, **1**:242; **5**:286
costs to create, **1**:237–39
organizational costs, **9**:241–42
traditional theory of rents and,
5:151–52
monopoly markets, **10**:21
monopoly-monopsony relations,
4:197–99; **6**:269
mergers and, **6**:416
monopoly of force. *See* coercion; police
monopoly prices, percentage above
competitive prices, **5**:14
monopoly profits, **9**:242
capitalized at moment of creation,
9:248–49
lack of, for current owners, **9**:249
Montague, Francis Charles, **8**:*45n. 54,
210n. 40*
Monte Carlo method, **4**:277, 280

Montesquieu, Baron de, **8**:135–36,
139–40
Montesquieu's theory of politics, **4**:122
Montross, Lynn, **8**:*125nn. 60, 61,
126nn. 62, 64, 65*
Moon, J. W., **1**:*140n. 11*
Moon, Reverend, **9**:351n. 31
Moore, Barrington, Jr., **8**:*105n. 69,
124n. 56*
Moore, John, **4**:*104n. 3, 307n. 7*
morality
changes in, **6**:332
as "higher goal" of government,
4:70–71
in organizations, **6**:25–29, 33–35
political effect of, **7**:190
relation with merit, **6**:20
science and, **7**:23
moral risk (insurance term), **7**:105,
106; **9**:109
morals
conflicts with efficiency, **9**:273
economic utility vs., **9**:381–82
efficiency considerations and,
9:265–66
inefficient institutions due to, **9**:265
law not based on, **9**:19
in politics, **2**:294
sex crime laws and, **9**:221
See also cost of conscience; ethics
Moran, M. J., **5**:*59n. 70*
more-rather-than-less-than hypothesis,
9:24
Morgan, J. P., **1**:242
Morgan, James M., **9**:*98n. 1, 100n. 5*
Morgenstern, Oskar, **1**:*111n. 14;
3:128n. 30; 4:323n. 5*
importance, **10**:445–46
mixed game strategy, **10**:443–44
theory of games, **2**:145, 157, 314
theory of games with side payments
allowed, **2**:178
Tullock's challenge of theory of
games, **10**:438

Moroccan government, **8**:302
Morris, Clarence, **8**:*225n. 1*
Morris, S., **5**:*245n. 6*
Morrison, Clarence, article on second
    best, **1**:47
mortgages, **9**:38
Morton, W. Scott, **8**:*64n. 4*
Mosher, Steven, **8**:*226n. 4, 243nn. 30,
    31, 243–44n. 32*
Mosher, William E., **4**:*196n. 22*
"Mosquito Abatement" (Tullock),
    6:*412n. 11*
mosquito abatement examples,
    1:378–86; **4**:49–67, 104,
    127
Moss, Richard L., **1**:*218n. 7*
Most, Robert, **8**:*194n. 5*
motivations of scientists
    effect on research results, **3**:110–11
    induced curiosity, **3**:24, 28–30
    monetary, **3**:169–70
    two basic, **3**:10, 32
motives
    of academic journal editors,
        5:20–21
    appellate court judges, **9**:417–18
    arbitrators, **9**:338
    for becoming informed voter,
        7:207–8
    boards of directors of corporations,
        4:174
    bureaucrats, **4**:194; **6**:296, 328
    charitable giving, **7**:7, 11
    of charity recipients, **7**:6
    civil servants, **4**:163
    for collective action, **10**:415–16
    college professors, **4**:39
    of dictators, **5**:127–29, 130; **8**:48–
        49, 56, 60–62
    doctors, **4**:40
    government programs with mixed,
        7:34, 38
    importance of knowing, **7**:39

income redistribution, **7**:25–26,
    27–29, 57–58, 64
individuals, **4**:70–71
of individuals in combat, **10**:407–9
insurance companies, **9**:378
judges, **9**:324–38
politicians, **4**:35, 123–24, 417–23;
    5:36, 240, 275; **6**:44–46,
    66–67, 328
preferences as, **4**:70
for present-day warfare, **8**:311
reference politicians, **6**:6
for revolution, **8**:164–65
of revolutionaries, **8**:182–85
special-interest groups, **7**:5
for theft, **9**:189
transfers, **7**:4, 24
transfers for reasons other than self-
    interest, **7**:64–68
transfers out of self-interest,
    7:59–64
universal-aid programs via transfers,
    7:168–70
universal public education,
    7:296–99
for violent crimes, **9**:218
voters, **5**:226
behind votes of congressmen,
    4:421–23
wealth equalization, **7**:53n. 12,
    55–57
well-informed voters, **4**:244
well-intentioned Machiavellianism,
    7:157
of workers, **4**:39
See also charitable motives; criminal
    intent; income insurance mo-
    tive; self-interest
motor vehicle offenses, **1**:441–49;
    9:137–46
MU (marginal utility), **10**:14
Mueller, Dennis C., **4**:*443n. 8*;
    5:*216n. 8*

bibliography of public choice literature, 4:220–21
Public Choice, second edition, 4:28
"voting by veto" system, 4:434
Muir, Ramsey, 8:*101n. 55, 108n. 3,
201n. 2, 202nn. 4, 7, 8, 10,
203nn. 12, 14, 15, 207n. 28,
250nn. 38, 41*
Muller, Edward N., 1:*341n. 5, 342n. 7,
344n. 10*
Muller, Herbert J., 8:*113n. 14, 116n. 24*
Mullineaux, Donald, 10:*383n. 10*
multiparty political systems, 4:389–90
advantages, 4:391–92
models for, 4:311, 386–87
three-party systems, 4:187, 189–91
See also coalition governments
multipeaked distributions, 1:102–3
multiple sovereigns, 6:109–14
definition, 6:56
diagram, 6:82
followers, 6:125–26
peers subject to, 6:119–21
readings about, 6:114
Mundell, Robert A., 1:*169n. 2;*
5:*17n. 11*
Munger, M. C., 5:*52n. 60, 54n. 66*
Munnell, Alicia, 7:*276n. 19*
murder, 9:215
example, 1:495–97
Pareto-optimal, 1:324
murderers, 10:70, 71, 72
Murphy, K. M., 5:*74–75n. 95*
Murray, Hugh, 10:*324n. 5*
Musgrave, Peggy B., 1:*195nn. 6, 7*
Musgrave, Richard A., 1:*195nn. 6, 7,
388n. 1;* 2:105, 189, 194;
4:*9n. 6, 68n. 1;* 8:*9n. 4*
Mustafa, Ahmed Abdel-Rahim,
8:*102n. 60*
mutations
effect on nonreproductive cells,
1:570–71

effect on reproduction of societies,
1:564–69
mutual disarmament. *See* disarmament
mutual gains, through bargaining,
4:90. *See also* contracts
Mwangi, K., 5:*128n. 6*

Nader, Ralph, 1:*444n. 4;* 4:158;
9:*140n. 4*
Namier, Lewis Bernstein, 4:*439n. 3;*
8:*41n. 38, 57n. 20, 136n. 92,
206nn. 24, 26, 207n. 27*
Namier, Phillip, 5:*161n. 1*
Nanson, Edward John, 2:315
Napoleon, 6:291n. 14, 369
Napoleonic legal system
Anglo-Saxon common law vs.,
9:451–55
pre-Napoleonic system, 9:356
relation of police with courts, 9:341
rules of evidence, 9:356–63
superiority to adversary system of
law, 9:339, 363
use of juries, 9:344
Nash equilibrium, 1:230
national defense, reciprocal externalities, 4:104, 105
national deficits, 1:29–30
National Fund for the Humanities,
1:578
national health service, for United
States, 4:40
nationalism, 8:159
income redistribution and, 7:48
Nationalist China
impact of inflation on currency,
10:316–17
monetary policy, 10:313–14
money supply and wholesale prices,
1937–1947, 10:309
nationalization of airlines by dictators,
8:57
nations. *See* countries

naturalistic fallacy, **10**:116
natural law, **9**:9–10, 227
natural laws. *See* laws of science
natural monopolies
of the majority, **1**:70–71
relation with externalities, **4**:111–13
techniques for dealing with,
1:69–70
natural rights, **2**:299
natural selection, **1**:543, 550–52,
569–70. *See also* evolutionary
theory
nature, improvability of, **1**:541–46
"Nature of the Firm, The" (Coase),
6:244, 252, 258
updates by Coase, **6**:*258n. 10*
naval conference agreement of 1922,
8:335–36
navigation and cartography, **3**:150–51
need, defining, **7**:225–26
Needler, Martin C., **8**:*92nn. 25, 28*
negative externalities, **4**:102
from property rights, **4**:77–78
negative incentives, **10**:417–19.
See also punishment
negative income taxes, **7**:114–16;
10:135
experiments, **7**:51, 107, 358
negative poll taxes, **10**:277–80
negligence–contributory negligence
rule, **9**:271–72, 364
costs involved in, **9**:384–86
efficiency of, vs. costs of accident
prevention, **9**:366–74
See also accidents
negotiation. *See* bargaining
neighborhood effects, **4**:67; **7**:65–
66, 82
neighborhood governments
collectives, **4**:140–41
Harlem, **4**:143–44
See also private local governments
Nelson, Douglas R., **1**:*290n. 23*

Nelson, Harold D., **8**:*65n. 10*
Nelson, Richard R., **3**:*18n. 14, 23n. 21*
neoclassical economics, view of social
cost of monopoly, **5**:14
nepotism, **1**:559, 565, 572–73;
10:188–96, 245. *See also*
altruism
neutrality during a coup, **8**:263–67
Nevsky, Alexander, **8**:119
Newell, J., **3**:*94n. 7*
Newhall, Richard A., **8**:*201n. 3,
218n. 53*
new ideas, **3**:148
application of, in social sciences,
3:154–55
degree of significance, **3**:27n. 16, 31
See also discoveries
Newing, R. A., **1**:*90–91, 95n. 12*
*Committee Decisions with Complemen-
tary Valuation*, **4**:*284n. 3*, 285
Newlon, Daniel, **7**:113–14
Newman, Donald J., **9**:*165n. 11*
newspaper articles, **1**:593
use for supervision of subordinates,
6:224–25
newspapers
lying by, **4**:266; **5**:46
political content, **4**:241
Newtonian vs. Einsteinian systems,
3:36, 37–38, 42
Ng, Yew-Kwang, **1**:425
90-per-cent-selfish hypothesis, **1**:14
Niskanen, William A., **1**:*21n. 7*,
268n. 14; **5**:*54n. 68*; **6**:244,
279; **7**:*312n. 25*; **8**:*169n. 4*
assistance to Tullock, **1**:179n. 15
*Bureaucracy and Representative Gov
ernment*, **4**:156–57, 201, 202,
220
career in government, **4**:201
"Peculiar Economics of Bureaucracy,
The," **4**:*133n. 17*
process efficiency, **5**:116n. 9

Tullock's review of book by, 1:*297n. 1*
view of bureaucracy, 5:55–58
Nixon, Richard, vs. Kennedy election, 4:217n. 35
Nobel Prize, 3:9
no-fault insurance, 9:100–101, 374, 388, 389
nondemocratic systems, 1:27; 4:37
  rent seeking and, 5:122–35
  See also despotism; dictatorships; monarchies
nonhuman societies
  absence of markets in, 10:200–202, 262
  differences from human societies, 10:197–200
  free riding in, 10:204–5
  hereditary behavior, 10:181–96
  wars, 10:239
  See also animal societies; plant societies
nonhuman species, preferences, 10:250–54
nonprofit organizations
  charitable giving to, 1:394–411; 7:90
  fund-raising, 1:396
  incentives to employees, 6:409
  structure, 6:346–48
nonscientific journals, importance to scientists, 3:66
"non-Tuism," 2:16–17
nonviolence, 8:26. *See also* pacifism
normative individualism, 2:xxii
norms. *See* legal rules
Norsworthy, J. Randolph, 1:*174n. 10, 454n. 13*; 9:*146n. 12*
North, Douglass C., 5:*54n. 67, 191n. 15*; 8:*36nn. 15, 17, 37n. 18*
Northern Ireland, 7:229–31
North Korean government, 8:98, 213

Norton, C. B., 9:*196n. 10*
Novak, Robert D., 8:*85n. 7*
nuclear energy
  debate over, 3:108
  history of atom bomb, 3:162
nuclear test bans, 8:344–45
nuclear war, 8:312, 331
nuclear weapons, 8:359, 361–67
Nutter, G. Warren, 1:*367n. 8*
Nutting, Anthony, 8:*89n. 16*
Nyerere, Julius, 8:65, 66–67
Nyrop, R. F., 8:*67n. 17, 69–70n. 24, 83n. 2*

occupational monopolies, 9:125
O'Conner, Edwin, 6:*45n. 3*
O'Dea, Thomas F., 8:*95n. 31*
OECD countries
  in cross-national sample, 10:397
  economic growth, 10:385–89, 395–96
Oechsli, W., 8:*130n. 78*
offenders
  incarcerated, 9:152–55
  innocent, 9:191–92
  juvenile, 9:128
  payment of wrongly incarcerated, 9:174–75
  punishment of civil vs. criminal, 9:186–88
  See also criminals; punishment
office politics. *See* reference politicians
oil price controls, 7:35–36, 330–31. *See also* gasoline price controls; OPEC
oil shortages in United States, 5:141n. 9
Okun, Arthur M., 7:50n. 8; 9:322n. 12
old age, 1:319
old-age pensions. *See* pensions
older poor people, 7:276; 10:301–3
oligarchy, 6:104–5; 8:112

oligopoly problem in political contests, **6**:103
Oliver, Henry, **2**:8, *19n. 5*
Olmstead, A. L., **5**:*141n. 8*
Olsen, E. A., **10**:*275n. 1*
Olsen subsidy, **10**:275–76
Olson, Mancur, **1**:*336n. 5*; **4**:*260n. 2*;
  8:*154n. 20, 181n. 6*
  criticisms of his theory about interest
    groups, **5**:54
  free rider proposition, **5**:48–49, 50,
    51–52
  insights related to rent seeking, **5**:52
  Logic of Collective Action, The, **4**:220;
    5:233; **7**:212, 213
  politics, **4**:18
Oman, C. W. C., **8**:*112n. 11,
  118nn. 32, 35, 133n. 84, 137–
  38n. 97*
Onate, Andres D., **8**:*303n. 17*
One Day in the Life of Ivan Denisovich
  (Solzhenitsyn), **6**:*400*
O'Neill, Richard, **8**:*228n. 6*
one-party governments. *See* single-
  party political systems
"On the Rationale of Group Decision-
  making" (Black), **4**:275
OPEC, **5**:138, 141, 142
  gains from U.S. price controls,
    7:172
  oil price controls after formation of,
    7:35–36
  See also cartels
OPEC countries, **10**:393–95
Opp, Karl-Dieter, **1**:*341n. 5, 344n. 10*
opportunistic behavior, **6**:260
opposition groups in government,
  1:76–77
optimal amount of public good,
  1:142
optimality, **2**:165
  in size of government, **2**:108
optimal outcome, **1**:468

optimal resource allocation and majority voting, **1**:61
optimal speed limits, **1**:444–47
"optimum" law, **9**:151
oral testimony, **9**:44, 74–75. *See also*
  written testimony
orders
  alternatives to giving, **6**:329–32
  bureaucrats' dilemmas when follow-
    ing, **6**:295–96
  carrying out superiors', **6**:300–302
  compartmentalization of, **6**:370–74
  elaboration of, by subordinates,
    6:354
  enforcing, **6**:197
  imposing uniformity on, **6**:195–96
  loss of control over, **6**:263
  military examples of issues over,
    6:322n. 8, 335, 354–55
  standing, **6**:322–23
  uniformity and simplicity, **6**:326
Ordeshook, Peter C., **4**:*181–82n. 12*,
  220, *234n. 12*, 347
Ordover, Janusz A., **1**:480–83; **4**:*39–
  40n. 12*; **9**:*303n. 8*
organ donation, **7**:97–99
organic society theory, **2**:11–12, 30–
  31; **10**:264
organizational cultures, **6**:42–44
  conformity, **6**:287–89
  general atmosphere, **6**:42
  large corporations, **6**:215–16
  reputation in, **6**:53, 289
organizational politicians. *See* reference
  politicians
organizational structures
  alternatives among, **6**:264–68
  experiment, **3**:140–41
  franchising, **6**:414
  hierarchical, **6**:39–42
  highly authoritarian, **6**:336–37
  internal, **6**:334–37
  military, **6**:230

See also crisscross system of supervision; functional organization of hierarchies; geographic organization of hierarchies

organizational theory, importance of human imperfection to, **6**:32

Organization of Inquiry, The (Tullock), **1**:37, *41n. 2*; **5**:20

organization of scientific community. *See* social organization of science

organizations

without central control, **6**:337

chief executive officers, **6**:155–57

communication in, **6**:191–96

control within, **6**:189–96

coordination in, **6**:162–67

diversity of human, **6**:252, 340–42

inefficient, **6**:141

information flow in, **6**:379–80

internal diversity, **6**:254

limits to size, **6**:162

military, **6**:319

need for some disorganization in, **6**:385–86

nongovernment and nonprivate, **10**:86

nonprofit, **6**:346–48, 409

perfection, **6**:127

plans by, **6**:388–91

radical change in, **6**:415

reorganizations, **6**:246–47

residual claimants, **6**:343

simple vs. complex, **6**:190

size, **6**:153–55

size and efficiency, **6**:203

staff, **6**:157–59

Tullock's model, **6**:5–6, 160–62

as way to exert influence over people, **6**:171–72

See also hierarchical organizations; organizational structures

organized crime, **8**:22; **9**:155

Oriental Despotism (Wittfogel), **6**:16n. 1, 250, 276

Orwell, George, **8**:*244n. 33*

Orzechowski, William Paul, **1**:*23nn. 9, 10, 304n. 7*

Ostrom, Vincent, **4**:*117n. 3*, 409; **5**:*76n. 96*

Oursler, J. Fulton, **9**:*84n. 6*

out-of-court settlements, **9**:70–72, 288, 389

Overcast, H. Edwin, **8**:*340n. 4*; **10**:*429n. 1*

overgrazing problem, **1**:428–29; **5**:249

example, **1**:542–46

Owen, David, **9**:272

pacifism, **8**:16–17; **9**:229–34. *See also* nonviolence

PACs (Political Action Committees), **5**:41–42

pain and suffering (legal damages), **9**:448

See also compensatory damages

pain from inflicted injury, **9**:31–32

Palvia, Chand Mal, **7**:*257nn. 12, 13*

paper money

in ancient China, **10**:321–25

Chinese government abandonment of, **10**:339–42

competition among forms of, **10**:359

See also Chinese coins

Papers on Non-Market Decision Making, **1**:36, 37; **5**:*20n. 17*

funding, **1**:38, 39

pricing, **1**:38

printed comments about papers in, **1**:41–42

production, **1**:38

refereeing, **1**:39–41

Tullock's creation of, **4**:14–15

See also *Public Choice*

"Paradox of Revolution, The"
(Tullock), **1**:341, 344
paradox of the liar, **1**:229
rent seeking and, **5**:89
paradox of voting, **1**:91, 124–29;
7:290
as applied to dictatorships,
5:131–32
See also cyclical majority
parasites, **1**:562, 571, 572
parasitic species, **10**:194–96, 204–5
Paretian welfare economics, **2**:8
Pareto, Vilfredo, **1**:*541n. 2*; **2**:8, 87;
4:18
optimality and, **2**:165–81
on voting, **7**:208–9
Pareto criteria, **1**:546n. 5, 548; **2**:87
applied to changes, **2**:166–67, 271
unanimity and, **2**:87–88n. 3
Pareto improvement, **1**:149
Pareto optimality
criterion of unanimity and, **2**:193
example where it does not work, **7**:40
externalities and, **2**:182–91
in government, **4**:344
income redistribution and,
2:182–91
indicating undesirable changes with,
9:11–12
justifying, **9**:12–13
in the large, **4**:246
majority rule and, **2**:165–79
side payments and, **2**:179–81
test for, **2**:89
three voter logrolling model, **4**:325,
334
Tullock's better idea, **1**:163
using, to evaluate biological systems,
1:541
See also quasi-Paretian rule
Pareto-relevant externalities,
1:551n. 8; **4**:109
collectivization and, **1**:349

Pareto rule applied constitutionally,
2:89–90
parking meters, **1**:443
parking regulations, **9**:138–40. *See
also* traffic courts
Parkinson's Law, **6**:145–47
parliamentary coups, **8**:276
parliamentary governments
advantages of multiple parties,
1:75–77
executive leaders, **4**:407; **8**:130
houses, **4**:414, 415
relationships among members, **6**:92
type of party organization under,
6:107
See also British Parliament
parliaments, advisory, **6**:225
parole, **9**:43n. 3, 171. *See also* probation violations
Parry, Stanley, **2**:*302n. 8*
particular curiosity, **3**:25–27
particular investigation
to establish a hypothesis, **3**:76–85
types, **3**:75–76
parties. *See* political parties
Pascal, Blaise, **10**:442, 443
passions, **1**:8. *See also* preferences
patents, **9**:251
patent system, **3**:18–20
discoveries that fall outside of, **3**:21,
168
in England, **5**:165
as a nonspecified reward for research,
3:168
relation with rent seeking, **5**:3–10
for social inventions, **3**:149–50
use by amateurs, **3**:181
See also inventions
paternalism
in charitable giving, **7**:95–96
of Social Security system, **7**:63–64
pattern recognition, **3**:95–96
induction as, **3**:96–101

methods used in, **3**:105–6
relation to hypothesis development,
    3:99–100
role in science, **3**:99–100
weak patterns, **3**:102
Pauly, Mark V., **7**:*117n. 1*; **9**:*102n. 6*
Pautler, Paul, **4**:*172n. 3*
Paxton, John, **8**:*78n. 38, 137n. 96*
Peach, Charles, **3**:178
Peacock, A. T., **5**:*60n. 73*; **9**:*447n. 17*
peers, **6**:115–21
  lying about, **6**:292–93
  reference politicians' relationships
    with, **6**:299
  subject to multiple sovereigns,
    6:119–21
  subject to single sovereign,
    6:115–18
Peltzman, Sam, **1**:*213n. 3*; **5**:*42n. 45,
    63n. 78, 69n. 89, 226n. 25*;
    6:*420n. 3*
  on subsidies, **5**:226, 227–28
  on transfers, **5**:34, 35
penalties
  to deter crime, **1**:496–97
  for income tax evasion, **1**:452
  not based on intent, **1**:448
  traffic court, **1**:447–49
  See also fines; sanctions
penalty taxes
  on consumers, **1**:419–24
  on industries, **1**:412–18
Penkovsky, Oley, **8**:*254n. 51*
*Penn Central Transportation Co. v. City
  of New York*, **9**:445
Pennington, Nancy, **1**:*507n. 17, 512,
    529n. 5*; **9**:*342nn. 8–11,
    345n. 18, 439n. 17*
Pennock, J. Roland, **2**:331
Pennock, James, **1**:*81*
Penrod, Steven D., **1**:*507n. 17, 512,
    529n. 5*; **9**:*342nn. 8–11,
    345n. 18, 439n. 17*

Penrose, Lionel Sharpes, **3**:*183n. 24*
pensions, **1**:582
  children as, **10**:40
  military, **7**:33–34
  taxation of, **10**:296–97
  "vested," **7**:126–27
  See also Social Security system
people
  motives, **4**:70–71
  recognizing, **3**:96–98
People's Republic of China, **9**:439
perception. *See* pattern recognition
Perez-Castrillo, J. David, **5**:95–100
perfect information models, **4**:231
performance evaluation, **6**:205–9
  of corporate lawyers, **6**:365
  in government agencies, **6**:324–25,
    362–64
  of government officials, **6**:364
  of judges, **6**:397
  random selection of things for,
    6:357–65
  using external checks, **6**:224–31
  using pseudo-accounting systems,
    6:217
  using simple objectives, **6**:325–26
  See also career advancement; promo-
    tions within organizations
performance measures
  Chinese government, **6**:325–26
  difficulties with, **6**:325, 335, 390
  limitations, **6**:219–20
  profitability as, **6**:210–11
  for reference politicians, **6**:300–301
  uniformity in, **6**:355–57, 359–60
  used by U.S. Department of State,
    6:361
Persian Empire, **6**:275
personal connections, **6**:42–43
personal expenditures by dictators,
    8:49–52
personal injury
  cases, **9**:98–100

personal injury (*continued*)
    compensation as measure of, **9**:13
    pleasure vs. pain concerning,
        9:31–32
    See also accidental injury
personal status, **9**:124–34
    of deceased persons, **9**:130–34
    protection of reputation, **9**:213
personnel. *See* employees
perspective, beginners', **3**:103–4
persuasion of subordinates, **6**:138–39
Peru, shining path, **1**:342–43
Peter Principle, The (Peter and Hull),
    6:303
Peterson, William, **6**:*219n. 1*
petition, right of, **6**:225–26
Pfaff, Martin, **7**:*256n. 9*
Pfeiffer, John E., **3**:*56n. 2*
pharmaceutical companies, **6**:419–20
    regulation, **4**:157–58
    research example, **10**:399
Philbrook, Clarence E., **4**:*257n. 14*
Phillips, Llad, **9**:255–56; **10**:*82n. 16,
    83n. 19*
philosophers
    approach to ethics, **8**:230–31
    effect on religion, **8**:229–30
philosophies of science, **3**:34–38
philosophy of law, **9**:9
Phoenician government, **8**:117–18
physics, pattern recognition in, **3**:99
pigeons, **10**:108–9
    falcons and, **1**:429
Pigou, Arthur Cecil, **1**:*253n. 5*;
    2:192–93n. 1; **4**:37, 68,
    68n. 2, 178n. 9; **9**:380;
    10:88–91
Pigovian method of subsidy, **4**:120–21
Pildes, Richard H., **4**:*442n. 5*
Pipes, Richard, **8**:*145n. 8*
Pirenne, Henri, **8**:*129n. 73*
plaintiff legal resources, **9**:310–13
planned economies. *See* centrally
    planned economies

planned science, **3**:6
    impact of patents on, **3**:19
    reason to avoid, **3**:105–6
    See also directed research; individual-
        ism of scientists
plants
    externalities, **1**:549, 550
    natural selection problem, **1**:550–52
plant societies, **1**:561–62; **10**:192
    cloning within, **10**:187
    territories, **10**:119
    See also lichens
Plato, **2**:297; **4**:33
plea bargaining, **9**:164–67
    in an inefficient legal system, **9**:434
    See also guilty pleas in court
pleasure from inflicting injury,
    9:31–32
Plotnick, Robert, **7**:*27n. 6, 241n. 19*
Plott, Charles R., **1**:*113n. 20*; **10**:100,
    101–2
Plumb, J. H., **8**:*206n. 25*
Podlesny, John A., **9**:*361n. 50*
point of minimum disappointment,
    4:184
Polanyi, Michael, **3**:xix, *6n. 4, 13n. 7,
    38n. 11, 122n. 21*; **6**:135
police, **6**:251
    bribery of, **9**:221
    compensation for searches by,
        9:175–76
    efficiency, **9**:174
    powers, under inquisitorial system of
        law, **9**:452
police force
    accuracy, **1**:510–11
    cost, **1**:177
    curtailing power of, **1**:320–21
    decision to use, **8**:20–21, 27–30
    effectiveness in crime prevention,
        9:269
    international force, **8**:343, 348
    intimidation of, by revolutionaries,
        8:197–98

use of violence or threats by,
8:18–21
using, to suppress revolutions,
8:188–96
See also coercion; illegal activities;
informers; law enforcement;
secret police
police services
charitable motives for, 7:139–41
costs, 9:191
optimum purchase of, 4:196–99
private, 4:204
privatization of, 9:269
protection from crime, 10:65–68
as proxy for rent seeking, 5:74
reciprocal externalities, 4:104–5
voting on, 4:182–86, 187–89
policy
of dictators, 8:53–61
economists' influence, 6:305n. 16
formation, by low-ranking personnel,
6:192
organizational constraints on, 6:13
politicians' costs from changing,
8:199–200
reasoning about, 6:206
Tullock's recommendation for U.S.
government, 6:235–38
See also United States government:
foreign policy
policy making using cost-benefit analysis board, 9:13–14
Polinsky, A. Mitchell, 9:*372n. 11*,
375n. 15
Political Action Committees (PACs),
5:41–42
political activism by economists,
1:597–98
political advertising, 4:248. *See also*
political persuasion
political advocacy, 4:251
through media, 5:45
political appointees, 1:23, 25
political asylum, 8:67

political candidates
alliances with other candidates,
6:104–5
allies, 6:104
campaign tactics, 5:40
decision whether to run, 6:100–103
"party differential," 4:234
platforms, 4:60, 129; 6:96–97
presidential campaigns, 6:118
spectators of presidential, 6:52–53
in systems with proportional representation, 4:385–86
in U.S. presidential races, 4:338–
39, 392–93; 5:276
write-in, 4:293
See also campaign contributions;
elections
political change, 4:257–58
political conservatives, 4:19
political correctness, 8:157–58
political corruption, 1:240–41
political costs of transfer mechanism,
1:194–98
political economy, 1:8
modern use of title, 1:37
Political Economy of Rent-Seeking, The
(Rowley, Tollison, and Tullock),
5:28
political equilibrium vs. social optimum, 1:376
political exploitation, 8:168–71
political freedom, 8:157–59
political information
lying to consumers of, 4:269
probability of accurate, 5:43
reasons for acquiring, 4:226; 5:39
sports information vs., 4:227
political negotiation, 5:281–83
political obligation, 2:294–95
political parties
advantages, 4:249
Britain, 4:341
coalitions, 1:77; 4:387
compared with sports teams, 5:39

political parties (*continued*)
  conflicts with U.S. president, **5**:62
  democracies without, **6**:101
  democratic, **8**:171
  difference from department stores,
    1:69
  Down's work on, **2**:9
  impact of persuasion on, **4**:252–53
  incumbent party advantage,
    1:74–75
  left-wing, **6**:106
  logrolling by, **1**:117–18
  "machines," **6**:104–5
  omission of, in *The Calculus of
    Consent*, **2**:xxii
  party differential between candi-
    dates, **4**:234
  platforms, **4**:60, 129, 338–39
  presidential nominating conventions,
    8:149–50, 297
  proportional representation by,
    4:383–84
  rebel groups within, **4**:308–10
  religious, **4**:342
  right-wing, **6**:106, 401
  as successful coalitions, **1**:165–66
  in systems with proportional repre-
    sentation, **4**:385–86
  transition to and from nonparty sys-
    tems, **6**:105
  types of alliances within, **6**:106–8
  in United States, **4**:335n. 1, 343,
    386, 387
  U.S. vs. British, **4**:340–41
  U.S. vs. European, **4**:420–21
  See also multiparty political systems;
    single-party political systems;
    two-party political systems
political persuasion, **4**:249–53
  direct or indirect, **4**:254–55
  equation, **4**:250, 252
  equation variables, **4**:234, 239
  maximizing, **4**:257
  by media, **5**:44–46
  relation to information, **4**:254
  short vs. long term, **4**:256
  See also political advocacy
political reform, to protect property
    rights, **5**:77–82
political relationships compared with
    economic relationships, **6**:6–9,
    250–51
political science, **2**:295–96
  differences with economics, **1**:10–11
  link with economics, **1**:5–6, 7–8
  methodology, **6**:40
  relation to public choice theory,
    1:16–17; **4**:16–20
political scientists
  difference from economists, **4**:124
  politics of, **4**:18–19
political strategy, **6**:97–100
political systems, ethical systems
    within, **6**:44–46
politicians
  bribery of, **5**:214
  characteristics of successful, **6**:21–23
  constituency work, **5**:40–41
  costs to, from changing policies,
    8:199–200
  in democracies, **4**:395–96
  "honest deception" by, **4**:260
  interaction with bureaucrats and
    special-interest groups, **5**:58
  job of, **4**:191
  knowledge of issues, **1**:18–19
  legal blackmail by, **5**:72–73
  lifestyle, compared with influence
    peddling by, **5**:215
  limits to power of, **5**:132–34
  local, **1**:75–76
  logrolling by, **1**:585–86; **7**:336–37
  lying by, **4**:267–68; **7**:168–69;
    9:212–13
  misinformed, **5**:309
  motives, **4**:35, 123–24, 417–23;

5:36, 240; 6:44–46, 66–67,
328
need for complex programs,
4:228–29
nonelected government officials vs.,
4:407
nonunitary motives of, 5:275
personal preferences vs. instrumental
actions by, 6:31
positions on issues, 4:186–87
public interest as motive of, 4:17,
191–92
reason for much talk and little
action, 7:361
relation with voters, 6:133–34
rent protection and, 5:71–73
reputations, 5:275
role in creating special interests,
4:239
role in rent seeking, 5:32–38
role in transfers, 9:411
self-interest, 4:174–75
study of behavior of, 6:90
types of dishonesty, 6:27
use of media, 5:45
use of poor people, 7:174–75
utility maximizing by, 6:29
view of transfers, 1:274
vote maximizing, 4:396
votes for detested, 5:299
vote trading, 4:396–99
who are good at logrolling,
4:336–37
See also elected officials; political candidates; reference politicians
politics
bartering in, 5:283–84
class interest in, 2:25–26
as class struggle, 2:25–26
compared with economics,
4:32–34; 6:14
cooperation in, 2:254
current U.S. legal system and, 9:401
developing predictive science of, 6:9
as economic exchange, 2:16–29
economic relationships in, 6:110,
114
economists' model of, 4:170
entry barriers, 1:69–77
externalities in, 2:41–44
fair labeling laws for, 4:129–30
gains-from-trade in, 8:3
of horizontal transfers, 7:187
importance of public interest, 1:577
influence on judges, 9:415
in the market, 6:16, 113–14
as moral matter, 4:17
as positive sum, 2:23
as power struggle, 2:22–23
public choice view of, 8:46–47
range of meanings, 6:13
relation with law, 5:81–82
as truth judgment, 2:4
Tullock's definition, 6:14
unmixed with economic considerations, 6:15–16
as zero-sum game, 2:23, 241–42
Politics of Bureaucracy, The (Tullock),
4:220; 6:243, 245, 263
Pollard, A. F., 8:*203n. 16*
poll taxes, 10:285–88
negative, 10:277–80
to raise government revenue,
10:284
pollution abatement
(chimney smoke) examples, 4:97–
101, 106–7, 159–61
economic experiments, 10:101–2
optimum amount of, 10:88–89
prisoners' dilemma, 10:203
pollution control, 1:412–14, 425–26,
549
Polo, Marco, 8:*99n. 45*
Polya, G., 3:*91n. 5*
Polybius, 6:*244*
polygraph tests. *See* lie detectors

Pommerehne, Werner W., 1:*24n. 11*;
6:*347n. 13*; 7:*257n. 11*
poor people, 10:301–3
amounts of charity and transfers to,
7:16–17, 23–24, 27
benefits received from universal-aid
programs, 7:250
data about, 7:120, 240–43
decisions about which to help,
7:345
externalities in charity to, 7:118
government aid to, 4:71–72
government employees among, 4:72
health insurance for, 7:364
impact of demand-revealing process
on, 7:48
impact of logrolling on, 7:233–38
impact of Social Security system on,
7:282–84
impact of universal health care on,
7:168, 306–8
impact of universalization of aid programs on, 7:253–55
income redistribution to, 7:29–33
income subsidies to working,
7.112 16, 357
income transfers to, 7:4
inefficiency of, in purchasing,
4:242n. 2
in-kind aid to, 7:133–41
insurance industry view of aid to,
7:105–6
older, 7:276
political power of, 7:255
political use of, 7:175
problems, 7:17–18, 156, 171–78,
244, 254
religious aid to, 7:57–58
research about, 7:120, 240, 243, 368
right to make own decisions, 7:347
Social Security system and, 7:275
transfers from, 7:159–60, 165–67
transfers to, 7:6–10, 64, 128–32

transfers to American vs. foreign,
7:359–60
transfers to nonvoting, 7:12–15,
83, 240
transfers to older, 7:125–26
transfers to voting, 7:15–18, 217–
20, 227–29, 232–33
value of health care to, 7:248
See also homeless people; means
tests; relative poverty
poor people in democracies
coalitions with other classes,
1:265–66
government transfers to, 1:262–64,
267, 285–86
transfers by rich people to, 5:24
transfers to rich people from,
5:225
poor people in other countries,
1:278–81
transfers to, 1:280–81, 282–83,
284
Popper, Karl R., 1:606; 2:*44n. 2*;
3:*33n. 2*, 40, *53n. 28*, *137*;
8:*132n. 80*
popular uprisings, 8:147
absence of, in history, 8:213–17
against despotism, 8:289–91
as mythology of revolution, 8:201
prevention of, 8:219–21
as split between ruler and legislature,
8:207–13
population explosion
fertility rates and, 10:52–53
in lesser developed countries, 10:50
population growth
economic growth in Africa, Americas, and Asia and, 10:391
economic growth in OECD countries and, 10:386
effect on economic growth of United
States, 10:390
size of country and, 10:395

pork-barreling, **1**:194; **2**:21; **4**:419;
   5:285–89
  getting rid of, **5**:177
  relation to transfers, **7**:203–4
  tax loopholes vs., **5**:175, 178
Porter, J. R., **3**:*120n. 19*
positive correlation fallacy, **1**:12–14
positive externalities, **1**:550–52
  from property rights, **4**:77–78
Posner, Richard A., **1**:*456n. 1*;
  5:*61n. 74, 62n. 76, 64n. 81,*
  74n. 94, 246n. 7; **9**:*307n. 17,*
  365n. 6, 399n. 1, 416n. 5,
  417nn. 7–10, 421n. 22, 434n. 9
  on arbitration, **9**:306, 308
  on bargaining, **9**:396
  economic view of legal process,
    9:449–51
  on efficiency of common law,
    9:270–72
  exact dissipation hypothesis, **5**:63
  on regulatory agencies, **5**:34
  theory about judges, **9**:418–19
  on transactions costs and govern-
    ment action, **9**:382–84
  on wealth maximization as objective
    of law, **9**:381–82, 395
  on wealth maximization in common
    law, **9**:431–32
  welfare criteria, **9**:380
possible deduction, **3**:90–91
possible hypotheses, **3**:94–96
Post Office bureaucracy, **4**:133
Potholm, Christian P., **8**:*63–64n. 2*
poverty. *See* poor people
power
  autocratic, **8**:49–50, 144–45
  within dictatorships, **5**:131–32
  division of, **2**:xxii
  holding on to autocratic, **8**:146–49
  of judges vs. juries, **5**:169–70
  maximization, in a bureaucracy,
    6:143

political, **8**:3
  real and apparent, **6**:142–44, 299
  transfers of autocratic, **8**:149–57
  See also balance of power among
    countries
Power and the Prize, The (Swigget),
  6:70
*Practical Guide for the Ambitious Politi-
  cian, A,* **4**:262; **6**:292, 293,
  304
Prall, Stuart E., **8**:*205n. 21*
Pratt, Robert W., Jr., **9**:*98n. 1, 100n. 5*
prayer in schools, **4**:255n. 11
precedent. *See* legal precedent
precommitment games, **1**:231–32
predictions by scientists, **3**:60
preference ordering, **1**:138–39,
  381–82
preferences
  altering after the fact, **6**:391–92,
    398–99
  assumptions about individual,
    9:18–19
  behavioralist research about,
    1:12, 13
  changed or imposed, **6**:332
  around charitable giving and trans-
    fers, **7**:8–10, 14
  before and after choice made, **8**:248
  about choices, **9**:20–23
  of computers, **10**:252–53
  costs of aggregating, **1**:152–53
  definition of terms involved in, **9**:18
  difficulty of ascertaining, **1**:10
  economists' approach to, **1**:9–10
  government maximization of indi-
    vidual, **4**:124
  within groups, **1**:13
  information and, **4**:89, 91–92
  inheritance of wealth and, **1**:258–60
  intensity, **2**:121–22, 126
  interdependence of, **1**:101–2,
    161–63

preferences (*continued*)
of married partners, **10**:38
maximization of, by reference politicians, **6**:401–4
method of aggregating, **7**:78
for more over less of something,
10:9
mosquito abatement example, **4**:57
motivating voters to state, **1**:135–36
as motives, **4**:70
of nonhuman species, **10**:250–54
nonindependent, **4**:434
pleasure vs. pain, **9**:31–32
policy making and, **9**:14
property rights and, **4**:78–80
relation with prices, **4**:73
revelation of, **2**:104–7
roots in human passions, **1**:8
science of, **1**:10
single-peaked, definition, **6**:96
sociologists' approach to, **1**:9–10
Tullock's assumptions about,
4:72–73
voting for one's own, **1**:124–27
See also aggregate preferences;
choices, independent prefer
ences; passions; single-peaked
preferences; tastes; transitivity;
utility maximization; voters
with strong preferences
preference weighting. *See* logrolling
premises of scientific theories, **3**:91
preponderance of evidence criteria,
9:201–2, 287–90, 410. *See also*
beyond-reasonable-doubt
criteria
prescription drugs
companies, **6**:419–20
regulation, **4**:157–58
research, **10**:399
present discounted value of income
stream maximization, **9**:24
presidential elections in United States,

4:430–31, 432; **5**:276;
8:149–50, 297
example, **1**:164–65
presidential logrolling, **1**:586n. 7
presidential role in rent seeking,
5:61–62
presidential systems of government,
4:414, 415. *See also* parliamentary governments
pressure groups, **2**:22–23, 269–80
ethics and, **2**:279–80
size of government and, **2**:272–74
See also special-interest groups
pretrial settlements, **1**:480–81, 499–
502
bargaining, **1**:503–4
frequency, **1**:502–3
preventative medicine, **7**:310
Price, H. Douglas, **10**:*371n. 10*
price controls, **1**:580–81, 594–95
in China, **10**:318–19, 320, 339
Chin dynasty in China, **10**:331
effect on barter, **10**:318
gasoline, **7**:171–73
ill-informed voters and, **7**:176–77
oil, **7**:35–36
oil and natural gas, **7**:330–31
using differential prices for life support, **7**:348–49
who benefits from, **7**:173
price elasticity and rational behavior,
10:103
price equilibrium, speed of approach
to, **10**:99
price indices, **10**:373–75
prices
comparison shopping, **1**:430–32
energy expenditures as, **1**:538
real world, **1**:432
relation with preferences, **4**:73
price supports involving no public
goods, **7**:319–20
Priest, George L., **1**:*500nn. 4, 6*

primary elections, **4**:227, 249
  U.S. presidential, **4**:431, 432
primates
  conflict among, **10**:164–65
  territoriality, **10**:165–66
  See also chimpanzees
primogeniture, **8**:218
principal-agent approach, **6**:245, 294,
  304
principle of the uniformity of nature,
  3:92
prisoners' dilemma, **10**:202–3
  bargaining as, **1**:184–85
  conflict studies and, **8**:4
  degrees of cooperation in, **1**:341–42
  of government transfers to the poor,
    1:272
  of how species become nonviable,
    1:566–69
  importance, **1**:343
  minimizing, **8**:6
  of mutually beneficial plants, **1**:552
prisoners' dilemma games, **10**:429–37
  with chosen partner, **10**:431–32
  played with changing partners,
    10:430n. 3
  police force example, **4**:105
prisons
  administrative routes to, **9**:167–71
  conditions in, **9**:261–62
  effectiveness, **10**:60
  offenders incarcerated, **9**:152–55
  punishment within, **9**:169–71,
    187–88
  See also criminals; debtors' prisons;
    parole
private enterprise in South Korea,
  10:355
private local governments
  condominium association constitu-
    tions, **5**:270
  condominium associations,
    4:42–43

Lake Geneva camp, **4**:140
  See also neighborhood governments
privately produced money
  in ancient China, **10**:325–26
  bank notes in ancient China,
    10:339–42
  on Mongol dynasty in China,
    10:336–37
private property
  animals vs. humans, **10**:119–20
  plants vs. humans, **10**:119
  in South Korea, **10**:354–55
  See also crimes against property;
    property rights
private rent seeking, **1**:238
private research vs. government research,
  3:20–21
private vs. public sector decisions,
  1:388–92. *See also* market vs.
  government problem
Private Wants, Public Means (Tullock),
  4:220
Private Wants and Public Needs (Phelps),
  4:20
privatization
  effect on economies of scale in govern-
    ment, **1**:80
  of government services, **1**:25
  of police services, **9**:269
  provision of public goods through,
    10:399–402
  reasons to choose, **4**:41
prizes for scientific discoveries, **3**:28,
  167–69
  compensation of scientists and, **3**:170
probable deduction, **3**:90–91
probate, **9**:130, 132–34
probation violations, **9**:168. *See also*
  parole
"Problem of Social Cost, The" (Coase),
  9:383
"Problems of Majority Voting" (Tullock), **4**:6; **5**:249, 271; **7**:231

problem solving, **3**:104
"process efficiency," **5**:116n. 9
production externalities, **7**:8
professional criminals, **9**:156–57
professional vs. amateur rate of errors,
    9:324–25, 439
profitability
    of corporate divisions, **6**:213
    measuring, **6**:300
    as performance measure, **6**:210–11
    of some government enterprises,
        6:281
profit distribution, **8**:4
profit motive
    businessmen who ignored, **6**:410
    reason for dominance of, **6**:398–99
progress
    defining, **1**:183–84, 548–49
    See also scientific progress
progressive tax systems, **1**:196
promise-keeping, rationality of,
    4:268–69
promotions within organizations,
    6:48–50, 123–24
    military, **6**:222–23
    by seniority, **6**:401
    See also career advancement; perfor-
        mance evaluation
proof of wrongdoing. *See* beyond-
    reasonable-doubt criteria; pre-
    ponderance of evidence criteria
property accumulation, **1**:314
property rights, **1**:309
    under common law, **9**:407–8
    definitions, **4**:75n. 8, 84
    difference from territoriality, **1**:556
    effect on trade, **1**:313
    in France and Russia, **8**:145
    to individual's own reputation,
        9:213
    justification for, **4**:74–77
    negative and positive externalities,
        4:77–78

political reform to protect, **5**:75–82
preferences and payments, **4**:78–80
quasi-private property, **4**:83
reduction of externalities and,
    4:146–49
relation to efficiency, **1**:464
rent seeking and, **5**:159
using bribery to support, **1**:325
U.S. Supreme Court defense of,
    9:445–46
See also housing examples; law of
    property
proportional income tax, **1**:375–77;
    7:50
proportional representation, **1**:31, 34,
    88–89; **5**:291; **10**:287
    in Europe and Middle East,
        4:326n. 10, 341–43, 384
    parties and candidates in, **4**:385–86
    pros and cons, **4**:382n. 1, 386–90,
        391–92
    reason for invention, **4**:381
    with single-party systems, **4**:390–91
    voting systems, **4**:432, 442–43
    See also voters with strong preferences
proprietary information, **5**:298
prosecutors, **9**:318
    in England vs. United States,
        9:178–79
    interest in convictions, **9**:162–63
    See also plea bargaining
prospectuses, **9**:211
prostitution, **9**:221
protective tariffs. *See* tariffs
Prothero, G. W., **8**:*33n. 3, 65n. 6,
    222n. 66*
protozoa, **10**:225–26
proximate cause, **9**:409
proxy fights vs. takeover bids,
    6:344–45. *See also* leveraged
    buyouts
Prussia, government in, **6**:157
Pryor, Frederic L., **10**:*164n. 5*

psychic income value, **1**:343
psychological research, **3**:139
"Public and Private Interaction under
 Reciprocal Externality"
 (Buchanan and Tullock), **4**:107
publication in economics, **1**:36–47,
 589, 593, 594, 598–99. *See also*
 academic journals; academic
 research
publication of scientific discoveries
 anonymous submission of papers,
 3:115
 by distribution of reprints, **3**:66n. 11
 importance of the discovery and,
 3:115–20, 121
 income from, **3**:67
 publicizing rejected papers,
 3:121–22
 relation to discussion among scientists, **3**:131, 133
 reputation of author and, **3**:119,
 120
 resubmission of articles, **3**:118–19
 through scientific journals, **3**:67–72,
 114
 See also scientific journals
Public Choice, **1**:42; **4**:171–72
 binding, **1**:44–45
 editorial policies, **1**:46–47
 founding, **4**:14
 funding, **1**:42–43, 44
 publication history of, **4**:*15n. 6*
 related products, **1**:47
 See also *Papers on Non-Market Decision Making*
Public Choice, second edition (Mueller),
 4:28
Public Choice Society, **1**:42
public choice theory, **6**:328
 academic journals for, **4**:16–17
 achievements, **4**:22–23
 bibliography, **4**:28–31
 confusion over name of, **4**:17

Duncan Black's role, **4**:301
 foundations, **4**:20–22
 four areas of study, **1**:17
 future of, **4**:27–28
 goal, **1**:17
 influence on public policy, **4**:25
 linkage with rent seeking, **5**:31
 numbers of scholars, **4**:24
 origin, **1**:16, 37; **4**:11, 15
 perspective on common law,
 9:411–12
 policy implications, **4**:32, 40–41
 problem of self-enforcing constitution, **8**:303
 problems in need of study, **1**:28–35
 promise of, **1**:26
 public interest theory and, **1**:587–88
 recent scholarship, **4**:24–25,
 220–21
 relation to economics, **1**:9, 16–17
 relation with social choice theory,
 1:42
 research methods, **1**:105
 view of human behavior, **4**:34–35
 view of politics, **8**:46–47
 See also economic approach to
 politics
public choice theory practitioners,
 7:334
 academic backgrounds of, **4**:19–20
 Marxists, **4**:15, 17
 organizations, **4**:15–16
 political views, **4**:15–16, 18–19
public education
 externalities in, **7**:366
 funding, **7**:295
 income redistribution and,
 7:365–66
 justifications for, **7**:296–97
 model of, **7**:294–96
 as moral indoctrination, **9**:226–27
 subsidies, **1**:269–70
 transfers for, **7**:297–99

public finance (field), **1**:9; **4**:169
public good, **10**:86–87
  argument applied to special-interest
    groups, **7**:212
  self-interest of civil servants vs., **6**:27
  See also public interest
public goods, **2**:33–35
  all or nothing characteristic,
    4:178–79
  argument for public provision of,
    1:588
  aspects of revolution, **1**:332, 334,
    336, 338
  costs, **4**:73–74
  definition, **1**:336–37; **4**:104n. 4
  demand-revealing example involving,
    7:145–46
  difference from market goods, **5**:282
  efficient and inefficient, **7**:194–97
  government-created problem with,
    1:388–93
  government procurement of, **4**:45
  household, **10**:31–32
  inefficiency in provision of, **10**:92
  literature, **8**:181
  military as, **10**.92
  money as, **10**:372
  multidimensional or multiple,
    1:147–48
  overconsumption, **5**:256–57
  paying for, **5**:280
  pork-barrel projects, **5**:289
  private goods vs., **7**:98–99
  as product of rent seeking, **5**:147
  provision of, through privatization,
    10:399–402
  rent seeking vs., **5**:258
  similarity to natural monopoly prob-
    lem, **4**:112
  for small groups of people, **1**:583
  from special-interest groups,
    5:233–34
  technological, **1**:581–82
  theft of, **8**:13–14

  uniformity in government-supplied,
    4:73
  wasteful, limited, vs. beneficial,
    5:288
  See also externalities; free riding;
    police services; public utilities
public goods aspects
  of coups, **8**:263–64, 270–71
  of revolution, **8**:174–76, 177–79,
    199
public goods problem, **10**:90
public health examples
  fluoridation of water, **4**:163–64
  inoculation, **4**:107
  smoking, **5**:198–200
public housing subsidies, **10**:275–76
public interest
  ambiguities, **2**:19n. 3
  damage done in name of, **5**:206
  democracy and, **2**:95
  determining what is, **2**:13
  as goal of governments, **4**:34–35,
    122–23
  government actions toward,
    4:177–78
  as motive of politicians, **1**:191–92
  Public Choice study of, **1**:577
  Public Choice view of, **2**:12
  relation to morality, **2**:294
  special-interest groups and,
    2:270–72
  vote trading and, **2**:263
  voting in the, **4**:237–38
  See also public good
public interest groups, **1**:18
public opinion
  about criminals, **10**:77
  effect on dictators vs. monarchs,
    8:151–52
  impact of mass media on, **4**:253
  pollsters, approach to voters,
    5:38–39
  rule by, **5**:131
  type dictator must maintain, **8**:296

public policy regarding prevention of
    monopolies, **9**:250–51
public sector
    pressure groups and, **2**:272–74
    side payments and, **2**:199–200
    size of, **2**:192–201
public transportation subsidies,
    4:356
public utilities, **4**:203–4, 401
    electric power production, **4**:112
public utility economics, **5**:297
public vs. private sector decisions,
    1:388–92. *See also* government
    vs. market problem
Pullman, N. J., **1**:*140n. 11*
punishment
    civil vs. criminal offenders,
        9:186–88
    Communist countries' reliance on,
        6:401
    as crime deterrent, **9**:252–62;
        10:76, 77–83
    for crimes of impulse, **9**:218–20
    of criminals, **10**:76–77
    economists' vs. sociologists' view of,
        9:257–59
    effect of certainty vs. severity of,
        10:80, 81
    effect of severity of, **10**:60
    to fit violent crime, **9**:217
    for fraud, **9**:208
    in prisons, **9**:169–71, 187–88
    relativity of, **6**:405–6
    by residual claimants, **6**:407–9
    rewards to subordinates vs.,
        6:400–401
    for speeding, **9**:144–45
    systems of rewards and, **6**:330–31
    See also death penalty; incentives to
        subordinates; negative incen-
        tives; negative poll taxes;
        sentencing of offenders
"Purchase of Politicians, The"
    (Tullock), **5**:300

purchasing function of corporations,
    6:398–99
pure research
    costs, **3**:183
    difference from applied research,
        3:10, 62–63
    discoveries by amateur scientists,
        3:181–82
    funding, **3**:15, 165
    importance of applied research to,
        3:16, 150–51
    interrelationship with applied re-
        search, **3**:43
    justifying, by its practical results,
        3:14
    marginal productivity of effort in,
        3:15–16
    prizes for, **3**:168
    separating it from teaching,
        3:171–72
    superiority to applied research,
        3:10–12, 14–15
    See also induced research
pure science journals, **3**:121
pure scientists
    advantage over applied researchers,
        3:26
    curiosity of, **3**:23–26
    dissemination of discoveries,
        3:115–22
    incentive to avoid error, **3**:132
    motivations, **3**:109–11
    self-education, **3**:64–75
    status, **3**:21–22
    unity sought by, **3**:63
    use of approximation, **3**:42
Purves, Robert, **1**:*477n. 2*

qualified majority rule, **2**:202–21.
    See also majority voting
qualified majority voting. *See* rein-
    forced majorities
quasi-Paretian rule, **9**:202
quasi-sovereigns, **6**:65–69

Quirk, Paul J., **5**:*216n. 8, 229n. 31*
quotas
  on consumption, **1**:419–24, 425–26
  taxes vs., **10**:101
  See also rationing

race, **1**:277–78
  governments within cities and,
    4:144
racial discrimination
  compensation to prevent, **4**:351,
    353
  against Jews, **4**:427–28
  voters with strong preferences and,
    4:427–28
  See also slavery
radical change, **6**:186
Rae, Douglas, **4**:349–50
Raiffa, Howard, **2**:*143n. 1, 155n. 10,*
  168n. 2, 170n. 3, 173; **3**:*128–*
  29n. 30; **10**:*441n. 5*
railroad crossing law example,
  9:383–84
Rajputs, **8**:35, 36, 38
Rand Corporation, **5**:295n. 1
R&D. *See* research and development
rape. *See* sexual assault
Rapport, David J., **10**:*109nn. 24, 25,*
  110n. 26
Raskin, David C., **9**:*361n. 50*
raspberry patch societies, **1**:561–62
Rather, Dan, **8**:*85n. 7*
rational behavior, **10**:8–10
  of criminals, **10**:58–60
  experimental evidence in economics
    of, **10**:95–102
  by insane people, **10**:102–5
  of rats, **10**:105–8
rational-ignorance model of voting,
  4:227–28, 232; **5**:42–43
  equations, **4**:234, 239
rationality, **2**:xxii, 30–37; **6**:30–32;
  8:6
  constitutions and, **2**:77–80

in game theory, **2**:154–56
of irrational behavior, **1**:310–11
irrational outcomes from, **1**:57
in market choice, **2**:32
revolution and, **1**:341–45
role of reason in economics, **1**:8
social choice and individual,
  2:30–37
social scientists' view of, **1**:10–11
See also human limitations;
  understanding, Tullock's
  use of
rationing, **1**:365–66. *See also* gasoline
  price controls; quotas on
  consumption
Rawls, John, **7**:*29n. 9*
  income redistribution proposal,
    7:78–79
  Theory of Justice, A, **7**:47
  "veil of ignorance" argument,
    1:282; **7**:32–33
  on wealth equalization, **7**:55–57
Ray, B. A., **1**:*113n. 21*
Read, Leonard, "I, Pencil," **6**:268
reading habits of scientists, **3**:70–71.
  See also literature searches
Reagan, Ronald
  campaign for president, **5**:276
  criticisms of, **7**:303n. 12, 332–33
  support for price supports, **7**:320n. 2
  tax reforms, **5**:178
Reagan administration, **9**:362
real estate agents, **5**:103–4
real estate development examples,
  4:92–95, 137–40
reality
  appearance vs., **3**:33–35, 49
  approximations, **3**:40–43
  of the universe, **3**:39–40
  See also investigation of reality
reason, role in economics, **1**:8. *See also*
  rationality
reasonable doubt. *See* beyond-
  reasonable-doubt criteria

reasonable-man rule, **9**:387–88
reasoning, **3**:98, 101–4. *See also*
    deduction; induction
reciprocal externalities, **1**:349; **4**:102
    nonsymmetrical, **1**:373–77
    numbers required for, **4**:104
recognizing human individuals,
    3:96–98
redistribution, **10**:86
    connotation, **8**:7
    as constitutional, **2**:188–89
    definition, **8**:9
    as insurance, **2**:185–91
    Pareto optimality and, **2**:182–91
    relation with distribution, **8**:5
Reed, Ritchie H., **10**:*41n. 2*
refereeing of academic journals,
    1:39–41; **5**:21
refereeing of scientific journals,
    3:67–68, 117n. 17
    anonymous, **3**:118
reference politicians
    conformity to type, **6**:47–48
    knowledge of own objectives and
        abilities, **6**:141–42
    maximization of own preferences,
        6:401–4
    motives, **6**:6
    need for hierarchical patriotism,
        6:46–47
    personal connections, **6**:42–43
    pleasing of superiors, **6**:282–83
    relationships of, **6**:41, 296–98
    relationships with allies, **6**:54–56,
        287–89
    relationships with peers, **6**:115,
        299
    relationships with spectators,
        6:51–54
    relationships with superiors,
        6:291–94
    relation with group sovereign,
        6:89–114
    single sovereign situation, **6**:70–88

skills needed for promotion, **6**:48–50
    sovereigns, **6**:57
    view of own hierarchy, **6**:284–94
    See also bureaucrats; career advance-
        ment; corporate executives;
        sovereigns; supervision
referendum on government policies,
    1:31, 584–85; **4**:182, 432
    pros and cons, **5**:41
    relation to logrolling, **1**:51–52
    rent seeking and, **5**:78–79
    with two alternatives, **1**:127–28
reform
    genuine, **6**:10
    radical, **6**:186, 415
regulation, **6**:419–20
    of automobile imports, **5**:263
    of banks, **7**:320–22
    of broadcasting industry, **4**:180–81
    as cost of rent seeking, **5**:114
    of dairy industry, **7**:184–86
    direct cash payments vs., **5**:301
    of drug companies, **10**:400, 401
    effectiveness, **10**:101
    hidden costs of, **7**:211
    improving, **5**:80
    of individuals to eliminate exter-
        nalities, **4**:149–51
    insurance and, **9**:114
    of land use for agriculture, **5**:219–20
    lobbying against, **5**:154–55, 157–59
    of prescription drugs, **4**:157–58
    of private markets, **4**:41–42
    protective tariffs vs., **7**:329
    "public interest" transfers vs., **7**:331
    of rent extraction measures, **5**:71–73
    of rent seeking, **5**:117–18
    that affects property rights,
        4:147–49
    transfers via, **7**:19, 35–36
    See also deregulation of industries;
        direct regulation; price controls
regulatory commissions, **5**:34–36;
    9:211–12

Rehnquist, William, **9**:417
Reich, Robert B., **5**:*214n. 3*
Reid, D. B. W., **10**:*109n. 24*
reinforced majorities, **4**:119–20,
    215–19; **10**:286–87
  combining with logrolling, **4**:349–
    50, 352–53
  80 percent majority rule, **5**:270
  share of costs borne by members,
    5:78
  above simple majority, **1**:31, 59
  variants, **5**:290–91
relationships
  buyer/seller, **6**:8, 269
  economic vs. political, **6**:6–9,
    250–51
  exchange vs. slavery, **6**:7
  between superiors and inferiors,
    6:285–87
  See also reference politicians
relative poverty, **7**:53–55, 226
  in India, **7**:343
  See also poor people
relief. *See* unemployment programs;
  welfare recipients
religions
  impact of philosophers on,
    8:229–30
  Marxism, **8**:255–56
  revolution and, **8**:216
  secular, **8**:256–57
religions and charitable giving,
  7:57–58
religious conversion, **3**:98n. 10
religious hierarchies, **6**:22, 418
religious political parties, logrolling by,
  4:342
Relles, Daniel A., **9**:*343n. 13, 350n. 29*
remainders, **1**:260–61
Rembar, Charles, **9**:*350n. 28, 353n. 34*
rent avoidance, **1**:239–40; **5**:112
  by businesses, **5**:118–20
  examples, **5**:114–15, 115–16

rent extraction, McChesney model,
  5:71–73
rent protection
  definition, **5**:69
  social cost, **5**:70–71
rents
  definition, **5**:104
  good, vs. bad, **5**:148, 154–58
  traditional theory of, **5**:148–54
  Tullock's discussion of, **6**:8
  types of investments that produce,
    5:109
rent seeking, **5**:284–89; **6**:375–86
  in adversary system of law, **9**:422
  advertising and, **5**:171–72
  applied to lesser developed coun-
    tries, **5**:27
  badly informed, **5**:206
  from bribery of public officials,
    1:241
  categories, **1**:594
  coalitions in, **5**:239
  from competition for jobs,
    5:110–12
  connotations, **1**:242
  in corporations, **6**:376–82
  data about returns on investment in,
    5:297–99
  definitions, **1**:237; **5**:9–10, 28–29,
    104, 171, 236; **6**:375; **7**:175
  in democracy vs. dictatorship,
    5:132–34
  drawing up of contracts and,
    5:191–93
  early beginnings, **5**:11–14
  economists' efforts to stop, **1**:594,
    597–601
  effect on voters, **5**:307
  effect on Washington, D.C., **7**:338
  effects of idea of, **5**:27–28
  equations, **1**:235–36
  equilibrium, **1**:222–23, 230
  ethical aversion to, **5**:234

as game of strategy, 1:230–33
games, 1:223–25, 226–27
general agreements to eliminate all,
   5:177–79
in government agencies, 6:383–86
through government regulation,
   5:117–18
hereditary monarchies and,
   1:227–28
Hillman strategy, 5:93–94
in historical England, 5:160–61,
   162–63, 164
in historical United States,
   5:168–69
ideological cover for, 5:122–24
impact of committees on, 6:382
impact of free trade on, 5:168
impact of juries on, 5:166–68,
   169–70
impact of transfers on, 5:31
importance of discovery of, 4:23–24
income redistribution and,
   7:174–78
inefficiency of rent transfers,
   5:215–18
inefficient policies from, 5:226–30
limits of Tullock's inquiry, 5:29–30
mathematical problems of, 5:85–87,
   95–100
measuring, 1:242; 5:241
minimizing, 1:228
minimizing, with selection bias,
   1:233–34
most desirable outcome, 5:66
necessary subterfuge in, 5:224–25
as negative sum game, 5:106–8
origin of term and concept, 5:25–27
of Parliament after Charles I,
   5:165–66
political market in, 5:30–32
problem with Tullock model of,
   5:88–94
property rights and, 5:159

protective tariffs and, 5:183
proxies for, 5:74
pseudo-equilibrium, 1:241–42
real loss from, 5:218–19
reduction of, successes in, 5:310
reduction of, via tax reform,
   5:181–82
relation with government transfers,
   5:147
relation with logrolling, 5:238, 239
relation with patents, 5:3–10
relation with rent avoidance, 5:117
resource investment in, 5:214–15,
   219, 231–35, 243–45, 300–
   306
returns on resource investments in,
   5:247, 248
role of bureaucrats in, 5:54–60
role of ill-informed voters in, 5:237,
   239–40
role of media in, 5:44–46
role of politicians in, 5:32–38
role of special-interest groups in,
   5:46–53
role of U.S. president and courts in,
   5:60–62
role of voters in, 5:38–44
severity of, in U.S. government,
   6:384
similarity of lawsuits to, 5:184,
   186–90
social costs, 6:376
by special-interest groups, 7:214–15
stock market and, 5:309
and theory of constitutions, 5:300
three types of investment in, 5:96
transitional-gains trap and, 5:68
zero dissipation result, 5:63–66
See also rent avoidance
rent-seeking costs
   Becker's view of, 5:52–53
   from bribery of government officials,
      5:112–13, 115

rent-seeking costs (*continued*)
  calculating, **5**:299
  costs for public goods vs., **5**:258
  data for estimating, **5**:295–96
  defining, **5**:204–5, 212–13
  efficiency vs., **5**:246
  empirical estimates, **5**:73–75
  from inefficient use of technology,
    5:222
  from logrolling, **5**:249–50, 251–52
  relation with risk premium on capital,
    5:155
  size, **5**:243, 296–97
  total size, **5**:298
  true total of, **5**:220–21
  types, **1**:240–42; **5**:236–40, 298
  in United States, **5**:114–15, 117–21
reparations. *See* compensation
repetition of scientific work, **3**:123–
    28, 133
reporters
  bias about government, **8**:232–33
  bias regarding revolutions,
    8:177–78
representation, **2**:116, 205–13
  definitions of, **4**:424–25
  in two-house legislature, **2**:224
representative assemblies, **6**:90–91
representative democracy, **1**:52;
    2:203–13, 205–13; **8**:143
  corporate shares as, **4**:440
  elections in, **6**:95
  leaving decisions to bureaucrats and,
    4:60
  making life-and-death medical deci-
    sions with, **7**:349
  minority of voters in, **4**:326
  models of political decision making,
    4:10
  nonpolitical examples, **4**:423–24
  perfect information model and,
    4:231
  voting for representatives in, **4**:122

See also democracies; proportional
    representation
reproduction of species
  ants, **10**:189–91
  bees, **10**:189–91
  hereditary behavior, **10**:187–96
  social insects, **10**:186–87, 223
  sponges, **10**:242–44
  termites, **10**:254–57
  See also cloning; eusociality;
    gemmulation
reproductive rate variations, **1**:543–44
  within animal societies, **1**:558–62
Republican Party, **6**:106
reputation, **9**:213; **10**:432–34, 435
  in hierarchical organizations, **6**:53,
    289
  See also personal status
reputation effect of purchases, **1**:400,
    401–2
research
  criminological, **9**:174, 252–54
  as example of environmental coordi-
    nation, **6**:338
  externalities from, **4**:108
  faking results of (*see* faking of re-
    search results)
  military, **8**:353
  pharmaceutical example, **10**:399
  secrecy in, **8**:350, 351–53
  theoretical and empirical, **10**:368
  See also scientific research; social
    science research
research and development
  by automobile manufacturers, **6**:414
  impact of lawsuits on, **6**:420
  See also directed research
research laboratories, **4**:261
residual claimants, **6**:343
  nonprofit organizations, **6**:346–47
  rewards and punishments by,
    6:407–9
  See also sovereigns

resource allocation
 for ill and injured people, **7**:345–51
 of limited goods or services, **7**:308–
  9, 341–42
 See also income redistribution;
  wealth equalization
responsibility in collective choice,
 2:36–37
restaurant menu choice example,
 1:81–83
Revel, Jean-François, **8**:*132n. 80*
revelation of preferences, **2**:104–7
reviews in magazines, **3**:73
revolutionaries, **1**:338–39
 concessions by government to,
  8:199–200
 expectations, **8**:184
 motives, **1**:333
 tactics, **8**:196–200
revolutions
 aims and effects, **8**:166–67
 arguments for, **1**:333–34
 bias in study of, **1**:332–33
 byproduct theory, **8**:184, 185
 after coups, **8**:287–88
 criteria for evaluating, **1**:329–32,
  334–35
 decision to participate, **8**:167–68
 definition, **1**:335; **8**:180n. 5
 differences from coups, **6**:59–60;
  8:267–72
 efficiency effects, **8**:164–66, 167
 as entertainment, **1**:332, 339, 343;
  8:185
 equations, **8**:176–77
 evaluation, **8**:179–82
 factors of participation, **1**:332
 geographically limited, **8**:289
 historical examples, **8**:208–13,
  290–91
 image of, **8**:177–79
 killing of losers after, **6**:53–54
 military role in, **8**:213

motives for, **8**:164–65, 182–85
 from outside the government,
  8:186–87, 261
 payoff for participation, **8**:174–77,
  180
 public good aspects, **1**:332
 rationality and, **1**:341–45
 reasons for success of, **6**:60–61
 religion and, **8**:216
 rewards for information about,
  8:188–96
 role of government officials,
  8:183–84
 romantic view of, **8**:163–64
 similarity to charitable activity,
  1:337
 theories of, **1**:336, 338–40
 three reactions to, **1**:329–32
 using police to suppress, **8**:188–96
 welfare costs, **1**:192–93
 what creates, **6**:61–62
 See also civil wars; conflict; coups
  d'état; popular uprisings
rewards
 punishments to subordinates vs.,
  6:400–401
 relativity of, **6**:405–6
 by residual claimants, **6**:407–9
 to subordinates, **6**:72–73
 systems of punishment and,
  6:330–31
 See also incentives to subordinates;
  punishment
rewards for scientific discoveries. *See*
 prizes for scientific discoveries
Reynolds, Morgan, **9**:*256n. 7*;
 10:*82n. 17*
Rhee, Syngman, **5**:114–15, 123–24,
 306n. 10; **8**:274n. 1
Rheinstein, Max, **9**:90
Rhode, P., **5**:*141n. 8*
Ricardo, David, **1**:8; **5**:148–54
 influence, **5**:310

Richardson, Louis F., **8**:317–18
Richmond, Phyliss Allen, **3**:*77n. 25*
rich people
  charitable giving to, **7**:26, 337–38
  coalitions of, **7**:189
  defined, **10**:11
  government subsidies to, **4**:346
  supplementary private services for,
    7:247–48
  taxing, **5**:181–82
  transfers from, **7**:123–25, 164–65
  transfers from, to the poor, **5**:24
  transfers to, **5**:224, 225
  U.S. Social Security system and, **7**:61
Ridgway, Matthew, **8**:*213n. 48*
Rigg, J. M., **8**:*122–23n. 50*
rights, **2**:44–45
right-wing political parties, **6**:106, 401
Riker, William H., **1**:*98n. 14*, *115n. 26*;
    2:*22nn. 10, 11*; **4**:*181–82n. 12*,
    234n. 12, 279n. 9, 329n. 11,
    390n. 5; **6**:*25n. 1*; **8**:*284n. 11*
  "Bargaining in a Three-Person
    Game," **4**:323n. 5
  criticism of demand-revealing pro-
    cess, **4**:366–72
  on efficiency of logrolling, **4**:347
  "game" characteristics of politics,
    2:143n. 2
  influence on public choice theory,
    4:13–14, 19
  *Introduction to Positive Political
    Theory, An*, **4**:220
  "Is a 'New and Superior Process'
    Really New?," **4**:366n. 1
  Theory of Political Coalitions, The,
    4:307–8
  on U.S. presidential nominating con-
    ventions, **8**:149–50
  "Voting and the Summation of Pref-
    erences," **6**:89
risk
  of being victim of crime, **10**:63
  to criminals being caught, **10**:72

risk aversion
  of criminals to conviction, **9**:161
  decision making and, **9**:30–31
  decisions about lawsuit involvement
    and, **9**:65, 68–70
  loss aversion of prosecutors,
    9:162–63
  present discounted value and,
    9:24n. 6
risk cost, **10**:12
risk of accidents, **9**:111–16
  pairing with liability, **9**:115
risk premium in capital investment,
    5:150–51, 153
risk reduction
  in court cases, **1**:500, 503, 517
  as motive for transfers, **1**:288
  tax evasion penalties and, **1**:454–55
Rizzo, Mayor Frank, **9**:362
road building
  by ants, **10**:220–21
  design safety, **9**:141–42
  reason for government to do, **4**:81
  in Switzerland, **4**:210
  U.S. interstate system, **4**:209–11
road repair, **7**:194–95, 196
  examples, **1**:53–54, 55–57, 199–
    203; **5**:272–74, 277
  logrolling coalitions for, **4**:344–45
  model for, **7**:198–202
  voting and financing, **4**:3–9, 118–21
  See also highway funding
robbery, **9**:189–203. *See also* burglary;
  theft
Roberts, Justice, **9**:416
Robertson, Dennis, **2**:27
Robins, Philip K., **1**:*284n. 13*
Rockhill, W. W., **10**:*321n. 1*
Rodgers, James D., **1**:*262n. 1, 276n. 2*;
    7:*29n. 10*, **8**:*9n. 4*; **10**:*138n. 8*
Rodzinski, Witold, **8**:*64n. 4*
Roe, Anne, **3**:*24n. 22*
Roett, Riorden, **8**:*92nn. 26, 27*
Rogers, J. R., **5**:*22n. 21*

Rogerson, W. P., **5**:*64n. 82, 65n. 84*
Rohr, Anders, **8**:*64n. 5*
Roman Empire, **6**:184, 243–44
Roman government, **8**:113, 137–38, 156
overthrow of republic, **8**:207–8
Romanian government, **8**:98
Roman law, **9**:180, 185, 291, 444
role of jurisconsultus, **9**:336
Romer, Paul M., **10**:380
Rommel, Erwin, **6**:*335n. 15*
Roose, Kenneth D., **7**:*278n. 1*
Roosevelt, Franklin Delano, **6**:97
Röpke, Wilhelm, **2**:*270n. 1, 273n. 3*
Rorvik, David, *In His Image*, **8**:246
Rose, Arnold M., **1**:*62n. 3, 63nn. 6, 7*
Rose-Ackerman, Susan, **9**:345
rosebushes example, **4**:86–90
Rosen, R. R., **10**:*110n. 26*
Rosen, Sherwin, **7**:*267n. 6*
Rosenbaum, E. P., **3**:*99n. 11*
Rosenberg, Nathan, **3**:*xxn. 4*; **4**:*70n. 3*
Rosenblum, Victor O., **9**:*395n. 27*
Rosenfeld, Arthur H., **3**:*99n. 11*
Rosenthal, Robert, **10**:*430n. 3*
Ross, M., **5**:*129n. 7*
Ross, V. B., **5**:*74n. 94*
Rosser, Richard F., **8**:*256n. 56*
Rostand, Jean, **3**:*124n. 22*
Rotenberg, Daniel L., **9**:*176n. 4*
Rothbard, Murray, **4**:37
Rothenberg, Jerome, **1**:62; **7**:6
Rothstein, Paul F., **1**:*517–18, 530n. 6*; **9**:*360n. 46, 434n. 10*
rotifers, **10**:109–10
Roucek, Joseph, **3**:*115n. 15*
Rousseau, Jean-Jacques, **2**:238, 303
Rowat, Donald C., **1**:*409n. 18*
Rowley, Charles K., **5**:*15n. 7, 16n. 9, 17n. 10, 20n. 17, 29n. 32, 31n. 35, 32n. 36, 51n. 58, 52n. 59, 53n. 63, 59n. 70, 61n. 75, 62n. 77,*

64nn. 80, 81, 69n. 88, 71n. 90, 77n. 98, 77n. 99, 77n. 101, 214n. 1, 224n. 20; **6**:*375n. 1*; **9**:*411n. 3, 417n. 6, 420n. 18, 432n. 5, 445n. 12, 447nn. 17, 18*
on *The Calculus of Consent*, **5**:299–300
on cleaning out oil tankers' tanks, **9**:272
"Gordon Tullock: Entrepreneur of Public Choice," **5**:*21n. 19*
Political Economy of Rent-Seeking, The, **5**:28
royal councils, **6**:94–95
Royko, Mike, **4**:*196n. 22*
Rubin, P. H., **1**:*220n. 11*; **9**:*418n. 11, 431n. 3*
Rugaber, Walter, **9**:*315n. 5*
rule of law, **9**:405–6
rules
agreement and, **2**:74
for collective choice, **2**:5–6, 60–80
constitutional, **2**:105
individual, **2**:93
rules of evidence, **9**:87–90, 319n. 10, 356–63, 434–37. *See also* facts in lawsuits and trials
ruling class, role in society, **1**:315–19
ruling class theory of state, **2**:12
Russek, Frank, **10**:*383n. 13, 384n. 16*
Russell, Bertrand, **8**:*107n. 2, 119n. 37, 137–38n. 97, 228n. 7, 256n. 53*
Russia
government in, **6**:335, 388–90
health care system, **7**:247–48
under Lenin, **6**:271, 371–72
See also Communists; Soviet Union
Russian Revolution, **8**:211

Sabine, George H., **8**:*121n. 45, 127nn. 68, 69*
safety in road design, **9**:141–42
Safeway examples, **6**:355–56, 358, 359

salesmen
  political methods of, **6**:16
  rent avoidance by, **5**:119
  See also customers
Samaritan's dilemma in charitable giving, **7**:102–3
Samet, D., **10**:440, 441
Samuelson, Paul A., **1**:*388n. 1, 588*;
    2:*183n. 1*; **4**:*6n. 5, 178n. 9*;
    9:*18n. 3*; **10**:*115n. 1*
  "Exact Consumption-Loan Model of
    Interest, An," **7**:264–65
  theory of constitutions and, **2**:330
  theory of public expenditure, **2**:105,
    194
  Tullock's variations on model of
    interest, **7**:284–85, 294–96,
    304–5
  on why government needed, **4**:37;
    10:92
sanctions
  discretion in fixing magnitude,
    1:463
  effective vs. nominal, **1**:459
  enforcement probability, **1**:459
  enforcement probability in relation
    to cost, **1**:461–62
  most efficient way to achieve, **1**:462
  why needed, **1**:457
  See also fines; penalties
Sanders, N. K., **8**:*118n. 33*
Sandmo, Agnar, **10**:*383n. 11*
Sarat, Austin, **9**:*341n. 5*
Sarton, George, **3**:*73n. 21*
Saudi Arabia, oil revenues, **5**:138, 139,
    140
Savage, Leonard J., **9**:*31n. 11*
saving
  definition, **10**:14
  impact of Social Security on,
    10:303–4
  taxes and, **10**:289
Sawers, David, **3**:*181n. 22*

Sayce, Archibald Henry, **8**:*116n. 27,
    117n. 30, 118n. 32*
Scammon, Richard M., **4**:*217n. 35*
scandals
  involving stockholders, **6**:348, 349
  nonprofit vs. corporate, **6**:347
Schattschneider, E. E., **5**:*184n. 1*
Schelling, Thomas C., **1**:*231n. 7*;
    2:147; **7**:25; **8**:*105n. 71*,
    278–79, 296–97
Schleifer, A., **5**:*74–75n. 95*
Schmidt, Wilson, **7**:*303n. 13*
Schneider, John H., **3**:*74n. 24*
scholarly journals. *See* academic
    journals
Schumpeter, Joseph A., **1**:606; **2**:325;
    4:302; **5**:153, 205–6; **10**:160
Schwartz, B., **10**:*314n. 11*
Schwartz, Gary T., **9**:*367n. 7*
Schwartz, Karlene V., **10**:*246n. 6*
Schwartz, N. L., **4**:*90n. 3, 98n. 1,
    109n. 10*
Schwartzman, D., **5**:*13n. 3*
science
  advantages over social sciences,
    3:147–48
  difference from inquiry, **3**:48,
    49–51
  difference from other activities, **3**:32
  dynamic web of, **3**:133–34
  higher-order, **3**:86
  as hobby, **3**:178, 184
  impact of secrecy on, **8**:353
  laws of, **3**:9
  morality and, **7**:23
  reality vs. appearance and, **3**:33–
    35, 49
  relation to economics, **3**:45, 52
  that is not science, **3**:110
sciences of choice and sciences of pref-
    erence, **1**:10
Scientific American, **3**:71–72
scientific backwardness, **3**:146

scientific community, **3**:5–7
  boundaries, **3**:7–8
  compared with markets, **3**:52
  impact of applied researchers on,
    3:131–32
  nongeographical nature, **3**:51–52
  relation to scientific method, **3**:9
  See also social organization of science
scientific curiosity. *See* curiosity
scientific discoveries
  accidental, **3**:8–9, 86–87
  by amateurs, **3**:178–84
  erroneous, **3**:123–28
  importance to new research,
    3:12–13
  monopolies on, **5**:8
  prizes for, **3**:28, 167–69, 170
  secrecy about, **3**:18–20, 112–13
  of tranquilizers, **4**:261
  See also dissemination of scientific
    discoveries; inventions; patent
    system
scientific education. *See* education of
    scientists
scientific experiments
  costs, **3**:183
  repetition of, **3**:123, 128
  to settle controversies, **3**:131
  See also laboratories; scientific
    research
scientific fields
  definitions of, **3**:49
  engineering fields vs., **3**:62, 63
  practical importance of research in,
    3:13–14
  relation to social studies, **3**:53
  that do not use patents, **3**:20
scientific journals
  citation counting of articles,
    3:*27n. 26*, 31
  dissemination of scientific discoveries
    and, **3**:114
  effect on induced research, **3**:46–47

effect on research, **3**:30
  errors and misunderstandings in,
    3:131
  functions, **3**:67
  impact on research, **3**:31
  levels of generality, **3**:71–72
  as news magazines, **3**:67–72
  prestige, **3**:121–22
  as source of self-education of scien-
    tists, **3**:66
  specialization among, **3**:117
  See also academic journals; editors of
    scientific journals; publication
    of scientific discoveries; referee-
    ing of scientific journals
scientific method, **3**:53–54, 136–37
  relation to knowledge, **3**:7–8
  relation with scientific community,
    3:9
scientific observation
  impact of discussion on, **3**:129
  repetition of, **3**:123
scientific papers. *See* publication of sci-
    entific discoveries
scientific progress, **10**:368
  proposals to slow or stop, **3**:159–61
  specific objections, **3**:161–63
scientific research
  association with higher education,
    3:171–72
  balance of power among nations
    and, **3**:160–61
  costs, **3**:182–84
  example, **10**:399
  funding, **3**:161, 163–65
  grant proposals, **3**:166–67
  impartiality, **3**:132–33
  importance of repetition to, **3**:122–
    28, 133
  inefficiency, due to patents, **5**:3–4
  inquisitorial system of law and,
    9:353
  progress too fast or too slow, **5**:3, 4

scientific research (*continued*)
projects for larger organizations,
3:163
similarity to nonscientific activities,
3:50
voluntary (unfunded), **3**:23
way to test importance, **3**:13
See also accuracy of scientific research;
applied research; faking of research results; funding for scientific research; government-
sponsored scientific research;
pure research; scientific
experiments
scientific terms, **3**:81–82
scientific tests. *See* verification of scientific discoveries
scientific theories, **9**:15
as approximations, **3**:40–42
choice of the simpler, **3**:37–38,
42, 43
correctness or incorrectness, **3**:88
developing new, **3**:58–62
disprovability of, **3**:39–40
methods for provisional acceptance,
3:45
pattern types and, **3**:100
philosophies of, **3**:34–38
predictive requirements, **3**:91
premises, **3**:91
repetition of work on, **3**:123–28,
133
theory of, **3**:37, 100
"truth" of, **3**:34–40, 48
untestable, **3**:100, 144
verification, **3**:112
See also hypotheses; scientific
discoveries
scientific training. *See* education of
scientists
scientists
attitudes toward applied and pure
research, **3**:21–23
attitudes toward errors, **3**:131–32

beliefs, **3**:45
commonalties with social scientists,
3:144–46
cooperative activities, **3**:4–5
decisions where to publish, **3**:68
depth of attachment to their subject,
3:26–27
desire for peer approval, **3**:27–28
education, **3**:56–64, 179–83
junior, **3**:28
level of compensation, **3**:170
lying by, **4**:266
methods of inquiry, **3**:43–45
morality, **3**:108–9
philosophical beliefs, **3**:33–35
predicting success by, **3**:91n. 5
predictions of, **3**:60
recognizing extraordinary, **3**:133
reputations, **3**:31
self-education, **3**:64–75
skepticism about theory, **3**:37
theories of their own behavior,
3:36–37
trustworthiness, **3**:5–7
See also academic researchers in science; amateur scientists; applied
scientists; motivations of scientists; publication of scientific
discoveries; pure scientists
Scitovsky, Tibor, **1**:*171n. 7*
Scott, Derek J. R., **8**:*109n. 5*
Scott, Robert E., **8**:*92n. 28*
Sculc, Tad, **8**:*34n. 7*
sea gulls, **10**:125
SEC (Securities and Exchange Commission), **9**:211
secrecy
about scientific discoveries, **3**:18–
20, 112–13; **5**:3
in voting, **4**:367–68
secret police, **1**:327; **8**:267–68, 269
in Communist countries, **1**:345
See, Richard, **3**:*77n. 26*
Seldon, Margery, **8**:*255n. 52*

selection bias as desirable, **1**:233–34
self-education of scientists, **3**:64–75
  individualism from, **3**:65
  three institutions used for, **3**:66
self-employed individuals, **6**:335
self-incrimination, **9**:435
self-interest, **2**:16; **6**:32–33
  academics and businessmen,
    4:173–74
  Adam Smith's theory of, **6**:3
  advancement of organizational goals
    vs., **6**:23–25
  in bureaucracies, **6**:27
  constitutional choice and, **2**:90–91
  of experts, **7**:254, 280, 281
  government and, **4**:39–40
  as human nature, **2**:26
  as motive for income redistribution,
    7:76–77
  as motive for transfers, **7**:59–64, 69
  net advantages, **4**:193n. 21
  of politicians and civil servants,
    4:174–75
  politicians and consumers, **4**:17
  of subordinates, **6**:402–3
  transfers motivated by, **7**:27, 187
  universal health care and, **7**:168
  as utility maximization, **2**:3
  in voting, **4**:173
  See also choices; "invisible hand"
self-sacrifice, **8**:228. *See also* altruism
self-serving attribution, **5**:129n. 7
Sen, Amartya K., **7**:30–31n. 15
seniority as tool of dictators, **8**:254
seniority systems, **1**:217; **6**:404, 413
sentencing of offenders
  by administrators instead of courts,
    9:167–71
  biasing proceedings for length of,
    9:287–89
  deterrence of crime and, **9**:258–59
  length of sentences, **9**:198–200, 343
  public opinion about, **9**:193
  reduction in, **9**:169–70

  reductions in return for information,
    8:195
  See also death penalty; parole; plea
    bargaining; prisons
Sesnowitz, Michael, **9**:257
settlements. *See* out-of-court settle-
  ments; pretrial settlements
Seward, Desmond, **8**:*100n. 53*
sex crimes, **9**:220–21
sexual assault, **9**:215, 221
sexual behavior among humans,
  10:168–69
Shadegg, Stephen C., **4**:*129n. 14*
Shaftsbury, Earl of, **10**:*146n. 8*
Shapiro, David L., **1**:*195n. 4*
Shapiro, Irving S., **5**:118
Shapley, Lloyd S., **2**:173
shareholders. *See* stockholders
Sharp, Lauriston, **6**:*267n. 6*
Shaw, C., **3**:*94n. 7*
Shepsle, Kenneth A., **1**:*115n. 24*;
  4:433
Sheridan, James E., **8**:*64n. 3*
Sherman, Paul W., **10**:*236n. 1*
Shiller, Robert, **1**:*434n. 9*
Shipley, J. J., **8**:*9n. 4*
Shipman, Len, **9**:*219n. 2*
Shleifer, Andrei, **6**:*376n. 4*
shoppers. *See* consumers
Shubik, Martin, **2**:*143n. 1*
Shughart, William F., II, **4**:*32n. 1*;
  5:*32n. 36, 53n. 63, 64n. 82*;
  8:*146n. 10*; **9**:*411n. 3, 418n. 12*
  on efficient rent seeking, **5**:88,
    90–92
sick people. *See* ill and injured people
side payments, **10**:416
  in majority voting, **2**:148–51
  Pareto optimality and, **2**:179–81
  public sector size and, **2**:199–200
  unanimity and, **2**:85–86
Siegel, Sidney, **2**:*100n. 1*; **3**:*137n. 3*;
  10:*99n. 5*
Sierra Club, **1**:548

Sieve, Jack E. B., **1**:*196n. 9, 263n. 6*
Silberberg, Eugene, **5**:*43n. 46*
Silver, Morris, **1**:*343n. 9*; **8**:*174n. 1, 182n. 8, 185n. 10*
Silverberg, Robert, **8**:*116n. 27, 117n. 30, 118n. 34*
Simon, Herbert A., **2**:*20n. 7*; **3**:94n. 7; **6**:416; **9**:166
Simon, Julian L., **6**:*417n. 2*
Simon, Rita James, **1**:*477n. 11*; **9**:*283n. 3*
Simons, Henry C., **4**:11; **7**:67, 125, 335
simple income transfers, **1**:206–7
Simpson trial, **1**:523, 532
Singapore government, **8**:137
single-member constituency system, **4**:386–90, 392
single-party political systems, **4**:387–88; **8**:108–11
    proportional representative democracies with, **4**:390–91
single-peak assumption about voting, **1**:20
single-peakedness, **2**:325
single-peaked preference curves, **1**:90
    for two dimensions, **1**:90–91
single-peaked preferences, **4**:54
    definition, **6**:96
    importance of Duncan Black's work, **4**:303
single sovereigns, **6**:70–88
    competition by peers subject to, **6**:115–18
Sinnigen, William G., **8**:*91nn. 21, 23, 92n. 24, 113nn. 12, 13, 15, 16, 125n. 59, 126n. 63*
Sirica, Judge, **9**:315n. 5, 329
Sjoquist, David L., **9**:*256n. 11*; **10**:*83n. 19*
Skinner, B. F., **10**:108
Skolnick, Jerome H., **9**:*166n. 13, 177n. 5*
slander, **9**:213

slavery, **1**:309, 312, 315; **4**:428–30
    relationship of, **6**:7
    selling oneself into, **9**:51–53
    in Spain, **7**:39–40
slaving ants, **10**:195–96, 199, 219
slime molds, **10**:144–45, 192, 246–49
slime mold societies, **1**:563–64
    example, **1**:566–69
small local governments, **4**:343
    advantages, **4**:399
    advantages of having many, **4**:145
    China, **4**:142–43
    contracting out by, **4**:404
    economic effects of welfare expenditures by, **7**:9
    economies of scale and, **4**:144–45
    income redistribution by, **7**:117, 132
    jurisdictions, and need for logrolling, **4**:343
    nonoptimal size of bureaucracy in, **6**:237–38
    officials who run, **4**:402–3
    problems with, **4**:145–46
    relative efficiency, **6**:385–86
    transfers by, **7**:122–23, 126–27
    transfers for charity by, **7**:359–62
    using for welfare and charitable giving, **7**:357–58
    wider use of, **6**:235–36
    See also local politics; neighborhood governments; private local governments
small-scale economic models, **7**:198
Smith, Adam, **3**:*5n. 2*; **4**:*32n. 2*; **5**:*123n. 2*; **9**:*446n. 14*
    on businessmen, **4**:260
    contribution to history, **5**:162–63
    discipline of continuous dealings, **10**:429
    distinction between economics and politics and, **4**:70n. 3
    on division of labor, **10**:209–10
    "History of Astronomy," **3**:xxn. 4

influence, **5**:310; **6**:252
interdisciplinary approach, **1**:7
interest in subjects besides econom-
    ics, **4**:169
justification for classical law of con-
    tract, **9**:444–48
on mercantilism, **5**:123–24
"natural sympathies" of, **9**:200
on protective tariffs, **5**:308–9
on reason and the passions, **1**:8
on self-interest and mutual gain,
    2:22, 238; **6**:3
Spinoza as precursor, **2**:298
view of human nature, **10**:181n. 1
Wealth of Nations, The, **1**:7, 8;
    3:5n. 3; **4**:33; **5**:160; **6**:252;
    10:3n. 1, 209, 220
writings about government, **4**:33
See also "invisible hand"
Smith, Dennis Mack, **8**:*88n. 14*
Smith, Jeffrey W., **4**:*173n. 3*
Smith, John Maynard, **1**:*427n. 1*
Smith, Peter, **8**:*304n. 20*
Smith, Richard J., **8**:*37n. 20*
Smith, Sydney, **9**:261–62
Smith, Vernon, **10**:95, *96n. 3, 97n. 4*,
    99–100
smoking, compensating those who
    refrain from, **4**:349–50
smoking, efforts to control, **5**:198–200
snails, **10**:108–9
Snow, C. P., **3**:*10n. 1, 108n. 4*
Snyder, J. M., **5**:236–37
Snyder, Richard C., **2**:*143n. 1*
Sober, Elliott, **10**:*159n. 2*
social change, **3**:154–55
    government role in, **3**:155
social choice and individual rationality,
    2:30–37
Social Choice and Individual Values
    (Arrow), **1**:90, 91, 103, 104,
    124–25; **3**:154; **4**:275–76,
    283
    second edition, **4**:275n. 2

social choice theory
    propositions of, **1**:20–21
    relation to public choice theory, **1**:42
    weaknesses, **1**:133
social contract, **2**:238–41, 295
    in Britain, **4**:206–7
    exceptions, **9**:229–34
    with government, **9**:407–8
social costs
    automobile design, **4**:158
    charity, **1**:185–87
    conflicts and wars, **1**:192–93
    of contracts, **9**:392, 423
    from fragmented political policy,
        5:37
    imposed by governments, **4**:156–59
    income transfers, **1**:177
    inefficiency of democracies in reduc-
        ing, **4**:162
    law enforcement, **9**:341
    lawyers, **5**:194–95
    litigation, **9**:441
    monopoly, **1**:242
    rent protection, **5**:70–71
    from rent seeking, **6**:376
    social costs of reducing, **4**:156–65
    tariffs, **1**:171
    theft, **1**:175–76
    votes by ill-informed voters on,
        4:159–62
    See also welfare costs
social dilemma, **8**:368
Social Dilemma, The (Tullock), **1**:341
social group behavior, **10**:8
social group structures, **3**:140–41
social inequality, **1**:315
social insects, **10**:225
    cells, compared with human cells,
        10:265–66
    haploidy theory of, **10**:143–44
    reproduction, **10**:186–87, 223
    social organization, **10**:143–44
    variable behavior, **10**:125–26
    See also ants; bees; termites

social inventions, **3**:148, 149–50
socialism, **6**:238
  control of capital accumulation and,
    1:249–50
  inefficiency, **5**:124
  as rent seeking, **5**:29
  rent seeking under, **5**:122–23
socialism and control of capital accu-
    mulation, **1**:252
socialist governments, **8**:252–53
socialized medicine, **7**:310–11. *See also*
    universal health care
social mobility in large organizations,
    6:19
social organization of science, **3**:4–5
  development of, **3**:7–9
  reasons for its success, **3**:6
  See also scientific community
social organization of social sciences,
    3:137
  effect on applied research, **3**:150–51
social provision area, **1**:363
social science research
  experiments, **3**:137–39
  funding, **3**:155–56, 161, 163
  unfavorable climate, **3**:148
  use of historical data, **3**:143–46
  See also applied social science research
social sciences
  advantages of science over,
    3:147–48
  coordinating research among, **1**:7–
    10, 14–15
  debates among fields within,
    1:10–11
  difficulty, compared with sciences,
    3:135–37
  general theory underlying, **1**:12–14
  impact of literature on, **3**:151
  nonscientific character of, **3**:122
  reasons for backwardness of,
    3:144–48
  relation to sciences, **3**:53

  social organization of, **3**:137,
    150–51
  spurious reasons for backwardness
    of, **3**:144–46
  See also social inventions
social science theory, **3**:141
social scientists
  arguments among, **3**:157
  commonalties with scientists,
    3:145
  methods of, **6**:18
  motivations, **3**:149–54, 157
  ultimate objective, **6**:6
  value judgments by, **6**:9
Social Security Act, **5**:266–67, 305
  amendment of 1977, **7**:288, 290,
    363–65
Social Security Administration, **6**:206
Social Security system, **10**:290–95
  benefits paid to civil servants, **7**:34
  benefits vs. costs, **7**:291–92
  benefits vs. taxes according to in-
    come level, **7**:288–90
  cuts to, **10**:296–99
  deferment of payout age, **10**:298
  effect on capital investment,
    7:62–63
  effect on GNP in United States and
    abroad, **7**:269–70
  effect on saving, **10**:303–4
  effect on upper-income groups,
    10:296–97, 300–301
  employer contribution, **10**:294
  historical development, **7**:278–84,
    285, 288, 292–93
  impact of income growth on,
    7:270–71
  impact of inflation on, **7**:287
  impact of population rate on,
    7:272–73
  inflation and, **7**:274
  as insurance, **7**:37, 60
  interest rates and, **7**:271–72, 274

models of, **7**:263–65, 266–68,
284–85
as national rather than local program,
7:122, 126
older poor people with and without,
10:301–3
paternalism in, **7**:63–64
as perpetual transfer from young to
older people, **7**:279
as Ponzi (pyramid) scheme,
7:62–63
poor people and, **7**:275, 278,
282–84
problem of credibility, **10**:295–96
problems, **7**:127, 363–64
size plateauing of, **7**:285–88
taxes, **5**:266–67; **7**:286–87
termination, **7**:265–66, 273–74
transfers built into, **7**:60–62
as transitional-gains trap, **7**:272
unemployment and, **7**:279, 281
for working women, **7**:282
See also pensions; Supplemental
Security Income (SSI)
social studies. *See* social sciences
social waste
from grants-in-aid, **1**:205–6, 211
from unionization, **1**:217–18
social welfare, **2**:80
social welfare function, **2**:13, 270
social welfare programs
compared with special-interest
groups, **7**:338
empirical research about, **7**:256–58,
259
for the nonpoor, **7**:363–66
See also Social Security system;
universal-aid programs;
welfare state
social workers, **7**:104, 111, 357
societies
characteristics of, **10**:174–76
definition, **10**:173

general theory of, **10**:145, 174,
175–79
of unrelated species, **10**:174, 193–95
See also human societies; nonhuman
societies
societies, elasticity of, **8**:134
societies, primitive
based on mutual defense, **1**:562,
572
based on reproduction, **1**:558–62
of cells, **10**:264–67
of commensals (paired species),
1:570–73
explanations of, **1**:558
impact of mutation on, **1**:564–69
of nuclei, **1**:564
of plants, **1**:561–63
self-sacrifice within, **10**:249
slime molds, **10**:144–45, 192,
246–49
of slime molds and sponges,
1:563–65
See also cellular animals; social insects
sociobiology, **1**:556–57; **8**:236–41;
10:115–17, 131–32
definition, **10**:142
economics and, **10**:133–38, 139–54
findings, **10**:118–20
general theory, **10**:143, 145
reason to practice, **10**:254
Sociobiology (Wilson), **1**:555; **10**:147
sociological view of transactions costs,
6:245
sociologists
contrasted with economists,
10:427–28
economists' view of crime and punishment vs., **9**:257–59
view of crime, **10**:73–77
sociology
contrasted with economics, **1**:9–11
nonscientific character of, **3**:122
solipsism, **3**:33

solutions
  in games of strategy, 1:230–31
  to government vs. market problem,
    4:50–51, 85, 95–96
  inefficient but optimal, 1:430–32
Solzhenitsyn, Aleksandr, 6:*400, 404*
Sophocleus, J. P., 5:*74n. 95, 246n. 7*
South Africa, 1:277–78
  economy, 7:43–45, 47
South America
  black (underground) economy,
    5:296
  bureaucracies, 1:300–301
  countries in cross-national sample,
    10:398
  economic growth, 10:391–93,
    396–97
  governments, 8:123–24, 251, 252
Southern Economic Journal, 5:20
southern states, voting block in United
    States, 5:273–74
South Korea, 5:114–15, 123–24,
    306n. 10
  adjustment to continuous inflation,
    10:343–49
  bank loans with negative rates,
    10:352–54
  Combined Economic Board Agree-
    ment with U.N., 10:349, 352
  compulsory sales of government
    bonds, 10:357
  fiscal problems, 10:355–57
  government, 8:137, 274n. 1;
    10:354
  ideological environment, 10:354–55
  legal system, 10:355
  money supply, 1945–1954, 10:352
  nonbudgetary sources of revenue,
    10:349–54
  possible remedies for inflation,
    10:358
  private enterprise, 10:355
  resale of foreign-aid goods in,
    10:351–52
United Nations developmental pro-
    grams, 10:356
  See also North Korean government;
    Rhee, Syngman
South Vietnam, 1:345
sovereigns
  aides and secretaries to, 6:84,
    321–22
  control vs. influence over subordi-
    nates, 6:369
  ideal, 6:132–33
  intelligence levels of, 6:80–82
  knowledge of subordinates' activi-
    ties, 6:74–78
  as above the law, 9:16
  limitations on time, 6:78–79
  maximization of power, 6:143
  overthrow of, 6:59–60
  pleasing one's, 6:70–72, 73–74
  principal problem in organizational
    efficiency, 6:152
  problem of flattery, 6:84
  quasi-sovereigns, 6:65–69
  real and apparent power, 6:142–44
  relationships with inferiors, 6:57–58
  rewards to subordinates, 6:72–73
  single, 6:70–78, 115–18
  ultimate, 6:64–65, 159
  vagueness of wishes, 6:86–88
  See also group sovereigns; multiple
    sovereigns; reference politicians;
    residual claimants; superiors;
    supervision
Soviet Union, 1:344–45; 8:14n. 1
  agreements with democracies, 8:349
  cold war with United States, 8:321
  government, 8:14n. 1
  Liebermanism, 4:82–83
  one-party system, 8:108–11
  overthrow of leaders in, 8:267–68
  succession of power in, 8:95–98
  system of voting, 1:88
  See also communism; Marxism;
    Russia

Spain, slavery in, **7**:39–40
Spanish Empire, **6**:276, 370
Spartan government, **8**:119–20
Spearman, Diana, **8**:*108n. 3, 122n. 49,*
    135n. 89
special-interest groups
  benefits to, **4**:398
  cartels as, **1**:212
  charitable giving to, **7**:26
  civil servants as, **4**:163, 406–7
  in common law system, **9**:450
  concerned with courts, **9**:414
  conflict within, **7**:94–95
  costs of competition for transfers by,
    5:52–53
  cost vs. efficiency, **5**:246
  danger of lying to, **4**:268
  desirable, **5**:206
  for disability issues, **7**:211
  for doctors, **7**:311–12, 364–65
  effect on information, **7**:177
  effect on public interest, **1**:578,
    583–85
  effect on voters, **1**:18
  free riding among, **5**:233–34
  governmental support of, **4**:421
  government officials and, **1**:580–81
  how they arise, **1**:212–15
  income tax law and, **9**:146–47
  income transfers to, **4**:229
  inelasticity of government privileges
    to, **5**:68–69
  influence on judges, **9**:414, 415
  information levels of, **4**:244
  interaction with politicians and bu-
    reaucrats, **5**:58
  of lawyers, **1**:475–76, 531–32;
    9:301
  legal privilege of, **9**:16–18
  legislation favoring, **9**:50–51
  lobbying on behalf of, **7**:175
  lying by, **5**:212–13
  methods of opposing, **1**:597–98
  model for, **4**:311

  motives, **7**:5
  organizational methods, **7**:213
  Pareto's view, **7**:208–9
  politicians' role in creating,
    4:228–29
  prisoners' dilemma of, **7**:215–16
  public good argument about, **7**:212
  public goods from, **5**:233–34
  reason for small number, **7**:211–12
  relation with intellectual community,
    7:336–37
  rent seeking by, **7**:214–15
  role in rent seeking, **5**:46–53
  role in transfers, **9**:411
  scandals involving, **5**:225, 230
  size of individual, **5**:300–301
  small, **5**:51
  social welfare programs vs., **7**:338
  tactics, **4**:259–60
  tariffs and, **3**:158
  tax reform and, **5**:176–77
  transfers by, **1**:327–28
  U.S. Supreme Court response to,
    9:445
  use of selective incentives to lure
    members, **5**:49–51
  vote payoffs for members, **4**:236–37
  why they persist, **1**:219–21
  See also lobbying; pork-barreling;
    pressure groups
specialization. *See* division of labor
special privilege, systems of, **9**:17
spectators
  boundary separating participants
    from, **6**:82–83
  definition, **6**:51–52
  numbers of, **6**:52
  reference politicians' relation with,
    6:52–54
speculation in stocks, **1**:435–36
speeding, **9**:140
  penalties, **9**:144–45
speeding violations, **1**:443–47
speed limit enforcement, **1**:447–49

Spence, Jonathan, **8**:*99n. 46*
Spencer, Herbert, **1**:553; **6**:10
Spiegelman, Robert G., **1**:*284n. 13*
spillover effects, **4**:67. *See also*
   externalities
Spinoza, Benedict, **2**:297–98
sponges, **10**:192, 240–46
   amoeboid cells, **10**:241–42
   colonies, **10**:241
   reproduction, **10**:242–44
   social organization, **10**:144–45
   sponge societies, **1**:563, 565
Spooner, L., **9**:*428n. 39*
spouse selection, **10**:35–36
Sproule-Jones, Mark, **4**:*172n. 3*
squirrels, **10**:119–20
Srinivasan, T. N., **5**:*27n. 28*
SSI (Supplemental Security Income),
   10:299–300
"Stability in Competition" (Hotelling),
   4:302
staff (crisscross) system of supervision,
   6:228–31, 316–20
staff type of organization, **6**:157–59
stagflation, **1**:304
Stahl, O. Glenn, **4**:*196n. 22*
Stalin, Joseph, **8**:146, 302
Standen, Anthony, **3**:*49n. 23*
standing armies, **1**:321
Stankovic, Slobodan, **8**:*79n. 45*
Staples, Ernest L., **10**:*282n. 4*
stare decisis, **9**:400, 401–2, 404
   why judges adhere to, **9**:419
Starosolskyj, Wolodijmyr, **2**:*64n. 2*
Starr, Chester G., **8**:*91nn. 21–23*
State Department. *See* United States
   government agencies: Department of State
state governments
   eligibility rules for welfare, **7**:131
   measures against rent seeking, **6**:385
   transfers among, **7**:359–60
   unemployment programs, **7**:129–31

vesting of unemployment benefits
   by, **7**:131
See also small local governments
states. *See* countries; governments
statistical methods
   of hypothesis verification,
      3:126–28
   in social sciences, **3**:145–46
status. *See* personal status
status quo and change, **2**:248–49
status system of law, **9**:124
statutes in criminal justice system,
   9:433
Stein, Herbert, **5**:203
Sterling, Theodore D., **3**:*126n. 27*
Stern, A., **9**:*365n. 6*
Stern, N. H., **9**:*256n. 9*; **10**:82
Sterne, Laurence, **8**:*54n. 9*
Stigler, George J., **1**:*212n. 2, 323n. 1*;
   2:*110n. 5*; **5**:*17n. 11, 48n. 51*,
      69n. 89; **8**:17n. 4
   on regulatory agencies, **5**:34, 35
   on special-interest groups, **5**:49–50
   on voting, **10**:287, 288
Stiglitz, Joseph E., **4**:*361n. 1*; **5**:262,
   268
Stillerman, Richard, **3**:*181n. 22*
stock exchange rules, **6**:349
stockholders, **1**:432–37
   compared with voters, **6**:348, 349
   conflict of interest and, **6**:350
   control of corporations, **6**:273–74
   diversification in corporations and,
      6:273
   incentives to management by,
      6:407–9
   large corporations and, **6**:262
   powers of, **6**:343–45
   scandals involving, **6**:348, 349
   as ultimate sovereigns, **6**:213n. 3
   See also corporate takeovers; invest-
      ments; stock market
Stockman, Alan, **10**:*383n. 8*

Stockman, David A., **4**:*419n. 14*;
   5:*277n. 7*
stock market
  example, **1**:432–37
  fluctuations, **1**:435–36
  honesty of members, **4**:261
  rent seeking and, **5**:309
  See also investments; stock exchange
    rules; stockholders
stock options for executives, **1**:433
stocks as votes, **4**:440. *See also* corporate takeovers
Stokes, Donald E., **7**:*343n. 5*
Storer, Norman W., **3**:*178n. 14*
Stout, L. A., **9**:*446n. 13*, *448n. 19*
strategies
  military, **10**:405–24
  mixed, **10**:442–45
  See also games of strategy
Strauss, Leo, **4**:17, 22, 33
strict liability, **9**:364, 370–79. *See also*
  broad liability
Strotz, Robert H., **9**:*30n. 10*,
  114n. 16
Structure of Scientific Revolutions, The
  (Kuhn), **3**:xix
Stubblebine, William C., **1**:*349n. 1*
student financial aid, **7**:60, 303
student protests, **1**:332, 339, 343;
  8:177, 184–85, 220–21.
  See also demonstrations;
  revolutions
subject of an inquiry, **3**:33. *See also*
  human subjects
subordinates
  actual desires of, **6**:402–3
  carrying out of orders, **6**:300–302
  checking up on, **6**:291–93
  communicating with, **6**:195–96
  control over, **6**:189–96, 353–61,
    391–99
  efficiency of, **6**:131–32
  firing, **6**:378, 383–84, 401, 407

  impact of incentives from superiors
    on, **6**:413
  importance to superiors, **6**:298
  incentives to, **6**:400–415
  insuring compliance by, **6**:197–204
  judging by results, **6**:205–9
  knowledge of superiors' desires,
    6:362
  lying by, **6**:403–4
  more intelligent than supervisors,
    6:169, 213–14
  motivating through environment,
    6:332–39
  with multiple superiors, **6**:228–31,
    302–4
  persuasion of, **6**:138–39
  pleasing of sovereigns, **6**:214
  ranking of superiors by number of,
    6:145–47
  relationships with superiors, **6**:285–
    87, 299
  reporting on other subordinates,
    6:201
  rewards and penalties, **6**:202
  robot model, **6**:313–14
  rotation, **6**:381–82, 385
  as slaves, **6**:7, 10
  sovereigns' knowledge of activities
    of, **6**:74–78
  superior to supervisor in abilities,
    6:*126n. 1*, 208–9, 313
  tradeoffs for higher/lower numbers
    of, **6**:155, 314–16
  types of obedience from, **6**:143
  "ugly genius," **6**:285
  See also superiors; supervision;
    supervisors
subsidies
  agricultural, **1**:218, 269, 583
  agricultural subsidies via foreign aid,
    10:352
  for charity, **5**:174
  to college students, **7**:301–3

subsidies (*continued*)
combining with cartels, **5**:258
direct cash payments vs., **5**:222–24,
229–30, 238–40, 301
effect on Tullock rectangle,
5:254–58
higher education, **1**:327–28
from higher to lower level of government, **5**:25
for housing, **10**:275–76
income subsidies for working poor,
7:112–16, 357
to increase capital accumulation,
1:251–52
inelasticity, **5**:68–69
via in-kind transfers, **7**:136–38
involving no public goods,
7:319–20
more efficient, **5**:226–27
as necessary evil once begun,
7:215–16
negative effects, **5**:219–20
Pigovian method, **4**:120–21
in private markets, **1**:354–55
public education, **1**:269–70
public transportation, **4**:356
taxes vs., **4**:155
transitional-gains trap and, **5**:67–69
See also agricultural subsidies; cartels;
income redistribution; transfers
Suh, John H., **7**:*323n. 3*
Summers, Robert, **10**:*381n. 4*
Summers-Heston data, **10**:381, 395
Sumner, William Graham, **4**:18
superiors
arts of persuasion, **6**:138–39
individual's way of dealing with,
6:403–4
influence over inferiors, **6**:171
multiple, **6**:109
personal assistants to, **6**:84, 321–22
relationships with inferiors,
6:285–87
as slave masters, **6**:7

subordinates' knowledge of desires
of, **6**:362
uses for committees, **6**:305–8,
310–11
See also sovereigns; supervisors
supermarket examples, **6**:355–56,
358, 359
superorganisms, **10**:130
supervision
allocation of time to, **6**:357–65
areas where relatively easy,
6:398–99
by committee, **6**:307–8
complaints from public, **6**:362
control issues, **6**:265–67
cost accounting for, **6**:210–16
crisscross system of, **6**:228–31,
316–20
by despots, **6**:322
ease of high vs. low level, **6**:221
judging subordinates by results,
6:205–9, 402
law of large numbers in, **6**:221–22
within military, **6**:321–23
optimal efficiency, **6**:387–88
of physical labor, **6**:102
by pressuring lower-level officials,
6:325–26
rewards vs. punishments in, **6**:400–
401
of routine tasks, **6**:321
by stockholders, **6**:343–45
structures with minimal need for,
6:395
techniques to help relax control,
6:365–67, 369–74
See also coordination of tasks; incentives to subordinates; performance evaluation; promotions
within organizations
supervisors
assigning tasks to subordinates,
6:391–99
central problem for most, **6**:191

criteria for judging subordinates,
6:199–205
decision about what to supervise,
6:357–59, 370–71, 374,
387–88
efficiency sought from subordinates,
6:131–32
ideal, 6:132–33
ignorance of area supervised, 6:169,
213–14
limits on what can be done by,
6:169–70
need to relax control over subordinates, 6:353–59
time allocated to supervision,
6:357–65
See also managers; subordinates;
superiors
Supplemental Security Income (SSI),
7:125–26; 10:299–300
supply and demand, 10:19–22. *See*
also demand; markets; supply
curves
supply curves, 10:13–14
supremacy of law, 9:405–6
Supreme Court. *See* United States
Supreme Court
surrogate mothers, 10:54
survival of the "fit." *See* natural
selection
survival probability, 1:311
Sweden, 1:279, 409; 7:44
Swedish legal system, 9:183
Swigget, Harold, *The Power and the*
Prize, 6:70
Switzerland, 1:31, 279, 584–85
government in, 5:78; 6:236, 413;
8:130
income tax, 7:124
social welfare programs, 7:257
voting system, 4:446
symbiosis, 10:193
symmetric contract, 9:57
synergetics, 1:70

Syracusan government, 8:133
Syrian government, 8:302–3
Szasz, Thomas S., 9:127
Szucko, Julian J., 9:*361n. 50*

Taft, William Howard, 9:417
Taiwan government, 8:137
takeover bids. *See* corporate takeovers
takings power, 9:407–8
Tallyrand-Perigord, 6:291
Tamagna, F. M., 10:*309n. 5, 315n. 12*
tariffs, 7:322–24
abolishing of, 6:186–87
arguments for, 3:157–58
combined with excise tax,
1:172–73
desirability of, 5:211, 212, 213
in dictatorships, 5:123, 124
economists' position on, 1:591
effect on academic disciplines, 4:18
as externalities, 5:267
lobbying for, 5:307–10
regulation of domestic industries vs.,
7:329
rent seeking and, 5:183
unemployment and, 5:124
welfare costs, 1:169–72
Tarr, David G., 10:*105n. 15*
tasks in hierarchies
assignment of, for increasing control,
6:391–99
complexity and efficiency, 6:197
deciding which to monitor,
6:357–65
limitations on, 6:134–36, 168–75
optimal span of control, 6:316
simple vs. complex, 6:190
supervision of routine, 6:321
See also coordination of tasks
tastes, 1:12, 14
impact of communication on satisfaction of, 1:83
See also preferences
Tax, Sol, 10:*147n. 9*

taxation as part of voting, **1**:137, 141–45
  Clarke tax, **1**:135–36
  composite tax, **1**:143
  excess revenues from, **1**:143, 145
  Lindahl taxes, **1**:159, 161
tax courts, **9**:149–50. *See also* income tax law
taxes
  on advertising, **5**:4–5
  beneficiaries of, **1**:268
  benefit principle in, **2**:277–80
  benefits from Social Security system vs., **7**:288–90
  coercion behind payment of, **8**:8, 11
  collectivization and, **1**:375–77
  cutting vs. increasing, **5**:175, 178
  earmarked, **10**:291
  evasion, **9**:137, 149–50
  excess burden from, **1**:358, 364–65; **4**:108–9
  excise, **5**:196–97
  exempting an individual from, **9**:230–31
  as externalities, **5**:269
  externalities and, **4**:99, 103–4, 106–7
  individual receipts compared with payments, **7**:16
  lobbying and, **1**:240
  maximization of revenue from, **8**:24
  optimal types of, **5**:179–82
  on pensions, **10**:296–97
  on people opting out of Social Security, **10**:297
  for police services, **10**:66–67
  quotas vs., **10**:101
  redistribution, **6**:272
  relation with benefits, **4**:117–18
  relation with savings, **10**:289
  in rent-seeking societies, **5**:114
  revenue from government-created monopoly vs., **5**:126–27
  social benefits/losses to payers, **1**:453
  Social Security system, **5**:266–67; **7**:286–87
  as sources of inefficiency, **1**:292–93
  special-interest subsidies vs., **1**:219–20
  subsidies vs., **4**:109, 155
  super tax, **4**:441
  tax farmers in France, **5**:127
  tax farming, **6**:282
  transfers to and from individuals and, **7**:24
  user taxes, **5**:180
  on wealth, **1**:253–54, 286–87
  See also income tax in United States; indirect taxes; inheritance taxes; penalty taxes; poll taxes; tax evasion; tax loopholes; tax reform; use taxes
tax evasion, **1**:441, 450–55
taxi company monopolies, **4**:113; **5**:67
taxi medallions example, **1**:213–15
taxing masters, **9**:314
tax loopholes, **5**:172–76
  closing, **5**:177
  desirable, **5**:174
  pork-barreling vs., **5**:175, 178
  for special-interest groups, **5**:177
taxonomy. *See* classification systems
tax reform, **1**:195–96
  definition, **5**:172
  lobbying and, **5**:174–76
  to reduce rent seeking, **5**:181–82
  special-interest groups and, **5**:176–77
tax-sheltered investments, **7**:124–25
Taylor, General Maxwell Davenport, **6**:403
Taylor, M. J., **4**:*284n. 2, 288n. 8*
teachers as political force, **7**:299
teams, theory of, **2**:10

technical progress. *See* inventions
technological advances, **7**:358
technological innovation
  in legal systems, **9**:307
  monopolies and, **9**:247–48
technology
  as cause of positive externalities,
    4:77
  choice of government vs. market
    solution and, **4**:50–51
  contracts as example of, **4**:91
  effect of changes in, on externalities,
    4:179, 180–81
  effect on collective decision-making,
    4:56, 59–60
  effect on optimum size of govern-
    ment, **4**:58
  impact of lobbying on, **5**:220–21,
    222–25, 228–30
  injury from introduction of new,
    8:28
  that eliminates externalities, **4**:113
  of voting, **4**:125–26
  See also computers; economies of
    scale
television. *See* cable television industry
television broadcasting regulation,
  4:180–81
Tella, Alfred, **7**:*107n. 19*
Tella, Dorothy, **7**:*107n. 19*
Teller, Edward, **3**:*163n. 2*
Temperley, Arnold, **8**:*205n. 21*
Temperley, H. W. V., **8**:*122n. 50*
temper loss, rationality of, **1**:310–11
tenure
  of academics, **6**:122–23, 220n. 3;
    9:394–95; **10**:111
  for judges, **9**:325
  for scientific researchers, **3**:171,
    172–75, 176–78
ten-voter rule, **4**:4
terminology changes and information
  retrieval, **3**:81–82

termites, **1**:559; **10**:225–31
  colonies, **10**:229
  difference from human beings,
    6:328
  differences from ants, **10**:226–28,
    229–30
  division of labor, **10**:230–31,
    256–57
  economic theory about, **6**:327–28
  environmental coordination, **10**:256
  information transfer among, **10**:257
  nests, **10**:228–29
  preferences, **10**:250–52, 253
  protozoa and, **1**:571, 572
  reaction to attacks, **10**:254
  reproduction, **10**:254–57
  responses to environmental factors,
    10:129–31
  similarities with ant social structure,
    10:230–31
  social organization, **10**:126–28
  swarming, **10**:222–23
  symbiosis with other species,
    10:193
  trade by, **6**:334n. 14
  See also ants; bees
terms of trade, **2**:96–97
territoriality, **1**:556. *See also* dominance
territories
  defense of, **10**:120–23
  economic model of, **10**:155–58
  of insects, **10**:120
  migrating, **10**:126
  of plants and animals, **10**:119
  shape of, **10**:157
  territoriality among species,
    10:165–66
testamentary disposition, **9**:130, 132
testimony
  of accused, **9**:357
  dishonest, **9**:429
  oral, **9**:44, 74–75

testimony (*continued*)
  written, **9**:74–75
  See also expert witnesses
"tests of truth," **3**:40
test subjects, 33. *See also* human subjects
Texas Railroad Commission, **5**:215,
  216, 248
Thailand government, **8**:123, 137,
  138–39
Thatcher, Margaret, **4**:207
theft
  incentives to engage in, **8**:13–14
  as involuntary transfer, **1**:187
  law enforcement, **9**:189–200, 201–3
  legalization of, **9**:268–69
  preference for, **9**:32
  prevention, **8**:14–21
  welfare costs, **1**:174–77, 178, 182,
    192–93
  See also burglary; robbery
Theodoracopulos, Taki, **8**:*223n. 67*
theoretical research. *See* pure research
theoretical vs. empirical science, **3**:49
theories, **9**:15
  of business behavior, **3**:36, 37
  theory of, **3**:37, 100
  See also scientific theories
"Théories de L'Interêt Général et
  La Problème Logique de
  L'Agregation, Les" (Guilbaud),
  4:*280n. 2*
theory approximation, use in applied research, **3**:42
theory of bureaucracy, **1**:21–24
Theory of Committees and Elections, The
  (Black), **1**:105; **2**:8, 127, 314–
  15, 318n. 9, 319–20; **4**:220
theory of constitutions, **1**:17; **2**:6–7,
  60–80, 296–97; **5**:300; **6**:89
  suggested reforms, **1**:24–26
  See also constitutions
theory of evolution, **3**:100
Theory of Justice, A (Rawls), **7**:47

Theory of Moral Sentiments, The
  (Smith), **1**:8
Theory of Political Coalitions, The
  (Riker), **4**:307–8
theory of political obligation, **6**:140n. 1
theory of political process, **6**:140n. 1
theory of relativity. *See* general theory
  of relativity, testability of
theory of the firm, **6**:5
thinking. *See* reasoning
think tanks, **4**:28; **5**:310
30 percent rule, **4**:218
Thomas, Alfred B., **7**:*39n. 28*
Thomas, Clarence, **9**:415
Thomas, Hugh, **8**:*296n. 8*
Thomas, Robert Paul, **8**:*36n. 17,
  37n. 18*
Thomas Jefferson Center for Political
  Economy and Social Philosophy, **4**:13
Thompson, Earl, **1**:*135n. 7*;
  9:*373n. 12*
Thomson, George, **3**:*10n. 2*
Thorndike, Lynn, **8**:*37n. 19*
three-party political systems
  model for, **4**:310–17
  voting in, **4**:187, 189–91
Thurow, Lester, **7**:*29n. 9, 33n. 21*, 52,
  221n. 2
Thursby, Vincent, **2**:xxv
Tideman, T. Nicolaus, **1**:*110n. 12,
  135n. 9, 153n. 2, 424n. 10*;
  4:*447n. 10*; **5**:*290n. 11*;
  7:*71n. 1, 142n. 2, 145n. 7,
  182n. 3, 195n. 16, 200n. 1,
  224n. 4*
  mathematical assistance to Tullock,
    1:236
Tiebout, Charles M., **2**:*105n. 5*
Tiffany, Lawrence P., **9**:*176n. 4*
Tito, Marshal, **6**:254, 299n. 7; **8**:50
Tittle, Charles R., **9**:*258n. 16*;
  10:*81n. 14*

tobacco industry lobby, **4**:355
tobacco taxes, **5**:196–200
Tobin-Mundell hypotheses, **10**:382–83, 387
Tocqueville, Alexis de, **8**:*210n. 37*
Tokagawa of Japan, **7**:335–36
Tolkien, J. R. R., **8**:*245n. 34*
toll highways, **1**:203, 204
Tollison, Robert D., **4**:*172n. 3, 443n. 8*; **5**:*32n. 36, 33n. 38, 53n. 63, 62n. 76, 64nn. 81, 82, 69n. 88, 77n. 101, 95n. 2, 122n. 1, 126n. 5, 162n. 4, 164nn. 6, 7, 165n. 8, 189n. 13, 214n. 1, 218nn. 11, 12, 221n. 15, 224n. 20, 226n. 24, 237n. 3, 241n. 2*; **6**:*375n. 1*; **7**:*174n. 4, 214n. 13*; **8**:*57n. 19, 154n. 21*; **9**:*411nn. 1, 3, 418n. 12*; **10**:*412n. 4*
 on efficient rent seeking, **5**:88, 90–92
 "Gordon Tullock: Creative Maverick of Public Choice," **5**:*19n. 13*
 Political Economy of Rent-Seeking, The, **5**:28
 Toward a Theory of the Rent-Seeking Society, **5**:28
 work on mercantilism, **5**:300
Tolstoy, Leo, **6**:*284*
Tolstoy, Nikolai, **8**:*50n. 8, 59n. 22, 69nn. 22, 23, 215n. 50*
Tombigbee Canal, **7**:236
tort, **9**:409. *See also* law of torts
torture, **8**:215–16
totalitarian governments, **8**:40–41
Toulmin, Stephen, **3**:*34n. 4*
Toward a Mathematics of Politics (Tullock), **4**:328
Toward a Theory of the Rent Seeking Society (Buchanan, Tollison, and Tullock), **5**:28
town meetings, **4**:182

Townsend, Peter, **7**:*54n. 13, 67n. 22*
Townsend plan, **7**:69
trade
 agreements, **8**:333n. 12
 ethics and, **2**:255–57
 in nonhuman societies, **10**:262
 terms, **2**:96–97
 whether mutually profitable, **8**:3
trading, **1**:308–13; **5**:261
trading of votes. *See* logrolling; vote trading
traffic congestion example, **1**:419; **4**:102–4
traffic courts, **9**:145–46, 173
 bias of, **9**:290
Tragic Choices (Calabresi and Bobbitt), **7**:97–99, 100–101, 339, 340–42, 346–51
training of scientists. *See* education of scientists
transaction model (Coase), **6**:244
transactions costs, **2**:85–86
 of bargaining, **9**:396
 bargaining without, **9**:381
 of efficient legal remedies, **9**:407
 existence of hierarchical organizations and, **6**:258–60
 five theories of, **6**:244–45
 government intervention to reduce, **9**:114–16, 382
 from monopoly-monopsony relations, **6**:269
transfers
 accidental, **7**:33–35
 actually observed in democracies, **7**:6
 built into Social Security system, **7**:60–62
 in cash, to well-off people, **5**:245–46
 for charitable giving, **7**:358–62
 charitable giving vs., **7**:65–66, 90–95
 coalitions involved with, **7**:189–91

transfers (*continued*)
　by competitive vs. negotiated bids,
　　1:292
　through compulsory insurance,
　　7:36–37
　conflict about, **8**:9
　connotation, **8**:7
　controlling consumption with,
　　7:136–42
　to correct monopoly resource mis-
　　allocation, **5**:12
　costs, **1**:173; **5**:22–25, 53; **7**:160–
　　65, 211, 338
　costs from possibility of, **1**:191–93
　decision making about, **7**:78
　definition, **8**:8
　desirable or undesirable, **8**:10
　from developed to poorer nations,
　　1:280–81, 282–83, 284
　driven by mixed motives, **7**:38
　effect of competition for, **1**:204,
　　206, 208–11
　effect on government, **1**:304–5
　effect on government subsidies, **5**:25
　effect on income within groups,
　　1:283 84
　effect on rent seeking, **5**:31
　efficiency, **7**:184–87, 194–97
　examples, **8**:8–9
　governmental budgets for, **1**:304
　via government regulation, **7**:19,
　　35–36, 329–30
　government role in, **7**:243–44
　for higher education, **7**:299, 301
　highly inefficient, **1**:289–90
　impact of government size on, **7**:6,
　　8–10
　importance of government motives,
　　7:39
　importance of self-interest, **7**:59–64
　individual taxes and, **7**:24
　inefficient, **8**:3
　information about, **7**:69, 240–43,
　　368

via in-kind aid, **7**:99–100, 193,
　209, 348
via in-kind aid less than market
　value, **7**:133n. 1
internal, **7**:181
international, **7**:8–9
involuntary, **1**:187–88
involving no public goods, **7**:319–
　20, 338
local government, **7**:122–23
local vs. national government,
　7:126–28
methods of, **1**:206–7
within the middle class, **1**:268–71;
　5:145–46
monopoly privileges vs., **1**:219
motives, **7**:4–6
motives of self-interest for, **7**:59–64,
　360, 362
motives other than self-interest for,
　7:64–68, 156–58
need for deception about, **1**:289–90
negative, **7**:145
nonexploitative, **8**:171
of oil revenues from cartels, **5**:136–
　42, 145
to older poor people, **7**:125–26
Pareto optimality in charitable,
　7:138
parties involved in, **9**:411
political costs, **1**:194–98
politician's view of, **1**:274
from poor people, **1**:386–87;
　7:159–60, 165–67
to poor people, **7**:7–8, 12, 23–24,
　64, 128–32, 240–43, 244
to poor people in United States vs.
　abroad, **7**:226–27
to poor people who vote on transfer,
　7:15–18, 217–20, 222–23,
　227–29
to poor who do not vote on transfer,
　7:12–15, 83, 240
preferences, **7**:9–10, 14

problems, **7**:93–96
progressive, **7**:61–62
rationale for inefficient, **5**:144–48
relation with government
    inefficiency, **7**:202
relation with lobbying, **5**:23
relation with pork-barreling,
    7:203–4
research about, **7**:368
from rich people, **7**:123–25,
    164–65
from rich to poor, **1**:197, 263–64
self-canceling, within middle class,
    5:24
social costs, **1**:177
social dilemma involved in, **8**:368
by special-interest groups, **1**:327–
    28; **4**:229
among states, **7**:359–60
supply and demand, **9**:411
of technologically private goods,
    1:582
types, **7**:204
among U.S. taxpayer groups,
    1:197–98, 267
for universal-aid programs, **7**:156,
    165–67
for universal public education,
    7:297–99
using coercion for, **7**:82
using demand-revealing process for,
    7:81–85, 224–25
using direct cash payment for,
    7:209–10
using Lindahl taxes for, **7**:71–76, 82
utility from, **7**:181
voting process for, **7**:6, 80
from wealthy to poor, **5**:24
welfare costs, **1**:180–91
to the well-to-do, **5**:224, 225
who receives, **9**:380–81
willfully ignorant decisions about,
    1:282
See also administrative transfers;

charitable giving; foreign-aid
    programs; horizontal transfers;
    income redistribution; subsi-
    dies; taxes; welfare recipients;
    welfare state; welfare transfers
    to poor; well-intentioned
    Machiavellianism
transfers within middle class
    examples of, **7**:125
    externalities in, **7**:7
    student financial aid, **7**:60
    See also administrative transfers;
        horizontal transfers
transitional gains
    from higher education, **5**:142–44
    from oil, **5**:136–42
transitional-gains trap, **1**:213–14;
    5:66–69
    examples, **1**:217–19
    reasons for, **1**:219–20
    recommendations, **1**:221
    Social Security system as, **7**:272
transitive nature of preference order-
    ings. *See* transitivity
transitivity, **1**:62
    without indifference, **1**:64–65
    indifference and, **1**:64n. 8, 65–67
    in market choices, **2**:32
    proof of, **1**:64
Trans-Jordan, **8**:142
treason, **8**:300, 302
treaties
    cheating under, **8**:337–38
    decision whether to cheat on,
        8:338–43
    detecting cheating on, **8**:345
    enforcement, **8**:344–48
    1922 naval, **8**:335–36
    nondisarmament, and war making,
        8:332–33
    secrecy and cheating on, **8**:349–53
    with "simultaneous performance,"
        8:345
    See also agreements; disarmament

Trebilock, M. J., **9**:*446n. 15*

Trevelyan, G. M., **8**:*75n. 37, 202n. 6*

Trevirannus, G. R., **8**:*127–28n. 71*

trial lawyers, **9**:422

trials

allowing bias in, **9**:264

choosing trier of facts for, **9**:180

enforcement of rulings, **1**:510

falsely charged defendants, **1**:461–62, 517

hearsay rule, **1**:518–19

information used in, **9**:73–79

likelihood of criminal, **9**:157–58

one-sided, **1**:500–501, 502–3, 505

outcomes of, **1**:500–502

shortening, **9**:90

Simpson trial, **1**:523, 532

votes needed for conviction, **1**:527

See also bench trials; courts; evidence of crime; illegal activities; prosecutors; verdicts

Trials on Trial (Tullock), **1**:497n. 3; **9**:265n. 5, 339, 343n. 14, 393

tribal societies, **10**:166, 167–68

trickle-down prosperity, **4**:*134n. 18*

trip insurance, **9**:112–16

Triver's reciprocal altruism, **1**:559n. 1

Trucial States (United Arab Emirates), **5**:140

trucking. *See* political negotiation

Trujillo, Rafael, **5**:127–28

Truman, David B., **2**:xvi, *9n. 15, 12n. 2, 21–22n. 9, 258n. 2,* 269–70

trusts for avoiding inheritance taxes, **1**:260n. 1

"truth" of scientific theories, **3**:34–38

as definition of science, **3**:48

logical problems raised by, **3**:38–39

"tests of truth," **3**:40

about the universe, **3**:39–40

See also faking of research results; hypothesis testing; reality

"truth" of social science theories, **3**:157

truth-telling, **1**:184–85

juries as arbitrar of, **1**:523

See also deception; lying

Trythall, John, **8**:*296n. 7*

Tucson, Arizona

Air Pollution Reduction Program, **5**:222–23

Central Arizona Project (CAP), **5**:250, 254–55, 277

Tullock, Gordon, career

Biographical Note, **1**:605–9

Buchanan's support, **1**:*541n. 2,* 607, 608; **2**:xix; **3**:xx

contributions to administrative theory, **6**:6

difficulty in publishing articles, **5**:19–20, 24

editorial experiences, **1**:36–47

education in economics, **9**:4

effect on his writings, **8**:304n. 21; **10**:307n. 1

intellectual influences on, **3**:xix–xx

invention of income insurance motive, **7**:67n. 23

Luddite attack on, **1**:6n. 3

Malthusian aspiration of, **1**:4

test for secret Communists, **8**:88

Tideman's mathematical assistance to, **1**:236

time spent in Far East, **5**:27

Tullock, Gordon, writings, **2**:*246–47n. 3*

"Altruism, Malice, and Public Goods," **10**:*115n. 1, 134n. 4, 145n. 6*

"Altruism, Malice, and Public Goods: A Reply to Frech," **10**:*115n. 1, 145n. 6*

"Altruism, Malice, and Public Goods: Does Altruism Pay?," **10**:*145n. 6*

"Another Part of the Swamp,"
5:*64n. 82*; 10:*440n. 2*
articles on biology, 10:141n. 2
Autocracy, 5:*29nn. 30, 31,* 132n. 11;
6:*350n. 17*; 8:*143n. 4*
"Avoiding Difficult Decisions,"
1:*281n. 10*; 7:97n. 10
"Back to the Bog," 5:*64n. 82, 65n. 84*
"Biological Externalities,"
10:*115n. 1, 133n. 1*
Calculus of Consent, The, 1:25, 108–
12, 264; 2:xiv, xxiii, xxiv, 8;
4:220, 230–31; 5:275,
299–300; 6:89–90; 7:38,
67n. 23, 231; 9:13; 10:287,
291n. 3
Calculus of Consent, The, cited,
1:*125n. 3, 129n. 6, 288n. 21,*
354n. 5, 388n. 1; 3:*73n. 22*;
4:*3n. 1, 10n. 8, 13n. 3, 56n. 6,*
65n. 11, 115n. 1, 119n. 5,
183n. 15, 210n. 31, 230n. 7,
249n. 5, 276n. 3, 347n. 1,
367n. 3, 392n. 6; 5:*33n. 37,*
46n. 48, 78n. 102, 176n. 2,
238n. 6, 290nn. 12, 13;
7:*78n. 2, 191n. 12, 197n. 19,*
236n. 13; 9:*11n. 1, 17n. 2*
"Charity of the Uncharitable, The,"
5:*226n. 24*; 7:*249n. 1,*
308n. 18, 360
"Coalitions under Demand Revealing," 7:*195n. 16*
"Coal Tit as a Careful Shopper,
The," 1:*541n. 1, 554n. 2*;
10:*108n. 21, 115n. 1, 133n. 1*
comment on "Asymmetry between
Bribes and Charges," 4:*90n. 3,*
98n. 1, 109n. 10
comment on Corcoran, "Long-Run
Equilibrium," 5:*88n. 1*
comment on Marglin's "The Social
Rate of Discount and the

Optimal Rate of Investment,"
7:*7n. 6*
comment on Riker-Brams article,
4:*347n. 2*
comment on "The Limits of Consensual Decision," 4:349n. 5
"Comment on 'The Physiological
Causes of the Evolution of Man
from Apes'," 10:*115n. 1*
"Competing for Aid," 5:25, *66n. 86*;
7:*359n. 2*
"Competing Monies," 10:*367n. 2*
"Computer Simulation of a Small
Voting System," 4:*320n. 2*
"Constitutional Mythology,"
5:*81n. 104*
contents of *Selected Works,* 1:611–21
Coordination without Command,
1:*570n. 11*; 10:*130n. 8, 145n. 7*
"Cost of Transfers, The," 1:*149n. 1*;
5:*22nn. 21, 22*
"Court Errors," 5:186; 9:*442nn. 4, 6*
"Courts as Legislatures," 1:*482n. 3*
"'Dead Hand' of Monopoly, The,"
1:*212n. 2*
"Defending the Napoleonic Code
over the Common Law,"
9:*428n. 40, 451n. 2*
"Demand Revealing Process as a Wel-
fare Indicator, The," 7:*89n. 1*
"Demand-Revealing Process, Coali-
tions, and Public Goods," 4:366
"Different Approach to the Repeated
Prisoner's Dilemma, A,"
8:*340n. 4*; 10:*429n. 1*
"Dynamic Hypothesis on Bureau-
cracy," 1:*303n. 6*
"Economic Approach to Crime, An,"
9:*137n. 1, 254n. 2*
Economics of Charity, The, 4:*173n. 4*
Economics of Income Redistribution,
The, 7:61n. 16, 63n. 18, 118,
160, 161

Tullock, Gordon, writings (*continued*)
*Economics of Income Redistribution,
The*, cited, **1**:*342n. 6*;
5:*59n. 72, 179n. 3*; **7**:*127n. 15,
148n. 9*; **8**:*216n. 52*
"Economics of Lying, The,"
9:*205n. 1*
"Economics of Primitive Societies,"
10:*189n. 8*
Economics of Redistribution, The,
9:*380n. 3*
*Economics of Special Privilege and Rent
Seeking, The*, **4**:24; **5**:*35n. 40,
42n. 44, 65n. 83*, 75, 236;
6:*375n. 1*
"Economics of the Media, The,"
7:*335n. 13*
"Economic Theory of Military Tactics, An," **10**:*425n. 2*
"Efficient Rent Seeking," **5**:95–100,
221, 231, 250–51, 297
"Efficient Rent Seeking," cited,
1:*238n. 3, 241n. 5*; **5**:*64nn. 81,
82, 65n. 84, 88n. 1, 90n. 5,
251n. 13*; **9**:*297n. 3*
"Efficient Rent Seeking Revisited,"
5:*65n. 83*, 85–87
"Elaborations on a Theme by Fried-
man," **7**:*90n. 3*, 91n. 5
Entrepreneurial Politics, **1**:*108n. 11*;
4:*121n. 7, 249n. 5*; **6**:90
"Excess Benefit," **4**:*109n. 9*; **9**:61
Explorations in the Theory of Anarchy,
1:*325n. 4*
"Externalities and Government,"
5:262, *268n. 2*
"Federalism: Problems of Scale,"
4:*117n. 3*; **7**:*195n. 17*
"Future Directions for Rent-Seeking
Research," **5**:*64n. 82*
"Games and Preference," **5**:*97n. 7*
"General Irrelevance of the General
Impossibility Theorem, The,"

1:*20n. 4, 106n. 2*; **4**:*283n. 1,
285n. 5, 304n. 2*
"Generalization of the General
Impossibility Theorem, A,"
5:*131n. 9*
General Theory of Politics, A,
2:325n. 23
on Harberger triangles, **4**:11–14
"Hawks, Doves and Free Riders,"
5:*99n. 9*
"Hyperinflation in China, 1937–49,"
10:*347n. 11*
"Inflazione Prolongata," **10**:*365n. 6,
369n. 5*
"Information without Profit," **1**:36;
5:*208n. 8*; **7**:*4n. 2, 69n. 25*,
101n. 15
"Inheritance Justified," **1**:*287n. 18*
"Inheritance Rejustified: Reply,"
1:*287n. 20*
"Intellectual Property," **5**:*4n. 2*
"Judicial Errors and a Proposal for
Reform," **1**:*495n. 1, 513n. 9*;
9:*442n. 5*
Law and Morals, **1**:*174n. 10*
"Legal Heresy," **1**:*524n. 2*;
9:*423n. 29, 431n. 2, 434nn. 8,
11, 437n. 14, 439n. 16*
Logic of the Law, The, **1**:495n. 1,
497n. 3; **9**:268n. 13, 389, 393,
394
Logic of the Law, The, cited,
1:*323n. 2, 456n. 1, 466n. 2,
486n. 2, 509n. 1*; **5**:*170n. 11,
186n. 3, 193n. 17*; **8**:*17n. 2*;
9:*263n. 2, 284n. 5, 291n. 2,
306n. 16*, 343n. 14, *365n. 5,
377n. 17, 381n. 5, 422n. 26,
425n. 33, 429n. 41, 430n. 42*
logrolling model, **4**:319, 327
"Measure of the Importance of Cyclical Majorities, A," **1**:*90n. 2*;
4:*280n. 1, 284nn. 3, 4, 291n. 10*

methodology used by, **6**:4, 9, 17–18, 241–42

methods of citation in footnotes, **3**:xx; **7**:7

model of competing currencies, **10**:360

"Model of Social Interaction, A," **8**:*167n. 2*

modification of welfare economics, **9**:11–14

"Mosquito Abatement," **6**:*412n. 11*

"Negligence Again," **9**:*385n. 14*

"New and Superior Process for Making Social Choices, A," **1**:*110n. 12, 153n. 2*; **4**:*366n. 2, 447n. 10*; **5**:*290n. 11*; **7**:*71n. 1, 142n. 2, 145n. 7, 182n. 3, 195n. 16, 200n. 1, 224n. 4*

New Federalist, The, **4**:*343n. 9*

"On the Adaptive Significance of Territoriality," **10**:*115n. 1, 155n. 2*

"On the Desirable Degree of Detail in the Law," **9**:*423n. 28*

"On the Efficient Organization of Trials," **1**:*223n. 2*; **4**:*39–40n. 12*; **9**:*291n. 1*

"Optimal Poll Taxes," **10**:*285nn. 1–3*

Organization of Inquiry, The, **1**:37; **5**:20

Organization of Inquiry, The, cited, **1**:*37n.1, 41n. 2*; **4**:*267n. 8*; **5**:*4n. 2, 14n. 6, 21nn. 18, 20*; **6**:*327n. 1*; **9**:*124n. 1*; **10**:*111n. 1*

"Paper Money—A Cycle in Cathay," **10**:*365n. 6, 369n. 5*

"Paradox of Revolution, The," **1**:*341*, 344; **8**:*174n. 1*

Political Economy of Rent-Seeking, The, **5**:28, *29n. 32, 64n. 81, 214n. 1, 224n. 20*; **6**:*375n. 1*

Politics of Bureaucracy, The, **4**:220; **6**:243, 245, 263

Politics of Bureaucracy, The, cited, **1**:*21n. 5, 299n. 2, 437n. 12*; **4**:*12n. 1, 306n. 3, 307nn. 4, 5, 7*; **5**:*54n. 68*; **8**:*40n. 34, 71n. 30*; **9**:*437n. 13*

"Polluters' Profits and Political Response," **1**:*425n. 1*

"Practical Problems and Practical Solutions," **5**:*290n. 11*

Private Wants, Public Means, **1**:*325n. 5*; **4**:*220*; **8**:*28n. 3*; **9**:*5, 381n. 4*

"Problems of Majority Voting," **4**:6; **5**:249, 271; **7**:231

"Problems of Majority Voting," cited, **2**:*127n. 1*; **4**:*3n. 2, 59n. 8*; **5**:*77n. 100, 176n. 2, 206n. 3, 249n. 10, 255n. 4*; **7**:*366n. 6*

"Public and Private Interaction under Reciprocal Externality," **1**:*177n. 13*; **4**:107

"Public Decisions as Public Goods," **1**:*476n. 6*; **4**:*39–40n. 12*; **9**:*302n. 7*

"Purchase of Politicians, The," **5**:300

"Rents and Rent-Seeking," **5**:*64n. 82, 220n. 14*

Rent-Seeking, **9**:*411nn. 2, 4*

"Rent-Seeking and the Law," **9**:*423nn. 27, 30*

"Reply to McChesney, and Ordover and Weitzman, **9**:*303n. 9*

"Revealing the Demand for Transfers," **1**:*154n. 4, 155n. 5, 160n. 10*; **7**:*89n. 1*

"Rhetoric and Reality of Redistribution, The," **7**:*108n. 21*

"Roots of Order, The," **8**:*129n. 75*

"Simple Algebraic Logrolling Model, A," **1**:*107n. 8, 264n. 10*

Social Dilemma, The, **1**:341

Tullock, Gordon, writings (*continued*)
  Social Dilemma, The, cited,
      1:*224n. 3, 344n. 11, 469n. 3;*
      8:*87–88n. 13, 105n. 71,*
      140n. 101, 214n. 49
  "Social Rate of Discount and the
      Optimal Rate of Investment:
      Comment, The," **1**:*248n. 2*
  "Sociobiology and Economics,"
      1:*556n. 7*
  "Switching in General Predators,"
      10:*109n. 23, 115n. 1, 133n. 1*
  "Switching in General Predators:
      Comment," **1**:*537n. 1, 541n. 1*
  "Theory of Government Punish-
      ments and Rewards, A,"
      1:*174n. 10*
  Toward a Mathematics of Politics,
      4:328
  Toward a Mathematics of Politics,
      cited, **1**:*17n. 3, 106n. 4,*
      112n. 17, 220nn. 9, 10, 392n. 5;
      4:*56n. 6, 74n. 6, 127n. 13,*
      129n. 15, 285n. 5, 293n. 2,
      443n. 6; **5**:*14n. 5, 39n. 43,*
      44n. 47, 226n. 23; **7**:*290n. 17,*
      343n. 6; **9**:*17n. 2*
  Toward a Science of Politics, **4**:*304n. 3*
  *Toward a Theory of the Rent-Seeking
      Society,* **5**:*28, 86n. 1, 95n. 2,*
      189n. 13; **6**:*375n. 1;* **7**:*174n. 4,*
      214n. 13, 319n. 1; **10**:*412n. 4*
  "Transitional Gains Trap, The,"
      7:*272n. 13*
  Trials on Trial, **1**:497n. 3; **9**:339,
      343n. 14, 393
  Trials on Trial, cited, **1**:*507n. 14;*
      5:*170n. 11, 186n. 3;* **9**:*264n. 3,*
      265n. 5, 342n. 7, 353n. 32,
      354n. 36, 377n. 17, 386n. 17,
      388n. 21, 392n. 23, 422nn. 23,
      25, 426n. 35, 439n. 18, 442n. 7,
      444n. 9, 453nn. 3, 4; **10**:*412n. 4*

  Trials on Trial Reconsidered,
      9:*422n. 24*
  "Two Gurus," **7**:*33n. 22*
  "Two Kinds of Legal Efficiency,"
      9:*364n. 2, 383n. 10*
  "Utility, Strategy, and Social Deci-
      sion Rules, A Comment," **6**:89
  view of human nature, **6**:35
  view of large hierarchies, **6**:9–10
  voting method for electing represen-
      tatives, **4**:382–83
  "Welfare Costs of Tariffs, Monopo-
      lies, and Theft, The," **5**:17–22,
      85, 221, 241, 296
  "Welfare Costs of Tariffs, Monopo-
      lies, and Theft, The," cited,
      1:*237n. 2;* **5**:*11n. 1, 22n. 21,*
      232n. 2, 244n. 4, 253n. 2,
      285n. 8; **6**:*375n. 1, 376n. 2;*
      9:*189n. 2, 254n. 2, 382n. 8,*
      411n. 4; **10**:*79n. 9*
  "What's Wrong with Editing,"
      1:*41n. 2*
  "Where Is the Rectangle?," **5**:252
  "Why Did the Industrial Revolution
      Occur in England?," **8**:*135m. 01*
  "Why So Much Stability," **5**:271;
      7:*191n. 11, 236n. 13;* **8**:294
  See also *Papers on Non-Market
      Decision Making*
Tullock Economic Development Plan,
      5:222–23
Tullock paradox, **5**:252
Tullock rectangle
  approximate nature of, **5**:297
  costs that exceed, **5**:252, 298
  empirical studies using, **5**:74
  Harberger interpretation of,
      5:18–19
  impact of subsidies on, **5**:254–58
  initial reactions to, **5**:286–87
  major way it appears in economy,
      5:249

Tulsa Oklahoma Ship Canal, **5**:250; **7**:203, 236

Tupamaros, **8**:197–99

Turbek, David M., **9**:*341n. 5*

Turkey, economic growth, **10**:389

Turkish immigrants, **1**:279

Turner, J. D., **10**:*109n. 24*

Turner, Paul, **8**:*105n. 68*

Turvey, Ralph, **1**:*349n. 1*

Twitchett, Denis, **8**:*89–90n. 19*

two-party political systems, **4**:187–89
  Anthony Downs's defense of, **4**:388–90
  disadvantages, **4**:391
  pressure toward, **6**:105–6
  single-member district model for, **4**:386–87
  United States, **4**:430–31

two-species ecology example, **1**:542–47

two-thirds majority vote. *See* reinforced majorities

UAW (United Auto Workers), **5**:228, 241

Udagawa, Akihito, **4**:16

Udall, Morris, **5**:251

Ulen, T., **9**:*407nn. 10, 13, 409n. 14, 441nn. 1–3*

ultimate sovereigns, **6**:64–65
  decision making by, **6**:159

unanimity, **2**:81–92
  bargaining costs and, **2**:57, 65–66
  as benchmark, **2**:6, 91–92
  compensation and, **2**:86–87
  as criterion, **2**:13–14, 87n. 3
  political exchange and, **2**:238–41
  See also consensus

unanimity rule, **2**:xxiv, 81–92
  bargaining costs and, **2**:103
  vote trading and, **2**:263–64

uncertainty
  in collective choice, **2**:35–36

rules and, **2**:74
veil of, **2**:74–75

underdeveloped countries, governments of, **8**:136–39

underground economy. *See* black (underground) economy

understanding, Tullock's use of, **6**:17–18

unemployment
  inflation and, **7**:279
  Social Security system and, **7**:279, 281

unemployment programs
  by state governments, **7**:129–31
  vesting of benefits from, **7**:131

unicameral legislatures, **1**:32

unionization. *See* labor unions

United Arab Emirates (Trucial States), **5**:140

United Auto Workers (UAW), **5**:228, 241

United Kingdom, economic growth, **10**:389

United Nations, **5**:268; **8**:45
  developmental programs in South Korea, **10**:356
  misunderstanding of South Korean fiscal system, **10**:352

United States
  economic growth, **10**:389–91
  historical rent seeking in, **5**:168–69
  rent-seeking costs, **5**:114–15, 117–21
  welfare losses from monopoly, **5**:11–13

United States Congress, **4**:334–35
  committee investigations, **9**:352
  effect on industries/products lobbied for, **5**:158
  House of Representatives system for debate, **4**:393
  power over judiciary, **9**:416
  procedures used by, **9**:353

United States Congress (*continued*)
  slipping bills through, **6**:237
  televising proceedings of, **5**:80
  voters' attitudes toward, **5**:38
  See also congressmen; elected officials
United States government, **9**:416
  bureaucratic cliques, **6**:43
  checks and balances in, **4**:388;
    5:60, 81
  cold war with Russia, **8**:321
  compared with Swiss government,
    6:413–14
  foreign-aid programs, **5**:267–68
  foreign policy, **5**:205–7, 306;
    6:180; **8**:328–31, 358–59
  foreign policy in Middle East,
    7:172–73
  foreign policy toward South Korea,
    10:343, 349, 351
  founding fathers, **4**:122; **5**:81–82
  income tax, **1**:195–96, 450–55
  logrolling, **4**:207, 212–13
  national health service, **4**:40
  need for constitutional changes,
    7:367
  opening of records, **1**:409
  organizational structure, **6**:275–76
  political parties, **4**:420–21
  presidential elections, **1**:164–65;
    4:430–31, 432; **5**:276;
    8:149–50, 297
  role in world, **8**:44–45
  severity of rent seeking in, **6**:384
  southern states' voting block,
    5:273–74
  treatment of Mexicans, **1**:278
  Tullock's recommendations,
    6:235–38
  See also Constitution of United
    States; federalism
United States government agencies
  Civil Aeronautics Board (CAB),
    1:212, 293
  Civil Service Commission, **6**:384
    Department of Health and Human
      Services, **7**:60
    Department of State, **1**:23; **6**:145,
      179–81, 280–81
      organizational structure, **6**:228
      performance measures, **6**:361
      See also Foreign Service of United
        States
    Federal Communications Commis-
      sion (FCC), **1**:293
    Food and Drug Administration
      (FDA), **6**:419–20; **9**:283
    Interstate Commerce Commission
      (ICC), **1**:293
    Securities and Exchange Commis-
      sion (SEC), **9**:211
    Social Security Administration,
      1:255n. 8, 269, 583, 585 (*see
      also* pensions; Social Security
      system)
United States legal system
  common law system, **9**:441–48
  compared with British system,
    9:85–86
  criminal justice system, **9**:318
  history of attorneys in, **9**:420–23
  history of juries in, **9**:425–27
  law enforcement, **9**:173–74
  size of, **9**:356
  Tullock's critique, **9**:451–55
  See also adversary system of law
United States Supreme Court
  as arbitrator of U.S. Constitution,
    5:81
  assumption of infallibility of,
    1:484
  decisions, **7**:130
  defense of property rights, **9**:446
  effect on the Constitution, **1**:35
  errors, **1**:514
  inadequacies, **9**:445–46
  packing bench on, **9**:416
  relation with Constitution of United
    States, **9**:10

role in rent seeking, **5**:61–62
rule by single precedent, **9**:185–86
sample selection example, **1**:486–89
suggested reforms, **1**:489–90,
    491–93
unity sought by scientists, **3**:63
classification systems and, **3**:82
universal adult suffrage, **1**:33
universal-aid programs
cost effects of transfers for,
    7:162–65
empirical research about, **7**:256–60
gains to middle class from, **7**:251–53
implementation via transfers,
    7:165–67
means tests vs., **7**:245–47
transfers for, **7**:156
types, **7**:247–48
See also public education; social wel-
    fare programs; welfare state
universal health care
arguments for socialized medicine,
    7:310–11
in Canada, **7**:258
characteristics, **7**:165
effect on poor people, **7**:306–8
effects of transition to, **7**:165–67
efficiency characteristics, **7**:311
examples, **7**:248–51
geographical distribution of care
    under, **7**:317
getting bill through Congress for,
    7:259
likely consequences, **7**:317–18
models of, **7**:304–5, 309
payoffs according to income level,
    7:251–53
quality of medical treatment under,
    7:314–16
resource allocation, **7**:308–9
for U.S. vs. foreign countries,
    7:303–4
See also British National Health
    Service

universe
logical order of, **3**:45
reality of, **3**:40
universities. *See* higher education
    institutions
University of Chicago Jury Project,
    1:477, 511
University of South Carolina,
    5:142–43
unpopular ideas, **4**:255–56
unsecured loans, **9**:133
urban renewal projects, **1**:269; **4**:94,
    141–42
Uruguayan Tupamaros, **8**:197–99
user taxes, **5**:180
use taxes, **10**:291
utilitarianism, **9**:431
utility
charitable giving as maximization of
    total, **7**:29–31
economists' perception of, **7**:95–96
marginal, **10**:14
negative utility interdependence,
    1:287
Paretian taboo on comparison of,
    1:183
from transfers, **7**:181
See also utility maximization
"Utility, Strategy, and Social Decision
    Rules, A Comment" (Tullock),
    6:89
utility maximization, **10**:16, 20
by politicians, **6**:29
in politics, **2**:25
See also preferences
utility theory as forerunner, **2**:314

values and value judgments, **1**:547–48
Van Doren, Carl, **2**:*205–6n. 2*
Van Lawick–Goodall, Jane. *See*
    Goodall, Jane
van Winden, Frans, **4**:*270n. 1*
variables
in decision to join revolution, **8**:175

variables (*continued*)
  used in this book, **9**:58, 206,
    235–37
Varian, Hal R., **7**:*267n. 6*
"veil of ignorance," **7**:32–33, 56, 78
veil of uncertainty, **2**:74–75
Velikovsky, Immanuel, *Worlds in
    Collision*, **3**:129n. 32
Venice
  Doge of, **8**:130
  voting system, **4**:437–38
venture capitalists. *See* capital
    providers
verdicts
  by judges vs. jurors, **9**:438
  unanimous, **9**:427
Verdier, Thierry, **5**:95–100
verification of scientific discoveries,
    3:122–33
  relation to dissemination of scien-
    tific discoveries, **3**:133–34
  workability test, **3**:40, 41, 43
  See also hypothesis verification
Vernon, H. M., **8**:*129n. 73*
Versailles, **5**:300
vested pensions, **7**:126–27
vested unemployment benefits, **7**:131
veto power, **2**:xxii
  in government, **4**:354–55, 408
  of U.S. president, **5**:62
  "voting by veto," **4**:434
Vickrey, William S., **1**:*253n. 5*; **7**:7
Vickrey's incomplete compensation
    mechanism, **1**:133–34
victimless crimes, **9**:220–21
Vietnam, equality of poverty in,
    5:124–25
Vietnam war, **8**:328–29
Vining, Rutledge, **2**:76n. 7, 201,
    313n. 3, 330
violence
  connotation, **8**:7
  desirable or undesirable, **8**:10–11
  necessity of, **8**:26

  as rational behavior, **8**:6
  romantization of, **8**:163
  theft prevention and, **8**:15–21
  threat of, **8**:11, 18
violent crime, **9**:215–22; **10**:68, 69,
    70, 71, 72
  pain and pleasure from inflicted in-
    jury, **9**:31–32
  punishment for, **9**:200–201
  See also crimes of impulse; sexual
    assault
Virginia School of Political Economy,
    1:608
Virginia State Lottery Commission,
    5:96
Vishny, Robert W., **5**:*74–75n. 95*;
    6:*376n. 4*
Vissering, W., **10**:*326n. 11*, *337n. 19*,
    341n. 26
vocabulary shifts and information re-
    trieval, **3**:81–82
Voltaire, **5**:160; **8**:*210n. 38*
Voltz, Charles L., **9**:*98n. 1*, *100n. 5*
voluntarism, **2**:50–51
  in government, **4**:402–3
voluntary action, **2**:50–51
voluntary charity. *See* charitable
    giving
voluntary labor, **1**:409
voluntary transactions, **1**:187
von Hayen, Victor W., **8**:*237n. 21*
von Neumann, John, **1**:*111n. 14*;
    3:*128n. 30*; **4**:*323n. 5*
  importance, **10**:445–46
  mixed game strategy, **10**:443–44
  theory of games, **1**:229; **2**:145,
    157, 312–14
  theory of games with side payments
    allowed, **2**:178
  theory of voting coalitions, **7**:189
  Tullock's challenge of theory of
    games, **10**:438–43
von Ranke, Leopold, **8**:*94n. 29*,
    121n. 44

Voslenskii, Michael, **8**:*50n. 4, 59n. 23, 87n. 14, 95nn. 32, 34, 96nn. 35, 36, 39, 109–10n. 6*
vote buying. *See* logrolling
vote-maximization model, **4**:306–7
  three party system, **4**:310–17
  vote-maximization position, **4**:307, 311
voters, **1**:19–21
  accuracy of judgment, **4**:235
  aggregate demand by, **1**:141
  better-informed, **4**:227n. 2; **5**:210
  bribery of, **5**:262
  casually informed, **5**:44–45, 46
  choice among options, **6**:99
  compared with consumers, **7**:177
  compared with stockholders, **6**:348, 349
  compensation of injured, **4**:64
  conflict of interest of, **6**:350
  consent of, as a resource, **4**:8
  Consumers Digest for, **4**:269
  costs of becoming informed, **4**:230
  costs of specialization of voting by, **5**:299
  cost to vote, **4**:235
  decision making, **1**:72–73; **4**:247
  definitions, **4**:429
  desire to receive transfers, **1**:288–89
  difference from consumers, **1**:391–92; **6**:283–84
  discouraging of, **4**:130
  effect on politicians, **4**:192
  extent of ignorance, **7**:207
  externalities from votes of, **5**:265–66, 269
  giving deceptive reasons for transfers to, **7**:156–60
  government bureaucrats as, **5**:54–55
  as group sovereign, **6**:133–34
  impact of mass media on, **4**:250, 252; **5**:44–45
  increasing the well-being of, **1**:52–53

influences on, **1**:18
information levels, **4**:126–28, 129
information levels, compared with consumers, **4**:36–37
kinds of issues voted upon, **4**:122, 126
lack of influence on voting outcome, **4**:127
lack of information, **7**:204–8
lack of selfish motives among, **1**:579–80
likelihood vote will make difference, **4**:235; **5**:43
"maximizer," **1**:55
motivating honesty in, **1**:134, 137, 143, 144–45
motivating public interest by, **1**:578
motivating to acquire information, **4**:131–32
motivating to vote, **1**:137
motives, **5**:226
number of decisions made by, **4**:121–22
payoff to a vote, **7**:205
poor, **1**:262–63
power of, **4**:35; **7**:360–62
predictability of voting by, **4**:246
preferences of, **4**:161, 232
reasons for voting, **4**:270–71
regard for others in own demand curves, **4**:373–77
restrictions on, **1**:33, 162
role in rent seeking, **5**:38–44
role in transfers, **9**:411
self-interest, **4**:173
specialization of voting by, **5**:203
strong opinions held by, **5**:303–4
tendency to play it safe, **4**:163–64
way to better inform, **7**:367
who change positions, **4**:227
See also elections; ill-informed voters; voting; voting process; well-informed voters

voters with strong preferences
  effect on politicians, **4**:191
  methods of measuring intensity,
    4:238–39
  model that includes, **4**:9–10
  use of demand-revealing process for,
    4:429–31
vote trading, **2**:36, 118–19, 257–61;
    4:396–99
  gains from, **2**:238
  in legislatures, **2**:224–25
  relation with rent seeking,
    5:33–34
  rules prohibiting, **5**:284
  unanimity and, **2**:263–64
  See also logrolling
Votey, Harold L., Jr., **9**:255, *256n. 11*;
    10:*82n. 16, 83n. 19*
voting
  actual size of total vote, **10**:287–88
  among alternatives, **1**:127–29
  Arrow's hidden assumption about,
    1:124–25
  charitable giving via, **7**:360–61
  for charity for oneself, **7**:12
  on choice of government services,
    1:84–86
  compulsory, **10**:277–80, 285–88
  costs and benefits, **10**:280–81
  costs of, **7**:205–6
  costs to individual of, **5**:43
  in democracies, **8**:143–44
  discontinuities in, **1**:93–94
  easing restrictions on, **10**:281–83
  geometrical model, **1**:93
  by government officials, **1**:23–24,
    218, 303–4, 580
  history of, **6**:277–78
  by illegal Mexicans in United States,
    7:46
  impact of demand revealing on
    abuses, **4**:367
  impact of logrolling on, **1**:53
  impact of poorly informed votes on,
    4:130
  impact of population size on, **1**:32
  importance of ideology in, **5**:226
  by juries, **1**:527
  "Kantian" median preference, **1**:54–
    55, 59
  "maximizing equilibrium," **1**:55–
    57, 58
  as means of collective control,
    4:181–92
  models, **4**:227–39; **5**:42, 43
  on multiple, continuous issues,
    4:285–88
  on multiple issues at once, **4**:60–61
  for other people, **4**:293–94
  payoff from, **4**:234; **5**:43
  private charitable giving vs.,
    1:271–72
  probability of "correct," **1**:486–89,
    493–94
  reasons for, **4**:270–71, 294
  reducing social pressure to engage
    in, **4**:130
  relationship to democracy, **8**:107–8
  in small systems, **4**:283–94
  technology, **4**:125–26
  tendency to median "consensus,"
    4:186–87
  on transfers by recipients of transfers,
    7:82–84
  unanimity, **5**:78
  universal suffrage, **1**:33, **6**:3
  See also decision making; logrolling;
    majority voting; poll taxes;
    reinforced majorities; voting
    process; voting rules
"Voting and the Summation of Preferences" (Riker), **6**:89
voting paradox. *See* cyclical majority
voting process, **6**:93–94
  agenda control, **1**:20, 21, *95n. 11*,
    106–7; **4**:435–36

Borda method, **1**:126–27

campaign contribution restrictions, **1**:228

changes in, before elections, **1**:32

contemporary, **4**:441–47

of corporate boards of directors, **4**:440–41

cost of unanimity and, **4**:345

demand-revealing, **5**:289–90

direct voting, **4**:417

effect on demand revealing, **4**:367–68

effect on minorities, **4**:427–30

efficient, **1**:88–89

historical, **4**:437–40, 442–43

impact of bureaucracy on, **1**:23–24

importance of, **1**:129

of legislatures, **4**:433–36

mathematical analysis and new theory, **6**:89

never-used methods, **4**:443–44

to obtain majority in legislatures, **4**:432

probability of cycling in, **1**:95–96

spatial models, **4**:284–85

suggestions for improving, **1**:24–25

for transfers from rich to poor, **7**:6

Tullock's, for electing representatives, **4**:382–83

two-party, **1**:107

in U.S. presidential elections, **4**:430–31

voting by veto, **4**:434

weighting votes, **7**:80, 82–85, 223–24

worldwide variations in, **1**:31–32

See also demand-revealing process; "English" system of voting; proportional representation; referendum on government policies; voting rules

voting rules

cost curve for, **4**:8

external costs for, **4**:6

ideal, **4**:3, 9

optimal, **4**:219

paradoxes, **4**:21

ten-voter rule, **4**:4

Vreeland, Nena, **8**:*86nn. 10–12, 98n. 43*

wage-price controls, **10**:67

Wagner, Richard E., **1**:*194n. 2*; **5**:*24n. 24, 53–54n. 65, 79n. 103, 82n. 107*; **7**:*79n. 3*, 213; **9**:187n. 7

Wagner's law of increasing government activity, **1**:367–69

"Wagner squared" hypothesis, **1**:305

Wagner-type lobbying, **1**:194; **5**:24

waiver of liability, **9**:54

Wakeman, Fredric, Jr., **8**:*64n. 4*

Wales, common law in, **9**:441–42

war

of aggression, **8**:354–67

in animal societies, **10**:164, 208–9, 239

cheating on allies, **8**:364–65

decision to start, **8**:323–26

defensive, **8**:311, 328

following death of dictators, **8**:89–90

impact of mutual disarmament on, **8**:326–27

as involuntary transfer, **1**:187

negotiation for peace during, **8**:328

with nuclear weapons, **8**:361–67

peace after, **8**:329–30

rate of economic growth after, **8**:323

rational reasons for, **8**:311–13

relevance of game theory to, **10**:446

role of small countries in, **8**:360–61

size of government and, **6**:412

war (*continued*)
  over small areas, **8**:365
  Tullock's equations, **8**:327–29
  Tullock's one-country model,
    8:313–17
  Tullock's two-country model,
    8:317–21
  Wars of the Roses, **1**:335
  welfare costs, **1**:182, 192–93
  why people go to, **8**:311
  See also civil wars; conflict;
    demonstrations; nuclear
    war; revolutions
Ward, A. W., **8**:*33n. 3, 65n. 6, 222n. 66*
Ward, Benjamin, **1**:*95n. 11*, 264;
  6:89; **7**:*94n. 7*
"War on Poverty," **4**:134
Warren, C., **5**:*81n. 105*
Warren, Chief Justice, **9**:339, 417
Wars of the Roses, **8**:42–43, 100, 201
Washington, Booker T., **4**:351
Washington, George, **2**:205n. 2
Washington Post, The, **7**:121, 150
wasps. *See* bees
wasp societies, **1**:558, 559–60
Watergate defendants, **9**:315
water projects, government, **5**:250,
  254–56, 277
Watson, Donald S., **5**:20
wealth
  decision making about distribution
    in society, **4**:80n. 9
  government protection of individual,
    8:170
  litigation as cause of redistribution,
    9:422
  relation with choice, **9**:23
  relative, and externalities, **4**:110
  word for the opposite of, **5**:218n. 13
  See also income
wealth equalization, **1**:252–53
  effect on inequality outside United
    States, **7**:50

impact of government on, **7**:174
inconsistent arguments in favor of
  equality, **7**:47
motives for, **7**:53n. 12, 55–57
for terminally ill, **7**:347–49
within upper income groups, **7**:48–
  50, 51–56
See also income redistribution
wealth maximization
  bargaining and, **9**:396
  as objective of the law, **9**:381–82
  Tullock's test, **9**:394
  utility maximization vs., **9**:395
Wealth of Nations, The (Smith), **1**:7, 8;
  4:33; **6**:252; **10**:3n. 1, 209,
  220
  historical context, **5**:160
  purpose, **3**:5n. 3
wealth redistribution. *See* income
  redistribution
wealthy people in democracies
  coalitions with the poor, **1**:265–66
  taxes on, **1**:286–87
  transfers from, **1**:267–68
weapons development, **3**:161–63.
  See also arms race
Weaver, Carolyn L., **5**:305; **7**:*255n. 8,
  259n. 16, 280n. 5*; **10**:*301n. 10*
Weaver, Richard M., **8**:*132n. 80*
Webb, Adrian L., **1**:*196n. 9, 263n. 6*
Weingast, B. R., **1**:*115n. 24*; **5**:*59n. 70*
Weinstock, Stefan, **8**:*105n. 67*
Weiss, Roger W., **9**:*115n. 20*
Weitzman, Martin L., **1**:480–83,
  481n. 2; **4**:*39–40n. 12*
Weitzman, Phillip, **9**:*303n. 8*
Weldon, Thomas Dewar, **2**:4, 60
welfare costs
  of monopolies, **1**:169, 174–79
  tariffs, **1**:169–74
  theft, **1**:175–77
  transfers, **1**:180–98
  See also social costs

"Welfare Costs of Tariffs, Monopolies, and Theft, The" (Tullock), **5**:85, 221, 241, 296
  Tullock commentary about, **5**:17–22
welfare economics, **1**:149; **2**:xxiii, xxiv, 87–92; **4**:64–65
  criteria used by Posner, **9**:380–81
  Paretian, **2**:8
  Pigovian, **2**:192–93
  revolution and, **8**:163–73
  Tullock's modification, **9**:11–14
welfare losses to monopoly
  challenge to theory of, **5**:14–17
  estimated magnitudes, **5**:11–13
  Tullock's work on, **5**:17–22
welfare programs, **1**:404; **4**:71–72
welfare recipients
  administration of programs for, **7**:238–39
  immigrants' ineligibility to be, **7**:130
  in-kind aid to, **7**:136
  reselling of in-kind aid by, **7**:138–39
  welfare system reforms, **7**:357–58
  work programs for, **7**:20–22, 109, 111–16
  See also social workers
welfare state
  failure to serve homeless, **7**:149–51
  position of poor under, **7**:16
  programs for the poor, **7**:125–26
  results of development of, **7**:122
  See also socialized medicine; Social Security system; social welfare programs; universal-aid programs; wealth equalization
welfare transfers to poor, **1**:263–64
welfare triangle, **9**:242–46
  relative size, **9**:246–47
well-informed voters
  definition, **4**:242
  ineffectiveness of, **5**:279

knowledge about income redistribution, **7**:70
knowledge of particular issues, **4**:245
lack of reason to be, **4**:240
lying to, **5**:44–45
motives, **4**:244
predictability of voting by, **4**:246
in simple logrolling models, **4**:329–30
See also ill-informed voters
well-intentioned Machiavellianism, **7**:156; **9**:264
  motives, **7**:157
  problems, **7**:246–47
  transfers to poor people out of, **7**:360, 362
Wellisz, Stanislaw, **1**:*413n. 2*
Wemelsfelder, J., **1**:*173n. 9*; **5**:*13n. 3*
Werstein, Irving, **8**:*138n. 98*
Wesley, John, **9**:225
West, Edwin G., **7**:*299nn. 8, 9*
West, Richard W., **1**:*284n. 13*
West Coast Hotel Co. v. Parrish, **9**:416
Western Economic Journal, **5**:20
Western legal tradition, **5**:81–82, 186. *See also* Islamic legal system
Westoff, Leslie and Charles, **10**:*44n. 5*
Wheatcroft, Andrew, **8**:*63–64n. 2, 110–11n. 7, 125nn. 60, 61, 131n. 79*
"Where Is the Rectangle?" (Tullock), **5**:252
Whinston, Andrew, **1**:*349n. 1, 413n. 2*
White, Leonard D., **4**:*196n. 22*
white corpuscles, **10**:129, 264
wholesale prices in Nationalist China, 1937–47, **10**:309
"Why So Much Stability" (Tullock), **5**:271; **8**:294
Wicksell, Knut, **2**:8, 79, 189, 278, 331
Wicksellian approach, **1**:418, 426
Wicksteed, Philip H., **2**:16–17

Wildavsky, Aaron, **4**:*233n. 11*
Willhoite, Fred H., Jr., **7**:*180n. 2*
Williams, B. R., **3**:*13n. 5*
Williams, G. C., **10**:*188n. 7*
Williams, L. Pearce, **3**:*64n. 8*
Williams, Roger J., **3**:*51n. 25*
Williamson, Oliver E., **1**:*84n. 4*;
    5:*308nn. 14, 15*; **6**:244, 260,
    269, 398, 416
Willit, Tom, **4**:*443n. 8*
wills (legal), **9**:131, 132–33
Wilson, David Sloan, **10**:*159n. 2*
Wilson, Edward O., **1**:*560n. 2*;
    8:*236nn. 16, 19*; **10**:*133n. 3,*
    191n. 10, 207nn. 1–3,
    246nn. 5, 6
  anthropomorphizing by, **6**:327
  on ants, **10**:128–29
  area of ignorance, **10**:143
  on conflict among animals, **10**:122
  effect on sociobiology, **10**:175n. 5
  influence of economics on, **1**:557
  on male dominance, **10**:116
  Sociobiology, **1**:555; **10**:147
Wilson, James Q., **9**:*167n. 15*
Winch, R. F., **10**:*35n. 6*
Winkler, R. C., **10**:*104n. 14*
Winters, R. F., **1**:*262n. 3*
Wintrobe, Ronald, **8**:*154n. 20*
wire tapping, **9**:177
Wisdom, J. O., **3**:*90n. 4*
witnesses in trials, **9**:75
  blood pressure tests of, **9**:362
  detecting lying by, **9**:90–97
  paying for, **9**:178
  rules concerning, **9**:89–90
  use of Fifth Amendment, **9**:357
  See also expert witnesses; testimony
Wittfogel, Karl A., **4**:*142n. 4*;
    8:*40n. 33, 147n. 12*
  Oriental Despotism, **2**:330; **6**:16n. 1,
    250, 276

Wolf, Charles, Jr., **8**:*174n. 2*
Wolf, Eric R., **8**:*127–28n. 71*
Wolff, Christian, **2**:302
wolves, **10**:122, 124, 125
women
  cartels of, **10**:18–19
  discrimination against, **10**:34
  effect of their vote, **1**:33
  U.S. Social Security system and,
    7:282
wood ants. *See* ants
Wookeun, Han, **8**:*65nn. 8, 9, 66n. 12*
Wooldridge, William C., **4**:*204n. 28*
Worden, W. L., **10**:*344n. 6, 352n. 17*
workability test, **3**:40, 41, 43
work by prisoners, **9**:187
workers, motives of, **4**:39
workmen's compensation, **9**:118
work organization. *See* coordination of
    tasks; labor
Worlds in Collision (Velikovsky),
    3:129n. 32
Wright, Arthur F., **8**:*89–90n. 19*
write-in candidates, **4**:293–94
writ system, **9**:406
written testimony, **9**:74–76. *See also*
    oral testimony

X-efficiency, **6**:245
X-inefficiency, **5**:14
  in firms, **5**:15–16
  in U.S. federal bureaucracy, **5**:58

Yamauchi, K., **10**:*208n. 4*
Yang, Lien-sheng, **10**:*324n. 6*
Yarbrough, Beth V. and Robert M.,
    6:244
Yohe, Gary W., **1**:425
Yonker, James A., **9**:*354n. 35*
Young, G. F., **8**:*100n. 50*
Young, L., **5**:*65n. 83, 74n. 95*
Yugoslavian government, **8**:98

Yugoslavian immigrants, **1**:279
Yule, Henry, **10**:*321n. 1*

Zajac, Edward, **1**:*433n. 8*; **6**:313n. 1
Zeisel, Hans, **1**:*477n. 9, 511n. 2,*
    528n. 3; **9**:*157n. 6, 185n. 6,*
    350n. 30, 437n. 15
zero-sum games, **10**:438–40

zero sum in politics, **2**:241–42
Zirkle, Conway, **3**:*107n. 2*
zoning, **2**:53–54
    external costs and, **2**:67
zoning laws, **4**:148
Zubrod, Donald E., **9**:*306n. 15*
Zulu South Africans, **1**:279
Zycher, Benjamin, **7**:*258n. 15*

The typeface used for the text of this book is Galliard, an old-style face designed by Matthew Carter in 1978, in the spirit of a sixteenth-century French typeface of Robert Granjon. The display type is Meta Book, a variant of Meta, designed by Erik Spiekermann in the 1990s.

This book is printed on paper that is acid-free and meets the requirements of the American National Standard for Permanence of Paper for Printed Library Materials, z39.48–1992. ∞

Book design by Richard Hendel, Chapel Hill, North Carolina
Typography by G & S Typesetters, Inc., Austin, Texas
Printed and bound by Edwards Brothers, Inc., Ann Arbor, Michigan